GRAND PASSION

A NOVEL
BY

SUSANNA SHEEHY

Elden Publishing

©2011 Susanna C. Sheehy

This novel is a work of fiction. Any references to historical events; to real people, living or dead; or to real locales are intended only to give the fiction a sense of reality and authenticity. Names, characters, places, and incidents either are the product of the author's imagination or are used fictitiously, and their resemblance, if any, to real live counterparts is entirely coincidental.

All rights reserved. This book is printed in the United States of America. No part of this book may be used or reproduced in any manner whatsoever without written permission except in the case of brief quotations embodied in critical articles and reviews. For information address inquires to:

Elden Publishing, LLC
susannasheehy.com
susannasheehy@susannasheehy.com

Interior Design by Elden Publishing, LLC
Book cover design by Elden Publishing, LLC
Editing by Elden Publishing, LLC

ISBN: 978-0-9789271-6-5
Copyright information available upon request

Other books by Susanna Sheehy

The Second Half Trilogy

Marking Time
Book 1

Second Half
Book 2

Crossed Lines
Book 3

Local Talent

Plastic Diamonds
An Elden Romance

Books are available at Amazon.com, BarnesAndNoble.com, in the Kindle Store, and are also available for order at local book stores.

Visit Susanna at:
www.susannasheehy.com

CHAPTER ONE

I climbed over the rail of my crib. They had lowered the mattress and made the rail into a guard just in case I rolled out of bed in my sleep. I could remember the conversation they had about it, my parents.

"Don't you think he's a little young to be roaming the house in the night?" Dad said.

"I don't think he'll go anywhere but to our room, Brian. He's only eighteen months old. What else would he do in a dark house in the middle of the night?" Mom said.

"I don't even want to think about that." They laughed and kissed each other.

"Anyway," Mom said. "I've found him teetering on the edge of the rail twice now. It doesn't matter how high it is. He's coming over it."

That was the last conversation I remembered them having.

I lowered myself from the rail to the floor. I could hear Mom downstairs in the living room. I was sure she was crying. Dad hadn't been home for a while. I couldn't figure how long. Then he came for a minute today. He told me that he would always be there for me if I needed him. He said he loved me.

I could understand all of this, but saying 'I love you too' was hard. I just couldn't make the sounds. It came out something like 'wub oo doo.'

When I got to the top of the stairs I turned around to crawl backwards down. Mom taught me that. We had practiced it over and over. She said, "Better safe than sorry." And she described in detail the pain of breaking an arm or leg. I sure didn't want to do that.

When I got to the bottom of the stairs I turned and peeked into the living room. She was sitting on the couch with her face in her hands. She was crying.

"Momma," I said. I was scared. She looked up at me and spread her arms out. I ran to them and let her scoop me into her lap.

"I'm so sorry, baby," she said. "I couldn't do it. I couldn't make him want to stay with us."

I looked into her tearstained face. "Who stay?" I asked.

"Your dad, honey. I'm so sorry. He's gone," she said. "You're the man of the family now."

She buried her face in my hair and sobbed. I couldn't say anything. I didn't know the words. I was only two years old.

✦

"Uncle Jeff?"

"What, David?"

"What does the man of the family do?" We were going to play soccer. My uncle Jeff took me on Tuesday afternoons. He was the assistant coach.

"The man of the family makes sure that everyone has what they need and provides protection," he said as he settled next to the soccer field with the cooler of Gatorade and cups. "Why?"

"I just wondered." How am I supposed to do that? I thought. I'm only six years old. Maybe when I turned seven I would be a grown man. Both Mom and Uncle Jeff said I was the man of the family now. At night I went to bed worried about what I would need to do the next day. So far Mom hadn't asked for much except hugs and kisses. But what if she needed something I couldn't give her. I'd worried about that for as long as I could remember.

"Are you ready to play ball, David?" Uncle Jeff said. I smiled up at him. He looked just like my dad. I could still vaguely remember what Dad looked like, and Mom still had his picture in a frame on her bedside table. He and Uncle Jeff were identical twins. Uncle Jeff was huge. He was tall and strong. I knew he had a landscaping business and he worked hard every day. Mom said that was why he was so strong. Dad was a lawyer.

"I'm ready," I said. Uncle Jeff spent a lot of time with me. He came to our house a couple of times a week, and we did a lot of stuff together. It was great, but I always felt funny when I called him Uncle in front of the other kids. They all had dads.

"Go on in then, son." He nudged my shoulder. "I know you don't particularly like playing the goal, but you're good at it."

"I'm good at other things too."

"Yes you are. I'll make sure you can play other positions."

I went to the goal and played the whole game there. My team won. At the six year old level, nobody really knew what they were doing. But I did. So they left me in the goal. Preventing my own team members from scoring on me was just as hard as preventing the opposite team from scoring.

3 / Grand Passion

"I don't think I want to play soccer next season, Uncle Jeff," I said on the way from the field. I was angry about never getting to play forward.

He stopped and looked at me. He reached down, picked me up, and settled me on his hip. He was so strong. I knew he was trying to take care of me, trying to make up for my dad leaving, but I resented him hauling me around like that.

"David, I know you wanted to play another position, but we didn't stand a chance without you in the goal."

"I know, Uncle Jeff." I looked down at the ground.

"Well, would you like to do something else next year?" he asked. "Would you like to play baseball or something?"

"No."

I think it was two years later that we started back packing. It was my idea. I had a friend in school that went backpacking with his whole family, his Dad, Mom, Sister, and younger brother.

Wow, I remember thinking. A whole family, mother, father, brother, sister, is there any such thing? I couldn't imagine it.

"Uncle Jeff, I want to go back packing," I said one day on one of his visits. He came every Tuesday even if I didn't want to play soccer.

"Backpacking?" he said. "You mean you want to carry all your food and any other needs on your back?"

"Yeah, for miles and miles ..."

"You know, David. That does sound like fun. We'll need to go to the outdoor store and get supplies. Do you want to join us, Charlie?" he asked my mom. He always called her Charlie, not Sharlie but Charlie. Her name was Charlotte.

"Oh, I don't think so, thanks." She wasn't really the outdoors type. "I'll stay home and take care of Pepper."

"Oh no, I want Pepper to come with us," I said. Pepper was my dog. He was a big old afghan hound. Mom loved that breed of dog. I really didn't care what kind of dog he was. He was my best friend.

"David," Uncle Jeff said. "I know you love your dog, but I'll have to object to that. I'm not that crazy about dogs. We'll let Pepper stay here with your mom. You can take him to the park when I'm not around."

Uncle Jeff just didn't understand some things. I really missed my dad then. He liked dogs. That was one thing I just vaguely remembered. I'd forgotten almost everything I knew about my dad. Sometimes I stared real hard at Uncle Jeff just to remember what Dad looked like. They were identical twins after all.

"I want to fit this young man and myself for a backpack." Uncle Jeff told the clerk at the outdoors shop. "And maybe you can guide us on the equipment we need."

It was so much fun shopping for the stuff that I forgot how sad I was at having to leave Pepper behind. I had to remind myself that I should be really glad that Uncle Jeff was willing to do this with me. After all, I'm really not his kid. I was pretty sure he just did this because he felt sorry for me.

"Now, let's get a book of hiking trips in Georgia. What do you think about starting in our home state and then moving on from there, David?"

"That's okay to begin with. I want to hike all the trails in Georgia, but I want to do the Appalachian Trail too."

"That's a pretty long trail. I don't think we can do it all at once. I can't get that much time off work." He rubbed the top of my head. I didn't like it when he did that. My hair always stuck up afterwards. It was embarrassing.

"I saw on discovery channel where a group of friends did it in short trips." I tried to smooth my hair. "After a while they had to fly to their starting point. Wouldn't you like to have that experience to talk about?"

"It does sound like a good thing to have in your experience file, but let's start with Georgia until we get in shape."

"Okay."

"Uncle Jeff." I called from my bedroom window when I saw him approaching the house.

"Hey, kid." He waved at me. "Don't lean on that screen. I don't want to be scraping you up off the walk way."

"I won't." I hurried down the hall and down the steps to the front door. "I've found the perfect hiking trail for our first trip," I said as I yanked the door open. "It's five miles long, and it has a difficulty rating of moderate. There are two camp sites at the end of it right next to a small waterfall and a swimming hole. Don't you think that sounds great?"

"It does sound great. Can we reserve one of the campsites or is it first come first serve?"

"It's first come first serve so we'd have to leave early. Can we go today? It's Saturday and it's early enough, isn't it?"

5 / Grand Passion

Uncle Jeff looked at his watch. "How far away is this place, David? It's already eleven o'clock. I doubt we'd get the spot if we left now, and we'd still have to pack," he said. "And besides, we're going to the retirement complex today to visit Gramma and Grampa Landrum. They're expecting us. It's plant the spring garden day."

"Oh yeah." I was so disappointed. Why did everything fun have to be planned in advance.

"Get me the book and let me have a look at this place."

I ran back up the stairs to get my Hiking Trails of Georgia book.

"Hello, Jeff, can I give you a cup of coffee?" I heard my mother say as I left the room.

"I'd love one," he answered.

They were in the kitchen when I came back down. I stopped to listen to what they were saying. Sometimes they said something about my Dad. I wanted to know anything about him, even the bad things.

"Will you come with us to the retirement complex, Charlie?" Uncle Jeff asked.

"Oh, I don't think so, Jeff. I'll just let you take David. They aren't my in-laws anymore. Even when they were they didn't like me very much," Mom answered.

"They don't like me very much either and they're my parents." Uncle Jeff laughed. "Brian is definitely their favorite."

"Yes, they're your parents so that means you have to go. I don't. I go to your Aunt Jeanne's for Christmas every year. I have to see them then. That's enough for me. "

"Lucky you." They both laughed. "David, where are you with that book. If we don't get going we'll miss the barbecue."

"Here I am, Uncle Jeff." I handed him the book and waited anxiously while he read the marked pages.

"I think it will take about two hours to get to this place. We'll go next weekend if that's okay with you, Charlie."

"Sounds great," Mom said.

"Are you sure you won't come along, Mom?" I worried about leaving her alone too much. She still cried sometimes. It always seemed to happen when I came home after being away for a while. "Maybe Uncle Jeff will let Pepper come if you come."

"No Pepper!" Uncle Jeff said.

"I'll be alright, David, but I appreciate your concern. You really have done a wonderful job of being the man of the family since your father left." She hugged me. "I'll arrange to have dinner with my friend Vanessa next Saturday. I'll be fine."

"If you're sure ..." I was angry with Uncle Jeff. Why did he hate Pepper so much?

"Let's go, kid. Gramma and Grampa are waiting for us."

◎

"David, come here and give me a hug."

Gramma Landrum put her arms out. Sometimes I didn't want to hug her. She always kissed me and her lips were wrinkled and cold, and her breath was bad.

"You are the image of your handsome father."

I liked it when she said that though. So I let her kiss me. People always said I looked like Uncle Jeff, but only Gramma said I looked like my Dad. Sometimes Mom did too, but it made her sad.

"What about me?" Uncle Jeff leaned down to kiss her on the cheek. "Aren't I the image of David's handsome father?"

"Hello, Jeffrey. You know I never believed you and Brian were identical twins. Your chin is weaker than his and your ears stick out more. It's a good thing Brian was the one that wanted to be a lawyer. You can't practice law with a weak chin and big ears."

Uncle Jeff laughed and put his arm across Grampa's shoulders. "Mom is just so good for my self esteem."

"You know I love you, Jeffrey. You take such good care of your parents," Gramma said, but I wasn't sure I believed she loved him very much.

"I wish you'd protect your skin more when you're out there working in the sun." Grampa said. "I swear it looks like leather."

"Well, are the two of you all slathered with sun screen? It's pretty hot outside and the sun is out," Uncle Jeff asked. "Where's Aunt Jeanne?"

"Here I am." We turned at the sound of her voice as she came breezing in. That was the only way to describe my great Aunt Jeanne. She breezed. It seemed like cool fresh air always surrounded her, even in the heat of summer.

"Aunt Jeanne." Uncle Jeff hugged her and she put her arms around him. I was always surprised at the way they hugged each other. They rocked back and forth in each other's arms. "MMMMhhhmmmm …" Uncle Jeff said. "It's always so good to see you."

"You too, sweetie." She kissed his cheek and turned to me. "Well, David, how about a hug for your great aunt. She put her arms around me. I didn't mind it at all. She smelled like flowers. I think it was perfume, but it wasn't very strong. She smelled more like fresh air.

Aunt Jeanne was my Grampa's sister. She was seventeen years younger than Grampa. I think she was closer to Uncle Jeff than either of his parents were. They always visited Gramma and Grampa together.

She hugged them and Uncle Jeff said, "Are we ready to garden?"

7 / Grand Passion

He was always so jolly. I know Mom wasn't like that when she was around Gramma and Grampa. I guess that was why she didn't see them very much.

Gramma wheeled her chair out toward the garden. Uncle Jeff took the handles and helped her get over the door sill. Grampa followed with his walker. Aunt Jeanne walked beside him. I was in the back of the line. I'd had my foot run over by the wheel chair or the walker enough times to want to stay clear.

We put gardening gloves on our hands. Uncle Jeff brought his own. The social committee at the complex never bought gloves big enough for him.

"Jeffrey," Gramma called from her chair. "Don't get too close to that pond. I don't want anyone to have to fish you out."

Uncle Jeff laughed. "Even if I fell in the pond, Mom, it only comes up to my knees."

"Well, I don't want you stirring up the fish."

The soil was prepared for the planting and the flowers and greenery were placed in the spots they wanted them planted. All we had to do was plant them.

"David, don't you have a birthday coming up next week?" Gramma asked when we had finished planting and were sitting down to lunch.

"Yes." I really didn't want to talk about it. I always got a card from my dad on my birthday. I got one on Christmas too. I loved those cards. Dad always said that he thought about me every day. He told me he loved me and he signed the card, DAD. For some reason I didn't want to share this with Uncle Jeff or Aunt Jeanne and my grandparents. I wanted to think it was because I didn't want Uncle Jeff to be jealous, but it wasn't only that. I just didn't want to share it with him.

"My birthday is Friday. Mom and Uncle Jeff are taking me to dinner at Chuck E. Cheese and on Saturday, Uncle Jeff and I are going backpacking. It's a five mile hike and there's a swimming hole at the end."

"Can Uncle Bill and I join you at Chuck E. Cheese for dinner? I have a little something I picked out for you," Aunt Jeanne asked.

"It's okay with me. Is that alright Uncle Jeff?"

"Absolutely, the more the merrier. You two want to join us?" he said to Gramma and Grampa. I held my breath. It would be embarrassing to have Gramma and Grampa there.

"No thank you, dear," Gramma said.

"Why in the world would I want to go to that place? It's so noisy it breaks up my hearing aid," Grampa said.

I laughed and Gramma said, "Maybe you could come by before you go so that we can say happy birthday to our first grandchild on his eighth birthday."

"Okay." I wondered how Mom was going to feel about that.

"So, you're going backpacking," Grampa said. "It's a little early in the spring time to go swimming in a mountain swimming hole isn't it?"

"We're not afraid of a little cold water, are we David?" Uncle Jeff ruffled my hair again. I wished he wouldn't do that.

"Nawww," I said. This always got a big laugh. After I ate I asked to be excused.

"Is it time for you to take your yearly dip in the pond?" Uncle Jeff laughed.

"I fell in last year."

"… And the year before," Grampa said.

"I just like to get close to the fish and the sides of the pond are slippery." I went out into the garden. I fully intended to fall into the pond.

It was the morning of the backpacking trip. I'd been up for hours. In fact, I don't think I ever went to sleep. I may have dozed a little, but I was too excited to really sleep. When Uncle Jeff got there I was waiting at the door with my pack on.

I had packed the night before. The birthday card I had gotten from my dad was tucked deep in the backpack. I didn't want it to fall out accidentally. I didn't want to show it to Uncle Jeff. I just liked having it with me.

I had the water bottle Aunt Jeanne had given me at my birthday dinner the night before. It was strapped to the side of my pack. The bandana Gramma and Grampa had given me when we stopped by on the way to dinner was tied around my neck.

"Where's your mom?" Uncle Jeff asked when he stepped into the foyer.

"She's still asleep."

"Well, we can't leave without telling her."

"She knows we're going. Why do I have to wake her up?"

"Because it's the right thing to do," Uncle Jeff said. "Go on. I'll wait here."

"I'm up," Mom called from the stairs. She was tying her bathrobe. She came down the steps and hugged me. She kissed my cheek. I felt something warm and wet on my face and looked up at her. She was crying.

"I'll be alright, Mom," I said. "If you want to come along we can wait until you get ready."

"What would I do without you, David?" She hugged me again then stood up and reached for a tissue on the table by the door. "You worry about me so much."

"You'll never know what you'd do without me because I'll never leave you," I said quietly. I could see Uncle Jeff out of the corner of my eye shifting his weight back and forth. He always got uncomfortable when my mom cried.

"Well, run on now and have a good trip." She looked up at Uncle Jeff. "Take care of my little man, Jeff. He's all I have."

"Take care of Pepper, Mom," I said. "You have him too. He's your dog too." I hugged my dog and ran out the door. There was a lump in my throat, but I didn't want to cry.

"I wish you liked dogs," I grumbled when we got into the car. It always helped if I get mad when I was sad.

"It's not that I don't like them, buddy roe. It's just that I haven't got any experience with them, at least not any good experience."

"Well, I do. I could teach you."

"You can only teach people what they want to learn."

"I guess so." Sometimes Uncle Jeff could get on my nerves, but he was the only person I had to go backpacking with. I wondered what it would be like with my dad. I thought about the card in my pack. He always said he loved me. Uncle Jeff only did this stuff because he felt sorry for me. He didn't love me. If he'd wanted a little boy of his own he'd have one, right?

"David, wake up, big guy." Uncle Jeff's voice seemed far away. "We're here. We're at the hiking trail."

I opened my eyes and sat up. Uncle Jeff drove a big truck with a bench seat. I was small enough to sleep lying down with my legs folded and still not put my head in Uncle Jeff's lap. He had brought me a pillow. I slept the whole trip.

"Can I have a Coke before we get started?" My stomach felt a little weird.

"Your mom doesn't like for you to have caffeine," he said. He tilted his head and looked at me. "However, you look a little green. I think we can break the rules this once." He went around to the back of the truck and opened a cooler to get a Coke.

"I brought this for the ride home. I think the ice will stay cold overnight. I'm sure we'll be happy to drink something other than water after our hike."

We sat at a picnic table and Uncle Jeff gave me a paper cup full of Coke and poured some for himself too. "I have some cheese and crackers. Want some?"

I nodded my head and took the package he handed me. "I'd rather have peanut butter," I said. "Do you have any peanut butter crackers?"

"Let's see." He dug through his back pack. "Sure enough," he grinned. "I got a variety pack."

I munched on the crackers and looked around the little picnic area. The trail started at the edge of the clearing and looked dark as it wound into the forest. There were sounds all around us. I guessed it was different types of birds and maybe squirrels made noise too.

"Look." Uncle Jeff pointed to a rabbit that approached us cautiously. "I guess they get fed a lot. He's awfully tame."

I was about to throw him a piece of my cracker, but Uncle Jeff stopped me. "It's probably better not to feed the wildlife, son. They need to be afraid of us. It's safer for them and for us too."

"Why do I need to be safe from a rabbit?" I asked.

"I guess you don't, but he needs to be safe from you."

I didn't quite understand that but I let it pass.

"You look a little better," Uncle Jeff said. "I guess the Coke was a good idea. Are you ready to start?"

I looked at the trail and nodded my head. Uncle Jeff helped me to put my pack on. "It feels heavier than it did this morning."

"Your legs are probably stiff from sleeping crunched up on that seat. They'll wake up after you walk for a while."

He put on his pack and we set off.

"You go in the front, buddy roe," Uncle Jeff said. "That way you can set the pace. My legs are a lot longer than yours. I don't want to wear you out too fast."

"You're not going to wear me out," I said. His remark irritated me. "I can go really fast." It sounded stupid even to me and that irritated me more.

"I know you can, son. I didn't mean anything by it. I'll go first if you want me to."

"No, I know the markers. I've been studying the book. I'll lead."

I started down the path. I could feel Uncle Jeff on my heels. I wanted to tell him to back off, but that would be rude. Mom hated it when I was rude, especially to Uncle Jeff. I reminded myself that I was lucky to have him to do this with. I wondered again what it would be like with my dad.

I rounded a switch back and sat down on a big rock on the side of the trail. "I need some water." I took the water bottle out of the side pocket of my back pack. "How far do you think we've gone?" I asked.

"Probably about a mile." Uncle Jeff sat down on the rock beside me and pulled his own water bottle out. "Maybe we shouldn't have started with five miles. Maybe we should have chosen a shorter trail for our first time."

"I'm not tired, are you?"

Uncle Jeff looked at me and grinned. He had a great smile. It always made me want to smile back, but this time that irritated me. It seemed like everything was irritating me today. My back hurt, my lungs ached, and my legs were so tired they felt wobbly. I looked at the trail and wondered how the stupid book could have described the difficulty of this trail as moderate. We had been going straight uphill the whole way.

"I'm pretty tired." He stood and stretched his arms. "But if you're not, we'll just keep on going."

I stood and started up the trail again.

"Finally, we're going downhill," Uncle Jeff said as we hit the top of the ridge and started down the other side of the mountain. "I think I hear running water, too. Maybe we're getting close."

"I think we're at least half way," I said. It was starting to feel good to be moving. "The air is much cooler up here than in Atlanta."

"Springtime comes later in the mountains," Uncle Jeff said. "David, watch your step ahead."

"A snake!" I stopped short, and Uncle Jeff put his hands on my shoulders.

"What kind of snake is that?" he asked.

"I think it's a rattler. See on the end of his tail. Isn't that a rattle?"

"It looks like one, doesn't it? Let's just wait until he leaves before we go on."

"I want a picture of it. Mom will never believe it if I don't have a picture." I pulled my camera out of another side pocket and aimed it at the snake. It slithered away as I snapped the shot. "I don't think I got anything but his rattle," I said. "I guess I didn't move fast enough."

"Well, if you were only going to get one shot I guess the rattle was the best thing to get."

"I can't wait to take it to show and tell." We started walking and Uncle Jeff stopped me again with his hand on my shoulder.

"Look through the woods," he whispered.

I followed the direction he was pointing and sucked in my breath. "A bear, that's pretty scary," I whispered back.

"Supposedly they're more afraid of us than we are of them." Uncle Jeff nudged me.

"I'm not sure I believe that," I said.

"Me neither." He laughed. "Keep walking."

I pointed my camera at the bear and snapped. The creature had been standing on its back legs looking at us, but at the sound of the camera it dropped to all fours, turned, and ran through the woods in the opposite direction. I smiled up at Uncle Jeff.

"I think I got a pretty good one that time."

"Good work, buddy roe."

✧

"It's funny, Uncle Jeff. After you've been walking for a while you don't want to stop." I pulled off my pack the way the guy at the outdoors store had demonstrated to me and propped it up against a tree.

"Yeah, I think they call that endorphins. The more you exercise the better it feels."

"Now that we're here though, I'll admit," I sat down on the ground and pulled off my shoes and socks. "When we first started this morning, I didn't think I'd make it."

"You know what?" Uncle Jeff was picking up small sticks for kindling for our campfire. "I thought I'd be carrying your pack by the time we got half way. Then when we were about half way I thought about asking you to carry mine."

I laughed as I put my feet into the pool of water. "Isn't this a great spot?" I called over the sound of the waterfall.

"It sure is. You can really pick 'em." He lit a match to the starter block he'd brought and stacked kindling on top of it. "I'll get a campfire going. Then, if you want, we'll take a little swim."

"Okay, I'm just going to wade in the water a little. I don't think it gets very deep."

"Well, don't go too close to the falls until I'm with you." Uncle Jeff was pulling things out of his pack. "I know you can swim like a fish, but currents can get tricky around a waterfall."

I tuned his warnings out as I walked across the swimming hole toward the bank next to the waterfall. It didn't get any deeper than my knees and the current was weak where the water flowed out of the pond and the stream continued down the hill.

I climbed up onto a rock next to the falls and looked behind the flow of water. There was a small cave behind the falls. I decided to wait to explore that when Uncle Jeff was with me, but there was a sort of stairway of stones that led up to the top of the falls. It looked pretty sturdy so I carefully climbed up.

13 / Grand Passion

When I got to the top I sat down. I had the most powerful feeling. The water rushed over the rocks with such force I felt like it was giving me energy. The breeze was cool. Actually it was cold, but it made me feel good all over. I smiled and lifted my face to the mist.

I looked down at the campsite and realized that Uncle Jeff was calling something to me. I couldn't hear over the sound of the falls so I tried to read his lips. He seemed to be pointing to something behind me. Suddenly I had the feeling that something was there. I remembered the bear we'd seen earlier.

I turned quickly to look. There was no bear, but the rock was slippery. I slid into the rushing water of the falls. It seemed like I moved in slow motion over the rocks. They were strangely smooth, covered with moss, I thought. The water carried me down to the pool below and held me firmly beneath the surface.

I felt panic at first. I would need to take a breath eventually, and struggle as I might, I could not get my head above water. I decided I would just not breathe. The thought of breathing water was horrible. So I held my breath. I started to feel a little dizzy, and I knew I was going to die. Poor Mom, I thought.

Suddenly there were strong arms around my waist, and I was hauled out of the falls and into the air. I was dangling a few feet above the surface. I took a deep breath of dry air and looked at Uncle Jeff.

He looked terrified. I felt completely calm. Then he wrapped his arms around me and held me so tightly to his chest that, again, I could hardly breathe.

"David, thank God. Thank God," he said holding me away from him so he could see my face. "Did you get water in your lungs? Did you swallow water?" he asked clutching me to his chest again. He was walking through the pond. It only came up to his knees.

I laughed. To think I was about to drown in two feet of water. I looked back over his shoulder at the falls. It might be deeper there.

"David, talk to me, son." He sounded frantic.

"I'm okay, Uncle Jeff. I decided not to breathe while was under there. So I didn't get water in my lungs."

"You decided not to breathe!" He started to laugh and sat down on a fallen tree. He was still holding me. He sat me on his lap and held me close to his chest. Any other time that would have bothered me, but he seemed to need to hold on to me right now.

"You decided not to breathe," he repeated. He was holding me so close that I could feel the bristles of his beard on my temple. "You're something else, David. You decided not to breathe."

"Well," I said. "Breathing water didn't seem like it would feel too good."

"Were you afraid?" He had stopped laughing now and he leaned back from me a little so he could look at my face.

"I was worried about Mom."

He studied my face. "What about yourself, David? What about me?"

"If I die Mom won't have a man of the family." He studied my face for a minute.

"David," he said. "Your mother loves you. I love you. Not because you're the man of the family but because you're you. I want you to value yourself as much as we value you."

"I thought if you wanted a little boy you'd have one of your own." I looked down at the ground. "I didn't know you loved me."

Uncle Jeff was quiet for a while. We just sat together on that fallen tree for I don't know how long. He kissed me on the temple and again on the cheek. This was unusual. He rarely kissed me.

"I do have a little boy of my own," he whispered. "His name is David."

✵

The next morning I got up before Uncle Jeff. We had changed into our sleeping clothes after my dip in the water the night before. We roasted hot dogs and baked beans over the fire and then crawled into our sleeping bags. It was really uncomfortable. I decided I would need a better inflatable mattress if I was going to do much of this.

Uncle Jeff fell sound asleep. I don't think he ever woke up again until morning. At least he didn't stop snoring once. I couldn't get comfortable though. I dozed on and off through the night. I emerged from the tent feeling like I was about to wet my pants and barely managed to get behind the first tree before I spent the next five minutes watching the pee splash around the base of it.

I looked around the clearing and breathed in the cool mountain air. I rolled my pants legs up and waded into the water.

"David," Uncle Jeff called from inside the tent.

"Don't worry." I smiled remembering the feel of him holding me yesterday. "I won't go near the falls again without you." It had been so nice to realize he loved me.

"Good, you shortened my life by about two years yesterday. I was planning to live to be a hundred. I guess I'll only make it to ninety eight now." He came out of the tent and headed for the same tree I'd just watered.

"I'm surprised you didn't scold me," I said as he joined me at the edge of the pond. "Mom would have scolded me."

15 / Grand Passion

"Well, I thought about it." He rubbed the top of my head.

I reached up to smooth out my hair and found that it was still a mess from sleep. "I hate when you do that," I said.

"You do? Why didn't you tell me?"

"I don't know. I guess now that I know you love me I can tell you a lot of things you might not like." I laughed and squatted down to splash my face with water.

"Oh, using my feelings to your advantage." He squatted down to splash his face too. "You're a smart boy."

We had a breakfast that came out of a bag. We mixed it with water and fried it up in our pan. It tasted kind of like eggs with bits of bacon in them. Then we packed up the campsite and headed back to the truck.

On the hike back we saw more wildlife. Across the stream we saw a long legged bird that took flight and must have been five feet in wing span. I planned to look it up when I got home. I snapped a picture of it and hoped it wouldn't be blurry. In fact I kept my camera in my hand all the way and I was glad because we saw a group of deer. I think they must call it a herd. I'd have to look that up too.

"Uncle Jeff, Jimmy Parnell belongs to a boy scout troop," I said on the drive home.

"Oh yeah, who's Jimmy Parnell?"

"He's my best friend at school."

"So what does a boy scout troop do?"

"They have meetings and they work on earning merit badges and they go on backpacking trips together."

"Sounds like fun. Why don't you join the troop?"

"Jimmy's dad is the troop leader. You can't really join with a mother."

"Do you need a dad to be a member? That doesn't seem fair."

"No, I can join. Jimmy's dad said he'd sponsor me. I was just thinking. I mean, I like backpacking with just you, but it might be fun to go with a group sometimes." I was resisting the urge to bite my fingernails. I always wanted to bite my nails when I was nervous.

"Can I join with you? Surely they'd take an uncle in the place of a dad."

"I was hoping you'd say that." Uncle Jeff put his hand on the top of my head then pulled it away.

"Sorry," he said. "I guess I need to break that habit.

CHAPTER TWO

"Call your mom." Uncle Jeff handed me his cell phone. "She'll be wondering about us. Tell her we'll be home in half an hour."

I dialed the number and pressed send. "Hey, Mom."

"David, I'm so happy to hear your voice. Are you guys okay?"

"Yeah, we had a great time. I took a bunch of pictures of wild life. We saw a rattle snake and a bear."

"Well, that's it." I could tell she was smiling. "No more backpacking for you."

"You're kidding, right?" I laughed nervously.

"Of course I am. When will you be home?"

"Uncle Jeff says we'll be home in about half an hour."

"Tell him I'll fire up the grill. He can stay for hamburgers if he wants. See you soon. Bye sweetie."

"Bye, Mom." I pressed end and handed the phone back to Uncle Jeff. "Do you suppose we could not tell mom about the waterfall incident?"

"I suppose we could ... not."

"It's just that she worries you know."

"I know, David, but I worry too. I want you to promise me you'll put a little more value on your life. I still can't believe you decided not to breathe." He chuckled.

"I didn't get water in my lungs, did I?"

"No you didn't. But please don't ever decide not to breathe again. I want you to fight for your life if you have to."

"I promise."

We pulled into the driveway of the townhouse that my mom and I lived in. She was standing on the front step waving. I jumped out of the truck as soon as it stopped and ran to her. She opened her arms and grabbed me. She picked me up and swung me around.

"I can hardly pick you up anymore, David." She set me back down on the ground and kissed both my cheeks. "I can't believe you're eight years old already."

17 / Grand Passion

"Well, I am." Remembering my birthday card, I went to the truck and retrieved my backpack. "I'll take this upstairs."

"I can get it if you want me to," Uncle Jeff said.

"No, I'll take it." I ran upstairs to my room and pulled the card out of the pack. I stuffed it under my pillow and hurried back down to the kitchen. Mom and Uncle Jeff were there. Mom was handing him a beer in a frosted mug.

"Where's Pepper?" I asked.

"He's in the back yard. He'll be happy to see you," Mom said. "He really missed you."

I ran out the back door and called to my dog. He jumped up from his bed in the pine straw and ran to me. He was a big dog. I didn't have to lean down much to hug him. He licked my face and I laughed.

Mom and Uncle Jeff came out onto the back deck and sat down. Pepper ran up to Uncle Jeff and wagged his tail.

"Hello, Pepper," he said, but he didn't pet him. "Everyone doesn't love dogs, David," he said when he caught me scowling at him.

"I wish you did," I said. "Everything would perfect if you just liked dogs."

"Sorry I can't be perfect." He and Mom both laughed. Mom stretched her hand out to Pepper and he came to her.

"I guess you'll just have to share that with me," she said.

"I guess so." I picked up Pepper's ball and threw it. He chased it and brought it back. The yard was too small for him, but he could still play fetch.

"I'm going now, David," Uncle Jeff called.

"You're not staying for hamburgers?" I threw the ball one more time then walked over to where Uncle Jeff sat with Mom.

"No, I'll grab something at home. I'm anxious to take a long shower." He put his hands on my shoulders and surprised me by kissing me on the head. I looked quickly at Mom. She was surprised too. "Thanks for going backpacking with me, buddy roe. Start looking for the next trail."

"I will," I said. I looked at my shoes for a minute while Uncle Jeff stood and walked to the back door. "Wait," I called.

He stopped and smiled back at me. I hurried over to him and put my arms around his waist. He leaned down and hugged me back.

"See you Tuesday," he said. "You can give me Jimmy Parnell's telephone number then. So I can call his dad."

"Okay."

✦

"It looks to me like you and your Uncle Jeff did some bonding on this trip," Mom said.

"What's bonding?" I sat at the table brushing Pepper. He loved to be brushed. It wasn't hard to remember to do it because he would bring the brush to me and nudge my hand with it.

"It's getting close to someone I guess." She was putting the burgers on the grill. She closed the lid and sat down beside me. "Tell me about the trip."

"Well, I slept all the way to the trail." I laughed. "I hardly slept at all the night before we went."

"I figured you didn't."

"When we got there and Uncle Jeff woke me up I felt kind of sick. So we sat down at a picnic table and had some peanut butter crackers and a Coke." I looked quickly at her. "I know you don't like me to have caffeine, but it settled my stomach."

"It's okay, honey. You can drink Coke now and then."

"Well, I didn't drink very much. We left the cooler in the car because you can't backpack with a cooler, you know. I drank Sprite on the way home." I watched her as she got up and went to the grill to flip the burgers.

Mom's name was Charlotte. I always thought it was a beautiful name. I always thought if I ever had a girl dog I'd want to name her Charlotte. That wouldn't work though, two Charlottes in one house. Of course, Uncle Jeff called Mom Charlie and I called her Mom. So maybe it wouldn't be too confusing.

Mom was very tall and very thin. She was shorter than Uncle Jeff but not by much. I asked her how tall she was once, and she told me six foot one. She said most women weren't that tall, and the ones that were usually slumped. Mom didn't slump. She had broad shoulders and long legs. I thought she was beautiful. Her skin was always a little tan. Her eyes were brown like her hair. She wore her hair very short. It was wavy.

"Go on." She sat back down next to me.

"We saw the first wildlife while we were sitting there. It wasn't very wild though. It was a rabbit. It came right up to the table. Uncle Jeff said that it must get fed a lot, and we shouldn't encourage it. He thought it wasn't safe if it was too friendly." I stopped for a second to concentrate on a knot on the back of Pepper's ear. "Why wouldn't it be safe, Mom?"

"Well, I guess some people hunt rabbits," she said. "If they're too friendly they won't run fast enough."

"Yeah, anyway, when we first started walking I was really cranky. My legs were stiff from sleeping in the truck, and the pack seemed a lot heavier than it did that morning. But the more we walked the better I felt. Pretty soon Uncle Jeff saw the snake and told me to watch my step."

"I'm glad he spotted it."

"Me too, it didn't rattle at us but we saw its tail. That had to be a rattle on the end of it."

I watched as she went to the grill and took the burgers off. She put them on a plate. "Let's eat inside. I don't want to bring everything out then take it back in."

I thought I would rather eat outside, but I didn't want to do all the work either, so I followed her into the kitchen. She pulled a bowl of potato salad out of the fridge. I love potato salad. She also had sliced tomatoes and lettuce. I wasn't going to eat any of that.

"When do you think we can get the pictures developed?" I asked when she put plates down on the table and sat across from me.

"I'll drop them tomorrow after I take you to school. I don't have to be at the shop until mid-morning."

"Can we get them in the afternoon after you pick me up at school?"

"I don't see why not." She took a bite of her burger. "So when did you see the bear?"

We walked Pepper after dinner. That was something we always did together before I took my bath and got ready to go to bed.

"Mom, you didn't walk Pepper alone last night did you?" It worried me to think of her outside in the dark all alone.

"I did, honey, but it wasn't dark yet," she said. "David, you don't have to worry so much about me. I can take care of myself."

Then why am I the man of the family? I thought. But I didn't say anything.

After our walk, I took a long bath and it felt great. My muscles were sore from all the walking I'd done. My shoulders ached a little from carrying the pack, but it was a good feeling, a good ache. Is there any such thing?

When I went to bed I pulled the card from my dad out from under the pillow. It said something about being proud to have a son like me. Of course, he signed it love, Dad.

"That card means a lot to you doesn't it." Mom stood in my doorway. She crossed the room and sat down beside me.

"Yeah," I put the card on the table next to my bed and crawled under the covers. "Do you suppose I'll ever get to go visit Dad?"

"I don't know, honey. I guess he's pretty busy with his career and his new family."

"He says he loves me. Do you think he really does?"

Chapter Two / 20

"Of course he does, David. I really feel kind of bad for him. He doesn't realize how much he's missing because he doesn't see you every day." She kissed me on the cheek and stood up.

"Go on to sleep, honey," she said. "Do you want a night light on?"

"No, I like the dark," I said. Sometimes I could actually remember what my dad looked like in the dark.

✦

The next morning I slowed my pace as I approached the kitchen. My mom was on the phone, and I wanted to listen. She was talking about my dad.

"I mean it's bad enough that he couldn't stay with me, but I can't believe he dumped David. Vanessa, it was heartbreaking. He asked me if I believed his father loved him."

I felt bad about breaking her heart. "Mom," I called to let her know I was coming. I didn't want to hear anymore.

"Good morning, David," she said. "I've got to go, Vanessa. I'll see you tomorrow night."

"Are you going out with Vanessa tomorrow night?" I asked. Vanessa was Mom's best friend. They'd known each other since high school. I liked her okay. She was a lot of fun, but she talked loud and sometimes the things she talked about were embarrassing. Like her period or her vibrator. I didn't know anything about periods and vibrators, but I could tell they were embarrassing subjects because my mom always shushed her.

"Actually, I have a date. Vanessa's boyfriend has a friend that's visiting from out of town. I'm going to have dinner with them. Uncle Jeff said you could stay at his house."

"Okay." I wished they would consult me. I didn't sleep that well at Uncle Jeff's house. He lived in a big three bedroom apartment over the plant nursery he owned. There was a display of ponds with waterfalls outside my window. It always made me feel like I had to pee. I was afraid to go to sleep because I'd be really embarrassed if I peed in the bed. I was always tired the next day at school.

It's funny, I thought. I slept fine by the waterfall, once I settled down anyway. I did really have to pee when I got up in the morning though.

"Do I have time for cereal?"

"No, we got up a little late so I have a breakfast bar and a juice box for you to eat in the car on the way."

"Okay." I got my school bag and went to the garage. Mom pulled the car out and we headed down the road.

"My first appointment is at nine, so I'll have time to drop the disposable camera to be developed before I go in." Mom worked as a seamstress. She had a little room in the back of the dry cleaning store up the street from the school. She did all her measuring and stuff there. Then she could do all her sewing at home. That way she didn't have to get a sitter for me.

✦

"Hey, Jimmy," I called as I got out of the car. "Bye, Mom," I said over my shoulder. I heard her say goodbye to me.

"Hey, David," Jimmy was getting off the bus. "How was the backpacking trip?"

"It was great! We saw a rattlesnake and a bear. I can't wait to show you the pictures."

"Cool, I've seen bears but I haven't ever seen a rattlesnake. Did it shake it's rattle at you?" Jimmy was always excited about things like that. That's one reason why I liked him so much.

"No, but that had to be a rattle on the end of his tail. You'll see when the pictures are developed." We walked into the door of the school and down the hall to our classroom. I was really glad we were in the same class this year. Last year we were in different classes and we hardly got to see each other at all. We were in the second grade.

"My Uncle Jeff said he'd join the scout troop with me," I whispered to Jimmy as we sat down at the table we shared with two other kids.

"Good, I'll tell my dad to call him."

Mrs. Brown, our teacher, cleared her throat. "We'll get started as soon as James Parnell and David Landrum have finished their conversation."

I smiled at Jimmy and we looked at the front of the room. Mrs. Brown always singled out a couple of people like that. The whole class was talking, but I guess that was just how she got our attention. I was tempted to keep talking since we hadn't exactly finished our conversation, but she might not think it was funny.

✦

At lunch Jimmy and I sat with some of the other kids that were in the troop.

"David's joining the troop with his uncle," Jimmy announced.

"Good," Rick Dillon said.

"I don't see why you didn't join before," Matt Colburn said. "I'm a member of the troop, and I don't have a dad." Matt's father died in a war.

"I have a dad." I felt defensive but I didn't know why. "He just doesn't live here. He lives somewhere up north. He looks just like my Uncle Jeff. They're identical twins."

"So we could have seen him and thought it was your uncle," Rick said.

"Yeah." I just wanted to change the subject.

"David, why did you quit soccer?" Matt asked. "The team was much better with you. We don't have a goal tender now. Nobody else is very good at it."

"I got tired of playing in the goal."

"If we promise to let you play forward sometimes will you come back?" This was Jimmy. He'd been trying to get me to come back to the team since I quit two years ago.

"Then your uncle could come back too. He was a good coach."

"He's joining scouts with me. I don't want to ask for too much of his time," I said. The truth was I didn't want Uncle Jeff to coach the team. I wasn't sure why, but I didn't. "Besides, there is no way he'd let me play forward."

"Well, come back without him," Jimmy said. "We really need you, David."

I was glad they wanted me, but I didn't know how I could go back without hurting Uncle Jeff's feelings. "I'll think about it."

◎

Mom was standing by the car when I walked through the doors of the school that afternoon. She waved and I started in her direction.

"My mom says your mom is a Amazon," Darla Bergquist said as I passed her on the walk way.

"She is not!" I turned around and scowled at her. "She's just tall and she doesn't slump."

"My mom says your dad left her for my Aunt Sharon because she was so big he was afraid of her."

"Your mom needs to shut up," I said and hurried past her to the car.

"Was that Darla Bergquist?" Mom asked when I got to the car.

"Yeah."

"You know your dad is married to her aunt," she said. "She looks like her aunt a little. She's a pretty girl."

"I think she looks like a duck, an ugly duck."

"That's not a nice thing to say, David." My mom patted my knee. "Is she mean to you or something?"

"I don't care what she says." I looked out the window hoping we could change the subject.

"You know when a girl is mean to a boy in school it usually means she likes him."

"Ahhhhh." I slumped down in my seat and covered my head with my book bag.

"You can't even see the snake." I was so disappointed. We'd picked up the pictures. I'd flipped through until I got to the one of the snake. It blended into the dirt and the leaves on the side of the trail. I had to really concentrate to see it.

"I can definitely see the rattle though." Mom pointed to the picture. The snake's tail was the only part that was still on the trail and the rattle was clear.

"You could blow that up and frame it. I think it would be a pretty cool picture."

"How could I blow it up?"

"I was at the camera shop this afternoon. They can do it for you." Mom pulled a package off the back seat. "I was going to wrap this up for you when we got home, but I guess this is a good time to give it to you."

She put the package in my lap and smiled at me. "It's a belated birthday present. It was on lay-a-way. I just couldn't quite get it paid for in time for your birthday."

I opened the bag and looked in. It was a camera. There was a case with a strap that I could wear around my neck. There was also a strap that I could attach to a back pack.

"I thought it would be good for your backpacking trips. It's digital," she said. "You can view the pictures as soon as you take them. If it's not good you can snap another one. I guess with wildlife you might not get the chance to snap it twice, but sometimes you will."

"Thanks, Mom." I stretched my arms out and hugged her.

"You're welcome. You can also edit the pictures on a computer." She started the car and backed out of the parking space. "Unfortunately, the computer will be on lay-a-way for a while longer."

"That's okay," I said. I was looking at the directions and turning the beautiful thing over in my hand. "This is great. Uncle Jeff has a computer. I hope he has the editing software."

"I hope so, but if he doesn't the guy at the camera shop says he'll be happy to help you if you need it. He says he can show you how to use the camera too."

"I can probably get most of the info I need from the directions."

"You're so smart, David." Mom patted my knee again. "Do you have a lot of homework?"

"I had a lot, but I finished most of it in study hall."

"Do you have study hall every day?"

"I usually do. They call it study hall when the kids that don't need help can do their homework while the kids that do need help get it. Some kids need more help."

"I'll bet you hardly ever do." Mom smiled.

"No, but Jimmy does. He just has a hard time understanding the directions. If I can tell him what to do he can usually do it. He just can't seem to understand directions if he has to read them."

"Do you help him?"

"As much as I can, Mrs. Brown doesn't like it when I talk in class."

"I guess not." She pulled the car into the driveway and opened the one car garage. "I was thinking we'd go to the deli and pick up some sandwiches for dinner. We can take Pepper to the dog park. He needs to stretch his legs."

"Okay." I jumped out of the car and went into the kitchen. Mom followed me. "I'll just take my book bag upstairs and finish up one little thing I need for school tomorrow. Then we can go."

"You don't cook much, do you, Mom?" I asked as we ate our sandwiches on the park bench at the dog park.

"I made hamburgers last night."

"Yeah, and your tuna casserole is good, but we do eat a lot of deli food." Mom looked down at her sandwich. She looked sad. I didn't mean to make her sad." That's okay," I said. "I like deli food."

"It's probably not the healthiest diet."

"It's pretty good." Me and my big mouth, I thought. "I mean we always get wheat bread."

"Why did you bring it up, David?" she asked.

"No reason. Mom, does it look like Pepper is limping to you?" I was glad for a reason to change the subject, but Pepper was favoring his back right leg.

She hesitated for a minute. Then she looked at Pepper approaching the bench. "It does. Do you suppose he hurt himself running around?"

"A couple of times lately in the yard he's limped too." I got up and went to examine Pepper's back right leg. "It's swollen down here." Mom looked at the leg and felt around the joint.

"You're right. I'd better take him to the vet. I'll call tomorrow and make an appointment."

✧

"Uncle Jeff is picking you up, remember?" Mom said as she dropped me at school the next morning.

"Yeah," I gathered my back pack. It was heavier than usual because it had my overnight stuff in it too. "Mom, don't forget to call about Pepper. Do you think you can take him today?"

"I don't think it's necessary, honey. I'm booked solid today. If it seemed urgent I'd cancel something, but I don't think I need to. Tomorrow will be soon enough. I'll make an afternoon appointment so you can come with me."

"Okay, good," I said. I hated worrying about my dog. He hadn't limped again since the day before. He was probably fine, but we needed to check it out. "I'd like to go along."

"Okay, I'll pick you up after school tomorrow afternoon. I love you, David."

I let her kiss my cheek then left the car. I hurried through the door of the school to try to catch up to Jimmy, but he was already in the classroom by the time I got there.

"You were almost late," he whispered to me as I sat down.

"I had to say goodbye to my mom. I'm staying at Uncle Jeff's tonight."

Mrs. Brown said, "When Darla Bergquist and Teresa Blake have finished their conversation, we'll get started."

The class became silent.

"The first thing on the list this morning is testing for the challenge program," she said. "I have three excellent students on my list. I know the whole class will be very proud of them."

Everyone was quiet when she called out the names. The challenge program was for the best students so they didn't get board when the other kids were doing ordinary stuff. Everyone wanted to be in it.

"Darla Bergquist," Mrs. Brown said and Darla made a squealing sound and ran to the front of the room. "Teresa Blake," Mrs. Brown continued. "... and David Landrum."

I waited, hoping by some chance she would call James Parnell next. But she didn't call anymore names. I looked at Jimmy. He was smiling sadly.

"That's great, David." He laughed. "I don't know how I'm going to make it without you though."

"It's only an hour in the morning, Jimmy. We'll be in class together the rest of the time."

"Hurry up, David. We only get the state testing once a year." Mrs. Brown said. "If you don't get it today your mother will have to pay for it separately or you'll have to wait another year."

"I'll be back by lunch." I told Jimmy as I got up to go down the hall to the counseling center.

✦

"So how was the testing?" Jimmy asked when we sat down to lunch. "Is the psychologist nice?"

"Yeah, she's really small though. I think she was shorter than me."

"She was shorter than you," Darla said. "And that makes her a midget because you're the smallest boy in the second grade."

"I am not." What was Darla's thing about how tall people were? I could feel it coming, she was about to call my mother an Amazon again.

"It's hard to believe you're so short when your mother and uncle are giants."

"Leave him alone, Darla," Teresa said. "Why are you so nasty to him?"

"Everybody knows he's white trash," Darla said.

"White trash," I repeated. I could feel a lump forming in my throat. I willed the tears to stay out of sight.

"My mom says the only reason you're here is because your mom tried to trap my Uncle Brian. She says …"

"Darla!" Mrs. Brown said from the front of the cafeteria. "I can hear your voice all the way up here. I suggest you mind what you say."

"Don't pay any attention to anything she says," Jimmy said. "I can't stand that girl. Nobody can."

I took a gulp of my milk and rubbed at my eyes. The words 'white trash' were bouncing around in my head. I didn't know what they meant, but they didn't sound good.

"Anyway," Jimmy continued. "I have to go to have testing this afternoon, me and Meryl Johnson."

"… For challenge?" I perked up. Maybe if Jimmy was with me it wouldn't be so bad having to be with Darla.

"No." He looked down at his plate and pushed the food around with his fork. "For special ed. Mrs. Brown thinks I might have learning disabilities."

"Did she say that?"

"No, she didn't have to. Why else would I need special ed?"

"You do okay when I help you. It's just the directions you have trouble with."

"Yeah, but they won't let you help me. Anyway, with you in Challenge in the morning you won't be able to help me."

"How was your day, David?" Uncle Jeff asked when he picked me up that afternoon.

"Not too good." I buckled my seat belt and sighed.

"Wow. That was a deep sigh. Do you want to talk about it?"

"Yeah."

"Okay, tell me what happened."

"Well, I got tested for the challenge program first thing in the morning."

"Really? That's a good thing isn't it? Don't they do all sorts of fun projects and go on field trips?"

"Yes, but Jimmy didn't get tested for challenge. He got tested for special ed classes. The teacher thinks he has learning disabilities." I looked out the window and leaned my forehead on the glass. "So if I go to challenge in the morning and he goes to special ed in the afternoon, we'll hardly see each other at all anymore. We might as well be in different classes like we were last year."

"I'm sorry. I know you and Jimmy are good friends."

"Yeah, at least we can still eat lunch together. Only we have to sit with Darla Bergquist. She says I'm white trash."

"She says what?" Uncle Jeff stopped the car at a red light and turned to look at me.

"She says I'm white trash. Mom says Dad is married to her aunt. Her mother says bad things about Mom."

"What bad things does she say about your mom?"

"Just bad stuff."

"You don't want to tell me?"

"I don't want to say it."

"You don't have to." Uncle Jeff turned back to the road when the light turned green. "Should I call the girl's parents or something, David? I don't want her saying things about you like that. Your mom's a great lady and you're a great kid."

"Thanks, Uncle Jeff, but I don't really care what she says. I just wish Jimmy and I weren't going to be separated so much in school. He's really smart, Uncle Jeff. I don't know why he has so much trouble."

"Well, maybe they can help him."

"Maybe." I doubted it.

"Maybe the test will show that he doesn't have learning disabilities."

"It won't. I'm sure he does."

"Maybe you won't make challenge."

"No such luck." I yawned. "I aced that test."

Uncle Jeff laughed and patted my leg. "You're so modest, David."

"I'm not sure what modest means, but it's true. I did ace that test. What are we having for dinner?"

"I was thinking I'd grill some salmon and corn on the cob. How does that sound? We could have a nice salad."

"I've never had salmon. I'm not that crazy about fish. I like corn on the cob okay, but I'm not eating salad."

"What do you feel like eating tonight, David?"

"Do you know how to cook?"

"I can follow a recipe. Why?" Uncle Jeff smiled over at me as he pulled into the garage at the nursery.

"I had turkey meat loaf at Jimmy's once when I stayed for dinner. Do you think you could make that?"

"I'm sure between the two of us we can. I can get a recipe off the internet then we'll go to the store and buy the ingredients."

We both got out of the car and went up the stairs to the apartment above. Uncle Jeff sat down at the computer in the kitchen. "I'll start looking for a recipe. What else do you want?"

"How about cheese potatoes and spinach soufflé," I said.

Uncle Jeff looked at me and raised his eyebrows. "You won't eat salad but you'll eat spinach."

"…spinach soufflé."

He laughed and turned back to the computer. "Go on to your room and freshen up, then we'll go to the supermarket."

"Remember last weekend when I said, now that I know you love me I can tell you things you might not like."

He turned around again and looked at me seriously. "What is it, David?"

"Sleeping in the room next to that fountain display makes me feel like I'm going to pee in the bed."

"Oh no!" He grabbed hold of me and pulled me onto his lap. "So you decided not to sleep." He laughed and tickled my belly.

I laughed. I didn't mind it this time. I usually did.

"I wondered why you always look so tired in the morning. I can turn off the fountains, but would you like to move across the hall to the back bedroom? That way you don't even have to think about those fountains."

"That would be great." I squirmed out of his hold and ran down the hall.

That was the night I discovered how much I liked to cook. Uncle Jeff and I found recipes for easy cheesy potatoes and Moroccan turkey meat loaf. We bought frozen spinach soufflé at the supermarket. We collected the ingredients. Then we took turns reading the directions and putting them together. The meal was fantastic. I decided that my first scout badge would be the cooking badge. Uncle Jeff could help. He wasn't half bad in the kitchen.

I slipped into the front seat of the car and into Mom's waiting arms the next day when she picked me up. She always seemed to miss me a lot when I'd been away from her for a while. I kissed her on the cheek then looked around to see if any of the other kids were watching.

"I waited down here by this tree so nobody would see me hug you, David." Mom laughed. She started the car and we moved away from the school.

"Thanks." I smiled and looked out the window.

"I talked to Uncle Jeff this morning. He told me about the testing. I'm very proud of you, David. You're so smart and you've adjusted so well."

"Adjusted to what?"

She looked at me seriously for a second. "Everything …"

To not having a father is what she meant. I continued to look out the window. "Anyway," I said. "Didn't you know about that testing? Didn't you have to sign something?" Sometimes it bothered me the way Mom and Uncle Jeff talked about me when I wasn't there, like they were comparing notes.

"Yes, remember, we talked about it right after Christmas break. It just kind of slipped my mind. I couldn't afford private testing so we had to wait for the school psychologist."

"It doesn't matter. I won't go into the challenge program until next year anyway. Mrs. Brown told us that today. I'm glad. Jimmy and I may not even be in the same class next year."

"Uncle Jeff told me about Jimmy too. I'm sorry you guys can't spend more time together in school. But now that you're joining scouts you'll see plenty of each other."

"What else did Uncle Jeff tell you?" I asked. I was feeling irritated. I don't talk about them behind their backs, I thought.

"Nothing." She glanced at me. "Is there something else to tell?"

"Well, we cooked dinner together last night." I was glad he hadn't told her about Darla poop head Bergquist. Jimmy and I had named her that at lunch today. We called her P.H. to her face.

"Really? What did you make?"

"We had Moroccan Turkey Meat Loaf, Easy Cheesy Potatoes, and Spinach Soufflé. I chose the menu. I had it at Jimmy's house once."

"Spinach Soufflé, I thought you didn't eat things that were green." We pulled into the driveway and stopped. "I'm just going to run in and get Pepper. We have an appointment at the vet in half an hour. Do you need to go to the bathroom or anything?"

"Yeah, and I think I'll take my pack upstairs too." I ran into the house. When I got back Mom was standing beside the car, and Pepper was in the back seat. He looked huge back there. Mom's car was small and the dog was big.

I locked the front door. We got into the car and drove away. I had to hold Pepper's collar over the back of the seat. He always wanted to crawl into Mom's lap.

✧

"Bone cancer ..." Mom sounded confused. We were looking at an x-ray on a lighted box. The doctor was a small woman with dark skin and black hair. She pointed to the leg bone. "You see all this irregularity here. That's the tumor breaking down the bone."

"Can you do anything? What does it mean?"

"Unfortunately, this kind of cancer moves pretty fast. It has probably already spread to the lymphatic system. There is chemotherapy for dogs. But it's very expensive, and we haven't had much luck with it. We could remove the leg. In most dogs that gives them another six months to a year of quality life. It would be worth it I think, except that we have another problem."

"We have another problem?" Mom's voice sounded far away. My ears were ringing.

"He has hip dysplasia." The doctor took down the x-ray and put up another one. She pointed at it. "If I take off one of the legs it's going to put so much more pressure on the other hip I don't think his quality of life would be very good."

Mom put her face in the soft fur of Pepper's neck. Her shoulders shook. I knew she was crying. I could feel the lump in my throat wanting to burst out. My eyes hurt and my nose wanted to run. I sniffed but I didn't cry.

"What should we do?" Mom's voice was muffled because she kept her face buried in Pepper's neck.

"Well, I can give him something for pain and you can take him home. If he's already limping he's probably pretty uncomfortable, but we can help him for a few days at least. When his quality of life is gone I think you should put him to sleep."

"A few days," Mom said.

"I'm sorry," the doctor said. She went to the door of the exam room. I'll give you a few minutes to digest it, and if you have any questions I'll be glad to answer them." She left the room. I put my arms around my mom and my dog. The lump in my throat didn't hurt so much now. I didn't cry.

"Eggs Florentine?" Mom sat up in the bed and leaned against a cushion. I had been up for an hour cooking her breakfast in bed. It was Mother's Day, and it was more than a week since Pepper's diagnosis. He was doing great.

"Yep," I said as I climbed up on the king size bed beside Mom. I had put a bed tray over her lap. I sat cross legged next to her. "I got the recipe out of a cookbook in the library at school."

"I can't believe you did this all by yourself."

"Uncle Jeff took me to the supermarket to get the stuff I needed." I cut a bite of the portion I had brought up for myself and put it in my mouth.

Mom took a bite of hers and said, "Mmmmm ... honey, this is delicious. Who'd have thought you would be such a good cook. I can't even boil water."

"You could if you wanted to. You just don't like to cook. I do."

"That's a really good attitude, David. You're so smart." She took another bite. "I'm still amazed that you like spinach so much. I never thought to try to feed it to you. I thought all kid's hated spinach."

"I still don't think I'd want to eat it in a salad." We laughed and looked at Pepper. He was lying at the foot of the bed. Mom always said she had to have a king size bed. You couldn't sleep with a full size Afghan in anything smaller. His nose was in the air, and he was sniffing at the yummy smells coming from the tray.

"I think the doctor was wrong," I said. "He still chases the ball even if he does have to run on three legs."

"She wasn't wrong, honey," Mom said. "We have to be grateful for every minute we have with him."

"I know." I stroked his furry head.

"I don't suppose you'll let me do the dishes," Mom said.

"Nope, but I have another surprise for you." I got down from the bed and lifted the empty tray. "Stay where you are."

I returned to the room a few minutes later with a steaming mug of espresso. "Uncle Jeff bought you a fancy coffee maker." I grinned and handed her the mug.

"He did? Why would he do that? I'm not his mother."

"He said you're the mother of his favorite nephew." I grinned. I loved it when Uncle Jeff called me that.

"He's so good to us." She sipped at the coffee. "It's delicious. I guess the machine froths the milk."

"Yeah, it's really cool." Pepper got up and jumped off the bed. He landed with a thud and disappeared below the edge of the comforter. Mom and I looked at each other, and I scrambled to the end of the bed.

"Oh no!" I screamed. He lay on the floor big brown eyes painful. His leg was bent at a wrong angle and the skin was broken. I could see the edge of the bone. I thought I was going to throw up at first. I swallowed a couple of times and scrambled to the floor to hold him still. He struggled to get up for a few seconds then relaxed with his head in my lap.

"Mom," I said surprising myself with how calm I sounded. She was on her hands and knees next to me. "Call Uncle Jeff and ask him to help us get Pepper to the car. It's time to let him go."

By the time Uncle Jeff arrived Mom had wrapped the bleeding leg in a towel. We had given him a double dose of pain medication. As stoic as he was, he couldn't hide the pain in his eyes. I hadn't moved from my spot in front of him. Pepper's head was still in my lap. Mom was sitting beside me. She had cried softly ever since Pepper fell. We heard Uncle Jeff come in the front door and up the stairs to the bedroom. My throat was trying hard to break open, but I swallowed it back.

"I'm sorry, Uncle Jeff," I said when he appeared in the doorway looking concerned. "I know you don't like dogs, but we need your help."

"Don't worry about me, David. I'm glad you called." Uncle Jeff came over to us. I was seated at Pepper's head. Uncle Jeff put his arms under Pepper's body and gently lifted him up. "We can put him in the back of my truck," he said.

"I'll have to ride back there with him." I stayed at Peppers head, supporting it and stroking it with my hands as we rose. My legs were stiff from sitting cross legged for so long, but I forced them to straighten out.

"Put him in my car. I don't want David riding in the back of a truck," Mom said.

"Alright." Uncle Jeff and I carried the dog down the steps. Pepper looked at me with eyes that said he knew he was going to die. He licked my face while I looked at him. I think he was worried about me. I swallowed and let go of his head only when Uncle Jeff had to lower him into the back seat. I hurried around the car and slid in. I pulled his head into my lap and started to stroke him. He looked up at me, then closed his eyes and sighed deeply. I think the pain pills were working.

It was only when Mom got into the passenger seat dressed in shorts and a t-shirt that I remembered I was wearing my pajamas.

"I have to get dressed."

"You look fine," Uncle Jeff said.

Mom looked back at me and studied my face for a few seconds. "You go ahead, David. I'll comfort Pepper while you're gone."

We had to go to the emergency clinic. It was Sunday and our regular vet wasn't open. It's all a kind of blur to me. Uncle Jeff laid Pepper on a table in an exam room. Then he stepped back the corner of the room.

Mom and I stood at Pepper's head while the doctor inserted a syringe full of pink stuff into his front leg. Mom cried and I gulped. My stomach was starting to hurt from swallowing so much air, but I was not going to cry.

Pepper licked me on the cheek then breathed real deep one time and went limp. He was dead. I knew he was dead. Mom started to cry and buried her face in his coat. Suddenly I had to get out of that room. I kissed Pepper one last time and ran.

I made it to the car with only a couple of tears spilling over. I scrubbed at my eyes and took several deep breaths. I was feeling light headed. I knew the car was locked and I couldn't get in. Then I heard the doors unlock and looked back at the clinic. Uncle Jeff stood just inside the door with the keyless remote.

I jumped into the front passenger seat as if it gave me privacy. It didn't. I willed the tears away and the lump in my throat to ease. It did and I looked over at Uncle Jeff.

He came out of the door and went to the driver's side of the car. "There's nothing wrong with crying over the loss of your dog, David," he said as he slid into the seat.

"I decided …" I had to stop to clear my throat.

"…Not to cry?" he said.

"...To be strong for Mom."

He put his hand on my arm and I pulled away. I didn't want anyone to be nice to me right now. I was only barely under control.

"You can't just decide not to live, David. You have to breathe, you need to sleep, and sometimes you have to cry."

I looked out the window. Mom was walking toward the car. Her eyes were red and her head was bowed.

I decided not to talk.

CHAPTER THREE

When I was ten years old my dad came to visit me.

Mom came to my room with her big black and tan Afghan hound. He looked exactly like Pepper. About a month after Pepper died she went to some rescue place and got a full grown Afghan with exactly the same markings as Pepper. Then she named him Pepper. It was the biggest argument we'd ever had before.

"You can't replace Pepper!" I shouted. It was the closest I had come to crying since he'd died. So I got really mad and the tears went away.

"I'm not trying to replace him, David. I want to remember him. If I have one just like him named the same thing it almost feels like he's still with me."

"That's not him. That dog doesn't have the same personality at all."

"You haven't spent one minute with this dog. You haven't given him a chance." Mom and I were in the kitchen after school.

"I told you I didn't want another dog." I packed up my books to take them upstairs.

"Well, I can't be happy without a dog. David, the world doesn't revolve around you. I deserve a little happiness too." She was mad now.

"I'll leave if you name that dog Pepper. I mean it. I'll go live with Uncle Jeff."

"You can't live with Uncle Jeff. He doesn't have any legal claim on you."

"Then I'll go live with Dad!"

"David he hasn't contacted you in …" She broke off the sentence and turned away, but it was too late. I knew she was telling me my dad didn't want me. I stormed out of the kitchen and up the steps. I slammed the door to my room behind me.

A few minutes Mom knocked on my door. "David, I'm sorry. I was mean to you and I shouldn't have been. Can I come in?"

"He has too contacted me," I said, but I didn't invite her in. "I get birthday and Christmas cards."

"Please let me come in, David."

"Okay." I sat on my bed with a shoe box full of greeting cards. "This one wasn't even for a birthday or Christmas." I held up a card. "He was just thinking about me."

"I'm sure he misses you very much. I'm really sorry, David." Mom sat down on the bed beside me. "The thing is. It hurts my feelings that you don't want me to have a dog. I love dogs. I'm just not happy without one in my life."

"I don't care about the dog, Mom. Just please don't name him Pepper."

"What should I name him then?"

"I don't care."

"Okay, I'll think of something." She put her arm across my shoulders. "Please forgive me, David."

"Okay." I kissed her cheek and she hugged me.

"Good, I'm taking him to the groom shop today. He has to be shaved down. He's all matted. Then you can help me keep his coat free of tangles. Won't that be nice? You know how you loved to brush Pepper."

"I'm not brushing that dog, Mom. He's your dog. You brush him."

"Okay." She kissed the top of my head and stood up.

"I'm sorry, Mom." I didn't look up at her.

Anyway, when I was ten years old she came to my room with her big stupid dog named Ruffles. It was a stupid name for a stupid dog. He wasn't anything like Pepper in any way but color. I wouldn't admit it to Mom, of course, but stupid dogs can be fun too. I mean, it wasn't his fault Pepper died.

"David, you're not going to believe who I just talked to on the phone."

I was sitting at the computer that Uncle Jeff had given me for my birthday a few months ago. I was editing a picture I'd taken on our last backpacking trip with the scouts. I had an album of all my trips into the woods. The ones I did with just Uncle Jeff and the ones we did with the troop.

"Who did you talk to?" I asked.

"Your dad!"

"Dad!" I turned around. "Why couldn't I talk to him?"

"You will. He wanted to run something by me first. He'll call back tonight to talk to you."

"Is he coming to see me?" For some reason my hands started to shake and my mouth went dry. I put my hand on my chest. I could feel my heart beat through my ribs.

"Yes he is." Mom smiled. She looked happy. She usually looked a little bit sad, even when she smiled. "He's coming to town for two weeks this summer. He wants to spend some time with his parents. They're getting a little old to travel up to see him anymore."

"Is his ... family coming?" I wasn't sure if I wanted them to or not.

"They'll be with him for the first week. Then they'll go back, and he's going to take you to Disney World. If it's okay with you that is."

I looked at her. She seemed happy about it. "Will you go with us?"

"No, he wants time with you alone, but he's coming to breakfast the day that you leave for Florida. The three of us can have a little time together then."

"Will you be glad to see him?"

"Of course I will." I'd never seen her look so pleased. For the first time I could remember I was mad at my dad.

"Do you still love him?"

She laughed. "You can't just stop loving someone. Not when you loved him as much as I loved your dad."

Then I remembered another time when I was mad at him. I couldn't have been more than a toddler, but I remembered my mother's sobs.

"I'm going to walk Ruffles. Do you want to come with me?" Mom headed for the door.

"No thanks, I want to finish up here." I turned back to the computer. When she had left the roo
m I closed my eyes and tried to remember what my Dad looked like. All I could see was Uncle Jeff.

✦

"Charlie, you should have said no." Uncle Jeff was in the kitchen talking to Mom. He'd come to pick me up to go visit Gramma and Grampa. My Dad was going to be there. Aunt Jeanne would be there too. Dad always stayed with Aunt Jeanne when he came. I wondered why he didn't stay with Uncle Jeff. When he didn't bring his family, I mean.

The assisted living complex was having a pie baking contest. I had baked my lemon chess pie. Mom said my Dad was bringing his famous pecan pie. Maybe that's where I got my love for cooking. The thought made me smile.

"I couldn't say no, Jeff. We have joint custody. He sends his child support on time every month. He even sends extra at birthdays and Christmas."

"Joint custody ..." Uncle Jeff said. "That's a laugh. How many times has he seen David in the last eight years?"

"I'm sure Brian has reasons for the way he handles David."

"Yeah, he has reasons. He a selfish ..."

"Jeff," Mom interrupted him. "Please don't talk about Brian like that. David might hear you."

I always heard them. I snuck up on them so they didn't know I was there. Otherwise they'd just talk behind my back.

"I'm sorry." Uncle Jeff sounded like he really was sorry. "I just hate what David must think."

"Maybe Brian can help with that. He's going to spend a whole week alone with him in Florida."

"I'm worried about that too," Uncle Jeff said. "How is Brian qualified to take care of David? He doesn't know anything about him. He doesn't know that he gets car sick when he sleeps in a car. He doesn't know what he likes to eat."

"He'll learn. He has two children with Sharon. He knows about kids."

"You're alright with this aren't you?"

"Yes, I can't wait to see Brian again."

I interrupted them at this point. I was ready for them to know I was there. "I'm ready to go, Uncle Jeff," I said as I came into the kitchen.

"Let's go then." He turned around and smiled at me. "Where's the pie?"

"Here it is." Mom took it out of the refrigerator and handed it to me. "Good luck."

My Dad won the contest. His pie was better than mine, but I was happy. I got second place and Gramma and Grampa were so proud of both of us. Aunt Jeanne brought a blueberry pie. She didn't place. I would have felt sorry for her, but she didn't seem to even care.

When we first got to the retirement place where Gramma and Grampa lived we left the pie in the dining hall and went upstairs to their apartment. When we went through the door I was almost afraid to look.

My Dad stood at the window looking at my Gramma. I don't remember even seeing anyone else in that room. I know Aunt Jean was there with Uncle Bill. Grampa was there somewhere, but I didn't see them. Dad turned and looked at me and my heart started to pound.

"Brian," Uncle Jeff said. He didn't sound too happy, but he extended his hand, and my dad shook it.

Then he looked at me. I was suddenly aware that I was standing behind Uncle Jeff. "David, son," Dad said. "Come here and give your old man a hug." I stepped in front, of Uncle Jeff. It was only then that I realized he had his hand on my shoulder. I was glad, but when Dad held out his arms to me, I moved into them and buried my face in his shirt.

I couldn't believe how much he looked like Uncle Jeff. I couldn't see any difference at first. Then as I kept my face buried in his shoulder I realized that he was softer than Uncle Jeff, and he smelled like cologne. Uncle Jeff always smelled like fresh air and dirt. Clean dirt, I thought, and smiled at the contradiction in terms.

When I was sure I had control and wouldn't embarrass myself by crying, I looked back at Uncle Jeff. My Dad was holding me off the ground like a child. Uncle Jeff had a strange look on his face. When I looked back at my Dad there were tears on his cheeks.

"Oh, David, I've missed you so much." He wiped at his eyes. "You know I've thought about you every day, every single day. You look great."

"Why am I so small?" I asked. I had no idea why. I didn't even know I was thinking that.

"Don't you worry about that, David," Gramma said. "Jeffrey and Brian were the smallest kids in their class too. Then when they turned about twelve years old they shot up like trees. Now come and give your Gramma a kiss."

I didn't want to kiss her this time. She had something gooey on her cheek. I made sure to kiss the other cheek. Then we went down to the dining hall. They were both in wheel chairs now. Grampa had a stroke about a year ago. He couldn't talk or walk anymore. Gramma didn't say anything about Uncle Jeff's weak chin and big ears this time, but I looked to see if it was true. The only difference I could see between them was Uncle Jeff's flat belly and Dad's sloping shoulders.

"I liked your pie better," Uncle Jeff said on the way home. "The judges were residents. Old people don't have good taste buds."

"Dad's pie was good." I smiled at him.

"You're a good sport, David."

"You don't have a weak chin and big ears, Uncle Jeff."

"Thanks, buddy roe." He squeezed my leg. "I appreciate you telling me that." He put his hand back on the steering wheel. "So how was your first visit with your dad in eight years?"

"It was good. I think he must love me like he says. He cried when we hugged." I could feel the corners of my mouth pulling up. It felt good to know he cared enough to cry.

"Of course he loves you. He'd be a fool not to."

"I always had the feeling you thought he was a fool." I could feel him looking at me. I kept my face turned away.

"I never meant to give you the feeling your father didn't love you," he said. "David." He put his hand on my arm when I didn't say anything. "Talk to me."

"It's okay, Uncle Jeff. I know you didn't mean that." I looked at him and smiled. "Anyway, I had a great day. I think I must have inherited my love of cooking from Dad."

"I guess so," Uncle Jeff said. He didn't sound very happy.

"How come Dad's family wasn't there?"

"He said they went home yesterday."

"I wonder why I didn't get to meet them. They hadn't been here a week. I thought they were going to stay a week."

"He said they had the chicken pox. He didn't want to expose you. That's why they had to shorten their trip."

"I had the chicken pox in the first grade. I don't think you can get it twice."

"I guess they just didn't feel well enough to meet a bunch of new people."

"I'm their brother," I said. My mood was going south. "Is he ashamed of me?"

"David, I have no idea why your dad does the things he does. But I'm sure he feels like he's doing the right thing. I'm sure he isn't ashamed of you."

"Okay,"

"Anyway, you won second prize. I can't wait to show your mom the ribbon."

"Yeah, and I saved a piece of Dad's pecan pie too. She'll be happy about that. She says it's her favorite besides my lemon. I need to find a recipe for pecan pie." I was trying to cheer up. After all, starting tomorrow I'd have my dad all to myself for a whole week.

"I'll bet your dad would share his with you."

"Yeah, I bet he would." I hoped he would.

"My dad will be here any minute." I was talking to Jimmy on the phone. It was Monday morning and we were going to have breakfast at the pancake house, my dad, my mom, and me. I couldn't wait. It would be like a real family.

"I just wish you weren't going to miss practice this week. The team needs work with us losing two players this year," Jimmy said.

I'd started playing soccer again last year when I was nine. I confided in Mom about wanting to go back but not wanting to hurt Uncle Jeff's feelings. He never said anything to me about it. I guess she talked to him.

"I'll only miss one practice. The season doesn't begin for another month. We'll be alright."

"Do you think your dad would like to be assistant coach? When Mark and Matthew moved away their dad went with them."

"No, he has to go back to Chicago. That's where he lives." I looked out the window and saw the rental car pull into the driveway. "I got to go, Jimmy. He's here." I hurried down the steps to the front door where my bag was already waiting.

"I guess you're ready?" Dad said as I pulled the door open and bounced up and down with excitement.

"I'm ready."

"Where is your mother? We're taking her to breakfast before we go, remember?"

"Here I am." Mom came into the room. Her smile was kind of shy but very big. She seemed to be sparkling. I'd never seen her look so beautiful.

"Well, Charlotte." Dad put his hands on her shoulders and looked at her at arm's length. "You're still that gorgeous Amazon I fell head over heels for all those years ago." He hugged her, and I watched my mom's eyes close over his shoulder.

"It's good to see you again, Brian," she said. She looked at me as they stepped apart. "So what do you think of our fine boy?"

"He's as good looking as his mother, and a good boy too. You've done a great job, Charlotte."

"I think so. But he looks more like his father."

"I didn't know I was that good looking." Dad smiled and rubbed the top of my head. I didn't mind it as much when he did it. I wondered why it bothered me when Uncle Jeff did.

"You called Mom an Amazon," I said. I had been so insulted when Darla P. H. Bergquist called her an Amazon. It sounded like a good thing when Dad said it.

"How many times do you see a six foot one woman walk tall and proud and beautiful?" Dad opened the front door for us to go through in front of him. "Her height is something I've always admired about her."

It made me feel good to hear him say that. He wasn't afraid of my mother. I wasn't quite sure I understood why he'd left her, but I knew it wasn't because of her height.

After breakfast we took Mom home. Dad got out of the car and picked up my suitcase from the foyer. He took it to the trunk of the car while I said goodbye to Mom.

"Will you be alright here alone?" I asked feeling suddenly panicked. After all, I didn't really know that man. I looked back at the car.

"I'll be fine, honey," she said. "David, I trust him to take care of you. Otherwise I wouldn't have agreed to let you go."

"I know." I hugged her. "Mom, don't walk that stupid dog alone after dark." I said as my dad came over and kissed her on the cheek.

"He worries about me a little bit too much," she said to Dad. I was surprised to see her blush and look away. "Take care of him." She went into the house. I'm pretty sure she was about to cry.

"You take good care of your mother, David," Dad said as we drove away.

"I'm the man of the family," I said. I watched the houses go by as we moved down the road. Pretty soon the uneasiness of leaving home was replaced by the excitement of the trip. I was going to Disney World ... with my dad.

"We're here, David." Dad was standing outside my car door. I sat up and immediately regretted falling asleep in the car.

I remembered Uncle Jeff's comment about getting car sick when I sleep in a car. I was irritated that it was true. Well, I just wouldn't tell Dad. "Can I have a coke?" I asked.

"Your mom said no caffeine. How about some lemonade? I have some in the cooler." He opened the back door and poured a cup. "I'll go in and check us into the hotel while you wake up a little."

Uncle Jeff would have waved the caffeine rule, I thought as I sipped my lemonade. The sweet tart flavor did help some. I wished I had some peanut butter crackers.

"Here, David," Dad said as he slipped back into the driver's seat. "They had some ginger snaps in the hospitality basket." He handed me a package of cookies.

"I don't think I ever ate ginger snaps before."

"Try them. They'll settle your stomach."

"There's nothing wrong with my stomach." I pulled open the package and stuck a whole cookie into my mouth. It was sweet and tart too. I was feeling a lot better now.

"I know what it's like to wake up after sleeping in the car. I always feel a little sick when I do that."

"I don't." I denied it again. Was he just not listening?

"Really? You looked a little pale. I guess it was just from waking up so suddenly. Here we are." He pulled into a parking space and got out of the car. "We're on the third floor." He handed me a key card. "I got two so we don't have to be completely dependent on each other."

I took the card and stuck it in my back pocket.

"Okay, what do you want to do with the rest of this day?" Dad asked when we had settled into our hotel room. I had explored the bathroom, checked out the soaps and stuff and looked through the fridge and cupboards in our kitchenette.

"What time is it?"

"It's six thirty. We'll have to eat dinner, but I thought we might benefit by a dip in the pool first. What do you think?"

"Is there a beach in Orlando?"

"No, we're in the middle of Florida. I thought we'd hit the beach on the way home. Maybe drive up the coast and stay a night or two somewhere."

"Okay, the pool sounds good. I'm a good swimmer."

"I can tell you are by the look of you, David."

We swam for about an hour then went to dinner in the hotel restaurant.

"Are you tired?" Dad asked when we got back to the room.

"No, I slept in the car. Can we watch a movie?"

"We can," he said. "But I was thinking maybe you'd like to see pictures of your brother and sister. I brought an album and a home video."

He wanted to show off his other family to me. I felt that angry feeling I'd had before. Funny, when I didn't know my Dad at all I was never mad at him. I thought of the album I had of my backpacking trips with Uncle Jeff. I wondered how Dad would feel about me showing him that.

"Only if you want to David, we can watch a movie if you'd rather."

"No." I tried to smile. "I'd like to." I sat down on the couch in the room.

"Want some lemonade? I think I'll have a beer."

Maybe that's why your stomach isn't flat like Uncle Jeff's, I thought. Then I remembered that Uncle Jeff drank beer sometimes too. "Lemonade's good," I said.

"We'll skip by the wedding pictures." Dad turned a few pages quickly. "They're pretty boring." I noticed as he flipped through that his wife was very small, not fat but maybe a little plump. She looked like Darla P. H. Bergquist except she had curly hair instead of straight. It was just as blond as P. H.'s, and she had dimples in her cheeks like P. H. too. She is pretty, I thought, but nothing like my mother.

"Okay, here's Kristina. She's four years younger than you. She's six now. In this picture I think she was about three." Dad smiled down at a picture of a little girl with blond curly hair but no dimples in her cheeks. "She has her mother's coloring but she looks more like me, like you." He smiled at me.

I smiled back.

"Here she's five." He flipped a page and pointed to a picture that I could tell was taken at school. "And this is your brother Andrew." The picture was of a baby. All I noticed was that his eyes were puffy, and he didn't have any hair. "He was about an hour old here." Dad smiled at me again.

I smiled back.

"He's four now and such a handful. He keeps your stepmother running."

My stepmother, I thought.

"Let's look at the video," Dad said. "Last winter the pond on our property froze. Well it freezes every year. The pool is winterized so it doesn't get damaged. But the pond freezes so we're able to ice skate."

They have a pool, I thought. They have a pond. I thought about the townhouse that my mom and I called home, the tiny back yard that I'd thrown a ball for Pepper in. It's a good thing Ruffles is too stupid to learn how to play fetch, I thought.

I watched the video of the happy family skating on the iced pond in their back yard. Andrew had curly blond hair like his mother and sister now, but he looked more like my dad in the face. He was cute. I'd like to know him, but I wouldn't ask now. It would be fun to have a little brother. I'd talk to Dad at the end of the trip when we'd had a chance to get to know each other.

For the next three days we were kept very busy in the amusement parks. We went to the Magic Kingdom one day. We went back to the hotel to eat dinner and rest for a little while. Then we went back to the park to watch the fireworks.

45 / Grand Passion

Dad got me up early to go to The Epcot Center. It was not as fast paced as the Magic Kingdom, but I liked it. We went back that night too. I guess all the amusement parks have fireworks.

On the third day we went to the Animal Kingdom on a Kilimanjaro Safari. It was great. The animals just roam around, and we got to feed the giraffes and rhinos.

"Do you want to go back for the night time show?" Dad asked after we ate dinner at the hotel restaurant.

"Sure," I said. I was stretched out on the double bed I'd been sleeping in all week. There were two of them in the room. Dad slept in one. I slept in the other one. I was glad we didn't have to share a bed. I didn't know him that well.

I thought about how different he was from my Uncle Jeff. I slept in the same tent with Uncle Jeff all the time. Once when I got scared in the night I even crawled into his sleeping bag with him.

Dad stretched out on his bed too. "I think I'll take a little nap," he said. "You've worn me out, David."

In a minute he was snoring. I looked over at him while he slept. His head was slumped forward on the pillow. He had a double chin. I guess being a lawyer doesn't require as much muscle as being a landscaper, I thought. Uncle Jeff didn't have an ounce of fat on him.

Why am I comparing him to Uncle Jeff? I thought. That really isn't fair. He's my dad, and look what he's doing for me. We really had been having fun.

"Wake up, David." Dad's voice sounded far away. I really didn't want to see anymore fireworks. I really just wanted to sleep for a while.

"Why don't we skip the fireworks tonight, Uncle Jeff," I said, then opened my eyes in surprise. I called my dad Uncle Jeff.

"I'm your dad." Good, he was laughing. "Not your uncle," he said. "And guess what. We already skipped the fireworks. It's morning. We both slept all the way through the night."

I was suddenly aware that I really had to pee. I jumped up and ran to the bathroom. I just barely got the seat up in time. The bathroom smelled like poop, but I didn't care. What a relief.

"That had to be a world record," Dad said when I came out of the bathroom. "I wish I'd timed the length of that flow." He wasn't looking at me. He had his back turned, and he was buttoning his shirt. I was glad. I could feel my face turning red.

"Where are we going today?" I asked.

"I only got a three day pass to the amusement parks." Dad turned around and smiled. He went over to the sink in the dressing area and combed his hair. "I don't know about you, but I think I've done enough around here. I was thinking we'd drive up the coast a little. Find a little beach somewhere to spend the next two days."

"That sounds good to me too."

"Great!" He turned around. "I'm going to drink a cup of coffee while you take your shower. Then we'll pack up and check out. We can grab breakfast on the road."

<hr />

"I was thinking we'd go up the Atlantic coast. The gulf coast is farther from here. It'll be fun to drive along the ocean. There's no ocean in Illinois."

"There's an ocean in Georgia," I said. "But it's a long way from Atlanta."

"Do you go to the beach much?"

"We went last summer. Uncle Jeff and I hiked the length of Cumberland Island. We stayed three nights. Mom stayed with a friend on Jekyll Island. She doesn't really like to camp."

"No, I can't see your mother camping. I'll have to thank Jeff for being so good to you."

"He likes to do it." That angry feeling was stirring inside again.

"I know he does and I'm grateful."

"I am too," I looked out the window. The ocean had just come in sight. "Could I roll down the window for a while?"

"It's pretty hot out there, but I guess it would be alright for a while."

I rolled down the window and put my hand out in the wind. "The air always seems soft at the beach," I said.

"I know what you mean."

"Will we stop in time to swim in the surf?" I asked.

"I was thinking we'd drive to St. Augustine. I think we'll get there just after lunch time. We had a late breakfast so we probably won't need to stop to eat. We can spend all afternoon in the surf then grab an early dinner and watch a movie."

"Good." I looked at him and smiled. "Thanks for coming to see me, Dad."

"You're welcome, son. I hope you've enjoyed yourself."

"I have." I had, but I was missing my mom right now, and I was missing my Uncle Jeff.

"I love you, David. You know that don't you?"

"Yes. I love you too Dad."

◎

We stayed at the beach for two nights. The surf was fantastic. Dad rented rafts the first day and showed me how he and Uncle Jeff used to ride the surf when they were kids. On the second day he rented surf boards, and we walked down the beach to a surf stand where you could take lessons. We had an hour lesson then practiced all day.

"That was the best day I ever had," I said when I collapsed onto my double bed that evening.

"The best," he said. He was laughing and he reached over to rub the top of my head. It was starting to bother me now, but I wasn't going to tell him. Nothing was going to ruin my time with my dad.

"Yep, I think when I grow up I want to teach surfing."

"Sounds like a good plan. Let's shower and go get dinner. We'll need to leave early in the morning. My flight leaves at eight tomorrow night."

"Oh yeah," I said trying not to sound sad.

"I'm sorry I have to leave, David. I've loved spending time with you."

"Dad, do you think I could come to Chicago some time. I want to meet my little brother and my sister too of course." I held my breath. It took all the courage I had to ask that question.

Dad sat down on the bed across from me. "David, I don't expect you to understand this, but I've decided that it would be better not to try to combine the families."

I felt my heart jump into my throat. I swallowed. For a minute I thought I was going to throw up, but I was determined not to. "Why not?" I asked.

"I've seen so many people try to do that. It never works. Someone always gets hurt. David, Sharon, your step mother, isn't open to it, and that's important."

More important than me, I thought. I swallowed again and stood up to go to the bathroom. I still couldn't believe he'd said no.

"David, son," Dad put his hand on my arm. "I'm going to do a lot better than I have up until now. I'll visit you more. We'll make more trips like this one. We haven't even seen half of Disney." He turned me to look at him. "I'm trying to protect you. You'll understand some day. For now, I just need for you to trust me on this."

"I trust you. More trips to Disney would be great Dad." I smiled. "Chicago is probably too cold for me anyway. I'm a southern boy."

"I don't want to disrupt your life. You've adjusted so well to your little family with your mother and your Uncle Jeff. David, now that I've discovered what a great kid you are, I won't lose you again. I'll call on birthdays and holidays instead of just sending a card." He was talking a little too fast now.

"That'll be great." I pulled gently away from him and went into the bathroom. My eyes and throat felt like they were about to explode. I looked at the toilet and thought about throwing up in it. I looked at the door. He'd hear me. I turned on the cold water of the shower and stepped in. With my face turned up to the cool water I felt better. I didn't cry.

The whole time we were in Florida my dad insisted that I eat seafood. I'd never been much of a fish eater, but I have to admit it was really good. Dad said you can't come to Florida and not eat the seafood. But that night I ordered a cheeseburger and chili fries. To hell with seafood.

The next morning we drove home. We didn't say much on the trip. When we got home my Dad kissed me on both cheeks and hugged me. I hugged him back but I didn't kiss him. He left for the airport after a short talk with my mother while I went upstairs to unpack.

When I came back down he was gone. My mother smiled at me, but she wasn't sparkling anymore. The sadness was back.

Two weeks later I went camping with Uncle Jeff. It was mid August and blazing hot in Atlanta. We had started the Appalachian Trail the year before so we had to drive a little bit longer to get to where we'd left off. It was nice and cool in the mountains.

This time we were hiking from where we had stopped last year to a little bit past Blood Mountain. I was excited because there was a place called the Walasi-Yi Center that was the only place on the whole Trail that actually went through a man made building. It had a place to sleep. They called it a hostel. They had cabins to rent too. There was also a store. We wouldn't sleep there, but I had saved my allowance and pet sitting money to buy a souvenir at the store.

"All set?" Uncle Jeff asked from the door of my room.

I was sitting at my computer.

I looked out the window and saw his truck at the curb. "I didn't even see you drive up." I laughed.

"You were concentrating." He smiled and I felt warm and comfortable. "I could see you in the window. What are you working on?" He sat down on the end of my bed and looked at the computer.

"I started a new album of my trip with Dad." I closed the file and switched off the computer. I had scanned all the cards I'd received from Dad over the years into the file. I still didn't want to share that with Uncle Jeff. I wasn't sure why. "I'm all set." I stood and picked up my pack. "Let's go."

We went down the steps to the foyer and my mom met us there. "I bought you some cookies for the trip." She handed me a paper bag.

"Thanks," I said and put my arms around her waist. She hugged me back and kissed the top of my head.

"The only person you haven't gone on vacation with this summer is me," she said. "But that's okay. I've had a good season at the shop. We'll be able to really outfit you for the coming school year. We'll go shopping when you get back."

"That'll be great," I said. I stood on my tiptoes and kissed her on the cheek.

"You're getting so tall," she said.

"I'm still the smallest boy in the class."

"Not for long." Uncle Jeff nudged me on the shoulder. "Let's get going. I wanted to get on the Trail this afternoon."

We got into the truck and headed north. "I'm not going to sleep on this trip," I said. "I always wake up carsick."

"I've got Coke and peanut butter crackers. That always saves you. You can sleep if you want to."

"No, I'll stay awake and talk to you."

"Good."

Then we didn't say anything for about an hour. I yawned and cleared my throat. "I guess I'd better start talking or I'll go to sleep."

"Talk," he said. "Tell me about your trip to Florida."

"It was great. Disney World is like another planet. The whole time you're there you can't remember being any place else."

"Did you have a favorite ride?"

"There are about a million roller coasters, but I liked Space Mountain the best."

"I seem to remember liking that one too."

"You've been to Disney World?"

"Yeah, I went with a group of friends when I was twenty."

"Did Dad go?"

"No, I went with some friends."

I looked out the window. We were starting to climb a mountain and the road was windy. "I don't get carsick when I'm awake," I said. "I wonder why."

"I think it's because you can look out the window at the view and all."

"Yeah, anyway, I think I had as much fun at the beach as I did at Disney World. Dad got us a surfboarding lesson. Then we practiced all day. I decided I'll teach surfing when I grow up."

"Your dad was always better at that than me. My sense of balance isn't as good as his."

"That's probably the only thing he's better at than you."

Uncle Jeff glanced at me. He didn't say anything.

"He's got a fat stomach and a double chin. His shoulders are softer than yours too."

"He sits behind a desk all day. I work outside in peoples gardens, takes a lot of muscle."

"I figured."

We drove in silence for a couple of miles. "I asked him if I could come to Chicago to meet my brother and sister."

"That'll be nice for you."

"He said no."

"He said no!" Uncle Jeff shouted. "... Son of a Bitch!"

"That's not a nice thing to say about Dad or Gramma." I laughed. Uncle Jeff's anger felt good to me.

He looked at me sharply again. "I'm sorry, David."

"About swearing?"

"No, about your dad saying you couldn't go to Chicago. Did he have an explanation?"

"Sharon isn't open to it and she's more important than me."

"Did he say that?"

"Not exactly,"

"She was always a bitch. Sorry, I guess I shouldn't have said that about my brother's wife."

"It's probably just as well. She might have been mean to me. Her niece Darla P. H. Bergquist is sure mean to me."

"What does the P. H. stand for?"

"Poop Head, Jimmy and I named her that."

Uncle Jeff laughed.

We hiked for four days and stayed three nights on the Trail. We fished in a pond at the bottom of a small waterfall the first night and caught two big trout. I cooked them over the fire and we ate them. They were delicious. Better then the fish I ate in Florida.

It was the third day that we hiked Blood Mountain. It was the highest peak of the Trail in Georgia, and it was the toughest hike Uncle Jeff and I had ever done. The first two miles were straight up. It was like climbing the side of a cliff except there was a path, a narrow, scary path.

"Are you sure you want to hike this trail?" Uncle Jeff said. "There's one about a mile around the mountain that's an easier hike. It is a little bit longer though."

"No, this is the one I want to hike, if you think you'll be alright." I looked up at him.

He smiled down at me. "Thanks for your concern, but I think I'll be alright. I have a feeling you and I are going to sleep well tonight though."

After the first climb the trail became a bunch of switch backs. It was not as hard to hike, but it was a little bit boring. Then we got to the summit. For a minute I couldn't breathe. The view was awesome. Uncle Jeff was silent too.

"Wow, what a view," he said and looked down at me. "Breathe, David." He patted me on the back. "Remember, you promised me you wouldn't decide not to breathe."

He was laughing, but I could hear concern in his voice. I took a deep breath and realized that I was a little light headed. "I gotta take a picture." I put down my pack and unhooked the camera Mom had given me from the side. I snapped about a dozen pictures before we sat down to eat some lunch.

"I'm not very hungry," Uncle Jeff said. "In fact I feel a little bit queasy."

I looked across the picnic table at him. He was pale. He had dark skin, so pale was unusual for him. "Do you want some peanut butter crackers?" I asked.

He laughed. "I think I'll be alright. Finish your lunch and let's get started." He sipped some Gatorade, but he didn't eat anything."

It worried me. I wasn't used to worrying about him.

We hiked down the other side of the mountain. It wasn't as hard going down but it was still pretty steep. My knees got a little bit sore. Uncle Jeff said his hurt some too. We stopped and he massaged my knees. I did the same for him.

Uncle Jeff seemed to start feeling better. He stopped to eat his sandwich about half way down.

At the bottom of the hill was the Center. They called it Mountain Crossings at Walasi-Yi. I stopped before we got there to take a good look and snap a few pictures. You went through it on a sort of covered walk way. They called it a breezeway.

"Let's hike through it, Uncle Jeff, before we go into the store."

"I think that's a good idea." He stood behind me with his hands on my shoulders. I turned around and hugged his waist.

He hugged me back, but he didn't say anything. I was glad because I had a lump in my throat, and I think I might have cried if I'd tried to talk. I don't know why I felt so weird.

"How about we hike another half mile or so and find a campsite. Then we can leave our packs there and come back without them. That way we can browse the store comfortably."

I cleared my throat. "Sounds like a good idea to me."

"You know, David," Uncle Jeff said as we put our packs down next to a stream and started to set up the tent. "I got a little choked up back there at the Center. I guess it was the strenuous hike and the spectacular views. Then seeing the Center and the work people put into it just to make it nice for hikers. It's nice to feel that emotional."

I didn't know if he was just saying that for me or if he meant it. But I was glad he said it.

We went back to the store at Mountain Crossings and shopped. I bought my Mom a pair of ear rings that had Appalachian Trail written on them with the symbol of a mountain.

"Do you think she'll wear them?" I asked.

"I know she will."

Uncle Jeff bought a water bottle that said Mountain Crossing. I bought one too, and I bought a patch to put on my pack. I figured I could transfer it if I got a new pack someday. I would probably outgrow this one.

That night we went into a small town in walking distance of the Trail and ate at a diner. We left the trail the next day. It was the fourth day. We met up with Jimmy and his dad at a hotel. They had hiked a different part of the trail and they hadn't been camping. We were hitching a ride with them back to our car.

"Hey, Don." Uncle Jeff shook Jimmy's dad's hand. "Hello, young James." He always called Jimmy that. He shook his hand and patted him on the shoulder.

"So how far did you go, David?" Mr. Parnell asked.

"We went twenty two miles," I said. I felt very proud. "We could have gone farther, but we like to stop and enjoy the trail along the way. I'll show you the pictures tonight after dinner. They're on my camera. It's digital. Blood Mountain was awesome."

"If you'd gone farther you would have had to hike back to meet up with us," Jimmy said. He looked a little grumpy. Maybe I was too excited about my hike. Maybe he wasn't so excited about his.

"How far did you guys go?" I asked.

"We went four miles yesterday and six miles today," Mr. Parnell said. "Your old man is in better shape than I am." He laughed and patted his stomach where it bulged a little over his belt. "We'll do Blood Mountain one day, Jimmy. I promise." He ruffled Jimmy's hair. I had the feeling Jimmy didn't like it any more than I did.

I looked at Uncle Jeff. Mr. Parnell had called him my old man. I guess he could be my old man even though he isn't my dad.

"There's a stream in the woods behind the hotel, David," Jimmy said. "There are some fallen trees across it. Come on, I'll show you." I followed Jimmy into the woods and Uncle Jeff and Mr. Parnell followed us at a walk. I looked back at them. They were talking. They were probably talking about the troop. I hoped it wasn't the soccer team. I didn't know what Uncle Jeff thought about that.

"Look what I found, Uncle Jeff." I held out my hand to him. He and Mr. Parnell were standing next to the stream where Jimmy and I had been climbing from rock to log for about an hour.

"It's a salamander," he said.

"I named her Sally." I laughed. "Sally Salamander. Do you think if I put her in a jar I could take her home?"

"I doubt that she'd live, David. She's a wild animal. You should put her back."

I looked down at the little creature in my hand. I was disappointed. I had planned a tank for her and everything.

"You can buy salamanders that have been raised in captivity," Mr. Parnell said. "But you'd better put that one back, David. She's already drying out."

I put my hand back in the stream, and the little creature slithered away.

"We can go to a fish store and buy you a pet when we get back, David," Uncle Jeff said on the trip home. "I just don't like the idea of taking a wild animal into captivity."

"I was thinking it might be nice to have a tank in my room. You could help me landscape it for a salamander."

"I've never done that kind of landscaping." He laughed. "It would be fun for a change. Let's do it."

"Okay. Uncle Jeff..?"

"What son?"

"We need a new assistant coach for the soccer team." I looked out the window. I didn't want to see his face right now. I was afraid he'd be mad at me or hurt or something. "I know it's a lot to ask, but do you think you could do it?"

He didn't say anything for a minute. Then he said, "I'd like to. I figured out what I did wrong the first time."

I turned my head quickly to look at him. "You didn't do anything wrong the first time, Uncle Jeff." He didn't look hurt or angry. He was smiling.

"Yes I did. I became too competitive for myself. I forgot I was doing it for you. I'm sorry, David."

"That's okay." I laughed. His smile was contagious and I was happy about what he said. "Mr. Parnell keeps me in the goal all the time too. It's okay though. I like it there now. I'm a pretty good forward, but I'm a better goal tender. We have a lot of forwards, but I'm the best goal tender in the league. We'd never win if it wasn't for me."

"I guess you've gotten more competitive as you've gotten older."

"Yeah, so will you do it?"

"I'd love to. In fact I'm really happy you asked me."

I looked at my Uncle and smiled. I was really lucky to have him. I felt a little ashamed. I always felt so sorry for myself because my dad left me. In fact I don't think he ever really wanted me. But I had Uncle Jeff. He wanted me.

"Mr. Parnell called you my old man. He was right. You're my real dad, Uncle Jeff." I laughed feeling awkward. "I guess that's a contradiction in terms."

He looked at me and smiled. "A contradiction in terms, David, you're only ten years old. Where do you pick up things like *a contradiction in terms?*"

"Vocabulary, we get a new list every week at school."

"*Contradiction in terms* was on a vocabulary list?"

"Probably not," I said and looked back out the window. Uncle Jeff always made me feel smart. "I must have picked that up somewhere else."

"Mom," I said that night at the dinner table. She had made her famous tuna casserole. She didn't cook anything that wasn't easy. "Jimmy's dog had puppies."

"You told me last week."

"Can I have one?" I asked. "Please, I'll give you my pet sitting money to help pay for it."

"You don't have to do that, David. I'm glad you want a dog. I'm sorry you don't like Ruffles." She stroked the big stupid dog's head. He sat at her feet every night when we ate, but he didn't beg. I figured he was too stupid to even learn that.

"I like Ruffles," I said, "even though he is stupid. I didn't want to like him, but how can you help it with that big goofy grin." I stretched my foot out under the table and rubbed the dog's back with it.

"What kind of puppies are they?"

"They're mutts. The mother is a chocolate lab, but they didn't breed her in time. They don't know what kind of dog the father is. I think it must be the next door neighbor's dog though, because it looks like a mop. It's smaller than the mother and all the puppies are kind of small and most of them have longer hair."

"Have you already picked one out that's your favorite?"

"Yeah, it's the only one that looks like the mother. It's a little small, but it has short hair and it's brown. It's a girl. I named her Charlotte."

"Oh, David," Mom looked at me. Her eyes were watering. "Come here and let me hug you. You are so sweet."

"Awww, Mom," I said, but I went around the table and put my arms around her.

The next time I saw my Dad I was sixteen years old. He came to my Grampa's funeral.

CHAPTER FOUR

When I was twelve years old I put my foot down to my Uncle. His birthday was on February 29. So was my Dad's, of course. But that didn't really matter. They only had a real birthday every four years. That year was leap year.

I insisted on cooking dinner for him, and my mom and I went to his apartment at the nursery to do it. I had a special gift for him that I'd bought with my pet sitting money. Well mostly. I didn't quite have enough and Mom pitched in. She also bought some camping gear for him and a new soccer ball.

He met us at the door of the apartment. "I'm really getting some special treatment tonight. You know it's your dad's birthday too," he said.

"I sent him a card." I hauled all my stuff into the living room. "I'm going to get stuff started in the kitchen. It won't take long. We'll eat first and then you can open your gifts."

"What's on the menu?" he asked as Mom poured him a chilled martini from a pitcher she'd mixed at home.

"Trout almandine on angel hair pasta with mornay sauce and a timbale of mixed greens, baked Alaska for desert."

"Wow." He sipped his drink and sat down at the kitchen table. "Thanks David. I'm a lucky man."

"And I'm a lucky woman," Mom said. "I had corn muffins for breakfast this morning. Last week he made blueberry. He's spoiling me rotten."

"Me too," Uncle Jeff said.

"I just hope he doesn't make me fat." She laughed and patted her perfectly flat stomach.

"Me too," Uncle Jeff said.

"I don't think that's a problem for anyone in this family." I prepared the meal and Mom set the table while Uncle Jeff sipped his drink. We ate and I think everyone really enjoyed it. That was one thing I was happy with my dad about. He taught me to eat fish.

"No, this isn't a fat family. In fact, David," Uncle Jeff said. "I do believe you're beginning your growth spurt. You're looking very tall and thin to me right now."

"He was five foot seven inches at his last check up," Mom said. "That was a month ago. I think he's even taller now."

"I'm almost the tallest kid in the class. Matt Kingsley is taller than me by a couple of inches. It's kind of weird going from being the smallest to the tallest."

"I remember that." Uncle Jeff pushed back his chair. "Can I open my gifts now?"

I took a deep breath. I was nervous. I didn't know how Uncle Jeff would react. "Okay," I said. "Mom and I will do the dishes when you've finished."

We went into the living room. I handed him Mom's gifts first. He opened them one by one. He kissed her on the cheek and thanked her. Then I handed him mine. He pulled the paper off and looked at the top of the line one man backpacking tent.

"I don't understand, David. Is my snoring too loud?"

"No, that flimsy tent won't help with your snoring," I laughed nervously. "Uncle Jeff, next summer we'll do our fourth stretch of the Appalachian Trail. I'm afraid I just can't do it without Charlotte." He looked at my mother puzzled. "My dog," I said.

"David, we've talked about this ..." He started.

"Uncle Jeff," I interrupted him. "I'm not ever going backpacking without my dog again." I stood and went to the kitchen to do the dishes. I could hear him talking to my mom in the other room. I couldn't hear the words, but his tone was angry. Maybe I shouldn't have done it on his birthday.

"Let's go, honey." Mom came into the room about the time I'd washed the last pan and dried it.

"Uncle Jeff isn't speaking to me?" I asked.

"Of course I'm speaking to you, David," he said. I turned around to look at him. His jaw was clenched the way he did when he was mad. He didn't usually get mad at me. But I'd seen him do that when we talked about my dad.

"Uncle Jeff, maybe I shouldn't have done this on your birthday, but this is important to me."

"I understand that it is." He took a deep breath. "But the dog will ride in a carrier in the bed of my truck, not in the cab."

"Okay."

"That's a really nice tent, David," he came over to me and hugged me. "I just hope I don't get scared in the night all by myself."

I smiled at him. "You'll carry the small one. I'll carry the two man tent from now on. You'll be alright, Uncle Jeff. I won't pitch my tent far from yours."

✦

"Mom," I asked on the way home. "Uncle Jeff is such a great guy in so many ways. Why do you suppose he doesn't like dogs?"

"Your Dad told me he was bitten by a stray when he was a kid. They couldn't find the dog so he had to have a series of rabies shots. It was painful and frightening. I guess he just never got over it."

"Charlotte won't bite him."

"I know she won't."

✦

I looked at my dog sleeping in her bed next to mine. I had tried since she was a puppy to get her to sleep in my bed with me. But she always ended up on the dog bed Mom had bought her.

She looked a lot like a chocolate lab like her mother, but she was smaller and a lighter shade of brown. At two years old, she weighed forty pounds. Her hair was like a lab's, but she had thin wiry hairs all over that stood above the rest. Mom wanted to take her to a groom shop and get them cut off, but I liked her the way she was.

She was the smartest dog in the world. Pepper had died four years ago and his memory was fading. I remembered that he was smart though. I taught him to play catch and to let me brush him. I taught him to come and to stay. He was smart and calm and gentle.

Charlotte was smarter. She was just as gentle, but she was not calm. Poor Ruffles didn't stand a chance. She would pull his tail with her teeth, and when he turned to snarl at her, she would lick his face. He would wag his tail and lick her back. Then she would run around him and pull his tail again. She would do that until she got bored or Mom or I made her stop. But Ruffles loved her anyway.

I took her to obedience class when she was eight months old. Mom and I worked with her together and she knew her commands perfectly. She always obeyed them too, not just when she wanted to. She could walk off leash. I kept her on one anyway because it was the law and also to keep her safe. Mom and I took her to the dog park with Ruffles twice a week. She was a happy dog.

"Are you ready to go, Charlotte?" I said as I picked up her small pack and mine. We'd been working with the dog pack for a couple of months to get her used to it. It was spring break at school and Uncle Jeff and I were going on a three day camping trip at Franklin D. Roosevelt state park. Even though we were going south, it was early spring and it would probably be cold at night. I knew she wouldn't sleep in my sleeping bag with me. She would need her own, and if I had to carry mine, she had to carry hers. It was the first time we'd taken her. I was a little bit nervous.

"All set?" Uncle Jeff said when I opened the front door.

"We're ready," I said. I handed him my pack and clipped the leash to Charlotte's collar. I looked up at Uncle Jeff. He was scowling at the leash.

"Alright then," he said. "Let's go." He headed out the door to his truck that was parked at the curb.

"Hey," Mom called as she came across the lawn. I was in the back of the truck putting Charlotte into the carrier that Uncle Jeff had in there. "You're not leaving without saying goodbye are you?"

"No." I checked to make sure that the carrier was anchored properly in the bed of the truck. Charlotte wasn't bothered by the crate. We'd crate trained her as a puppy. She still had a crate in the kitchen. She went in it when there were thunderstorms.

"It's a nice crate," I said as I jumped out of the bed of the truck.

"I know," Mom said. "It's an airline crate. She'll have shelter if it rains too. I couldn't stand the thought that she might get rained on. But she still has good air circulation."

"Your mom insisted on paying for it." Uncle Jeff came to where I was standing next to my mom. "The dog will be comfortable." His smile was reluctant.

"Take care of him," Mom said to Uncle Jeff. She always said that when we left. She hugged me then kissed Uncle Jeff on the cheek. She didn't always do that.

We got into the truck to leave. I watched my mom wave to us until we were out of sight. When I was little I had this fantasy that Mom and Uncle Jeff got married. Then it would almost be like he was my Dad. He would be my stepdad. I couldn't call him Dad because I had always thought of his brother that way. Maybe I could come up with another name, like Pop, or something.

I knew that wasn't going to happen though. I wasn't sure why. They seemed to really like each other. They'd raised me together. But they never dated. They never did anything together unless I was there. My mom was dating someone now. His name was Vern. I guess that's short for Vernon. I suspected that Uncle Jeff was dating someone too.

"You sure are quiet, David," Uncle Jeff said. "Is everything okay?"

"Yeah," I said. "Uncle Jeff ..?"

"What ..?"

"Do you have a girlfriend?"

He looked at me sharply.

"I saw you kiss a lady on the mouth the other day when you picked me up after school and we stopped by the nursery on the way to the soccer field," I said.

"Yes, I guess she's my girlfriend, although we've only been seeing each other for a little while." He seemed uncomfortable. "Does that bother you?"

"I guess not. Mom is seeing someone too. It just sort of complicates the family image."

"I guess it would."

"I used to wish you and Mom would get married. I guess that was silly."

"I don't think it was silly, but it wasn't realistic. Your mom is one of my very best friends, but I couldn't feel romantic about my brother's ex-wife, and she couldn't feel romantic about her ex-husband's brother."

"I guess not."

"How do you feel about Vern?"

"He's okay. He doesn't have any kids so he has no idea how to talk to me. He seems to be nice to Mom though. I know he'll spend the night while I'm gone. That bothers me a little bit."

"Why is that?"

"I'm not sure."

Uncle Jeff was quiet for a little while then he said, "David has your mother told you anything about …um …sex?"

"She took me to see a movie at the public health department."

"Oh, did you understand everything? Do you have any questions to ask?"

"No, it's pretty clear. At first I thought it was gross, but I'm starting to notice some of the girls in school are getting prettier. I'm not too grossed out anymore."

"Good, so any particular girls, the pretty ones I mean?"

"Well, I hate to admit it, but P.H. is shaping up pretty good. She's blond and she's stacked."

"She's stacked?"

"Yeah." I cupped my hands and put them in front of my chest.

"Oh."

"Jimmy has a crush on her. I'm not having anything to do with that woman though. Of course, she wouldn't have anything to do with me either. I think I'll go in the brunette direction. I like Teresa Blake."

"Have you told her?"

"No, I'm not ready for that yet."

Uncle Jeff smiled and looked at the road.

We got to the park and I took Charlotte out of the carrier. She seemed fine. I had worried about her on the trip, but I didn't say anything to Uncle Jeff. Mom said it was a compromise, and she'd make sure Charlotte had sufficient travel accommodations. I had to be happy with that.

I took her on leash to the woods beside the picnic area. She peed and pooped. I picked up the poop in a plastic bag and threw it into the trash can. Uncle Jeff was spreading stuff out on a table and we joined him there.

"I don't sleep in the car anymore, Uncle Jeff." I laughed. "I'll be thirteen years old in two weeks remember." He had peanut butter crackers and Cokes in the cooler.

"It's always nice to start a hike with something to eat, don't you think? Does …uh … Charlotte need anything? David, I have to say I always feel a little strange calling that dog by your mother's name. Are you sure that isn't an insult?"

I laughed. "Mom didn't think so. When I told her I named the dog Charlotte, she cried and hugged me. She said I was soooo sweet. Yuck!"

Uncle Jeff laughed. "It's hard to understand women sometimes."

"Yeah." I drank some Coke and opened my crackers. "I'll give Charlotte some water. She won't need anything to eat until tonight."

We spent three days on the trail and two nights. The first night, we pitched the two tents right next to a stream. I didn't seem to have a problem sleeping next to a stream. I never peed in my sleeping bag. Of course, I was almost thirteen years old, but even when we first started it didn't bother me.

Whenever we were camping we pretty much went to bed with the sun and got up with it. So I crawled into my tent with Charlotte just after dark. She nestled into her canine sleeping bag, turned a couple of circles, and curled into a ball. It always amazed me how a dog can just close her eyes and be asleep. I crawled into mine and fell pretty quickly to sleep myself. Hiking is very tiring. I had to really appreciate Uncle Jeff for carrying that tent for all those years. It really added some weight to my pack.

"Grrrrrr …" I woke up to the sound of something big moving around outside my tent. Was that what growled, I wondered. "Grrrrrrr …" It was Charlotte growling. Was there a bear outside the tent?

"David ..." Uncle Jeff's voice came from just outside the door of my tent. "It's me," he whispered.

"Why are you whispering?" I whispered back.

"I don't want that dog to bite me."

"Charlotte, no!" I said out loud and she quieted. "What's going on, Uncle Jeff?"

"I want to come in there and sleep with you. I don't like having my own tent."

"That's funny." I laughed. "I kind of liked having mine."

"You have company," he said as he unzipped the door to the tent.

I put my arms around Charlotte. She had come out of her sleeping bag and was standing in a protective stance next to me. She wagged her tail and relaxed when she saw Uncle Jeff's face appear in the doorway.

He pulled his sleeping bag inside and stretched it out beside mine on the opposite side as Charlotte. "I can't believe I'm sleeping with a dog," he grumbled as he crawled into it and turned his back to me.

I smiled. It was dark. He couldn't see me. "Uncle Jeff, don't you like your birthday present?"

"I hope it doesn't hurt your feelings, but I think I'll trade it in on a four man tent. We've pretty much outgrown this one."

"It won't hurt my feelings."

We didn't even pitch the small tent the next night. "I don't think you can take this one back now that you've pitched it in the woods," I said.

"No, we'll sell them both in your mother's next garage sale."

On the ride home it started to rain. I tried not to look back at the bed of the truck where Charlotte was hunkered into her carrier. But when a loud crack of thunder sounded, I couldn't help it. I glanced back.

I settled back into my seat knowing she was safe and at least fairly dry. But I hated her having to be back there all by herself in this storm.

We rode for a couple more miles. Suddenly Uncle Jeff pulled off the highway into a rest stop and jumped out of the cab. It was still pouring rain. I watched him run around the truck and climb into the flat bed. He hurried back just a few seconds later with a dripping Charlotte in his arms and jumped into the driver's seat.

"She was dry when I pulled her out of there." He put Charlotte in my lap. "The whole cab smells like wet dog," he grumbled and put the truck in gear to pull out of the rest stop.

"No it doesn't." I buried my face in Charlotte's coat to hide my smile. "It smells like wet human."

He looked over at me. His eyes were scowling, but the corners of his lips were twitching. "Very funny," he said.

"David," Mom said that evening when I'd bathed and unpacked my pack and come down for dinner. "I hope you didn't wine or wheedle your uncle into letting Charlotte ride in the cab today. Remember, we talked about the importance of compromise."

My mouth was full so I couldn't say anything, but I looked up at her with my eyes wide and shook my head.

"He was so grumpy," she continued. "He didn't even come in to chat like he usually does. He just unloaded the truck and left."

I swallowed and drank some milk. "I don't think he was grumpy, Mom. He was just soaking wet. He wanted to go on home and change his clothes."

"That's another thing. Why was he soaking wet? Did you make him go out in the rain to get her?"

"No, Mom." I couldn't help smiling at the memory of him running around that truck. "I didn't whine or wheedle, and I didn't make him go out in the rain. All I did was glance back at the carrier when there was a loud clap of thunder. At first I didn't think he saw me, and I pretended I wasn't concerned." I laughed and dipped an oven fry in ketchup. "Then suddenly he just pulled over and ran out in the rain."

"You're kidding," Mom said around a mouthful of turkey burger.

"Nope, he grumbled a little about the smell of wet dog. I teased him about the smell of wet human." I popped the fry into my mouth.

"David, you're terrible." She was laughing when she said it. I went to bed that night thinking everything was right with my world.

When I was fourteen I won the state champion spelling bee. My mom and Uncle Jeff were there to watch me.

"How did you know how to spell all the proper names and places of Georgia?" Uncle Jeff asked.

"I read on the internet that that's what usually stumps kids in spelling bees. So I made a point to learn them."

"How did you get to be so smart, David?" he asked. "It must come from your mother because it sure didn't come from my side of the family."

"Dad's a lawyer."

"Yeah, but he's not all that smart." He had his hand across my shoulders. I was almost as tall as he was these days. I hated that. When I first became the tallest kid in the class I liked it. But now I was a tower over everyone, and I was so skinny. Mom always made a joke about not letting me go out in a high wind. I hated that.

"Let's get some refreshments," Mom said. I had received my award, and now there was a social in the auditorium. It wasn't my high school, but I'd been there a few other times for soccer games. Jimmy and I played on the school team now.

We went into the auditorium. There were kids there from all over the state. I was taller than all of them.

"Mom," I said. "I think I'm ready to go home."

"You can't win the championship and then just go home." She laughed. "You're a celebrity."

"I've got a lot of studying to do."

"Your mom is a little worried about you, David," Uncle Jeff said. "She says all you do is study since you quit scouts."

"I don't have time for scouts anymore. I'm studying for the SAT and the soccer team at school takes up a lot of my time." The truth was that I didn't want to go to scouts without Jimmy, and he had all sorts of tooters and special ed classes after school. His dad had to give up the troop. His mom had to go to the school and fight to get them to let him be on the soccer team. The only reason they let him was because I said I'd stay on the independent team with him if they wouldn't.

"Well David, it wouldn't be right to just take the award and go. You have to socialize for a little while. People may want to ask you questions." Mom wasn't going to let me leave so I agreed.

We stayed for about an hour. People did want to ask me questions. Mostly they wanted to know how tall I was. I lied. I said I was six one. I was six two and still growing. I hated it.

"Didn't you already take the SAT in middle school?" Uncle Jeff asked on the way home.

"He did," Mom said. "And he did very well on it."

"That was with the gifted program though. It doesn't count. Besides, I can beat that score. I'm looking into getting through high school faster than most kids."

I was sitting in the back seat of the car. Uncle Jeff looked at me in the rear view mirror. "You don't have to be in such a hurry."

"I hate high school. It's boring.

✦

I was practicing soccer after school in the fall of my senior year in high school. I was only fifteen years old. I had taken what accelerated classes I could and tested out of some of the core curriculum. This was my last year in high school, and it was going pretty well.

Teresa Blake and I were dating. She was a year behind me in school now. We'd been in the gifted program together since second grade. She was tall for a girl. Still she was a good head shorter than me. I was six foot four now and prayed every day that I had stopped growing. I was as tall as Uncle Jeff, taller than my mother, and Uncle Jeff said my dad was six foot three. That meant I was taller than him too.

I wouldn't know, of course. I hadn't seen him in five years. Sometimes I lay in bed at night and remembered all those promises he'd made to me when we were in Disney. Why did he do that? Did he feel guilty? I guess feeling guilty was better than feeling nothing at all.

"Hey, David," Teresa said as she approached the bench where I had gone to get a bottle of water. She was smiling. She looked so pretty. Her dark hair was blowing in the fall breeze and a little piece of it was stuck in her mouth. I reached over and pulled it free.

She grinned at me and I grinned back. "Hey, Teresa," I said.

"I wondered if you had a ride home from school." Even though I was a grade above her she was older than me. She had just gotten her driver's license. I wouldn't get mine until spring.

"My uncle is picking me up. I'm staying with him for a few days. Mom went on vacation with her boyfriend."

"You don't sound happy about that."

"I don't care." I was sorry she could hear the irritation in my voice. But I really didn't like Vern.

"You don't like Vern very much, do you David?" she asked.

"Vern has no personality," I said. "What's not to like? What's to like?"

"Here comes your Uncle." Teresa was looking behind me. "Who's that with him?"

I turned to see my uncle and a tall elegant looking woman in a suit walking toward me. "I have no idea. I've never seen her before."

"David," Uncle Jeff called to me. The woman smiled at me when I waved. She followed him over to where I stood with Teresa. "Hello, Teresa," Uncle Jeff said. "Mary Ann." He took the woman's arm and propelled her to the front of him. "I want you to meet my nephew, David and his friend, Teresa."

"It's nice to meet you, David." The woman looked up at me. She was pretty. She had brown hair and brown eyes like my mother. But she wasn't nearly as thin.

"When Jeff said he wanted me to meet his fifteen year old nephew I didn't expect to be meeting a young man as tall as he is." She laughed.

I rolled my eyes. "Yeah, yeah, I'm tall." I reached for my book bag.

"David." Teresa squeezed my arm. "That was rude."

"Yes, it was." Uncle Jeff sounded angry. I looked back at him, trying to look bland.

"I'm sorry," I said, not sounding like I meant it. "I get tired of people commenting on my height."

"I apologize then," Mary Ann said. "I didn't mean to offend you."

Uncle Jeff was staring at me with a very stern look.

"I'm sorry too. I shouldn't be so sensitive," I said.

"Apology accepted, now could we start over on a new foot."

Uncle Jeff said, "Mary Ann is a real estate agent and we're going to look at a house. I wanted you to come along. Since you'll be living in it some of the time I need your opinion."

"You're buying a house? What's wrong with the apartment over the nursery?"

"I just think it's about time I live like a grown up." He laughed. "Would you like to come along, Teresa?"

"No thanks, Mr. Landrum. I've got tons of homework to do. See you tomorrow, David." She walked away. I followed her with my eyes. I hadn't gotten to kiss her because of Uncle Jeff and Mary Ann. Ever since the first time I kissed Teresa I'd thought of little else. I just wanted to kiss her all the time, that and a whole lot more.

We went to the house. It was ordinary. It was a three bedroom brick ranch. There was a big fenced back yard and a big lawn in the front yard, in a word, boring.

"Let me take us all to dinner so we can talk about what we thought," Uncle Jeff said. He was acting so cheerful. What did he want me to say? Yipee!

"Is it alright with you, David?" Mary Ann asked. "Maybe you'd like to talk with your uncle alone."

"I don't care." I sounded surly even to myself. "After living above a nursery that house is boring but whatever makes you happy, Uncle Jeff." I walked to the back door of Uncle Jeff's truck and waited for him to hit the keyless remote. When he didn't I looked over at him. He was glaring at me. Mary Ann was saying something to him. I felt a twinge of guilt, but I opened the door when I heard it unlock and got in.

"David," Uncle Jeff said after we had dropped Mary Ann at her house. "You were rude to my friend today. I love you kid, but you're trying my patience."

"I thought she was just a real estate agent."

"We've actually been dating on and off for a couple of years, but that's beside the point. David, everyone deserves to be treated with respect. Even if she was just doing a job you shouldn't have been rude."

"I'm sorry," I said, again not sounding sorry. "That's probably all I say these days. I'm sorry. I should get a button to press that says 'I'm sorry.' Save my voice."

"When did you get to be such a smart ass?" Uncle Jeff asked. He didn't look too happy.

We were silent for the rest of the ride to the nursery. I got out of the car and went up the stairs and straight to my room in the back of the apartment. Sometimes I wondered if I might not be happier in the room over the fountain display now. After camping by mountain streams for so many years the sound of running water was soothing. I guess it didn't matter anymore. We were moving.

I took a cold shower to wash off the sweat from soccer practice and to cool the burning feeling in my belly that always happened when I didn't get to kiss Teresa. Then I went out to the kitchen where Uncle Jeff was sitting in front of his computer.

"I'm really sorry I acted like such a jerk," I said as I pulled a cola out of the refrigerator.

"I'm not sure if a cola is a good idea this late in the day."

"God, I can't make any decisions on my own. I'll graduate from high school this year and go to college in the fall. Then who's going to tell me how to live."

"I'm sorry, David, you're right. You know if you can handle a cola. Old habits die hard."

I took a deep swallow and sat down at the table. "Uncle Jeff, how can you date someone on and off?" I said. "You're as bad as Mom and Vern. It's been years. Why don't they just get married and make it official?"

"I had the feeling you didn't like Vern too much."

"We don't have anything in common, but what difference does that make. She's still seeing him. How many women do you date on and off? That's one thing you have to give Vern. He's the only man Mom goes out with, and I doubt anyone else would go out with him."

"David, what's bothering you? You've never asked me to explain my social life to you before."

"Nothing's bothering me." I stood and went into the living room to turn on the television.

Uncle Jeff followed me in. "What colleges have you heard from, David?"

"It doesn't matter. I got into Harvard and that's all I care about."

"Your mother says she can't afford it, and she won't let me pay."

"She'll give in," I said not taking my eyes off the television screen. I didn't even know what was on. "Dad will help. She can't say no to him."

"Have you talked to your dad?"

"No, but I will."

"David, you're a brilliant young man," Uncle Jeff said. "I don't think you've ever gotten a B in a class at school, have you?"

"If I got a B, I'd kill myself." I heard Uncle Jeff's sudden gasp. He made that sound whenever I said something that startled him. I flicked off the TV with the remote control and stood up. I gulped down the rest of my drink. "I think I'll go on to bed."

That night at two in the morning I regretted the caffeine. And like everything else, that made me angry.

✻

That year the soccer team went to the state championship. I got my picture in the paper for being the best goal tender at the high school level. I also got my picture in the paper for being the star student of Georgia.

I made love for the first time with Teresa Blake. I told her I loved her and asked her to stay faithful to me when I went to Harvard in the fall. She would still be in high school for another year, but I'd see her on breaks and holidays. She agreed that ours was an everlasting love.

It was a great year. I worked very hard. I had too many courses to finish before graduation, but with the help of the internet I could do it. I worked late some nights. Some nights I never even went to bed.

"He just doesn't sleep." I heard my mom say to Uncle Jeff when he'd come to pick me up for a backpacking trip. When we hiked the Appalachian Trail now we had to use most of the first day driving. We needed more time for that. This was spring break and we were just doing a Georgia trail.

"He'll sleep on the trail, Charlie. He always does. I wouldn't worry about him too much," Uncle Jeff said. "He's just a very driven young man."

He was trying to soothe my mom's nerves, but I knew he was worried about me too. The truth is. I was a little worried about myself. Lately, I just couldn't seem to turn off my brain. Even if I'd stopped working on my school work at night I wouldn't have slept.

"All set?" I said. I wanted to let them know I was coming so they'd stop talking about me. I'd been sneaking up on them like that all my life and they still weren't on to me.

"All set." Uncle Jeff stood up from the kitchen table where they'd been having a cup of coffee. I wondered how many times over the years I'd walked into that scene. The thought gave me a strange fluttery feeling in my chest. I didn't like it.

I snapped the leash to Charlotte's collar and went out the front door.

❖

"David, wake up," Uncle Jeff nudged my shoulder. I was asleep in the truck with my forehead resting on the window. I sat up. There was that nausea again. It had been a long time since I'd fallen asleep in the car. God, I hated this.

"Don't worry." Uncle Jeff laughed. "I've got Coke and peanut butter crackers."

"Uncle Jeff, I'm not a kid. I'm fine." I got out of the car and went around to the bed of the truck to spring Charlotte. I took her to the woods at the edge of the picnic area and thought about ducking behind a tree to throw up. No way was I giving him the satisfaction.

"David," he said when I went back to the table where he'd put out snacks. "Don't be stubborn. You're white as a sheet."

"I'm fine!" I sat down and took a sip of the Coke. I felt the fizzy refreshment of it, and the nausea started to ease. I tore open the crackers and put two of them in my mouth. He's always right, I thought. It made me angry.

"You must have really needed the sleep. Your mom says you've been studying hard."

"Yeah, it's a good thing for the internet," I said. "I can do class stuff any time of the night or day. Otherwise I probably wouldn't finish."

"Why is it so important to you to finish fast, David?"

"I'm bored. I don't want to go to high school anymore. I want to go where I can study what I want. Not what someone says I have to study."

"You know there will be some core curriculum you have to complete."

"Yeah, I know, but I figure I can do that stuff on the internet like I did this year. I plan to finish college in three years tops."

"You're something else."

❖

"This is the first trail we ever hiked, isn't it?" I said after we'd been walking for a couple of miles. "Yeah, I thought it might be fun to come back. You were eight years old then, or were you seven? You'll be sixteen next week so it's been at least eight years. They've worked on the path a little, but it still looks pretty much the same."

"That's right. This is where we saw that bear, remember?" I looked at the spot in the woods where the bear had stood on its hind legs looking at us. "You know, Uncle Jeff, when I was up on that waterfall and you were signaling me from below, I thought the bear was behind me." I laughed.

"I wondered why you jumped backwards into that waterfall." He laughed and I started to relax.

"I thought I was jumping away from a bear. Then I slipped and went over the edge. What were you signaling me about if there wasn't a bear?" We were both laughing. I actually felt like there was weight coming off my shoulders.

"I wanted you to move away from the falls."

We walked into the clearing where we'd camped before, and I looked up at the spot where I'd been perched eight years earlier. "It had the opposite effect," I said.

"It sure did." Uncle Jeff put his pack down and started to set up camp.

I took off my pack and my shoes and my outer clothes. I was wearing my swimming trunks under my hiking shorts. I waded into the water. "Ahhh …" I looked back at Uncle Jeff. "I don't remember it being so cold. Stay, Charlotte," I said as she waded into the pond behind me. She stopped and watched me as I went deeper.

Uncle Jeff laughed. "Be careful this time, David. I'm not sure I can haul you out of there anymore."

I made a face at him then continued over to the waterfall. "Uncle Jeff, look." I called out over the rushing of the water.

He looked back at where I stood in the falls. The water of the pond came only to my upper thighs. I stood with the falls running over my head. Uncle Jeff's face registered surprise and then something else. I think it was fear. Then he relaxed and smiled.

I remembered his strong arms hauling me out of these falls all those years ago. I remembered his cries of fear and relief. I also remembered thinking I was going to die and not being upset about it.

I thought about Mom. She'd have been upset. I thought about Teresa and making love to her. Neither of us had known what we were doing, but we figured it out. I would hate to have missed that.

I waded back to the campsite. "Thanks for saving my life, Uncle Jeff," I said as I looked for my towel in my pack. It was cool in the mountains, and I was shivering so hard my teeth were chattering.

He looked at me over the tent he was pitching. "Thanks for sharing it with me."

※

The next week I turned sixteen and got my driver's license. I also had a seizure.

※

Mom bought me a ten year old Chevy Cavalier. It was red. Uncle Jeff gave me a stereo system for it with a CD player and fantastic speakers. I drove to school and parked in the student parking lot. The other kids mostly had fancier, newer cars. I didn't care. I was happy.

I got out of the car and shook my head. There was something strange about the way I felt. I'd had this feeling a few times before. It was like I wasn't really there, like I was dreaming. It cleared in a minute and I went on to class.

There was only one more week of classes at school for seniors. I'd have my on-line classes done by the middle of May. Then I was out of this place.

When I got to the class room the feeling returned. When the teacher started to talk, I realized I was in trouble. Her voice sounded like it had an echo. I stood and walked straight toward her.

"Go back to your seat, David," she said, but I kept walking until I got to her. "Is something wrong?" I could see her looking into my face. It seemed like I was looking through a telescope or something.

I opened my mouth and a sound came out. I didn't recognize it. Then things got kind of blurry.

"Sit down right here." Mrs. Epstein guided me to a chair and pushed me into it. She looked into my eyes as if she was trying to see through them into my head. I noticed that I was so tall, and she was so small, that when I was sitting and she was standing, we looked eye to eye.

"Does anyone have a cell phone?" she called to the class.

"I do." Teresa ran to the front of the room and handed her phone to Mrs. Epstein. "What's wrong with him?" Her voice was shaking. I could feel her hand on my shoulder. "David." She was crying. "What's wrong?"

I looked in the direction of her voice and I heard myself say, "I need ... help." It sounded like someone else said it, but I knew it was me.

"We'll get you help, David," Mrs. Epstein said. "Someone run to the office and tell them what's happened. Tell them I've called 911."

"What's happening to him?" someone said.

"I'm not sure, but I think he's having a seizure."

Mrs. Epstein rode in the ambulance with me. The principal followed in her car. My muscles were twitching. I could feel them at some point, but I didn't stay conscious the whole time. I woke up at the hospital emergency room. My mom was there. I started to cry when I saw her.

I couldn't remember the last time I lost control enough to cry. I grabbed the sheet that was over me and covered my face until I could make the tears stop. Then I rubbed my face until it was dry.

"What happened?" I asked. My voice was normal now.

"Oh, David." Mom got up from the chair she was sitting in and ran over to me. She took my hand and pressed it to her face. "Thank God you're awake."

"What happened?" I asked again. My voice was crackling. I cleared my throat.

"You had a seizure."

"I never had a seizure before," I said. "What's wrong with me?"

"The doctor didn't want to talk about it until you woke up. He said you might sleep for hours and we should let you sleep."

"Well, I'm not asleep now, and I want to know what happened." I tried to sit up, but my mom held me down by my shoulders.

"Take it slow, David," she said. "I don't know what happens with a seizure. Maybe you shouldn't sit up."

"He can sit up." I looked at the door where a man in a white lab coat stood. "Like I said before, Mrs. Landrum, it was a mild seizure. It only lasted a couple of minutes."

I sat up in the bed. I was still fully dressed. "How could it have only lasted a couple of minutes? I had time to get here in the ambulance."

"What you experienced at the school was what we call an aura. It's kind of a warning that a seizure is coming on."

"So that weird feeling in my head and the changes in sight and sound were a warning?"

"That's right. You didn't actually have a seizure until you were in the ambulance. By the time you reached the hospital you had pretty much come out of it."

"I don't remember getting here."

"It's not uncommon to sleep very soundly after a seizure."

I looked at my mom. She was still holding my hand and looking at the doctor.

"I'm sorry. I didn't introduce myself." He came over to the bed and shook my hand. "I'm Dr. Farmer. I met your mother earlier."

"I assume," he continued, "that you are not epileptic or diabetic since we didn't find a medical ID on you."

"No."

"Dr. Farmer, he's never had a seizure before," Mom said. "He's really never been sick, except the usual childhood things. What happened?"

"I'm not sure I can tell you," he said. "But I will tell you that these things happen sometimes with no explanation and then never happen again. We call it idiopathic."

"What does that mean?" I asked.

"Exactly what it sounds like, we're idiots. We have no idea why you had a seizure."

"So what should we do? Just hope and pray?" Mom asked.

"That's a good start." He laughed. "But I would also recommend a complete neurological work up. Let's make sure there isn't a medical reason for this."

"And if there is?" Mom asked.

"Then there is also a treatment."

"And if there isn't a medical reason?"

"Then there is probably a psychological reason."

Mom looked at me. Her eyes were shining with tears. She brushed my hair away from my face.

"Cut it out, Mom," I said, pushing her hand away.

"Be nice to your mother, young man," Dr. Farmer said. "You scared her to death today."

I looked down at the sheet in front of me. I didn't want to look at my mom. I was afraid I'd cry.

"Stress can cause these things," Dr. Farmer continued. "It could be as simple as learning stress management. Have you been under a lot of pressure lately?"

"No," I said too quickly and looked at my mom sharply. She didn't say anything.

"Well, we'll get to the bottom of it," he said. "Now, I'm going to discharge you. I'll send someone in with papers for you to sign, the referral for a neurologist, and a list of things for you to avoid that could bring one of these episodes on. You won't have any more seizures today. I feel pretty sure of that." He left the room then looked back around the door. "Just to be safe though, David, don't drive anywhere today."

✦

"No David," Mom said in the car on the way home. "We are not going to the school to get your car. It will be there in the morning when I drop you off. You can drive it home tomorrow."

"Come on, Mom, it's not safe in that parking lot over night. You heard the doctor. I won't have another seizure today."

"I also heard him say don't drive anywhere today. If you want I'll call Uncle Jeff. He can go get the car."

"No, I don't want him to know about the seizure."

"Why not, honey? He cares about you."

"I just don't want him to know, Mom, please."

"Alright,"

"I don't want Dad to know either."

"Honey, I understand with Uncle Jeff, but your father has a right to know."

"Why does he have any rights? He's only biologically my father. It's bad enough he has a son he doesn't want. Now he's got one that's defective."

"David!" We pulled into the driveway and stopped. "You are not defective, and your father does too want you. He sends his child support on time every month. If he didn't want you he wouldn't send those cards every year. He's never missed a single one."

"And all that keeps his conscience clear!" I shouted. "He doesn't want me any more than he wanted you. Don't tell him about this, Mom. I mean it."

I jumped out of the car and ran to the front door. I'd seen my mom's hurt expression. I hated myself for saying that to her, but I had to say it, and she'd better not tell him about this.

I unlocked the front door and ran through the house to the back. Charlotte jumped at the back door, and I let her in. I scooped her up in my arms, closed the door in Ruffles' face, and ran up to my room.

CHAPTER FIVE

"So what did the doctor say?" Teresa asked.

"He said I'd be fine if I had sex at least twice a day, preferably three times."

We were in the back of my car. If I pulled the seats down between the back seat and the trunk even I could almost stretch out. We had spent the last couple of months since my birthday getting to know each other's bodies.

"Well, we've taken care of the first time. You won't get the second unless you tell me what he really said." We were lying together on our sides, her back to my front. I had my face buried in her thick soft hair.

"They took about a hundred pictures of the inside of my head and my spine and did all sorts of blood work. You won't believe what they found."

"What is it, David?" She turned over so she was facing me. Her eyes looked concerned.

"Nothing,"

"Nothing?" she asked.

"Nope, not even a brain. My head is completely empty."

"Shut up." She leaned forward and kissed me "We all know better than that."

I rolled onto my back and put my hands under my head. "There isn't anything wrong. It was just stress. There was a list of things I should avoid to keep it from happening again. The only one that I think matters is caffeine. I was drinking a lot of Coke to stay up studying at night. I won't do that anymore."

"That sounds a little too simple to me." She started to pull on her clothes. "That was a pretty scary thing that happened to you."

"I wasn't scared. Why are you getting dressed? What about round two?"

"Sorry," she laughed. "You only said that about needing sex twice a day because I'm so good in bed."

"I have no idea how good you are in bed. I only know about the back of a car." I slapped her bare bottom. She was sticking it up to pull her pants over it.

"Get dressed, David. I have to go home. I'm sitting for my little brother tonight."

✦

I pulled my car into the driveway up to the garage. The town house only had a one car garage. Vern's car was at the curb. I figured Mom's was inside. The front door opened and Vern came out. He wore his usual white short sleeved button up shirt. I couldn't believe the way he always had it buttoned all the way up to the top.

"You are a surly little snot!" he said to me.

I laughed since that was the most interesting thing he'd ever said to me. "It's nice to see you too, Vern." I thought it was funny him calling me little. I was at least a foot taller than him. My mom was taller than him.

"Your mother just gave me my walking papers, and I'm sure it had something to do with you."

"You don't think maybe she just got tired of waiting for you to propose?"

"Considering the first time I asked her to marry me was over a year ago. No, I don't think so." He turned toward his car. "We'll I'm better free of you, even if it means losing her too."

I didn't watch him go to his car. Who cares, I thought. I went to the house and found Mom in her little sewing room off the kitchen.

"S, Vern says it's my fault that you gave him the boot," I said. "Is that true?"

She looked up from her sewing machine. "I can't figure out why he thinks that."

"So why did you give him the boot?"

"He's leaving town, moving away. I don't want to go with him."

"So you don't love him."

She smiled. "You start every sentence with so."

"So?"

"It's hard to say I don't love him. He's very nice to me. He was good company. He never made my insides quiver like your dad did, but he stayed around."

"So," I said. "I guess he was more of a friend than anything else."

"I guess." She pressed the peddle and the machine whirred quietly. It was such a familiar sound.

"You slept with him," I said. She looked up sharply. Then she looked back down at the table.

"Yes, not that it's any of your business. It brings up another point though." She continued. "David, I want you to assure me that you understand the importance of safe sex."

"So, my sex life is your business but yours isn't mine."

"I'm your mother, David. It's my job to make sure you understand this. You are aware that it isn't just pregnancy that you are trying to avoid?"

"Mom, in this day and age, everyone on earth is aware of the importance of safe sex. I don't want to talk about it anymore." I left the room and ran up the stairs to take a shower. Could she tell somehow that I'd spent the afternoon in the trunk of my car with Teresa?

"David," Mom called through the bathroom door. "Your Uncle Jeff is on the phone. He wants to know if you'd like to go look at a house with him tonight."

"Sure," I called. It was something to do. Teresa wouldn't let me help her babysit. She said she had to wash her hair. "Tell him I'll be ready by the time he gets here."

✦

"It's the first house we looked at." Uncle Jeff said when we were in the truck. "You remember the brick ranch, an acre and a third of property. I think I'm going to buy it."

"I thought that house was boring."

"I look at it more like a blank canvas. I guess that's the artist in me."

"Well, that's great for the landscaping, but who's going to make the place livable."

"Mary Ann does a little interior decorating on the side. That's what she really likes to do. I think selling real estate just supports her habit."

"You mean she can't make a living decorating?"

"I think she probably could, but it's easier in real estate."

"Are you still dating her on and off?"

"More on than off now." We pulled into the drive and up to the garage. Uncle Jeff stopped the car and we both got out.

"Isn't Mary Ann going to be here?"

"No, I asked if you and I could look at it without her this time. Get the feel of the place with nobody looking over our shoulders." He went to the front door and unlocked it. We went inside.

There were two bedrooms on the front of the house. The master was on the back.

"I was thinking I'd take the wall down between these two bedrooms. Make a second master suite here. I'll take this bedroom. I'm planning to put a pond with a fountain out front. I know you don't like to sleep next to running water."

"Wrong again," I said.

"What do you mean wrong again, David. Didn't you change rooms because of that at the nursery?"

"I was eight years old, Uncle Jeff. I'm sixteen now. Besides how many times have we camped next to running water? I like the sound of it now." I turned and went down the hall toward the kitchen.

He followed me. "Well you can have the front suite then if you want it."

"Just choose where you want to live, Uncle Jeff. Then make the other room a guest room. You really don't have to plan your house around me. I'll be having my own house pretty soon."

"You'll always have a place in mine, David," he said. "No matter how mean you are." He went out the back door to the yard beyond.

"I'm sorry," I said when I followed him out.

"Charlotte, will have a blast running around out here. There's almost a full acre fenced in."

"You never let me bring Charlotte to your house," I grumbled.

"There was too much trouble for her to get into at the nursery. It would be a shame to waste this yard though." He walked toward the wooded area in the back. "I guess Ruffles could come over too if you want."

"I'm afraid with a whole acre Ruffles wouldn't be able to find his way back."

Uncle Jeff laughed and put his arm across my shoulders. We walked back toward the house.

"David, I wanted to talk to you about something," he said.

"What? Uncle Jeff, I've already committed to going to Harvard in the fall. You're not going to tell me you can't pay for it after all. I finally got Mom to agree."

"Of course not, David, I made a commitment to you. I started putting the money away when you were two years old." He opened the back door, and we went into the kitchen. "I'm planning to take the wall down between the dining room and the kitchen too. I think it'll be nicer if it's more open."

"So what did you want to talk to me about?" I leaned against the counter.

"You've been seeing Teresa pretty steadily now. I think it's been about a year that you've been going out."

I took a deep breath and rolled my eyes.

"I know you get tired of hearing about safe sex, David, but when you're young you think you're invincible. I need to know that you understand the dangers. Honestly, David, pregnancy isn't the worst of them."

"Why does everyone in the world think my sex life is their business?" I was yelling. My voice broke. It hadn't been doing that lately. It infuriated me even more.

"David ..."

"No Uncle Jeff, stay out of my business." I stormed to the front door and slammed it behind me. He came through a minute later and locked the door. We both walked to the car in silence. When we got in I said, "You're dating Mary Ann. You've been dating her on and off for years and you've dated other women. Do you know the importance of safe sex, Uncle Jeff?"

"Yes, I do," he said. "And I appreciate your concern."

"I'm sorry I yelled."

"I remember what it was like to be sixteen, David," he said. "I thought my parents were as stupid as you think I am."

When we got to the house, Mom was waiting for us on the front porch. She came to the driver's side of the car and Uncle Jeff rolled the window down.

"Jeff," she said. "I wanted to catch you. I was afraid you'd drop David and leave without coming in."

"Is something wrong?"

"Yes, I just got a call from your mother. Your father died this afternoon."

That was the first time I'd seen my Uncle cry. It was oddly disturbing. He just sat there in the driver's seat for a minute and stared at Mom.

"Come inside for a minute, Jeff," she said and opened his door. She took his arm, and he got out of the car. I got out of my side and followed them to the house. We went to the kitchen, and Mom led him to the table.

"Why don't you sit down for a minute? I'll get you some ginger ale." She stood in front of him and looked into his face. "Jeff, are you alright?" That was when he started to cry. His face just kind of crumpled. Mom put her arms around him. He seemed to just collapse onto her shoulders. They stood like that for a few minutes. He was sobbing. His shoulders were shaking.

After a minute he sat down at the table. He put his head down on his crossed arms and cried some more. I put my hand on his back and he sat up and looked at me. My eyes were dry. I was angry with myself. With all the times I choked back tears, why couldn't I find some when I needed them. I had visited my Grampa once a month from as far back as I could remember. He'd been nice to me, but in the past few years since his stroke he couldn't talk or anything.

"Decided to be strong again?" Uncle Jeff said.

I nodded and said, "I'm sorry."

"I guess I need to go see my mother. I wonder what else I need to do. I guess I'll need to find a funeral home and make arrangements. I suppose Mom has already called Brian." Uncle Jeff sipped the glass of ginger ale Mom had just put in front of him. "Why does ginger ale taste so good when you're crying?" He laughed weakly.

"I don't know," Mom said. She handed him a box of tissue. He took two of them and dried his eyes and blew his nose.

"It was time. He was old, and he never came back from that stroke. Mom was able to come back from the stroke she had a few years back. She never walked again but she could communicate."

"I guess your Dad just had more brain damage," Mom said. I got up and poured some ginger ale for myself. "I'm sorry, honey," Mom said. "I forget that you're grieving too."

"I'm okay. Uncle Jeff do you want me to go to Gramma's with you?"

"I'd appreciate it, David, but bring your own car. You may want to leave before I do."

"He just went to sleep in his wheel chair by the window. He did that a lot so I didn't think anything of it." Gramma was looking at the ground in front of her. Uncle Jeff was sitting in a chair next to her with his arm across her shoulders. When we first arrived, they had held each other and cried together. I was mad at myself again. All I could think of was that my Dad would come. He'd come to see them before and not contacted me. He couldn't avoid me this time.

"When they came to get us for dinner we couldn't wake him up. He still had a heartbeat at that point, but he was gone by the time the paramedics got here."

"I'm sorry I wasn't here, Mom."

"You're a good boy, Jeffrey." She put her hand on his cheek. I looked at her hand. It was so old. Would my Mom's hand look like that some day? I looked at Uncle Jeff's hands. They were weathered, but they didn't look old.

"You were never our favorite when you were growing up, but you're the one that's taken care of us in our old age," she said. "I'm sorry if we were mean to you about your work."

"You weren't mean, Mom. You didn't like what I wanted to do, but you put me through school. You helped me when I needed it."

"And now you've helped us when we needed you. We're lucky to get a visit from Brian twice a year."

He comes here twice a year? I thought.

"Brian helps with money, Mom. He's a busy man, and he lives far away. Is he on his way here?"

"Yes, he'll arrive late tonight. He'll stay with your Aunt Jeanne."

"I guess I need to call her. He was her brother after all."

"She was here this afternoon. She left just before you arrived."

"It's getting late but I'll call her. Do you need to come home with me tonight, Mom? I've got plenty of space and David can help me get your wheel chair up the stairs. I can carry you. You're light as a feather."

"That would be nice, honey. I don't want to be alone tonight."

"David, you're huge." My dad put his arms around me and held me close to his chest. I put my arms around his back for a second then pulled away from him.

"The last time I saw you, you asked me why you were so small." He smiled at me looking slightly upward. "Remember?"

"Yeah," I said and stepped back a little.

"I guess you're the tallest in your class now."

"I was," I said. "I don't know how tall people will be at Harvard." We were at Uncle Jeff's apartment getting ready to go to Grampa's funeral. I had opened the door when the bell rang. Uncle Jeff was still in his room. Gramma was sitting in the living room looking out the window at the fountain display.

"Brian!" Uncle Jeff said from behind me. My dad looked around me. He put his arms around Uncle Jeff. I'd never seen them hug. More distressing than that, they both started to cry. I stepped back and bit my lip. It was the first time I'd felt a lump in my throat since Grampa died.

"I can't believe he's gone." Dad pulled away first and took a tissue from the box on the foyer table.

"Are those my beautiful sons?" Gramma called from the living room. Uncle Jeff led the way to where she sat in the living room. Dad and Uncle Jeff knelt on either side of her. They all three hugged each other and cried. I swallowed the lump in my throat and went to the bathroom to head off the tears. I was not going to cry.

When I came back they were all dabbing at their eyes with tissue and talking about Grampa.

"Are you about ready to help me get Gramma down to the car, David?" Uncle Jeff said.

"I'll carry you, Mom," Dad said. He picked her up out of the wheel chair then put her back down. "I forgot. I hurt my back a few months ago. I guess you'll have to do it, Jeff. I'll help David with the wheel chair."

"If you can just carry the cushions, I can get the chair," I said.

Once we had Gramma settled in the truck I started to climb into the back of the extended cab.

"Why don't you ride with me?" Dad said.

I frowned and looked at Uncle Jeff. I didn't want to ride with my dad.

"I need David to help me when we get to the funeral home, Brian."

"We'll be right behind you," Dad said.

Uncle Jeff looked at me and shrugged. He really couldn't help me. I went to the passenger side of my dad's rental car and got in.

"David," Dad said when we pulled into the traffic. "After the funeral, I'd like to take you to lunch. My flight back to Chicago leaves at 6:00 pm. I'll have to head to the airport by about three to get through security and all. But I think we have some time to spend together."

"You're leaving tonight? You only got here yesterday."

"I know, son, but my schedule is full. I have to go back."

I didn't say anything.

"I don't like it anymore than you do," he said.

"I don't have a problem with it, Dad. I completely understand." I looked out the window. "Lunch would be really nice. Maybe we could take Mom."

"I'd really like to spend a little time with just you. I'm so proud of you. Harvard is an incredible accomplishment."

"I think I just test well."

"Oh come on, David." He laughed. "You're only sixteen years old. You shouldn't have even finished high school yet. You are definitely an over achiever. You know, I told Jeff I'd help with tuition, and I want to set up a monthly allowance for you."

"Thanks."

"Aunt Jeanne says you have a lovely girlfriend. Will I meet her at the funeral?"

I looked over at him. He acted like this was some kind of social event, some kind of party. "No," I said. "She wanted to come but I asked her not to. She didn't know Grampa."

"She wanted to be here to support you."

"I needed to do this alone." The truth was that I didn't want her to see me cry. I was pretty sure I could maintain control, at least until I saw Dad. Until then I hadn't felt like crying. If I did cry though, I didn't want her to see. "So why isn't your wife here to support you?" My heart thumped when I said that. I hadn't planned to, and I knew it wasn't very nice.

He didn't say anything.

I spent an hour and a half with my dad that day. We talked about what I planned to study in college. We talked about Teresa. We talked about my dog and a very little bit about my mom.

I smiled a lot. I wanted him to believe that I was happy without him. I was happy without him. My life was perfect. Why did I need him?

"Do you want me to take you back to Aunt Jeanne's house? I know the family is meeting there this afternoon. I guess it's kind of a wake or a memorial for Grampa," he asked. "Or would you rather I take you home so you can pick up your car."

"Take me to Aunt Jeanne's," I said. "Uncle Jeff will give me a ride home." The truth was, I wanted to be there when Dad left. I also needed some time with my Uncle. I didn't want my own car.

"David," he said when we were approaching my Aunt and Uncle's house. "It isn't that I don't believe your mother and your uncle have done a good job with you, but I need to ask you something."

Oh shit, I thought. I knew what was coming, and for the first time, I was glad about it. It meant he cared.

"I'm so happy that you have such a good relationship with Teresa, but I need to know that you understand the importance of safe sex."

I smiled and looked out the window. I didn't want him to see me laugh. "I know the importance of safe sex," I said. I sounded angrier than I'd thought I would.

"I know you don't want to talk about this," he said. "But I need to be sure that you understand that pregnancy is the least of the dangers. There are diseases and …"

"Dad!" I stopped him. "I've been to all the films. I've talked to all the adults. I know about safe sex. Now I don't want to talk about it anymore." I was angry, and the anger felt good. It felt better than knowing he cared.

"Alright," he said as we pulled up behind a car parked at the curb in front of my Aunt Jeanne's house. "It looks like there are a number of people here already."

"A lot of people loved Grampa," I said and reached for the car door handle.

"David." Dad stopped me with his hand on my arm. "Like I've said a million times before, I think about you every day. I love you very much."

I looked back at him but said nothing.

"I know it's hard. It's hard on both of us, son. I want you to trust me on this. It wouldn't work to try to combine the two families."

"I trust you on that," I said. "I think about you every day too, Dad." I didn't tell him about the anger, the feelings of abandonment. I pulled the door handle and opened the door. "I love you too," I said as I got out of the car. I felt that lump in my throat again. It was true. I did love him.

✺

The next time I saw my dad, I was eighteen years old. He came to my Gramma's funeral. We had lunch together.

✺

"I'm glad we didn't have to call off the backpacking trip," I said. We were sitting at the beginning point of the Trail.

"Your Grampa wouldn't have wanted us to do that. He was having a great time plotting our progress on the Trail. He started when we started and took great pride in showing us the map he was drawing. Remember?"

"Yeah, until he had that stroke. He just didn't come back from that stroke. Too much damage I guess."

"Are you sure you don't want to stay in a hotel tonight, David?" Uncle Jeff asked. "The drive to Tennessee took a little longer than I expected. It's seven miles to Clingman's Dome. We won't want to go that far tonight."

"No," I said. "If you don't mind I'd like to get on the trail. It's funny. I can't seem to sleep anywhere but in the woods anymore. Clingman's Dome will be more spectacular in the morning anyway. Don't you think?"

"Probably," he said. "We can camp a few miles before it and hike to it in the morning."

"I understand it's the highest peak on the Trail." I stroked Charlottes back and stood up. She smiled up at me. "Stay," I said and dropped the leash to put on my pack.

"That's right, 6,640 feet." Uncle Jeff stood and pulled on his pack. "I'll bet it feels like you're on top of the world."

We started up the trail with Charlotte scampering ahead sniffing the ground.

"Your mom was telling me you don't sleep well, David. She says she wakes up in the middle of the night and your light is still on. I haven't noticed it of course." He laughed. "I sleep like a rock."

"Yeah, and snore like a chain saw." I laughed with him. "It's funny though, your snoring doesn't bother me at all in the woods."

"Does it bother you at home? Maybe we could get some kind of soundproofing when I renovate the house."

"I don't think that's necessary, Uncle Jeff. Mom doesn't snore, and I can't sleep there either."

"What is it? Are you worried about something? Is it anxiety?"

"It was when I was in school. Well some anxiety, but mostly it's like I just can't get my brain to turn off. You know I've got all these projects I'm doing on the computer, and I'm putting together a cookbook of all my favorite recipes. Before I know it the night is gone. I usually get an hour or so before daylight. But when the sun comes up, so do I."

He laughed. "Do you feel tired all the time?"

"No, but I feel tense. It just seems like sleep would be a nice break from thinking. I think too much."

"Maybe you should try meditation or something like that. You can take lessons you know." He tapped me on the shoulder. "Look." He pointed to three deer standing on the path ahead of us. One was a buck sporting a good size rack of antlers.

"I've never seen a buck that old before." I picked up the camera that hung around my neck. "Something tells me this trip is going to make a great chapter in my hiking album."

"How about this for a stopping point?" I said to Uncle Jeff when we came around a corner of the trail that opened onto a wide spot in the stream we'd been following. "That's a great looking bathing pond. I could use a bath tonight. Riding in the car always makes me feel grimy."

"Looks great to me," he said. "I figure we've done three miles and in the morning we'll have a little less than five to reach the dome. I can't wait to see it. I've read that it's a spectacular view."

We set up our camp. We'd gotten it down to perfection after seven years of camping. We had all the comforts of home.

"I know my snoring didn't keep you up last night, David." Uncle Jeff crawled out of the tent that we shared. I was coming out from behind a tree after emptying my very full bladder. Charlotte followed me toward the stream after emptying her own full bladder.

"No, I don't think you snored last night."

"Who could tell with all the noise you were making." He laughed and disappeared behind another tree.

"Did I really snore?" I stooped by the stream to brush my teeth and wash my face. Charlotte lapped at the water then sat on dry ground to wait for me.

"Like a chain saw," he said as he joined me.

"I'm sorry."

"Not to worry, buddy roe. I was glad you were sleeping."

"I always sleep well in the woods. I need to simulate the forest in my bedroom somehow." I laughed. "Let's not stoke the fire, Uncle Jeff." I stopped him as he started to stir at the coals.

"You don't want breakfast?"

"Let's get some coffee on the camp stove then head for the dome."

"Okay," he smiled. "You look really excited."

"Amazing what a good night's sleep can do for you."

"I brought decaffeinated coffee if you want it," he said.

"No, I think I'll drink the real thing this time. I'm not too worried about it."

We drank our coffee while we packed up the site. Uncle Jeff had some dried fruit and nuts for us to munch on. Trail mix I guess you'd call it since we actually did eat it on the trail. It was light but energizing as we hiked the last few miles to the Dome.

"I think you could definitely call that a strenuous hike," I said as we neared our destination.

"The whole thing has been. Yesterday we really maneuvered some rough terrain. Then this last rocky climb, I'm just glad they've maintained the Trail so well." Uncle Jeff was a little bit out of breath.

"Yeah, I'm glad for the steps and hand rails." I stopped as we came on to the open area of the dome. The scene was breath taking. For as far as you could see everything was below us. "Look Uncle Jeff, there's a platform that leans over the mountain and a bridge to get there." I turned to look at him and gasped. "What's wrong?! You're white as a ghost!"

He swayed and I jumped to his side. He put his hand on my shoulder and steadied himself. "I don't feel right, David. I need to sit down."

I found him a bench near the foot bridge and helped him to sit.

"I was feeling queasy for the last mile or so. Then when we climbed that last set of steps, I felt light headed." He sat down and put his head between his knees. He sat up quickly. "Nope, that makes me spin worse," he said.

"Uncle Jeff, lie down on the bench." I pulled off his pack and helped him lie down. I put the pack on the end of the bench and propped his feet on it. Then I went to his head and stooped down next to him. "If you puke, puke in the other direction, okay?" I said.

He smiled but didn't open his eyes.

"Maybe this strenuous of a hike is too much for an old guy like you. Have you been to the doctor lately?" I wanted to lighten things up a little, but I had to admit I was nervous. I'd never seen my Uncle look like that before.

"I'm fine, David. My checkup was fine this year, and I'm in good physical condition. I think I just didn't nourish myself properly this morning." Now he opened his eyes and looked up at the clear blue sky. "I'm starting to feel the blood coming back into my head now."

"Yeah, I'm seeing the color return to your face. I've never seen a person turn that color before," I said.

He slowly sat up and put his legs over the side of the bench. I sat down beside him.

"It was probably the color I turn every time I go to sleep in the car." I reached into my pack where it was sitting on the ground beside me and pulled out a package of cheese and crackers. "I know you prefer the cheese." I handed it to him.

He smiled and opened the package. He bit into one of the crackers and chewed slowly.

"Kind of a reversal in roles isn't it?" I said. "It's kind of fun."

"It wasn't fun for me," he said, but he was smiling.

"I guess not." I pulled out my water bottle and handed it to him.

Uncle Jeff insisted on walking out to the viewing deck. The scene was spectacular. I took a bunch of pictures, but we didn't stay on the dome long. We were planning to cover a good bit of ground this year. Not only that, but Uncle Jeff didn't recover completely until we were hiking back down the hill.

We were on the trail for five days. We saw deer, a mother bear with cubs, and a bald eagle. When we came off the trail my camera was full of pictures. I couldn't wait to get to work on my computer.

"We did some serious hiking this week," I said when we got on the bus to take us back to our car. "Next year let's go another couple of days maybe another week. We can finish up Tennessee and get into Virginia."

"Sounds great," Uncle Jeff said. "You look great, David, more rested and excited than I've seen you in a long time."

"I feel good too. I love backpacking."

✧

"In two weeks you leave for Harvard," Uncle Jeff said as we pulled into my driveway.

"Yeah, I'm really excited."

"You'll be the youngest student there."

"Oh, I don't know. There are probably other kids who finish high school early."

"I'm going to miss you, son. You'll still backpack with me at spring break won't you?" Uncle Jeff's voice broke. For a minute I thought he was going to cry. I didn't know what to do.

"Here comes Mom," I said when the front door opened and she hurried over to the car. "Sure, I'll be home at spring break. We'll backpack then." I got out of the truck to hug Mom and Uncle Jeff got out too. I looked closely at him. He didn't look like he'd been about to cry. Maybe I imagined it.

✧

"Hey." I answered my cell phone. It was on vibrate because it was 1:00 am. I looked at the caller ID. It was Teresa.

"I thought you'd still be up."

"So what's going on?"

"I wanted to come over and show you something." She sounded mysterious.

"Why don't you come over and show me everything." I teased.

"Very funny, we're not going to make love tonight. I wanted to turn you on to something else."

"It can't be as fun as sex."

"Meet me outside."

"Okay." I hung up the phone and left my room. I looked into Mom's room. She was sound asleep with Ruffles stretched out beside her.

Charlotte was beside me. When I got to the front door I took her leash off the hook and clipped it to her collar. If I tried to leave her behind she'd make a racket.

Teresa's car was creeping down the street with the lights off. What kind of silliness is she up to now, I wondered. She was always doing something to try to surprise me. She pulled up behind my car at the curb and got out.

"Let's take a walk," she whispered.

"At 1:00 in the morning?"

"Yeah." We started down the street. She pulled a hand rolled cigarette out of her pocket and a lighter.

"Is that marijuana?" I asked.

"Yeah, a bunch of the kids at school are smoking it. It's fun, David. Try it."

"I don't think so, Teresa." I leaned down to stroke Charlotte. She trotted along beside me in a perfect heel.

"It'll help you sleep."

"Nothing will help me sleep."

"David, you're just too intense. That's why you have so much stress. You just can't stop thinking. This will help you. I'm sure of it. If you can just learn some way to relax I'm sure you'll never have another seizure."

"I'm not going to have another seizure anyway."

"One puff, David," she said. She lit the joint, took a long drag, and started to cough. She handed it to me and I did the same.

It hurt going into my lungs. I coughed and looked back at the house. We had gone far enough that Mom couldn't have heard anything. I took another puff. This time it didn't burn so much. It almost felt good. We walked along and Teresa started to talk.

"I'm going to miss you so much when you go away," she said. "You'll probably find someone else and you won't want me anymore."

"You know that's not true." I put my arm around her waist and pulled her close to me. I kissed her cheek, and she turned her mouth to mine. She put her arms around my neck. "We'll be together forever, Teresa. I love you."

"I love you too."

"Let's get into my car and go somewhere so we can make love," I whispered.

"There isn't any place we can go. I only snuck out for a minute. They'll realize I'm gone if I stay away too long. I have to go back."

I felt very relaxed. She was right. That stuff made me feel good. I wanted to make love to her in my bed and then drift off to sleep holding on

Chapter Five / 90

to her. What a thought. How many years would it be before we could do that?

"We'll have to wait until tomorrow." She turned and started walking back to her car.

"I don't want to wait." I put my arms around her from behind and nibbled her neck. "I want you to come back to my bed with me, and we'll just forget about the rest of the world."

"I can't," she giggled. When we got to her car she put her arms around me again and kissed me deeply. Her tongue teased mine and she ran her hands through my hair. Then she pulled away and got into her car. She smiled out the window, started the motor, and pulled away.

I could feel myself standing there with a goofy grin on my face and a raging erection. It was hot outside in August in Atlanta, but it felt good right now. The air felt soft on my skin. I went to the door of my house and opened it quietly. Charlotte followed me in and startled me as she brushed my leg. I looked at the leash in my hand. I'd forgotten I was holding it. I laughed then put my hand over my mouth and looked in the direction of my mother's room.

I went upstairs, took off my clothes and crawled into bed. I don't remember falling asleep. When I woke up in the morning my computer was still on. "Oh man," I said out loud. "I didn't even save my work." I went to the computer, saved my work, and logged off.

"Wow," I said as I went into the bathroom to take a shower. "It's nine thirty. I never sleep that late." I realized I was talking out loud to myself and stopped. I felt so rested. The only other time in my life that I felt that refreshed in the morning was when I was backpacking. I wondered where I could get some more of that stuff.

Teresa was crying and holding on to me. I felt that familiar pain in my throat and my eyes wanted to explode. I'd felt that feeling so many times over the years I knew how to deal with it. I swallowed and laughed.

"Don't laugh at me." Teresa pulled away and buried her face in a tissue. "This hurts too much. Please don't go, David."

"I wasn't laughing at you, Teresa. I was laughing at myself. If I laugh I won't cry."

"Why don't you cry? Don't you have feelings?"

"I have feelings. I wish you could come with me. I don't know what I'll do without you, but men don't cry." I felt stupid saying that. I'd seen my Uncle and my Dad cry. I knew men cried.

"That's just stupid." She sniffed. "Besides, you're not a man. You're only sixteen years old."

"I've been the man of my family since I was two years old." I pulled her close to me again. It felt good to hold her. She was a tall girl. Her head rested easily on my shoulder so that I could put my face in her hair. It always smelled like peppermint.

We just stood like that for a minute. We were on her front porch. Her parents were unusually absent. They'd always watched us pretty closely when we were at their house. Today I was leaving for school. I'd come to say goodbye.

"I have to go." I reluctantly pulled away from her. She walked down the walk with me to my car.

"Why aren't you taking your car to school with you?"

"Mom won't let me. She said we'd see about it next year. I think she's afraid of the winter driving."

"I hadn't thought about that. Be careful, David. Don't let anything happen to you up there."

"I won't, and you be careful down here. I'll call you as soon as I get there." We kissed one last time, and I got into my car to go home. I looked back and she was standing in the driveway waving. Her mother came out of the house and put her arms around her. I held that picture in my mind. I wanted to have it with me. I was feeling the first pangs of homesickness before I'd even left.

Mom and Uncle Jeff were going up with me. We'd shipped my stuff off the day before, and our flight left in a couple of hours. Charlotte and Ruffles were at the kennel. I hated that. They'd never been boarded before.

We went to my dorm room first. My roommate was there. His name was Richard Barrett. He was a small kid with a big head and horn rimmed glasses. I looked like a giant next to him, but I figured I'd get used to that. I'd been taller than everyone for a couple of years at least. I was definitely skinnier than him too.

"If you go out in a high wind, David, stay close to Richard," Mom whispered while we were carrying my trunk into the room.

"Funny," I whispered back.

"Hello." A man who looked very much like Richard put out his hand to Uncle Jeff. "I'm Richard Barrett Sr.," he said. "And this is my wife Kaye."

I noticed that Kaye was taller than either one of the Richards.

"We're Richard's parents."

Kaye smiled and shook my mother's hand. "David," she said. "You look exactly like your father." She looked at Uncle Jeff and smiled.

I had the feeling that the smile was somewhat flirtatious.

"Except for the eyes," she said. Yours are brown, and your father's eyes are a very nice shade of blue," she said.

Yep, definitely flirtatious, Uncle Jeff smiled back, but he didn't tell her he wasn't my father. I didn't either.

"I don't know," Mom said. "Your son looks pretty much like his father."

"He's my stepson."

"Oh." Mom turned to me. "David, I think we'll go check in at the hotel and freshen up. We have the parent student orientation dinner in a couple of hours. Do you want to come to the hotel with us?"

"No," I said. "I think I'll stay here and get acquainted with Richard. I need to unpack all this stuff too."

"I guess we'll walk out with you," Richard Senior said. "We'll see you tonight, son, at the orientation dinner."

✦

"The letter said that you're one of the younger students too." Richard said when the parents had left. We were unpacking our trunks and setting up either side of our room. There were two beds, two desks and two bedside tables.

"Yeah, I graduated from high school a year early," I said.

"I did too. I'm sixteen, but I'll be seventeen on September fifth."

"I won't be seventeen until next spring."

"I was a little disappointed," he said. "The whole reason I worked so hard to graduate early was to get away from punks like you."

I turned and looked at him. He was trying to move his desk into a slanted position under the window and struggling with the weight. He looked at me and laughed. His smile was genuine. His whole face lit up with it.

"Could you give me a hand here?"

I laughed and crossed the room. I took the other side of his desk and helped him carry it to where he wanted.

"I heard your mother tell you to stay close to me in a high wind."

"I'm sorry."

"Not a problem. I have a Mom too. You know Miss Kaye isn't my mother."

"I heard her say that."

"My Mom is the one I'll miss. I haven't really spent much time with my Dad. Since he's paying for school he got drop off privileges. I had to leave Mom at home since they can't be in the same room with each other without friction." He laughed.

At least your dad wanted drop off privileges, I thought.

"People call me Rich. Do people call you Dave?" he asked.

"No one ever has. I don't really care though."

"Maybe I'll call you Dave if it fits."

"Okay." I could tell I was going to like Rich. I was glad. I needed a friend. I could feel the homesickness starting. I wanted more than anything to go home. Why did I do this? Why didn't I just go to State like Mom wanted me to? Then I could have lived at home.

"Hey, let's go over to the student center." Rich said. "Find out what people do for fun around here. I plan to spend most of my time studying, but at first I need to have some fun. Otherwise, I'm going to get depressed."

"Me too," I said. I was amazed that he wasn't embarrassed to admit it. I'd have never told him I missed my mom and my uncle.

"That was very nice," Mom said as we left the dining hall where we'd had the orientation dinner. "Are you sure you don't want to come back to the hotel with us tonight, David. Uncle Jeff has two double beds in his room, and I'm right next door."

"No, I might as well get used to my new bed, my new room, and my new roommate," I said. I really wanted to go back to the hotel with them and then back to Atlanta with them the next morning, but I wasn't going to admit that.

"Well, if you need anything, honey, we don't leave for the airport until around ten. Just call." We got to the car and Mom turned to me. She brushed tears away from her cheeks and put her arms around me. I held her and she cried for a minute.

"I love you, David. You're everything in the world to me. Please take care of yourself."

"I will, Mom. I promise. I already have my plane ticket to come home at Thanksgiving. It won't be that long." I was surprised I didn't feel like crying. I thought I would when we said goodbye.

Mom pulled away from me and slid into the passenger side of the rental car. Uncle Jeff put his hand on my shoulder and turned me to face him. His face was crumpled like it had been when Grampa died. He sobbed a little then wrapped his arms around me in a crushing hug.

"God, I'll miss you, David," he sobbed.

I looked around a little to see if anyone was watching. I could imagine how ridiculous two six foot four men must look holding each other like this. Luckily everyone was pretty caught up in their own dramas.

"I'll miss you too, Uncle Jeff."

Chapter Five

"David," Uncle Jeff said as he eased the pressure and moved slightly away from me. "Promise me you'll value yourself." It was almost a whisper in my ear.

I pulled a little further away from him to look at his face. It was almost dark outside, but I could see his concern.

"I will."

"I mean for yourself, David, not just for your mother and me."

"Don't worry," I said. Suddenly I noticed that there were blank spots in my vision. I blinked my eyes. They didn't go away. I needed to get away from here. "I promise to take care of myself." I turned and walked away. "I'll call you in the morning at the hotel before you leave." I called over my shoulder.

"Alright," Uncle Jeff said. I turned to wave at him. He waved back and walked around the car to get into the driver's seat.

The spots were still in my vision. In fact, there was something like a hole in the center of it. What could that be? I wondered if it could be another seizure. But it wasn't the same as the aura I'd had before the seizure.

✧

"That was brutal," Rich said when I got to the room. "My dad actually cried." He shook his head as if to clear it. "I'm going over to the student center. There's a movie playing, and a couple of the guys we met this afternoon are going to meet me there. Want to come along?"

"No," I said. "I've got a headache. I think I'll read a while and turn in early."

"Okay, I'll try not to disturb you when I get back."

I tried to read but the vision problem prevented it. I turned out the light and tried to sleep, but my head pounded too hard. I wished for a joint. Teresa had gotten me an ounce before I left, but I couldn't chance bringing it on the plane. So I hid it in my room. I was sure a joint would cure whatever was bothering me now.

Rich came in at midnight. There was a curfew for freshmen. I pretended to be asleep. He turned on his light and read for a little while, then went to sleep. I was disappointed to find out that he snored, worse than Uncle Jeff.

The headache got worse and I began to feel nauseated. I got up and got dressed. The house mother met me in the lobby of the dorm.

"What are you doing up?" she asked. "What's your name?"

"I'm David Landrum. I feel really sick. I can't see and my head aches. I'm starting to feel nauseated."

"Do you have something that you usually take for migraine headaches?"

"I've never had a migraine headache."

"Oh." She looked into my eyes. "I think you're having one now. Let's get you to the infirmary. I'll drive you."

"That's okay," I said. "Just tell me where it is. I'll walk."

"If you can't see, I'm not going to let you walk all alone in a strange place at night," she said. "It isn't much of a walk. I'll go with you." She locked the door and we went out into the night.

I took a deep breath of the cool night air. It wasn't cool even at night in Georgia this time of the year. I shook my head and pain shot through it. Migraine headaches, seizures, I thought, I'm falling apart and I'm only sixteen years old.

CHAPTER SIX

"Where did you go?" Rich asked when I returned to the room at nine the next morning.

"I spent the night in the infirmary. I had a migraine headache," I said.

"Really, Dave, did your dad cry too?"

"No, my dad didn't cry. Speaking of which, I told them I'd call before they leave. I'd better hurry."

I pulled out my cell phone and dialed the number to the hotel.

"Hey, Mom," I said when she answered.

"Hi, sweetie, how was your first night at college?"

"Great, I'm really excited. Today I go to see my counselor. We'll plan my schedule and then I'll register. I can't wait."

"That's wonderful. I know how much you like to study but remember to have some fun too. Make some friends."

"I will, Mom. I like Rich a lot. I already have a friend. I'll make more."

"Good, honey, we're about to leave. Uncle Jeff has taken the bags down to the car, and I'm on my way down the steps. Here he is. I'll let you say goodbye to him. I love you, David."

"I love you too, Mom," I said. I talked briefly to Uncle Jeff then hung up the phone.

"You didn't tell them about the migraine," Rich said. "Do you get those things a lot? My older sister gets them. It doesn't look like much fun."

"I've never had one before and I plan to never have one again. I don't see any reason to worry my parents," I said. "Oh, by the way, that man you met isn't my dad. He's my uncle. Even though my dad is helping to pay for this, he didn't want drop off privileges."

"You're kidding, Dave." It felt funny being called that. It made me want to laugh every time he said it. "I can't believe that guy isn't your dad. You look just like him."

"He and my dad are identical twins. My Uncle Jeff raised me, along with my mom of course."

"So you don't know your dad very well either."

"I've only seen him a few times in my whole life. He lives in Chicago and has another family. He doesn't think it's a good idea to combine the two families. He says someone always gets hurt." I gathered up my shaving kit and soap for a shower and went toward the bathroom.

"I wish my dad felt that way. We have combined the families and it's a mess. My half brother is a brat, and Kaye can hardly stand the two weeks my sister and I spend with them every summer. I'm just grateful that we don't live close enough for him to get every other week end. That would suck."

I looked at Rich. He seemed to really feel that way. I hadn't thought about it in that kind of detail. I'd always just felt rejected. Maybe Dad was right.

"What are you staring at?" Rich broke into my thoughts.

"Nothing," I said turning back toward the bathroom. "I'm going to take a quick shower and get ready for my appointment. It's at eleven o'clock."

"Mine's at eleven too. I think a group of us go into a big room and wait for our councilors. We can walk over together."

"Good."

The homesickness was excruciating. Rich struggled too. He would go into the bathroom and stay there sometimes for half an hour. He'd come out with his eyes all red and puffy. He really missed his mom.

I missed mine too. I had expected to miss her though. It was Uncle Jeff that brought me the closest to tears. I was surprised about that. I hadn't expected to miss him so much. We didn't live together full time, and when we spent time together he tended to get on my nerves. But I couldn't wait to see him.

Thinking about Charlotte was just too painful. So I tried not to. I even missed big stupid Ruffles. I didn't cry though, and I didn't have another migraine headache.

I talked to Teresa three times a week in the first month. At night I tried to remember touching her. It was the only way I could go to sleep. I didn't sleep much though. I kept my plane ticket home for Thanksgiving under my pillow. Sometimes I got four or five hours but there were a lot of nights that I didn't sleep at all.

Some of the kids in the dorm smoked pot, but I decided I'd better stay really clean until I learned my way around this place. So I took my books and my computer into the bathroom to study until I discovered that Rich could sleep through a cannon blast. Then I just sat at my desk.

The big difference in Harvard and High school was the competition. In high school I was the smartest person in the class. That was not the case here. Everyone was smart.

"Man, I have to work really hard to keep up here. I never had to do that in high school," I said to Rich in early November.

"I know what you mean," he said. "I was always waiting for the slow students in High school. I mean some kids weren't smart and some had learning problems. I was just tapping my feet until I figured out how to go to school on line."

"Me too. My best friend at home has learning disabilities. The weird thing is that he's not stupid. He's really smart. He just can't follow written directions."

"You know what though, Dave," Rich sounded serious so I looked up at him from my computer.

"What?"

"I'm worried about you. There are all these frat parties going on and other stuff too. You never go to any of them."

Rich came in from parties a bunch of times. I could always smell beer on him. A few times I smelled pot on him too. "I drank too much beer once at home in the woods with some friends. It made me sick. I don't really like the stuff."

"You don't have to drink enough to make you sick, Dave. You'll like it if you take it slow. There are some really pretty women at this place. There's a party tonight, go with me."

"I told you. I have a girlfriend."

"It's still fun to talk to pretty women. You don't have to go home with any of them." He stood up and picked up his jacket. Boston was cold in the beginning of November. "Have a little fun, Dave."

As always it made me feel like laughing when he called me Dave. "Alright, I'll stop in for a little while. We're way underage though. How do you get beer?"

"Nobody's paying attention. Come on. Let's go on over."

"Okay." I logged off my computer and shut it down. I took my coat off the peg and went across the campus to the party with Rich.

He was right. There were a lot of very pretty women there. None of them wanted anything to do with me. I was only sixteen years old and built like a six foot four flag pole. I drank a little beer and felt a pleasant buzz. I waved the joint on when it came my way, and I left at a little after ten o'clock.

I slept that night for six hours.

The next morning I started marking the days off my calendar. In two weeks we would have mid-terms. The next week it was home for Thanksgiving. I couldn't wait to see Mom and Charlotte and Uncle Jeff. I couldn't wait to actually put my arms around Teresa. I was missing her even more these days since I hadn't been able to get in touch with her for a while.

Her mother said she was very busy with school and cheer leading.

✦

I got off the plane on Saturday afternoon before Thanksgiving. Some people had exams on the Monday and Tuesday of the next week, but I had finished my exams on Friday.

Uncle Jeff and Mom were at the security gate waiting for me. They were smiling so big I couldn't help but laugh. I was disappointed to see that Teresa wasn't with them. I tried not to let it show.

"David, my baby boy, I have missed you so much." Mom threw her arms around me and I hugged her back. It startled me how tall she was. I guess I'd forgotten my mom was an Amazon. She kissed both of my cheeks then stepped back a little so Uncle Jeff could greet me.

He held out his hand and I shook it.

"Oh, hell," he said and swept me into a bear hug. He swayed back and forth for a minute then stepped back. "A handshake just wasn't enough." He laughed.

"I like your teddy bear," Mom said, pointing at the stuffed toy I had in my left arm.

"I brought this for Teresa," I said looking around. "I thought maybe she'd come with you guys."

"She couldn't. She had something at school, cheerleading practice I think."

I thought Mom looked disappointed. Maybe I should have brought her a stuffed toy. I couldn't have carried two though. It was big.

"I brought something for you too," I said. I didn't think she'd be as happy about the decal I'd gotten for her car. "You too, Uncle Jeff," I'd gotten them both one that said Harvard Parent.

"That's great, son. Let's get your bags. I'm sure you can't wait to get home and see Charlotte and Ruffles." Mom turned in the direction of the baggage claim and I followed. I couldn't wait to see Charlotte. But it was Teresa I wanted to see most.

✦

I knew there was something wrong when she answered the phone.

"Teresa, what's going on?" I asked. "You don't sound very happy to hear from me. I can't wait to see you."

"I'm happy. I can't wait to see you either," she said, but she didn't mean it. I had the strangest feeling. I knew it was over without even seeing her. I had the feeling that I'd known it for a while. But it was the first time I'd had the thought, even though I hadn't been able to talk to her for a couple of weeks.

"No you're not," I said. "You can't fake it with me, Teresa. Tell me what's going on."

"Not over the phone, David. Could you maybe come to my house? We could sit on the back porch."

"No, tell me now." I wasn't going over there if my premonition was true.

"David."

"Tell me. Who is it? Who are you seeing?"

"Dexter Bradshaw. David, I'm sorry. I didn't plan for this to happen. It just did."

"What happened to I'll love you forever, David?" My heart was pounding against my ribs, and I felt like I was going to throw up.

"I will, David. I do love you, as a friend."

"Fuck that!" I was going to throw up. But damn the lump in my throat, I would not cry. "You couldn't be happy with a nerd like me. You just had to have the captain of the football team. Hell, I don't even play football. I'm just a wimpy soccer player."

"David, that's silly. It just made sense for Dexter and me to go to dances together since I'm the captain of the cheerleading squad and he's the captain of the football team. Things just happened."

This all sounded so high school. I hated high school. "You fucked him, didn't you?"

"I'm not talking to you anymore if you're going to say things like that," she said.

"All the time I was avoiding parties and pretty women," I said. I felt a pang when I remembered that none of those pretty women had even noticed I was there, and I'd only gone to one party. "And you were down here screwing around with that stupid jock. I can't believe this, Teresa."

"That's it, David. If you want to talk to me about this you'll have to calm down. Call me when you've done that." The phone line went dead, and I stared at the device in my hand. I wanted to fling it across the room, but I didn't. The urge to puke passed, and the lump in my throat eased. I'd be okay.

"David." Mom called through my bedroom door. I was still sitting at my desk looking at my cell phone. I don't know how long I'd been there.

"Yeah, come on in," I said. "You want this stupid stuffed bear?"

"What happened?" she asked, but I could tell by her voice that she already knew.

"Why didn't you tell me? Maybe I wouldn't feel like such an idiot if you'd warned me."

"I wasn't sure." She sat down on the bed. "I saw her a couple of times with that big football player. I think you've been in school with both of them since kindergarten."

"No, Dexter didn't come around until the fourth grade. He's a Neanderthal."

"I'm sorry, honey. I know you really love her."

"She loves me too," I snarled. "Like a friend. I hate it when girls say that. Do they really think it's going to make you feel better?"

"I don't know. I don't think I ever said that to a guy." She smiled and put her hand on my arm. "Let's take the dogs to the park."

I looked at Charlotte. She sat at my feet looking up at my face. She obviously adored me. I loved the little dog so much. I thought about what I felt for Teresa. "I guess maybe I didn't really love her."

"Well, you thought you did anyway. What do you feel for her now?"

"It's hard to tell with all the anger and humiliation." I reached down and scooped Charlotte into my arms. "Right now though, I'm sure I love Charlotte more." I thought about it for a minute and laughed. I looked into the dogs big brown eyes. If I'd ever had to choose, I'd have chosen Charlotte. "Yep, this is my lady love." I looked at my Mom. She smiled. "My dog and my mom, the loves of my life," I said. "Let's take the dogs to the park."

"So, did you stay faithful to her?" Jimmy Parnell asked the next day. He had come over to see me after church, and we were sitting in the back yard throwing the ball for Charlotte and watching Ruffles spin around in circles trying to figure out where it went.

"That is a very stupid Dog." Jimmy laughed.

"Yeah, but you've gotta love him." I ran my hand along Ruffles' long back and picked up the brush that my mom had left on the table. I ran it through the silky hair and had a distant memory of Pepper.

"Well, did you?" Jimmy persisted.

"Yeah, I stayed faithful to her. Not that I had any temptations. I'm the baby of Harvard, remember? Everyone is older than me and way cooler."

"But even if you'd been tempted you'd have stayed faithful. You're just that kind of guy."

"Yeah, I'm the kind of guy that doesn't fit into high school and doesn't fit into college either. Is there a place in this world for me, Jimmy?" I laughed, but I didn't sound happy.

"I don't know, David, but I'm really sorry about Teresa. I knew it was going on. I just couldn't bring myself to tell you. I mean I didn't want to mess up what you were doing in school. I was afraid you wouldn't be able to concentrate."

I looked at him. "You're a good friend, Jimmy. I'm glad you didn't tell me." I leaned back in my chair and crossed my arms. "So what's going on with you? Are you dating P. H. yet? I know you wanted to."

"That's just a dream, frequently a sloppy one." He looked down at the ground and grinned. The skin on his neck turned red.

I laughed when the blush traveled up his face.

"She won't even talk to me," he said.

"She was always a snob."

"Not anymore, David. She's gotten really nice." Jimmy came to her defense and it surprised me. "I mean she will talk to me. She just isn't interested in me romantically. We're friends."

"You're madly in love with her and you know it." I sat up as Mom came out the door. "Hey, Mom?" I asked as she set down a tray with lemonade and cookies on it. "Can I have a beer?"

"No." She looked at me sharply. "You're underage. I brought you lemonade."

"I didn't think you'd say yes but it was worth a shot." I took the glass she handed me. "Are these store bought cookies?"

"Of course, they are." She laughed. "I haven't started cooking while you were gone."

"I'm grateful for that." I teased as I picked up a cookie.

Mom sat down. "I'm not that bad a cook." She laughed. "How are you doing, Jimmy? Do you have any plans for college next year?"

"No, school doesn't work for me. My dad and I looked into some apprenticeships. I'm trying to decide between pipe fitters and HVAC."

"What's HVAC?" Mom asked.

"Heating Ventilating and Air Conditioning," Jimmy said sounding proud of himself for knowing. "I'm leaning toward that. It's a good business to be in here in the southeast."

"It sounds like it would be," I said.

"I just hope they accept me. I don't test very well and there is a classroom segment to it. You know how bad I suck at school."

"Whenever you have a problem, Jimmy," I said. "Email me or call. I think I helped you in school better than any of those LD classes."

"You could always explain things better than anyone else. Sometimes it almost seems like you understand what I'm having trouble with and nobody else does."

"Yeah, you always did better when we worked on things together."

"I'm so glad you guys are such good friends." Mom got up. "David, I'm going to the supermarket. Do you want anything?"

"Six pack of beer," I said.

"I hope you're not drinking at school. It's against the law, honey. Don't get yourself in trouble."

"I won't, Mom." I laughed as she went inside.

"There is a party at Matt's house tonight." Jimmy said when Mom had closed the back door. "His parents are out of town, and his older brother is getting a keg. Why don't you come along?"

"I don't think so. Teresa and the Neanderthal will probably be there, and I don't want to see them."

"You still live here, David, even though you go away to school. You'll have to face them some time." Jimmy stood up. "I'll pick you up after dinner. Things won't really get started before that."

"Oh alright, I guess I need to get it over with. See you tonight." Jimmy left and I put Charlotte on a leash. A good run in the park was just what I needed.

❁

I saw them come in from across the room. Teresa's eyes stopped their search of the room when she saw me. I could see she was disappointed. She had clearly hoped I wouldn't be there. She put her hand on Dexter's arm and said something to him. He looked across the room and met my eyes.

I concentrated on not looking away. I wanted to. I wanted to just leave the room, but Teresa was coming toward me, and Dexter was watching me from his place by the door.

"You didn't want your boyfriend to talk to me?" I said when she stood in front of me. "I'm not planning to hit him, Teresa. I'm taller than he is, but look at his muscle. I can't take him. I'm not stupid."

"I thought you and I needed a little time alone and Dex understood."

"Dex understood, so why is he giving me that 'touch her and I'll kill you' look."

"I'm sure he isn't," she said, but she glanced over her shoulder to see for herself. "Well, he does get really jealous." She turned back to face me and lowered her voice.

"David," she whispered. "I told him I was a virgin." She looked up at me and smiled sweetly. "Please don't tell him we slept together."

I laughed. It wasn't a nice sound so I stopped. "He believed you? He's dumber than I thought."

"He isn't dumb, David. Don't be vindictive." She scowled and looked over her shoulder again. Dexter stood where she had left him. He was talking to Meryl Johnson. He glanced back at us but continued his conversation.

"He got into the University of Georgia. We're going there together in the fall."

"Do you think I care or something?" I laughed again.

Teresa looked back me. This time the look on her face was hostile. "If you say you slept with me I'll deny it."

"What, do you think I'm going to brag about my conquests?"

"All I'm saying is you just better not say anything. Everyone will hate you if you do. You'll never be popular with these people if you spread nasty rumors."

"Popular!" I laughed loud this time. "God, I hate high school. Teresa, I never was popular with these people. I don't give a damn about it now."

"Shhhh ... David ..." She looked around. The expression on her face was fear. I had a sudden rush of feeling. She looked like a trapped animal.

"I'm not going to say anything, Teresa," I said. "Surely you have a higher opinion of me than that."

"Well, I know you're angry." Her voice trailed off and her eyes looked teary.

"No..." I touched her cheek. She flinched and looked at Dexter. He had his back to us now. She was clearly relieved. "He doesn't hurt you does he?" I had the most horrible feeling.

"No, but he gets very jealous. You shouldn't touch me." She shifted uneasily. "I'm really sorry, David. I meant to stay faithful. I don't know. Things just happened."

"It's okay, Teresa. It just wasn't meant to be I guess." I put my hand on her arm when she turned to leave. She flinched again and looked at Dexter. He was looking at us again. His expression was bland.

"Teresa," I whispered. "You told me you were a virgin too. Was it true?" I knew that it was, but for some reason I had to ask.

"Of course, I wouldn't lie to you about something like that."

I released her arm and she went across the room. Dexter greeted her with a smile and they moved off toward the keg together.

"She wouldn't lie to me about something like that, but she would lie to him." I wondered out loud.

"Are you talking to yourself, David?" I turned around at the sound of my name and found myself looking down into the china blue eyes of Darla P. H. Bergquist.

"P. H.," I said startling myself with the use of the nick name Jimmy and I had given her in the second grade.

"That's not a nice thing to call me, David. I haven't said anything mean to you in years." She laughed and showed dimples in her cheeks. My god she was beautiful. No wonder Jimmy was so crazy about her.

"It stands for Pretty Hair," I said lifting a lock of the long straight blond silk that hung over her shoulder to her waist.

"It does not." She laughed. It sounded like ice cubes tinkling in a glass or maybe wind chimes. "Jimmy and I are very good friends these days. He told me what it really means."

"That's right. I told her." Jimmy approached with Meryl Johnson. He held two plastic cups full of beer and Meryl held two. She handed one to Darla and I took one from Jimmy.

I sipped my beer and held the cup. "I don't like to drink too much of this stuff," I said. "I can't get any work done the next day."

"You're on vacation," Darla said. "Relax. I told Jimmy we should stay here for a while and then go to my house. I've got a game box. It'll be fun. My parents are home, but they won't be a problem."

"I don't know." I couldn't believe she wanted me to come to her house. "Doesn't your mother hate me or something?"

"Don't be silly, David." Darla put her hand on my arm and I looked down at it. "My mother won't be rude to you. It isn't your fault that my uncle married your mother."

I looked at her face. She was sincere. I still didn't want to go to her house. "I don't think so." I turned to Jimmy. "If you want to go over you could just drop me at home on the way."

"No, I want to spend time with you. You won't be here that long." Jimmy looked at Darla. "Let's go to my house, P. H. I've got a game box too. I know my dad would like to see David."

I couldn't believe this exchange. Jimmy called Darla P. H. even though he'd told her what it meant. They really had become friends. What was really interesting was that as Jimmy stood there talking to her he had taken Meryl's hand and was holding it pressed to his chest.

Meryl smiled up at me and I looked at her for the first time in years. She was lovely, dark curly hair and brown eyes. "I've been telling Jimmy that he was going to marry me since second grade," she said.

Jimmy smiled at her. "And she was right. I am going to marry her."

"You're a little young to be making decisions like that, don't you think?" I couldn't believe he was talking about marriage. "You have that apprenticeship to do and all, Jimmy. You can't support her yet."

"I'm pretty sure I can't do it without her," he said and they kissed each other.

"Okay, let's go to Jimmy's house," Darla interrupted. "I'm sorry you're so uncomfortable with my family, David. But I guess I don't blame you when I was so mean to you."

"Your family thinks I'm white trash." I said, but I was laughing. "I'll never forget the day you told me that."

"I won't either, and I'll never forget the look on your face. I hate myself for doing that." Darla drained the last of her beer. "Let's go." She put the cup down. "We can take your car, Jimmy. Meryl and I came with Teresa and Dexter. You can give us a ride home, can't you?"

"Sure," Jimmy said. He put his beer cup down. He hadn't touched it.

"I hope you didn't drink and drive last night." Mom said when I came down to breakfast the next morning.

"I didn't have my car."

"How did you get home? You didn't get in until midnight."

"Mr. Parnell brought me home. He and I played a game of chess while some other kids played with the game box. It was good to see him. He took everyone home."

"Does he let you drink beer? I smelled it on you when you got home." She frowned and put the coffee pot down on the table.

"Mom, you aren't around to smell beer on me when I'm in school. I guess you're just going to have to trust me." I was glad she hadn't smelled the joint I'd smoked in the back yard with P. H. We had snuck out for a minute. Jimmy and Meryl declined. It was great. I remembered the pleasant feeling I'd discovered last summer. I slept that night too.

"I just worry, David."

"Well, don't. I'll take care of myself. I know about the dangers of driving under the influence just like I know about safe sex." I laughed and she reluctantly laughed too.

"It's hard watching you become independent." She stroked Ruffles' head and smiled sadly. "It was easier when I could just make sure you were safe all the time."

I thought about the time I'd fallen down that waterfall. I was glad I hadn't told her about it.

"I'm going to be alright, Mom." I looked at my watch and stood up. "I told Uncle Jeff I'd come over to see his new house. Apparently he's having the two front bedrooms made into one for me. I told him he didn't have to do that but he insisted."

"He regards you as his family, David."

"And I regard him as mine." I kissed her on the cheek and picked up my keys. "I'll be home for dinner unless Uncle Jeff wants me to eat with him. I'll call, and Mom, don't worry about me, okay." I took the leash off the hook and put it on Charlotte's collar.

"I'll try," she laughed. "Are you sure you should take Charlotte over there. You know your Uncle and dogs."

"When we looked at the place one of Uncle Jeff's selling points was how much Charlotte would enjoy the back yard. I'm just testing his resolve."

I pulled up the driveway to Uncle Jeff's new house, stopped the car, and got out. He was working in the front yard and I noticed for about the millionth time in my life how muscular he was. You could actually see the muscles of his shoulders working under his shirt.

He waved and finished up what he was doing. Then he wiped his hands on his jeans and came over to where I was standing.

I opened the passenger door and let Charlotte out. She bounded toward him then stopped, apparently recognizing him. She sheepishly came back to me to sit by my side.

"I've never seen you work in the yard without gloves before," I said.

"I wasn't planning to work when I came out here." He picked up a cup of coffee from a stone bench beside what looked like the beginnings of a goldfish pond. "I guess I should know better than that by now." He smiled and walked toward the front door. I followed.

"You're already starting the pond. You work fast. How long have you been living here?" He hadn't closed on the house when I left for school.

"I got in here in about the middle of October. Unfortunately your room isn't finished yet. So you won't be able to stay with me this time, but at Christmas I demand at least one night. Maybe you should take Charlotte around the house to the back yard."

"I will if you want me to, but if she walks through your house she won't contaminate it or anything."

He frowned and looked down at my dog. "I guess not," he said, not sounding too sure. He opened the door and we were met by the smell of new wood and saw dust. I liked it. "Since it's Sunday, there isn't any work going on in here. You can get a general idea." He guided me down the hall to the first door on the right. Charlotte padded along beside me, and Uncle Jeff didn't say anything.

"This is going to be the bathroom. This part will be sort of a powder room for visitors and people in the living room. Then back here …" he went through an adjoining door. "…Is your shower and bath. The toilet will be behind that wall and a small sink and mirror for your privacy."

I followed him through the construction. "Then through here is your bedroom. It will also open onto the hallway over there. And here …" he pointed to the window and raised the shade. "…is your fountain. Or at least it will be when I get the pond finished. He turned and looked at me. He was beaming with pleasure. I realized he'd designed this all with me in mind.

"Uncle Jeff, you didn't have to do all this just for me." I smiled my gratitude.

"I wanted to. I know your mom's house is home, but I hope you feel that way about my place a little bit too."

"I do. I've been staying with you since I can remember."

"Good, because I want you to look at some color panels with me. I thought we'd stick with the hardwood floors, but I'll want to put in an area rug. I'll need your opinion on what you like best. Let's go into the living room and have a look."

"What about the rest of the house? Don't I get to see your bedroom?"

"Well okay, but I haven't done anything with it yet. Mary Ann has all sorts of ideas, but I've been so caught up in your room and the pond I haven't paid much attention."

"You'd better be careful, Uncle Jeff. You'll end up with a pink room with polka dot curtains if you don't pay attention." We both laughed and continued the tour of the house. When we went through the kitchen I let Charlotte out the back door. She looked around for a minute as if she didn't know what to do with such a big yard. Then the wind blew up a swirl of fall leaves and she launched herself at them.

I watched her for a minute then followed Uncle Jeff into the dining room. The table was covered with paint panels and small pieces of fabric.

"I have no idea about this kind of thing, Uncle Jeff." I sat down feeling lost.

"I didn't either, but I'm starting to figure it out with Mary Ann's help. She puts everything in groups, wall color, floor color, rugs, and curtains. Here's what she's suggested for your room. That over there is ours. I mean mine."

"Ah hah…" I laughed. "So she's living here with you."

"No, but she spends a lot of time here." He looked down at the table. "Look, no pink and polka dots."

"Uncle Jeff, you're blushing. Even with your dark skin I can see the blush." I teased him.

"Knock it off, kid." He was laughing. "Now which combinations do you like for your room?"

We studied the swatches for about an hour then Uncle Jeff suggested we go into the kitchen and have lunch.

"I got sandwiches from the deli, and I have beer and soft drinks in the fridge," he said.

"Uncle Jeff, are you offering me a beer?"

"Yeah, I figure you probably drink at school. It wouldn't be honest to pretend differently. It's not legal though, so I hope you won't turn me in to the police."

I laughed. "I won't but Mom might." I opened the refrigerator and took out a ginger ale. "You want a beer?" I asked.

"No, I think I'll have a ginger ale too." We sat down at the table that Uncle Jeff had just covered with wrapped sandwiches and a container of potato salad.

"Did you get to go out with Teresa last night?" he asked.

"No, she dumped me earlier in the day over the phone."

"She dumped you," Uncle Jeff said around a mouthful of sandwich. "Stupid girl!" He sound so outraged I laughed.

"That's what I thought, but it seems that she and the captain of the high school football team have struck up a relationship." I took a bite of my sandwich.

"I'm sorry, David. I know you love her."

"I thought I did." I looked out the window to the back yard. It was breezy and the fall leaves were blowing in little swirls around the yard. Charlotte was chasing them happily. "Maybe I didn't. It really doesn't hurt that bad."

"Have you seen her at all since you got home?"

"Yeah, she and Dexter were at a party I went to last night. She asked me to keep our relationship a secret from him. I had a bad feeling."

"What kind of bad feeling."

"About the two of them, I got the feeling that she was afraid of him."

"Oh no, really?" Uncle Jeff studied my face for a minute. "David, there isn't anything you can do."

I looked at him. "How did you know I was thinking I should help her some way?"

"I know you. The look on your face was a dead giveaway. David, you can't do anything. You can't take care of the whole world."

"I guess not." I finished my potato salad and gulped down the last of my ginger ale.

"So did you have fun at the party anyway? Did you see some old friends?"

"Yeah, we didn't stay too long. We went to Jimmy's house. I played chess with his dad. Jimmy is dating Meryl Johnson. I never really noticed how pretty she is. They're talking about getting married."

"They're only sixteen years old." Uncle Jeff sounded so shocked it made me laugh.

"Actually, they're both seventeen. I'm the baby of the group, remember?"

"Seventeen isn't much older."

"Jimmy isn't going to college. He's going to an apprenticeship. Meryl is going to cosmetology school. They say it's different for people like them."

"I still think it's a little young."

"Yeah, so do I." I opened the back door. "I'm going outside with Charlotte."

"Put on that sweatshirt on the coat rack," Uncle Jeff said. "It's cold out there."

"B!" I knew Uncle Jeff and Mom could hear me outside when I screamed out loud about my grades. "I made a fucking B!" I could feel tears welling up in my eyes and rubbed so hard that I couldn't see for a minute after I stopped.

We had come by to get Uncle Jeff on Thanksgiving afternoon, and I came in to check the computer to see if my grades had been posted. I had checked before we left the house, but our internet connection was down because of the rain.

They were waiting in the car when I stormed out the front door and locked it. I hurried to the car and climbed into the back seat.

"David, we heard you yell, honey," Mom said.

"B is a pretty good grade in a school like Harvard," Uncle Jeff said.

"I wanted to graduate with a 4.0 GPA. If I blow it in the first semester I might as well just quit."

"I don't think that was a very realistic goal, David. You were the smartest person in your public high school. You aren't the smartest in a place like Harvard," Mom said. "Honey, calm down and be realistic. Besides, that was only the midterm exam, maybe you can bring it up."

They both looked at me for a minute.

"What are you looking at," I said. "We'd better go or we'll miss Thanksgiving dinner at Aunt Jeanne's. Then she'll cry like a baby."

"If you're going to be nasty, David, you can just stay here," Mom said.

"Fine, I'll stay here." I got out of the car and stormed over to the front door. Uncle Jeff was right behind me. "What are you doing?" I demanded. "Aunt Jeanne will cry if you aren't there. She doesn't care about me."

"Now David, you know that isn't true. For one thing Aunt Jeanne won't cry, but we'll both get the tongue lashing of our lives if we don't show up to her Thanksgiving dinner. And besides that, you told me once that if you ever got a B you'd kill yourself." He had unlocked the door and pushed it open. "I'm not going to leave you alone."

"I didn't mean that, Uncle Jeff. You know I'm not going to kill myself over a stupid grade. Besides, like Mom said, that was just the midterm exam." I was standing on the front porch in the rain and he was in the foyer.

"Ever since you fell over that waterfall and decided not to breath, I've worried about your self value. I'm not leaving you alone." He crossed his arms.

I laughed. "I didn't get water in my lungs."

"No. But you can't live without air, and you didn't seem to care about that."

"Okay," I said and started back down the walk toward the car. "Let's go to Aunt Jeanne's. I don't want to get a tongue lashing on top of a B. That would suck."

"What test did you get a B on?" Mom asked when I got back into the car.

"Algebra ..."

"Math was never your best subject. You always struggled with it."

"I struggled with it to get an A."

"David, it's not the end of the world to graduate with a B average."

"No," I said. "It's not the end of the world." I was picturing the joint I had in my pocket and wondering if I could get away for a few minutes this afternoon to smoke it. I wouldn't mind the B so much then.

✦

"David, over here." I heard Darla's voice across the crowded airport. The call was immediately followed by her tinkling laugh. I smiled. I looked in the direction of her voice and spotted Jimmy and Meryl smiling and coming toward me through the crowded airport. Right in front of them P. H.'s hand was waving in the air. I caught sight of the top of her blond head as she jumped up and down hurrying to catch up with me and Mom and Uncle Jeff.

She hurried over and threw her arms around my waist. I couldn't believe how small she was. I was always surprised by it when I saw her. She had such a big personality for such a tiny person.

"We've come to see you off." She smiled up at me as she stepped back. "Not that it was easy to get these two lazy bums up and on the road this early. Why did you take such an early flight and why Saturday? You don't have to be back in class until Monday do you?"

"No, but I need to get back in time to get prepared." I didn't say I was going to study nonstop for the rest of the semester to pull up that B.

"Well, I wish you could stay another day." Darla pouted and she looked adorable. I wondered why she cared when I went back to school. It didn't matter. It was nice to have friends seeing me off.

"David," Mom broke into my thoughts. "What a nice surprise to have your friends come to say goodbye."

"Darla, you've met my mom haven't you?" I said. I noticed that I stood slightly blocking my mother from view. I was feeling something like embarrassed. Mom was so tall. Wasn't it Darla who'd called her an Amazon?

Uncle Jeff stepped up and extended his hand. "Hello, Darla," he said. "You've grown into a beautiful young woman."

I closed my eyes and prayed that Uncle Jeff didn't have dirt on his hands or his clothes. Then felt a blush moving up my neck from the thought.

"Hello Darla," Mom said. "Jimmy, Meryl, it's nice to see you." She stepped around me and stood next to Darla. She had to be at least a foot taller than her. The contrast was startling.

"Well," Uncle Jeff said. "We'd better get you through security, David. You don't want to miss that plane."

CHAPTER SEVEN

"Man, did I ever mess up my midterms." Rich was sitting on his bed when I got back to the room.

"Me too." I put my bag down and sat on my desk chair.

"What did you make?"

"I did alright in everything except algebra. I got a B on the exam. I made A's on all the other tests though, so I think I can pull it up." I turned pulled my laptop computer out of the bag and put it on the desk.

"That's nothing. I have Cs in everything. I haven't made above a C on any test all semester. I can pull it up but not to an A. God this is humiliating. I never made below an A in anything up to now. I guess college is a different story than high school."

"I guess so," I said. My computer screen was lighting up, and I had turned to face it.

"So how was the trip home? How's Teresa?" Rich grinned.

"She's fine." I didn't turn to look at him. "She dumped me over the phone. She's dating the captain of the football team."

"Aw man," he said. "That sucks. I'm sorry, and after you sat in this room for three months staying faithful to her."

"It wasn't that much of a sacrifice, Rich, since none of those beautiful women out there were interested in me." I laughed.

"You didn't give them a chance, Dave. Now that you don't have a girl friend you have to get out more. There's a party tonight at that big house on the edge of campus where all those seniors live, you know the one. It's walking distance so it doesn't matter if we drink too much. Come with me."

"No, I plan to study nonstop from now until the end of the semester, Rich. I intend to graduate from this place with a 4.0."

"Well, I'll be happy with a 3.0. I don't think you're being realistic about that. But I'm not going to argue that point. I'm going to argue the party point. I'm not giving up until you agree to come, at least for a little while."

That's how I ended up at a party off campus that night. I'm not going to go into much detail here. This was probably the most humiliating night of my life. I didn't like to drink too much, but I guess the accumulation of too much bad news on my trip home was getting to me. I quickly lost track of how many times I filled up at the keg.

Stupidly, I shared a joint that went around the room, and before I knew it I was spinning like a top. Rich took me outside, and I promptly puked up at least half of the beer I'd drunk.

I went to the bathroom and washed my face and rinsed my mouth. Then I went looking for my coat. It was cold in Boston in late November. I remembered putting my coat on a bed in someone's room when I'd arrived so I started checking bedrooms.

After opening two doors to find the bed's occupied by tangled naked bodies, I found a pile of coats at the end of the hall. I searched through it to find mine and pulled it on as I walked down the hall to the front door of the house.

"Wait, David," I heard a feminine voice behind me and turned to see a tall shapely brunette coming toward me. "I'm leaving too. I don't live far from here. It's on the way to your dorm. Can I walk with you? It's kind of creepy walking alone at night."

She knew my name so I guessed I'd met her sometime during the party. "Sure," I said. "Although I'm not much protection. You have to hold on to me in a high wind." I laughed awkwardly. I felt stupid using my mother's joke."

"There's safety in numbers." She handed her coat to me and I helped her put it on.

We walked out into the cold night. It had been snowing when I got to the party. Now there were a couple of inches of new snow on the ground and the wind had picked up. It was hard to see as we trudged through the snow.

"Well, here we are?" The girl said. We had arrived at a small row of apartments. "David, did you get sick? I saw you heading around the back of that car port with Rich."

"I don't drink very often." I laughed stupidly. "I don't think I'll ever drink again."

She laughed with me. "Listen, why don't you come in for a while? You could even sleep on the couch if you wanted to. My roommate is still at the party, but she wouldn't mind. You can have a Coke. It'll settle your stomach."

"No thanks, I think I'll just go on back to the dorm." I looked around. I wasn't sure which direction to go, and I felt very tired. The word weary came to mind.

"Come on, you don't even know where you are in this driving snow. If you get lost out there you could freeze to death." She pulled me to the stairs and we went up to the second flight of apartments. She unlocked a door and we went inside.

"I'll get you a Coke." She led me to the couch and disappeared into the kitchen of the small apartment.

When she returned I looked up at her and realized that my vision was still blurry and I couldn't quite see her face. I also realized I didn't know her name.

"I watched you all night." She sat down beside me and handed me the Coke. I popped the top and took a sip. It did make my stomach feel better. But I still couldn't quite get my eyes to focus. I shook my head. It didn't help.

"It's that pot," she said. "It's really strong." She ran her hand along the back of my neck and across my chin. I jumped and pulled away.

"Don't worry," she whispered and pulled me closer to her. "My boyfriend isn't back yet. He won't come back until tomorrow night."

"You have a boyfriend?" I cringed as she leaned close to me and kissed my ear.

"Yeah, but don't worry." She whispered in my ear. "We can have this night all to ourselves. You looked so good all night. I love tall men."

"I thought you said you had a roommate." I looked down at my crotch and realized that the tightening that I'd always felt so quickly when I was with Teresa was not happening with this girl. I looked at her. She was still a blur. Maybe she was ugly.

"My roommate was doing pretty well with one of the guys that live in that house. She won't come home. Anyway we have our own bedrooms."

She put her hand on my soft pants. I guess she noticed that I wasn't hard because she said. "Don't worry about that. I know some tricks." She pulled me to my feet and we went into her bedroom. She shut the door and started unbuttoning my shirt.

"I'm only sixteen," I said, immediately wondering why.

"Ohhhh..." she laughed. "Statutory rape, how exciting."

She pulled my shirt over my shoulders and slid to the floor on her knees in front of me. She unbuckled my belt and pants and pulled them open. I looked down horrified. My penis was completely limp, and with the cold weather I'd just come out of, it was tiny.

She put it into her mouth and laughed again. "It's so tiny for such a big boy."

117 / Grand Passion

I grabbed my shirt from the floor beside me and pulled up my pants. I ran out of the bedroom and almost out the front door before I remembered my coat. I guess I didn't want to die as much as I thought I did.

I don't remember how I got home. I vaguely remember pulling my clothes on in the freezing night and looking back at the door of her apartment when I heard her laugh. I only know that I woke up in the morning in the throes of another migraine headache. My mouth tasted like manure. Rich was snoring and each vibration felt like a chain saw going through my head.

I ran to the bathroom to vomit. Then turned on the cold water of the shower and stepped in.

I still have no idea who she was. I don't know what she looked like, and I never knew her name. Sometimes I felt like I could feel a girl looking at me funny and I'd wonder. But I never knew.

"Hello." I answered my cell phone and looked at the clock. It was 6:00 on a Thursday morning in late May. The school year was almost over. I had two final exams the following week. Then I was flying home.

I'd been back home for Christmas and spring break. Uncle Jeff and I had taken an overnight backpacking trip. I'd spent some time with Mom. Most of my friends were off in Florida for the break so I came back to school without seeing them.

"David," Jimmy's voice was frantic. "Didn't you get my email? I'm sorry to call you so early, but my exam starts in one hour. I'm sure I can't do it without talking with you first. I can't remember the rules."

"Calm down, Man." I cleared my throat when it sounded like a grizzly bear. "Calm down, Jimmy. We've been over this so many times I'm pretty sure you've got it."

"That's easy for you to say. This exam could ruin all my plans. I've just barely got a B in that class and the apprenticeship won't accept a C. My whole life could be over today."

"Jimmy, even if you don't get a B your life won't be over. There is always another direction to go in."

"Not for me, David. I've about exhausted all my options."

"No you haven't. Now repeat after me," I said. "'I'll do fine. But even if I don't, everything will be alright.'"

"I can't say that if I don't believe it. Now go over the rules with me again."

"Not until you say it."

"David ..."

"Not until ..."

"I'll do fine. But even if I don't, everything will be alright. Now please, tell me the rules."

I laughed and heard an echo of laughter on the other end of the line. "You tell me," I said.

"I've arranged with the teacher to exempt the time limit."

"That's good. That's what the learning disabled status is for. I'm glad you've finally started letting it work for you. Go ahead."

"I've arranged to have a spare scratch paper. They have to inspect it on the way in, but that's okay. It's just a blank sheet."

"And where are the algebra equations that you'll need?"

"They're in the rap song you and I wrote. I think I've got it pretty well memorized."

"That's right. Remember, there's no rule against tapping or moving your head to the rhythm while you write them down on your scratch paper."

"Right ..."

"Okay Jimmy, that's rule number one. Assemble your equipment. What's rule number two."

"Never read the directions myself."

"That's right. Again, you're letting your LD status work for you. Have the teacher explain the directions to you."

"Right, and rule number three is break down the work into parts."

"You've got it. You can even draw lines between every ten problems if you want to." I was sitting up in bed now.

"There are a hundred problems on the test, David. I have an attention span problem. I'll never make it."

"You just broke rule number four."

"Don't think ahead." He sounded defeated.

"Concentrate on the problem you're working on and never think any further than the group of ten you're on now."

"It's hard." Jimmy was as stressed as I'd ever heard him. He and I had been working together long distance ever since Thanksgiving. He'd done well, but there was a lot at stake with this test. This course had been his hardest struggle.

"I know it's hard, Jimmy. But if you stay calm and follow the rules, you'll do okay. I promise."

"I don't know what I'd have done this year without you, David. You're a good friend."

"You're a good friend too. Let me know how things go." I hung up the phone and stretched. I got up and booted up my computer.

"You have a way with handicapped people," Rich said from his bed. It was getting light outside, but seven o'clock was early for him.

"I have a hard time thinking of Jimmy as handicapped. Sometimes he seems smarter than anyone I know."

"I think learning disabled falls under the category of handicapped though." Rich yawned and pulled the covers up over his head.

"I'm sorry I woke you up," I said. "Jimmy was in a state of panic."

"I could tell." He rolled over and looked at the wall. "I suppose you're getting ready to study some more. How do you keep your focus?"

"I wish I could break my focus."

"That's why you smoke pot isn't it? You don't do it to party. You haven't partied since that time after Thanksgiving break. You still haven't told me what happened that night."

"That's because I can't remember." I lied. I gathered my shaving kit and started for the bathroom.

"So why do you take that pot walk every night around midnight. How do you get past the house mother?"

"She's in bed and the janitor's door isn't locked. Walking stops my brain from working so I can sleep. So far it's the only thing that works."

"You know what, David. I think you have the opposite of ADD."

"I don't think there's any such thing." I went into the bathroom and took my shower. Maybe I've invented a different type of learning disability, I thought. No I guess it wouldn't be called that since I'm about to finish my first year at Harvard with a 4.0 GPA, just as planned. I smiled and dipped my head under the icy cold water. I loved cold water.

"Over here, David," Uncle Jeff called to me from the crowd in the airport.

I looked over at him and waved. He and Mom were there. I could see the top of Darla's blond head and her eyes as she jumped up and down waving at me. Jimmy stood behind her smiling and holding Meryl's hand. Jimmy wasn't as tall as me of course, but he was at least six feet. He looked about even with my mom. Meryl was probably about five foot eight.

"How tall are you, P. H.," I said as I leaned down to hug her. I picked her up off her feet and swung her a little then placed her back on the floor. "Hey Mom." I gave my mom a hug then shook Uncle Jeff's hand and Jimmy's.

"That's not good enough, remember?" Uncle Jeff swept me into a bear hug.

"Not good enough for me either." Jimmy grabbed me around the neck and squeezed.

"Everyone sure is happy to see me. Is something going on I need to know about?"

"I got an A on that exam." Jimmy was dancing around and Meryl was laughing. "It pulled the whole grade up, David. Can you believe it? I got an A in algebra."

"That's great, man." I shook his hand again and hugged his shoulder. "I knew you could do it."

"I didn't." We walked over to the baggage claim and started pulling my luggage off the carousel.

"I was worried when you said you wouldn't tell me your grade until I got home."

"How did your exams go, David?" Mom asked.

"Good, 4.0, just like I told you." She kissed my cheek. I looked down at Darla. She was frowning at me. "What?" I asked. "What did I do?"

"You asked a question then didn't give me a chance to answer." That was definitely a pout she had on her face, a pretty one too.

"Well, how tall are you?"

"I'm five feet two inches and that's doing pretty well. You've seen my family. We're all short."

"That's true." I squeezed her shoulder. "Why did you come to welcome me home, P. H.? We've never really been friends."

"Oh, I'm glad you're so happy to see me." She squared her shoulders and walked in front of me toward the doors of the terminal. "I guess I won't bother anymore." She called back to me.

Biting my tongue for being so clumsy, I looked at Jimmy. He was frowning.

"Sometimes I wonder about you, David," he said. "She's been so excited to see you, and you say a thing like that."

"Why is she excited to see me?"

"She like's you. I don't think she's in love with you or anything. She just likes you like a friend."

"Yeah, girls seem to want me to be their friend." I watched as she went through the doors to the warm Atlanta summer.

"Is this all your luggage?" Uncle Jeff asked.

"Yeah, that's it."

"Okay, your mom and I will put it on this cart and bring it outside," he said. "You go apologize to Darla for being such jerk."

"I'm not a jerk." I looked at him quickly. He was laughing.

"No, you just act like one sometimes," Mom said. She was laughing too.

"Shut up." I smiled, but I hurried to where I could see Darla disappearing into the crowd.

"P. H. wait," I called out to her. "I was just kidding. I guess it wasn't very funny. I'm sorry."

She turned around and put her hands on her hips. All five feet two of her looked formidable. I couldn't help but smile.

"I'm not a poop head," she said.

"No, but you have pretty hair." She stood looking at me for a minute. "Come on, forgive me. I'm a jerk. Uncle Jeff just told me so. Mom says I only act like one sometimes."

"Well." Her face softened and she smiled showing the dimples in her cheeks. "Okay, I guess I'll forgive you. I was pretty mean to you when we were kids. Maybe you're just getting me back."

"Maybe," I said. "Did you ride here with Uncle Jeff and Mom or did you ride with Jimmy and Meryl?"

"I came with Jimmy and Meryl, but I could ride home with your parents and you. Jimmy and Meryl are coming to your house too."

"Okay, good. Here they are with my bags." We walked to the parking lot and loaded the bags into Mom's car and went home.

"How about I start up the grill and we have some hotdogs and hamburgers?" Mom said when we'd gotten home, and I'd taken my stuff up to my room. "We can have a celebration. I'm so happy to have you home."

We were sitting on the back deck. I was holding Charlotte in my lap. Ruffles was standing in front of me with that stupid grin on his face. I was happy to see both dogs. I was happy to see my family and friends.

"I think that's a great idea," Darla said. "Can I run out to get some potato salad or something?"

"No, believe it or not," Mom said. "I made potato salad this morning. I was hoping something like this would come together. I even baked cookies for desert."

"Uh oh," I said.

"I tasted them, David," Uncle Jeff said. "They're not bad." We both laughed.

"You two are so funny." Mom was enjoying the teasing. I think she liked the attention.

"I guess you were kind of lonely this year, Mom." I'd missed her, but I hadn't thought of her being lonely, just me. Some man of the family I was. "I'd forgotten that Vanessa moved away. Old Vern was gone too."

"I was lonely but I did alright. I actually made a new friend at work. The dry cleaners changed ownership, and the woman who bought it has become a good friend." She went inside to get some chips and dip.

"I sure am glad the new owner didn't fire her or anything."

"Well," Uncle Jeff said. "Your mom was afraid of that, but you know she doesn't work for the people. She just rents space. It's her own business. It would just be a matter of changing locations."

"I guess that's true." It was the first time it had dawned on me how really alone my mom was. She didn't have a husband. She didn't have a friend. She didn't have an employer. All she had was me, and I spent nine months of the year away at school.

"I'm going to go in and call my parents to let them know Meryl and I are staying for dinner," Jimmy said.

"Ask them to come over," Mom said coming out of the house with a tray of chips and peanuts. "We'll make a regular celebration of it."

"I'll ask my parents too." Darla said. Everyone stared at her in silence.

"Of course," Mom smiled. "Please do, honey."

Darla's parents had other plans. Thank God. Sometimes I wondered if Darla even remembered that they hated me and my mom. She seemed so innocent about these things.

"I'd like to say a few words if it's alright with everyone." Jimmy stood up. We were all gathered in the small back yard of our townhouse. Jimmy's parents came over when he called them. His dad and I had a nice conversation. His mom helped my mom get the hot dogs and hamburgers cooked, and we all sat in folding chairs and ate with our plates on our laps.

"You have the floor," I said. "I mean the lawn."

"I want to toast to David's summer vacation." Everyone lifted their glasses and drank lemonade. "I also want to congratulate him on his 4.0 average in his first year at Harvard."

"I'm a nerd, Jimmy." I could feel myself blushing. "All I did was study."

"Well, that's not entirely true, because you helped me get through my senior year with a 3.0 average. In fact it was a 3.4." He held up his glass and everyone drank more lemonade. "And I want everyone to congratulate me on that."

The group laughed. Jimmy extended his hand to Meryl, and she stood up next to him. "I'd also like to make an announcement. Meryl has agreed to marry me."

"Ohhhh..." Darla squealed and stood up to embrace them both. "When? Will it be a long engagement?" She was bouncing up and down.

"No, we want to do it this summer, before Meryl starts school in the fall. My apprenticeship doesn't start until the fall either. I will be working for the union, but I'll be able to take a long weekend for a wedding and a short honeymoon."

"Oh honey," Mom stood and hugged Jimmy. "I worry with you being so young, but if you two really want to do this, I'm happy for you."

Jimmy's mother got up and hugged both of them. She opened her mouth to say something but couldn't talk. She started to cry. Mom put her arm around her and handed her a napkin.

"Mom, we already talked to Dad about moving into the basement apartment. Would that be alright with you?" Jimmy said.

"Of course," she said. "Meryl." She hugged her. Meryl looked nervous. "I'll love having you so close."

Jimmy's dad and Uncle Jeff got up and shook hands with Jimmy and congratulated him. They took turns hugging Meryl and then everyone sat down again.

"You haven't said anything, David," Jimmy said. "Aren't you happy for us?"

I didn't know what to say. I wasn't happy for them. I hated them for being so happy with each other. I didn't have anyone who wanted to spend their life with me. Anyway wasn't this supposed to be my party?

"David, I want you to be my best man."

Darla punched me in the arm and said. "Stop scowling like a spoiled child and congratulate your best friend, you stupid oaf."

I stood up and extended my hand. "I'm sorry. I guess it just took me by surprise." I tried to smile but it felt like my face would break. "I mean you're only seventeen. What's the hurry?"

"We'll both be eighteen in the fall."

"That's still young to be getting married."

"Life is different for people like Meryl and me, David. We function better when we do things together. If you don't want to be my best man I'll find someone else."

"No, no, I want to do it." I turned to hug Meryl. "Are you sure you want to marry this bozo?" I teased. "You haven't given me a chance."

She smiled and took Jimmy's hand. "I always told Jimmy he was going to marry me. You never had a chance."

Chapter Seven

"Oh, I'm so excited." Darla was jumping up and down again. Her tinkling laugh was rolling out. I wasn't sure I was happy about this, but I couldn't help but smile. "Will I be your maid of honor?" she asked.

"I was hoping so. It won't be a big wedding. My parents don't have a lot of money."

"Don't worry about that, Meryl. The bride's maid always buys her own dress. I can't wait to start planning."

✦

"You didn't seem too happy about the big news," Uncle Jeff said when he and Mom and I were alone after everyone left that night.

I stroked Charlottes head. She was lying next to me on the couch. "I'm jealous. Isn't that awful? Some friend."

"You don't think they're too young?" Mom asked.

"Well, yeah, but more than that, I'm jealous that they have each other, and I don't have anyone. I didn't plan to marry Teresa until we'd both graduated from college, but I did plan to marry her then."

"You still miss her?" Mom asked.

"Not her really, I miss having a girlfriend."

"Find another one, buddy roe," Uncle Jeff said. "You're a nice looking boy and you're a nurturer. That's rare in a man. What about Darla? She seems to like you."

"As a friend …" I sounded disgusted. Mom and Uncle Jeff both laughed.

"Don't you hate it when a girl says that to you?" Uncle Jeff stood up. "I love you like a friend."

"Yeah, like it's going to make you feel better." I stood too. "I'm tired, and I haven't unpacked anything. I think I'll go on to my room."

"It's good to have you home," Uncle Jeff said. "We'll get together in the next couple of days to discuss our stretch of the Appalachian Trail for this year."

"Good, I guess we'll have to plan it around the wedding date."

"I'm sure we'll manage. I'm going home." He left. I stood looking at the front door for a minute after it closed behind him. I looked back at Mom and sat back down.

"Do you need to talk to me about something, honey?" she asked.

"Mom, why don't I have two sets of grandparents? Where did you come from?"

"I don't know exactly." She sat back and took a deep breath. "I wondered when you'd ask about that."

"I'm such a selfish bastard. I never noticed it before today."

"Don't call yourself that. You are a wonderful caring boy. There is no reason you should have noticed that I didn't have parents before this," she said. "Don't call yourself a bastard."

"That brings up another question." I was remembering when we were kids and Darla said my mom had tried to trap my dad by having me. "How long had you and Dad been married when I was born. Am I a bastard?"

She took another deep breath and looked angrily into my eyes. "You were born a month after our first wedding anniversary. I did not try to use you to get your father. I know certain people have accused me of that, and I deeply resent it."

I closed my eyes and gripped the arms of the chair. "I'm sorry, Mom. I should have known better." I opened my eyes and leaned forward. The anger was gone from her face and she smiled at me.

"So why don't you have parents?"

"Like I said, I don't know. I was abandoned at birth. Apparently my mother just walked out of the hospital and left me there. She was indigent so they didn't have any way of tracking her." She stood and went over to the small wet bar in the corner of the room. "I'm going to have a glass of wine. Would you like to join me?"

"Yeah," I said. "I thought you weren't going to serve alcohol to me under age."

"I've changed my mind." She poured two glasses of wine and brought me one.

"So where did you grow up?"

"Mostly in a girls home,"

"An orphanage?" I asked. "I didn't think the government ran those things anymore."

"This was a church home, a catholic one." She sipped. "I lived in a few foster homes that were government sponsored, but they didn't work out. I always ended up back with the sisters."

"Were they good to you, the sisters?" I was feeling a lump forming in my throat. It surprised me. I was not going to cry.

"Some were, some weren't. Nuns are just people. Some of them are very good people. Some of them aren't."

"It sounds lonely."

"It was, but I learned how to survive alone. It's a good thing because that's the way I've lived most of my life. Sometimes I think it must be God's plan for me."

"You're not alone now, Mom. You have me."

"Yes I do, and I thank God for you every day." She leaned forward in her chair and took my hand where it rested on my knee. "But you will form your own family. It won't include me, and David, that's alright. I'll be fine."

"Any family I ever have will include you, Mom. It will include Uncle Jeff too. As long as we have each other none of us is alone." I stood up and handed my full wine glass to her. I had only taken a couple of sips. "I'm going up to bed. I love you Mom." I kissed her cheek.

"I love you too, David."

I scooped up Charlotte and ran up the stairs.

Jimmy and Meryl were married on the fourth of July. It was on a Wednesday so Jimmy only had to take two days off to have a five day weekend. I stood up with him, and Darla marched down the aisle in a blue dress that was strapless and floor length. She was beautiful, but not as beautiful as Meryl.

I was shaken to the core. I wanted this. I wanted to marry someone that I was completely in love with. I wanted to know the future I craved. It would be so nice to be so sure of something.

Meryl's smile was radiant. Jimmy looked so happy. There was that stupid lump in my throat again. I was becoming a sentimental fool.

Darla and I stood side by side and blew bubbles at them as they came away from the reception that had been held at the Parnell's house. They climbed into the small Jeep that Jimmy's dad had given him for graduation and took off to honeymoon at Calloway Gardens, a resort south of Atlanta.

"I wish they could go some place more exciting," I said.

"I don't think they care where they go." Darla laughed. I smiled like I always did at the sound.

"Well." I turned to her. "Do you want to go to a movie or something tonight? We could grab a bite to eat too."

"Thanks, David, but I have a date tonight."

"You have a date?" I looked down at her.

"Well, don't sound surprised. You don't have to escort me everywhere. I can get a date."

"Who are you going out with?"

"You don't know him. It's a guy I met at work. You know I'm working for the summer at my dad's department store."

"That's right." I smiled trying to look like I didn't care. "I guess I'll go home then. I can't wait to get out of this tuxedo."

"See you later, David." Darla hurried back into the Parnell's house to say goodbye. I got in my car and went home.

"You're sure you don't want to come along this time," I asked my mom for about the hundredth time. "We don't have to hike far. Uncle Jeff and I will carry everything."

"I'm not a camper, David." She kissed my cheek. "And you don't have to go back to Boston for two weeks after you get back so we'll have plenty of time together. Don't worry about me so much."

It was one of the last times we'd be able to drive to our starting destination. After this it would take too long to drive. We'd have to cut off whole days of hiking time.

Charlotte was seven years old and in excellent condition, but she was creeping up in years. I didn't know how many more trips she'd be able to go on. I wanted her to come along every time if possible.

"Ready to go?" Uncle Jeff called from the front door.

"All set." I bounced down the stairs and clipped the leash on Charlotte.

"We'll see you in a week, Charlie." Uncle Jeff kissed her on the cheek.

"Take care of my boy, Jeff." How many times had I heard her say that? She was standing on the steps smiling down at us.

"I always do." We went out the door and put Charlotte into her crate. I waved to my mom as we pulled out of the driveway.

"I always invite Mom to come along," I said absently when we were out of sight. "And I always hope she says no. Is that wrong do you think, Uncle Jeff?"

"No, and I don't think you really worry that she's going to say yes. She'd hate camping."

"Yeah, and she'd slow us down. We're going to reach Virginia this time."

"If we don't get that far it won't be a failure." Uncle Jeff looked concerned. "This isn't a competition, you know."

"We'll make it. We've got almost three weeks." I leaned my head on the glass of the window and watched the passing scenery.

"I can't believe that at seventeen years old I still can't sleep in a car without getting carsick." We were sitting at a picnic table at the start of the Trail segment drinking Coke and eating peanut butter crackers.

"Have I ever told you that your dad was like that too?" Uncle Jeff asked.

"No, but I think he did when we went to Disney a hundred years ago."

"That's right. Are you feeling well enough to get started?" he asked. "We can stay in a hotel tonight if you want."

"No, I'm fine," I said. "Coke and crackers does it every time. It's decaffeinated coke too." I looked at the can.

"I know you've stayed away from caffeine for the past few years."

"I drink it now and then," I said. "You ready, Charlotte? Let's go."

"Uncle Jeff," I asked. "Are you still seeing Mary Ann?" We'd walked in silence for about a mile. I'd been thinking about my mom's lonely existence and remembered that Uncle Jeff hadn't had a partner most of his life either.

"No," he said. "She wanted more than a casual relationship. I just didn't think I could give it to her."

"So she dumped you?"

"It was a mutual agreement. It isn't fair for me to expect her to just coast along with me when she wants a home and a family."

"She dumped you."

"Yeah, but I didn't mind too much." We both laughed. We walked in silence for a while longer.

"You were married once. I remember vaguely. What happened?" I asked.

He didn't say anything for a minute.

"I guess it's none of my business. You don't have to answer that."

"No, I want to answer you. I'm just not sure I know what the answer is." He was quiet for a little while again. I didn't say anything else.

"I think I really did love Cynthia," he finally said. "She was a tall kind of willowy woman with blond hair. I don't think it was naturally blond, but I don't suppose that matters. She had a wicked sense of humor. But just like with Mary Ann, she wanted a family."

"So you really didn't want a family. You just got stuck with me."

"You know that's not true."

"I'm kidding, Uncle Jeff. I've known you love me ever since you hauled me out of that waterfall."

"I enjoy everything I do with you. You're probably the reason I haven't been lonely."

"Good, now go on. Why didn't you want a family with Cynthia?"

He was quiet again for a while. "It's terrible to say, but I don't think I minded the idea of a family as much as I just didn't want to hang out with her as much as she wanted me to." He laughed. "You know I've always loved my work."

"So why did you get married?"

"I think I just thought I should. Your dad had been married twice by that time. He'd already left you behind. I'm sorry." He turned to look at me behind him on the trail. "I shouldn't have put it that way."

"It's okay." I laughed. "How old are you now, Uncle Jeff?"

"I'm forty one."

"And you don't wish you had a family?"

"I do have a family, David. I have you. I still have a mother and no one could have better roots than Aunt Jeanne and Uncle Bill."

"That's true. But you don't wish you had a partner of your own?"

We walked in silence for about a mile. I didn't push. This was the kind of thing you had to talk about at your own pace.

"I think I did wish I had my own partner. I think that's why I bought that house. I wanted a home. That's why I pursued Mary Ann. But that didn't work."

Uncle Jeff stopped at a camp site that had been recently used. We were beside a stream like I always wanted us to be. "I think we've gone about eight miles. How's this spot? We'll go further tomorrow. We got a late start today."

"This looks great." I took off my pack. I took off my shoes and socks and sat on a rock with my feet in the stream. "I love this part of backpacking."

"I do too." Uncle Jeff sat down on another rock beside me and put his feet in the stream. "The truth is I love every part of backpacking. This was your idea, David, and it's been a great project."

"It's hard to believe we haven't even hiked a quarter of the Trail."

"Well, we started slow to get in shape and now we travel farther each trip, but we're busy people. We only go once a year."

"That's okay. I'm not in a hurry."

"Me neither." Uncle Jeff tossed a stick into the water and we watched it make its way down the stream. "I plan to live to a hundred, remember?"

"Ninety eight since I fell down the waterfall." I laughed.

"Oh that's right." He smiled.

"So, even though Mary Ann didn't work out, do you still wish you had your own partner?"

"No, I'm feeling more settled now. You know I've always loved my work, and I'm having a lot of fun working on that house. How did you like your room when you stayed with me last week?"

"It was great, and the fountain is really coming along too."

"Maybe all I needed was a real home of my own," he said. "Why all the questions, David?"

"You know when I got home from school this summer, for the first time I wondered why I didn't have two sets of grandparents. Can you believe that, Uncle Jeff? I'm seventeen years old. I've lived with my mother all my life, her exclusively, not my dad. You too of course, but mostly her, and I've never wondered where she came from."

"There's no reason you should."

"Yes there is. Did you know she grew up in a Catholic girl's home? She really has no roots."

"Yes, I knew that. She's a mate for lifer too. She'll never stop loving my brother," he said. "...Your dad."

"Her life just seems so lonely."

"And mine does, too? We're both okay you know, David."

"I guess."

"But you don't want to be lonely."

"I told Mom. As long as we have each other we won't be lonely. That's right, don't you think, Uncle Jeff?"

"I think that's right, David."

The Trail was the most mountainous part we'd hiked so far. It seemed like we were hiking up and down mountains all the time. I made a list of the mountains and peaks for my album. The scenery was spectacular. I took about a hundred pictures, maybe more. We camped next to streams a couple of times. Sometimes we stayed on the top of a mountain. There aren't any streams on the top of a mountain. I enjoyed the cool night breeze almost as much.

Charlotte was in her prime, and it was a great pleasure to have her with me. She trotted along beside us up the hills, rarely panting very much. She carried her pack with ease. I could let her off leash some of the time when we were in remote parts of the Trail. I leashed her when people were around. She wouldn't bother anyone, but it was the right thing to do.

Uncle Jeff seemed okay with it. We still slept in the same tent. Charlotte slept on the other side of me. I slept in the middle. He never really talked to her. I did see him stroke her back a few times when he thought I wasn't looking.

"Let's stay tonight in the shelter on Roan High Knob." Uncle Jeff broke the silence of about three miles. "We're seven days into this trip, and even though we stayed at that hotel the other night, I'm too tired to pitch a tent in the rain. Look at the sky. I think we've just got time to get there before the bottom drops out."

I looked up at the sky. Sure enough, there was a black thunder head moving slowly but surely our way over the ridge of the next mountain. We were about half way to the top. "Sounds good to me," I said. "It'll be a good entry for my album anyway. It's the highest shelter on the whole Trail. I'll have to get some pictures of it."

We hiked the rest of the trail at almost a run as the wind picked up, and we started to hear thunder. Charlotte stayed close to my side. She was afraid of thunder. I kept her on a leash. I didn't know what she'd do if she panicked.

At first it was a distant rolling sound. Then it moved closer until we were seeing lightning streak across the sky, and the thunder was more of a cracking sound. Charlotte was so close to my leg now I had to be careful not to trip on her.

I was in front. Suddenly Charlotte stopped and pulled the leash backwards. I turned to look back. Uncle Jeff had fallen behind. I was approaching another switchback, but he was all the way back at the last one. He had his hands on a tree and was looking down at the ground. I started back down in a hurry. He seemed to be swaying.

"What's wrong, Uncle Jeff?" I put my hand on his shoulder. It was shaking.

"I don't know. I feel like I'm going to throw up."

I stepped back a little and took my hand off his shoulder.

He looked at me and smiled weakly. "Don't worry. I think I can control it." He was white as a sheet. "Do me a favor, David. There's a roll of mints in my side pocket. Would you get me one? I have to hold on to this tree. It's swaying." He laughed, again he sounded weak.

"Okay." I fumbled in his pocket and found the mints. I handed him one then I eased his pack off of his shoulders. He put the mint in his mouth and sucked loudly on it for a minute. Then he turned and sat down on the ground with his back up against the tree.

There was another loud crack of thunder. The storm was getting closer. "I'm sorry, kid. If you want to go on to the shelter it's okay. I think it's only a couple of switch backs up. I hate for you and the dog to get wet waiting for me."

"No way I'm leaving you here by yourself." I sat down beside him. "What's the matter? You don't have pain in your chest or anything do you?"

He laughed sounding a little bit stronger. "No, I'm not having a heart attack. In fact I'm feeling a little better now. Let me drink some water. Then I think we can go on."

We slowed down after that. Even though the clouds were directly overhead the rain was holding off. Uncle Jeff stumbled a couple of times along the way. I held his elbow and he didn't object. He was right though. It was only two switchbacks to the shelter. When we got there I took off my pack and snapped the leash off of Charlotte's collar so she could pee if she needed to. She stayed glued to my leg.

Uncle Jeff sat down on the porch of the shelter with his pack on. His color had changed from white to a strange shade of gray. I was really starting to feel panicky.

"You know what, David." He looked up at me and his eyes were blood shot." I've figured this out. It's altitude sickness. I read about it somewhere. It feels the same as that time I got sick at Clingman's Dome."

Just as the first drops of rain started to fall, he struggled to stand up with his pack on and started toward the path that led down the other side of the mountain. "I'm not staying here. I'll pitch a tent in the rain."

"Wait for me, Uncle Jeff." I picked up my pack and snapped Charlotte's leash back on.

He turned around but kept walking backwards. "No, you get some pictures. I'll wait at the bottom of the third switchback." He turned and hurried down the trail.

I figured I could take a few pictures. I wanted them for my album, and we would probably not come back here.

The next night we stayed in a bed and breakfast in the mountains. We'd stayed in a hotel the week before after the fourth night of hiking. Most of the places on the Trail were dog friendly. It always felt great to take a shower and eat at a table in a restaurant. Sleeping in a real bed was nice too.

The next day we hiked Grassy Ridge which is the longest grassy bald in the Appalachians. I took pictures even though it wasn't as exciting as some of the other scenery. I wanted the whole Trail documented.

We hiked mountainous terrain for several more days. I was getting exhausted and thought maybe Uncle Jeff was right. Maybe we didn't have to go all the way to Virginia.

We stayed at another bed and breakfast on Tuesday of our last week. We cleaned up and met at a restaurant a few blocks from the Inn. I sat down at the table Uncle Jeff had already claimed. He looked tired too.

"Well, David," he said. "This is the longest we've ever hiked. Are you ready to quit? We can get a bus from here and we won't have far to hike to Virginia the next time we go."

"I'm thinking about it."

We ordered dinner and ate in relative silence. I think we were both too tired to talk.

"Let's head home, Uncle Jeff."

"That's okay with me. You won't feel defeated will you?" He sounded concerned.

"Maybe a little bit," I said. "But I'll just blame it on you."

We both laughed. We finished our desert and stumbled back to the Inn where we slept until late the next morning.

I went back to school to a single room. I had requested my own room in the dorm. Uncle Jeff said he didn't mind the extra expense. That way I could study all night without bothering anyone.

Rich didn't come back to school. I don't know if he didn't do as well as he thought on his exams or if he just didn't want to. I never saw him again and I missed him.

Of course, I wasn't there very long that year. I got caught smoking marijuana on campus. I got arrested and put in jail. My dad and my uncle managed to get me out of jail and off the hook with a slap on the wrist. Harvard expelled me.

I like to tell myself I did it on purpose because I was worried about my mother. She was all alone at home. So was Uncle Jeff. They needed me.

How true do you think that is?

CHAPTER EIGHT

"David." I heard my name called across the crowded cafeteria of Georgia State University. I thought I recognized the voice and turned around. Teresa was waving to me from a table across the room. I went over to her and put my tray down on the table across from her.

"I thought you were going to UGA," I said as I sat down.

"I thought you were going to Harvard."

"Things change." I wasn't going to talk to her about that.

"Yeah they do," she said. "The food here is pretty good. There are also a bunch of restaurants around. We should try some of them together."

"That would be nice, but I'm planning to work really hard. I want to get through as fast as I can."

"So you won't have time to hang out with me," she said. "That's the David I remember. Maybe that's why I couldn't wait for you. You were never able to give me enough time."

I looked at her and wondered why I was sitting there. "Speaking of not waiting for me, how's old Dexter?"

"I wouldn't know. He's still at UGA. I flunked out in the first semester."

"Really? Why, Teresa? You're so smart. We were in the challenge program together all through school."

"Dex was so insanely jealous. I couldn't concentrate on anything but staying away from all the other boys."

"I was worried about that the last time I saw you." She was right, the food in the cafeteria was good. I made a mental note not to bother with restaurants. It was cheap here too.

"I finally gave in to one guy's moves. All we did was kiss. Well, we were really kind of making out under the steps in the library. Dex caught us and he beat me up. He didn't touch the guy. He just hauled me over to his apartment. You know his parents rented him an apartment, and he beat the crap out of me."

I looked up at her. "I hope you had him arrested!" I couldn't believe it.

"I wouldn't do that. I thought I loved him at the time." She continued to eat. I looked down at my plate. I'd lost my appetite.

"So," I said. "Are you still with him? I mean do you get together on weekends?"

"No, he wouldn't forgive me. I tried to explain that he'd driven me to it with his jealousy. It didn't matter. He wouldn't forgive me. He's dating some junior at UGA now."

"I'm not quite sure I understand how his jealousy drove you to make out with some guy under the library steps," I said. "But he shouldn't have beaten you. You should have charged him. He'll just do it to someone else now."

"Not my problem."

"Well, I need to get to class. I've got calculus across the street in Kell Hall, and then I have a biology lab."

"David, wait." She put her hand on my arm. I looked down at it. "I heard what happened at Harvard and I'm sorry. I feel responsible. I turned you on to that stuff."

Her hand felt clammy on my arm. I wondered why I'd ever thought I loved her. "Teresa." I got up effectively breaking the connection. "It was my fault not yours, but thanks for the concern." I took my tray to the trash receptacle and scraped the contents in. Then I stacked the tray with the others. When I turned around there were a group of boys at Teresa's table. One was nuzzling her neck. They all were laughing. I turned and walked out of the cafeteria.

I shivered as I hurried across the street to my calculus class. It was mid February. I'd brought my jacket, but in my rush to get out of the cafeteria, I hadn't put it on. I got to the classroom just before the professor started and sat in the nearest desk. I pulled my book and notebook out of my backpack and prepared to listen.

As usual the professor's explanation made perfect sense. I felt comfortable with the material. Then he gave us a problem to do. The concepts seemed so different than the reality to me. I struggled through the problem which included a formula that was at least a page long with all sorts of squiggly symbols that I didn't really understand.

After about ten minutes the professor said, "David."

Oh, shit! I thought.

"What was your answer?"

I looked up at him and said, "I haven't gotten one yet." It was a lie, but I wasn't confident with my results.

"Alright," he said. "Luther, what is your answer?"

I looked at the man who sat in front of me. He'd been there since the semester had started two weeks ago, but we hadn't spoken. He was older than the rest of the students. He recited his result to the problem.

"That's right," the professor said. "How many of the rest of you got that?"

I looked at my paper. Not even close. I sighed deeply and started packing up my stuff to go to my biology lab.

"I can help you with this stuff." I looked up as Luther spoke to me. "I'm pretty good at it."

I looked at him but didn't respond. I was usually the one helping people in school. I'd never needed a tutor before, but I was struggling. "How much do you charge an hour?" I asked.

"Well, since I'm taking the same class I don't know if it would be right to charge. I'm learning too."

"I'd need to pay you something." My pride was hurting about the calculus. I didn't want to be a charity case too.

"Okay, whatever you think," he said. "I was going to the library after my next class. Would you like to meet there?"

"I have a biology lab. It's an hour and a half long."

"That's okay. I'll get us a study room. Ask at the front desk. They'll tell you where I am." He walked out of the room ahead of me. He was short. I noticed a balding spot on the back of his head. He was definitely older than me. That didn't mean much. I was still about the youngest student in the school.

"My name is Luther Wendall," he said.

"I'm David Landrum." We parted then and went different ways.

Biology lab was fun. I sat down at one of the lab tables. My lab partner came in a little late and sat down next to me. Amy was a tall brunette. She was pretty. Her teeth were a little too long for my taste. That really didn't matter. I had no intention of asking her out or anything.

"Are you ready to test your urine?" she asked.

I laughed. "I'd forgotten that was what we were doing today." We all went to the bathroom and peed in a cup, then performed all the exercises the lab instructor gave us. Amy had a brilliant sense of humor and kept me laughing the whole time.

After lab I pulled on my jacket and went over to the library. I found out where Luther was and joined him. We worked together for about an hour then Luther suggested we go and get something to eat.

I looked at my watch. "It's four thirty," I said. "I need to go. I'm riding the train home, and I don't want to be late for dinner."

"You still live at home with your parents?" he asked and I felt uncomfortable.

"My mom," I said.

"Well, if my mom would still let me live with her I would," he said. "When I turned thirty she threw me out." He laughed and put his hand on my shoulder. "Come on, I'll walk with you to the station. I'm going home that way too."

We started down the road. The wind had picked up. I zipped my jacket higher. "Where do you live?" Luther asked.

"A little north of Buckhead."

"Some fancy places up there. I live a little south of midtown. Not so fancy."

"We're pretty much in the low rent district." I laughed.

"I didn't know there was one up there," he laughed too. "Listen, David, I don't mean to be corruptive, but this calculus stuff for someone like you is going to be easier if you get high when you work on it."

I stopped walking and he stopped and turned around to look at me. I know I looked shocked. He laughed and put his hand my shoulder encouraging me to continue to walk.

"I didn't mean to shock you, but I've seen minds like yours struggle with this before. You are just too intense. You need to relax a little and let it flow."

I walked beside him in silence. There was a prickling feeling on the back of my neck. Was it fear? I looked at the man beside me. He looked innocent enough, but what was he doing in college at thirty years old.

"Luther, do you work or are you just going to school?"

"I tend bar at Tattle Tails, that strip joint in midtown. Don't be afraid of me, David. I can see it in your eyes that you are. I'm going to school so that I can get a real job. I'm tired of night life."

We entered the station, bought tokens, and got on the same train. "David, my apartment is on the way. Stop in for a minute. I have an album I want you to hear."

"I never paid you for the tutoring," I said stupidly.

"Pay me for the album if you like it. I'll sell it to you."

I knew he was talking about marijuana. The prickling feeling on the back of my neck had returned. I knew I should say no, but I hadn't smoked anything since I'd been back, and I was craving sleep. I followed him like a zombie to his apartment. I left with a bag of weed stashed in my book bag.

Amazingly enough, calculus was easier for me when I was high. My midnight walks resumed. Charlotte became so used to them that she'd come to get me at my computer when it was time to go. That was good because sometimes I lost track of time.

❂

"David." it was Darla's voice I heard when I answered the phone.

"Hey, P.H.," I said.

"I'm coming over and get you. We're going to a movie with a bunch of my friends and then we're going to a pub that will serve us for a beer and a snack."

"I can't tonight, P.H.," I said. "I have a calculus test on Monday and math is not my best subject."

"That's right. You only get an A- in math, not your usual A++." She laughed and the sound of ice tinkling in a glass made me smile.

"That's right, and to get that A- I have to study all the time."

"Well, its Saturday night and you have all day tomorrow. I'm coming over to get you, and if you refuse to come I'll pester you until you change your mind."

"Okay, I'll go," I said. "I know when it's a losing battle." I could never change Darla's mind about anything. Luckily she did seem to care about what was right for me. I hadn't gone out with friends in a while. I probably needed some socializing.

I went downstairs to my mom's sewing room off the kitchen. "Mom, I'm going out with Darla and some of her friends in a little while. Is that alright with you?"

She turned and smiled at me. "Honey, you don't have to ask permission. I'm glad you're going out. Please stay out of trouble though." Her expression registered concern.

"Mom, forgive me okay. I did a stupid thing. I'm not going to repeat it." I hated having this stigma following me around. Couldn't they just forget about it? Of course, I did have a bag stashed in my room, but I knew how to be careful now.

"I'm sorry, David. It's hard for me." She turned back to her sewing machine and the familiar whir of it started again.

"I'm sorry. I shouldn't snap at you. It's my fault." I put my hands on her shoulders and kissed the top of her head. "I'll stay out of trouble. I promise."

Darla picked me up. Meryl and Jimmy were in the back seat. "We're meeting Jan and Matt at the theater," she said.

I always had a hard time sitting through a movie, but this one was good. An adventure film, I don't think I ever knew the name.

We went to a nearby pub afterward. One of the places in town that we knew would serve us underage. We just had to sit in the back. Darla was designated driver so she didn't drink from the pitcher. I poured myself a glass but barely touched it.

"Don't you like beer?" Jimmy asked.

"Yeah, I do like it, but it's a little late for me. I like to drink beer in the afternoon. I'll just have to get up to pee all night long if I drink it now." I laughed and Darla kissed my cheek.

"What was that for?" I smiled down at her.

"I'm just glad you're here."

"So why aren't you drinking beer, Meryl?" Matt asked from across the table where he sat next to Jan with an arm over her shoulder. "You usually drink like a fish."

"I do not." Meryl blushed and looked down.

Jimmy took her hand and looked at the people around the table. "We're going to have a baby," he said.

My heart thumped in my chest and I felt short of breath.

"Oh, Meryl!" Darla squealed. "I'm so excited. When are you due?"

"My due date is October 6th."

"Wow, that's a long way off," Jan said. "I guess you don't know if it's a boy or a girl yet, do you?"

"No, I'll find out at my next ultra sound. That's two weeks away. I'm not sure I want to know though. Maybe we'll just be surprised like the old days."

"I want to know," Jimmy said. He was smiling proudly and twining his fingers with Meryl's on the table. "I'm hoping for a girl that looks exactly like her mother."

"I agree," Darla said. "Not about it being a girl. I don't care which one it is. I just want to know. It'll be easier for me to make plans."

"What plans are you going to make?" I surprised myself with my question. My voice sounded squeaky and high. I cleared my throat.

"Whoa," Darla looked up at me. "You were almost growling. Aren't you happy for Jimmy and Meryl?"

"They're only eighteen years old." I could hear the anger in my voice, and I wondered why I was so upset about this.

"We'll be nineteen when the baby is born." Meryl squared her shoulders in a defensive gesture.

"We don't have to justify ourselves to him, Meryl," Jimmy said. He turned to look at me. "You're just jealous, David, because I have what you want."

I flinched at the truth in his statement and looked away from him. My eyes landed on a corner booth. I sucked in my breath in shock. Teresa leaned back against the booth. The boy next to her was kissing her neck and his hand was in her shirt.

"Shit!" I said and stood up just as a gust of cold air came from the front of the pub. Dexter came in and looked around. He stormed over to the booth and yanked the boy off of Teresa.

Chapter Eight

"Dex!" she screamed. "Don't hurt him."

"It's not him I'm going to hurt." He pulled Teresa out of the booth by the arm and dragged her across the room to the door.

I started after them.

"David!" Darla pulled on my arm. "There isn't anything you can do."

I looked at her hand on my arm. It was small and white. I put my big hand over hers and lifted it to my mouth. I kissed her knuckles then turned and went to the door. I was hardly aware of the cold when I went outside. I looked around the crowded parking lot. Dexter and Teresa were struggling next to a red mustang convertible. I put my hands in my jacket pockets and walked over to them.

"Fancy car, Dex." I leaned on the hood.

"Get out of here, Landrum." He snarled. "This is none of your business."

"I'm not going to let you hurt her." My voice sounded ominous even to myself. Fancy that, I thought. I think the slight smile on my face worked in my favor because Dexter shifted uncomfortably.

"What's it to you anyway. She dropped you over a year ago."

"We're still friends, aren't we, Teresa?"

"Have you been messing around with him again?!" Dexter demanded of Teresa. He grabbed her by the arm and pulled her roughly to face him. "I know he had you before I did." Now he was growling.

Faster than I knew what I was thinking, I grabbed both of his arms and twisted them behind his back. He shrieked and Teresa grabbed my arm.

"Don't hurt his arms, David. He's a quarterback," she cried.

I looked down at her. Then I looked at the hands I had twisted into a painful position. "If I ever hear of you hurting her again," I said. "I'll break them both. I swear I will." I let him go and he fell to his knees. I stepped back. Teresa rushed in and put her arms around Dexter.

I wanted to vomit. "David," I heard Jimmy's voice from what seemed like a distance. I felt something on my arm and looked down at Darla's hand. She and Jimmy were standing on either side of me.

"You still love her?" Darla sounded sad. I looked at her pretty face.

"I never did love her," I said feeling the truth of it. "I just don't like to see people beat up on each other."

"He'll beat up on her anyway," Jimmy said. "And she'll leave him. Then she'll go back. It's been going on all year. It's not your problem, David. There isn't anything you can do."

"So I just walk away?"

"That's right."

I pulled on a stocking cap and gloves along with my jacket and clipped Charlotte's leash to her collar. The middle of the night was cold. I'd even seen a few snowflakes in the glow of the street light. I opened the front door and stopped, surprised. Jimmy's utility truck was parked at the front curb. He stood leaning against it.

I walked down the path to the sidewalk. He fell in line beside me and Charlotte.

"I wanted to talk to you," he said.

"How did you know I'd take a late night walk?"

"I didn't. I was trying to decide whether to throw a rock at your window or call your cell phone."

"I take a walk every night about this time."

"I guess this is when you smoke."

I looked at him, startled.

"I know you haven't quit. I don't think you can. David, I think you're an addict."

"You don't get addicted to marijuana," I said, putting the joint in my mouth and lighting it up. I offered it to him.

"No, the union drug tests," he said. "Besides, I don't like the stuff."

We walked in silence for a minute while I smoked. "David, most people don't get addicted to pot, but that's because they smoke it recreationally. You smoke because you need it. It's self medication."

"Okay, I'll go with that," I said. "So what else should I do? Just not sleep, never relax. Try living that way, Jimmy."

"No, I suggest you go to your doctor and tell him about the problems you're having with sleep and relaxation. You know there are different types of attention span problems. Being too focused can be a problem too. There are legitimate ways to deal with it."

"I can get addicted legally."

"Not necessarily drugs, there are therapies too."

"Hmmm ..." I dragged the last of the joint and threw it on the grown to crush it. I pushed it into the drain on the side of the road and turned around. "I'm handling it fine, Jimmy. Give me a break. I'm not going to get in trouble again."

"Teresa says you've been seen with a known drug dealer at school."

"You still talk to Teresa?"

"She's still a friend."

"Do you tell her she's being an idiot?"

"Yes, she doesn't listen to me either. But David," He took a deep breath and turned to look at me. We were back at his truck and he took out his keys. "If you continue like this I can't be your friend anymore."

"What!" I raised my voice then glanced at the house. "Jimmy, after all I've done for you. You just won't be my friend because I have a vice."

"I'm getting ready to be a dad, David. I don't want you setting a bad example for my kids," he said. "Not to mention that I can't stand watching you destroy yourself."

"That's another thing. You give me shit for taking a midnight walk when you're about to have a baby at nineteen years old. Do you really think that's wise? You haven't even finished your apprenticeship."

"I'm married, David. It's legal. Besides, we didn't plan the baby, at least I didn't."

"So do you think she tricked you?"

"Maybe, it doesn't matter. I love her and I love our baby. I have a paying job, and she'll have finished cosmetology school and have a job too by the time the baby comes." He walked around the truck to the driver's side door and looked across the hood. "I'm serious, David. If you keep hanging around with thugs and taking midnight fix walks I can't be your friend anymore. Make your choice." He got into the driver's seat, started the car, and drove off. He turned on the lights just as he turned off my street.

The next morning I woke up feeling like something was wrong, something was missing. I remembered my conversation with Jimmy last night and felt a wave of depression. I rubbed my eyes and sat up.

Charlotte's bed was empty. I looked around the room. She wasn't there. She'd never slept anywhere but in my room before. Had I left her outside? I tried to remember what I'd done when I came in from my walk. Charlotte had gone into the kitchen to drink from her water bowl. I came upstairs alone. I left the door open so she could get in when she came up.

I got out of bed and pulled on my bathrobe. I went into the hall and looked over the banister. Charlotte lay at the bottom of the stairs on her side. My heart began to pound. Was she breathing?

"Charlotte," I said. She picked up her head and looked at me. Her tail thumped on the carpet and she struggled to her feet. She held her back left leg above the ground and cried softly as she put her front foot on the step and pulled it away.

"What's wrong, girl?" I hurried down the steps to where she stood. The leg was bent at the knee. When I touched it she cried out. I had visions of those last painful days with Pepper, and my heart began to pound. "Mom," I called.

My mom came to the stairs in her bathrobe and looked over. "What's wrong?"

"Charlotte can't use her leg. I need to take her to the vet."

"Let me get dressed," Mom said. "It's only 6:00 am. We'll have to go to the emergency clinic. They probably can't do much about this, but they can tell us who can." She hurried away.

I picked Charlotte up gently and carried her up to her bed. I laid her down. "Why didn't you call me girl?" I hurriedly pulled on blue jeans and a t-shirt. I picked her up again and hurried out to the car. Mom got into the passenger seat of my Chevy and we were off.

"It's a torn cruciate ligament," the doctor said after examination and x-rays.

I couldn't say anything for a minute my relief was so great. He hadn't said cancer. "Can it be fixed?" I stood beside the table Charlotte lay on and stroked her soft fir.

"Yes, I can give you a referral to a specialist. There are several in town or you can go to the University of Georgia. It will cost less there, but you'll probably have to get on a waiting list."

"How much will it cost?" Mom asked. I looked at her, startled.

"I would guess about fifteen hundred dollars at the University. More like two thousand at a specialist in town."

"I can't afford that," Mom said. "Is there an alternative to surgery?"

"Mom!" I couldn't believe my ears. "We have to fix it."

"David," she said. There were tears in her eyes. "I don't have the money. I can't do it. You don't have any money. How can we do it?"

"There is an alternative for some of these cases," the doctor said. "You can confine her for a couple of months and do some physical therapy. But in this case she hasn't even put that foot down again. I think it will require surgery. Otherwise, she'll just be a three legged dog. That really isn't an option because then the other knee would go bad from the pressure."

"Would it be better to put her down?" Mom asked.

"No." I scooped Charlotte off the table and carried her out to the car. I put her in the back seat and got into the driver's seat.

Mom came out the door and tapped on the driver's side window. "David," she said. "I have to pay the bill. Don't you dare leave me here."

"How could you even suggest that, Mom?"

"I don't want to put her down, David, but I don't have the money to pay for the surgery. It would be cruel to make her walk around on three legs for the rest of her life. You heard what the doctor said. That would probably make the other knee go."

"I'll find the money," I said.

She put her hand on my arm. "I'll see what I can do to help." She went into the building and came out with a referral to a specialist and the number for the University of Georgia.

"I can't believe that you would call me and ask for money after the mess I pulled you out of only a few months ago." The anger in my dad's voice was just barely controlled. "It's a good thing you didn't call me at home," he continued. "Sharon would be furious."

To Hell with Sharon, I thought, but I said. "It's not for me, Dad. It's for my dog. You like dogs. She's a great little mixed breed, and she's too young to die or be permanently crippled." There was silence on the line. "I'll pay you back. I promise."

"How are you going to pay me back?"

"I'll get a job."

"Two thousand dollars, you said." I could tell he was softening. "Why didn't you ask your Uncle Jeff? He's usually pretty indulgent toward you. That's probably your problem."

I took a deep breath. I had to humble myself to him. I needed him right now. "He hates dogs," I said.

"He refused to help you?"

"I didn't ask." The line was quiet for a while.

"Two thousand dollars," he repeated.

"The University of Georgia couldn't take her for four weeks, and it didn't save any money anyway with the treatment she'd require in the meantime. The specialist can do it next week if I can come up with the money."

More silence.

"Alright," he finally said.

I let out a breath I wasn't aware of holding.

"I do like dogs, David. I'm still furious with you, but I do like dogs. Give me the number to the veterinary specialist. I'll arrange payment."

"Thanks Dad," I said. "I promise I'll pay you back."

"You had damn well better," he said and hung up the phone.

I never told my Uncle Jeff where I'd gotten the money for Charlotte's surgery. He didn't ask. I guess he just didn't think about it.

My mom was pleased that my dad had been willing to do that. The surgery was a success but recovery time was long, so when Uncle Jeff and I went backpacking for spring break, Charlotte couldn't come along. We went back to Cumberland Island. It was a good time to go there. They don't allow you to bring pets onto the island anyway.

✦

"I love the sea breeze in my face," Uncle Jeff said as the boat pulled away from the dock.

"Me too," I held my face up to the wind. I had a flash memory of surf boarding with my dad when I was ten years old. It made me smile. I had planned to teach surfboarding when I grew up.

"I've got a friend who's the caretaker of the small private island to the north of this one. Those are all privately owned homes. This part is open to the public. There are ruins from old plantations. There are all sorts of feral animals. Do you remember? It's been a while since we camped here."

"Yeah, I remember."

Uncle Jeff tapped my arm. "Look," he pointed to the open sea. There was a school of dolphin ahead of us. Their fins danced above the surface then ducked below.

When we reached the dock at the island we unloaded our gear and went to a safety orientation that all campers, backpackers, and hikers had to go to.

"I'm glad they did that," I said when we came out of the building and put on our packs. "I'd thought about snakes. I'd forgotten about alligators."

"We'll be fine if we just stay out of the freshwater ponds."

"The hiking is a lot different on flat ground isn't it?" I said after we'd walked about a mile.

"A lot different," he paused. "David, I wanted to tell you that I'm proud of the way you've picked up the pieces and moved on after what happened at Harvard."

"I'm trying to forgive myself for that."

"You're not still smoking that stuff are you?"

I didn't say anything. We walked another mile in silence.

"David," Uncle Jeff persisted. "I know it's none of my business but it really isn't worth it. If you get caught again you'll probably go to jail."

"Uncle Jeff, I never smoked it for recreation. It was the only way I could sleep."

"So you are still smoking it."

"I didn't say that. Maybe I'm just not sleeping."

"You're not going to answer my question are you?"

"No."

We hiked four miles the first day. We had started late and when we got to the campsite we settled in and changed into our swimming trunks. The beach was a short hike over the dunes. We had a quick swim while there was still daylight. Then we went back to camp, pan fried the cat fish we'd caught in the surf, and went to bed.

I hadn't brought any pot with me. We could hear the ocean from our tent. I slept like a baby for five nights. I got a good six to seven hours a night and felt great when I got back on the ferry to go to the mainland. I smiled as the sea wind hit my face. Jimmy is ridiculous, I thought. I'm not an addict.

✦

"Oh no," Uncle Jeff said as we pulled into the driveway. Mom was weeding around the hedge in the front yard. She stood and walked toward the car. "She was waiting for us."

"Gramma?" I said through my open window as she approached. She nodded.

Uncle Jeff got out of the car and walked into her waiting arms. I got out and stood behind him. He cried again. I'd never noticed his parents, my grandparents, being very nice to him; but he loved them. I put my hand on his shoulder, and he turned and put his arms around me. I held him while he cried for a few minutes, then we all walked to the house and sat at the kitchen table while my mom got us three glasses of ginger ale.

"She died quietly, Mrs. Simmons at the nursing home said." Mom told us. "Mrs. Simmons said that when the last nurse visited her she told her she'd just like to be alone for a while. She said some people prefer to die alone. When she went back to check on her she was gone."

"Sounds like my mother," Uncle Jeff said. "I guess I need to call the funeral home."

"No," Mom said. "I called and they've received the body. If you want to view it you can in the morning. We have an appointment to make the arrangements at 10:00."

"Has anyone called Brian?"

"I thought you would want to do that," she said. "Jeff, why don't you stay the night tonight? The guest room is made up and you don't need to be alone right now."

"No thanks, I think I'll go on home."

"I'll go with you," I said. "Just give me a minute to pack a bag." I looked at my backpack. "A clean bag," I said.

"Bring your own car, David." He stood up and put his arms around me again. He kissed my cheek which was rare. "I'll go on home. Thanks, David. Thanks Charlie." He touched Mom's cheek and went down the hall and out the front door.

"You'll be alright, Mom?"

"I'm fine, sweetie."

I let myself into the garage with the remote that Uncle Jeff had given me. I also had a key to the front door. I could hear him on the phone in the living room. I waved as I went by on the way to my room. He put his hand over the receiver and said, "It's your dad. Come back as soon as you can. He may want to speak to you."

I hurried to my room and put down my bag then hurried back to the living room. Uncle Jeff was hanging up the phone.

"He needed to go. There'll be time to talk when he gets here. He'll call back to give me his itinerary."

"Sure," I said controlling the disappointment on my face.

"It was kind of a shock to him," he said. He was studying my face. I turned toward the kitchen.

"I don't know why it would be a shock," I said. "She's been dying for years."

"Well." He followed me into the kitchen. "He was always her favorite. He was Grampa's favorite too, but it showed mostly with her. He was a kind of a mamma's boy." He laughed and sat down at the kitchen table. He studied me while I poured myself a glass of lemonade.

"I'm sorry, David," he said. "He should have taken the time to talk to you."

"It's okay, Uncle Jeff. He's mad at me. I don't blame him. I'm mad at myself."

"Don't be mad at yourself. Life is too short."

"Life seems too long to me. Sometimes I wonder if I'll get through it."

He studied me while I looked through his pantry and refrigerator. "You scare me to death sometimes, David. I don't think you understand how much I love you."

"I don't mean to scare you," I said. "I'm supposed to be keeping you company in a rough time. Let me cook you a gourmet meal."

"I'm not sure I could eat it."

The phone rang and he answered it. He talked for a minute then hung up and said, "Go ahead and cook. Aunt Jeanne and Uncle Bill are coming over."

I went to the funeral home with Uncle Jeff and Mom the next day. We planned gramma's memorial service then went to the airport to meet Dad. He walked off the plane and hugged Uncle Jeff. They both cried. It was unnerving to watch. Then he turned to me. He scowled for a minute then put his arms around me and hugged me stiffly.

I touched his soft shoulders with both hands then we pushed away from each other. He looked into my eyes and said, "I'm working on forgiving you, David, but it's hard."

"I know it's hard," I said. I wondered if he had any idea.

We had the service on the following day. Afterward I went to lunch with Dad. I suggested that we include Mom or Uncle Jeff, or both. Dad insisted on us going alone. He made a point of telling me that he hadn't seen a penny of the money I'd borrowed to fix Charlotte's leg.

"I expect you to start paying me back, David," he said.

"The job I have at the bookstore at school really only covers the money I need for books, Dad."

"Then get another job."

"I can't work two jobs. I take a double load of hours at school. I want to finish in two more years. Why can't I pay you back when I get out and have a career? It's not like you need two thousand dollars to live on or anything."

"That's not the point. I know you think I'm being unreasonable, but someone has to teach you some responsibility. Apparently your mother and uncle aren't doing that."

"You have no right to criticize them. They've been great. None of my shit is there fault."

He sat back and looked at me. "I suppose you're telling me it's my fault because I haven't been there for you."

"No, it's my fault. I'm not just a monkey on a string that does what I'm told, Dad. I'm a person, separate from Mom, separate from Uncle Jeff. I think and act on my own."

"Stupidly," he said.

I took a deep breath. "Yeah, stupidly, I'll pay you your money. Now get off my back." I stood up quickly, knocking over my glass of water into his lap. I jumped back startled and knocked over my chair. My damn body was so long I didn't even know where it was so I knocked over a coat rack with my knee when I rushed out the of the restaurant door. It fell across the doorway, and I tripped onto the sidewalk. I scrambled to my feet and ran down the street and around the corner.

I walked to Darla's house. It was probably about four miles away so it took me a while. That was fine. I needed the walk. I called her cell to tell her I was there then went to the front door. She opened it and flew at me wrapping her arms around my waist.

"Thank God, you're alright!" she cried.

"Why wouldn't I be alright?" I said prying her hold off me and looking down into her eyes. They were wet with tears.

"Your parents have called everyone. Your dad said you ran away hysterical."

"I ran away from him. He was being a shit. I was not hysterical. I was just clumsy. I guess I should call my mom." I pulled my cell phone out of my pocket and started searching for the number. "I was wondering if you'd give me a ride home."

"Sure come on in. I'll get my keys."

"Your mother doesn't like me, Darla," I said. "I think I'll just stay out here."

"David ..."

"Please, P. H., I've had enough drama for one day."

"I'm not a poop head," she said, but she closed the door and returned a minute later with her purse and keys.

I smiled down at her. "No, but you have pretty hair."

"Hey, David ..." I heard my name across the library courtyard and recognized Luther's voice. The hairs on the back of my neck prickled like they always did during encounters with him. I ignored it and turned around.

"I've got one more CD for you to deliver. You just have to go to a burger place over on fourteenth and sit there. Have a burger. It's on me." He handed me a bill. I pushed it away.

"I'm not hungry," I said. I'd been working for him since my encounter with my dad. He gave me a cut for delivering pot to customers. I'd paid off about five hundred dollars of my debt to my dad doing this. I didn't feel like it was very dangerous. It was only as much as could be packed into a CD case, sometimes a couple of CDs. That wasn't enough to go to prison for. At least I didn't think so.

"When you get finished with this come by my apartment, I have something to talk to you about. I think you'll like it. It would pay your bill to your old man completely off and you'd be finished. Then you can retire." He smiled and I felt that familiar prickle.

"Okay," I said. "I can only stay for a minute. It's my birthday, and I have to meet my Mom and Uncle and some friends for dinner."

"Ohhh." He smiled sarcastically. "Are you all going to Chuck E. Cheese?"

"No," I snarled. "We're going to grill out in my uncle's back yard." Why was I explaining this to him? I took the CD from him and headed for the train station. If I was going to get all of this done and not be late for dinner, I'd better hurry.

✦

"Happy birthday to you ..." They sang. My mom was there, Uncle Jeff, Darla, Matt and Jan, and of course, Aunt Jeanne and Uncle Bill. Jimmy and Meryl were conspicuously absent. He hadn't spoken to me since the night we'd talked. I missed him. I'd called him a couple of times and left messages. He'd refused to return my calls.

I'd talked to Meryl. "How can he just drop our friendship?" I asked. "We've been friends since kindergarten. I've helped him in school."

"I'm sorry, David. He won't budge," Meryl said. "I love him, but I think he's wrong about this."

"Don't you think he'll come around, Meryl? I'm not just evil."

"You need to forget about him and find a new best friend, David. He won't come around."

God it hurt. I can't live without Jimmy, I thought.

"Blow out your candles." Darla's voice brought me back to the present, back to my eighteenth birthday party. I blew out the candles and Mom cut the cake.

After everyone left and Darla and I had helped Mom clean up, I clipped Charlotte's leash onto her collar, and Darla and I took her for a walk.

"She's doing pretty well after the surgery," Darla said.

Charlotte hardly limped. She scampered a few yards ahead on the extendable leash then came back to us.

"I'm pleased," I said. "I'm not sure she'll be doing any more of the Appalachian Trail, but that's okay. She's alive. We can take walks together."

"I love you, David. You're so good at looking at the bright side of things," she said as she put her arm through mine.

I flinched at the endearment. I hadn't quite gotten a grasp of our relationship. We were definitely very good friends, but romance wasn't part of it. I looked down at the top of her head. She was beautiful. Sometimes when I looked at her in a bathing suit or short shorts I felt a tightening in my pants. She was hot, but something was missing.

"Are you having any luck in the dating department, David?" she asked.

I laughed. "I was just wondering the same thing about you."

"Well, I'm not," she said. "I was hoping for a knight, you know, a grand passion."

"A grand passion?"

"Yeah, you know swept off my feet, head over heels."

"Have you dated anyone?"

"Yeah, you remember. I went out with some guy from work, and there was that guy that I met at the concert a few weeks ago." She laughed. "Men ask me out all the time. Some guy in the grocery story last week followed me around all the way through, then when we had both checked out and were walking to our cars he said, "Now that we've bought dinner together, why don't we eat it together."

I laughed again.

"How can you expect a positive answer to a come on that lame."

"No grand passion there," I said.

"Have you dated anyone?"

"I've been out a couple of times with girls from school." I shook my head. "No grand passion." We walked in silence for a while then turned around to come back.

"I don't think we have it either," she said.

"You don't love me?" I laughed.

"Of course I do, and it would be so great if we could be boyfriend and girlfriend, don't you think?" She stopped and looked up at me.

"Yeah ...but ..."

"We can't." She smiled showing the dimples in her cheeks. "Well, you come in handy when I need a date and don't have one, or have one and don't want one."

I laughed. "I know what you mean."

"In fact, I have a date this weekend that I'm not anticipating to be *the one*. Can you come along?"

I laughed and hugged her to my side. "I hate to miss it, but I'm going to Birmingham on Saturday. I have to take a camper to a friend."

"You have to take a camper to a friend?" She looked puzzled.

"Yeah, he bought a camper from someone here. The guy's license is suspended for speeding so I said I'd deliver it. I don't think I'll be back in time for your date."

"Oh," she looked concerned, but we turned back to the sidewalk and went to the house. "Well, be careful on the road."

"I wouldn't ask you to do this if I didn't think it was safe," Luther said on Saturday when I got into the truck with the camper attached to the tow bar on the back. "I'd do it myself, but I've got that suspended license."

I got into the cab of the truck and drove away. I returned to Atlanta in a police car with handcuffs on. I went to jail that day. My mother wouldn't pay bail so I waited for trial. She didn't tell my dad or Uncle Jeff until I'd been sentenced to six years for possession with intent to sell ten pounds of marijuana.

Uncle Jeff and I had planned to hike the Appalachian Trail to Virginia that summer. We were going to take all three weeks this time. We couldn't go.

After they'd sentenced me they gave me two weeks to arrange my affairs. I couldn't leave the state.

CHAPTER NINE

The first few months of prison were agony. I'll never forget the tearful parting with Mom and Uncle Jeff.

I'll never forget the cringing of my spine at the sound of two metal doors closing and loudly locking behind me as they took me to my cell. The word cell is a bit dramatic. I was in a new modern minimum security prison. The rooms were like dorm rooms rather than cells.

I remember the claustrophobic panic I felt at the thought that if there was a fire or flood, I was at the mercy of the guards. I couldn't save myself.

The most vivid memory though, is the crushing homesickness. My first month at Harvard pales in comparison.

Then I met Lenny. I had two cell mates in the first month. The first told me that I was beautiful. He said that I shouldn't be surprised if I woke up one night with him buried deep inside of me. I reported it to the guard. Nothing happened.

I told my mother and Uncle, and in a week he'd been removed from my cell to a higher security section of the prison.

The next cellmate was a nice enough guy, but his stories of demons creeping into his body through his penis were disturbing. When he started to pace back and forth between our bunks and talk to someone other than me, I reported him to the guard. Nothing happened.

I told my mother and Uncle, and in a week he'd been removed from my cell to a higher security section of the prison.

Apparently, my parents had found avenues of influence. I was grateful.

That's when Lenny became my third cellmate.

"Hello, David." He offered his hand as he entered my cell. "I'm Lenwood Jones," he said.

I shook his hand. "It's nice to meet you. I'm David Landrum." That was stupid, I thought. He obviously knows my name.

"Dan tells me you've had some bad cellmates just like I have."

"Who's Dan?" I asked.

"Let me introduce you." He turned to the guard that had escorted him into the cell. "Dan, this is David Landrum. Apparently you haven't been as friendly with him as you have with me."

"I think it's the other way around." The guard laughed as he went to the cell door. "You're the friendly one, Lenny." He turned to me before he went out. "It's nice to meet you, David. I hope you do okay with this nut. He's not your average guy." He laughed as he went out the door. I heard him lock the door and move down the hall.

"What does he mean by that?" I asked, cautiously. "You don't have demons in your pants or anything do you?"

He laughed. "No, I guess you have had some bad cellmate experiences. I don't have demons in my pants. I just like to make the best of all situations. What are you in here for, David? I know it's none of my business, but I think we should be able to talk about our mistakes together. We'll be a better support system that way."

I looked at him. He was sitting on the edge of his bunk. His elbows were resting on his legs, and he was leaning forward looking at me sincerely. He was small, maybe five seven or eight. His hair was brown and his eyes were green. He was thin to the point of wiry.

"Don't stare, David," he said.

I laughed. "I drove a truck with a camper on it over state lines for a friend who had lost his license. It had ten pounds of marijuana in it, the camper not the truck."

"You were duped."

I laughed again. "Wish I could say so, but I knew there was stuff in it. I didn't know how much. But I knew it was there."

"So you made a stupid decision."

"That's right," I laughed again. It was the first time since I'd gotten here that I didn't feel horrible.

"I have a very similar story. I won't bore you with it." He stood up and started to pace back and forth between the bunks.

It made me nervous because of the last guy. "You know the last guy that I bunked with here paced like that. Then he started to talk to someone that wasn't here. At one point he pulled a watch out of his pocket to look at the time. The thing was there wasn't a watch in his pocket," I said. "Lenwood, are you alright?"

He stopped and looked at me and laughed. "Lenny, call me Lenny. I can't believe my parents named me Lenwood. I'm fine," he said. "But you'll need to get used to me pacing. I can't sit still, ADHD, attention deficit hyperactive disorder." He paced a few more steps. "That's what they called it in school."

"Okay," I said. "I can deal with that, as long as you don't start chasing imaginary rabbits or something."

He whirled around and sat down on his bunk. He laughed and looked me straight in the eye. "No rabbits, I promise. So, David," he said. "Have you figured out how we'll survive in here?"

"I just plan to do whatever they tell me. I'm okay with the farm work," I said. We farmed for the entire Georgia Department of Corrections. All the prisons did. We were the agriculture unit. It was nice for me being raised by a plant lover.

"I don't mind it either," Lenny said. "It takes your mind off things. You know what though? I like to write, and I've found out that you can get a college degree while you're in this place."

"That's right," I said. "I arranged for that before I got here. They gave me two weeks to get my affairs in order. I arranged to continue classes on line through the school I was going to before."

"Yeah? I was going to a small community college in South Georgia. I don't think they have anything on line."

"Well, I think I can help you at the counseling center. You can get your transcripts sent to State."

"Oh man, I'm glad I got hooked up with you. I'm going to get a degree in English. I want to be an editor. Well actually, I want to be a novelist, but I'll support myself with editing." His face was so animated that I felt some of the crushing depression I'd dealt with lift. Maybe this wouldn't completely ruin my life.

"What's your sentence?" Lenny asked.

"Six years, possibility of parole in three."

"Me too." He stretched out on his bunk and put his hands behind his head. "We're only going to be here for three years, David."

"I hope so," I said.

"I know so."

Mom and Uncle Jeff came to visit me every weekend. Sometimes Uncle Jeff was only there on Sunday. Mom was there for the whole weekend. Uncle Jeff's business wasn't as flexible as hers. There were only certain hours that we could spend together. Luckily I was only an hour and a half drive from Atlanta. On Saturday Uncle Jeff's nursery was open. Now and then he had to be there during the time they could be here. Mom could sew at any hour of the day or night.

There was a large room where families gathered to spend time with their inmate members. They brought picnic baskets and children, no pets. That was sad for me. I missed Charlotte.

Mom and Uncle Jeff brought me picnics of deli sandwiches and salads. Mom brought cookies. Uncle Jeff always had a flower arrangement for the table. It was nice. I looked forward to these visits.

I hadn't heard from my dad since I'd been sentenced. He'd expressed his displeasure with me. We hadn't spoken since.

When I'd been there for three months I was in the field working. Dan, the guard Lenny and I had befriended the most, came to tell me I had a visitor.

"Who is it?" I asked. I was worried that something bad had happened to Mom or Uncle Jeff. It was mid week, and although we were allowed visitors at that time they usually didn't take us off work duty to receive them. No one had ever come to see me mid week anyway.

"Some guy named James Parnell," Dan said. He looked uncomfortable. "He seems to be upset."

I didn't press him. He was clearly uncomfortable so I just fell in before him. That was the accepted way for the guards to escort us around.

"We're going to the visiting room," he said.

"Alright," I walked ahead.

When I got there I went to the table where Jimmy sat. "What's going on? Is everything alright?"

He was staring at his hands folded in front of him. "No," he said and jumped up to face me.

My heart started to pound. He wouldn't have come about Mom or Uncle Jeff. "Is Meryl alright, Darla?" My voice sounded frantic.

"They're fine, David." He lunged toward me and wrapped his arms around my shoulders. He buried his face in my neck and sobbed. "It's me," he cried.

"What's wrong, Jimmy? The baby …"

"The baby's fine. She isn't due for another month." He continued to hold me and sob into my shoulder. "Please be alright, David. Don't kill yourself. You'll get through this. You'll get through this."

"Jimmy …" I tried to pry his arms away from me, but he held tight.

"I'm sorry." His tear streaked face looked up at me. "I shouldn't have cut you off. You're my best friend. I love you, David. Please don't kill yourself."

"Jimmy." I pried his arms away from me and held him at arm's length. "Some of the guys in here might give me a hard time if they saw you wrapped around me like this." I laughed uneasily.

He jumped away from me and looked around the room.

"I have no plans for suicide." I looked straight into his eyes. They were red and swollen. "You don't look so hot."

"I haven't slept a night since you left." He sat down and rubbed his face.

"Jimmy, you should have contacted me. I didn't call you because I thought you didn't want to talk to me." I sat down next to him. "I never was mad at you. You should have called."

"I couldn't. I hate myself for the way I acted." He looked down at his hands. "You made me what I am. I never could have gotten this far without you." He looked up and I smiled.

"Yes you could. You're a brilliant man, Jimmy. You'd have found a way."

He smiled sadly. "I know I'm not stupid, but I could never have fit in anywhere without you. The professionals don't have any idea how to help people like me. Meryl either, she was just lucky she was happy with who she is."

We sat in silence for a minute.

"So, the baby is okay and due in a month," I said. "Have you decided on a name?"

"Heather," he said and when he looked up at me his eyes were bright with excitement. "Heather Darlene, for Darla, you know Meryl and P. H. are best friends."

"She's not a poop head," I said with a smile.

"No, but she has pretty hair." He stood, we embraced again, and he left.

✦

"What was that guy's problem?" Lenny was at the cell when I came back from the visitor center. "I was going to counseling and I saw him slobbering all over you."

I laughed. "He's been my best friend since we were kids. Six months before this happened he told me he wasn't going to be my friend anymore if I kept going in the direction of drugs."

"Oh, so he's feeling guilty."

"I think so. He didn't speak to me for the whole six months." I sat down on my bunk. "Too bad I didn't listen to him."

"Well, then you'd never have met me. Look at the bright side, David."

I laughed again. Lenny was such a nut I found myself laughing all the time. "You never sit still do you, Lenny?" I watched as he did pushups on the side of his bed.

"I sit still when I write. I got a lot done at the counseling center today. I'm about half way through my first novel."

"That's great," I said as I got into position beside him and started doing pushups. "Do I get to read it?"

"Sure, I need an opinion." He looked at me as he crossed the room to the bar above the door and started doing pull-ups. He had to climb to get to it. I walked over and took hold of the bar. There was room for two.

"I'm going to be in great shape when I get out of here." I bent my knees so that I could pull up. "I'll give you an honest opinion."

"I didn't say I wanted an honest one. I want a good one."

"Even if I have to lie?" My voice sounded strained as I pulled up for the fifth time.

"Even if you have to lie."

The days went by quickly. Honestly, in prison I was not miserable. I hated that I was there. But with no distractions I whizzed through my college courses. I never made any trouble, unlike about half the population. So I got more freedom to pursue my own interests.

Lenny did too. I don't know what I would have done without him. He was a constant source of energy. He motivated me to graduate quickly, and I helped him on the farm. He didn't like getting his hands dirty.

"Landrum." The big guard broke through my concentration. I was sitting at the computer reading my email. I got regular letters from Darla and Jimmy. Meryl wrote less often, but when she did write I got a photo of Heather. She was an adorable baby.

I looked up. He was new. I had been in here for over a year, but I hadn't seen him until about a week ago. He was usually in the higher security section so I only saw him in passing.

"Yes, sir," I said.

"You've got visitors." It made me nervous when someone came to see me during the week. It almost never happened, but when it did, it was usually some kind of bad news.

I moved in front of him like we were instructed to do, and we went to the visiting center. "What is your name, sir?" I asked as we walked along.

"Al Braxton," he answered shortly.

"Can I call you Al?"

"You can call me Mr. Braxton." He was stern. "If you ever have reason to call me at all."

"Yes, sir." I didn't attempt conversation any more. We arrived at the visitor's center and I went through the door. Something was definitely wrong.

"Mom!" I hurried to where she and Uncle Jeff stood. Her eyes were red from crying. Uncle Jeff looked uncomfortable. "What's wrong?"

"David, I'm so sorry." She started to cry again. I looked at Uncle Jeff.

"Charlotte died," he said softly.

"Charlotte died." I looked back and forth between them. It couldn't be true. "But she was only nine years old. What happened?" I felt the familiar lump in my throat growing and my eyes stung. I swallowed and sat down.

"Charlie," Uncle Jeff said to Mom. "He doesn't have to know all the details."

"Yes he does," Mom said and sat down beside me.

"Yes," I said. "I do. Tell me."

She took my hand and held it between both of hers. "I think she died of missing you, David."

"Why do you say that?"

"She died in her sleep. She was sleeping on your bed."

"She never slept on my bed," I said. My voice sounded hollow. "When I was a kid I tried to get her to sleep on my bed with me. She wouldn't." I looked up at my mom's swollen eyes. I looked at my Uncle.

"I'm sorry, son," he said. But I knew he didn't understand how bad it hurt. I wouldn't cry though. I'd become good at getting rid of the tears.

"Ruffles misses her so much," Mom said. "I'm worried about him. He won't eat."

"He'll be alright," I said and stood up. "When did this happen?"

"I found her yesterday morning. I couldn't get here before now, David." Mom was apologetic. "I had to cancel appointments and all."

"That's okay." I kissed her cheek and turned to the door. I tapped for the guard and left. I didn't say goodbye to them and they didn't call me back.

"Do you want to go back to the computer room?" Dan was the guard that opened the door. I was glad to see his friendly face.

"No, can I go back to my cell?" I asked. "My dog died. I have some grief to process."

"I'm sorry, son." Dan put his big hand on my shoulder.

"Thanks Dan, but don't be too nice to me." I laughed. "I might crumble."

"That would be alright, David. There's nothing wrong with grieving for your pet."

"I guess not." I didn't say anymore as we walked back to my cell.

I had my elbows propped behind me on the bars on the wall doing leg lifts when Lenny came in. "I've rubbed off on you," he said and pulled up beside me to join in.

"It's amazing what it does for you."

"Yeah, not just the health benefits," he said. "I think it's good for your soul."

"I would agree with that. Have you seen that new guard?"

"You mean the one that's over in maximum security."

"Yeah, I asked him his name today. He said it was Al Braxton. He said I could call him Mr. Braxton if I ever had reason to call him at all."

Lenny was lifting his legs. He started to laugh. He jumped down from the bar and sat on his bunk. "You can't do that and laugh too," he said.

I got down and sat on my bunk.

"Why were you in maximum security?" Lenny asked.

"I wasn't. I had visitors, Mom and Uncle Jeff. Braxton came to get me. I guess he was the only one available."

"Oh, well I've decided on a new challenge. I'm going to make that guy laugh. Every time I've ever seen him he looks like he's at a funeral."

"Have you been in maximum security?" I asked.

"No, but he's been out in the yard a couple of times when I've been out there. How long do you think it'll take me to make him laugh? Maybe I'll get a little bet going with the guys."

I didn't tell Lenny about Charlotte. I was pretty sure he wouldn't understand, and I was equally sure he'd make some kind of joke out of it. I wasn't going to cry, but I wasn't going to laugh about it either.

✦

P.H.

You're really the only person I want to talk to about my grief. Charlotte died. I don't know if I can stand it.

I let her down, P.H. I took great care of her all her life, and in the end I let her down. I haven't told anyone this, but the reason I drove that truck and camper to Alabama was to make the money to pay my dad back for Charlotte's surgery.

So you see. I let her down. I managed to get her knee fixed. Then I abandoned her. I was sure she'd

still be there when I got out. I fully intend to make parole, but she won't be there.
She died of a broken heart.
I don't know if I can stand it

David

I hit send then put my face in my hands. It was the first time I'd talked about it. It had been two weeks and the pain was still piercing. I kept seeing her big adoring brown eyes looking up at me. I dreamed about our midnight walks. She loved them because it was just the two of us.

She'd been my faithful companion through so much. She was less needy than my Mom, more understanding than Uncle Jeff, and definitely more loyal than my dad. I couldn't believe I'd never see her again.

I looked at the computer screen and saw an answer from Darla. She must be at her computer at work. I opened it up and read it.

David,

I am so sorry. I hadn't heard. I usually have lunch with your mother on the first Wednesday of each month, but she cancelled this month. I guess she was going to tell you the news.

I know how much you loved Charlotte. David you didn't let her down. I know you'll feel that way anyhow, but you didn't.

She loved you, and you gave her the best life she could have.

I love you too. I'll come to see you on Sunday. I have something to tell you.

Pretty Hair Darla

I smiled. I was glad she was coming to see me. I wondered what she wanted to tell me. Probably what color she had her toenails painted or something like that.

She was so funny.

I returned to the visitor's center with a new wave of inmates. Mom and Uncle Jeff had left about an hour before. It was Sunday evening, and I was beginning to think that Darla wasn't going to show.

Chapter Nine

I flinched at the sound of the double doors closing behind me and the group of prison garbed people I was with.

Darla stood next to a table for two. It had a table cloth on it and a basket. I winced. I was stuffed from the picnic lunch I'd eaten with my parents. I smiled and returned her wave. I crossed the room to her. She threw her arms around my waist the way she always did. I leaned down and kissed the top of her head.

"You look pretty good for a guy grieving his pet." She tilted her head back to look up at me. Then she stepped back and looked me up and down. "In fact, David, you look great. Don't tell me this place is working for you."

"Actually, it's not so bad, Darla. I have so little control that I don't even have to think about what I should be doing. I'm not driven like I used to be."

"No." She examined my face. "In fact you look relaxed and ...what else?" She tipped her head to the side. "Rested, you look rested."

"Yeah, it's strange. I sleep like a baby at night. I still only get about five or six hours, but it's quality sleep." I sat down at the table. She sat across from me.

"You were always so worried about everything at home, your mom and all."

"I can't be the man of anyone's family in here. I have no control."

"You're still going to school though, right. And you're clearly working out. Do they have a gym?" Darla opened the box that turned out to be a small cooler. "I brought peanut butter crackers and Coke, decaffeinated," she said.

"Good, I'm not very hungry, but I can find room for that." I opened a package of crackers and smiled across the table at her. "I am still going to school. In fact, I'll be finished a good year before I get out of here. I think I'll just take some courses in finance at that point."

"You still plan to graduate with a marketing degree?"

"Yeah, I really love working up the plans and then simulating the execution of them. That's about all I can do in here." I sipped my Coke. "School is different in here. It's a privilege, not something I have to do, and I can only do as much as they allow me to."

"Sounds like you've been allowed to do a lot if you're going to graduate so fast."

"I don't cause any trouble. They like me pretty well around here." I looked across the table at her. She was small and blond and beautiful. She'd become a really good friend.

I looked a little closer. "Is something wrong, P.H.? You have dark circles under your eyes."

"I'm just not very happy, David." She looked down at the unopened package of crackers in her hand. "I need to make a change."

"What kind of a change?" The crackers had gone very dry in my mouth. I sipped my Coke again.

"I'm moving to New York City," she said.

"Has someone hurt you, Darla?" Has she been dating someone bad, I wondered?

"I wish." She popped the top on her unopened Coke. "I'm just not going anywhere, David. There just isn't anything in Atlanta for me, and with you not there, I don't even have any fun anymore."

"I'm sorry," I said. "Maybe it's time for you to try school. I'm sure your dad would still pay for it."

"That's what I'm going to do in New York. I'm going to acting school."

"Acting school," I laughed. "You weren't even in the drama club in high school. I didn't know you wanted to act."

"I didn't either, but one of the girls I've made friends with at work is going to this school too. So I applied and they let me in and I'm going up there. My dad's department store has a branch up there. I'm going to work in the administration end, secretarial of course. Daddy is paying for school."

"Wow!" I said reaching across the table to put my hand on hers. "I'll miss you, but I hope you do great. Maybe someday I'll be able to say, see that Broadway star, I knew her when …"

"That's what I was thinking. I'm not shy you know, David. I don't think I'll have any trouble with acting."

"I'm sure you'll be great." I smiled sadly. "I'll miss you."

"I'll still email. I don't get down here to see you very much anyway." She looked away from me, and I thought her eyes clouded up.

"Are you sure everything else is alright, Darla. I'm not used to seeing you look so sad." I pressed.

"Meryl is furious with me. She says I'm abandoning her and little Heather. And my mother washes her hands of me. She's disgusted."

"I'm not surprised about your mother. She's a little bit of a snob you know."

"I know, but I hate disappointing her. I've been a disappointment to her from the beginning."

"You have not. You're beautiful. You were in the gifted program all the way through school." I squeezed her hand. "She'll come around." I leaned back in my chair. "I am surprised about Meryl though. That sounds really selfish. I never thought of her that way."

"Well, she's pregnant again and Jimmy is mad at her." She put her hand on her lips. "I guess I shouldn't have told you that. Has Jimmy mentioned it?"

"No, and they were here about a month ago with Heather. She's adorable. She's a perfect combination of her parents."

"Yeah, she is." Darla smiled and showed the dimples in her cheeks.

"Why is Jimmy mad at Meryl?"

"Because she got pregnant again without his permission. He thinks she tricked him."

"He thought that about Heather too. But hey, it takes two."

"Yeah, but she did trick him. Meryl knows what she wants out of life, and she'll have it her way." She looked down at her hands and then up into my eyes. "Wouldn't it be nice to know exactly what you wanted out of life, David?"

"Yeah, it would."

❖

"Is that your girlfriend?" One of the inmates I didn't know very well asked as I watched Darla carry her small cooler out of the room. Her waist length platinum blond hair danced with the sway of her voluptuous hips.

"No, she's just a friend."

"Are you gay?" The young man stepped slightly away from me. "If you're not there's something wrong with you."

I looked down at him and smiled. "I'm not gay," I said and looked back in the direction of Darla's exit. She pushed the door shut with her small bottom. "So there must be something wrong with me."

❖

When I look back at my time in prison, I don't feel embarrassed or ashamed. The truth is that I'm grateful. I'm not suggesting that breaking the law is the means to an end, but my time there gave me a new perspective.

My days were spent with study and field work on the farm. Lenny and I worked out at the gym during designated times, but we spent most of the leisure time we had in our cell, working out and talking about our hopes for the future.

I went into prison a troubled kid trying desperately to do the things that should come natural, like sleep. Sleeping should be easy, but I had resorted to drugs, not even prescribed drugs, to do it.

By the time I left the place I was a man. I had topped out at six feet five inches. I was taller than most of the inmates and all of the guards. My shoulders had broadened and become muscular. My stomach was flat and my legs were strong from running on the prison track and working on the farm.

I had a degree in marketing and had studied post grad finance. I hadn't decided if I'd go ahead and get my masters or if it was really necessary. I was stronger for the experience, and to a large part, I had Lenny to thank for that.

He was a driving force. He couldn't sit still for a second, and he had all sorts of plans for the future. He wrote books that entertained me when I took a minute to read.

His antics with the guards, especially Al Braxton, were a source of entertainment for the entire prison population. With all of his carrying on, it took until just before we were paroled for Lenny to make Mr. Braxton smile. When he did, it was a fleeting thing. If you weren't looking you'd have missed it.

But the news spread throughout the prison, inmates, guards, and admin. Lenny was greeted with congratulations for weeks.

He was my inspiration. I won't say that many of the people I met in prison were good people. Most of them were just plain bad. They were certainly nobody I'd want to meet without guards. You could feel the evil in some of them. I had the feeling that most of them would be back time and again until finally they did something that would keep them there forever.

I knew I'd never be back, and I knew Lenny wouldn't either. We were paroled only months apart. Lenny first, he went back to Valdosta, Georgia where he was from. We stayed in touch.

The two and a half months I waited after he got out was the hardest part.

I arrived home on a Friday evening. Mom and Uncle Jeff had come to pick me up after the parole hearing. I didn't have much to bring home. We weren't allowed a lot of personal effects.

Mom brought me a change of clothes. They were new and uncomfortably tight. My shape had changed, for the better of course. I walked into the front door. Ruffles struggled to stand up from his bed in the living room.

"Hey, old man," I swallowed the lump in my throat. "How old is he now, Mom?"

"He's fourteen years old. He was a year old when I brought him home." She stroked his sleek bony head. "He's done well."

I looked around. The place hadn't changed at all, which made the ache for Charlotte more painful. "Well," I said. "I guess I'll go upstairs and see about going on with my life."

"David," Uncle Jeff said. "I'm going home. Call me if you need me for anything. I've got some work to do. I thought I'd come over tomorrow. Maybe we can plan to pick back up on the Appalachian."

"Sounds great, Uncle Jeff, I don't need anything right now. It was great to see you waiting for me outside those gates. Thanks for coming."

"Welcome home, David." He hugged me and left.

I went up to my room, sat at the familiar computer desk and booted up my computer. I looked out the window at the familiar landscape.

Uncle Jeff and Mom had been completely faithful. Mom and I had fought at the time of my arrest. She'd refused to solicit help from Uncle Jeff or Dad. I suppose I could have contacted them on my own, but somehow I knew I needed to pay the price for what I'd done.

Darla was gone now. She emailed but she was in New York. I wondered if I'd ever see her again.

Jimmy and Meryl had two children. Heather was almost three years old and James, Jr. was six months. Whatever differences they'd had seemed to have been smoothed over. They were a beautiful family. I liked babysitting for the kids. It gave Jimmy and Meryl time to get off by themselves, and I discovered that I enjoyed the company of children.

My Dad sent me Christmas and Birthday cards all the time I was in prison, but I hadn't heard from him directly since I'd been sentenced. Not a word. I sent a letter to his office telling him about my parole. He sent his congratulations in a card.

I was twenty one years old, and even with all my preparation, I had no idea what my future held.

CHAPTER TEN

"We don't have to do this in the summer or at spring break anymore, Uncle Jeff." I said as we picked our way along a rocky path in Virginia.

"No, I guess it's just become traditional to take the time now," he said.

"Well, spring time is alright," I said. "But I was thinking, since we don't have to work around my school schedule anymore, maybe we could push the summer hiking to fall. The weather is nicer."

"That's true," he said. "We'll plan it for October next time." He sat down on a log. I took a good look at him.

"How old are you now, Uncle Jeff?"

He looked up at me and laughed. "Why? Do I look like I'm struggling?"

"No, you look more fit than I am. I just wondered." The truth was that I was wondering if he was going to make it to the end of the Trail in Maine with me. It was over two thousand miles long, and we hadn't even made it half way.

We had started going twice a year to the Trail. We needed to make up for the lost time in prison. I'd been out for almost four years now. I was about to turn twenty five years old and we were almost through the five hundred and forty four miles of the Trail that were in Virginia.

The thing we'd enjoyed the most about the stretch in Virginia, besides the incredible scenery, was the wild blueberries. The bushes were everywhere and the berries were plumper and sweeter than the cultivated ones you bought at the store. I'd even managed to make a crumble with a dried desert we'd bought at the backpacking store. We wouldn't get any on this trip though. They didn't ripen until summer.

"Don't worry, David. I think I'll make it." Did he read my mind? "I'm only forty seven and my work keeps me in shape."

"Yeah," I sat down beside him. "I wonder how Dad's doing. He was looking kind of soft last time I saw him. That was six years ago. Have you seen him lately?"

"No, not since your gramma died." He put his hand on my knee. "I'm sorry, David."

"I don't blame him, Uncle Jeff. He never wanted to have anything to do with me before. I think the only reason he ever did spend time with me was guilt. I guess screwing up like I did gave him a good excuse to write me off."

"He's a horse's ass."

I laughed. Uncle Jeff was always on my side.

"Actually, I shouldn't insult horses that much," he said.

"I'm sure he has his reasons for what he does." I stood up. I hadn't taken my pack off when I sat down so I grabbed a nearby branch to pull up with. I extended my hand to Uncle Jeff and pulled him to his feet.

"I think we've gone about ten miles today," he said. "There are camp sites about a mile from here. According to the map they're beside a stream. Do you want to camp or go on another three miles to a bed and breakfast?"

"Let's have a look at the campsites. If they're private it would be nice to sleep next to running water."

✧

I opened the door to the apartment above the nursery. I had moved into it two years ago. I put my pack down and looked at the answering machine. The red light was on. I had messages. I pressed play and went to the refrigerator to get a glass of lemonade.

"Hey, David, this is Jimmy," the voice said from the machine. "I wasn't sure if you were due back from your hike on Friday or Saturday. This is Friday. Give me a call when you get in. Nothing important, just wanted to talk to you about a soccer team we're starting up at the union. You don't have to be a member to join. When was the last time you played soccer?"

"Soccer," I said out loud to myself. When you live alone you talk to yourself. I fought it at first then just gave in. "I wonder if I'd still be any good." I was on a team at Harvard and when I went to state, but I hadn't joined any of the games at the penitentiary. I'm not sure why.

"David," the next message started. "This is Darla." She'd been crying or else she had a bad cold. "Give me a call when you get a chance. I need a friend."

"Hmmm ..." I'd better call her, I thought. I started flipping through my directory when the next message said:

"David, I just talked to Meryl. She told me you were backpacking and wouldn't be back until tomorrow." It was Darla's voice again. "I still want you to call me, but I'm okay after talking to Meryl. So don't worry about the tears on the last message."

I smiled to myself. This was typical of her. I wouldn't be surprised if there was another message from her. The machine crackled and her voice sounded teary again.

"I was wrong. I'm not alright. Please call me as soon as you get in."

I picked up the phone and dialed. "What's up, baby?" I asked when she answered.

"I feel better now. I was just about to call and leave another message for you not to worry," she said.

"Worry about what?"

"You won't believe it, David. I get stage freight."

"No way!"

"I do. I even threw up, twice. What am I going to do? I finished school, and I've worked so hard to get something on stage."

"You didn't have a problem when you were doing those commercials."

"No, but that's different because they film it, and if you mess up they just film it again."

"I thought you said it was usually the other actors that messed up."

"That's right. I never messed up. That's why I thought I'd be good on stage. I got this great part."

"I remember. You told me about it. You're a girl thinking about committing suicide."

"Yeah, doesn't that sound like fun?"

I laughed. It didn't sound like fun to me.

"And I've learned my lines so well. Two nights ago was opening night. I wanted you to come, but you'd already left for Virginia when we got our schedule for the theatre."

"I wish I could have been there."

"No you don't." She sniffed. I could tell she was crying again. I'd actually never seen her cry, so she was really upset.

"Don't tell me you threw up on stage," I said.

"No, of course I didn't. But I threw up in my dressing room right before, and when I got on stage I was shaking like a leaf. I'm sure everyone noticed."

"I'm sure they didn't."

"Well, I'm sure they did because the reviewer talked about it in the newspaper."

"I'm sorry, P.H."

"Thanks for calling me that because I feel like a poop head right now. Guess what happened the next night?"

"You did fine."

"No, I threw up in my dressing room again, and when I got on stage I passed out. They had to carry me off on a stretcher."

"Are you alright, P.H.? Have you been to a doctor? This doesn't sound like you."

"The president of the theatre company made me go to a doctor. I'm fine. I think they were just covering their asses before they fired me."

"They fired you?"

"Yeah." She wasn't crying now but she sounded defeated. I'd never heard her sound that way. Then I remembered the day she came to prison to see me. She was sad that day.

"So go back to doing commercials, Darla. There's nothing wrong with that."

"It isn't what I had in mind."

"I'm sorry."

"Well, thanks for calling," she said. "I've got a date so I have to go take a shower. I feel better after talking to you. I miss you, David."

"Do you have any plans for a visit?" I asked.

"Maybe in the summer. Gotta go, bye."

I looked at the silent telephone in my hand and hung it up.

"Happy birthday, David," Mom said as I came through the door of the townhouse. Uncle Jeff was there and Aunt Jeanne and Uncle Bill. They all hugged me.

Mom poured me a glass of wine and I sat down. It was pouring down rain. The spring time was always rainy in Georgia. We'd had more than usual this year. I couldn't remember ever having to celebrate my birthday inside before.

"I'm sorry we couldn't have a barbecue like we usually do," Mom said. "But I made your favorite among my specialties, tuna casserole." She laughed and everyone laughed with her. The doorbell rang and she went to open it.

"Surprise!" Darla ran in and wrapped her arms around my waist. I leaned down and kissed the top of her head.

"What a great surprise. I didn't even know you were in town," I said. Jimmy and Meryl came in behind her. They each had a child by the hand.

"Happy Birthday," Meryl hugged me and Jimmy handed me a package.

"Happy Birthday, Uncle David," Five year old James, Jr. stretched his hands up to me. I picked him up and put him on my right shoulder. "Thanks, Jamie," I said.

"Me too, me too," seven year old Heather said. I swung her to my left shoulder, and put my arms straight up for them to hold on to.

"Don't try to leave the foyer, David," Mom said. "You're too tall to go through the door. You'll scrape them right off."

"Duck, guys," I faked a step to the doorway and they both squealed. I bent my arms and said, "Hang on tight." Then I lowered them to the ground.

"I can't believe you can still do that with them," Jimmy said. "They've gotten so big."

"I'm just a lot bigger," I laughed. "Come on in and have some wine." We all sat down to dinner and Mom passed the casserole. She also had spinach soufflé, frozen of course, and a salad.

"You don't have to eat the salad if you don't want, David," she said. "I just made it for our guests."

"Thanks, Mom," I passed the bowl without taking any.

"He's never been a salad eater." She smiled maternally and I felt good inside.

"David tells me you guys have started a soccer team at the Union, Jimmy," Uncle Jeff said.

"That's right, I asked David to join us as the goal tender and he came to practice with the team last week. He hasn't lost a thing. He's still the best."

"I was worried," I said. "It's been a long time since I've played but I did okay."

"More than okay," Jimmy said around a bite of casserole. "He still excels at everything."

"Not everything," I said.

"Do you need an assistant coach or anything?" Uncle Jeff asked.

Jimmy looked at me cautiously. I smiled. "Do we, Jimmy? It would be fun to work with Uncle Jeff on a team with us again. Don't you think?"

"Yes, I do. I wasn't sure he'd want to."

"I'd like to talk to the coach about it anyway," Uncle Jeff said. "Would that be alright with you, David?"

"Absolutely," I said.

"David," Darla interrupted. "I was wondering if you'd take me to a dinner party tomorrow night. It's kind of business. There's this theatre company in Atlanta. It's pretty small, but I was thinking that if I could get a part with them, maybe I could get the companies in New York to give me another chance."

"They haven't black balled you or anything just because you threw up a couple of times. I mean I'd think that kind of thing is pretty common in acting," Jimmy said.

"Jimmy." Darla looked down as her fair skin turned pink. "I really didn't want to talk about that at David's birthday dinner."

I laughed and she looked up at me.

"It's okay, P.H. Sure I'll go, but please tell me they didn't black ball you for something like that."

"Well no, I'm just afraid to try again in New York. Maybe if I start small it won't be so scary. I applied to read for a part here. That's one reason why I came." She looked anxiously at me. "Your birthday was the main reason of course. They've given me an appointment to read for the part on Wednesday. The woman I talked to said I should go to this dinner party with the cast tomorrow night. I really need an escort."

"I'd love to go," I said. "Imagine that, hobnobbing with stage actors."

"Oh good," Darla said as she stood to help Mom clear the table for the birthday cake.

✧

Uncle Jeff and I helped Mom clean up after everyone left. Then we sat down in the living room to relax for a minute together. This had become a tradition over the years. We always enjoyed it.

"Tell me how things are going, David," Uncle Jeff asked. "How's your computer business?"

"It's doing okay." When I first got out of prison I applied for jobs in the marketing field. People didn't want to hire an ex-con.

"I was very proud of the way you forged on like that when you couldn't get a job," Mom said.

"Thanks, Mom."

"I was too, David," Uncle Jeff said. "A lot of people would have had a hard time not getting depressed."

"I had to work at it," I said. "But then I got excited about building my web-page, and the thing I always liked about marketing was making a plan and then making it work. So I did that for myself and other people. Most of my customers are artists. That's fun. So many artists just fade away because they don't know how to get their work in front of people."

"What kind of artists do you work with?" Mom asked.

"Mostly writers, they can write a book or publish a magazine, even a column. But they don't know how to sell it. I do."

"So you're happy with how things are going?" Uncle Jeff leaned forward and rested his elbows on his knees. "David, why do you deliver pizza in your spare time?"

"You're delivering pizza?" Mom sat up and looked at me.

"Artists don't have a lot of money up front. Once they start to sell they don't need me anymore." I looked at my hands in my lap. "Are you trying to get me back for that birthday that I forced Charlotte on you, Uncle Jeff?"

"No, son, I didn't plan to bring it up tonight. I'm sorry. A friend of mine, actually a new employee of mine, ordered pizza the other night, and she was amazed at how much the delivery boy looked like me."

"I'm sure there are other people that look like you. You're not that unique."

"That's what I thought at first. Then she went on about it for a while and said the only difference was that my eyes are blue and his were brown."

"I'm not going to deny it, Uncle Jeff. I deliver pizza. It makes good money. It's an honest job." I stood up. "I think I'll go home," I said, then remembered that I didn't really have a home. I was living in my uncle's apartment. I sat back down.

"What are you thinking, David?" Uncle Jeff asked.

"I pay rent." I sounded defensive.

"Yes, you do, David, and what's mine is yours. You don't have to feel bad about living where you do. You don't have to feel bad about delivering pizza to make money. But I think that if you weren't already feeling bad about it you wouldn't have tried to hide it from me."

"David honey, why did you hide it from us?" Mom asked.

I couldn't say anything. I wanted to deny that I'd hidden anything, but I knew that wasn't true. I hadn't wanted them to know.

I looked up at them. They were both looking at me with concern. I wanted to scream at them to get out of my life. But these two people were totally loyal to me. All either one of them wanted was for me to be happy. I thought about the birthday card I'd gotten from my dad. *I think of you every day. I love you, Dad.* It said the same thing every time. Did he care if I was happy? He'd never indicated that he did.

"I'm discouraged," I said quietly, looking at my hands.

"Wheww ..." Uncle Jeff said. "I didn't realize I was holding my breath."

"Me neither," Mom laughed.

I looked at the two of them. They were smiling. I smiled back. "I like the internet business," I said. "It's fun and it makes okay money. But I think I've done about all I can do with it. I mean I'd like to actually be able to think about having a family or at least my own apartment. I don't pay you half what that apartment is worth." I held my hand up when Uncle Jeff tried to object. "I can't support any of that with this business, and I don't want to do it delivering pizza."

"Would an investment help? I'd be willing to invest in your business. Maybe a little more money in it would get it off the ground," Uncle Jeff said.

"It doesn't need more money. It needs more paying clients, and I don't think there are any. Besides, I want to work on a team. All the time I was studying that's how I saw myself, working for an organization with different people doing different jobs and pulling it all together for a common goal."

"I don't know if there's anything I can do to help you with that."

"There isn't," I said. "But I feel better having talked about it. It was hard getting all of that rejection when I first got home. I guess I should have known I'd have to face the stigma of my past. But the truth is, it caught me by surprise."

"So what are you going to do?" Uncle Jeff stood up and stretched.

"Start applying for positions again. Eventually someone will hire me. I just need to brace myself for the rejections."

"I'm proud of you, son." Uncle Jeff kissed me on the cheek. "I'm going home. Great party, Charlie," he said to my mom.

"Thanks, Jeff." The door closed behind him. Mom reached down and stroked the neck of her new afghan hound. Caramel was the color of her name. I guess Mom had stopped trying to replace Pepper. Ruffles had died peacefully in his sleep a couple of years ago.

"David," she said. "Remember Vanessa?"

"Yeah, your friend that moved away a while back." I frowned. "She's the one that introduced you to Vern. He's not back is he?"

"No," she laughed. "The last I heard he got married and has a young family."

"So, why did you bring up Vanessa?"

"She and her husband and daughter have moved back to Atlanta. She got her daughter a dog, a black lab, and she didn't get her spayed in time. I scolded her about it of course."

"I know where this is going, Mom. I don't want one of the puppies."

"David, it'll be a lab mix, just like Charlotte. Honey, please forgive yourself. You love dogs."

"I think we argued about this same thing when you tried to replace Pepper. I can't replace her, and I don't want to let another dog down."

"I'm not saying you did, honey. But if you feel like you let her down you won't do it to another dog. That's how we learn by our mistakes."

I stood and went to the door to leave. She followed me.

"No more dogs for me, Mom. Now please stop trying to force one on me."

"Alright, I won't bring it up again." She pulled on my shoulder to turn me around. We looked at each other almost eye to eye. "Happy birthday, please don't go home mad at me."

I smiled. "I can get mad at you, Mom, but I can't stay mad at you." I kissed her cheek and went back to the apartment over the nursery.

"I don't know why you don't move up here," I said on the phone to Lenny the following week. "You could move in here with me. We could pay Uncle Jeff a little more rent that way. I'd feel better about that."

"I don't know how I'd pay him rent. I can't talk anyone into hiring me."

"So your internet editing business isn't doing so hot."

"Probably about as good as your internet business."

"Not so hot, how about your books? Isn't my marketing plan working?"

"Yeah, actually they are selling pretty well. I guess I just really want to work on a magazine or a newspaper."

"Then you really should come up here. I'm sure the opportunities are better in Atlanta than Savannah." I missed Lenny. We talked almost every week. He'd been such a source of energy in prison. I missed his enthusiasm.

"Yeah, but I'm closer to Valdosta here. I have to go home to see my mom a lot. She took that prison thing pretty hard. I need to make it up to her."

"I can understand that, but Valdosta isn't that far from Atlanta. You might not have better luck up here, but at least we could hang out some."

"I'll think about it, David." He sounded depressed. He had the last few times I'd talked to him. It wasn't like him. I was worried.

"Are you alright?" I asked.

"I'm struggling. I'm sure it's just a passing thing. Anyway, like I said, that marketing plan worked great. You've done a lot for me since we got out. You even designed my web page."

"We've got to stick together, Lenny."

"But I haven't done anything for you. What can I do to help you?" His voice was shaking and I wondered if he was crying. Poor guy, this was really getting him down.

"You help me by being my friend. Besides, I don't think I'd have made it through all three years at the penitentiary without you. Don't worry about it. I'll tell you if there is anything you can do."

"I feel like I'm sinking, David. Maybe if I could do something valuable for you I'd feel better."

For the life of me I couldn't think of any assignment I could give him. I just had no need for his skills. "Move up here then. We could work together like we did in prison."

"I'll think about it." He was definitely depressed. "I've got to go," he said. "I have to take my aunt to the doctor. That's who I'm living with here in Savannah. I drive her around for rent. I'll call you next week."

I turned to the computer screen after he hung up, but I couldn't concentrate. I was uncomfortable about Lenny's state of mind. Maybe he needed some medical help or something.

The phone rang again and I jumped. I looked at the caller ID. It was the nursery number. It must be Uncle Jeff. I picked it up. "Hey."

"I'm coming up for a minute."

"Okay, I'm in my office. Just come on back." I had made the master bedroom into an office for my internet business. It had a great view of the greenhouses and growing field. I slept in the room over the fountain display.

I heard the front door of the apartment open and close. I stood up and went into the hall. "What's up?" I said as I motioned for Uncle Jeff to follow me into the kitchen. "Have you had breakfast?" I asked when the timer on the oven started to sound.

"I had a protein drink about an hour ago, but I'll have some of whatever smells so good in here." He poured himself a cup of coffee and sat down at the table. "This coffee is so good, David. How do you make something like plain old coffee taste better than anyone else's?"

"It isn't plain old coffee." I smiled as I took two of the muffins out of the pan and put them on a rack on the table. "These are harvest muffins. Have one." I put down plates and butter, then pulled a bowl out of the refrigerator and put it on the table with spoons.

"What's that?" Uncle Jeff looked into the bowl.

"Dried fruit compote," I said and laughed at his cautious expression. "It's delicious. Try it."

"You really do love to cook, don't you, son?"

"I really do." We ate in silence for a minute, and I sat back to sip my coffee. "What's up?" I asked again.

"I don't want you to get your hopes up too high about this, David. I have a friend that is starting up a magazine. She has a position open for someone with marketing skills. The magazine is targeting middle age and older. I don't know if you'd be interested in that at your age."

I sat up and leaned forward. "Really, I don't care about the subject. Of course, I'm interested."

"She says that the position would benefit by some knowledge of finance. I told her I'd be willing to put you through some post graduate courses if she wanted me to." He reached for the bowl of fruit. I handed it to him.

"Uncle Jeff, I took all sorts of graduate finance courses after I finished my bachelor's degree. I'm not far from a Master's Degree in it." My heart was beginning to pound in my chest. Could this be my break?

"Really?" He sat back and looked at me just as he put a spoonful of fruit into his mouth. His eyes registered surprise, I guess at the excitement on my face or maybe it was at the taste of the fruit. He started to cough.

"You okay?" I leaned further forward.

He tapped his chest with his fist. "I'm fine. I was just startled by the look on your face. Please don't get too excited about this, David. I told her about your past. She's willing to talk to you. That's all. There are no guarantees."

"You told her about my past. I was hoping maybe that since she's just starting up she might not do a background check."

"You know you can't hide that kind of thing, David," he said. "You have to be up front with it."

"I know. You're right." I leaned back in my chair. "But she's willing to talk to me."

"Yes, I thought I'd go by there this afternoon and get her contact info. She's just moving into some office space over by the mall. We're pretty good friends. We cycle together on Sundays. I talked to her about it last Sunday and she agreed to talk to you. I don't know if it would be politically correct to give you her home number yet. So I'd better find out about her business phone."

"Okay." I couldn't help but smile. "Thanks, Uncle Jeff. If she hires me, I won't make you sorry. I promise."

"I never thought you would, son." He stood and took his plate to the sink. "Thanks for the breakfast. That compote stuff was delicious, so were the muffins." He ruffled the hair on the top of my head as he walked by. I laughed and he did too. He turned when he got to the kitchen door.

"I'll let you know about the contact info," he said. "Her name is Jane Winslow. She's been in the information tech field for a while. You can probably look her up on the internet. Find out a little bit about her.

"Great, I think I'll do some research on the magazine business too."

※

"I'm so excited, Mom." I had stopped by home on my way back from the interview. "This lady is fantastic. She's beautiful, probably late fifties or early sixties, and still absolutely beautiful."

Mom laughed and turned from her sewing machine to look at me. "You sound so surprised. Old people can be beautiful too."

"I know you will be when you get old." I could feel myself blushing. I was surprised I'd been so impressed by the way Jane Winslow looked. "She's not just beautiful though. She's dynamic. I could feel the energy in the room."

We went into the kitchen, and I sat down at the table. Caramel put her floppy head in my lap. I stroked the silky fir. "Don't drool on my good suit, girl. It's the only one I have."

"I guess you'll need some more suits. I'll get started on your new business wardrobe right away. Would you like a cup of coffee?" Mom picked up the coffee pot.

"No thanks, I'm buzzing from too much caffeine already. I usually drink decaf." The truth was her coffee was really bad.

"I'm glad." We had never talked about that seizure I had in high school again, but I knew she worried. I was glad I'd never told her about the migraine headaches.

"I wouldn't start on a wardrobe yet. She hasn't hired me, and I don't want to jinx it." I grinned. I could feel the happiness on my face. "I'm not usually superstitious, but just to be safe."

"Okay, just give me the word." Mom came over to me and put her arms around my neck. She leaned down and kissed my cheek. "I'm so proud of you, David. You've grown into such a wonderful man."

"Thanks, Mom," I said. "Anyway, after meeting Jane Winslow, I don't think she'll be requiring very formal attire. I imagine it will be business casual."

"Okay, I can do that."

※

"How do you spend a whole day riding bikes with her and keep from ravishing her, Uncle Jeff?" I asked when I stopped by his office after I left my mom's house. "Jane Winslow has got to be the most beautiful woman I've ever seen."

He jumped and looked at me. There was a look on his face that I'd never seen before. "Don't talk like that, David. Jane and I are just very good friends. Besides, she's romantically involved with someone else." He turned back to his computer and started typing furiously.

"Sorry," I said. "I didn't mean to hit a sore spot."

"I don't have sore spots," he snapped without looking at me.

I sat down in the chair next to the desk. "Don't you want to hear about my interview?"

He turned around quickly. The expression was gone and had been replaced by wide curious eyes. My stomach kind of lurched. There was something wrong with Uncle Jeff. I didn't know what it was, but something wasn't right.

"You had your interview? How did it go?" He was almost demanding.

I shook my head to clear the uneasy feeling. I smiled cautiously. "I think it went well. We got the prison thing out of the way first. Then we talked about the magazine. I did my research well. I think I impressed her."

"Good, son." He turned back to the computer and started to work again.

"Uncle Jeff," I said. I felt strangely cautious. "You don't usually spend so much time in the office. You usually do more in the field. Is everything alright?"

"Are you watching me or something?" When he looked at me I saw that look on his face again. "I hope she hires you so you can get a place of your own and stop sticking your nose into my business."

I sucked in my breath. He'd never talked to me like that. "I can move back in with Mom in the meantime," I said, hearing the anger in my voice. "I didn't know it was bothering you, and besides, I don't give a damn about your business. I was just concerned."

He turned around again and the wide eyed expression was back. Was he losing his mind or something? Maybe I was losing mine. I stood up and started for the door.

"I'm sorry, David," he said. For a minute I thought I saw his eyes cloud up. "I bit your head off for no reason. I'm becoming a grumpy old man." He stood and came around the desk to put his hands on my shoulders. "Forgive me, please. I've been snapping at my friends lately too. I think I need a vacation."

"Why don't you take one," I said. The anger was receding, and again I was feeling concerned.

"I will." He let go of my shoulders. "So will you forgive me?" He looked into my eyes sincerely.

"Of course I will." I didn't tell him I was worried again.

"Come to dinner at the house tonight," he said. "Please, there's something I want to show you."

"Alright."

"I think I'll ask your mom to come. I want to show it to her too." He smiled and looked like his old self again. "You're not going to believe it. You're just not going to believe it."

✦

"This is going to be the greatest soccer team." Jimmy was practically jumping up and down. His hair was slicked back with sweat and water he'd dumped over his face from a water bottle.

I laughed. "You look like such a goon."

"Thanks, David." He grinned boyishly and punched at my shoulder.

"Daddy, Uncle David," James, Jr.'s young voice piped from behind Jimmy. I watched the boyish look vanish and a fleeting look of regret crossed his face. Then he turned to scoop up his son.

"Hey, kid," I said. "Where is your sister?"

"She's in the car having a fight with Mom. I didn't want to stay there."

"I don't blame you," Jimmy said putting his son back down on the ground. "What are they fighting about this time?"

"I don't know. All the sudden they're fighting." James Jr. shrugged his shoulders and looked at me. "I wanna be a goal tender like you, Uncle David," he said.

"Don't jump into that too fast," I said. "I didn't like it much when I was a kid."

"But you like it now, right?" He tugged at my hand and I looked down at him. I looked at the goal I had just finished defending.

"Yeah, I guess I do."

"Can I ride on your shoulders, Uncle David?" It never ceased to amaze me how fast this child could change the subject. I wondered, not for the first time, if he had some of the learning problems that his father had struggled with.

"Sure you can, Jamie." I swung him up to my shoulders and started toward the parking lot where Meryl and little Heather were emerging from the car looking angry.

"You're even bigger than Daddy." James Jr. piped. I started to jog and the child squealed.

"Don't let him fall," Jimmy said from beside me.

"I won't." I laughed at my friend's concerned expression. "You're such a dad, Jimmy."

"Yeah, well that's what happens when you have kids."

"I guess I wouldn't know about that, would I?" I said feeling a little depressed.

"Hold on tight," Meryl said to James Jr. as she approached us. "It's a long way down. Hello, David. Did you enjoy the practice?"

"Yeah, this is great. I'm glad to be playing soccer with Jimmy again. We make good teammates."

"I'm glad too. He needs to have some recreation. He works too hard," she said.

"Hey, guys, I'm standing right next to you. Don't talk about me like I'm not here," Jimmy said.

"Sorry, honey," Meryl stretched up to kiss him. "Did you enjoy practice?"

"Yeah, I did."

"Did you hear about Darla?" Meryl asked looking at me.

"What about her? Did she get the part?"

"No, she won't be coming home. She didn't get the part. She plans to go back to doing commercials. She's too afraid to try the stage again in New York."

"Oh, man," I said. "I was hoping she would come back to Atlanta. I miss her. She's probably upset. I'd better call her."

"I was planning to call her tonight. Why don't you come to dinner and we'll call her together?" Jimmy said.

"I can't. I'm going to Uncle Jeff's for dinner." I swung James Jr. down to the ground and picked Heather up in my arms. She put her little arms around my neck and kissed my cheek. I kissed hers back. "Your cheek is so soft I can barely feel it on my lips," I said. There was that sadness again.

"Oh, well, another time then," Meryl said as she took the children's hands and led them toward the car.

"I'm hoping in another year we'll be able to afford to buy her a car," Jimmy said. "Then she won't have to drop me and pick me up all the time. I have no independence." He slapped me on the shoulder and followed his family to the car.

"So, what did you want to show me?" I asked when I arrived for dinner at Uncle Jeff's house. My mother's car was in the driveway.

"Come on out back. Your mom is already out there. Grab yourself a drink on the way through the kitchen."

I pulled a beer out of the refrigerator and popped the top as we went through the back door to the patio.

"Hey Mom." I kissed her on the cheek and then looked in the direction she was watching. "What are we looking for?" Just as I said it I saw motion in the wooded back part of the lot, and something that looked like a deer bolted out of the woods.

"Wow," I said. I looked closer. It was a dog, a greyhound. "What a beautiful dog." It was carrying a ball. It ran up to Mom. She took the ball and threw it back out into the yard. The dog scampered after it.

"Whose dog is that?" I asked.

"Mine," Uncle Jeff said. "His name is Gabe. I've been dating a woman who has a rescue facility for these dogs. I just adopted him."

I looked at him with my mouth open. He laughed. I looked at Mom and she laughed too. "People change," she said.

"You wouldn't let me take Pepper camping," I finally said. "And Charlotte had to ride in the bed of the truck."

"Gabe rides in the bed of the truck." Uncle Jeff laughed. "In fact I bought a camper top and cut a piece of carpet for him. I'm thinking about buying a Jeep. That might be more comfortable for him."

I felt a wet nose on my hand and looked down at the dog nudging me. I stroked his neck and patted his side.

"If you want we can go to her facility and have a look, David," Uncle Jeff said. "Don't you think it's time for you to get another dog? Charlotte's been gone for years."

I pulled my hand away from the dog. I took the ball he was holding and threw it into the woods. "No thanks, I'll just hang out with Gabe sometimes."

I saw, out of the corner of my eye, the look that my parents exchanged. The dog ran for the ball. I looked straight ahead.

"I got the job, Darla," I said into the phone receiver. "I can't believe it. She apologized for the low salary. It's twice what I'm making now, even with delivering pizza."

"That's fantastic, David!" I could hear the genuine happiness in her voice. "I knew it was only a matter of time, and working on a magazine, how exciting!"

"It is exciting and Jane Winslow, my new boss, said that she was going to arrange some profit sharing opportunities since she can't offer big salaries." I sounded like an excited child even to myself. "That makes it like my own business."

"You already have your own business."

"Yeah, but here I'll be working with a team, people that I'll talk to face to face every day. Not just emails." I took a deep breath. "Man, I can't wait to get started."

"I'm happy for you, David." She sounded sad. I had just hung up the phone with Jane Winslow when she called. Darla was the first one I'd talked to.

"I'm sorry, Darla. I didn't even say hello did I?"

"I don't blame you. You had big news."

"Is everything alright? Why did you call?"

"I just wanted to hear your voice."

"Something is bothering you. I can tell."

"Well, I'm doing okay with the commercials. It pays the rent, but I'm thinking that if I can't get started in the theatre in the next year, I'll crawl back home defeated as usual."

"You're not defeated, P.H. You make great commercials. I loved the detergent one. You were great."

"I went to school to be on stage, not on television commercials."

"Well, get on stage then. I'm sure you can do it. Go ahead, try," I said. "You'll get your break. I got mine."

"You sure did. When do you start?"

"Tomorrow, Jane said I could start next week or even the next week if I wanted, but I want to start right away. Mom is even making me a new wardrobe. That reminds me, I haven't told Mom and Uncle Jeff."

"You'd better go tell them."

"Are you alright?"

"I'm fine. But you're right, I need to go out and try. Like I said, though, one year, then I'm crawling back home."

"You're not going to crawl."

"She offered me the job, Uncle Jeff," I said from the door of his office. I couldn't even remember going down the steps from my apartment.

"Did you accept?" he asked without looking up. I was disappointed. I wanted him to jump up and down like me.

"Of course I accepted. Aren't you excited for me, Uncle Jeff?"

He looked at me then. "I'm sorry, David." He got up and came around the desk to hug me. "I was caught up in what I was doing. I'm thrilled for you. Let's get your mom and go out to dinner to celebrate."

"Okay, but I want to go tell Jimmy first, and I need to call Lenny. I'm so excited. I already have plans. Jane says first I have to organize my department. You know, buy supplies and go over resumes for assistants. Man, I can't believe it." I looked at Uncle Jeff and noticed circles under his eyes. That was the first time I'd seen anything like that. He was smiling at me, but the smile didn't reach his eyes.

"I knew you'd get a break, son. You deserve it," he said. "Go tell your friends. I'll make reservations. Let me know if you want to bring anyone else along."

"I wouldn't have gotten this break without you. Thanks, Uncle Jeff. Thanks for believing in me, even still."

"More than ever, son, you're a good man."

✦

At midnight that night I took my usual walk. I had resumed my midnight walks as soon as I got out of prison. There was something about the cool night air that soothed me. It was fun walking around the nursery. There was a growing field behind the place. There were paths through it for the gardeners. They made a nice walk way.

As I was coming back I noticed Uncle Jeff's truck in the parking lot. The light was on in his office, so I tapped on the window.

"Ahhhhh …" he yelled and jumped. I smiled and leaned closer to the window to make sure he recognized me. He laughed. "Come on in. The alarm is off." He called through the closed window.

I let myself into the front door of the store and crossed to the office. I had a key and a code, but I never came into the place at night.

"There goes another year off my life." He laughed when I came into the office.

"So you're down to about ninety five now. I'm sure the prison thing was worth at least two." I took off my sweater and sat down. It was late September. The days in Atlanta were still warm, but the nights were starting to cool off.

"Yeah, I still think I'll finish the Trail with you." He shut down his computer and turned to look at me.

"Come upstairs with me and have some hot chocolate," I said.

"I don't think so." He patted his flat stomach. "I'm still full from dinner."

"Yeah, thanks for paying for the whole thing. Thanks for including Jimmy. I think it was nice for him to get out without the family for a while."

"I worried that he was starting a little young. They seem to be happy though."

"Yeah," I said. "He works really hard. They're planning to buy a house, and he's hoping to be able to get a second car soon. He really plunged into adulthood, but I think he's happy."

"His children are beautiful." Uncle Jeff looked sad.

"Is everything alright, Uncle Jeff? You don't usually come in to work at midnight. I'm not watching you," I said quickly. "But living upstairs and taking a midnight walk every night, I think I would have noticed."

"So you're still taking a midnight walk every night?" He changed the subject. "Are you still smoking that stuff when you go out?"

I stood and turned to go out the door. "The cool night air can be very soothing," I said.

"You didn't answer my question." He stood behind me and switched off the light. He put his arm across my shoulders, and we walked out of the store together.

"You didn't answer my question either," I said.

CHAPTER ELEVEN

I'd worked on the magazine for about a month when I decided to ask my new boss if I could hire Lenny. I continued to worry about him. We talked more often now. Lenny just seemed to need to talk a lot. I was sure he was sinking into a serious depression.

I'd thought about bringing him on to the magazine from the start. But I thought I should hold out for a while, establish myself with my new employer first. I hoped I had won her trust by now. I really didn't think I could wait much longer. Lenny needed to get a break.

She agreed to talk to him. I told her how we met of course. Uncle Jeff was right. You can't hide that sort of thing. Jane Winslow was a very tolerant person.

Within minutes of being in the office he'd managed to make the dour secretary laugh, and Jane was smiling comfortably. Lenny was a charmer. She hired him the next day to edit and select articles and short stories for the magazine. The group of us got to work producing the sample product. It was supposed to be on the stands by December first. So we had our work cut out for us.

"David." Lenny appeared at the door of my office.

"Hey, Lenny." I smiled at him. It was so nice to see him everyday again. We'd shared a cell for three years. I missed him. "Come on in. I can take a break for a few minutes." I turned away from my computer and rubbed my eyes.

"Stop doing that," Lenny said. "You'll look like an old man before you're thirty."

"Sorry." I smiled. Lenny always gave me a hard time about rubbing my eyes.

"What's up with the dress designer?" he asked.

"Anna Smart? She keeps pretty much to herself. I haven't had much interaction with her."

"I've asked her to lunch twice and she just says, No thank you. Have I developed bad breath or something?" Lenny had his hands on my desk and was doing pushups against it.

I stood up and started doing pushups against it across from him. I laughed. "I'll get into better shape with you around."

"You're in pretty good shape already," he said. "That workout room you have at the apartment is pretty well equipped."

"I'd rather make monthly payments on the equipment and own it than make payments to a gym."

"Which reminds me." He stretched his arms out in front of him and started to do deep knee bends. I followed suit. "I've found an apartment. I can actually afford to rent a place of my own now. I'll move out at the end of the month. I won't have to sleep on the couch in the office anymore."

"I told you we could move the office into the living room and you could make that your bedroom. It's a pretty nice room. It's the master. I've just lived there since I was a kid, so I'm more comfortable in my own room."

"I know, David, and I appreciate it, but I'm hankering for my own place."

"I guess I can understand that."

"Anyway, have you noticed how beautiful the dress designer is?"

"Anna?" I laughed at the speed with which Lenny could change the subject. We were still doing deep knee bends. I lost my balance and fell on my butt on the floor. I started to laugh. Lenny laughed too.

He offered his hand to help me up. I let him pull me to my feet. I was always surprised at how strong he was. He was half my size.

"I'm going to get her to go out with me. Want to place a bet on how long it will take?"

"I'm just a little uncomfortable betting on something like that, Lenny. How about I just wish you good luck," I said as I settled back into my desk chair.

"Thanks." He sat down in the chair across the desk. "I guess I'd better get back to work. David, I'm really happy in this job. It's great. I like the work and the people too. Thanks for doing this for me. I still wish there was something I could do for you."

"It's just nice having you around, Lenny."

He looked disappointed. "Good." He stood up to leave.

"Oh, Lenny," I said. "Thanks for the workout."

"I'm sorry, David," Jimmy said as we walked off the soccer field. "I can't stand that guy. I don't even want him around my kids."

"Oh, come on, Jimmy, you're just being prejudiced because you know where I met him." I was surprised by his reaction to Lenny. "You don't mind me being around your kids. I was there too."

"You are a decent person who made a mistake. It was a stupid mistake I'll admit. But it was a mistake all the same."

I shivered and reached for my jacket on the bench beside the field. It was late October. I didn't remember it getting this cold yet. When we were working out on the field I was fine. Now I was cold.

"I wasn't the only decent person in there that made a mistake you know."

"I'm sure you weren't, David, but I'm also sure Lenny wasn't one of the others."

I looked at Jimmy. He had a sulky expression on his face and it suddenly dawned on me. "You're jealous because he and I are so close."

"I am not." He pulled on his jacket with exaggerated movements and turned to walk toward the car where his family waited.

I hurried to catch up with him. "Jimmy, you can't replace a lifetime of friendship with a few years. You'll always be the best friend in my life."

He stopped and looked at me. He smiled slowly. "I guess some of it might be jealousy. He's smarter than me too."

"Nobody is smarter than you, Jimmy. Don't talk like that or I'll get mad, and you know what happens when I get mad."

He laughed. "No I don't. I don't think I've ever seen you get mad." He looked at me puzzled for a minute, then he became serious again. "Still, when he came to dinner the other night the kids thought he was the greatest thing in the world. I had a really uneasy feeling."

"It's just because he can't sit still. He's just like a kid."

"My kids can sit still, David. When we were kids we could sit still."

"What's your point, Jimmy," I asked. There was something really bothering him.

"I'm not sure." He turned and walked toward the car. "I just don't want him around my kids, okay David?" he called over his shoulder.

"Okay Jimmy, they're your kids."

"He's the only person that's ever reacted that way to Lenny." I told my mom at dinner that night. I ate with her once a week. I usually insisted on cooking or else I'd request something that I knew I could stand. She'd never really learned to cook.

"You're probably right. He's jealous. He's never really had to share you with anyone. I know you and Darla are good friends, but that's different. They're good friends too. You haven't even had a girlfriend since Teresa."

"No, and I really want one." I shook my head. "Anyway, I guess I'll respect his wishes. I was going to take the kids to the amusement park next weekend. Jimmy and Meryl need to get away together for a while. I thought I'd take Lenny with me. I guess I won't."

"I think that's probably the right thing to do."

Working in the startup phase of a magazine was as exciting as I had hoped it would be. So much depended on my marketing plans and abilities, but I didn't struggle with the pressure of it. The stress drove me. I had never worked so hard.

It was different than the frenzy I'd put myself in to get out of high school fast. I never felt anxious. I didn't sleep much, but when I did, I slept soundly. I think the fountain display below my window helped, but I planned to find my own apartment soon anyway. I guess I'd just have to put an indoor fountain next to my bed.

Lenny started dating Anna, and I started noticing how beautiful she was.

"I think I might be falling in love with her." I told my mom. "And that won't work. She's dating Lenny. I can't interfere with that."

"I guess not, but maybe that won't last. You said she's a black girl didn't you? Lenny's from a small town in South Georgia. Do you think his mother will approve?"

"Probably not, but I don't think Lenny cares that much about that."

"I don't know. He visits his mom regularly."

That was true. Lenny went home for a weekend almost once a month. He had already used up his vacation days for this year to spend a week at home. I hadn't used any of mine. Uncle Jeff and I had skipped our Appalachian Trail trip. I had plans to skip it in the spring too. I hadn't told him that yet.

"So tell me about Anna." Mom interrupted my thoughts.

"Well," I thought about it. "Her skin looks really soft. I've wanted to touch it, but that wouldn't be okay at work."

"I guess not." Mom laughed.

"It's very clear. There are no marks on it anywhere. You can't see veins or muscles. It's perfect." I smiled at myself. "And her figure is perfect. She's very small and very trim. I think she's about the same height as Darla, but her body is completely different. She doesn't have the large breasts and small waist and flaring hips."

"Sounds like you've noticed Darla's figure too. I didn't know you were so interested."

"I'm not interested," I said. "Darla and I are just friends, but I'm not blind."

"I think Darla has a beautiful figure."

"So do I. I'm just using it as a comparison. The change from her breasts and her waist and her hips is so extreme. It's voluptuous, dramatic. Anna's just kind of flows, like water over rocks or something. Her small breasts taper to a smaller waist. Then her waist tapers out again to a subtle flare of hips. Darla's bottom is flat too. Anna's is round." My voice had faded almost to a whisper. "Her hair is cut very short and sculpted to her head. It's just tiny little black curls. But the most beautiful thing is her voice. I can't even listen to the words when she speaks in our meetings." I suddenly felt self conscious about telling all this to my mom. I cleared my throat and straightened my shoulders.

"Don't worry about it, honey." Mom read my thoughts. "It does sound like love to me. If it is, you can't just let it go."

"She's seeing Lenny." I shook my head. "I know how bad Dad hurt you when he left for another woman. I'm not having anything to do with anything like that."

Mom didn't say anything. She got up and cleared the dishes from the table.

"Are you going to Aunt Jeanne's house for Christmas this year?" I changed the subject as I helped her wash the dishes.

"I guess so." She sounded sad.

I started the New Year in a new apartment. I was living in the same complex as Lenny. That was nice. Lenny had a tendency to drink too much on Friday night. He didn't drink often, but when he did he went a little overboard. I figured it had something to do with him being so small. It didn't matter. He could just walk home from my house. I usually walked with him. I just incorporated it into my midnight stroll.

"Hey, Victoria," I said to Uncle Jeff's assistant when I went into the nursery. She'd also written the gardening article for the sample magazine that had come out at the beginning of December. So we'd worked together.

"Hey, honey," she said. She was an older, kind of motherly, type of person. "I'd be careful if I were you." She pointed to the closed door of Uncle Jeff's office. "He's been growling all morning."

"Is he alright?" I asked. "He used to be a much nicer person."

"He's going through the change." She laughed at my startled expression. "Believe me it happens to men too." She went off with a customer who had approached her for help, and I reluctantly went to knock on the office door.

I peeked in. "Uncle Jeff," I said.

He looked up from the plans he had spread out on his work table. "Why are you looking so sheepish?" he asked. "I haven't bitten your head off today."

"Only because I haven't been here," I closed the door behind me. "All your employees are walking around without heads."

He laughed and sat down behind his desk. "I'll buy them lunch. In fact, let me call Vic in here and tell her so she can get everyone's order and call the restaurant of their choice."

He picked up the phone and tapped in three numbers. He told Victoria to order lunch then hung up and looked at me. "Do you want something? She'll be coming in with a menu any minute now."

"No, I have to get back to the office. I was just driving by on my way from an appointment, and I thought I'd stop in and say hi."

"That's nice. Tell me about the apartment. You've been in it for what, two weeks now?"

"Yeah, you know it's really the first home of my own." I raised my hand when he started to object. "I know home is with you and mom, but it's the first place I've supported myself. It's a gratifying feeling."

"I'm glad for you, son. Jane says you're doing great at the magazine. I'm proud of you. Of course I've always been proud of you."

"I love that job, Uncle Jeff. I'm good at it too. I've gone all over the southeast making sure I have that sample copy in every waiting room. I've got us on subscription lists and we're selling like crazy. I know magazines don't survive on subscriptions. They survive on advertising. But people don't buy ads in magazines that don't have a big distribution."

"I can hear your enthusiasm in your voice, son." He smiled but it didn't reach his eyes. "I wish I could feel some enthusiasm for something again. I can't remember the last time I was excited about anything."

"That's one of the reasons I came by, Uncle Jeff. I'm worried about you."

"Don't worry about me, David. I'm fine." He snapped and turned back to study his computer. I didn't say anything. A minute later he looked up at me and smiled weakly. "Well, there went your head."

I smiled and waited for him to go on.

"I guess I should be glad someone cares enough to be worried about me."

"Uncle Jeff," I said. "Have you seen a doctor? You're not sick or something are you? There's no terminal illness you're keeping from me is there?"

He laughed and ran his hand through his hair. I always liked the way he could run his hand through his hair and it fell perfectly back into place. "I suppose life itself is a terminal illness, isn't it," he sighed. "It always ends in death."

"You're depressed, Uncle Jeff. There are medications that can help you through this."

"I hate pills. I just need a vacation, but I can't take one. You won't go anywhere with me because of work, and I can't really leave things here at the nursery anyway. I mean I need more than a week or two. I think I need sort of a sabbatical. I need a business partner, but I don't have one. I just feel so trapped."

"I'm sorry. Maybe we could get away for a long weekend. Your friend Sam with the airplane could take us to the Trail."

"That would be nice." He looked up at me. I was startled by the hopeful look on his face. I felt guilty. I'd neglected him.

"I'll see how much time I can get off." I stood up. "Let's aim at the first weekend in February." I put my hand on his shoulder. "It's not enough. I know you need some real time off, but maybe it'll help a little. I love you, Uncle Jeff."

"I love you too, son." He put his hand on mine. On the drive back to the office I felt very uncomfortable. I'd never seen him like that.

I woke up to the sound of my cell phone ringing. I fumbled around on the bedside table and wished I had a cradle to put it in so it would be easier to find. "Hello," I said when I found it. I hoped I wasn't too late.

"You have a collect call from a correctional institution from…" It was a recording. "…Lenny." His voice was muffled. "Will you accept the charges?" The recording again.

"Yes." I sat up and turned on the light.

"David, thank God. I'm in jail. You've got to come and get me out."

"What's going on, Lenny?" I demanded.

"I'll tell you all about it when you get me out, but hurry. We have to find Anna. I don't even know if she's alright."

My heart started to pound. "What happened to Anna?" I could hear the growl in my voice.

"I wrecked the car trying to get away from the police. I had stuff, David. I had to get away."

"What happened to Anna?" I demanded again.

"I don't know. She was unconscious when they pulled me out of the car. They called an ambulance and took her away. We have to find her."

I couldn't feel anything but rage. "You son of a bitch, you don't have a car. Were you driving hers?"

"I'm not sure. I can't remember. David, come and get me."

"Like hell I will," I shouted. "I gave you a chance and you've ruined it. You've probably ruined my chance too, you bastard. God knows what you've done to that beautiful brilliant woman. I hope you rot in prison this time. I hope you rot." I hung up the phone and looked at the clock. It was 2:25 am. I jumped out of bed and pulled on my clothes. I didn't know where I was going, but when I got there I was at Uncle Jeff's house.

I hurried to the front door, let myself in with the key and called out his name. In only minutes he appeared in the foyer and folded me into his arms. I cried like a baby on his shoulder. It was the first time I'd cried since I could remember. I didn't think I'd ever stop.

At some time during the night my mom joined us. We were on the phone calling the police and all the hospitals in town. When we found Anna she was at a hospital that was not far from Uncle Jeff's house. They told us we couldn't see her yet. They wouldn't elaborate on her injuries. Her condition was serious but stable.

The police wouldn't give us details either. Eventually we discovered that Lenny had stolen a car. He'd gone to Anna's house and they had argued. The neighbors called the police. That's why he was running away. He'd been arrested for grand theft auto and possession of cocaine.

By the time we'd made these discoveries and my parents had calmed me enough to face my employer it was late morning. I typed up a letter of resignation, and Uncle Jeff and I went to see Jane.

She refused my resignation and assured me that it was only Lenny that was in trouble. She sent me home to clean up. Then I had to go to the hospital and face Anna. I wanted to throw up, but I didn't.

I knocked on the door of the hospital room and said, "Anna, it's me, David." For some reason I was whispering. "Can I come in?"

"Just don't turn on the light."

I went into the room. I put down the flower arrangement I had bought at the gift shop in the lobby, and walked to the side of the hospital bed. Her left arm was lying across her stomach. There was a cast on it. I looked at her face. There was a huge bruise on her temple and one eye was swollen. She looked up at me. This dynamic woman who always seemed so in control looked small and frightened. There was a squeezing feeling in my chest. I took her right hand in mine.

"I'm so sorry, Anna. This is my fault."

"No it isn't." She squeezed my hand back. "It's my fault. I seem to attract people like that. As soon as I found out about the drugs though, I broke it off. That's why he was so mad."

"When did you find out about the drugs?" I asked. I sat down on the chair beside the bed, still holding her hand. "I had no idea. We were friends. You'd think I'd know."

"I found out about a week ago," she said. "He offered me some. I told him I wouldn't say anything to anyone if he'd leave me alone. I guess I should have told someone."

"He wouldn't leave you alone?"

"He did at first, but you know what drugs do to people."

"That drug," I said and she looked at me puzzled. "I thought he was a pothead." I smiled sadly.

"No, not a pothead," she said and a tear leaked quietly out of her eye and rolled down her cheek. "I thought I was falling in love with him. What happened to my radar? I can usually recognize a drug addict."

"Why can you recognize a drug addict?"

She sniffed and smiled, shaking her head. "No reason. Thank you for coming to see me, David. I don't hold you responsible for this at all. I'm tired now. I need to sleep."

"I'll leave then," I said. "When will you go home?"

"Tomorrow, they want to keep me for another night to make sure about the head trauma. I'll be back at the office next week."

"I'll take you home tomorrow."

"That isn't necessary, David. I can take a cab."

"Please, Anna, let me take you home."

She looked at me and smiled weakly. "I'll call you when they discharge me."

A week later I sat in my apartment feeling especially lonely. I hated to admit it, but I was actually feeling sorry for myself. It was Friday night, and there was no Lenny to go to the local sports bar with and watch hockey. I wouldn't get to listen to him wax eloquent on some obscure subject while he drank himself silly when we got back to my place. Then there was no Lenny to walk home at midnight. I would have to take my midnight walk by myself. I wasn't used to that.

The buzzer on the wall of the apartment sounded. There was someone at the front gate of the complex. I looked at my watch. It was 11:45 pm. I pressed the button on the intercom and said hello.

"David, it's Jimmy." I smiled at the familiar voice. "I know it's late, but this is pretty much the only time I can get free these days. Can I come in?"

"You bet." I pressed the button to open the gate and went into the kitchen to warm the hot chocolate I had just finished a cup of. I was glad I'd made enough to add to my coffee in the morning.

The knock sounded on my door and I opened it up. "You're here just in time to take my midnight walk with me," I said.

"It's pretty cold out there," Jimmy looked over his shoulder at the sound of the cool breeze.

"That's okay. I've got hot chocolate heating for when we get back." I pulled a hat and scarf off the coat stand I had by my door and put the hat on Jimmy's head. I wound the scarf around his neck. "You just need to dress more warmly, that's all. Do you have gloves?"

"Yeah." Jimmy pulled gloves out of his pockets. He pulled them on as I got my jacket on and bundled up for the cold night air. "You're more of a mother hen than Meryl."

"I'm surprised she let you go out like that." I locked the door behind me after ushering Jimmy out. We turned and walked down the steps from my apartment to the complex walking trail.

"I left her a note," he said as he followed me into the park. "Is it safe to walk around here in the middle of the night?" He looked around at the dark shadows.

"It probably isn't. But it's a gated community, and I'm six foot five. We'll be alright."

"You're not planning to smoke any of that stuff are you?" Jimmy asked. "They drug test me at work. I don't even want to be standing next to you when you smoke that stuff."

I held out my empty hands. "I won't do that tonight, Jimmy."

"But you do it other nights?"

I stared at him. I couldn't see his features clearly in the moonlight, but I could detect the scowl. "Did Uncle Jeff send you here tonight?"

"You didn't answer my question."

"It doesn't deserve an answer." I started down the trail. Jimmy didn't move. For a minute I thought he might not join me. Then he hurried to catch up with me and we walked in silence for a minute. I breathed the cool night air and felt the usual relaxation of my shoulders then my back.

"You really love these midnight walks, don't you?" Jimmy broke the silence.

"I do, even if it isn't safe. I risk it."

"Maybe I should start taking midnight walks. The only problem is that most nights I'm in bed by ten thirty."

"Did you stay up especially for me tonight?" I asked.

"That, and my first service call in the morning is at 9:00 instead of 7:00, so I can sleep in a little."

"Is everything alright, Jimmy?" I asked. "Why the mid-night visit? Is everything alright at home? You seem stressed lately."

"Well, it's hard being the man of the family," he said.

"Tell me about it!" I said under my breath.

"What?"

"Tell me about what's bothering you?" I said louder.

"Well, nothing I guess. I mean it's just worrying about paying the mortgage every month. And the kids college, even though that's a long way off, and Meryl already has trust funds set up for them."

"Sounds like heaven to me, Jimmy, two beautiful children and a beautiful and loving wife. Here I am feeling lonely, and here you are wishing you had a little more alone time. Ironic, Lenny might have called that. He loved irony."

"You're right. I'm a happy man. I do worry but I'm not lonely. I worry about money, but I'm not alone in that either. Meryl brings in extra money with her hairdressing business. She can do it at home, so we don't need daycare. I do feel kind of trapped sometimes though."

"Yeah, I might not be there but I can see how you would." We walked in silence around the fountain in the middle of the park. We couldn't have talked anyway; the fountain was too loud.

"That's not why I came though," Jimmy said and smiled. "Well, that's not the only reason."

"Why did you come?"

"I wanted to see how your grief process was going?"

I stiffened. I knew what he was leading up to, and I didn't want to talk about it with him. "What grief process?"

"The one over Lenny."

"I don't want to talk about that with you, Jimmy. You figured him out from the beginning. I really don't want to hear you say I told you so."

"You trust me more than that, David. Come on."

I didn't say anything. I looked straight ahead as we walked toward the steps to my apartment. I could feel him looking at my face.

"He isn't dead." I broke the silence. "You can't grieve for someone if they aren't dead."

"Yes you can. You have to." We were climbing the steps now and I unlocked the door. "A few minutes ago you said Lenny would have called it irony. Lenny loved irony. You talked about him in the past tense, David. He's dead to you. Even if he isn't really dead, the relationship is."

We went into the apartment. It smelled like hot chocolate. I went into the kitchen to pour two cups of it. Jimmy sat on a bar stool across the counter.

"I understand this." He sipped his chocolate, "Because I had to grieve for you."

I looked up at him, startled. "I'm not dead to you."

"No, because I was wrong. You were worth holding on to, no matter what. I thank God I realized that every day."

"But Lenny isn't." I sipped my chocolate. "How did you figure him out, Jimmy? I spent three years living in the same quarters with him. I don't know how I'd have made it without him. When we both got parole I thought most of the guys in that place would be back. But I wouldn't, and I believed that Lenny wouldn't either. How did you see it when I didn't?"

"Gut instinct," he laughed. "Us stupid guys are long on gut instinct. Besides, I didn't need him like you did."

"You're not stupid." I put my empty cup down. "Everything about Lenny wasn't bad you know. He was a very talented man and a hard worker. He had a fantastic sense of humor."

"I'm aware of that, David. And that's part of the grief process. First you'll get angry."

"That's established."

"Then you'll get depressed. Then you'll start remembering the good stuff. Then you'll resolve whatever you have to and move on. I researched it," he said. "I wish I could talk to the woman about it too. I think she probably needs a friend right now."

"Anna?" I was surprised Jimmy would think about her. To my knowledge he'd never met her.

"Yeah," he said. "You're in love with her, aren't you, David?"

I looked at him and smiled. "Can you actually see inside my head?" I laughed.

"I've known you for a very long time, David." He stood and put on his coat. He stopped at the door and looked at me. "It's none of my business to give you advice, but David, she doesn't need a lover right now. She needs a friend." He left closing the door behind him.

I went around the counter to the door and locked it. I looked across the room to my bookshelf. I had a collection of albums that I'd made starting when I was a kid. I had a good desk top publishing system and software. I'd found a good print on demand company to produce them. There was one on my hikes with Uncle Jeff. It wasn't finished yet of course. It got so long I had to publish it. I figured that one would come in volumes.

I had the one of my dad with all the birthday and Christmas cards and the trip to Disney. I figured there wouldn't be any more volumes on Dad.

I had several volumes of Mom and me, Jimmy and me. There was one of Teresa and me. There was one of Charlotte and me.

I sat down at my computer and opened a new file. I titled it, *Lenwood Jones.*"

When I was twenty five years old, I used the greatest patience I'd ever had to woo the love of my life, Anna Smart.

My Uncle Jeff went away on his sabbatical. I can't believe how much I missed him, and he was only gone for three months.

And my Dad came back into my life full time.

"I'm really sorry about that, David." Uncle Jeff ushered me into the hotel room. He pulled the greyhound on a leash behind him. "I know you wanted to get on the Trail tonight, but I didn't expect Gabe to get airsick."

"I didn't expect to get airsick either," I said, looking fondly back at the dog. "I've flown all over the place since I've been working on the magazine. I've never had a problem before."

"You probably wouldn't have if Gabe hadn't vomited on you. You were looking a little green, but you were holding on until that happened."

I looked down at my soiled clothing. "I'm glad I had a barf bag. I'd hate to be wearing that too. I hope the hotel has a laundry room so I can wash this stuff."

"It does, I asked at the front desk. Go into the bathroom and take a shower. Throw your clothes out. I'll get them started," he said. "I've got peanut butter crackers and decaffeinated Coke for you when you finish."

"Thanks, Uncle Jeff," I called as I shut the bathroom door behind me and turned on the cold shower. I had taken off a Friday and a Monday in late March so that we could fly to our starting point on the Maryland border. Uncle Jeff's friend Sam had a private plane. It only had two seats but a fairly large baggage area in the back. I sat cross legged leaning against the wall of the plane, and Gabe curled next to me with his head on my knee. We were fine until we both fell asleep, always a mistake.

"That was quick." Uncle Jeff let himself back into the room with his key. I was dressed and sitting on the edge of the bed putting on my shoes. "I've got your stuff in the wash. The laundry room is right down the hall. Here …" He opened his bag and pulled out a variety of crackers. There was a small cooling section in his backpack and he pulled out regular Coke and decaf.

I sat down at the small table by the window and he did too. We opened our crackers and popped the lids on our Cokes. They were such familiar sounds that it made me smile. I stuffed the first cracker into my mouth and enjoyed the salty taste that always settled my stomach.

"I know you wanted to get started on the Trail right away," Uncle Jeff said around a mouthful of cheese cracker. "We still can. It's only three o'clock. We could get a three or four mile start before it gets dark. The days are getting longer now."

"What about the hotel room?" I took a deep swig of my Coke.

"We can check out early. They don't care if we pay for a night we don't stay here."

I thought about it. I looked at Uncle Jeff. His eyes looked tired. They looked that way a lot these days. He was still grouchy more often than I'd ever known him to be. I was concerned about him. That's why I'd taken this trip. I was enjoying my job so much I really didn't want to leave it.

"Where will you sleep better, Uncle Jeff?"

"I can sleep anywhere, David. You're the one with a sleeping problem."

I looked at the two double beds in the room. There was a fountain in the square outside the hotel. I could hear it clearly. The carpet was soft for the big dog. He was already comfortable on it. I looked back at Uncle Jeff. He was rubbing his eyes.

"There's a trail at the entrance to the hotel parking lot. I noticed when the cab dropped us off," I said. "Did you see it?"

"No, I was concentrating on not being squeamish about the way you smelled."

I laughed. Gabe nuzzled my hand from where he lay on the floor between Uncle Jeff and me. "You've washed Gabe too." I looked down at the wet dog.

"I hosed him off outside. He got most of it on you. He wasn't so bad. I'm going to give you both motion sickness meds on the way back." We laughed.

"Let's wait until the laundry is done," I said. "Then we can hike that trail for a couple of hours, do a little exploring, and have dinner at that restaurant down the street with quaint balconies, my treat. We'll get a good night sleep here and start early on the Appalachian Trail in the morning."

"That sounds good. Will you sleep alright in here with me snoring like a buzz saw?"

"I'll be fine, Uncle Jeff. I think I'll ask the management to keep that fountain turned on though."

✧

"Your new assistant, Victoria, says you're going through the change." I laughed as we stone stepped our way across a stream.

"Men don't go through the change," Uncle Jeff said. He jumped to the bank on the other side of the stream and stretched out his hand to me. I took it and he pulled me to the shore.

"I probably could have done that myself," I said.

"Old habits die hard."

"Victoria said you'd deny it, but she assures me that men go through menopause too."

"Victoria talks too much." We started up a steep incline toward a path we could see along the ridge of the mountain.

"Yeah, but she sure is a lot of fun to listen to," I laughed again. I was feeling relaxed and glad that I'd come after all.

"She is," Uncle Jeff said thoughtfully. "And that brings up something I've been meaning to talk to you about."

He sounded so serious it worried me. "What is it?" I asked.

"I'm planning to offer Victoria a partnership in the nursery." We reached the top of the hill where the path flattened out along the ridge. He turned to look at me. I don't know what he saw on my face, but it seemed to concern him. The truth was that it was relief. I was afraid that he was going to tell me he was sick or something.

"Don't worry, David. Your inheritance is safe. You'll always be my first concern, but right now I need a partner. Someone I trust." He was talking too fast.

"I'm not worried, Uncle Jeff. I'm alright with this. I'm just a little surprised. That place has always been your life. It defines you."

"When you were growing up I planned to partner with you. But I don't think you're interested in the nursery. I mean it's not what you want to do with your life, and I want you to have your own dreams."

I put my hand on his shoulder as we walked down the path. "It's okay, Uncle Jeff. You're right. I loved working there as a kid during the summer, but I'm doing what I want to do now, largely thanks to you. You're right. It isn't the nursery."

We walked together quietly for a minute. "So are you planning your sabbatical?" I asked.

"I am. I've got a bike trip planned for next fall. Victoria will have time to get used to the management end of the business by then. I'm going on a trip to the Machu Pichu in Peru."

"On a bike?"

"Well, I'll fly there. Then I'll be on a bike. It's an organized trip. I found this travel group on the internet. I'll be there for about a month. Before that I'm going to go to Little Cumberland Island and be the caretaker for a month. Remember I told you about my friend Randy, who retired to take care of the place. He wants to go on vacation to France with his wife and daughter. Imagine that."

"So you'll be gone for two months."

"Yeah, I really need it," he said. I felt sad. I'd miss him. But it was more uncomfortable than that. I was afraid of losing him. I was afraid he wouldn't come back.

"Too bad we couldn't sit on the balcony, but it really is too cold out there," I said. We sat across from each other in the restaurant in the quaint little town at the beginning of the Trail.

"When the sun was out this afternoon it felt warm enough, but it is late winter after all," Uncle Jeff said. "I'm just glad we brought our winter camping gear. It's been so warm in Atlanta we might have been fooled."

"You never get fooled, Uncle Jeff. You're always prepared."

He sat back and looked at me with a sad smile. "You have a completely different image of me than I have of myself."

"I guess that's understandable."

The waiter came and we gave him our orders.

"David," Uncle Jeff said. "Jane tells me that she thinks Anna Smart, her dress designer, is getting over that Lenny mess pretty nicely. She says it's mainly because of you."

I sipped at the beer the waiter had just put down in front of me and looked at him. I didn't say anything.

"Of course, Jane is very discreet. She didn't give me any details. I just had a feeling that maybe you were becoming romantically involved with her."

"Would that bother you?"

"Why would it bother me, David?"

I didn't say anything.

"Because she's black?" he asked. "Not in the least. Because she's older than you? I've dated women older than me. I dated Jane."

"I suspected you had. Why didn't it work? She's beautiful and brilliant and rich. What more do you need?"

"Don't deflect, David. I'm talking about you and Anna, not me and Jane."

"If you're about to give me that safe sex lecture again I can assure you that I've got that down. I even know that pregnancy isn't the only thing I'm trying to avoid."

He leaned back and sipped at his beer. He smiled and said, "I'm not going to lecture you. I guess I'm asking how your love life is going because I'm worried about you being so alone. A handsome, caring young man with a good job shouldn't be alone."

"Look who's talking." I laughed and leaned forward to look at him. "You've never dated anyone seriously since you were divorced at, what age was it, twenty six?"

"Twenty seven." He looked down at the plate the waiter put in front of him. His skin was very dark so it was hard to see, but I'm pretty sure he blushed. I laughed.

"Tell me about your love life, Uncle Jeff? Are you still seeing that woman with the greyhound rescue facility?"

He looked into my eyes and smiled. "Not romantically. We're still friends, but she's a good bit younger than me."

"Who cares? I've noticed that younger women seem to get the hots for you. I think it's the burly physic." We laughed.

"I think sometimes they do, but it doesn't last. In the end I'm still an old man, even if my work keeps me in shape."

"How old are you now, forty nine? I don't think that's old." We ate in silence for a while? "So what happened with Jane?" I asked.

"I'm aware that you've manipulated this conversation from you to me, David." He looked at me and smiled.

"What happened with Jane?"

"Our friendship got in the way. Then she found someone else."

"But the romance was gone before she found someone else?" I asked. I didn't want to be angry at the new boss that I thought so much of.

"It was. She didn't dump me for him. She's still a very good friend." He leaned back in his seat and looked me in the eyes again. "It's your turn to talk. It's only fair, David."

"I'm pretty sure I'm in love with her. Anna," I laughed, "not Jane. Although, I'm pretty sure I do love Jane, but not that way."

"Yeah, Jane's pretty lovable. How does Anna feel about you?"

"She's coming around. You know she's very stand-offish. I think she has a painful past that makes her stay away from people. But we helped each other through the grief process with the Lenny thing, and I think she's opening up to me. We've had lunch a few times, and I'm planning to ask her to celebrate my birthday with me. It's on a Friday night this year, so I can catch her before she goes home. She can't say no when I tell her it's my birthday. Good plan, don't you think?"

"Sounds good, I'll keep my fingers crossed for you. Your mom and I will celebrate with you on Saturday."

"David." I woke up to Uncle Jeff's voice and the sinking of the bed as he sat on the side of it.

"What?" I sat up quickly and my head spun. I shook it to regain balance. "Is something wrong?"

"You sure are jumpy lately, David. You're always worried."

I noticed that the light on the table in the corner was on. There were some papers on it and an open book.

"Read this." He put the open hotel information notebook in my hand.

"The light is too dim. Flip the switch on the bedside lamp."

"Okay." He turned to do that, then looked back at me. His face looked different than it had yesterday. He seemed excited about something. I hadn't seen him look that way for a long time.

"What time is it?" I asked.

"It's five o'clock. I've been having a hard time sleeping lately." He pointed to the notebook in my lap. "Read it."

Thru-hikers who have hiked the Trail to this point from either end have gained enough endurance to take on what we call the Maryland Challenge. Hike the whole 41 mile stretch of the Trail in one day.

If you keep your room for another night we'll pick you up at the end of the Trail and bring you back for a small fee of ten dollars a person. When you get back here you'll have a hot meal and a comfortable bed. Try it! It's exhilarating!

"Don't tell me you want to do this." I looked up at him. I was shocked by the way his expression fell at what I'd said. "The furthest we've ever gone was 25 miles, and we were really tired at the end of that day."

He stood up and went back to the table. His shoulders were slumped and his head hung forward. He sat down at the table and looked at me. "I guess it was unrealistic," he said.

I looked back down at the notebook. "You know they say it's an easy hike. It might be fun." I looked back at him. His expression was brightening again. Definitely male menopause, I thought. "If we keep the room, we could take the day packs with plenty of water. We could take our sleeping bags in case we don't make it. They're light weight. We could pack plenty of water and lunch and dinner. We have the dried food from the hiking store. The load would be light. Do you think Gabe can keep up?"

"Sure he can." He rubbed the top of the dog's head. "He's a thru-hiker too."

"Let's do it."

He stood, pulled his day pack out and started to pack it. "You'd better get up and shower, David. We need to hit the trail soon or we won't get back until after dark."

Believe it or not we made it, all three of us. It was easy terrain, so we even managed to have some pretty good conversations. The weather was cool. We got back to the hotel and skipped the hot meal. We'd already eaten on the trail.

When we got back to the room, Uncle Jeff turned the television on. We both woke up late the next morning, only because Gabe needed to go out. The television was still on.

CHAPTER TWELVE

I stood at the entrance to Anna's work cubical. I loved the look of her work space. She had half of the desk turned into a drafting board. Her walls were tacked with pictures of clothing designs. There was one picture of a handsome young man. I had asked about the picture, and she'd told me he was her younger brother. When I pressed for details she changed the subject. I didn't push.

"Hey," I said. She looked up. I had the familiar urge to stroke her smooth cheek.

"Hello, David." She stood at the end of the counter space collecting her things to leave for the day.

"Anna." I sat down on the stool. I was nervous. My knees were shaking. I didn't want to embarrass myself by crumbling to the floor. "I was wondering if you'd go out to dinner with me."

"Oh, I don't ..."

"It's my birthday," I said it quickly. "I'm alone tonight. Please come and celebrate with me."

She stopped with her hand on her lunch bag and looked at me. She smiled. "I don't celebrate my birthday," she said. "But I always make a big deal out of Anthony's." She looked fondly at the picture of her brother.

"I'm an only child. I make a big deal out of mine." My heart was pounding. She'd revealed a small part of her life to me. It was hard to get past the shell she'd built around herself. But I was making progress.

"Why aren't you celebrating with your family, your uncle and your mother?"

I had a lie prepared, but I said, "I am, tomorrow night. Tonight I wanted to celebrate with you."

She took a deep breath and sat down on the desk chair.

"We've been through a lot together in the past few months, Anna. Lenny's betrayal hurt both of us. I'm coming through it," I said. "I hope you are too."

She nodded her head. "I'm doing well, David. You've been a big help in the grief process."

"Then come out and celebrate my birthday with me, please?"

"Can I go home to shower and change first?"

"Sure, I will too. I'll pick you up at seven thirty. How's that?"

"That's good." She rose and I followed her down the hall. When we got to my office I went in and picked up my keys. I turned around to turn off the lights and close the door. When I turned back she was gone. When I reached the reception area I saw her car pull out of the parking lot. I stood at the glass door and watched as it disappeared from sight.

"She agreed to go out to dinner with me to celebrate my birthday," I said to Amanda, the secretary.

"I suppose that's good."

I turned and looked at her. She was very different from Anna, but in one way she was the same. She was older and very plain. She dressed and acted like the stereotype of an old maid. Anna was beautiful and fashionable. But they both were unusually reserved. I knew they were friends. They spent more time with each other than either of them spent with anyone else on the magazine team, except Jane of course.

"You suppose that's good?" I asked.

"Just be careful, David. She could hurt you without meaning to."

"I'm a big boy," I said, trying to be playful. "I've been dumped before. I can take it if it happens." I laughed.

"Good." She smiled and looked back down at her desk. "Happy birthday, David," she said without looking up again.

"Thank you." I left the magazine feeling a combination of excitement and ambivalence. "I won't analyze it right now," I said to myself. I hurried home to shower and dress.

"You look beautiful." I stood at Anna's door as she slid through it and closed it firmly behind her. She fumbled with her keys. I took them from her and locked the door. I handed them back.

She hadn't asked me in I noticed. I wondered how long it would take to get her to trust me enough to let me come into her apartment. I looked at her as I took her elbow and guided her to my car. She was wearing a dress that draped smoothly over her rolling curves. It was a deep purple interwoven with black thread. It shimmered as she moved. She carried a matching jacket over her arm.

I'm up for the challenge, I thought. I opened the passenger side door for her and she hesitated for a moment. She seemed nervous. I stepped away from her to walk around the car. By the time I'd gotten into the driver's seat she was seated neatly beside me.

"You make all of your own clothes, don't you?" I laughed. "I've never seen any of them anywhere before, not even on our models in the magazines."

"It's kind of my signature." She smiled and looked out the window. "My clothes are unique."

"My mom is like that. She makes her own clothes. They're different than anything she tailors for anyone else. She alters her patterns to fit her own body. She's very tall, you know."

"I've seen her when she comes to visit you. She's a very distinguished looking woman."

"Isn't that great?" I smiled proudly. "And she's a seamstress that works out of the back room of a dry cleaning store."

"That's a respectable occupation."

"Absolutely," I said as I pulled into the parking lot of the new formal dining establishment not far from Anna's apartment.

"Oh, David, I've heard this place is very pricey. I was going to insist on paying the bill, but I'm not sure I can afford it."

"There's no way I'd let you pay for it anyway. It was my idea. It's my birthday, and I want to eat here."

"I won't try to insist then." We both laughed and I got out of the car. By the time I'd walked around to open Anna's door she was already out of it and standing on the sidewalk.

"You're very independent," I said.

"David, I've been getting in out of cars for a long time."

We laughed again. She had such a dry sense of humor. "I guess that's a silly tradition."

We went into the restaurant. The lights were dim and the atmosphere was quiet. I was glad. I wanted to be able to talk. I chose the booth I wanted us to sit in. It was in the corner. We sat across from each other. The table was small, so we weren't shouting distance away.

"I like the ambiance of this place," I said after the waiter took our drink orders. Anna ordered sparkling water. I had planned to order a martini. It was so fashionable, but I didn't. I ordered water too. "I hate the noisy trend in restaurants these days. You can't have a conversation."

"I've noticed that. I rarely go out. When I do I like a soothing atmosphere."

I leaned back and looked at her. "Anna, I know you don't like to talk about yourself much, but I'd like to hear about your brother. I know you love him. I can see it in your eyes when you look at his picture."

She smiled and looked down at her empty plate. "I'm just crazy about him. I'm more like his mother. I raised him." She held up her hand. "Don't even ask. I'm not going to talk about her."

"I didn't ask. I wouldn't. I know better."

She met my eyes and smiled. "Anthony is ten years younger than me," she said still holding eye contact. "He's twenty years old."

The waiter approached our table with our drinks breaking our stare. "Are you ready to order?" he asked.

Anna looked down at the menu in front of her.

She's five years older than me, I thought, big deal. Will she think it's a big deal?

"I'll have the stuffed chicken breast," she said.

I looked at the menu. It was the least expensive thing on it. "Anna, don't be frugal," I said. "It's a celebration."

"I like chicken." She smiled. There was something familiar about her smile. I wasn't sure what. I smiled back at her.

"So do I. I'll have the chicken too." I said to the waiter. "Should we order a bottle of wine?"

"I'll only drink one glass. Unless you want the rest, I think we should order by the glass."

"I'll have a glass of chardonnay, this one." I pointed to the wine list. I wasn't even going to try to pronounce it. "And one for the lady?" I looked at her. She nodded. We gave our menus to the waiter and he left us alone.

"So, go on about your brother," I said.

"He's in college in New York State. He's studying pre-Law and doing very well. I'm proud of him."

"I guess you would be. Is that why you're so frugal about everything?" I asked knowing I was getting too close. "Is all of your money going to putting him through school?"

I sucked in my breath at the trapped look that came over her face. "I'm sorry," I said. "That's none of my business."

"No it isn't," she said.

I wanted to punch myself as I watched her compose her expression. As the composure came over her features the defensive wall descended, and I knew she wouldn't talk about herself anymore tonight.

"Anna, please forgive me," I said.

She smiled a bit stiffly and the familiar look was gone. "You're forgiven," she said. "Now tell me about you. How old are you today, David?"

I took a deep breath. "I'm twenty five."

She didn't flinch. "Happy twenty fifth birthday." She raised her glass of water and held it forward.

I raised mine and we touched them together.

"Well, I had a wonderful time," I said as I pulled into a parking space at her apartment complex. "Even though I made you mad by asking a question that was none of my business."

She glanced at me quickly. "I wasn't angry, David. I'm just a very private person."

"I understand that. I'll be more careful in the future." I took the keys from the ignition and grinned at her.

"Don't flash that boyish grin at me." She laughed and her smile was familiar again. "You remind me of Anthony," she said.

I made an exaggerated effort to straighten my features. "I don't want to look boyish," I said. "I'm afraid you'll think I'm too young for you."

She sobered and opened her door and got out. I met her at the back of the car.

"You are too young for me. We're just friends and colleagues, David. You do understand that."

"Of course, I do," I said quickly and watched her features soften. I thought I might be getting to her. "Can your friend and colleague come in for a minute? We could have some coffee, or tea, do you drink tea?"

She laughed and looked toward the building. She hesitated for a minute then said, "I don't think so tonight, David. Thank you for taking me to dinner and Happy Birthday." She started toward the building. I followed her.

"David, I said not tonight."

"I know. I'm just walking you to the door. That's the proper etiquette isn't it?"

"I believe so." I saw the slight smile that pulled at the corners of her lips.

"Anna," I said softly. We approached the door and she took out her keys. "May I touch your cheek?"

She sucked in her breath and looked up at me.

"Please," I said. She didn't move. She just held my stare. I raised the back of my forefinger and stroked down her cheek to her jaw. "Soft as silk," I whispered and before I'd even thought about it my lips were touching hers. She responded. My heart started to pound as I realized that she was kissing me back. It only lasted a few seconds. Then she pulled away and unlocked her door.

"Anna,"

Chapter Twelve / 210

"Thank you for dinner, David," she said and the door shut behind her. I turned and walked toward my car. I felt like I was walking on a cloud. My hip collided with the handrail of the short flight of steps that led to the parking lot.

She responded to me. That was all I could think about.

✦

"Who could this be?" I called into the intercom. The buzzer from the front gate had sounded at six am. It was a Monday morning. I was sitting at my breakfast table waiting for my French toast casserole to come out of the oven.

"It's Jimmy." The intercom buzzed the voice. "I'm sorry to wake you up, David. Could I come up for a minute? I won't keep you long."

"You didn't wake me up." I buzzed the gate open. "You're just in time for French toast."

I had taken the casserole out of the oven by the time he knocked on my door. "You have got to be kidding," he said as he came into the apartment. "You cook before you go to work?"

"Breakfast is my favorite meal." I laughed at his expression.

"Did you take your midnight walk last night?" Jimmy poured himself a cup of coffee and sat down at the counter.

"Of course I did." I set the casserole down and went back to the stove. "I made a blueberry syrup, but I know you don't like blueberries, so let me get some maple." I poured the blueberry syrup into a cream dispenser and turned back to the refrigerator. I poured maple syrup into a dispenser and put it in the microwave. Jimmy was staring at me with amazement.

"You walked late last night then got up early this morning to cook a gourmet breakfast. I'm worried about you, David."

"I slept in between," I said. I felt defensive. The truth was that I hadn't slept much at all.

"Meryl isn't even up yet. I usually just drink a glass of orange juice for breakfast. She says I should eat some walnuts too, but it's more trouble than it's worth."

"That's not healthy, Jimmy." I sat down across from him at the counter and cut the casserole into pieces. "The health nuts aren't kidding when they say breakfast is the most important meal of the day."

"Well, I'm not going to get up earlier to fix it. Meryl has to get the kids up and off. I can't ask her to do it."

"Then you should come by here every morning. I always cook."

Jimmy looked at me as he took a bite of his casserole. Then he just dug in. I poured myself a cup of coffee and sat down to eat with him.

"This is decaf," I said. "I hope that's alright with you."

"I've already had caffeine," he said. "Meryl has a coffee maker that she can set up the night before. It's ready when I get up in the morning."

"There you go. She's taking care of you."

"Yeah ..." He smiled happily. I noticed the contentment on his face. "She takes good care of me."

We ate in silence for a while, only talking to ask for something to be passed. "So, why the early morning visit, Jimmy," I said, getting up to clear the plates. "It's almost time for me to shower and dress for work."

"I just wanted to check in with you. We haven't seen each other in a while and I had time before my first service call this morning," he said.

"You could have slept late."

"I would have if I could have," he laughed. "It's becoming impossible for me to sleep past five thirty. So... anyway, David, how are things going with Anna?"

"I think they're going well." I could feel the grin on my face. "I kissed her on Friday when she went to dinner with me for my birthday. She still wouldn't let me into her apartment, but she didn't reject my kiss. In fact, she kissed me back."

"That's good, David. I wanted to tell you how impressed I am with your patience. It's been months since that mess with Lenny and you haven't given up."

"I think I'm in love with her, Jimmy. I can't wait to see her every morning and I can't stop thinking about her all day long, and all night."

"Sounds like love," he said. "I mean as far as I can remember. I'm sure I felt that way about Meryl, before all the distractions I mean."

"You did. Anyway, she's coming to watch the soccer game on Saturday. It took a lot of talking to get her to agree, but she said she'd come. She won't let me bring her, so I'm keeping my fingers crossed. Knowing her, though, I think if she said she would, she will."

"Great, I hope we win. Maybe that will encourage her to come back."

"Will Meryl and the kids be there? It might be nice if Meryl sat with her in the stands so she wouldn't feel alone."

"No, since we got the second car Meryl doesn't come to many of my games. Heather has some kind of a dance rehearsal. Jamie wanted to come. He hates going to dance class with Heather, but Meryl says he's too young to sit in the stands by himself. She says I'd be distracted in the game too. But I think he'd be alright." He shrugged and stood up. "No matter, she won't let him come."

"Maybe Anna could watch him. She raised a younger brother. I could ask her?"

"It's taken months for you to get this far with Anna. Are you sure you want to subject her to hurricane James?" Jimmy stood and picked up his keys.

"Let me ask her and gauge her reaction. It might be just the right thing to keep her from feeling out of place."

"Alright, I'll run it by Meryl. I don't think she'll object."

"Good, see you Saturday, if not before," I said as he went out the door.

Anna's reaction to the suggestion that she watch James, Jr. during the game was exciting. I had thought she might enjoy it since she had a younger brother, but I thought she might not want the responsibility. I was wrong. Her face lit up at the prospect so much that I felt a brief stab of jealousy.

It didn't seem fair for a five year old boy she'd never met to get the light in her eye that I wanted for myself. Still I was happy she had agreed. It was assurance that she would indeed be at the game.

"David." The voice over the phone was Uncle Jeff's. It was Friday evening, and I was on my way out of the office when it rang.

"Hey, Uncle Jeff, you just caught me. I was on my way home."

"I'm glad I did. I have a meeting with a client in North Highlands this evening. I didn't want to bother you too late."

"You know there's no such thing as too late for me."

"Unless I call at midnight, then you'll be out walking. I hope you're careful out there, David."

"I carry a machete." I laughed.

"That won't do much against a gun."

"Parents never stop worrying do they?" I laughed, but I was starting to feel irritated. Uncle Jeff had an attitude of gloom and doom these days. "I'll be fine, Uncle Jeff. What can I do for you?"

"I seem to have misplaced my schedule. I have got to get some organization to this office. It's just too small with Victoria and me both working in here." He was grouchy as usual. "When is the game tomorrow?"

"It's at 11:00 am."

"I know it's bad for the assistant coach to have to ask, but anyway…"

"Not a problem, Uncle Jeff." I hung up the phone. I was worried about Uncle Jeff.

I was up at six am on Saturday morning. I never slept late. I often wished I could, but when my eyes opened they stayed that way. I got up and started breakfast. I had a muffin recipe I wanted to try. Breakfast had become my favorite meal to cook.

I loved the smell of the coffee brewing first thing and fresh muffins baking in the oven. I was really good at biscuits too. I loved fruit. I had recipes, mostly of my own creation, for cooked fruit dishes, fresh fruit salads, and a combination of the two. I had egg casseroles and bread casseroles. A lot of times I'd take my leftovers into the office. People gathered in the break room and feasted on my artwork.

I liked cooking at dinner too, but breakfast was the best.

I finished ladling my batter into the muffin tin and slid it into the preheated oven. I turned to look out the sliding glass doors to my balcony.

"Oh no," The dawn had been barely breaking when I'd gotten up, but it hadn't gotten much brighter outside in the half hour I spent starting breakfast. It was clearly daylight, but there were dark clouds covering the sky, and a fine mist had started. A brisk wind was making the trees of the park dance. "Don't you dare ruin my carefully laid plans," I said.

The buzzer on the intercom sounded. I pressed the button. "Who is it?"

"It's your mother, and coincidentally, your Uncle Jeff is behind me in his own car."

"I'll let you both in," I said. "Signal him to follow you."

I pressed the button to open the gate, then went to boot up my computer so that I could check on the weather. Before the boot had finished the buzzer sounded again.

"I told Mom to signal you to follow her through," I said. I felt a little edgy.

"Where is she?" Jimmy voice crackled through the wire.

"Is that you, Jimmy?" What's going on? I thought.

"It's me and Jamie. We couldn't sleep, or I guess I should say, Jamie couldn't sleep. He's too excited about going to the game today. I figured you had breakfast on, so I suggested we come over here."

"Mom and Uncle Jeff just came through the gate. They weren't even together. I'll buzz you in." I pressed the button to open the gate again then went to open the front door at the sound of the knock.

"What's going on?" I asked. "Is this some kind of a surprise party? What's the occasion? My birthday was last week."

"Not a surprise party, honey," Mom said as she came through the door and kissed me on the cheek. "I wanted to see you before I left for my appointment in Macon. I'm so sorry I have to miss your game, but this is a wedding, and the bride actually has to be sown into her dress. They're paying me a lot."

"Mom, I'm a grown man. It's just an amateur team and not even a special game. I think I can handle it."

"I know you can, David." She patted my cheek. "But I'm still sorry I have to miss it." She went into the kitchen to pour herself a cup of coffee. "Besides, she called over the bar. "I didn't want to stop on the road for breakfast when I knew you'd have a gourmet meal set up here."

"I don't think she cared that much about the game." I laughed and turned to Uncle Jeff. I stepped back when I saw his angry face.

"Of course she cared about the game, David. Your mother is not shallow."

"I was kidding." I saw Jimmy getting out of his car with James, Jr. "Uncle Jeff, if you're mad at me about something this isn't the time. Jimmy is here with his son and I don't want you to scare him."

"I'm sorry." His face fell. He looked defeated. He looked old. "I didn't mean to snap. I'll behave." He smiled, but the smile didn't crinkle his eyes like it usually did. "Can I come in and have some of that gourmet breakfast too?"

"Of course, but why are you here? Do you need me for something?"

"Just company," he said as he took the cup of coffee Mom offered him.

"That's decaf; I'll put some real stuff on." I went around the counter. "You greet Jimmy and Jamie for me, would you?"

Once I'd gotten the second pot of coffee brewed and taken the muffins out, I arranged the food in buffet style on the counter. Mom and Uncle Jeff and the James's sat at the bar chatting and drinking coffee. James, Jr. had a juice box that his father had brought. I was glad. I didn't know what I would have offered him.

"Let's serve ourselves and sit at the dining table. I think I can find enough chairs," I said. "Jimmy you can help Jamie. The counter is a little high."

"I can fix my own plate," James, Jr. said.

"Okay." I was beginning to wonder if I'd made a mistake. Was Jamie going to offend Anna?

"This is nice." I smiled as I sat down at the table and looked around at my little gathering. "You know breakfast is the most important meal of the day. I'm glad you all joined me."

"I probably shouldn't eat all this stuff," Uncle Jeff said. "My cholesterol was high at my last check up."

"Are you alright, Jeff?" Mom asked before putting a forkful of strata into her mouth.

"Yeah, it wasn't too high, but I'm pretty much supposed to stop doing anything fun. You know, eat vegetables, fruits, whole grains, yuck!" He took a spoonful of fruit salad.

"I don't suppose this stuff counts as fruit, does it David? It tastes too good," Jimmy said.

"It's not too bad for you, but I have some very healthy recipes too. I could have made them if you'd told me you were coming, Uncle Jeff. I mean if I'd known you had special needs."

"I don't have special needs." He snapped, but looked quickly at Jamie who was stuffing a piece of muffin, dripping with butter, into his mouth. The child hadn't noticed anything.

"No, of course you don't," Mom said. "However, I do. My cholesterol was high too, and my blood pressure is up. Getting old is not for sissies."

"That's the truth." Uncle Jeff leaned back and took a sip of his coffee. "Are you alright, Charlie?"

"Yes." She grinned and the tension in the room relaxed. I loved the way she could do that. "It's just time for some lifestyle changes."

"I'm just sure there has to be a way to make it fun," I said. Jane had hired a dietician for the magazine a few weeks ago. I made a mental note to talk to her.

"Well, I've got to run, David." Mom stood and kissed the top of my head. "I'll wash my own dish. You have enough cleaning up to do. Oh look, David." She pointed to the window. "It's clearing up. I think it's supposed to be a warm spring day, a great day for a game."

I looked at the window. The clouds were moving out and the sky behind them was clear blue. "How did you do that?" I asked her as she picked up her bag and opened the front door.

"Magic!" She laughed and closed the door behind her.

"The weather report predicted it, David. Your mother isn't magic." I looked at Uncle Jeff's face. Was he pouting?

By the time we got to the soccer field I was a nervous wreck. Uncle Jeff and I had spent the morning washing and drying dishes while Jimmy and James, Jr. argued over just about everything.

Jimmy wanted James, Jr. to help with the dishes. Jamie very adroitly pointed out that there was not room in the kitchen for any more people.

"It's alright, Jimmy," I said, trying to diffuse the situation. "He's right about that. Maybe the two of you could just get the stuff off the table and put it on the counter." Then, of course, they had to argue about that. Jamie dropped a fork on the carpet, which sent his father into a frenzy of trying to get the grease out of the rug before it set in.

Jimmy told James, Jr. to finish clearing the table while he cleaned up his mess, and to be sure not to drop anything else.

Jamie picked up two plates and tripped over something that nobody could see. Both plates turned upside down on the carpet, which of course enraged his father. Jimmy's reprimand sent James, Jr. into tears. He ran into the kitchen to hide behind my leg, smearing butter and muffin crumbs all over my clean soccer uniform.

"I'm **sorry**." The child squealed and ran out of the kitchen into the bedroom.

"Jimmy," I said as I dabbed at my soccer shorts with a wet cloth. "You've got the kid hysterical, and you're not much better yourself."

"If he was mine I'd turn him over my knee," Uncle Jeff grumbled from his spot at the kitchen sink.

"Right, big shot," I said. "You forget you raised me, and you never turned me over your knee."

He grumbled something else. I ignored him and looked down at the floor where Jimmy scrubbed viciously at the spot in the rug. I put my hand on his shoulder. "What's going on? I've never seen you and Jamie at each other's throats like this."

"I..." he looked back down at the spot and started to scrub again.

"Wait," I said. "I've got this great spray stuff that gets that kind of thing right out." I went to the closet and got the stuff and the two of us started to clean the spots in the rug.

"He doesn't want to sit with Anna," Jimmy said quietly. "I've tried everything, bribery, threats. Nothing is working."

My heart started to pound. I had a panicky feeling that by setting this up this way I'd ruined all of my efforts. Would I lose all of my progress today? I looked at my bedroom door. It was shut. I could hear Jamie's muffled cries behind it. I looked back at Jimmy. His shoulders were hunched and he looked pale.

"He doesn't have to then," I said. I was angry, not at the kid or Jimmy, not even at Uncle Jeff. I was angry at myself for being so desperate.

Uncle Jeff came out of the kitchen and picked up the dishes from the floor. "He can sit on the bench with me," he said as he cleared the rest of the table and went back to the kitchen.

"I don't think that would work any better in your present mood," I said. My heart was pounding. I could feel a headache coming on. I said a silent prayer of thanks that there was no visual aura. It wouldn't be a migraine.

Uncle Jeff turned and bristled. "Oh come on," he said. "Am I really that bad?"

"Worse," Jimmy and I said together. Then I started to laugh. I sat down on a chair at the table. My laughter was becoming hysterical. I wished my mom would come back.

Jimmy started to laugh too. "You okay, David?" he asked between chuckles.

"No, I'm hysterical."

Uncle Jeff came out of the kitchen and sat down beside me. He put his hand on my shoulder. I felt his calming influence right away and dabbed at the tears in my eyes with a napkin.

"Let's see if we can pull this day out of the fire," he said. "Jamie!" He called to the closed bedroom door. "Come out here."

"I don't want to sit with Miss Smart." He sulked as he looked around the door.

"Why didn't you say so in the first place?" I said. My heart pounded again at the sound of her name. Uncle Jeff squeezed my shoulder, and I took a deep breath.

"It was the only way to get Mamma to let me go to the game instead of the ballet rehearsal. I hate ballet."

"So you made a bargain. You said you'd sit with Miss Smart if you could go to the game," Uncle Jeff said.

"I didn't mean it."

"So you lied."

James, Jr. glanced quickly at his father. Clearly they'd discussed lying before. There was a punishment. "No, I just changed my mind."

I looked at Jimmy. His face was set in angry lines. He moved toward his son, but Uncle Jeff put his other hand on Jimmy's shoulder. "So you want to go to the Ballet rehearsal. I'll take you." Uncle Jeff stood up and walked over to the counter to get his keys. "I needed to go home and change before the game anyway." He leaned down and took the little boy's hand.

"No!" James, Jr. cried and ran to his father. "I'll sit with Miss Smart. Please Daddy." He dissolved into a fresh torrent of tears and clung to his father's neck.

Jimmy reluctantly put his arms around him. "I'm mad at you, Jamie. You've made this morning miserable for me, and you've turned Uncle David into a nervous wreck." He pulled the child into his lap where he sat cross legged on the floor.

"I'm sorry." Jimmy looked up at Uncle Jeff. "Thank you. I got so caught up in the power struggle, I didn't think about reasoning with him."

I looked at Uncle Jeff. He was really smiling for the first time in a long time. I was glad the three of them were feeling so much better. I was still a mess. How could I inflict that little brat on Anna?

"Apologize to Mr. Landrum and Uncle David," Jimmy said. "You ruined their mornings too."

"I'm **sorry**," he said. He didn't sound sorry.

"Jamie, if you don't cooperate I'll take Mr. Landrum up on his offer. He can run you to the ballet studio. It's right on his way."

"It sure is." Uncle Jeff jingled his keys.

"I'm sorry, Mr. Landrum." He looked up this time with big round eyes like his father's. "I'm sorry, Uncle David. I'll sit with Miss Smart." He looked at me. I smiled. I couldn't help it.

"You'll be polite to her, won't you?" I said.

"I'll be polite." He opened his eyes a little wider, a little too wide, I thought. Jimmy and Uncle Jeff were both smiling triumphantly. I wasn't so sure.

✦

I pulled up next to the parking slot Jimmy had just pulled into, and Uncle Jeff pulled into the one next to me. We had gone our separate ways for about an hour before the game. I had quickly washed and dried my soccer uniform.

Uncle Jeff had gone home to change. Jimmy had taken James, Jr. home to get a sweater since a cool wind was blowing. The sun was hot though. It was a perfect day for soccer.

I looked around for Anna's car and spotted it at the other end of the parking lot. I pulled out the soccer balls I'd brought and two water bottles and hurried to the stands. I wanted to get there ahead of Jimmy and James, Jr. I didn't know if I should warn her or not, but I wanted to greet her first.

She was sitting on the first row of the bleachers all alone. Her tight black curls ruffled only slightly in the breeze. She was looking across the field to where our opponents were warming up. She turned to look my way as I approached and smiled. I was always amazed at how she could smile without really moving any muscles. It was like her face just flowed into a smile. Like some kind of special effect.

"Hey," I said. I leaned down, kissed her lightly on the lips and felt her stiffen. I pretended I didn't notice. "I hope you haven't been here long."

"Only a few minutes, where's the little guy?" She looked around me to where Jimmy and James, Jr. were coming across the grass. They were loaded with sweaters and water bottles and juice boxes.

"Here they come," I said. My stomach was fluttering. "He hasn't been in the nicest mood this morning. If he gives you any trouble just let Uncle Jeff know. He'll take care of it."

She looked up at me quickly. I wondered if she sensed my anxiety. "Don't worry, David. Believe me I know how to handle little boys. We'll be fine."

"Anna." Jimmy arrived beside us and took her hand. "It's nice to see you again. I'm glad you came to watch the game. I hope my performance is good. There's no question about David. He's the best. Did you know he won the title of best goal tender in Georgia on the high school level?"

I felt myself blush. "Jimmy, cut it out."

"I didn't know that." Anna glanced at me with a quizzical smile. "You never mentioned it."

"I hardly remember high school." I shifted nervously.

"This is James, Jr.," Jimmy said.

We all looked down at Jamie. He looked at the ground in front of him.

"Jamie, say hello to Miss Smart," Jimmy said.

"Hello." He didn't look up.

My heart started to pound, and I looked at Jimmy. He looked like he was about slap the kid. Oh please don't do that, I thought.

"Where do you want to sit, James?" Anna asked. "I don't have a problem with heights if you want to sit at the top, but if we sit down here we'll be closer to the field."

"I don't care," James, Jr. continued to look at the ground.

"Well, I'll choose then," she said. "We'll sit down here so we can be close to your dad, your uncle, and Mr. Landrum. Hello, Mr. Landrum," she said. I looked around to see Uncle Jeff approaching.

"Hello, Anna, it's nice to see you again. Please call me Jeff." He put his hand on James, Jr.'s shoulder. "Remember son." He leaned down to talk in the child's ear. "I'm just the assistant coach. I can leave any time if there's some place you need to go."

"I'm gonna sit with Miss Smart." James, Jr. hurried over to stand beside her. "I was thinking we'd go just a little higher," he said.

Anna looked at Uncle Jeff. She looked puzzled. Then she looked at me. I shrugged. The whistle blew indicating we had to get in our places to kick off. "Uncle Jeff will be right here, if you need any help," I said to her.

Anna smiled and followed James, Jr. up to the spot he chose in the bleachers. "James," I heard her say. "Call me Anna."

"Okay, Miss Anna," he sounded sulky.

"Drop the Miss. I hate it."

As I walked out to the goal I turned and looked up to where they were in the bleachers. Anna was talking, and Jamie was looking at her with an expression something close to awe.

I smiled and turned my attention to the game.

It was one of those boring soccer games. It's a low scoring sport, but if there's no scoring what's the point?

We broke for hydration at the half. Anna stayed in the stands. Jamie ran down to talk to his dad and me while we were wiping the sweat from our faces and drinking water. I waved to her and she waved back, but she didn't come down

We played most of the game with energetic drive to both goals. It was unusual to score against me. The goal tender of the other team was good too though. I wanted to blame it on the offence, but they were playing hard and smart. I could feel my anxiety rising as we neared the end of the second half with no score.

Anna would never want to come to another game. She'd be bored to tears. I glanced up to the stands where she sat with James, Jr. They were talking. They were both animated. I'd never seen Anna that animated. She was gesturing with her hands and Jamie was too.

The whistle blew, and I returned my focus to the field. The game moved toward the opposing goal and then back toward me. I stopped a ball that was heading for the top left corner. Our team got it on the rebound. I glanced up to the stands just as the small crowd jumped and cheered. Anna and James, Jr. were cheering with them. She held the child by the arm as he jumped up and down. Anna's other arm waving in the air.

I looked down the field. We'd scored a goal. The team was congratulating Jimmy. I was up. I had to defend us. There were only minutes left in the game. The score was one to nothing. The opposing team volleyed the ball down the field. They were good. It was getting close. I glance up to the stands. Anna and James, Jr. were standing, watching. They each had one forefinger pointed at me. Jamie's was laid across Anna's. Their hands were joined.

"Uuufff..." I gasped as the ball plowed into my middle. I tried to pull a breath but my lungs were lock. My whole body was locked. I fell to my knees on the grass and looked up to the stands. I couldn't breathe. Anna picked Jamie up, propped him on her hip, and ran down the bleachers. She didn't use the steps but jumped from bleacher to bleacher. She almost tossed James, Jr. into Uncle Jeff's arms. He was coming toward me too, at a less frantic pace. I smiled and fell forward onto my face.

"David, David!" I was looking at the ground. I could smell dirt. I'm sure I never lost consciousness because I could hear Anna's voice calling my name. It couldn't have been more than a few seconds after my face hit the ground that she got to me.

Something pulled on my shoulder and rolled me over. I looked up at the sky. It was blue and beautiful. Then I looked up at her face. There were tears in her eyes. She looked scared. Don't be afraid, Anna, I thought. But I couldn't say anything. The air still wasn't coming into my lungs. I'd had the breath knocked out of me before. I knew I just had to wait a minute.

"He's alright, Anna. He's just had the breath knocked out of him." I heard Uncle Jeff's confident voice come from somewhere over my shoulder. "Move over and let me have a look."

Shut up, Uncle Jeff, I thought. She's holding me in her arms. God, I wish I could talk. I closed my mouth and pulled slowly at the air through my nose. I made a wheezing sound as I drew it slowly into my lungs.

"Uncle David," Jamie's excited voice broke through my efforts. "That was great. We won. The last seconds ticked off while you stood on your knees with your mouth open. It was great. What a save."

I was aware of small feet leaving and landing on the ground in front of my face.

"I don't think I've ever seen you make a save that way, David." Jimmy was laughing. I took a deep breath through my nose and then another. Okay, I was breathing again. I put my hand to the left side of my rib cage. I was sure broken ribs hurt more than that, but they were definitely bruised.

"Take your time, kid." Uncle Jeff's voice was at my right ear. His hand was on my shoulder. The back of my head was nestled between Anna's small firm breast, and I could feel her sweet breath next to my left ear. Shut up, Uncle Jeff, I thought. Go away. I hoped I hadn't said it out loud.

"David, please say something," Anna whispered into my right ear. "You're scaring me."

I looked up into her dark eyes and smiled. "I'm..." I croaked. "I... just need ...a second."

"Did you hear what I said, Uncle David?" Jamie's voice piped. "We won. Me and Anna have a secret handshake. It brought you luck."

I took another deep breath and cleared my throat. I sat up slowly, instantly feeling the loss when I pulled out of Anna's arms. "It did ... Jamie ... good luck." I took another deep breath and looked around at the circle of heads above me, my team, my family, my friends, and Anna. I took another deep breath, rolled onto my knees and stood up. Anna moved in beside me and put her arm around my waist. I looked down at the top of her head. She was so small, but she was going to carry me back to the bench.

I sat down and took the bottle of water she handed me. I looked at Jimmy. "You said we won. I... I don't have to go back in."

"We have a goal tender on the bench," he laughed. "You still wouldn't have to go back in, but yes, we won. There were only seconds. The other team got the ball and dribbled it, fumbled, time ran out."

"And you were on your knees watching the whole thing, Uncle David." Jamie was standing still now. I looked at him. Anna stood behind him with her hand on his shoulder. "I can't believe you knew what was gonna happen."

I met Anna's eyes and smiled stupidly. She smiled back.

"Okay then." I stood up. "I guess it's time for us to go on back home and go to bed." Even I knew I was disoriented.

"No way, Uncle David, it's the middle of the day. Anna said we could go to the amusement park. I told her I couldn't go without Heather, and she said Heather could come too."

"James." Anna's smooth cultured voice answered. "Sometimes plans have to be changed. Uncle David isn't up to it today. We'll do it another day."

I looked up at Jamie expecting a protest. I encountered a resigned pout.

"I think the amusement park sounds great," I said. "And if we take Heather, your dad and mom can have a little time together. What time is it anyway?" I looked at Uncle Jeff.

"It's one o'clock, David. You should definitely eat something first, maybe lie down for a minute."

"We'll eat at the amusement park. I don't want to lie down." I stood, trying not to wince at the pain in my left side. I gathered my soccer balls, towels, and water bottles and looked at Jimmy. "You take Jamie home and pack anything in a bag you want him to take. We'll pick them both up in an hour."

"David..."

"We'll pick them up in an hour," I put my arm around Anna's shoulders. She put her arm around my waist. "You don't mind if we take them do you, Jimmy?"

"No. I mean, if you're sure. You took that soccer ball to the belly pretty hard."

"I'm fine."

"We'll be along, Jimmy," Anna said. "Make sure they have anything they need."

◊

"David, please just let me take you home," Anna said as she pulled into the parking lot of her apartment complex and parked beside my car. "I can't believe you insisted on driving your own car home to change and then coming to pick me up."

"I'm fine, Anna." I felt really foolish. When we'd left the soccer field, I'd insisted I wanted my own car. The field wasn't far from my apartment. I showered and changed, but when I got into the car to go to pick her up I realized I was really not comfortable driving. I drove to her apartment, admitted it to her, and she agreed to drive the kids to the amusement park. We argued again about whether I should go at all. I was determined, so I won.

"I'm glad you didn't talk me into staying home. I had a great time." I leaned across the seat and kissed her. She kissed me back for a minute. Then she pulled away and got out of the car.

I took the keys out of my pocket and turned to my car. "Thanks for coming today, Anna. I loved having you there." I fumbled to find the key to the car door.

"David," she said. "Why don't you come in for a little while? We'll have a glass of wine. If you don't want to drive home I can take you, or we'll call you a cab."

I looked at her standing beside me with her hand on my arm. "You want me to come into your apartment?"

"Yes, but be prepared. It's humble."

I followed her to the building, up the stairs, and into her apartment. It was actually very homey. It was a lot like mine as far as layout but it was an efficiency apartment. The kitchen was a small corner of the room. There was a bed at the far end and an easy chair with a matching foot stool next to the big window. The walls were covered with shelves full of books, no knick-knacks, just books.

"Sit down." Anna motioned to the chair. "I'll get us a glass of wine. Are you hungry?" She had already turned to the small kitchenette.

I sat down and looked out the window. The view was nice. It was a corner apartment that looked out onto the forest behind the complex.

"David." She stood in front of me with a glass of white wine. "If you're hungry I can make you a sandwich. I have ham, and of course, peanut butter and jelly."

I pulled my eyes from the view and looked at her. She was beautiful. "The hamburger and fries we had at four o'clock is still sitting at the bottom of my stomach," I said. I took the glass from her and looked back out the window. "I like the view."

"Yeah." She walked to the window and stood looking out. "I got a special deal on this apartment because of the dumpster outside the window."

I looked around and saw the dumpster in the corner of the parking lot. "I didn't even notice," I said.

"That's because of the way I've arranged the chair." She laughed and sipped her wine.

I looked around the room. "There's only one chair."

"I usually only need one," she said.

I put my glass of wine on the side table and stretched out my arms. "We can both sit in it."

"David." She turned her back to me to look out the window. "I can't give you what you want. Please don't push me too hard. I don't want you to get hurt. I don't want to get hurt."

I dropped my arms. "I just want you," I said. "I just want you to sit with me for a minute. I promise I won't push anymore."

She looked at me then moved silently into my lap, into my arms. My ribs protested. I shifted her small weight a little and they were fine. We sat silently for I don't know how long. I sipped my wine. She sipped hers. I felt her relax. I relaxed and yawned.

"You're tired, David," she said. "Let me call you a cab to take you home."

"What time is it anyway," I asked, remembering roller coasters, pirate rides, soccer games, breakfast fights. "I can't even remember getting up this morning."

"It's ten o'clock," she said.

"You're kidding." I laughed weakly. "I haven't been asleep before one am since I was ten years old. I haven't even taken my midnight walk yet."

"You don't sleep much?" she asked. "Anthony had a problem sleeping. Come and lie down, David." She stood up and pulled me to the bed.

"As soon as I lie down, Anna, I'll wake up. I won't be able to sleep."

"I know."

She pulled me to the bed and helped me take off my shirt and pants. My heart started to beat. I couldn't believe it. She was seducing me. We crawled under the covers. I was only vaguely aware that she was still dressed. I tried to kiss her, but she turned me around so that my back was to her front.

"Anna, I want…"

"Shhhh..." she said. "You want to sleep." She was behind me again. The back of my head was nestled between her small warm breasts again, and she was softly stroking my temples.

"Sleep, David," she whispered into my right ear, and I slept.

Sometime during the night we made love. We never spoke. I don't think I ever came fully awake, but the memory is solid, not clear, nothing I can put into words, but it's permanent. It never fades. It never will. I felt her soft hands on my body and my hands on hers. Our mouths came together, and my big, clumsy body fit to her small, graceful one like two matched pieces of a puzzle. We were perfect. When we had both found release she lay with her head on my chest. I was vaguely aware that she was naked. I don't remember her taking off her clothes. All of her skin was as soft as her face. As I drifted off again I knew; I had to make this work.

CHAPTER THIRTEEN

I looked up at the sound of a knock on my office door. I had come in early and put a full breakfast spread in the break room. I talked with a few of my co-workers over coffee and muffins. Then I came in to my office to get to work.

"Come on in," I said cheerfully. I was feeling pretty good about life. The door opened only a crack, and Anna's pretty face peered around it.

"Can I see you for just a second, David? I won't take up much of your time."

"Sweetheart, you can have all my time." I smiled at her as she came into the room and closed the door behind her. I stretched my arms out to her. "Come here and sit in my lap."

"I'm not going to sit in your lap at work, David." She scowled, but she didn't look really mad. "We've talked about this."

"I was kidding." I rocked my chair forward and put my elbows on the desk as she sat down across from me. "What can I do for you?"

"I wanted to show you the clothing tag that Mark in design worked up for us. She put a piece of paper with a drawing on it on the desk and pushed it across to me."

I turned the page around so that it was right side up and studied it. "It's good, but I want your name bigger. The Second Half Magazine logo swamps it. You're the designer. People need to know that."

I looked across the desk at her. She was grinning widely. I had that feeling of familiarity again. I just couldn't quite grasp what was familiar about her smile.

"The clothing line belongs to Second Half, David."

"Yes it does, but your work needs to be recognized." I picked up the drawing and put it in my desk organizer. "I'll talk to Mark about it myself. You're too humble." I raised my hand when I saw her about to object. "I'll clear it with Jane. Don't worry."

"I'm so excited about signing the contract this afternoon. I can't believe I'm actually going to have a clothing line in a nationwide department store chain. You're a marketing genius." She smiled again. "I told Anthony about it and he's so proud. He's told all of his girlfriends to buy my clothes."

"He should be proud. We do great things together, Anna." I reached across the desk and took one of her hands. "In the office and out."

"David..."

"I know," I said quickly. "You don't like for me to talk about it. Come to lunch with me today," I said. "I was thinking of going to the food court at the mall."

"Not today, David. I brought my lunch." She stood up. "But I was thinking of coming to your apartment this evening for dinner. I haven't had one of your gourmet meals for a while."

My heart started to pound. She never stayed the night at my place. She let me stay at hers from time to time though. It was late July. We'd been seeing each other romantically since the night of the soccer game. It was still touch and go. She insisted she couldn't give me what I deserved in a partner. I insisted she could.

The phone on my desk rang, interrupting my thoughts. I watched her move toward the door then looked at the caller ID. It was Lenny. He called me from time to time. I didn't answer any calls I got from a correctional institution.

"I'm just going to let it go to voice mail." I stood and walked with her to the door. "Around 6:00?" I said.

"I was thinking 7:00 so that I can go home and change."

"You look wonderful."

"I'll want a shower."

"You can take one at my house."

"David, you're terrible," she said. She was laughing. "I'll see you at seven."

I closed the door behind her as the phone started to ring again. Lenny, I thought, stop calling me. I'm not going to talk to you. But when I looked at the caller ID, it was Uncle Jeff.

I picked up the phone. "David Landrum."

"David, I'm leaving in a few days for my trip. I wondered if we could have lunch today. I wanted to ask you something, and in case I don't see you before I go, I want to say goodbye."

"Sure." He sounded grumpy like he always did these days. "Do you want to meet me here at the magazine?"

"No," he snapped. "I was thinking we'd meet at the mall."

"Okay." I said goodbye and hung up the phone. I dialed up my voice mail. A recording said "A call from a correctional institution from *Lenny.*" I heard his voice and my throat ached. "Will you accept the charges?" No, I thought, as I erased the message. I did have an errand to run at the mall though. I'd ordered Lenny's latest book, and the book store had called to tell me it was in.

I pulled my keys out of the drawer and left the office.

The mall was crowded. In the heat of Georgia July, a lot of people used the air conditioned mall as a place to walk. I didn't have to meet Uncle Jeff for an hour at the restaurant. He didn't want to go to the food court. It was too loud. I wondered what he wanted to talk to me about.

I headed straight to the bookstore. I figured I'd look at the competition in the magazine stand, then pick up the book, then meet Uncle Jeff. After I had picked out a couple of magazines, I went to the customer service counter and got the book. I turned it over in my hand. He did his own cover design. I flipped through the pages. He did his own interior too. I guess he didn't have a lot else to do in prison.

There was a picture of him on the back cover. My throat got that swelling feeling again, and I turned the book back around. I looked up at the sound of angry voices and a child crying. There was some kind of commotion going on in the children's book department.

A very pregnant woman with shaggy dark hair and a bruise on her shoulder was struggling with a stocky boy who looked to be about three years old. She was holding him by the arm pit, and he was kicking her legs and swinging his small fists at her. My heart skipped. It was Teresa. I hadn't seen her in years, but I knew her instantly.

I left the book and the magazines on the counter and hurried over to her. "Don't treat mother that way, young man," I said to the child. He stopped his tantrum for a moment to look up at me. I guess my height frightened him because for a second he hid behind Teresa's legs.

"Sir, I can handle my own child," she said, then recognized me. "Oh, David, I didn't realize it was you."

When the child realized I wasn't a threat, he resumed his tirade and landed a fist firmly on his mother's swollen belly. He turned to swing at me. I caught his small fist in my large hand and held it so that he couldn't get away.

"Don't hurt him, David," Teresa said.

I looked at her, shocked. "Of course I won't hurt him, Teresa." I looked back at the boy. "What's your name, young man?"

"Dexter." He spat the name at me like venom.

"Oh." I straightened up but didn't let go of the child's fist. "Junior…" I smiled at Teresa. She looked tired. She smiled back and nodded. "You shouldn't hit your mother's tummy," I said. "She has a baby brother or sister in there for you."

"I don't want a brother or sister." The child pouted. "And I don't want to read any stupid books."

"Books aren't stupid, Dexter. Only people can be stupid."

He looked at me, clearly not understanding. I laughed. I wasn't sure I understood either. "Let go of my hand," he whined.

"Only if you promise not to hit your mother anymore."

"I'll hit her if she tries to tell me what to do." His tone was defiant.

"Well, I guess I can't let go of your hand then, can I?"

His eyes widened and he looked at his mother for help. "Mommy…"

"David, you're scaring him."

I released the child's hand, and he moved behind his mother. Then he was distracted by something on the bookshelf, and he moved away. I looked down at Teresa. She was my age but she looked ten years older. Her face was drawn. Her once shining, dark hair hung limp and dull.

"I can see finger prints in this bruise on your shoulder." I touched her arm. "Why do you let this go on, Teresa?"

"I have to David." She looked up at me. "You don't understand."

"No, I don't."

"Ma'am," A store clerk approached her with Dexter, Jr. by the hand. "I need for you to control your child. He's disturbing the other customers."

Teresa took the child by the hand and pulled him out of the store. She didn't look back. I watched her leave the store then returned to the counter to collect my purchases.

"Hey David." Uncle Jeff slid into the booth opposite me. "I hope you haven't been waiting long."

I had arrived at the restaurant early and gotten a table. I sat down. Ordered a glass of water and started to read Lenny's book.

"Is that Lenwood's latest book?" Uncle Jeff asked. "I have to admit he writes well."

"He's a brilliant man, Uncle Jeff." I closed the book and put it aside. "You know, I don't know how I'd have gotten through those years in prison without him. It came as a complete shock to me that he couldn't live in the outside world."

"It's a puzzle," Uncle Jeff said. "It's hard for you, isn't it? You look sad."

"The thing with Lenny is hard for me. I'm handling it. What's really got me down now is that I ran into Teresa at the bookstore." I rubbed my eyes. "Uncle Jeff, she's my age, but she looks like an old hag. She's hugely pregnant, and she's got this horrible little brat. She had bruises on her arm that were clearly finger prints, and the child is beating on her too. I can't believe I ever thought I knew her. I wanted to marry her and she prefers this?"

"David, I know it's not my place, but I hear things. She isn't completely innocent. It takes two."

"She cheats on him, doesn't she?"

"It seems that way."

"That doesn't justify violence."

"No, it doesn't, but it does play a part in the dynamics of the thing."

I took a drink of my water and ran my hand through my hair. "There's nothing I can do," I said.

"No, there's nothing you can do."

The waitress came and took our orders. "What did you want to talk to me about?" I asked.

"I was wondering if you'd stay at my house while I'm gone. I leave in just a few days, and I'm starting to feel panicky about leaving the place. It's close enough to your apartment that you could go back and forth."

"Sure, that might be fun," I said.

"You wouldn't have to stay every night. I just thought two months is a long time for a house to be empty."

I looked at him. He looked tired and stressed. "I can't believe you'll be gone for two months. I'll miss you."

"I doubt that, with as grumpy as I've been lately. Hopefully I'll come back feeling refreshed." He smiled weakly. "Are you sure you don't want me to leave Gabe with you? He's good company."

"No." I looked down as the waitress put down my plate. "He's better off with Victoria. She has other pets, and I work long hours."

I got home at five thirty. I left the office a little early so I could get dinner started. I planned to make my favorite spaghetti sauce with stuffed mushrooms and a spinach timbale. I put Lenny's book into a drawer in my desk. I didn't want Anna to see it. While she was healing we had talked about him a good bit. We both felt betrayed by him. We were both healing. But lately we'd focused on each other. I didn't want to rock the boat.

I had a few minutes before I had to start cooking so I sat at the computer and typed Lenwood Jones into the search engine. The results revealed a web site. It was amazing what you could do from prison. I double clicked on it and the site came up.

"Well, will you look at that," I said to myself. There was a picture of Lenny holding the hand of a female prison guard. Under the picture was written. "To anyone who cares, I'm getting married. Meet my bride, Carmen Varone."

I added the web site to my favorites, then logged off and shut down the computer. I'd add those pictures to his album later. I went into the bathroom and got into the shower. "I hope it works for him," I said into the cool spray of the water. "I hope he can make a life for himself."

The phone was ringing when I got out of the shower. I looked at the caller ID. It was Darla.

"Hello."

"Hey, David," she said. It was nice to hear her voice. We hadn't talked for a while.

"What's up?" I asked.

"I wanted to give you my big news. I don't think I'm going to have to come crawling back home after all. I got a part in a play. It's a small part. I think it's best for me to start small."

"That's great, P.H. Tell me about it." I glanced at my watch. I really needed to get dressed.

"I'll tell you about it later. I don't have much time and I wanted to talk to you about your grand passion."

"My grand passion?"

"Yeah, Meryl says you're in love."

"What a grape vine, is there no privacy among friends?" I said, but I was smiling. It was nice to know they cared enough to talk about me. And it was nice to know they'd all accepted Anna.

"So tell me about her, David."

"She's beautiful and she's brilliant. I think about her all the time. I miss her when she's not with me, and I can't wait to see her when we get together. She should be here any minute now. She's coming for dinner."

"Wow, you are in love. I'm happy for you."

"How are you doing up there in New York. Have you found your white knight yet?"

"No, but I'm going out tonight with a new guy. He's one of the actors in the play I'm in. He's really cute, good looking, and funny. I'm hopeful."

There was a knock at my front door. I looked down at the towel wrapped around my waist. "Darla," I said. "I've got to go. Anna's here. Can I call you later?"

"Sure, call me tomorrow. I'll be at home during the day. I'm taking a day off from the department store to learn my lines. Have a nice evening, David."

I hung up the phone and answered the door dressed in a towel.

✦

"I had a letter from Uncle Jeff," I said as I served myself some of my mom's potato salad. It was one thing she did well, potato salad, cole slaw, and burgers. It was late September and still warm enough to eat on the back deck. I was over for my weekly dinner with her.

"I've had a few letters from him since he's been gone. He's becoming very poetic in his dotage."

"If he's in his dotage, so are you." I took a bite of my burger and chewed thoughtfully. "He says he isn't coming back for another three weeks. He's met a woman down there, and he's going to visit her parents in Ecuador. You don't suppose he'll stay down there do you?"

"I didn't have the impression it was a romantic relationship," Mom said. "I guess you'd miss him if he did stay down there."

"Wouldn't you?" I looked up, surprised. I thought of these two people as my family. It always surprised me when they didn't think of each other as family.

"Of course I would, honey. But if he found happiness down there, I'd want him to do what's right for him." She put her hand on my arm. "I'm sorry, David. I didn't mean to upset you."

"It's okay." I looked down at my plate. I'd lost my appetite. I suddenly missed my uncle painfully. "I guess I'm just used to having him there for me whenever I need him."

"Do you need him now?" Mom looked concerned.

"No." I laughed. "I was just thinking, just in case." I took another bite of my burger. My appetite was returning.

"Anyway, I doubt that he'd stay down there even if it is a romantic relationship. I think he'd bring her here." She laughed as she started to clear the table. "Can you see him giving up his precious nursery? He loves that place."

"Yeah, but I didn't think he'd sell forty percent of it and take on a partner either. I sure never thought he'd get himself a dog, and did you know he bought a horse that he keeps at a stable about an hour north of here?"

"All of that was surprising. I'm going in to get the desert," she said. "I got ice cream sandwiches. Do you think it's too cool to eat them outside?"

"Yeah, I'll come in with you." I picked up the last of the dishes from the table and followed her into the house. "I'll tell you what though. I don't want to stay in that house by myself anymore. It's just not the same there without him."

"You should have kept Gabe." She stroked Caramel's head. The big fluffy dog lay on the rug beside the back door. "David, don't you think it's time for you to get another dog?"

"No Mom." I sat down and took a bite of my ice cream sandwich.

"So tell me how things are going with Anna?"

I smiled. "Thanks for changing the subject."

"Anna is a subject that always makes you smile."

"Yeah, I'm crazy in love with her."

"I know you are. How does she feel about you?"

I licked the melting ice cream from the edges of the cookie and thought about her question. "I think she loves me back. She certainly acts like she does."

"But she doesn't tell you she loves you."

"She's said it reluctantly a few times." I popped the last of my desert into my mouth and smiled, knowing that I had ice cream all over my face.

Mom laughed and handed me a napkin.

"She always tells me that she can't give me what I want in a partner. But all I want is her. I'm determined to convince her of that." I wiped my mouth and put my elbows on the table. I leaned toward my mom. "There is some dark secret in her past that makes her afraid to love anyone. I'm never going to push her to tell me what it is. I think that will make her trust me. Then she'll be free to love me."

"How long do you think that will take?"

"I don't know. I don't care. I'm not in a hurry." I stood up to leave. "If I hurry I'll lose her. If I lose her I'll die."

"David." She stopped me before I got to the front door. "Maybe Anna could come to dinner with you some time. I'd like to get to know her a little bit."

"You've met her at the magazine." I was mad at her for pushing until I turned and looked into her eyes. They were filled with worry and I softened my tone. "I was thinking when Uncle Jeff gets back. Maybe we could all go out to dinner. You know …neutral ground."

"That would be nice, honey." I kissed her on the cheek and left.

I was standing at the mailbox at Uncle Jeff's house when his big truck pulled into the driveway. He smiled and waved at me as he drove by. He didn't stop until he'd opened the garage and pulled in. I ran up the driveway and wrapped him in a bear hug as he came out of the truck.

"Whoa," he laughed. "What a greeting." His arms were wrapped around me. For a second I felt like a little boy again. Even though I'd topped him by a full inch of height, he always seemed bigger than life to me.

"I really missed you, Uncle Jeff." I stepped back. I felt a little awkward about my unbridled show of affection. "I was starting to think you weren't coming back."

"I missed you too, son." He walked around to the bed of the truck. It was covered with the camper top he'd bought when he got Gabe. "Look what I've got." He let down the gate and pulled out a large plastic container with holes punched in the top. He opened it and a small turtle stuck its head up and blinked its eyes.

"It's a sea turtle," Uncle Jeff said when I looked confused. "His name is Ned."

"When I was on the island I watched a bunch of them hatch. They have a project that goes on down there every year to protect them." He picked up the small turtle and looked at it. I'd never seen Uncle Jeff's eyes so soft. I could see the affection in them. It startled me. I felt a stab of jealousy. Jealous of a turtle, I thought. Idiot!

"This one was too small to make it to the sea. I wasn't going to let the raccoons have him." He placed the little creature back into the water in the box. "Help me unload some of this stuff, will you, David?" He picked up the box with the turtle in it and headed toward the house.

I pulled a big box I assumed was his mountain bike out and carried it in behind him. "I was worried that you'd found the love of your life on your bike ride, and you wouldn't want to come home."

He looked at me and studied my face. I put the box down in the living room and shuffled uncomfortably.

"I mean..." I was rambling. "You said you were going to Ecuador to meet some woman's parents."

"Oh that. No she was just a friend I made on the bike trip. She fell in love with another friend of mine. No romance for me, as usual." He sounded sad. "Let's go get the rest of my stuff."

"Well," I said as I followed him out to the truck. "I don't mind if you fall in love. I just want you to stay here."

He turned and looked at me again. "I'm not going anywhere, David. I won't leave you like your father did."

So that's what's bothering me, I thought. "I wasn't worried about that," I said, feeling my ears burn as I lied. "I'm a grown man. I don't think about things like that anymore."

"Good." He slapped me on the shoulder. "Grab that last bag. Do you want to ride with me over to Vic's to pick up Gabe? I can't wait to see him."

"No, I think I'll go on home. I'm cooking dinner for Anna tonight, at her place. I want to change before I go."

"So you're still seeing the dress designer. Good for you, David."

Uncle Jeff looked rested. He wasn't as grumpy as he'd been before, but something was still wrong. I couldn't quite describe it. He was anxious about something. I mentioned it to my mom, but she wasn't as tuned in to him as I was. She hadn't really noticed anything.

He'd only been back a day or two when I decided I'd talk to my boss about it. She was a good friend of his. In fact, he came to the magazine to see her as much as he did to see me. I knocked on her office door first thing on an early morning.

"Come in," she called. I opened the door and stepped into the office. I was always a little bit awed at the sight of her. She had married shortly after starting the magazine changing her name. Jane Fox was a striking woman. Her hair was snow white. She wore it long. She was tall, even sitting behind a desk, and she always looked completely in control.

"Good morning, David." She leaned back. "What's that you've got in your hand?"

"What? Oh." I looked down at the steaming mug in my hand. I'd forgotten I was holding it. "I brought you some of my pumpkin latte." I put the mug on the coaster on the desk.

"How delightful." She lifted the mug to her shapely lips and sipped. "In keeping with the fall season, I love it." She smiled. I sat down stupidly in the chair across from her. "You look troubled. What's bothering you?"

I don't think troubled is exactly the way I looked. I was thinking more like moronic. "I'm concerned about Uncle Jeff. He's certainly rested from his trip and all, but something is bothering him," I said. "I know you and he are close friends. I wondered if you knew anything."

"Hmmm..." She sipped her coffee again. "Actually, I do, but I'm not at liberty to talk to you about it. Your Uncle will have to do that."

"Oh... you're right ... I don't know why I thought..." I was stammering.

"I'm glad you came to me, David. Don't feel bad. It was astute of you to notice your uncle's distress. I love how close you and Jeff are." She stood and came around the desk to stand beside me with her hand on my shoulder. I took a deep breath and began to relax. "I can't talk to you about the details of your uncle's problem, but I can assure that he's alright. He isn't sick or anything, not physically anyway." She laughed. I smiled up at her. "And he will work it all out."

"Good, I'm glad. I think I'll go over and talk to him tonight."

"I think that's a great idea. It's always better if you talk to the people you care about. It eases the stress of any situation."

The phone was ringing when I returned to my office. It was the front desk, Amanda, our secretary.

"What's up Amanda?" I asked. "I was just up there a second ago."

"Your father is here."

I sat down hard in my desk chair. "You mean my uncle don't you?"

"No, David. It's a Brian Landrum. He says he's your father."

"I'll be right there." I hung up the phone and hurried down the hall to the lobby. What could be wrong? Had something happened to Uncle Jeff or Mom? Why would my dad be here?

"What's going on, Dad?" I burst through the door to the lobby. Amanda looked startled. Dad was looking out the glass door. He turned around. There were circles under his eyes. He looked tired. He looked old. Oh my God, I thought, it's him. Something is wrong with him. "Are you alright?" I demanded.

"I'm alright, David." He smiled weakly. "I just wanted to see you. It's been so long. It's been too long. Could we talk in your office?"

"Sure, I'm sorry." I took a deep breath and felt my pounding heart begin to slow. "I... I guess I over reacted." I stepped back and gestured for him to follow me down the hall to my office.

"I don't know why you would over react." He sounded so sad. "It's only been what, eight years?"

"Something like that," I said as I closed the door to my office behind us. My dad reached out and grabbed me around the shoulders. He buried his face in my neck and started to shake. Was he crying?

"Dad!" I put my arms around him and once again noticed the softness of his flesh, the sagging of his shoulders. "What's wrong?" I was really worried now. "Talk to me." I pushed him slightly away and looked at his face. There were tears in his eyes. I guided him to a chair and sat down in one beside him.

"All I could think about all the way here, David, was putting my arms around you. I wish I could go back twenty five years. I wish I could do it all over again. I'd do it better this time."

"You did fine, Dad." It sounded lame even to me.

"You're being kind." He wiped his eyes with the back of his hand and smiled at me.

"You're scaring me to death, Dad." I laughed. "Tell me you don't have some terminal illness or anything like that."

He looked down at his hands. "I guess life is a terminal illness."

"Uncle Jeff said the same thing last summer. I guess twins really do have some kind of telepathic connection," I said. "So does that mean you don't have cancer or anything like that?"

"I'm not sick, David. But thanks for caring. I don't know why you do."

"You're my dad." I shrugged. "It's unconditional."

He looked up and studied my face for a minute. "Yeah, it's unconditional." He stood and walked to the window to look out at the parking lot. "I'm here for a year, David. I've taken a sabbatical from my law practice. My young partners are thrilled, and I still have a good income from it. I may stay forever. I don't know right now. Sharon and I are separated. The kids have both gone on to their next stages of life." He turned and looked at me again. "David, can you and I try to work on a relationship? I want to be a part of your life. I know it's late but better late than never, right?"

I took a deep breath. "All I ever wanted in my life was your love," I said. "I had these two fantastic parents, and all I wanted was you."

"I'm sorry, son."

"You're ... sorry." I repeated and walked over to the window to look out. "Uncle Jeff is here," I said, and Dad turned to look out the window again. We watched as my uncle got out of his truck and stalked toward the front of the building. He looked determined about something. I wondered what.

"Still a farm boy," Dad laughed. "I've got amends to make with him too."

"Grampa used to call him a glorified farmer."

"I know. That's where I got it." He turned and looked at me. "I love you, David. I love my brother. I still have feelings for your mother too. I've just buried all of that for so many years it's overwhelming me now. Please give me another chance."

"There will be issues."

"We can handle issues."

"We can handle most issues, Dad, but you need to know one thing. You hurt Mom again like you did before. There will be no relationship for us. I'm the man of her family now, and I've been playing that part for a long time."

He smiled and I was reminded of Uncle Jeff. "I'm proud of you, son," he said. "Come on. Let's go out to the lobby and confront your uncle."

◎

"David." It was Uncle Jeff on the phone. I was sitting at my desk again contemplating a lunch without Anna. She was working through, so I figured I would too. She wouldn't have dinner with me either. I felt a pout coming on. She had some phone conference after hours. What kind of phone conference could she have?

"Hey Uncle Jeff, what's up?"

"Let's have lunch. I've got something to tell you."

"Okay, do you want to meet at the mall like last time?"

"No, I'll come by to pick you up at the magazine."

"I hope this isn't going to be more family dramatics. I think I've had about all I can take right now." I was picturing the scene in the lobby with my dad and my uncle. At first I thought they were going to kill each other. Then I thought they were both going to cry.

He laughed. "I don't think this will be too upsetting. Your dad's arrival on the scene has been somewhat traumatic though, hasn't it?"

"To say the least."

"To say the least," Uncle Jeff laughed. "I love the way you talk." He sounded really happy for a change. Maybe his news was good.

"I have an appointment at eleven. It may run a little past noon. Is that alright?"

"Not a problem."

◎

"I'm sorry I'm late, Uncle Jeff. Are you ready to go?" I entered the lobby and stopped short. Uncle Jeff was looking fondly at our pregnant secretary. I remembered back to the day of his confrontation with my dad. When we'd come into the lobby they'd been talking quietly and seriously. Hmmm...

"All set," he said and moved to the door.

I pulled on my jacket and followed him to his truck.

"I was really impressed with your idea to introduce Anna to all three of your parents at dinner the other night." He laughed as we sat down in a booth at a restaurant around the corner from the office.

"Yeah, whose idea was that anyway?" I laughed too. Uncle Jeff was definitely feeling better. His usual sense of humor was coming back, and it was contagious.

"I hate to tell you, David, but it was yours. I tried to talk you out of it, so did Anna." He sobered. "I hope it didn't do any damage to your relationship with her."

"I don't think so. She's a pretty good sport."

"So how are things going with your dad?" I looked at my uncle and saw the conflict of feelings on his face.

"Okay, I feel kind of bad for him. His life is all turned upside down." I leaned back in the booth. "But like I've said before, you're the man that raised me. You'll always come first with me."

"Thanks for saying that, David. I know I was fishing. I'm jealous as hell and I need reassurance." He laughed again and I felt warm inside.

"I'll give you reassurance as many times as I need to, but that's not what you wanted to tell me is it?"

"No..." He leaned back and looked away from me. "What I wanted to tell you is that you were right. I have found the love of my life, but I didn't find her in South America." He looked back at me and leaned forward with his elbows on the table. "I'm in love with Amanda."

"And you're the father of her baby. I figured that out about fifteen minutes ago when I saw the two of you talking in the lobby."

"I'm the father." Was that pride I saw on his face?

"She announced to the whole magazine when she found out she was pregnant. She told us in a meeting, just like a piece of business on the agenda. We all thought she was inseminated."

"I'm the father," he repeated. "And there are two of them, twins, girls."

"Well, what are you going to do about it?" I don't know why I was feeling angry. He just seemed a little too casual about this.

He held up his hand in a defensive gesture. "Calm down, David. You sound like her father or something."

"Well, someone has to look out for her. She's alone in this world you know."

"She's not alone anymore, David. Like I said, I'm in love with her. Even if she wasn't carrying my babies I'd want to marry her. The problem is she doesn't want to marry me. I asked her. She said no."

"Hmmm..." I relaxed. "I've never thought of her as stupid before."

He looked up and smiled. "Thanks for saying that. You're very reassuring today." He took a deep breath. We ordered our lunch and gave the waiter the menus.

"I'm not giving up though. She says she won't object to me being a part of the girl's lives. So if it takes the rest of my life, I'll convince her to marry me."

"Good for you. You know she and Anna are friends, the closest thing to a friendship that either one of them will allow, that is."

"So you and I are kind of working on the same thing. Imagine that."

"So, how did this happen with Amanda without me even suspecting?" I asked. Now that I looked back at his grouchiness of last summer, some things were starting to fall into place.

"She's a very private person and I respected that. I wanted to pursue a formal relationship last summer. She didn't. I have to say that when I left here in August, my heart was thoroughly broken."

"I'm sorry," I said and picked up my sandwich to eat. I munched thoughtfully for a minute. He did too.

"So ... Uncle Jeff..." I said seriously. "It was just the part about getting pregnant that you didn't understand about the safe sex lesson."

He choked on his sandwich, tapped his chest and took a drink of water.

"I can explain it to you if you want. Lord knows you've explained it to me enough times."

"Don't be a smart ass, David." He cleared his throat. He was laughing.

My uncle married Amanda Green on Christmas day. It was a small ceremony but very moving. My eyes burned with tears I refused to shed as I watched him say his vows to her. He looked happier than I'd ever seen him. My mother was there, my dad, Aunt Jeanne and Uncle Bill.

I looked down at Anna's soft black curls. She stood at my side. She hadn't thought she should come to the wedding, but I insisted. She had let out one of her brides maid dresses to fit a very pregnant Amanda. It was a beautiful shade of green that looked perfect on her.

I just kept seeing Anna in a wedding gown. We were getting close to the point where I would feel comfortable asking her. Even if she said no, I would persist. It paid off for Uncle Jeff, didn't it?

I guess she felt my eyes on her because she looked up at me and smiled. Just like the first time, I didn't even think about kissing her. I just touched my lips to hers, even as Uncle Jeff touched his lips to Amanda's.

There was a knock on my office door and I looked at the clock. It was 6:00 pm. I glanced out the window. It was dark outside. It was late January. The month had been busy. We were planning our annual fashion show and I'd had to make a couple of marketing trips around the country to sign contracts. The magazine was growing and my work was exciting.

"Come on in," I called and reached into my drawer for the keys to my car. "Hello, sweetheart," I said as Anna came into the room and closed the door behind her. I reached for her but she dodged me.

"I need to talk to you, David."

"Let's get dinner. I don't want to cook tonight. We could just go to that new Mexican place near your apartment."

"No, David, please sit down. I have something to tell you."

"Are you alright?" I looked closely at her face. It was set in a lack of expression I'd seen before. "Is Anthony alright?"

"Anthony is fine. I'm fine. David, please sit down."

I sat in the chair across from my desk. She sat in the one next to it.

"David," she said. "I just gave Jane my notice. I'm leaving the magazine in one month."

"You're leaving the magazine?"

"Yes," she said firmly. "I've found an agency that will represent me. I'm starting my own line of clothing. This one will bear my name, not Second Half Magazine."

"That's great, Anna," I laughed, but I had an uneasy feeling. "That's even more reason to go out to dinner. We'll celebrate, but not at a Mexican place. Let's get steak, good steak."

"David." She looked away from me. "I'm going to New York. It's where I'll need to be. That's where the agency is."

"You're going to New York." Why was I repeating everything she said? "How long will you be gone?"

"Forever, David. I'm moving up there. I'm sorry."

"You're sorry." I did it again.

"I'm sorry. I can't continue in this relationship, David. It isn't your fault. It's mine."

"I'll go with you." I could hear the panic in my voice.

She looked up and smiled that familiar smile. It only lasted a minute. Then she looked serious again. "I knew you'd say that, but no, David. There is really no place in my life for you. I'm sorry."

"You're sorry. Anna, I can market you. Look how well we've done together. Come on, you can't just leave. I love you."

"I can leave, David, and I'm going to. I care about you too, but I've told you all along that I can't be what you want in a partner, what you deserve."

"All I want is you."

"And you and I want different things out of life. I see how much you enjoy Jimmy's children. David, I don't ever want to have children."

"I don't need children. Anna, all I need is you. I'll get my fill of kids with Jimmy's, and now Uncle Jeff is having twins."

"And you're so excited about it you can't sit still." She stood. "No, David, I'm going to New York. If you follow me I won't see you. So don't bother. It's over. I'm sorry if you're hurt. I really am."

"How can you just leave me like this? I guess you really never did love me. You said you did. Not very often, but you did say it. Were you lying?"

"I don't lie. I do love you. I love you enough to leave you so that you can find someone who wants the same things you do. I hope you'll believe that some day." She opened the door and she was gone.

The phone on my desk rang. I looked at the caller ID. It was my dad. I sure didn't want to talk to him. I'd just been abandoned again. The story of my life, I thought.

I left the office in a daze. I wasn't aware of the cold or that I held my jacket in my hand instead of wearing it in thirty five degree weather.

I didn't know where I was going until I got there. I was at Amanda's house. Uncle Jeff had moved in there after they were married. His house was for sale.

He wasn't there. I talked to Amanda for a few minutes. Then I lost control.

I could count on one hand the number of times in my life I'd cried, but these tears would not be denied. Then Uncle Jeff was there. His strong arms were around me, and I knew I wouldn't die from this. I wanted to, but I wouldn't.

CHAPTER FOURTEEN

Two things stand out about that winter, the birth of my little cousins and the backpacking trip on Cumberland Island that I took with my dad.

Besides those two things, I went through the winter in a daze. The month I had to work with Anna before she left was agony.

The annual fashion show in early March went off without a hitch even without Anna. That's strange because I planned it and arranged it, but I don't remember how.

"I told you when you called last night I wouldn't have any breakfast for you," I said as I opened the door to my apartment. Jimmy stood on my doorstep with two steaming take out coffees and a bag in his hand.

"I brought breakfast." He pushed past me and set the bag and coffees down on the table. "You won't even have to wash dishes. I have plastic stuff." He leaned back. "Man," he said. "You look as bad as you sounded over the intercom when I buzzed from the gate."

"You're so uplifting." I sat down at the table. I was fully aware of my ragged t-shirt and boxer shorts. I also knew I had three days of beard growth. It was Monday morning. I hadn't shaved on the weekend. I hadn't even gone out once, so I didn't need to shave. I sipped at my coffee through the hole in the top of the cup.

"It's 7:00 am. Shouldn't you at least be showered and shaved. What time do you have to be at work?"

"I don't punch a time clock, Jimmy," I said as I started to rummage through the bag. "I'm management, remember?"

"You asshole!" He walked to the door. "I think I'll leave. I was trying to be a supportive friend, but I'm not sure you even deserve one."

I looked up startled as he put his hand on the door knob. "Wait, Jimmy, I didn't mean that. I am an asshole." What had made me attack him like that? "Please don't go."

"Are you sure you want to sit at the table with a lowly HVAC technician?" He looked sulky.

"I doubt you want to sit at the table with a starchy buffoon."

He scowled and took a deep breath.

"Please, don't go. I really do need a friend right now. I'm not doing so hot." I watched the expression on his face soften. He came over to the table and sat down.

"You really hurt my feelings when you said that," he pouted. "If it hadn't been for you, I wouldn't even have made it this far. I thought you were proud of me."

"I am, Jimmy, and you really did it on your own. You're happy with what you do, aren't you?" I took the breakfast sandwiches out of the bag and handed one of them to him.

"Yeah, I really am. I go to so many different jobs all week that I never get board."

"Good." We both dug into our sandwich and ate in silence for a while.

"Are you sleeping at all?" Jimmy finally asked.

"No."

"Not even for an hour or two."

"No."

"What do you do all night, David?"

"This." I got up and went to the bookshelf. I pulled out my latest album and handed it to him. It was of Anna and me. I had pictures of us at the soccer field, the amusement park, and other places we'd been together. I had articles that had been written about her clothing designs, tickets to the Circ de' Soleil, pictures of the fashion show.

"This is nice." Jimmy looked across the room at the bookshelf. "Are those all albums you've made?"

"Yep."

"And that's what you do all night?"

"Yep."

"I guess if you were smoking pot, you'd be sleeping."

I gave him an expressionless stare.

"You never answer that question."

"It doesn't deserve an answer." I got up and took the trash into the kitchen.

"David, I'm sorry about what happened with Anna."

"It's no big deal."

"It is too a big deal." He came around the counter and put his hand on my shoulder. "You won't heal until you grieve for the loss of the relationship. We've talked about this before."

"Since when did you become such an expert on grief?"

"I'm not an expert. I just know that this kind of hurt doesn't just go away. You have to work through it."

"You've never had your heart broken, Jimmy. Anna's the second woman who's dumped me. Then of course, there was my dad."

"I've had my heart broken, and yes, my dad is still around, but I've always been a disappointment to him. You have to grieve that stuff too."

"Your dad thinks you're great." I turned to look at him. I hated to admit it, but it felt good to have company in my pain. "Who broke your heart?"

"Darla."

"Really, you and Darla dated?"

"No, we didn't have to."

"I'm sorry, Jimmy. I knew you were attracted to her. I didn't know you loved her."

"I loved her. I still do, but I worked through the pain of her rejection, and I'm happier with Meryl than I could ever have been with Darla."

"She never told me that you two had been involved."

"She never knew."

I laughed but Jimmy didn't. "I'm sorry."

"I'm okay, David, because I worked through it. You aren't okay. Take a good look in the mirror when you go into the bathroom to get ready for work. You need to stop acting like it doesn't hurt and just feel the pain for a while. That's the only way you'll ever get over this." He looked at his watch. "I have to go." He put on his jacket and went to the door.

"Thanks for coming by, Jimmy. Thanks for the breakfast."

"David..." It was Uncle Jeff's voice on the phone. It was Sunday evening at about eight thirty, the first day of March. "I'm a dad." No wonder he sounded so excited.

"The twins are here?" I stood up and stretched. I'd been working on my computer all day. My back was stiff.

"Yeah, you know they discovered a heart problem in one of them just before they were born. She just got out of surgery. She did great. She's going to be alright."

"That's great! Can I come by to see them? Can I come to see you and Amanda?"

"Tomorrow, Manda's asleep, and I'm stretched out in this weird chair that folds out into a bed. It's been such a big day. I haven't had time to call anyone. I just wanted to tell you before I go to sleep. I'm going to call Jane too. Maybe you two can come tomorrow morning."

"Okay, I'll get in touch with her. Uncle Jeff…"

"Yeah."

"Congratulations. I'm really happy for you. What are their names?"

"Evelyn and Alice," he said. "Alice is the one that had surgery. You'll have to see her through the nursery window, but Evelyn is here with us. You can hold her and everything."

"That's great," I said. "I can't wait." I hung up the phone. He sounded so happy. I sat down at the computer and opened a new file. It would be another long night for me, but I had a new album to start. I typed the document name in: Evelyn and Alice. I hit save and started to search the web for the history and meaning of their names.

"Hello, David," I heard Jane's voice behind me as I stood at the hospital nursery window looking at my little cousin. I was reluctant to turn around. I'd seen the circles under my eyes that morning when I shaved and got dressed to come to the hospital.

"Hey, Jane," I glanced sideways at her. If she noticed my eyes she didn't let on. "That's Alice, she had surgery yesterday. Looks pretty good, doesn't she."

"She's beautiful," Jane said. "Have you been in to see Jeff and Amanda and Evelyn yet?"

"No, I wanted to get a look at Alice first," I said. "I have the strongest urge to call them my sisters, but they're my cousins."

"Those are some confusing feelings." She linked her arm through mine and we walked down the hall to the hospital room. "I'm sure you'll work it out though."

We got to the room and read the names on the sign. Jane tapped on the door and we went inside.

"David, Jane, look at my baby girl." Uncle Jeff's face was lit like a Christmas tree. "Did you see Alice?" He held a small bundle in the crook of his arm. Amanda sat in the bed looking just as radiant as Uncle Jeff did.

Aunt Jeanne was there. She stood next to Uncle Jeff. "Hello, David," she said. "Come and meet your sissy." I laughed. My great aunt

Jeanne was such a southern lady. "Evelyn," she crooned. "This is your bubba."

"We saw Alice and she's beautiful." Jane stretched her arms toward the baby and Uncle Jeff handed her the bundle. "David, I think bubba and sissy are the perfect solution to your problem. You don't have to call them your sisters or your cousins. They're your sissies and you're their bubba." She looked down into the sleeping baby's face and smiled.

"That is a good solution," I smiled at Aunt Jeanne and she looked at me. I could see the concern on her face. She didn't hide it like Jane did. She was worried about me. "I'm fine, Aunt Jeanne," I said before she had a chance to comment.

She bit her lip. Then she kissed me on the cheek. "I need to go, honey. Come to dinner next weekend, David. It's been too long since we've spent time together."

"Aunt Jeanne …"

"I won't take no for an answer. I'll call to remind you." She kissed Amanda's cheek then Uncle Jeff's and left the room.

"Here, David," Jane handed me the baby. "Hold your little sis."

I took the tiny bundle and looked down into the little pink face. Every feature was so small. It was like a miniature face. The little pink lips and bump of a nose were so soft looking. I ached to squeeze her but didn't dare. She opened her eyes and started to whimper.

"Amanda," I said looking at the baby's mother. "What should I do?"

"I don't know, David. I've never done this before." She held out her arms and I handed her the baby. I turned just in time to see Jane struggling to hold my uncle up. His head was rolled forward, and he had gone limp.

"Help me, David," she said. "The big guy is going down."

I caught him and lowered him gently to the floor.

"Are you sure you're alright?" Mom asked Uncle Jeff for about the fourth time.

"I'm fine. I made it through the deliveries, no problem. I just wish I hadn't looked at that mirror that one time."

We were having dinner at my mom's house that night. Mom had come to the hospital and insisted that Uncle Jeff come to dinner. She said Amanda needed a break. I have to admit, Amanda looked relieved when we left the room with Uncle Jeff reluctantly in tow.

"I just can't believe you went into the delivery room and didn't watch the birth of your children," Dad said. I was amazed at how easily the four of us sat around Mom's table. It was like we'd been doing it all along.

"I just wanted to be with her," Uncle Jeff said. "I'm a little bit squeamish about blood and stuff like that."

"I'm sure Amanda would have understood if you wanted to wait in the lobby," I said.

"Oh, that's where she wanted me to wait, but I just knew I'd go crazy out there. I begged her to let me come into the delivery room."

"But you didn't want to watch the birth?" I laughed.

"Nope, wish I hadn't looked at all." He rubbed his eyes.

"I watched the birth of all three of my children," Dad said.

I looked up. That included me. Mom was smiling at him. She still loved him. It was written all over her glowing face. She always had. She always would. My heart flopped against my ribs.

"I remember," she said. "You didn't take your eyes off that mirror. You held my hand. I'm not sure who was squeezing harder."

"I think it was you," he laughed. "In fact, see that dent." He held out his hand and they both laughed.

"Well, I know Manda squeezed the hardest," Uncle Jeff said, oblivious to the touching scene in front of him. "My hands are so sore I won't be able to work on the landscape team for a month."

"Maybe you can get some of that dirt out from under your finger nails during that time," Dad teased.

"Talk about squeamish." Uncle Jeff stuck his big weathered hand under Dad's nose. "I clean my fingernails every night, and I wear gloves. There is no dirt under my finger nails."

"Yuck." Dad pushed Uncle Jeff's hand away and grimaced. They were bantering like kids. Suddenly I was very uncomfortable.

"What's for desert?" I stood and took my plate and Mom's over to the sink. "...ice cream sandwiches?"

"No, apple pie, can't you smell it?" Mom got up and went to the oven.

"You baked a pie?" I teased. I wanted to feel close to her, closer to her than Dad.

"Yes I did." She laughed and kissed my cheek. "Right after I took it out of the package and thawed it out."

"You still don't cook?" Dad joined us at the sink with his and Uncle Jeff's plates. "I had to do all the cooking when we were married." He laughed as he rinsed the dishes.

"She makes great tuna casserole," I said. I could hear the sulk in my voice. I sat down at the table. Uncle Jeff put his hand on my shoulder and squeezed. I looked at him. He was smiling at me. How did he always know what I was feeling? I looked at the pie Mom put down in front of me. I didn't feel like eating pie.

"Am I jealous, P. H.?" I was talking to Darla on the phone. It was two weeks since the twins were born. I didn't see much of Uncle Jeff. He was spending most of his time at home with his new family.

"It would be understandable if you were, David. But I doubt that your feelings are that clear. This has to be very confusing for you."

"Yeah, confusing, I'm just one raw nerve. I walk around with a lump in my throat all the time. I don't like Dad being so close to Uncle Jeff or to Mom. But I still just crave his attention like I did when I was a kid."

"And your heart is broken at the same time."

"My heart is broken." I rubbed my eyes. It was ten o'clock at night. Soon the restlessness would start. I'd take my midnight walk, but I still wouldn't be able to sleep. I'd work on my computer on Darla's album. She was in another long running play and doing pretty well.

"I'm really happy about your success, P. H." I changed the subject.

"I am too, but I'm not going to let you stop talking for just another minute. I know what you're thinking, David."

"How do you know what I'm thinking?"

"You've said it to me before, and I don't believe it's true. You were not just a rebound for the dress designer. I believe she really loved you. I went to her first fashion show here in New York, the one where the agency introduced her new line of cloths. I got tickets through the theatre group. I could see sadness in her eyes, David. Her heart is broken too."

"She's sad about a lot of things, but I'm not one of them. She was in love with Lenny. I just came along when she needed someone. I think I knew that all along. I've tried to convince myself that I'm just humiliated. But the truth is I really love her. I'll never love anyone like I do her."

"Then go after her."

"No," I said firmly.

There was silence on the line. "David, I'm sorry. You know I love you too. You're my best friend."

"I don't know what I'd do without you, P. H."

"I'm not a poop head," she laughed.

"I know."

"Do you remember when we did that surf boarding, David?" Dad asked. We were sitting on the ferry crossing the sound to Cumberland Island. We were going on a backpacking trip for a week, just the two of us. We would hike the interior of the island in five to six mile segments, camp at sites along the way. Then we would come back on the beach. The island was only fifteen miles long, so it would fit nicely into a week.

"Yeah, I remember." I was as excited about this trip as I'd been about the one we took when I was ten years old. That made me furious. I'd been grouchy as a bear on the whole trip to the coast. I'm not sure Dad noticed.

"That was a great week. It's etched in my memory like a statue in stone."

I looked sideways at him. He was smiling and looking out to sea. My heart pounded at his happy face. Maybe it had meant something to him to be with me.

"You sure are poetic today." I sounded surly. "I'm amazed how much you and Uncle Jeff are alike. He's gotten all poetic in his middle age too."

"Well, we are identical twins." He was oblivious to my foul mood. "Look, David." He pointed at the back of the boat. The sea gulls were gathering in the breeze above the wake. "I guess they think we're a shrimper or a fishing boat." He laughed and looked straight at me.

I looked away at the gulls. "I guess so." I tried to smile. I'm pretty sure I didn't succeed.

The boat slowed down and we approached the dock. There were people in forestry uniforms on the dock to greet us and to help dock the boat. I got up to throw out one of the lines. We gathered our gear and climbed out of the boat. We went with the other campers, packers, and day visitors to the welcome center to hear their safety session and to gather our campsite passes.

"Hope I make it all the way," Dad said as we pulled off our packs at the first site. It had only been a four mile hike. We planned to do six and a half the next day.

"You'll make it," I said. I pulled my bottle of water out of my pack and handed it to him. "You kept up just fine. Don't forget we drove down from Atlanta this morning. It's been a long day."

He drank deeply, swallowed, and drank again. "It was a beautiful day. I can't remember enjoying a day so much, even though you were furious with me about something. Are you ready to tell me what it is?"

"I'm not mad at you." I pulled the tent out of my pack and started connecting the poles. "Get on the other side of this with me. It's easier to set up if you have two people." I tossed him the rolled up tent. We had hiked in relative silence. We only talked to comment on the landscape or to point out wildlife to each other. My tension had started to ease at about the last mile.

It had started to get dark about an hour ago. It was almost completely dark now. Luckily there was a full moon so we could still see without the lantern. We set up the tent. Again, we only talked when he had a question or I had an instruction. Then he set up the stove and prepared to cook our dinner while I started a campfire.

"They said we had to hang our food from a tree or the raccoons would get it," Dad said after we'd eaten. "I think we'll need the lantern for this."

"I'll get it going," I said and set to work. We bagged all the food we had in our packs and hung it in a tree a good distance from camp. Then we sat down cross legged in front of the fire.

"It's cold. The day was warm, but when the sun goes down it's cool."

"It's only the beginning of April," I said.

"I thought it would be warmer down here at the coast."

"It usually is. This is just a cool year."

"David," he said. "Please tell me what's bothering you."

I looked at him across the dying fire. "Mom never stopped loving you," I said.

He was quiet. He seemed to be studying my face, even though I knew he couldn't really see me in the dark with the fire dwindling. "I never stopped loving her either," he finally said.

"Why did you leave her then?"

"I'm pretty sure I can't explain it to you, David."

"Was it a mistake, something you wish you hadn't done?" I couldn't believe how much I wanted him to say yes.

"No, it was something I had to do, for myself. I had to go with Sharon. She was my life's dream. I'd always loved her. We'd known each other since childhood. We dated all the way through school. She was away at college in New England when I met your mother. She had written me that she was seeing someone else. I didn't think she was coming back."

"So you don't regret leaving us for her even with the way things are now?"

"I don't regret it for myself. I had a very good marriage with her for a long time. I have two beautiful children with her. No, I don't regret it for myself. I regret that you and your mother had to be hurt. I regret that I didn't spend more time with you while you were growing up, but I don't regret my life with Sharon."

I swallowed. My throat was swelling and my eyes ached. I took a deep breath to steady myself. "How could you have loved Mom if Sharon was your life's dream?"

"I don't know but I did. I still do." I could see him smile in the shadows. "I'll never forget the first time I saw her. There was this dance club in mid-town. I'd gone there with some friends. I was just getting ready to graduate from college, home for spring break. I'd already been accepted to law school.

The door opened and everyone turned to look. You know, we wanted to see if any new girls were showing up. We'd already tried to dance with a few of the one's that were there, but they all had dates.

In walks this gorgeous Amazon. She was with a group of girls, but I didn't even see them. Your mother was a sight to behold." He looked toward the darkened forest. He seemed lost in time for a moment. Then he snapped back to me. "She still is. Anyway, none of the guys with me dared ask her to dance. They were all half a head shorter than her." He got that dreamy look on his face again. "Of course, I was always, Giganto." He laughed. "I asked her to dance. We started seeing each other and the rest is history."

"Yeah," I said. "I don't understand."

"Neither do I." He looked down. "I never stopped loving her." He continued after a few minutes of silence. "That's one of the reasons I didn't come around more. It hurt so much to see her, to see what I'd done to her. I loved you, David, but it was too painful."

"It was too painful." I remembered the years of craving his love, craving his attention.

"I hid from it. I hid from the pain, and of course, Sharon encouraged that. I was weak."

I took a drink of water hoping to wash down the lump in my throat. "What about now. She'd take you back, no questions, if you asked her to."

"I know she would." I could feel the sadness in his voice.

"Why don't you ask?"

"I might. It's too soon to tell. We're going to take it slow this time. The first time was like a whirlwind."

"Suppose Sharon changes her mind and wants you back?"

"That won't happen. She already has a new boyfriend. I wouldn't be surprised if they get married as soon as the divorce is final."

"What if it doesn't work?"

"I'm pretty sure my marriage with Sharon is over, David."

"You're pretty sure."

"I can't give you a guarantee, David, if that's what you're looking for."

"You mean you still can't make a commitment to Mom."

"I've made a commitment to you. I'll never cut you out of my life again. What's between your mother and me is between your mother and me."

I took another deep breath. The lump in my throat was gone. My eyes were dry. I suddenly had a desperate need to move. I stood up. "I'm going for a walk before we turn in," I said.

"David, you can't walk around alone in the jungle in the middle of the night."

"Oh yes I can. Don't forget, I'm a grown man. I'll be fine." I hurried to the road. It was only yards from our campsite. I could see it in the moonlight. If I stayed on the road I wouldn't get lost.

"Mom," I called as I came in through the front door of the townhouse.

"I'm up here, David," she called from upstairs. "I'll be down in just a minute. Fix yourself something to drink if you want."

"Okay." I went into the kitchen and opened the refrigerator. There was lemonade and beer. I looked in the door and pulled out a Coke.

"That's caffeinated." Mom came into the room behind me.

"I can handle it, Mom. I've never had another seizure you know." I knew I sounded snappy. "I'm sorry."

"Don't worry, David. I know you're sensitive about that. I can't help but worry about you though. No matter how old you get, you're still my baby."

"Yeah." I sat down at the table and watched her pour herself a glass of wine.

"Your dad and I are going dancing." She sat down across from me and sipped. "We used to love to go dancing. We still move pretty well together."

"He told me you met at a dance club," I said. "We talked a little on the backpacking trip."

"He told me you did," she smiled. She looked so happy. I'm not sure I'd ever seen her look so happy. It made me furious. "I'm glad you and your dad are getting this chance to get to know each other."

"We could have gotten to know each other a long time ago if he'd wanted to." I could hear the anger in my voice. Mom's face fell. Her smile turned to a frown. She looked sad. I hated that I had done that to her. That made me even madder.

"I hoped you wouldn't have to deal with much hostility in this new relationship you have with him. I guess that was hoping for too much."

I put my hand on hers. "I'll probably have to deal with some, but I shouldn't put it on you. I'm sorry."

"I can stand it, sweetheart." Her smile was back, not as brilliant, but still warm. "Did you have a good time other than that? Your dad said that he kept up pretty well. He was relieved about that. I don't think he believed he would. He hasn't kept up with his conditioning as well as your Uncle Jeff has."

"Uncle Jeff had me around," I laughed. "I kept him in shape."

"That's right." She squeezed my hand. "Was there something you wanted to talk to me about?"

I took a deep breath. "Yeah." I stood and walked to the window. Caramel came to the back door, and I let the big floppy dog in. "Hey, ladybug." I stroked her furry head. "The first night on the trail I talked to dad about his relationship with you. I didn't like his response to my questions."

"Did he tell you it was none of your business?" I could hear the edge in her voice.

"Is that what you're telling me?"

"Yes." She raised her chin in defiance.

I laughed. "Mom, I'm the man of your family. I have been for a long time. It's my job to protect you."

"David, you can't know how many times I have regretted saying that to you. You were just a baby. I didn't think you understood. You were only two years old. Can you actually remember it?"

"Yes, I remember it. I don't remember the incident clearly, but I've always known inside that I was the man of the family. I've always needed to take care of you."

"You were a baby, David. I didn't expect you to take the weight of this family on your shoulders. I didn't expect you to think you had to take care of me."

"I'm a man now."

"You're a man, but you aren't responsible for me. I can take care of myself."

"I asked him what he would do if Sharon changed her mind and wanted him back. He couldn't tell me. He doesn't know, Mom. You need to know that before you get too involved with him again."

"Oh David." She took a deep breath and stood up. She walked to where I stood by the back door looking out the window. She kissed my cheek. "Of course, he doesn't know. He didn't know he would leave me for her the first time either."

"Why are you still seeing him?"

"Because I love him, I've loved him since the first time we danced together. I'll love him until the day I die."

"He might hurt you again."

"I'll survive it if he does. I survived it before. But maybe he won't. Maybe he'll stay this time. I doubt she'll come back anyway. It sounds to me like their marriage is over."

"And that's alright with you, not knowing what he would do."

"That's alright with me." She put her hand on my shoulder. "David, I have the opportunity to spend time with the only man I've ever loved, the only one I ever will love. It will be wonderful if we grow old together now. But even if we only have a little while and he leaves me again. Even if I have to let him go and I grow old alone, I'll be glad I took this time with him. I'd hate to grow old alone knowing I had the opportunity, even for a little while, and I didn't take it because I was afraid of the pain of losing him."

"God, Mom, I wish I could find someone who loved me like that."

She put her arms around me. "Honey, you're still hurting over Anna. That's why this upsets you so much. I'm alright. I know the chance I'm taking and I'm willing to take it." She let go of me and went to the sink to rinse her glass and put it in the dishwasher. "Don't worry about me, David. Heal yourself. Deal with your own grief."

The sound of the front door opening stopped the conversation. "Hello, beautiful." My dad's voice sounded down the hall. "Hey, David," he said as he came into the kitchen. "I saw your car out front." He looked from my face to Mom's. "Am I interrupting something?"

"No," I said. "I was just leaving." I tapped my dad on the shoulder as I went by. "I'll see you on Sunday for dinner, Mom."

"I love you, David." She called as the front door closed behind me.

"So, I was thinking we'd go around the end of May," Uncle Jeff said. We'd had dinner together. It was a Friday afternoon and he'd come by the office to check on me. He insisted on taking me out to eat. It was clear that people were worrying about me. Jane, my boss, had commented on how tired I looked a couple of times. Even Uncle Jeff's new wife, our secretary, had told me I looked like I wasn't getting enough sleep. That's a laugh. I wasn't getting any sleep.

"I don't think you've heard a word I've said."

"What?" I looked across the booth at my uncle.

"David, do you want to go to the Appalachian Trial this summer? We'll be crossing the half way mark. I think the girls will be old enough by then that Amanda will be able to handle them by herself. We could take a long weekend."

His voice was kind of echoing in my head. I didn't feel quite real. "Uhhh, sure," I said. "I can't believe we're half way. That's more than a thousand miles."

"We've been hiking this Trail for over fifteen years, David. I can't believe we're not further along."

"I guess so."

"You okay, son?"

"I'm good," I said looking down at my untouched plate. "I'm just too tired to eat."

"I thought you said the doctor gave you some sleeping pills." His concerned expression swam somewhere before my eyes. "Are you still not sleeping?"

"Yes, I'm sleeping. The pills are helping," I lied. "I just haven't caught up yet. I need to sleep a lot to catch up." I smiled and pushed the food on my plate around with my fork. "I think I would like to go home now though. I'm feeling pretty tired. Maybe I could get to bed early for a change."

"Okay, we'll talk about the trip another time." He signaled the waiter for the check.

I yawned and looked at the clock. It was three o'clock in the morning. I winced. I'd lied to Uncle Jeff when I told him I was sleeping. I usually didn't lie to Uncle Jeff. I'd taken a sleeping pill about two hours ago, but again, it didn't work. Sometimes they made me drowsy, and I could actually sleep for an hour or so. But lately they weren't even doing that.

In fact, I think they made me more depressed. I shut down my computer. I'd just finished the album of Anna and me. There was an article in a fashion magazine about her that I'd put in as a dramatic end to that episode in my life. I planned to follow her career, but that would be another album.

I went to the refrigerator, pulled out a beer and popped the top. I had to go to work in just a few hours. Maybe the combination of the alcohol and the sleeping pill would make me sleep.

"Maybe I should take another pill," I said out loud. "That one didn't do anything. I opened the bottle and downed a pill with the beer. I took off my shoes and pants and got into the bed. I sat there for a few minutes with the lights off then took off my shirt. That was the last coherent memory I have of that night.

I have a flash of getting up to get another beer and vaguely of opening the pill bottle again. Then the sleepiness moved in. At first I was glad. Then I was panicked. That's all I remember.

Apparently I called Uncle Jeff in the middle of the night, because I woke up the next morning in the hospital. My throat was sore. My stomach was raw, and there was a nurse with a clipboard asking me questions.

Mostly they wanted to know if it was a suicide attempt. I said no, over and over again.

"It was an accident," I said. "Uncle Jeff." I looked at him where he stood in the corner of the hospital room. "You have to believe me. It was an accident. I just couldn't sleep. I wasn't thinking clearly."

"I believe you." He came over to the side of the bed and took my hand. "But it doesn't matter what I think. The hospital has to protect itself. It looks like a suicide attempt, and they have to send you to a facility where they can watch you for three days. It's the law, son."

"I can't do that, Uncle Jeff. I don't have time. I have to get to work." I looked at the clock on the wall in the room. "Shit!" I sat up in the bed. "I'm late."

"Your job will wait three days, sir," the nurse said. She put the pen on the clipboard and left the room.

"You don't have a choice, David," Uncle Jeff said. "Maybe you'll get some rest. You need a break."

I closed my eyes and lay back on the pillow.

"David," Uncle Jeff said, almost in a whisper. "Was it a suicide attempt?"

"No." I didn't open my eyes. "It was not!" Would I have minded dying, I thought. No! I would not!

CHAPTER FIFTEEN

When I was twenty six years old I met my brother.

"David." Amanda's voice sounded over the phone on my desk. "Jimmy Parnell is here to see you. Can I send him back?"

"Sure, send him." I smiled. This was the first time I'd seen him since I got out of the hospital. I braced myself. I had no idea how he would react or even if he knew about it. I had asked my parents, all three of them, to keep it quiet.

"David!" Jimmy flew across the room at me and wrapped me in a bear hug. "Thank God you're alright."

"You know what happened, right," I said, resigned.

"Darla told me."

"I asked her not to."

"She tried but I knew something was going on. You know how she is if she's pressed."

I laughed. "I didn't really think she could keep her mouth shut. It wasn't a suicide attempt, Jimmy."

"I'm not sure I believe you. I've always thought you had that tendency."

"I know," I said. "So are we going to have to discuss this? Is that why you're here?" I sat down and motioned for him to sit too.

"No." Jimmy looked nervous. "I need your help, David."

"You need my help?" I leaned forward. "What's wrong? Do you have to take another test?"

"No, it's James, Jr."

"Is everything alright, Jimmy? Is he sick or something?" My heart was thumping.

"He's just like me, David. The school system has already put a learning disabled tag on him. They take him out of class and don't help him at all, but the rest of the kids think of him as a retard. He's just like me and I hate myself for it."

"Jimmy," I took a deep breath and relaxed. "Being like you is a good thing. You're the best man I know. Jamie will be just fine."

"Heather is perfect. Not too smart but smart enough. She's not like you. She won't become neurotic about her grades. She isn't that smart. She's very main stream. Everything is easy for her. But Jamie struggles with everything. I try to remember all the ways you helped me, but I can't reach him. It's too emotional for me."

"I love being neurotic." I laughed. "Let me work with him." I hated to admit it, but for the first time since Anna left I felt excited, energized.

"That's what I was hoping you'd say." Jimmy looked relieved. "He doesn't have a friend in school like I had. In fact he's having a problem making friends. I'm going to coach his soccer team. I'm hoping that will make a difference, but he's not the most athletic kid either."

"Maybe soccer isn't the way then."

"I don't know what else to do."

"How old is he now? I hate to have to ask. I've been a little preoccupied with self pity lately." I laughed.

"He's about to turn seven. I was eight years old before they labeled me. I guess they pick up on these things earlier these days."

"When can we get started?" My mind was churning with ideas. I needed to sit down and organize them. First I would need to try to remember how I'd worked with Jimmy. Then I had to get a feel for where James, Jr. was struggling. I could do this. I could help this kid.

"Meryl was hoping you could come to dinner this Saturday night. Darla is in town and she'll be there. I was hoping maybe you could take a few minutes alone with Jamie then. I haven't said anything to him about it. I wanted to check with you first."

"You know I want to help if I can."

"I hoped so. Also, Meryl has hired tutors. They've been pretty useless, and Jamie hates them. I don't know how to approach him without causing a problem between the two of you."

"I'm not going to be a tutor. I'm going to be a friend."

✣

"David," Darla ran to me when I came through Meryl and Jimmy's front door on Saturday night. She wrapped her arms around my waist and buried her face in my chest. I leaned down and kissed the top of her head. This was our traditional greeting. I loved it.

"I'm so glad to see your face, David. I wasn't going to be comfortable until I did. Are you feeling better?"

I winced. The whole hospital thing was embarrassing. "I feel better when I'm not feeling humiliated."

"I won't say another word about it. You look great. Are you sleeping now?"

"I sleep a few hours a night, without sleeping pills. I won't even have them in my house anymore."

"Good." She wrapped her arm around my waist, and we walked into the living room together.

"You will drink beer though, won't you?" Jimmy said from behind a small wet bar in the corner.

"I'd rather have a glass of wine if you have one. I have to admit I've been a little off beer since the incident."

"Sure." He poured me a glass and handed it to me.

James, Jr. sat in the corner at a child size table working on a jigsaw puzzle. He looked up at me. He was obviously unhappy. In fact he looked angry.

"What's up, Jamie?" I asked.

"I hate tutors," he said and looked back down at his puzzle. I looked at Jimmy.

"Meryl told him you were going to tutor him. I guess I forgot to mention that might not be a good idea."

"I'm not going to tutor you, Jamie. Your dad and I just thought I might be able to help you with the problems you're having in school." I thought about the notebook full of ideas I'd decided to leave in the car. I was glad I hadn't brought it in.

"Jamie," I said feeling cautious. "You've never hated me before. Why should this make a difference?"

"I hate tutors. I hate school." The child jumped to his feet and wiped furiously at his tears with the back of his hand. "I don't ever want to go back to school. I'm not going back!" He shouted and ran out of the room.

I started to go after him, but Darla stopped me with a hand on my arm. "Leave him alone for a minute, David. Let him stew on it for a while."

"Maybe I won't be able to reach him," I said. I looked at Jimmy and Meryl. Meryl looked hurt. Jimmy looked angry.

"Of course you'll reach him," Darla said. "You just have to remember that it's not the same as when you helped Jimmy. You two were in the same setting. Jimmy wanted your help. To James Jr. you're bigger, older, and in the position of authority. You have to work your way to his level."

"How the hell do I do that?"

"You'll think of a way."

"Uncle David," Heather called from another corner of the room. "Come over here and look at the picture I'm painting for art class."

I looked at Jimmy.

"Go ahead," he said. "Let Jamie cool off for a minute."

When dinner was served Meryl went into James, Jr.'s room and brought him out. He didn't look tear stained like I expected him to. He sat down to dinner with us and studiously avoided my eyes.

"Well, David," Darla broke the silence. "I'm crawling back home. Did Meryl tell you?"

Her statement effectively pulled my attention away from Jamie. "What do you mean? I thought you were doing well on stage in New York."

"I puke before every performance. I'm tired of throwing up," she said. She dished herself a large serving of potato salad and handed the bowl to me.

I looked at the salad and put the bowl down on the table.

"I'm sorry. I guess that wasn't a very appetizing thing to say." Darla laughed.

I hadn't heard her laugh in a while. I'd forgotten what it sounded like. I used to think it sounded like ice tinkling in a glass or wind chimes. I smiled and served myself some salad. "You don't think it's worth it? I mean acting on stage."

"Definitely not, besides, I only get small parts, and try as I might, I just can't seem to get anything better. I have to work at Dad's department store to make ends meet. Everything is so expensive in New York." She took a piece of chicken and handed me the platter. "I'm tired of the whole thing. I'm going to secretarial school. I start in the fall."

"Secretarial school..." I laughed.

"Here in Atlanta..."

"Well," I looked at James Jr. toying with his food but not eating. "It will be nice to have you back in town. I wouldn't call it crawling back, P. H. I'd call it making a career change."

"That's easy for you to say Mr. big shot executive."

I laughed and nudged her with my elbow. "Jamie," I addressed the sulking boy. "Are you excited about your dad coaching your soccer team?"

"I'm not very good at soccer."

"Nobody is until they learn how to play. Is this your first year?"

"I played at the beginning of the year. I can't run as fast as the other kids."

"How about the goal, you always told me you wanted to play goal tender."

"His mind wanders," Jimmy said. I saw James Jr. look at him out of the corner of his eye.

This kid feels defeated at age seven, I thought. How do you deal with that? I wished I was his age. He'd listen to me then, like his father had. I needed to get him alone. We needed to talk. Maybe I could get an idea of what to do for him if we did.

"Did your parents tell you I was going to pick you up tomorrow afternoon, Jamie? They have something to do with Heather, and I thought it might be fun for you and me to take a hike together. Have you been to the trial on the Chattahoochee River?"

"I've been to a bunch of trails on the river." He was on to me. I could tell.

"Where are we going?" Heather asked her parents.

I looked across the table at Meryl and Jimmy's blank faces and raised an eyebrow.

"We're going to the aquarium. Remember, Jamie didn't want to go and you did."

"I went there with my class," James, Jr. said. He sounded happier. "It was boring."

"I thought you said we couldn't afford it right now," Heather said.

"We scraped around and found the money," Meryl improvised. "It'll be a great day."

"Thanks, David." Jimmy was smiling. He looked relieved. I didn't feel relieved. What now?

◊

The buzzer from my front gate sounded at 10:00 am the next morning. I pressed the button for the intercom and said hello.

"David," it was Dad's voice. "Can I come in? I have someone with me that I'd like you to meet."

"Sure," I pressed the button to open the gate. "Give me a minute when you get to the door. I just got out of the shower and I need to put on some clothes."

"We'll wait," Dad sounded happy.

I pulled on a clean pair of jeans and a polo shirt, pulled on some socks and running shoes. I ran a brush through my hair and went to the door, tucking in my shirt as I went. I opened it to my dad and a young man with curly blond hair. He was shorter than my dad and me, and he had a more delicate frame. I knew immediately who it was.

"David," Dad was beaming. "This is your brother Drew, Andrew actually, but I've always called him Drew." I looked at my brother and then at Dad. He was proud of both of us.

I held out my hand. Drew was smiling too. He looked a little shy but happy to see me. "It's nice to finally meet you, Drew," I said.

"You're huge!" he said taking my hand and shaking it energetically. "I'm short like my mother. I always wished I was big like Dad."

"You aren't short," I said, surprised at the comfort I felt with a brother I'd never seen except in pictures, pictures of a little boy. "What are you, about six one?"

"Six feet even." He came into my apartment and looked around. "This is a pretty cool apartment. My roommate at school and I are going to try to get an apartment next year."

"It's okay. I'm going to give it up when my lease comes up though. I'm moving into Uncle Jeff's wife's house. That sounds so strange. I guess I should call her my aunt now. Have you met Uncle Jeff?"

"Yeah, the first day I got here."

"How long have you been here?" I asked. I had only been out of the hospital a couple of days. I had an uneasy feeling he knew about it.

"I've been here five days. I have to go back tomorrow. I wanted to meet you before, but you were in the nut house. What was it like in there with all the kooks?"

I looked at my Dad. He shuffled his feet and looked away. "I'm sorry, David. I had to explain why you couldn't meet him right away."

"I guess you might as well know what a misfit your brother is," I said. I went behind the counter to my kitchen and poured some coffee. "Can I get you some coffee? The muffins will be out in a second. Do you want some scrambled eggs?"

"I'll have some coffee," Drew said.

"Is it decaff?" Dad asked.

"No, it's real coffee." I poured three cups and put them on the counter. I put the cream and sugar down and pulled three spoons out of the drawer.

"I don't know, Drew. Do you think you should have caffeine?"

"Seriously, Dad, do I ask your permission to drink coffee when I'm at school?"

"No, I guess not." Dad sat down on a stool and pulled one of the mugs toward him.

"Does he treat you like that?" Drew asked.

"No," I turned to take the muffins out of the oven. "He doesn't."

"I have curly blond hair like my mom too." Drew chattered. "I always wished I had straight brown hair like Dad. You have it. You're eyes are brown though. Dad's are blue."

"Actually," I set the muffins down on the counter and got out plates and butter. "Other than those few differences, I'm surprised how much you and I look alike." I guess this was what Drew wanted to hear because he smiled broadly at me.

"Yeah," he said. "We do. Don't you think so Dad?"

"You both look beautiful to me. I wish your sister was here, but there'll be time enough for that."

I smiled at him and he smiled back. "We were hoping we could spend the afternoon with you, David," Dad said. "Drew has to go back tomorrow. His classes start on Tuesday."

"I'm sorry. I have something I have to do this afternoon. I'd cancel it, but it's a delicate situation. I don't think it would be a good idea to back out."

"Could you join us for dinner at least? I'd really like for you to spend some time with your brother. Drew says he wants to spend the summer here with me this year, but that's a couple of months away."

"Sure, dinner sounds good. Drew spending the summer with us sounds good too. Maybe you guys could join Uncle Jeff and me when we go to the Appalachian Trail this year. We're passing the half way mark."

"Have you hiked it to the half way mark?" Drew was impressed.

"We have, but it's taken a long time. We started when I was eight years old."

"Wow, could we go, Dad?"

"I wouldn't want to slow you guys down." Dad looked concerned.

I punched him playfully on the shoulder. "You did great at the island. You'll do fine."

"The island was flat. You're talking about mountains."

"Dad, you look much better than the last time I saw you," Drew said. "You're getting into shape. By then you'll be ready."

"Thanks son," Dad laughed. "I can't believe I was so bad you can see a difference."

"Well, you sat on your butt behind a desk for a long time." Drew took another muffin. "I thought you were going to scramble some eggs," he said.

"Right," I laughed and got up to go to the stove.

"Can you tell us about what you have to do today?" Dad asked. "I mean if it isn't too personal. It sounded mysterious."

"Not mysterious, just delicate. I don't know if I've told you about the problems Jimmy Parnell had in school. You know Jimmy, my best friend. He was learning disabled."

"You mentioned it."

"I'm not so sure I would call it disabled. I think he just didn't fit into the system very well, but anyway that's the way they labeled him. They've put the same label on his son James Jr. Jimmy is having a hard time with it."

"I guess he would. I'm sure he feels guilty."

"He does, and I think with his own difficulties, he can't help much. They've hired tutors, but I remember with Jimmy, those people haven't got a clue how to help."

"So they've asked you to help," Dad smiled. "That's a great idea."

"I thought so at first. When Jimmy asked me I was excited about it. It's the first time I've felt excited since…" I looked at Drew. He was concentrating on his muffin and not paying too much attention to what I was saying. I met my dad's eyes and he smiled reassuringly.

"Anyway," I continued. "I'm not so sure now. I went over there for dinner last night, and James Jr. was not friendly toward me. Meryl told him I was going to tutor him and he hates tutors."

"So you're going to spend some time with him today?"

"Yeah, we're going hiking. Maybe I can bring him back around. We've always gotten along so well."

"Why don't we come along?" Dad said. "That way it won't seem like you're just trying to get him alone."

"Yeah, and Dad can get some practice with hills," Drew said.

I smiled. I guess he was paying more attention than I thought.

"I was hoping to get some ideas about his interests. I thought maybe that would be a good way to reach him."

"We'll head off on our own from time to time. We'll make sure you get some time alone with him."

"Okay," I said. "It might just work out fine." I looked at my watch. "I need to pick him up in about an hour. Do you guys need to go home and get anything? I don't think your shoes are right for hiking." I looked at the dress shoes my dad was wearing.

"Yeah, we'll go change and meet you back here in forty five minutes."

"I think I'll just wait here with David, okay Dad? My shoes are fine."

Dad met my eyes again. I nodded and he left.

We pulled up to Jimmy's house an hour later. Drew and I had talked the whole forty five minutes that Dad was gone. The kid was not at all shy. I liked him. I don't know what I had expected, but I didn't expect to have this warm feeling of recognition right away. I wondered if it would be the same way with my sister.

"I'll go get Jamie," I said. "Would you mind sitting in the back seat with Drew, Dad? I don't want Jamie to feel intimidated."

"Not a problem." Dad got out of the car and climbed into the back seat.

"Ready to go?" I said when Jamie met me at the door with his backpack on.

"Who are those people with you?" He peered around me at the car in his driveway.

"That's my dad and my brother. They're going to come along if that's alright with you."

"I didn't know you had a brother." Jamie looked pensive.

"I knew I had one, but I met him today for the first time. I'm glad you're coming on the hike with us. I won't feel awkward or shy with you along."

He squared his small shoulders. "Is he nice?"

"He seems to be." I took the small hand in my large one and walked him to the car.

"Hey, aren't you even going to say hello?" Meryl called from the front door. She looked surprised when she saw the passengers in my car.

"I'm sorry, Meryl," I said. "I should have come in to tell you we were leaving. Come and meet my brother. You've already met Dad."

Meryl came to the car with Jimmy and Heather behind her. I buckled James, Jr. into his seat and walked around to the driver's side. Everyone said hello and commented on how much Drew and I looked alike. I enjoyed that.

"I thought you were going to get him alone to talk to him," Jimmy said when Drew had gotten back into the car, and Meryl and Heather had gone into the house.

"I just met Drew this morning. He's leaving tomorrow. What could I do? Besides, this seems like less of a set up. It'll work, trust me."

"Alright." He leaned down to look in the window as I got into the driver's seat. "You be a good boy, Jamie."

"I will, Dad."

"It's a loop with a path up the middle," Dad said. He was studying the map of the trail. "Why don't we hike up the middle path together, then when we get to the top, you and Jamie can go one way and we'll go the other? We can see who gets back here the fastest."

"That sounds like a good plan," I said. "What do you think Jamie?" He'd been very quiet all the way over. We'd tried to draw him out. Drew had asked him about video games that I'd never heard of. He talked a little about that but not much.

"I guess that would be alright," he said. I was starting to feel panicky. How would I reach this kid if he wouldn't even talk to me? I looked at my dad. He smiled reassuringly and started up the path. Drew went after him, and Jamie and I started up behind them.

The trail started in an uphill direction. Pretty soon it moved into switch backs of trail to cut the steepness of the climb. Jamie walked beside me for the first quarter of a mile or so. Then he pulled away from me and climbed the bank beside the trail.

"Jamie, be careful," I said. "Don't fall off that bank. Your dad will kill me if you get hurt."

"I have a feeling that young James can handle that terrain just fine," Drew said. "In fact, it looks more fun than walking on this flat trail." He grabbed the root of a tree and swung himself up to the ledge in front of Jamie.

"Now that's the benefit of having a smaller more wiry build," Dad said. "David and I couldn't get these gigantic bodies up there if we tried."

"Speak for yourself." I laughed and grabbed the root of the tree. I looked at Jamie and Drew tight roping along the edge of the bank and decided I should stay on the ground below. "I guess you're right." I let go of the root and walked on positioning myself below Jamie so I could catch him if he fell.

"Can you do this, Jamie?" Drew rounded a tree that grew close to the path and pulled up to its lowest limb. He stood on the limb about two feet off the ground and then jumped to the ground and continued to walk. James, Jr. did the same thing.

"Shit!" I said under my breath.

"Just watch the kid, David," Dad whispered. "We'll catch him if he falls."

"Look over here, Drew." Jamie was warming up to the challenges now. "There's a stream." He hurried down a slope to a stream that ran down the hill and crossed under a bridge on the path. He leaped onto a large rock that was in the middle of the shallow but rushing water. I hurried to the bridge only to realize that if he fell in the stream I wouldn't be able to reach him from there.

He didn't fall in the water. He balanced himself for a minute then leaped to another stone. Then he was across the stream and standing on the stump of a fallen tree. Drew was right behind him laughing. My brother jumped onto the fallen tree and started walking it like a balance beam.

Jamie followed him and the two of them walked one foot in front of the other, their arms swinging in a balancing motion. They walked the length of the tree then jumped together onto the path.

"You can see his short attention span," Dad said. "Drew has the same thing. Walking on a trail bores them stiff. They need an obstacle course."

"Is Drew ADD?" I asked, surprised.

"They said so in school. We put him in a private school. It was good for him. He did great. So far he's done well in college. I think he's learned how to work with it."

I looked at my brother, then at Jamie. He looked so much like his father. "Some kids don't have the option of a private school," I said.

"I know. That's why James Jr. is lucky he has you."

"I hope I can reach him."

"You will, just watch and listen closely to him. That's all you have to do."

I went to mass with my mother that night. I hadn't been to church since before I went to prison. She was surprised when I showed up just as she was leaving the house. She always went to 5:30 mass. I usually came over for dinner after she got home. That night we went together. Dad and Drew came over for dinner after we got back.

The next morning all four of us went to the airport to see Drew off. He hugged and kissed my mom. He said he was glad to finally meet his step mother. This brought a smile to my mom's face.

He shook my hand. Then I pulled him into a bear hug. He hugged me back for a minute before hugging Dad and going through security. He smiled and waved as he walked to the escalator. We waited until he was out of site before we went back to the car.

Two weeks later, Darla and I sat on folding lawn chairs next to a soccer field. Jimmy stood in the middle of the field with a gaggle of seven and eight year old boys gathered around him.

"Look at James, Jr.," Darla said.

"I wish I could take my eyes off him." He squatted with his back to the group drawing designs in a muddy spot on the field.

"Jamie!" The irritation in his father's voice could be heard to the edge of the field. "Listen up, kid." Jamie stood and turned around wiping the mud off his finger onto his white soccer shorts.

"Jimmy has no patience with him," Darla rubbed her face with her hands. "Meryl won't even come to practice with him. She can't stand to watch it."

"Have you talked to him about it? I mean, how can he have no patience? Can't he remember what he went through?"

"He played soccer. He was good. Jamie isn't, and I hate to say it, but he isn't ever going to be good. I've tried to point that out to Jimmy. He just can't accept it."

"The homily in church last week was about the sins of the fathers. I wonder if this applies."

"You're going to church? Don't tell me you've found religion?" Darla laughed and nudged me with her shoulder.

"It's time spent with my mom."

"Maybe I'll join you tomorrow. Or would that interfere?"

"No, I'm sure she'd love it. I'd like it too."

"The game's starting," she said. "He's got Jamie in the front, forward, poor thing."

Jimmy walked off the field. His head was bowed. The expression on his face was unreadable. I got up and went over to him.

"He doesn't even listen to the game plan," he said.

"Jimmy, I'm not trying to piss you off, but remember back about fifteen years ago. You couldn't read directions."

"But I could listen." Now the anger was clearly evident. "You coached me on that. I couldn't follow written directions. You told me to insist that the teacher explain everything to me in words, remember?

I looked at his scowl, and for the first time in my life, I felt furious with him for his handicap. Was he really so stupidly rigid? "Jimmy, these things manifest themselves differently in different people. Surely you can see that."

"Oh, stop with the big words, David." He looked out at the field. "I wish I hadn't asked for your help. God, look at him. He's a forward and he's behind the damn defense."

I looked around. A number of the parents were squirming in their seats. "Jimmy, you'd better watch your language. I think a children's soccer league is the wrong place for swearing. I doubt they'll put up with it for long."

"Get off my back, David."

I watched him go to the bench and mop his brow with a towel. It wasn't hot in May in Georgia, but he was sweating. I turned back to the field. Jamie was running with the team, but if the ball came near him he studiously avoided it. I looked at his face. He was scared to death.

"Come back to the stands, David." Darla tugged on my arm, and I walked backwards with her to sit down.

"I'll get Jimmy to put him in the goal," I said. "That way I can be his personal coach."

"It won't help," she said, but she didn't say why.

I shrugged and went to the bench to talk to Jimmy. The miserable half ended. The kids all walked off the field to drink Gatorade and congratulate each other on their expertise. Nobody knew the score, nobody cared, and nobody recognized James, Jr.'s distress.

I walked the unhappy child to the goal and stooped to talk to him. I put my hand on his arm, and he immediately looked up at me. For a second I could see the raw pain in his face. Then he smiled sadly and took a deep breath. I squeezed his arm lightly, and he smiled a little more warmly. He liked to be touched.

"Jamie, the goal can be a challenge. The hardest part is watching the game while you're not playing. You have to always be ready if the ball comes your way. It's important to concentrate on what the rest of the team is doing." He was looking at me while I talked, and I had the feeling he was listening. I took my hand off his arm and stood up. The change in his expression was so subtle I would have missed it if I hadn't been looking for it. He needed to be touched. I put my hand on his shoulder, and he cocked his head back to look up at me.

"We have a few minutes before the game starts. You go over there. I'll kick the ball to you a few times. Let's get your reflexes warmed up."

He was sharp one on one. He stopped almost everything I kicked at him. His reaction time was great. By the time the game started I was feeling confident. I returned to the stands where Darla was sifting through a cooler.

"I brought tuna sandwiches. Do you want one?" she asked.

"Sure." I took the sandwich she unwrapped and put in my hand without taking my eye off the field. The other team kicked off. They went straight by our defense and stormed the goal. Jamie made a spectacular save. They recovered the ball and attempted another goal. It was wide. It wouldn't have gone in, but Jamie was there anyway and kicked it back into play. Our team got hold of it and carried it up to the other end of the field. I stood and waved at Jamie as he beamed in my direction. I sat back down and took another bite of the sandwich.

"What do you mean he won't be able to play goal?" I said. "He's great."

"I think you should wave with your other hand, David," Darla whispered in my ear. "That lady in front of us has tuna on her hat and she doesn't know it."

I looked at the glob on the hat in front of me and extended my hand to wipe it off. The woman turned around and glared at me when I touched her head.

"I got tuna on your hat," I said, extending a napkin toward her. She took it and moved away. "Sorry," I called after her.

"Look." Darla tapped my arm and pointed at the goal. The play was moving toward it. James Jr. was stooped with his back to the action, drawing lines in the mud again.

"Oh shit," I said.

"Watch your language," the man next to me said.

Jimmy was jumping up and down on the side lines signaling to his son. The coaches weren't allowed to shout. The ball hit Jamie on the back and bounced into the goal.

I watched Jimmy and James, Jr. walk off the field when the game was over. Both of their heads were bowed. Young James was crying, and I could swear I saw steam coming out of his father's ears. He walked a few steps ahead of the boy. He was saying something to him. I didn't want to know what it was. They were the picture of defeat. The tuna sandwich sat like a lead weight in the pit of my stomach.

"Soccer isn't going to work for him, Jimmy," I said the next day. We were moving me into my new house. When Uncle Jeff got married he had lived here with Amanda for a while until the twins were born. Then they bought a big house with property in an equestrian community about 20 miles north of Atlanta. They both had horses now. Man! I was starting to look forward to midlife.

"Nothing's going to work for him, David. He's a mess and it's my fault."

"Well." I put down the couch we were carrying. Jimmy stopped short, barely catching himself from falling over it. "Saying that about the genetic part would be just plain stupid. I never thought of you as stupid before. I'll tell you what though. If you don't stop being such a shit head the rest of it will be your fault."

"Thanks for the support, David. I wish I hadn't asked you for help with this. You haven't done a thing for Jamie, and you've pounded on me the whole time. In fact, you can just move yourself into this damn house. I'm taking my kid and going home." Jimmy turned to leave just as James, Jr. came running into the house. They collided and Jimmy raised his hand as if he would slap the boy.

"If you hit him I'll deck you, man," I said.

He dropped his hand. "I wasn't going to hit him."

"I'm sorry, Dad," James, Jr.'s small voice piped. His eyes were round with fear. He was almost cowering.

Jimmy took a deep breath. "It's okay, Jamie. You just startled me. Come on, we're going home."

"We haven't unloaded the truck yet?"

"That's right, Jimmy," I said putting my hand on the child's shoulder and feeling the current that ran between us. "Are you going to abandon me just because we had a little disagreement?"

"Did you and Uncle David have a fight," Jamie asked. "Cool." He grinned and I laughed.

Jimmy smiled reluctantly. "I'm hungry," he said, looking at his watch. "Isn't it about lunch time?"

"That's right." I squeezed Jamie's shoulder. "I forgot your dad gets grouchy when he's hungry."

"Yeah, mom always knows when to feed him," Jamie hurried to his father and took his hand. Jimmy shook it off, and I watched the child's face fall. He recovered quickly. "Do you have anything to eat, Uncle David, or should we go somewhere. We could go to burger doodle."

"No burger doodle," I said. "I don't want to move the rest of this stuff while suffering from heartburn. It just happens that I went to the deli before I picked you guys up this morning. I got sandwiches and salads. I also got a six pack of your favorite Canadian beer, Jimmy."

"Good," James, Jr. said. "I'll have a beer." He rubbed his belly.

"I got lemonade for you." I laughed. Jimmy was standing near the kitchen door looking reluctant to give up his anger. "Come on," I said. "Let's see how we feel after a good lunch." I went into the kitchen, Jamie on my heels. His father joined us reluctantly a minute later. He sat at the table we'd brought in earlier, and I unpacked my deli bag.

We ate in silence except for James Jr.'s chatter. He was excited about the front yard. There were shade trees with low branches so he could climb. There was a pond with big stones that he could walk across, and there was a wooden bridge that went over it just beyond the fountain.

"I didn't see any goldfish in the pond," he said.

"Uncle Jeff's wife loves her animals. She got attached to the goldfish and took them with her when she went. They all had names." I laughed.

"Are you going to get more?"

"Maybe," I doubted it. I didn't want the responsibility. Jamie finished his sandwich and went out the back door to the deck. There was a rail around the deck. In a flash he was standing on it and walking it like a balance beam.

"Whoa." Jimmy jumped up. "That deck is a story up. I'd better get him down." He headed for the back door.

"Leave him alone, Jimmy, he's fine. There are shrubs below him. Even if he falls he won't break anything and besides, he isn't going to fall." Jimmy stopped at the door and watched his son pivot to turn around and move back along the rail balancing with his arms.

"He has an incredible sense of balance. He's really coordinated," I said.

"I wouldn't have hit him." His voice was almost a whisper.

"I didn't think you would, but even if you had, at least you would have touched him. You don't touch the kid, Jimmy, why?"

He looked at me, surprised. "I touch him. What are you talking about?"

"Ever since you told me about the problems you were having with him I've been reading articles about learning disabled children. They need to be touched. In fact one of the reasons that they're thinking it happens more in boys than girls is because boys don't get hugged and just touched as much as girls."

"And they shouldn't." He turned to look out the window.

I dropped my jaw. "I can't believe you just said that. Why shouldn't they?"

"They'll grow into men. Men have to be strong. They're the breadwinners, the providers, the protectors."

I walked to the window and stood beside him. "I can remember at least two times when you wrapped your arms around me and cried on my shoulder."

Jimmy stepped away from me a little bit. "Those were times of extreme emotion," he said.

"Jimmy, life doesn't proceed by a set of rules. And besides, I'm sure even cavemen hugged their children, boys and girls. Listen," I said. "I can feel Jamie's response when I touch him. Try it."

"Where are you touching him?" He demanded. His eyes narrowed.

"Oh come on, Jimmy, I'm not molesting your son. I'm caring about him. I'm communicating with him. Jeez!" I looked out the window. We stood in silence and watched as James, Jr. hopped from the rail to an iron table and onto the ground. He stooped and looked at the deck floor in front of him.

I took a deep breath and reached across Jimmy's back, hanging my hand off his far shoulder. He tensed and looked at me. I smiled and looked back out the window. He relaxed slowly. James, Jr. had started to draw lines in the dirty surface of the deck.

"That kid can draw circles for hours. He can draw in sand, dirt, mud. He comes home from school with designs drawn all over his papers.

If he can keep his mind on that, why can't he keep his mind on anything else?" Jimmy asked.

"He can, we just haven't figured out what it is yet."

"It's not soccer," Jimmy opened the door and we both went out.

"It's not soccer." We're making progress, I thought.

That evening during mass, I remembered the feeling of Uncle Jeff's hand on my shoulder. I remembered his fierce hugs after my near death experience with the water fall, and I remembered the self conscious embraces when I went away to school. I remembered the hugs and kisses from my mother at night as a child and still as a grown man whenever I saw her. I remembered the fierce hug and the tears on my dad's cheeks when we saw each other for the first time in years, when I was ten years old and again less than a year ago. For the first time in my life, I was truly grateful, and I knew how lucky I'd been. I looked up at the high ceiling of the cathedral. I was blessed?"

"Hey, Uncle Jeff," I called from his back deck. He was on the other side of the swimming pool. The new place he had bought for his new family was really very grand. I was glad. He'd lived a very humble life up until now. He deserved to indulge himself and his new happy family.

"David," he called. "Join us." He signaled. He held a baby in one arm. Another one sat on a blanket in the shade of a flowering fruit tree of some kind. I'm sure he knew what kind. I started toward him. The lawn on the other side of the pool was long and rolling. There were other trees around the outside of it. I was sure they produced some kind of fruit too. Some of them probably just produced pretty flowers. Uncle Jeff liked both kinds.

At the end of the lawn I saw Gabe. The big greyhound was picking up a ball. He stopped and looked back at us, the ball in his mouth. He was beautiful.

"I wish I had a camera," I said.

Uncle Jeff looked in the direction of my gaze. "He's a beautiful dog," he said. "He's gentle with the girls too. I'm glad."

"Is that one gentle?" I asked as a massive Rottweiler bounded out of the small patch of forest in the corner of the walled back yard. Amanda had brought the dog to the family with her.

"She's a marshmallow," Uncle Jeff laughed as the big dog dropped to the side of the blanket where the baby sat and rolled over for a belly rub. The infant leaned forward to pat the large dog and squealed with delight.

"Okay, that's Evelyn." I laughed. "She has her name embroidered on the back of her shirt. What a great idea."

"Yeah, Alice too," he said, setting the baby down on her belly on the blanket so I could see the back of her shirt. "Amanda finds a way to distinguish them. I think as they get older they'll look more different from each other, like me and your dad. At this age it's hard to tell by the way they look. Their voices are different, and their personalities, but not the way they look."

"How are their personalities different?" I took the ball from the anxious greyhound and tossed it to the far end of the yard. Gabe bounded after it.

"Well, it's hard to describe. Their development is different too. For instance, Evelyn sits on her fat ass just fine. Alice will fall over if you put her on her butt. However, she can crawl like a racer. You really have to watch her or she's overturning plants and dumping drawers. Evelyn isn't moving around much, but if she's next to a solid piece of furniture she'll pull up to her feet. I have a feeling she's just going to take off on foot. I think she'll skip the crawling stage."

"Wow, this whole thing sounds like fun."

"It is. It's also exhausting. I'm sleeping like a baby at night." He took the ball from Gabe this time and threw it. "You sleeping alright?" he asked, cautiously.

"I'm doing okay," I said. I was sleeping three to four hours a night, an improvement from a few months ago.

"Still walking at night? You know, living in mid-town like you do now, it might not be safe."

"I'm okay, Uncle Jeff,"

"Are you smoking that…"

"Drop it, Uncle Jeff," I interrupted. Gabe had put down the ball and was lapping at a bucket of water by the deck.

"Sorry." He sat down on the blanket with the babies. I joined him. Amanda came out carrying a basket of sandwiches and chips. There were a couple of beers and some Cokes in an icy bucket and two Sippy cups for the girls.

"You guys hungry?" she asked. I looked up at her. Seeing her reminded me of Anna. They had been friends. There was a fluttering feeling in my chest. I wanted to ask if she'd heard from her, but I didn't.

"I could eat," I said. It was late September and the weather was cooling off but still warm. I bit into a sandwich and Uncle Jeff did the same. Amanda busied herself with the girls and their Sippy cups.

"How are things going with James, Jr.?" Uncle Jeff asked.

"I don't know. Sometimes I think we're making progress. Then something happens and we're back at square one."

"I heard the soccer season was a disaster."

"Where did you hear that?"

"…From your mom."

"You guys are still talking about me when I'm not around?" I was surprised. They didn't have anything in common except me.

"We check in with each other on a regular basis." He sounded defensive. "You're still our mutual concern, even though you are a grown man."

"Wow," I said. I looked across the yard at the dog stretched out in the sun. Uncle Jeff followed my gaze. "He'll get a second wind in a minute." He laughed. "We'd better finish our sandwiches."

"So go on and tell us about what's happening with James, Jr." Amanda said.

"Well, we got through soccer season. Jimmy insisted that James, Jr. finish the season with the team."

"That was probably not a bad thing, David. You can't let your teammates down."

"I'm not sure staying with the team was any better. Anyway, that's what we did. After that was over we built an obstacle course in the back yard of Jimmy's house. Jamie has a great sense of balance. It was my suggestion, and I had to fight to get Jimmy and Meryl to agree. I'd have put it in my yard, well yours, Amanda," I said. "But there really isn't room."

"So how did it work?" Uncle Jeff asked.

"Building it was good. Even Jimmy helped. We did it during the summer. Meryl and Heather got into making sure we all had enough to drink. I got to thinking it was kind of pulling the family together." I chewed thoughtfully and swallowed.

"But…" Uncle Jeff prompted.

"Yeah, but… When it was finished Jamie got on it, and we worked up a routine for him to run. It was great and he's fantastic. His balance is good, and he can run the tires perfectly every time. He hits the bars and walks along them on his hands. I wish you could have seen it, Uncle Jeff."

"So where does the 'but' come in?"

"He practiced the routine and got his parents out to watch him when he'd perfected it. They got into a big fight."

"I'm sorry."

"Jimmy says it won't do him any good to do that. What can he do with it? He can't be a gymnast. He's going to get too tall. You know Jimmy is six feet and Meryl is five ten. Her dad is taller than me."

"I guess you don't see many tall gymnasts, but running an obstacle course is not useless. It'll keep him in good shape."

"I think Jimmy is having a hard time letting go of the soccer thing. You know it was his passion when we were growing up. I think it's what kept him from feeling completely defeated as a child."

"He was good too," Uncle Jeff stood up and stretched. "Not as good as you, of course."

I laughed and stood up with him. "Of course," I said. "Still, there is some truth in what Jimmy says. James, Jr. needs a passion. Like Jimmy had. School started last week. I'm working with the kid on that now. I can't help but pick up on the hopelessness he feels."

"Does he listen to you at all?" Amanda asked.

"Yeah, and he's doing okay, but it'll always be an uphill battle. He needs something on the side that takes his mind off the struggle. I just haven't figured out what it is yet."

She picked up the babies and settled one on each hip. "I need to take them in for a change and a nap."

"You go ahead," I said. I watched her walk to the house holding both babies. "What have you done to Amanda, Uncle Jeff?"

"What do you mean?" I looked at him. He was following her with his eyes too. There was a smile on his face that I could only describe as content.

"I used to think she was plain, with her crooked teeth and severe hair style. She isn't plain. She's beautiful."

"Yeah." His smile widened. "Well, it's more what she's done. She doesn't tie her hair back anymore. She dresses better. I always liked the crooked teeth. They're sexy. I guess all I've done is love her." He looked away from her, and we both watched as Gabe got up from his bed on the ground and went looking for his ball.

"So, can Jamie play any games at all?" Uncle Jeff continued the conversation. "I mean is it competition that doesn't work for him?"

"No, I played ping pong with him the other night and he's fantastic. It's a fast game. He focuses on that ball beautifully. It never stops unless the point is over. I beat him a couple of times. He's not a bad loser. But there aren't any ping pong teams."

"There probably are, but they might be hard to find. I guess it wouldn't be kids anyway."

"He's talented really." Gabe handed me his ball. I threw it for him, and he bounded off. "I mean his balance is great. He's agile to the point of wiry. His hand to eye coordination is fantastic."

The big dog bounded back to me, and I took the ball from him again. It was wet and I looked down at it with distaste. "Whoa," I said. I was holding a tennis ball. "I have an idea."

Uncle Jeff looked at the ball in my hand. "Yeah," he said. "Gabe," he stroked the dog's side, "you're a genius."

"Tennis!" Jimmy didn't sound excited. "That's a rich kid's game. David, don't encourage my kid to put on airs."

"That's dumb, Jimmy. Tennis isn't a rich kid's game. They teach it in the public high schools. We took it, remember?"

"I hated it."

"It wasn't your game."

"So why would it be Jamie's game?"

"He's your son, stupid, not your clone."

"That's the second time you've accused me of being stupid in the last five minutes. It's starting to get on my nerves." Jimmy turned his back to me and picked his towel up off the bench. We were at the soccer field. The practice season had just begun.

"I have to go to field five," Jimmy said. "Heather's first practice of the season is over there in about fifteen minutes. She plays soccer like a champ."

"That's great," I said, fighting the urge to be irritated with him. "So you get to coach one of your kids in soccer after all."

"Yeah, imagine that, my daughter, not my son."

"Stop feeling sorry for yourself, Jimmy. Heather is just as much your kid as Jamie is, and they're both great kids."

He walked away shaking his head. I ran to catch up with him. "I've found someone who will coach him in tennis. Can I go ahead and sign him up?" I asked.

"I can't afford tennis lessons," he said.

"It's only forty dollars an hour. Heather said she quit ballet because she likes soccer better. How much did you pay for the ballet lessons?"

Jimmy stopped and looked at me. He took a deep breath.

"I'll pay for it, Jimmy," I said. "Please give me permission to sign him up."

"Have you talked to him about it?"

"Not exactly," I knew I looked guilty so I quickly said, "I did take him out to hit balls back and forth the other day after our lesson. I dug up a couple of racquets out of Mom's basement. I think he's a natural. I know he enjoyed it."

"Alright," Jimmy looked so defeated I felt terrible. "Sign him up, I'll pay for it." He dropped the soccer ball he was holding to the ground and dribbled it down the field.

CHAPTER SIXTEEN

I arrived at the office at 7:00 am on the day of my twenty seventh birthday. Jane had given me the day off, but what would I do with it. It was a Monday. Uncle Jeff was working. Dad was in school studying to be a dog groomer. I smiled at the thought. It was nice having him in my life, and as hard as I tried to stay mad at him for leaving me, I couldn't. I not only loved him. I liked him too.

Mom would hang out with me, but she had another out of town job to go to. She was doing a great business on wedding attire. She was getting some paid trips around the country too. This time she was in Las Vegas. I couldn't see my straight laced mom enjoying that too much. I'm pretty sure she wouldn't gamble, and since she goes to bed at 9:00 pm, I couldn't see her enjoying the night life.

I knew all of this because my dad had asked me to go out to dinner with him after work that night. He'd be with her if she was in town. He'd been living with me at the house in midtown. A few weeks ago he had moved into Uncle Jeff's apartment at the nursery. He did this, I knew, so that I wouldn't realize how many nights he didn't come home, how many nights he spent with my mother. I'm sure there was no way he'd live in that apartment. He hated the smell of dirt.

We'd celebrated my birthday with mom the night before after Mass. Uncle Jeff and Amanda were there with the girls. They were growing so fast. They were both walking now. You had to scramble to keep them out of trouble. Darla had come over and Jimmy and Meryl and the kids. I frowned at the thought. Jimmy still hadn't accepted James, Jr.'s tennis lessons. I had to take the kid to the courts every week because Meryl worked out of the house on Monday afternoons.

The phone rang on my desk startling me out of my thoughts. I sat up straight. I was sitting in my desk chair. I hadn't even taken off my jacket. It had been a cool spring this year.

"Hello," I said into the receiver.

"David." It was my dad. "Can you get away a little early this afternoon? I've got a surprise for you."

"Sorry, Dad, I'm already leaving early to take Jamie to his tennis lesson. I really can't cancel it at this late date. His father would be furious with me if he had to pay for a lesson the kid didn't get."

"Let his father take him then."

"I can't do that, Dad. They fight about tennis. It's a real mess that relationship."

"David, I don't like to get involved in your business, but…"

"You do too." We both laughed.

"Okay, maybe I do. What I was going to say was, maybe it's time for you to step back a little and let them fight it out."

I thought about that. Maybe he was right, but I couldn't let Jamie miss tennis. It was doing wonders for his self esteem. He was really good at it. "I'll see what I can do. Don't count on me too early."

"Alright, just try to get there a little bit early so we have time before the reservation. I made it for 7:00. I want a few minutes with you before we leave."

"This sounds mysterious. I hope you didn't go too far out on my birthday present."

"You got your birthday present last night."

I looked at the watch he had given me. It was almost 8:00 and I hadn't even started work. I had a lot to do. "I really like the watch, Dad, but looking at it just reminded me I have a meeting across town in half an hour. I have to go. Should I meet you at the nursery before dinner?"

"No, meet me at the house. I still have my key. I'll let myself in. Try to get there before six, okay?"

"I'll see what I can do. See you later." I hung up the phone and picked up my keys. I had a sales call across town. My friend and colleague had set it up for me. The ads in the magazine were selling well. I loved this about my job. In fact, I loved my job.

I arrived at Jimmy's house at 4:30. I had called Meryl. She said she couldn't take Jamie to tennis. She had a customer coming to get her hair and nails done. Jimmy had come home early to help with the kids. "He'll just have to do it," she said. Why did that make me so nervous?

"Uncle David!" Jamie met me at the door. His face was tear stained and he hiccupped as he wrapped his arms around my waist. "I'm so glad you came. Dad says he won't take me to tennis. Mom's fighting with him now, but she won't change his mind. He hates me! He hates me!"

"He doesn't hate you," I said. I scooped him up and hugged him. "He's just acting like a big baby. He didn't get his way so he's having a temper tantrum." I laughed and Jamie sniffed and wiped his wet face on my shirt.

"I tried to play soccer. I wasn't any good at it." I closed my eyes. I could remember the feeling that I wasn't good enough for my father. I realized at that moment that I'd always believed he left me because I wasn't good enough.

I could hear the angry voices of Jimmy and Meryl in the other room. Heather came in and frowned at me. "This is your fault, Uncle David!" Her face was tear stained too. Should I have just stayed out of this? I didn't mean to start a family feud. Maybe Dad was right. Maybe I needed to back off and let them work it out.

"It isn't his fault, Heather." Meryl came into the room and sat down on the arm of the chair that her daughter was in.

"No, it's my fault," Jimmy said from the doorway to the kitchen. "If I hadn't supplied faulty genetics everything would be just fine."

"I don't know why you say that." I was angry. I couldn't stop myself. "Your kids are great, brilliant and talented people, despite the fact that they have a jackass for a father."

"You know what, David." My best friend turned to me. His face was red with anger and he sneered. "Get the hell out of my house. You've done enough damage here."

I put James, Jr. down on the floor. "Please take me to tennis, Uncle David." He wrapped his arms around my waist again and buried his face in my shirt.

I pried his arms away from me and looked into his face. "You're growing up so fast, son. You're so tall I can look into your face without stooping." I smiled, but Jamie just looked down.

"Please take me to tennis," he repeated.

I took a deep breath. "I can't. Your dad is right. I've done too much damage here already. My interference has caused a family rift. I need to back out now."

Jamie put his hands over his face and crumbled to the floor sobbing. I thought for a minute how nice it would be to just fall to the floor when you were hurt. I didn't even do that when I was a kid.

"I'll cancel my appointment and take you, honey." Meryl sat down cross legged on the floor and scooped Jamie into her arms.

I looked at Jimmy. He was standing behind Heather with his hand on her shoulder. She was scrubbing at her eyes. Jimmy wasn't looking at her. He was looking at his wife and son on the floor.

"I'll take him," he said. "Just let me get my keys and my jacket." He turned and went back into the kitchen.

"Jamie," I said. "Go give your dad a hug."

"He won't hug me. He hates me."

"No he doesn't," Meryl said. "He loves you. Sometimes I think he loves you too much."

"You can't love someone too much," I said. "Go on, Jamie, he's made the first move. He's taking you to tennis. It's time for you to do something now. Go and give him a hug." I pulled Jamie to his feet and nudged him in the direction of the kitchen. He looked over his shoulder at me, then at his mother.

"Go on," she smiled encouraging him. He ran after his father. I left the house and got into my car. I didn't want to see my own father right now, but I knew he was waiting for me at my house. I thought about stopping at Darla's for a minute. Maybe she'd go have a beer with me somewhere.

No, I thought. Dad is waiting for me. I'd better go home.

"I'm here, Dad," I called as I came up the stairs from the garage. I opened the door that led into the kitchen. "It's just a little after five and..." I stopped as I came into the room. Dad sat at the kitchen table with a very lovely young woman with curly blond hair. I knew without introduction that she was my sister. She looked very much like my brother.

"Kristina?" I asked.

"David?" She smiled, and I saw the same dimples that made me smile at Darla.

"I knew you'd recognize each other." Dad was beaming. "This is your sister, David. She's come to visit for a while. I was hoping she could stay here. I really hate for her to stay at that apartment over the nursery." He turned back to look fondly at Kristina. "She's pregnant again, The smell of dirt might make her sick."

"Dad, I told you I'm fine." She blushed. Her skin was fare, not dark like Dad's and mine. "I can stay at the nursery, David. It's okay. We wanted to surprise Dad so we didn't tell him we were coming. I would have given you some warning if I'd known he was going to make you keep us." She dimpled at me again and I smiled in reflex.

"No, I'd love to have you stay here. We can get to know each other that way. How long will you be here and how many of you are there?"

"Just five days. My husband is at a conference here so he'll be staying too. And, of course, there is the baby." She looked up as we heard a baby fussing in the room above us. "Speaking of the devil, he's awake. That's a lot of people to be in your house, especially since we're total strangers."

I felt unexplainably relieved that her husband would be staying too. "Not a problem. I only have one spare room though. It's the one that was Uncle Jeff's girl's nursery when they were born. It's pretty big. And you're not a stranger. You're my sister." I laughed.

"I guess that's true." She smiled and left the room.

"What is the baby's name?" I asked dad as I went to the refrigerator to pour myself a glass of wine.

"Brian Eliot, he's named after the two grandfathers," Dad was beaming again. "They call him Ely though." He frowned but didn't really look unhappy. "I call him Bri."

"I'll call him Bri too." I sat down. The intercom buzzed from the gate at the front of the house. "Who's that?" I said as I went to the intercom on the wall.

"It's your Uncle. He and Amanda are coming to babysit for Bri while I take you and Kristina to dinner. Steven, the husband, has to work late tonight, so he couldn't do it."

"I hate to leave them at home," I said. "We don't have to go out."

"I want to take my two kids out on my firstborn's birthday. I don't think Jeff minded. He didn't seem to when I asked him."

"Come on in, Uncle Jeff," I called through the intercom and pressed the button to unlock the gate.

"A minute later the front doorbell rang and Dad went to answer it.

"Bubba..." Both girls rushed into the room on stubby legs with stubby arms raised toward me.

"Hello, ladies," I scooped them up and settled them each on a hip.

"Bubba?" Kristina laughed as she came down the steps holding a baby that looked to be a little over a year old.

"They call me bubba." I felt myself blush. "It's a southern thing. I was supposed to call them Sissy, but that never worked for me, so I call them ladies. I don't call them by their names much because I haven't figured out which one is which yet." I laughed and set the squirming girls down on the floor. I checked the basement door, and turned the lock so there wouldn't be any accidents.

"Alice is in the blue," Amanda said. "And Evelyn is wearing yellow today." She smiled shyly at Kristina. "I have to color code them for their father too. I guess this is Bri." She held out her hands to the baby that my sister was holding. He immediately started to cry and buried his face in his mother's shoulder.

"Sorry," Amanda blushed. "I should have known better."

"He just woke up from his nap. He'll warm up after his bottle." Kristina pulled out a bottle and put it in the microwave. "I'll just feed him,

Dad. Then we can go." She sat down in a chair and both girls toddled over to look at the baby."

"...cute," Alice said.

"...baby," Evelyn said.

"Cute baby," I laughed. "That's what the big girls say."

"Big ... gor..." Evelyn pointed at Alice and we all laughed.

I opened the envelope I had picked up at the mailbox that morning as I left the house for work. I recognized the return address as Kristina's. She had started corresponding with me through the mail after she left my house last spring. It was mid July and I had received three notes from her. We communicated via e-mail on a more regular basis, but she said she liked to send cards if she found one that made her think of me.

I laughed at the picture on the front of the card, then again at the caption. Her note was short. She just saw this card at the supermarket and it made her think of me. It's funny, I thought, Dad does that too. I wondered if some people just like to hang out on the greeting card aisle. I never went there unless I had to.

Drew was in Atlanta for the summer. He had opted to spend the summer here with us. He was staying with me like Kristina did. Dad didn't really live in that apartment over the nursery. Did he think he was fooling us? Dad and Drew and Uncle Jeff and I were all going to fly up to the spot on the Appalachian Trial where we'd start this year. We were over half way now.

I finally had a place in my Dad's family, well, his other family. My mom and dad and I had become a family in the past couple of years. I felt myself frown and pushed the card to the side of my desk. The relationship between my parents made me nervous. I'm not sure if I worried that he'd hurt her again or what, but somehow I wasn't comfortable with it.

There was another thing that bothered me. I hadn't met Sharon and I had an odd craving to. It worried me. Why did I want to meet the person who had taken my dad away from us? It was more than that. I wanted a relationship with her. I wanted to know my stepmother.

"That's stupid," I said out loud and was glad when the phone rang to distract me from my thoughts. I looked at the ID. It was the front desk. "Hey Celia," I said to the girl that did that job. Amanda only worked part time these days, and she only helped out up front when the job got too much for Celia. Amanda was working mostly in the design department now.

"David, there's someone named Teresa here to see you. She wouldn't give me her last name. She says you'll know who she is."

Hmmm, I thought. I only know one Teresa. Why would she be here? "You can send her on back, Celia, thank you." I put down the phone.

"Come in, Teresa." I called when the knock sounded on the door. She opened the door slowly and peered around it. She was smiling and I noticed right away that her hair was freshly cut and shined with lighter streaks against the dark.

"You've changed your hair," I said. I stood up and held out my hand to her. "It looks nice."

She ignored my hand and put her arms around my neck. She was tall. I'd forgotten one of the things that attracted me to her was her height. I hugged her back briefly then pushed her gently toward a chair. "Sit down," I said. "What can I do for you?"

She sat down and crossed her legs. Her skirt was short showing a generous portion of shapely legs. She'd lost weight since I'd last seen her. Of course, she'd been pregnant then, but she'd been heavy too. I had a memory flash of the two of us naked in the trunk of my first car. I cleared my throat and cleared my head at the same time.

"I guess you've heard that Dexter and I are divorced."

"Didn't you get married to him again?" I laughed.

"...and divorced again," she said. "It'll stick this time. He'll never forgive me now. My daughter isn't his. He did a test."

"Oh." I was puzzled. Where is this going? I thought.

"I knew she wasn't his as soon as I looked at her. She looks like her father." Teresa looked out the window. She looked embarrassed. I felt bad for her.

"I see."

"David, I'm sorry about leaving you the way I did." She looked at me now, and I thought I saw sincerity in her eyes. "I don't know what happened. Dex was like some kind of a drug. I just couldn't stay away from him."

"Will you be able to stay away from him now?"

"I have to. He's getting married to someone else."

"You'll still have to see him sometimes. He'll have joint custody with Dexter, Jr. won't he?"

"Actually, he got sole custody. I guess they don't give custody to adulteresses. I have visitation rights. I guess we'll see each other then. Or maybe his wife will bring him. Her name is Cindy." She said it with a sneer.

"Oh, I see." Didn't I say that before? I thought. What does this have to do with me?

"David, I know I was your first heart break, but I was thinking maybe we could try again. I really did love you. I wondered if you'd come to my house for dinner tonight. My mom is keeping the baby. I think it might be fun."

I smiled. So that's what she wants. I looked at her. She'd dressed nicely. She was still beautiful, and I had been planning to make a family with her once. I took a deep breath. She hadn't really broken my heart. She'd embarrassed me and disappointed me, but I remembered the pain when Anna left. It hadn't hurt like that when Teresa left.

"My dad dumping me was my first heart break, Teresa." I said, though I'm not sure why.

"You've let him back into your life, David. Don't you think you could find room for me?"

"Only as a friend," I saw the pain on her face when I said it and remembered the pain I'd felt when she said it to me. "I'm sorry," I said and stood. "I'll have dinner with you tonight if you want, but not at your house. We'll go out somewhere. How do you feel about Mexican food?" I walked to the door hinting broadly for her to leave.

"We'll go out as friends." She stood. It wasn't a question. It was more of a statement.

"Sure, friends go out to dinner together."

"I want a boyfriend."

"It won't be me, Teresa. I'm flattered, but I just don't have those feelings for you anymore."

She smiled sadly and went to the door. "Never mind then."

I buried myself in my work that day. I wrote a report on the magazine marketing that I was to present at the next meeting. It was two weeks away, after I got back from my backpacking trip. It would be nice to have it already done. I told myself. I really wanted to keep my mind off of Teresa. It was depressing to know how desperate she was. I wondered how I could ever have thought I loved her.

The phone on my desk rang and I looked at the clock. It was 3:00 in the afternoon. I had buried myself pretty deeply. I'd missed lunch. I looked at the ID. It was Amanda at the front desk this time. "Hey, Amanda, what's up?" I asked.

"Darla Bergquist is here to see you."

"It's a day for visitors from my past," I said. "I had one this morning too. Send her on back. Amanda, how are Uncle Jeff and the twins? I need to get over to see them. I haven't been by for a while."

"I was thinking the same thing. Why don't you come for dinner on Saturday? Come in the afternoon and swim. Then we can barbecue. The girls will be so excited to see you."

"Sounds great, I'll put it on my calendar." I hung up the phone just as Darla appeared at my door.

"Come on in," I said, motioning to a chair next to my desk. "Sit down. What's up?"

"I want you to come to my house for dinner tonight. I have an idea I want to run by you and something I want to show you."

"Sounds mysterious, give me a hint."

"No, but please come. I think you'll like it."

"Will Jimmy and Meryl be there?"

"No, just you and me, you aren't afraid to be alone with me are you?"

"Maybe I am a little bit." I laughed. "I never know what you've got up your sleeve."

"That's the way I like it. I keep people guessing so they won't get tired of me." She laughed and I smiled. No matter how bad I felt. Darla's laugh always made me smile.

"I can't imagine anyone ever getting tired of you, P. H." I got up as she did and walked her to the door. "By the way," I said as we went into the hall. "I love your new haircut." I hoped it was a new cut. It was in layers all around her face. It seemed to me that the last time I saw her it was all one length and about down to her waist.

"Thanks, I can't believe you noticed it. I had to tell Jimmy. I swear his head is in the ceiling all the time."

I laughed and breathed a sigh of relief that I'd been right about her hair. It was a day for noticing hair. I'd noticed Teresa's too. "He's always in the ceiling thinking about heating and air conditioning."

"Yeah, or about little Heather and James, Jr.,"

"Yeah, I'm pleased with the way he and Jamie are getting along. I really made a mess of things there. Have you seen them lately?" We were in the lobby now. I opened the front door, and we walked out into the hot Georgia summer.

"Yes, I saw them yesterday. They're growing up so fast. You didn't make a mess, David. You did exactly the right thing. You even backed off at the right time."

"That's why I was hoping they'd be there tonight. I was hoping to get to see the kids and kind of check up on things without being too obvious."

"Another time," She stood on her toes and pulled my head down to kiss my cheek. "Seven okay with you? That way you can go home and change if you want."

"Sounds good, I'll see you then." She got into her little sports car and waved at me as she screeched by.

"She really drives that little car." Amanda said as I came back inside the building.

"Scares me to death," I said. "I'm going to have to talk to her about that."

✦

"Hey," Darla met me at her front door. She looked beautiful in a blue dress. Her hair was pulled back on one side with a blue ribbon that matched her dress. I always loved the way she looked in blue.

"Come on in." She stepped back and motioned for me to go into the living room of her apartment.

"It smells great in here."

"I made Lasagna, the kind they make in the north of Italy, not the kind with a lot of Tomato sauce and cheese."

"I didn't know there were two different kinds." I lied.

"You're going to love it." She turned and her skirt swished on the leg of my pants. I smiled at the way her white blond hair bounced when she walked.

"Come on into the kitchen and pour us a glass of wine," she said.

I followed her in and picked up the cork screw on the table. "So what's the occasion? What's this idea you wanted to run by me?"

"Pour the wine and let me put the bread in to warm. Then we can go into the living room and talk."

I sipped my glass and watched her as she put the bread into the oven and set the timer. Then I followed her into the living room. We both sat down on the couch and she turned sideways to look at me.

"I want to ask you something, David?" She smiled. I loved the dimples in her cheeks.

"Ask me," I said.

"Will you marry me?" She reached behind the cushion of the couch and pulled out a ring box.

"What!" I laughed and leaned away from her in surprise.

"Will you marry me?" She repeated then leaned forward. "Don't say anything else right now. Just let me explain." She rested the hand that held the ring box on my knee.

"I know you were in love with that dress designer a while back. So you don't have to worry that I expect to be your grand passion or anything."

"Darla…"

"Don't say anything yet." She tapped my knee with her wrist. "I know she broke your heart when she left, and I'm really sorry about that." She held up a hand as I started to interrupt. "I keep waiting for my knight in shining armor, my own grand passion." She continued. "But I just don't think there is one for me." She laughed and I checked the smile that always came so fast at the sound.

"P. H. you can't just ask me to marry you because …"

"I said don't talk!" Her voice was commanding and this time I did laugh. "David, I'm twenty seven years old. I'll be twenty eight in October. I know you won't be twenty eight until next spring, but that doesn't matter. I want a family, and I think you and I are the perfect genetic compliment."

"Genetic compliment," I laughed. "You're so romantic."

"Well." She sat back leaning her shoulder against the cushion of the couch. "I don't think romantic is going to work for me, and it doesn't look like it's working for you either." She smiled. I smiled back and took a sip of my wine.

Why not? I thought then shook my head. What a crazy idea.

"Don't you want a family, David? I see how much you enjoy Jimmy and Meryl's kids. I see how much you love your little cousins. You work with the big brothers organization. Wouldn't you like to have some of your own?" She cocked her head sideways and looked at me. "You're thinking about it, aren't you?"

I sipped my wine and took the ring box out of her hand. I opened it and laughed. "It's for you."

"Of course, it's for me. Men don't wear engagement rings."

I took the ring out and looked at it. The diamond was big, at lease a carrot and there were smaller ones all around the band. It must have cost a fortune.

"The wedding ring matches. It has diamonds too," she said. "After we're married the jeweler will fuse them so they won't be so easy to lose." She smiled. I looked her in the eyes. "I got you a plain gold band."

"You chose and bought your own engagement and wedding ring."

"Yeah, well I charged it. I figure you'll pay it off."

I laughed again. "I sure am having fun tonight, P. H." She rolled to her knees on the couch beside me and kissed my mouth. I put my hand behind her head and deepened the kiss. She tasted sweet and smelled like something spicy.

"Me too," she whispered as she pulled back. She kissed me quickly again then took the ring from my fingers. I'd forgotten I was holding it. She put it back in the box and said. "Let's go eat this meal. I'm sure that bread is just about ready."

The timer sounded just as she stood up. I stood and followed her into the dining area of the small apartment.

"Say yes," she said when she had served desert. "You want to, don't you?"

"Yyy…" I stopped myself before I said the word. "I think I do want to, but I'm not going to say yes without thinking it through."

"Well, let me make a case for it then."

"P. H."

"I'm not a poop head." She laughed and I laughed too.

"No, but you have pretty hair."

"David, you have a good job. You can support me, and even though I'm managing to keep this apartment going, I hate my job. I'm just a secretary, and I don't want to be. You could support me."

I laughed so hard this time it took a minute to say anything. "So you just want to marry me for my money."

"Well, I'd be lying if I said I didn't care about having a husband that can support me. I want to be a stay at home mom, David. I want our children to be raised by their mother and their father. No day care, no nanny, us, you and me."

I sobered at her earnest face.

"Not only that, I think I'd excel at home making. I've got all sorts of interior decorating ideas, and you like the way I cook. Wasn't this meal good?"

I looked down at my empty desert plate and realized that, even though I couldn't remember tasting anything, I'd cleaned my plates, even the salad. "I like to cook," I said stupidly.

"I know you do, and you do it well. You can cook any time you want, but you won't have to because you'll have a wife who can do it for you after a long day at work." She flashed her dimples at me. "Say yes."

"What about sex? I tried a one night stand once when I was at Harvard. I couldn't do it. I didn't love the girl. I didn't even know her. I failed. It was embarrassing."

"But you do love me, David. I'm glad you couldn't have a one night stand. Our marriage will be based on love. I know I love you." She paused and played with her fork for a minute. Then she looked up at me and said. "If you tell me you don't love me, I'll drop the subject."

I looked at her pretty face and the memory of her childhood taunting flashed in my mind. I remembered the pain the words 'white trash' inflicted. It wasn't just because of what she said. It hurt because *she* said it. She was my stepmother's niece, the prettiest and smartest girl in the class.

"I do love you, P. H."

"Can I put on the ring?"

"What about your family?" I asked. "What about mine?"

"They'll deal, David. They all want us to be happy." She opened the ring box. "Your mother and uncle want you to be happy. Truth is I think my dad will be thrilled to know that someone else will be supporting me from now on."

"My money again," I laughed.

"You make a good living, David, and don't worry about the sex. You're a really good kisser, almost as good as Teresa."

"You've kissed Teresa?"

"Everyone has kissed Teresa." She laughed. I thought about my conversation earlier that day with Teresa and frowned. "I'm sure you'll be at least as good in bed as she is."

The comment shocked me. "You've had sex with Teresa?"

"Everyone has had sex with Teresa."

Darla got out of her chair and sat in my lap. I pulled her close to me and we kissed again. I could feel myself responding. She squirmed in my lap telling me that she could feel it too. "I was the first," I whispered between kisses.

"The first what?" Darla was unbuttoning my shirt and nibbling my neck.

"To have sex with Teresa."

"I know. That's why I know you'll be such a good lover. Now don't think about her anymore. Think about me."

We made love all night long. Sometimes I think back on it and can't believe I had that much stamina. But P. H. was right. We were great together. I couldn't get enough of her, and she seemed to feel the same way.

I woke up in the morning tired, a little bit sore, and very certain about my future. "Put on the ring," I said when I had finally stared Darla awake.

She smiled and reached for the box on the bedside table. I opened it and slipped the ring onto her finger.

"Hey Mom," I stood in the doorway of the little sewing room off the kitchen.

"Ahh..." She jumped and looked up at me. She smiled. "I didn't hear you come in. You startled me." She stood up and came over to kiss my cheek and hug me.

"I'm sorry," I said. "I guess I should have rung the doorbell or something."

"No, you don't ever have to ring the doorbell. This will always be your home." She went past me to the kitchen. "Would you like some coffee?"

"That would be nice." I sat down at the table and rubbed Caramel. The afghan hound lay under the table."

"Is everything alright?" Mom said as she sat down with two cups of coffee. "I don't usually see you at this time on a Wednesday morning. Are you sick?"

"No." I laughed. For a minute I thought she was going to put her hand on my forehead to feel for fever. "I called work and said I'd be late. I need to talk to you about something."

"All right," she said. "I'm all ears."

"No, you're mostly legs." I laughed. She smiled. "Mom, Darla and I are getting married. I wanted you to be the first to know. I need to know you're okay with it."

She looked into my eyes and studied me for a minute. "You didn't tell me you were going to ask her. You usually talk to me about things like this before the fact."

"I didn't this time." I felt irritated. How did she know that Darla had asked me and not the other way around? Sometimes I really thought she could read my mind. She looked at me for a few seconds more then took a sip of coffee.

"Are you happy about it?"

"Very, I love Darla. Besides Jimmy she's the best friend I've ever had. I think she's good for me." I was rambling. Why did I feel the need to justify this?

"Then I'm very happy for you, honey. Why would you think I wouldn't be?"

"Well, her aunt did run off with your husband."

"Oh yeah, that." She laughed. "Well, I certainly can't hold that against Darla, can I?"

"No, but it may make family politics a little difficult." I put my hand on hers and squeezed.

"That's true, but that will be harder for you than it is for me. Remember, your father isn't with Sharon anymore. He's back here in Atlanta, and he spends a good bit of time with me." She smiled and I could see the raw happiness in her eyes.

"Uncle Jeff always said you were a mate for lifer." I smiled back. "Why haven't the two of you remarried?"

"We don't need to. We're happy the way things are." She picked up my hand and kissed the back of it. "When will you and Darla get married?"

"She wants to start a family right away." I laughed. "She says we're the perfect genetic compliment."

Mom laughed with me. "Oh, I think I'm going to enjoy that little daughter-in-law of mine."

"She really is something else." I felt happy for the first time in a while. "She wants to get married in a month."

"So that would be around the beginning of September. Has she given you a date?"

"Yes, September fourth. She's going to have a Matron of Honor, Meryl, of course. I'm torn. I think I should ask Jimmy since I was his best man, but I'd like to ask Uncle Jeff. Of course, that would hurt Dad's feelings."

"Oh honey, it's your wedding. Don't worry about other people's feelings so much. If you want to ask Uncle Jeff, ask him."

"Yeah, I guess you're right. I'm going to Uncle Jeff and Amanda's for dinner on Saturday night. I thought I'd ask Amanda if I could make it an engagement party. She's getting more comfortable with groups of people. Could you be there?"

"Of course, honey."

"Good." I stood up and took my coffee cup to the sink. "I'm on my way to the nursery now to talk to Uncle Jeff. I didn't want to make an announcement. I want to tell people in person."

"You're such a caring person, David." She kissed my cheek as I left. "I raised you right." I could hear her sewing machine start up as I closed the front door.

◊

"How did your mother take it?" I asked Darla at dinner that night.

"She cried and ran to her room." She laughed and handed me a napkin. We were on the back deck of my house. I had barbecued chicken and Darla had tossed a salad.

"She didn't expect you to marry white trash?"

"Don't tease me, David." She laughed. "I've already apologized for that stupid comment."

"You were only parroting her."

"That's true, but I think that she cried more because I'm her only child, and she hoped I'd stay a baby forever. My dad, by the way, was thrilled. He said you had established yourself well enough to be an excellent provider."

"My money again," I laughed.

"Speaking of only children, David, I don't want to have one."

"I thought you said we were doing this so we could have children."

"That's right, children. I don't want to have an only child. I want four."

"Four," I gasped. How was I supposed to support four kids? How would I educate them? "P.H. I can't have four kids. I mean you have to put them through school. We'll probably want them to go to private schools. I don't make that good a living."

"There is no reason for private school. We didn't go to private school. I want four kids, David."

I looked at my plate and suddenly had no appetite. "I was thinking two kids. Jimmy and Meryl only have two."

"Not anymore, Meryl told me today. She's pregnant."

"Oh really?" I looked up. She laughed and I looked down at my plate to keep from smiling. "Maybe this isn't going to work out after all."

"Oh come on, David. We can work this out. I promise you four kids won't be too much."

"I only want two." I stirred my salad with my fork and remembered how much I had hated salad as a child. Now sometimes it was the best part of the meal. What was happening to me?

"How about we compromise and only have three."

Three sounded like a better number but it still seemed like a big responsibility. "Three is an odd number," I said.

"It's perfect, three seats in the back of a car. I'm okay with it. David, cheer up, I didn't mean to upset you." She bit into a piece of chicken. "Besides it's really up to God. Maybe I won't be able to have any at all. Then we'd have to adopt. Waiting lists for adoption are long. We might not be able to adopt three children."

"This conversation is scaring me to death," I said.

"We'll change the subject then." She ate quietly for a while. I took a few bites. Then I noticed her eyes wandering around my kitchen. "This house will do for a while, but we'll need a much bigger place in the long run."

"Oh shit!" I put down my fork.

There was only one awkward moment at the engagement party. Darla and I arrived early. My mom was there helping Amanda. Uncle Jeff opened the door to us. He put his arms out to Darla and she moved into them. He picked her up off the ground which was the only way to get a true hug from her since she was so small.

"I hope you'll call me Uncle now," he said as he set her back on the floor.

"I sure will." She smiled exposing those adorable dimples. I thought, if we have girls, I hope they have dimples. "Where are Amanda and Charlie?"

"They're in the kitchen, but you're not going in there right now. The girls are in the play room, and they want you in there as soon as you get here."

"Oh, a command performance,"

"That's right." Uncle Jeff led us into the play room and two squeals of joy met our entrance. My twin cousins toddled in my direction. I scooped up one and Darla picked up the other. I was always amazed at how much they looked alike. Dad and Uncle Jeff looked alike, but fifty years and different lifestyles had put distinguishing marks on them. At two years old, identical twins are truly identical.

"Which one do I have?" I asked.

"That's Alice, she's wearing green today. This is Evelyn in the pink." He kissed the head of the baby Darla held. "Amanda tells me the color code every morning when she dresses them." He laughed.

"How does Amanda know them apart?" Darla asked.

"Alice has a scar on her chest from surgery, remember."

"Oh that's right? How is she doing?"

"Everything looks great. It looks like the problem was solved." Uncle Jeff put his hand on the head of the toddler in my arms. "I wish they'd get some hair." Both girls were almost completely bald.

"I'm sure they will," Darla said. "You and Amanda both have thick hair. Look," she ruffled the top of Evelyn's head and said. "I see a little coming in."

I looked at Darla holding the baby. She looked so right in that position. I wondered what our own children would look like in her arms. I felt warm all over. Maybe I could support three kids. I smiled. She looked at me and smiled back.

"Bubba," Alice put her chubby hand on my lip and pulled it. I looked down at her. She was smiling, exposing slightly crooked baby teeth.

"They're both getting braces as soon as we can put them on," Uncle Jeff said. "Crooked teeth are way too sexy." He put his arm across Amanda's shoulders as she came into the room with Mom. "My girls are getting their teeth straightened." Amanda blushed and we all laughed.

"Let's go into the living room and wait for the rest of the guests. When Jimmy and Meryl get here we can all go swimming," Amanda said. "Your family is coming a little later. They didn't want to swim. They're just joining us for dinner."

"Thank you for inviting them. I've instructed them to be on their best behavior." Darla laughed, and I noticed that everyone in the room smiled at the sound.

"We're not worried honey," Mom said.

"Hey, where is everyone?" I heard my dad's voice from the kitchen. He came into the playroom making the space just a little too crowded. Everyone moved toward the living room. "I went out to clean up the grill, and when I came back I was alone," he said.

"Would anyone like some champagne?" Uncle Jeff asked.

"It's a little early for that," Mom said. "Let's have some lemonade?"

"Do I get a hug from my beautiful niece and daughter-in-law?" Dad approached Darla.

Darla smiled and moved into his arms. He picked her up, cradling her like a child. I had a feeling he'd held her that way before. They had a relationship that had nothing to do with me. The old longing came back for a minute. I swallowed and followed my mother into the kitchen for lemonade.

"I know it's hard for you to see evidence of your father's life without you," Mom said. She was pouring lemonade into glasses and putting them on a tray to carry to the living room.

I didn't say anything. The familiar lump was in my throat. I splashed cold water on my face from the sink. Cold water always seemed to help. "I'm a grown man, Mom. Why does it still hurt so much?"

"I'm afraid emotional wounds don't go away with age. Things like that never stop hurting."

"Does it hurt you too?"

"Very much," She put her arms around me and I leaned into the embrace. We held each other like that for a minute then separated. I felt better. She picked up the tray and went into the living room. I followed her.

"I told Darla to call me Dad now, but she says she doesn't think she can break the Uncle habit." Dad laughed. He was taking the best man thing pretty well. I hoped it didn't hurt him. If it did, maybe it should.

"I've got it," Darla said. "I'll call you Uncle Dad."

Jimmy, Meryl, and the kids arrived in time for lemonade and cookies.

"I understand congratulations are in order," I said to Jimmy.

"Yeah, well," he said. "It wasn't really planned. I sure hope we can handle a third child."

"You'll do fine, Jimmy." I looked at Darla and she smiled somewhat triumphantly up at me. I stuck out my tongue at her and she laughed.

"Don't stick your tongue out at me unless you intend to use it."

"Okay, you two wait for the honeymoon," Meryl laughed.

After our lemonade I put on my bathing suit in the room Uncle Jeff had designated as my room, even though I'd only spent a couple of nights in it. It was full of soccer trophies and pictures of backpacking trips. I smiled when I looked around it. Uncle Jeff had made it look like a room I'd grown up in. He had a wife and children of his own, but I was still as much a part of his family as they were.

I got into the pool. The water was cool, but the babies were already in and bouncing around in their floating bathing suits.

"Dad, Uncle David, watch," James, Jr. called from the diving board. He ran to the end and jumped grabbing his knees and landing in the water in cannonball fashion. The spray hit me in the face. I looked over at Jimmy. He was dripping wet and scowling at his son.

"Jamie, that was…"

"Don't yell at him, Jimmy. He's a kid. We're in a swimming pool."

"Yeah, you're right and you were right about tennis too. He's really good. I've started taking lessons. That way we can play together." He smiled reluctantly. "I'm way too hard on that kid. He's doing pretty well in school. Thanks for tutoring him even though I acted like a jerk."

"You can't help it." I jabbed him with my elbow. "You are a jerk."

He laughed. "Thanks for being so understanding. I guess I'm a little on edge about the new baby and all."

"Are you worried about having a third child?"

"Yes, I told Meryl I didn't want any more babies. She tricked me again."

"Hey Jimmy, it takes two," I said. Just then Meryl and Darla came out of the house in their bathing suits. I watched the expression on Jimmy's face change from a frown to a smile. His eyes widened and he moved across the pool toward his wife. Meryl had maintained her tall slender figure even after two kids. She wore a one piece bathing suit. Her belly was barely showing signs of the child to come. She sat down on the side of the pool and Jimmy put his hands on her waist to draw her into the water and into his arms.

I looked at Darla as she made her way to the end of the pool where Heather was getting ready to go down the steps into the water. The sight of her took my breath away. Had I purposely chosen to marry a woman so totally opposite of Anna? Darla's hair looked like white gold in the sunlight. It was perfectly straight and silky. Her skin was fair, almost translucent, and perfectly clear. These were the obvious differences of race. But her body was voluptuous, not subtly curved like Anna's. Her breasts were big and the cleavage that showed at the top of her bikini was smooth and round. Her waist was small and her belly was flat. Her bottom was flat too, and her legs, though shapely, were thin with tiny delicate knees and ankles.

"David," James, Jr. tugged on my arm. "Throw me, okay."

We had played that game since James and Heather were small. I looked down at my best friend's son. "I'm not sure I can any more, Jamie. You're so big. How old are you now?"

"I'm eight and you're a lot bigger than me. So throw me."

I picked the child up and cupped his small bottom in the palms of my hands. I tossed him up into the air and watched him land in the water. I turned and waded through the water to where Darla and Heather were just getting to the bottom of the steps.

"My turn." Heather hurried over to me and I tossed her too. "I guess if Jamie is eight that would make Heather ten, right?" I leaned down to kiss Darla and pressed my tongue lightly to hers.

She smiled. "So you did intend to use it."

"We're falling behind. We need to have some babies."

We all had a wonderful time in the warm Atlanta summer. As long as you stayed in the water it was fine, but it was too hot to stay outside when we were finished swimming. We all got dressed and met in the cool living room. We were enjoying our first glass of champagne when Darla's parents arrived.

"Please come in," Amanda said in her soft voice. "I'm so glad you could join us to celebrate this happy occasion."

Darlene Bergquist came into the room. She certainly had a sour expression on her face which definitely worsened when she saw my mom sitting on an overstuffed loveseat next to my dad.

"Thank you for inviting us," she said and sat down on a straight back chair. Jason Bergquist stood behind his wife and smiled looking a little nervous.

"We've had a lovely afternoon in the pool," Uncle Jeff said. "Will you have some champagne with us? I was just about to propose a toast."

"Do you have sparkling water?" Darlene asked.

"Yes, I'll get you some," Amanda said. "Do you prefer water, Jason?"

"Yes, he'll have sparkling water too," Darlene said,

"No, I'd love some champagne," Jason said. Uncle Jeff handed him a glass and poured champagne into it.

Darlene sneered. Amanda came back into the room with a champagne glass filled with sparkling water.

"Alright," Uncle Jeff said. He held his glass up. "To Darla and David, I hope you have a long happy marriage and happy healthy children."

"I don't know if I can toast to my daughter marrying a convicted felon and cross breeding with the son of an Amazon," Darlene said. The room fell into a crushing silence that seemed to last for hours.

"Darlene," Dad stood up and crossed to her chair. He pulled her to a standing position. "I don't have any problem planting my foot in the seat of your pants as I kick you out that door."

"Mother," Darla finally moved forward. "I told you that if you couldn't refrain from doing that you couldn't come to this party."

"Since when do you tell me what I can and cannot do, young lady?" Dad was pulling Darla's mother to the door and she said. "Jason, are you going to let this man abuse me."

"What am I going to do about it, Darlene? He's huge and I'm not." He looked around the room. "There are three of them and they're all huge."

"There are four of us," Jimmy said. "I'm not huge, but I'm not a lightweight."

Everyone had stood up. It looked like there was going to be a fight. I looked at Darla. Our eyes met. There were tears in hers. I stuck out my tongue at her. She dissolved into laughter and I whispered. "And I do intend to use it."

"Dad," I said. "Let Mrs. Bergquist go. She does have a point. I am a convicted felon."

"David, we said we wouldn't talk about that," Darla sobered again.

"You said we wouldn't talk about it. It's part of my life. I can assure you I'll never forget it. So let's talk about it." I turned to Darla's mother. "I'm a really nice guy though. I make a good living. You won't have to support Darla anymore."

"That's right," Jason Bergquist smiled and slapped me on the shoulder. He had to reach to do it.

"Oh for crying out loud," Darlene said. "Why do men make such a big deal about who brings home the money."

"No Mama, it isn't just men. One of the reasons I chose David is because he can support me."

"She's marrying me for my money." I put my arms around Darla's neck from behind and leaned down to kiss her on the top of her head.

"Not entirely," she smiled up at me. "I want your genetics too."

"This brings us back to another subject." Mom took my arm. "I am definitely an Amazon."

"I think this family needs a little height," Jason said. Then he lowered his eyes at his wife's glare.

"You're a gorgeous Amazon." Dad kissed Mom on the cheek. Darlene Bergquist huffed and Dad said. "Darlene, try to remember that it was your sister that left me."

"But she didn't expect you to go running back to her." Darlene pointed to Mom as her face crumpled and she started to cry. "It's humiliating, like you never even loved Sharon."

Mom picked up a box of tissue off the table and handed her one. "Darlene, it sounds to me like your problem is not with David. It's with his father." She smiled at Dad. "And maybe a little bit with me. Don't you think it would be better to deal with that in another time and place?"

Darlene looked around the room. "I want to go home now."

"Well, I don't," Jason said. "I want to celebrate my daughter's engagement." He lifted his glass in solute and took a sip of champagne. "Although, I have to say one thing, David."

"What's that, sir?"

"The proper way to do it would have been to ask me for my daughter's hand in marriage before you proposed to her."

"I'm sorry, sir. I would have if I'd proposed to her. The truth is, she proposed to me."

There was another moment of silence before the room erupted in laughter. I gently took Mrs. Bergquist's arm and guided her into the dining room.

"I guess I should have asked you for your son's hand in marriage. Sorry Charlie, Uncle Dad," Darla said to Mom and Dad as they followed us.

"That's my girl," Darlene muttered as I seated her at the table.

CHAPTER SEVENTEEN

At my wedding I met my stepmother.

Four weeks from the time we first made love, Darla and I got married. She had moved in with me already. It only took her about a week to get her small apartment neatly incorporated into my small house. I was in the process of buying the place from Amanda.

We were married at three o'clock in the afternoon on Sunday, September 4th. The priest at my mother's church did it. I'd been confirmed as a child and so had Darla. I wasn't sure we needed a priest, but it made Mom happy.

The cathedral was grander than I remembered it from going to mass, maybe because of the vows that we were taking on that day. I walked to the front of the church where the priest waited for me. Uncle Jeff was at my side. As we passed the last pew I saw my mother and father sitting side by side. Across the aisle was an older version of Darla. My breath caught in my throat. I knew I was looking at the woman who had taken my dad from me, the woman who had kept my dad from me.

She sat next to Darla's mother. My brother and sister sat further down the pew. Uncle Jeff put his hand on my shoulder and squeezed. I realized I was staring. I took a deep breath and felt grateful for my uncle's touch.

Then the music started. I looked back as Heather, dressed in pink, and young James in a very small tuxedo, started their procession up the aisle. They were beautiful. Then Meryl followed in a blue dress. She was lovely. Her pregnancy showed only slightly and the folds of the dress had been artistically arranged over it. I looked at Jimmy where he sat next to my parents. He watched her with a smile that reflected pure love.

Then the music stopped and the wedding march began. The rest of the ceremony is a blur. Darla appeared in the door on her father's arm and the lights of heaven seemed to shimmer around her. Her white gold hair was swept up off her neck, and a veil of lace fell to the ground behind her. As she walked up the aisle toward me, the lights danced off the folds of her gown.

"Oh…" I heard myself say on a breath.
"You're a lucky man," Uncle Jeff whispered in my ear.
"I'm a lucky man."

I sat down at the table that was set up for the bride and groom. The reception was at Uncle Jeff's house and the yard was full of people. It was almost time for Darla and me to leave. The limo was waiting and Darla had gone in to change her clothes.

"It was a beautiful wedding, David." My shoulders stiffened at the voice from behind me. I turned and looked at Sharon as she sat down at the table beside me.

"I guess you know who I am," she said.

"We met in the reception line."

"But you knew who I was before that."

"Yeah." I looked away from her at the people forming a path for us to walk through while they threw bird seed at us and blew bubbles. "I'm surprised. Darla looks more like you than she does like her mother."

"Not really, Darlene just let her hair go grey. I didn't." She sipped the glass of champagne she was holding. "Don't you have any hostile words for me, David? I'm the person your father left you for."

"There is no hostility in me today." I looked around for Darla. I wanted her to rescue me.

"I also kept him away from you. He thought about you a lot you know."

"That's what he tells me."

"You look like him." She brushed her hair away from her face. I looked at her. She didn't actually look like Darla. She looked sad. There were no dimples in her cheeks. "I hated that. Our children look more like me."

"They look like him too. I'm surprised to see a family resemblance in the three of us."

"I suppose." She looked across the yard, and I saw my brother tap my sister on the shoulder. He pointed toward us, and they both started in our direction.

"So," I said. I had mixed feelings. I had craved some kind of contact with this woman. Maybe I really didn't want to be rescued. "Where's the new husband?"

"There's no new husband," she said. "That didn't work."

My heart started to pound, and I searched the crowd for my mother and father. "Does that mean you've come to reel him back in?" I demanded.

"I thought you said there was no hostility in you today." She laughed and for just a second it sounded like Darla. It didn't make me smile.

I relaxed when I spotted my parents. They stood in the line. Mom held her bubble maker to her lips. Dad had bird seed in one hand and the other hand on her waist.

"Look at that." I heard the sadness in her voice and saw that she was watching them too. "He left her for me. He was a good husband to me, a good father to our children." She looked up into my eyes. "I was his ideal. But she was always his grand passion." I looked at her and then back to my parents.

"Did we get here in time to stop the fireworks?" Drew's voice interrupted.

"Is everything okay, David?" Kristina sounded concerned.

"Everything is great," I said. "I'm glad to be getting to know my stepmother after all these years."

"They're very protective of you, David." Sharon stood up. "Far more protective of you than they are of their own mother."

"You take care of yourself pretty well," Drew said. "David doesn't know you. He's a babe in the woods."

Sharon laughed and I saw a different expression in her eyes, not sadness anymore.

I wasn't sure what it was but the expression unsettled me. Can you feel bad for someone you've hated all your life, I thought. Actually I hadn't hated her. I'd just wanted to. She put her arms around my brother and sister and went to the lines of waiting people.

"Are you ready to go?" Darla put her arm through mine. I looked down at her and forgot the whole incident. She took my breath away again. I smiled. "Let's go, wife." I could feel the grin on my face.

Five years later, I pulled into my driveway after work and stopped to look at the view. We had moved from the small house in midtown that I had bought from Amanda. I offered it back to her because I knew it had meaning, but she tearfully refused. She and Uncle Jeff had a solid family now. My little cousins were seven years old.

"I can't believe how fast my life is going by," I said out loud. Then I looked across the rambling lawn in the front of my house. It was a two story with columns in the southern style. It sat on an acre and a half of land. The house was slightly downhill from the road and the yard rolled toward it. We had lived there for four years and Darla had been hard at work building pathways through the yard that circled small to medium sized flower beds. There were flowering and fruit bearing trees and bushes. It was spring time, so everything was blooming and it was my thirty third birthday.

My eyes wandered across the pie shaped yard to the far corner where I saw my two daughters standing on either side of what looked to be a beach ball. The beach ball rolled a little in my direction then waved at me. It was Darla. My tiny little wife was perfectly round. Today she wore a pair of orange shorts and a t-shirt that was alternating panels of white and green and white and blue. Beach ball was a perfect description.

My five year old daughter, Charlotte, bounced up and down and waved in my direction. Her three and a half year old sister Veronica followed suit. I watched as Darla stood and took her gardening gloves off. She put them in the pouch that hung around her middle. She took the girl's hands and started toward the house. I drove the car down the hill and around to the back of the house to the three car garage.

"Happy birthday, Daddy." My daughter's sang in unison as I came through the garage door.

"Thank you, ladies." I scooped them both up in my arms and settled them on my shoulders.

"Be careful, David," Darla said. "Don't whack anyone's head again."

"I only did that one time," I laughed. "Will you ever forgive me? Charlita has." I hadn't planned to have pet names for my kids. I'd never shortened the twin's names, but it wasn't long after each of my girls was born that I shortened their names. Charlotte was Charlita, I pronounced it with a Ch not an Sh, and Veronica was Vroom.

"Charlotte will forgive you anything." Darla laughed, and I stopped seeing a beach ball and smiled at the tinkling sound. "I probably won't."

I put the girls down and embraced my soft sweet wife. She kissed me. "Happy Birthday, David," she said.

"Thank you." I put my brief case on the table and went to the refrigerator to pour myself a glass of lemonade.

"I want some lemonade, Daddy," Charlotte said. "... Lemonade, Daddy," Veronica parroted.

"How about apple juice," Darla said. "Lemonade gives you girls a tummy ache, remember."

Charlotte pouted but accepted the glass of juice when Darla poured it. I was reminded of how much she looked like my mother. She had wavy brown hair and soft brown eyes and she was tall. She was surely going to be an Amazon just like Mom. Veronica had straight blond hair like her mother. She had blue eyes like her mother too. Other than that she looked like my mom. Her facial features were Mom's. She was a year and a half younger than her sister and almost as tall. I wouldn't be surprised if they grew up to be as tall as me, a worrying thought. Neither one of them had dimples in their cheeks.

"You'd think these girls were Mom's, Darla. They look just like her."

"They do." She smiled as she took something out of the oven and set it on the counter. "I'm glad. I've always thought your mother was beautiful, strikingly so with her height."

"I wanted dimples," I said.

"Sorry." Darla looked up at me. "Maybe next time."

Our youngest was three and a half years old and we hadn't talked about a third since she was born. Charlotte was born eight months after we were married. I was glad we'd had such a short engagement. Veronica came a fast sixteen months later and Darla was so tired after that, she hadn't talked about number three at all.

In the past three months she'd made little comments that indicated she may be getting ready. Even though I'd fought the idea, I found myself hoping she would want to go ahead and have a third. I guess family life agreed with me.

"Go change your clothes, David. Uncle Jeff and Amanda are coming tonight with the kids. The pool isn't open, so there won't be any swimming. But if the thunderstorms hold back, I was hoping for a back yard picnic. The girls will be thrilled to see their cousins."

"Mom called me at work," I said. "She and Dad are taking the girls home with them tonight."

"Yeah, she said you and I should celebrate your birthday alone together. I'm glad. There's something I want to talk to you about anyway."

"I'm glad too." I headed toward the back stairway to the bedrooms on the second floor. I hoped I knew what she wanted to talk about. I hoped she was ready to work on baby number three. I loved both of my girls. I didn't really care if I had a boy or not, but I really did hope this one had dimples.

After I showered and changed my clothes, I poured myself a glass of wine and went out to the back yard. The pool was off the back deck. It was still covered for winter. There wouldn't be any swimming. Beyond the pool was a small stretch of back lawn before the yard rose in a dramatically steep hill of forty three feet. I had measured it before we bought the place. I was trying to talk Darla out of buying. What in the world would we do with that hill?

Uncle Jeff settled the debate by saying the hill would take care of itself, and he was right. The natural flora of Georgia had taken it over. Besides having to pull out the occasional kudzu vine that wanted to take up residence; we hadn't had to do much at all. It did shorten the back lawn a bit though. That was nice for mowing, but there wasn't room for a proper badminton net. We managed to squeeze one in anyway. We had to take it down, though, if we wanted to do anything else back there.

"Bubba!" Alice ran out of the back door and flung herself around my neck. I spilled my wine before I could put it down. I wrapped my arms around her and accepted the kisses she wet my face with. "Sorry I spilled your wine," she said, not looking sorry at all. "I'll go get you another glass."

"Bring me out a towel when you come." I set her down on the ground and rubbed at the spot on my shirt. "Where is the rest of the family?"

"They're poking along behind. They move like turtles." Alice lived life in full gear. She had always been the go getter. Evelyn was quiet and bookish. I loved her just as dearly, but she was the more grounded one. It seemed odd to me that Alice had entered the world without a guarantee that she would even have a life. The heart condition that had been repaired at birth had been life threatening, but she was the one with the tremendous energy. Maybe she was just grateful to be alive.

"Happy Birthday, David," Uncle Jeff came out the door and wrapped me up in one of his great bear hugs. "I can't believe how old you're getting. You don't suppose that means I'm getting old too do you?"

I looked at his familiar smiling face. Well into his fifties at this point, he looked great. His hair was completely white, and the smile lines around his mouth and eyes were prominent. But his skin looked healthy, and he moved easily and without stiffness.

"No," I said. "I think you're getting younger as I get older."

"Happy Birthday, David," I turned to Amanda. She looked the same as always. I suppose her hair had a few more highlights. She looked happy. They both looked happy.

"Thanks, Amanda," I kissed her on the cheek. "Where is Evelyn?"

"Darla had some books she'd brought from the school library to look at. She brings her some every time she volunteers at the elementary school. That's so nice. She'll be out in a minute."

Just as she said it, the back door opened and Evelyn came out with a book in her hand. "Happy Birthday, Bubba." She put the book down on the table and stretched her arms up to me. I leaned down for the hug and picked her up off the ground. She kissed me softly on the cheek, and I noticed the sweetness of her lips and the softness of her cheek against mine.

"What a nice greeting. I loved your sister's greeting too, but she almost knocked me over. She spilled a glass of wine on me, drowned me in kisses, and ran back into the house before I'd even gotten a chance to kiss her back."

"I think Alice has ADHD," Evelyn said as I set her back down on the ground. The back door slammed as Alice hurried out the door with a glass of wine in one hand and a towel in the other. She watched the wine glass closely as she walked as fast as possible without spilling. A few drops slopped over, but I had an almost full glass when she handed it to me.

"ADHD means Attention Deficit Hyperactive Disorder," Evelyn continued after we had all watched Alice's progress across the lawn.

"I make good grades, and I'm not a disciplinary problem, so they aren't going to test me. I don't have ADHD." Alice raised her shoulders and puffed out her chest as she said this to her sister. I thought they were going to fight. My two girls came out the door with their mother and ran toward us. Darla carried a padded basket.

"Those are some pretty big words for a seven year old," I said. I put my hand on Evelyn's shoulder.

"I know those words too," Alice said.

"They're smart like their Bubba," Uncle Jeff smiled.

"Evelyn, Alice," Charlotte called. "We have kittens, come see."

"Kittens?" Uncle Jeff looked at me.

"Darla thinks the girls should have pets and someone she volunteers with at the school had a litter, so we have kittens. Their names are Soft and Furry. I wanted to insist that they give them real names, but Darla said Soft and Furry were fine names."

Uncle Jeff smiled. My mom and dad came out the back door with glasses in their hand and came toward us.

"Happy Birthday, honey," Mom said. She kissed my cheek.

"Happy Birthday, son." Dad put his hand on my shoulder and squeezed.

"Honey, Darla says she wanted a puppy and you said no."

"Kittens are better. Cats are easier so they can each have their own pet."

"You know what concerns me, David. I know you loved Charlotte, but you can love another dog."

"That's right, David," Uncle Jeff said. "When Gabe died last year it really hurt, but after a few months I went back to the greyhound rescue and got another one. I'm crazy about Dolores. She's a great dog."

"Gabe didn't die of a broken heart," I said. "I don't want to talk about it."

"David," Mom said.

"Leave him alone, Charlotte," Dad said. "You too, Jeff. He'll work through this his own way."

"That's right." I looked at the basket with the kittens in it and the girls gathered around it. "Now I'm going to go play with the other kids and the kittens." I walked away from my three parents ignoring the looks of concern on their faces.

✧

"The girls have no trouble going home with your parents. Charlie says they don't get separation anxiety until they're getting closer to preteen years. I don't think ours will ever have a problem," Darla said after we had said goodnight to our children and our guests.

"I don't either. They've been staying with grandparents since they were weaned." I went into the kitchen to rinse my glass and put it in the dishwasher. Darla came into the kitchen behind me, and we started on the dishes. We had used paper plates so there wasn't much clean up.

"You don't think Alice really has an ADHD problem, do you, David? You're pretty familiar with it since you've helped the Jameses," she laughed.

"Yeah, and most of the kids I've worked with in the big brothers program have had ADD of one form or another," I said. "No, Alice is fine. She just has a lot of energy. You saw how she concentrated on that glass of wine. I thought at the time, maybe it isn't good training to have a kid bring me booze."

"It's not like she was carrying liquor to a drunk, David. It was the only glass of wine you had all evening."

"Yeah," I dried my hands and went into the living room. Darla followed me and we sat down, me in my easy chair, her on the couch. "I'm tired," I said. "It's been a long day. I'm glad it's Friday and I don't have much to do tomorrow."

"Me too, and I'm glad the girls are with your parents."

I rested my head back and closed my eyes.

"Don't go to sleep yet. There's something I want to talk to you about."

"I'm not sleeping," I said not opening my eyes.

"I saw my OB/GYN earlier this week."

I opened my eyes and looked at her. I could feel my grin. "You're pregnant? I was just thinking it's about time for number three."

"I thought you didn't want more kids."

"I've changed my mind. What a great birthday present." I stretched my arms out toward her. She didn't move.

"Well, settle down. I'm not pregnant."

"Oh." I dropped my arms to the chair. I was surprised at the disappointment I felt. "So why did you go to the doctor? You're alright aren't you?" My disappointment became concern.

"I'm fine but I'm fat. Dr. Rhomert said that he didn't want me to conceive again until I'd lost thirty pounds." She frowned and I laughed. She pouted just like Charlotte.

"It's not funny, David. You wouldn't believe how mad I was at him for saying that. Of course, it's true."

"When I pulled into the driveway today, I thought the girls were standing on either side of a beach ball." Shit, I thought, why did I say that?

She jumped up from her seat on the couch. "I can't believe you just said that to me."

"I can't believe I did either," I muttered.

"You're no lightweight yourself, Mr. Potato Head. Have you noticed this lately?" She poked at my belly with her finger. I looked down. It was true. I sat behind a desk all day. I had stopped working out. I used the excuse that I needed to be with the family in the evening, but we had a workout room at the house. I could find the time.

Uncle Jeff and I still hiked, but I'd noticed myself slowing down the last few times. I even quit playing soccer after Charlotte was born. Jimmy had stopped after their little girl, Marissa, was born too. Maybe it was time to look for another team.

"You're a good cook, Darla." I said and rubbed my belly.

"I know I am. That's why we both have to lose weight. You're as fat as I am." She turned like she was going to leave the room.

"Well, I don't think I'm as fat as you are."

"Ahhh… I can't believe you said that." She whirled around and glared at me. I held my arms out to her again.

"I'm sorry," I laughed. "I'm just trying to lighten things up. Please come and sit in my lap, baby. I'd get up and come to you, but I'm too fat."

She looked at me and narrowed her eyes. "If I'm so fat, won't I cut off your circulation?"

"Beach balls are big and round, but they're very light." I kept my arms extended toward her. She looked at me sideways, but I knew I had her. I was seeing evidence, however small, of the dimples in her cheeks. She moved toward me and took my hands in hers. I gently pulled her toward me. She climbed onto the easy chair. My legs were stretched out on the stool. She straddled my hips with her knees and sat back on my lower thighs. It was a familiar position. We enjoyed sitting this way with each other.

"It's actually nice," I said. "The padding on your butt keeps the bones of your flat ass from sticking into my legs."

Her mouth and eyes went round, and she started to struggle to get off my lap. I put my arms around her and pulled her to my chest. "I'm kidding," I laughed. "Don't struggle so hard. Our bellies get in the way when you do." She settled down and put her head on my chest. I kissed her silky hair. Her arms went loosely around my neck and I held her close. "I don't care about the weight," I said. "You're still sweet to hold."

"Well, I don't care about your belly either," she said. "But I do care about having a healthy pregnancy, and I guess it isn't healthy for you to have a gut either. We have to do something." She sat back and took my face in her hands. She kissed my lips. "So I joined both of us in a weight loss group that meets at the school on Wednesday nights."

"Oh man, I don't want to go to a weight loss group."

"I figured you wouldn't, but I need your support. There was a meeting on Tuesday, but I know that's when you work with Jamie. Meryl says he's doing very well by the way. So Wednesday night is it."

"Thirty pounds?" I said. "How long do you think that will take?"

"I don't know. I never had to lose weight before." She smiled and climbed off my lap. "You really want baby number three don't you?" She pulled me up. "I can't stop the birth control pills until I've lost the weight, but we can still practice." She pulled on my hand, and I struggled out of the chair.

"I hope our bellies don't get in the way," I laughed.

"I think we'll manage."

✧

I watched my tiny wife volley the soccer ball down the field. She had lost her thirty pounds and we had joined a co-ed soccer team with Meryl and Jimmy. Things were looking up.

"Did you play soccer when you were a kid, P.H.?" I asked as she and Meryl walked off the field.

"Yes, I can't believe you didn't know that. I was on the field next to yours most of the time." She picked up the towel and wiped her face with it. I handed her a bottle of water and she drank half of it in one move.

"I was concentrating on my team," I said. "You know how focused I am."

"Yeah, I do." She smiled.

"I guess you and Meryl were on the same team?"

"I can't believe you didn't notice them, David," Jimmy said as he handed Meryl a water bottle. "I mean girls in shorts when we were in high school. Focused is one thing, man. You must have been wearing blinders."

I laughed. "You're right."

"So do you guys want to come to dinner tonight?" Meryl asked. "Jamie got straight A's on his report card so I'm fixing his favorite. I even baked a flourless chocolate cake, also his favorite. It'll be a celebration."

I looked at Darla.

"Sounds great," she said. "That way I don't have to cook. I don't feel much like cooking these days."

"Let's say six thirty," Meryl said. "That way I've got time to assemble the meat loaf and make the mashed potatoes."

"Meat loaf and mashed potatoes," I said. "It sounds like heaven."

"So when are you going to tell me about the baby," I said on the drive home.

"I guess I don't have to tell you." She reached for my hand and squeezed it.

"How far along are you?"

"Ten weeks, I stopped birth control when I reached the twenty pound mark."

"You didn't tell me."

"I didn't want you to feel any pressure." She looked out the window.

"I don't generally mind that kind of pressure." I squeezed her hand again. "Is everything alright?" I asked when she didn't squeeze back.

"Yeah, Dr. Rhomert says everything looks good. I'm sicker with this one though. Remember, I never had morning sickness with the girls."

"What does that mean?"

"Dr. Rhomert says it doesn't mean anything. It looks like a healthy pregnancy. My weight is good. The blood work is fine. My energy level is good." She smiled and looked at me. "Hey, I can still play soccer."

"Maybe you shouldn't play soccer."

"I'll quit when it doesn't feel good anymore. I actually feel better when I'm moving around."

"I didn't notice you being sick in the morning," I said.

"How would you have noticed, David? You're out of bed by 5:00 every morning. I don't get up to get the girls off until 7:00."

I looked at her. She had looked back out the window. Was she unhappy about my early hours?

"Besides," she said. "It isn't morning for me. For some reason I start to feel bad in the afternoon, right about this time of day. In fact, David," her voice had gotten higher. "Pull over, hurry!"

I pulled the car to the side of the road and she opened the door just in time. She vomited into the gutter for a couple of minutes then dry heaved for a couple more. She looked up at me when she was finished. Her eyes were big and wet. She laid her head back on the seat and closed them.

"I'm sorry," she said.

I handed her a bottle of water and a sweaty towel. "I'm the one that should be sorry," I said. "Are you finished? Can I go on now?"

"Wait just a minute." She took a drink of the water, swished it around in her mouth and spit it into the gutter. "I guess I made a mess in front of someone's house."

"Don't worry about it. There's a thunderstorm coming. It'll take care of it."

"I hate this. It starts just about the time I have to pick the girls up from school. I take a trash can with me just in case. So far I've made it home each time."

"How long has this been going on?"

She looked at me and smiled weakly. "It started the next day."

I laughed and she laughed with me. "You didn't tell me."

"You don't get home until I've started feeling better. I wanted to make sure the pregnancy was alright before I said anything. I'm superstitious I guess. And the truth is, it's embarrassing."

"You don't have to be embarrassed in front of me." I looked at her. She was looking out the window again. Her cheeks were a little flushed. Was it because she'd been sick or was she blushing?

"David!" Her voice was high again. "Pull over, hurry!"

"I wanted to call and cancel, but she insisted on coming. I hope she won't puke at the dinner table." I said to Meryl when we arrived at their house.

"If I thought I would do that, David, I would have let you cancel."

"So you finally told him about the baby." Meryl ushered us in the door and guided Darla to a chair.

"He already knew. I couldn't have kept it from him this afternoon even if I'd wanted to."

"I had to pull over twice on the way from the soccer field to pick up the girls. Then she stayed in the bathroom for half an hour at Mom's."

"I feel fine now. I took a cool shower and brushed my teeth. I'm fine. I'm hungry." Darla did sound perky. The color in her face was good.

She'd gone between white as a sheet and flushed for the last couple of hours. Now her cheeks were rosy and her lips were pink.

"Well, I'm glad you're hungry because we have a big meal prepared." Meryl sat down on the stool in front of Darla's chair and took her hand. "I do think it might be time to quit playing soccer though."

"I think you're right," Darla said. "I hate letting the team down right in the middle of the fall season."

"We'll be lost without our best forward, but we'll manage." I put my hand on her shoulder and squeezed. She put her hand over mine.

"Hey Uncle David," Jamie came into the room in tennis shorts holding a racket. At fourteen he was tall and thin. He hadn't reached his father's height yet, but he didn't have far to go. He was about as tall as his mother. "Dad and I were just getting a quick game in before the big dinner. Did you hear about my report card?"

"I heard and I'm impressed."

"I am too." He smiled and looked at the front door as his father came through holding his own racket and a basket of balls. "I told Mom and Dad not to get too comfortable with it though. It may never happen again."

"Hey," I said. "We take it as it comes."

"Yeah, I'm going to take a quick shower before dinner." Jimmy headed down the hall to his bedroom.

"So is Jamie," Meryl said.

"I'm okay, Mom. I don't stink or anything."

"Yes you do." Meryl nudged her son in the direction of the hallway. "Make it quick. She turned back to us. "Heather should be here any minute. She's bringing her boyfriend."

"Her boyfriend," I said. "Isn't she a little young for a boyfriend?"

"She's sixteen years old, David. So is the boy," Meryl said. "It scares me to death."

"Is he driving her around?" I asked. I had a fleeting memory of Teresa and me in the trunk of my first car. "Shouldn't you keep a closer eye on her? I mean she's just a kid."

"We're pretty strict, but we can't forbid her to ride with him. She'll just do it anyway. I like the boy. I think he'll drive safely."

I wasn't worried about his driving.

"Would you like a beer or some wine, David? Do you want a ginger ale, Darla?"

"That sounds good."

"I'll have a ginger ale too," I said.

✦

"I don't think you should work in the dark, David." The light of my office switched on startling me and making me blink my eyes. "It can't be good for your vision. Don't you get a headache?"

"No," I said. "Turn it off, my keyboard and screen are lit. Turn it off." I put my hand over my eyes.

The overhead light went off, and I looked at the clock on my monitor. "Wow," I laughed. "It's 2:00 in the morning. Did I disturb you, baby?"

Darla sat on the stool next to my desk chair and yawned. "No, I just woke up and you were gone, like usual," she said. "I decided this time I'd come and find out what you were doing."

"I'm working on my Lenny album."

She looked at the monitor. "Lenwood Jones.doc." She read. "I try not to pry into your scrapbooking. I know it's private."

"Nothing's private from you, P.H." I said thinking of my three volumes of Anna Smart albums and hoping she wouldn't ask.

She went over to my book shelf. I had published all of my albums and had them displayed on the shelf. She read the backs of the covers. I felt a prickle on the back of my neck as she reached for one of the books. She took it off the shelf and came back to sit on the foot stool.

It was the first volume on Lenny. There were pictures of us in prison. I wasn't thrilled about her seeing them. I guess if I wanted to be secret about it, I shouldn't have put it in an album. I took a deep breath. At least it wasn't Anna's.

"You do beautiful work, David," she said as she flipped through the book, stopping to look at certain pages. "Whatever happened to that internet business you had before you went to work at the magazine?"

"It was marketing, not scrapbooking. I still do a little on it. I have just a few customers who think nobody else can market them."

"Really," she looked up. Her eyes were wide. "When do you work on it?"

"Usually in the middle of the night like this. I either work on my scrapbooks or my fiction marketing."

"Do you market Lenny?"

"No, I don't have contact with Lenny." I turned back to my computer to save the file and close it down. The room was dark now. "Are my nocturnal habits bothering you lately, Darla?"

"A little," she said. "I've always known that you go to bed with me then get up and work, after your midnight walk of course. When do you sleep, David?"

"I usually doze off right after we have sex for a couple of hours." I smiled at her. She smiled back. I could see her dimples in the light of the full moon through the window. "Then I grab a couple of hours before I get up in the morning."

"Is that enough sleep?"

"It must be. I seem to function alright. I have enough energy to do my job, play with the girls in the evening, and play soccer on the weekends. I'll tell you a secret."

"What?" She yawned again.

"I catch a half hour power nap on my couch after lunch."

"Oh, sounds sexy. Maybe I should join you some day."

"I don't think that would be a power nap, but I'd be willing to make the sacrifice."

"Maybe after the baby," she yawned again.

I stood up. "Let's go to bed." I took her hand and pulled her to her feet.

"After all that you cook a delicious and healthy breakfast," Darla said the next morning as she walked into the kitchen. She had bathed the girls and they were getting dressed for school.

"Don't make me sound like some kind of superman, Darla. I just like to cook."

"I know. You're good at it too. You've been handling dinner since it makes me throw up. You even pack the girls lunches." She sat down at the table and propped her chin on her hands. "I'm useless," she said.

"What?" I turned away from the stove surprised. "I've never heard you say anything like that before. What's going on?"

"I'm useless. I can't do anything."

"That's not true," I said. "You take care of the girls. You get them ready for school. You take them to school. You pick them up."

"No I don't. Meryl picks them up when she goes to get Marissa. She even goes to a different location to get Veronica from preschool. She's such a good friend. But I don't know what I'd do if she couldn't do it. I keep throwing up."

She was crying. Her face was buried in her hands and she was sniffing loudly.

"Is this the pregnancy, P.H.?" I asked. "I don't remember you acting like this with the other two."

"Of course it's not the pregnancy." She was shouting now. I put my finger to my lips.

"Don't get the girls upset before school."

"I'm just good for nothing." She continued in the same loud voice. "I didn't even know what you did in the middle of the night until now. How long have we been married, seven years?"

"In September," I sat down on the chair beside her. I put my hand on her arm. She shook it off.

"Don't be nice to me, David. I don't deserve it."

I opened my mouth, but I was afraid to say anything.

"I didn't even know you still had an internet business. I didn't know you took a power nap at lunch. I didn't know you had no contact with Lenny. What kind of wife am I? All I focus on is myself, my kids, and my home."

"Our kids, our home," I said. "That's what you're supposed to be doing. That was the deal. I make the living. You make the home."

"A deal," She looked at me with red eyes. "A marriage isn't supposed to be a deal."

"It's a partnership."

She picked up a napkin from the table and wiped her eyes. She went to the sink and washed her face. I busied myself with flipping the almost burned pancakes.

"Buckwheat," Darla said. "You've even made things healthy since we've been on our diet."

I didn't say anything. Was she trying to make me feel bad about the good things I do. Should I try to point out something bad about myself? I didn't say anything.

"I'm fourteen weeks along now and I still throw up in the afternoon."

"I'm sorry. That's got to be hard."

"The doctor says I'm fine."

"It's hard to be fine when you don't feel fine."

"Stop saying the right things, David."

"I'm sorry."

"I have an appointment to have another ultrasound this morning. I had to make it in the early morning so I don't throw up on the doctor or the ultrasound tech. I can't take the girls to school."

So that's what this was all about, I thought. "I can't take them today, Darla. I have a meeting."

"Cancel it," she said. "What's the matter are you afraid your co-workers will find out you're not perfect?"

"I can't just cancel business meetings at the last minute. Why didn't you tell me before?" I didn't really care about the meeting. My irritation seemed to be helping her mood.

"I didn't think about it before. I guess you'd better hurry," she said as she left the room.

"What's wrong with Mom?" Veronica said as she came into the room with her preschool pouch in her hand.

"She's just having a little tantrum," I pulled the chair at the table back for her. "Here, have some pancakes and fruit."

"Charlotte is having a tantrum too. I decided to just come on down and ignore her."

"Good plan," I smiled at my pretty little girl. "We'll give her ten minutes." I looked at my watch. "If she isn't down by then I'll go up and get her. In the meantime, tell me what you're doing at school."

◊

"Hey Amanda," I picked up the phone on my desk when I saw it was the reception phone. "What's up?"

"I know you're about to lie down, but your wife is here."

"How do you know I'm about to lie down?"

"She told me."

I guessed Darla's mood hadn't changed since this morning. "Send her on back," I said.

"Sorry I gave away your secret, David." Darla said when she came into my office a minute later. "I really didn't mean to. It just blurted out."

"That's okay, but if you're planning to join me on the couch people might figure it out."

"I'm not planning to join you." She reached up to put her arms around my neck, and I leaned down to kiss her lightly on the mouth. "I've come to apologize."

"For what?" I tried to sound innocent.

"Very funny, I'm sorry I acted so stupid this morning. This pregnancy has been so much harder than the other two. I'm not handling it very well."

"I understand. How'd the ultrasound go?"

"Well, I found out why I've been so sick and so ... hysterical."

"Why," I felt a buzz of anxiety. "What's wrong?"

"Nothing is wrong. At least I hope you won't think it's wrong."

"You're killing me here, P.H."

"Twins, we're going to have twins." Her eyes held mine, daring me. What was she daring me to do?

I stood staring at her with my mouth open for a minute. Then I sat down in my desk chair and rocked back. I covered my face with my hands and laughed. "You always get your way. You wanted four. I wanted two. We compromised at three. How did you manage twins? You even waited until the third pregnancy."

Chapter Seventeen / 318

"This is not my fault," she said. "There isn't a set of twins in my family as far back as we go. Your family is full of them. You can't blame this on me."

I looked at her and smiled. "I'm happy about it, baby."

"Oh, thank God." She sat down in the chair across from my desk. "I was so afraid you'd be mad."

"I'm sorry I made you think that. I'm not mad. You have to admit it's kind of funny though."

"Yeah, it is." She flashed her dimples at me.

"Come over here and sit in my lap." I reached toward her.

"The door is open. Someone might see."

"I don't care." She came around the desk and climbed into my lap, crossways this time.

"I noticed that you got fat faster with this one than either one of the girls."

"You shouldn't say something like that to a pregnant lady. It might make her cry."

"I don't think you want to cry right now."

"No, I don't."

"Are you two alright?" Amanda peeked around the door. "Darla seemed emotional when she came in."

"Congratulate us, Amanda. We're having twins," I said.

"That's wonderful." She came into the room and behind my chair. She put a hand on each of our shoulders and kissed the tops of each of our heads. It was an unusual display of affection for her. "Can I tell your uncle or do you want to."

CHAPTER EIGHTEEN

"All set?" Uncle Jeff said as I let him into the front door of my house.

I smiled at the familiar question. We were going back packing on the kid's spring break from school. It was a late break that year. That was good because the weather in April in Pennsylvania was pretty nice, highs between seventy and eighty, lows in the lower fifties and upper forties. Pretty soon we'd have to change our trips to early summer. We were getting to the northern part of the Trail. We had passed the midpoint a few hikes back. It's also in Pennsylvania. Uncle Jeff, Dad and I had split the cost of an air taxi to our destination on the Trail.

The twins were eight years old and this was the first time we'd included them on the Appalachian. We'd packed small trails in Georgia with them and they'd done well. Evelyn was crazy about camping, but Alice wasn't sure. She wouldn't be left behind though. It was the first time I was including six year old Charlotte too. Darla wasn't happy about it. This time we'd move slower and catch up on mileage in the fall when we'd leave the kids at home.

"If you really object, P.H., I won't take her." I said when I saw Darla bite her bottom lip as she hugged her daughter.

"You're not leaving me," Charlotte called over her shoulder as she ran to Uncle Jeff's truck to climb into the back seat of the cab with her older cousins.

"You can't leave her now," Darla said. "I just wish you'd never suggested it to her."

"She's camped with us before. She does fine."

"But this is for a whole week, David. What if she gets homesick?"

"It's only five days and she's with her father. I won't let her get homesick or hurt. I kissed Darla on the cheek. I'm more worried about you and these guys." I brushed my hand over her bulging belly. "Don't be shy about calling Mom if you need anything." I looked over to where my mom stood beside the open back window of the truck saying goodbye to the girls.

"I won't. I have my parents too, and Meryl and Jimmy. I'm not sick anymore either. So don't worry about me."

"I want to go, Dad."

I looked down at my younger daughter. She tugged on my hand, and I swung her up into my arms. "I know you do, but I couldn't take both of you away from your mother for that long the first time. Next year you'll both go."

"That's not fair. I never get to go by myself."

"Charlita isn't going by herself either. Alice and Evelyn will be there."

Veronica narrowed her eyes at me, and not for the first time, I had the feeling she could see right through me. "You're too smart for your own good, kid." I kissed her loudly on the cheek and put her down. "Next year, I promise." I kissed Darla again and went to the truck to climb into the passenger seat. I kissed my mom through the open window and we pulled away.

"Take care of my boy," Mom said to Uncle Jeff. I laughed.

I waved out the window until we were out of sight, then I turned to look at the three girls in the back seat. "You guys excited?" I asked.

"I am," Evelyn and Charlotte said together.

"I suppose," Alice said. "Will we stay in a motel at least one night?"

"Yes," Uncle Jeff said. "On the third night we hike by the small town of Boiling Springs. I've made reservations at a bed and breakfast. We'll all be happy to have a shower and sleep in a real bed by that time."

"A bed and breakfast," Alice said. "I want to stay at the Ritz and eat in the dining room."

"Not this time, Alice," Uncle Jeff said. He sounded irritated.

I looked back at my young cousins. "Why are they brunettes?" I asked. "I don't think any member of our family has had hair that dark."

"Bubba," Evelyn said. "Don't talk about us like we're not here. We're brunettes because we want to be."

I looked at Uncle Jeff. He shrugged his shoulders. "There's your answer."

"Well, you look beautiful with the dark hair and the blue eyes," I said.

"We planned it that way." Alice lifted her head like royalty.

I laughed and watched the smile spread over Uncle Jeff's face.

"Aren't Uncle Drew and Grampa coming?" Charlotte said.

"They're meeting us at the airfield."

❖

"David didn't throw up this time," Alice said as we unloaded the small air taxi and put our packs into the back of two cabs.

"You've never seen me throw up."

"No, but Dad told us you did. He said that his dog threw up on you and then you threw up on the dog."

"I had a barf bag. I didn't get any of it on the dog." I looked at Uncle Jeff.

"Sorry, I forget about the parroting problem," he said.

"A barf bag, David," Alice said. "Gross."

"How come you're calling me David?" I asked as I took the pack she handed me and wedged it into the full trunk.

"Bubba is a stupid name. Aunt Jeanne is just too old south. I'm so glad you don't call me Sissy."

"It never worked for me, but I'll miss Bubba."

"No you won't," Evelyn said. "You'll always be Bubba to me."

"Good." We all piled into the two cabs and headed for the Trail. We planned to do only a couple of miles tonight. Then we'd camp and go a little further the next day.

"Don't fall asleep in the car, Bubba," Evelyn said. "Dad says you get carsick if you fall asleep in the car."

"Your dad talks too much." I laughed. Uncle Jeff smiled and looked out the window.

"I'm going to wander up this side trail for a while." My brother Drew said after we'd set up camp beside a widening in a stream. "Anyone want to come with me?"

"I'll go," Dad said.

"Me too," Evelyn ran up the trail behind Drew.

"Can I go, Dad?" Charlotte asked.

"You guys think you can handle them all?" I called up the trail as Charlotte ran to join them. "I'd like to stay here with Uncle Jeff and help get supper started." I pulled out my folding fishing pole. Uncle Jeff was already knee deep in the water with his lightweight fishing boots.

"No problem," Drew said.

"They don't have to handle me," Alice said. "I've had enough hiking for one day. I'm staying here."

"Are you alright, sweetie?" Uncle Jeff sounded concerned. "We didn't work you too hard today did we?"

I sometimes forgot about the problem Alice had with her heart when she was born. Obviously Uncle Jeff didn't.

"I'm fine, Dad," she huffed. "My stress test was perfect. I'm not tired. I'm tired of hiking."

"I'm sorry but I'm your father. I can't help worrying."

"Well, I think I'll walk around the side of this pond. It's too cool to go into the water without wading boots. I didn't know it would be this cold in April." She sounded disappointed. "It's warm in Atlanta."

"We're a lot further north." I cast my line into the deep part of the pond.

A few minutes later I pulled in a big mountain trout, took it off my line, and put it into the bucket that Uncle Jeff had already put two in. We fished in silence for probably fifteen or twenty minutes. I added two more trout and Uncle Jeff added one. I was just getting ready to fold up the fishing pole and go back to shore when a shrill sound caught my attention.

It caught Uncle Jeff's attention at the same time because we both looked in the direction of the sound.

Alice hung from a limb that stretched across the rushing part of the stream where the pond continued its downhill flow. Her legs flailed wildly in the air. Her mouth was open in a continuous scream. Uncle Jeff tried to run, but his wading boots caught him, and he fell face first into the water.

I was out of my boots so fast I don't know how I did it. I ran through the water toward the spot below Alice. With my long legs I was able to straddle the water standing on the two large rocks on either side of the opening of the stream. I held my arms up to her just as she lost hold of the branch and fell. I caught her and turned myself to cushion her fall as we plunged into the stream.

The water was deep. The rush of it tore her from my arms. I struggled to pull myself above water to take a breath. As the water carried me down stream I grabbed a fallen limb to stop myself. I pulled up onto a rock and looked frantically around for Alice and Uncle Jeff.

I caught sight of him plunging into the stream as it curved around a small hill. Then seconds later he surfaced with a gasping Alice. I stumbled across the stones and wet sandy ground until I got to the spot where they sat, Alice clutched to Uncle Jeff's chest. I fell to my knees and wrapped my arms around them both.

"Oh God, Alice, baby, are you alright? Alice talk to me," Uncle Jeff gasped.

"I'm okay." She sounded surprisingly calm. Water was running down her face and dripping off her nose. I brushed her hair out of her eyes.

"I held my breath," she said.

Uncle Jeff looked at me and I smiled, "Smart kid."

When we got back to the camp site, Uncle Jeff took Alice into the tent they were going to share with Evelyn. I could see in the dimming light of the day that he was toweling her dry. I could hear him murmuring something to her and her short responses, but I couldn't hear the words. I hoped he wasn't scolding her. Should I interfere? I wondered.

I quickly changed and started a fire while they were in the tent. It was getting pretty cool with the sun going down. I didn't want Alice to get a chill.

They came back out dressed in dry clothes. Uncle Jeff went to the line I had stretched across the clearing to hang their wet clothes next to mine. Alice and I sat down next to the fire, and I started to clean the fish.

"Did he scold you?" I whispered.

"No, I wish he had," she whispered back. "He just lectured me about valuing myself as much as he and Mom value me."

"Oh, I've heard that one."

"It makes you feel guilty." She sat up straight as we heard the rest of the group coming down the trail. "Dad, David," she said. There was a panicky sound to her voice.

"What's wrong, baby?" Uncle Jeff hurried to her side.

She rolled her eyes in my direction. "Could this be our secret? I mean could we not tell anyone about the falling in the river thing?"

My eyes met Uncle Jeff's and we smiled at each other.

"We just all bathed after our long hike," I said. "Right, Uncle Jeff?"

"That's right," he said. "And we did it in our clothes for the sake of modesty. I don't know about you two, but I'm really refreshed after my bath."

"Me too," I said.

"Good," Alice sighed in relief. "Then we don't have to tell Mom either. She'd never let me out of her sight again."

I smiled at Uncle Jeff. He smiled back.

The next morning I hurried out of the tent to pee. The rushing stream increased the urgency, and I barely made it behind the first large tree. I heard a rustling in the woods and looked up to see Uncle Jeff coming toward me zipping up his jeans.

"You made it a little farther than I did," I said.

He laughed and went to the stream to wash his face. He took his tooth brush out of his pack and brushed his teeth in the stream. I went to the tent I shared with Charlotte to get my overnight kit. She was still sleeping.

"Did you get up in the night with her to pee?" Uncle Jeff asked when we had finished our morning routine and sat next to the fire to drink our coffee.

"Twice," I said. I don't think she sleeps very well on the trail. "Funny, I've always slept better out here."

"Yeah, but you weren't a lot older than her when you moved across the hall to get away from the fountains. Remember?"

"You're right. They made me feel like I needed to pee. She'll probably get over it. I did."

"The twins only got up once, but they did it at separate times. So I was up twice. I didn't want them to go into the woods alone."

"I guess it's tough having two of them at the same time."

"Looks like you'll be experiencing it pretty soon," Uncle Jeff smiled and gripped my shoulder. "It's not so hard. Amanda and I were old when we did it and we survived." He looked over at the tent where his daughters slept. He shivered. "So far; Alice took a few years off my life last night."

"Don't let your life get too short," I said.

He laughed and took a sip of his coffee. "So, one of the twins is a boy."

"Yep," I smiled. "We've got a girl and a boy. I'm happy about the boy, but I'm just as thrilled about the girl. I love my daughters. I hope this one has dimples like her mother."

"That would be nice, but your daughters are beautiful even without dimples."

I smiled and looked in the direction of my tent. "They are aren't they? Charlotte just looks exactly like Mom."

"Veronica looks like your mother too, with Darla's blond hair and blue eyes. I think they'll both be tall."

"I think they'll be very tall." I worried about that a little bit. "I hope they're proud of it. I hope they don't slump."

"With your mother setting the example they wouldn't dare."

We laughed.

"I'm glad you're going to get to raise a son, David. Raising boys is nice too. I enjoyed it."

"It took a few years off your life." I smiled.

"I don't know. I think all this backpacking and soccer and stuff put some years back on. I'm probably going to break even."

We had hiked a little over two miles when Charlotte started to wine.

"I'm tired, Daddy. When will we get there?"

"Charlotte if you say that again we'll never get there."

"What do you mean?"

"Every time you ask when we'll get there it makes it ten minutes longer. Isn't that right Grampa?" I looked at my dad for confirmation.

"That's right," he laughed.

"I don't believe it." Charlotte pulled at the straps of her backpack. "It doesn't make any sense."

"Here," I helped her take off her pack. "I'll carry your pack for you." I hooked the small nap sack I'd packed with her pajamas and toothbrush on the side of my pack. She wasn't really carrying anything. I just wanted her to get used to having something on her back.

By the end of the day I had Charlotte on my shoulders. Uncle Jeff had Alice's pack on the back of his own. Evelyn hiked like a trooper insisting on taking her own pack the whole way.

"Well, I guess we've got at least one backpacker in the crowd," Uncle Jeff said as he helped Evelyn take her pack off. "I was a little worried about you toward the end, Ev," he said. "You looked a little pale."

"I'm okay, Dad." She stretched her shoulders. The gesture made her look older than her eight years. "I'm tired, but I'm healthy tired."

"Well, I'm not healthy tired," Alice grumbled. "I'm stiff and sore and I don't like this at all. I want to stay in a hotel."

"Do you see any hotels around here, Alice?" Uncle Jeff huffed as he pulled the tent out of his pack. "Come over here and help me assemble the Ritz."

"That's not the Ritz. That's a stinky old tent. I'm not helping you do another thing. I hate backpacking."

"Me too," Charlotte crossed her arms over her small chest. "I want to go home. I want Mommy." Her chin started to quiver and she burst into tears. "I want Mommy!" She cried again.

"Oh, Charlita," I said picking her up to cradle her in my arms. "Maybe your mom was right. Maybe you're just too young for this."

"I'm not too young. I just hate it." She kicked in my arms and I was forced to put her down. "You didn't tell me about it right. It's not fun. It's awful." I could see a tantrum coming on, and I rolled my eyes.

"Excuse me," Drew said as he came around the turn in the path. He and Dad had gone on a different trail to explore a cave. They were just arriving at our planned campsite. "What's going on here, David? Are you torturing the kid again?"

"Don't be cute, Drew," I snapped. "If anyone is torturing anyone, it's her torturing me. I carried not only her pack, but her fat little body for the last two miles. Now she wants to go home. She wants her mommy. I was trying to comfort her and she kicked me." I stopped talking when I heard the sound of my own tantrum coming into my voice.

"There's steam coming out of your ears," Dad said as he slid his pack to the ground.

"Yeah, well," Uncle Jeff stormed over to his pack to pull out his tent poles. "Look at her highness over there." He pointed to Alice who sat on a log with her arms crossed looking haughtily in the opposite direction. "Princess Alice wants to stay at the Ritz tonight."

"Will the two of you stop acting like babies and go fishing," Dad said. "Drew and I will pull things together here."

I pulled my fishing pole out of my pack and headed down the path to the trout pond below the campsite. Uncle Jeff followed close behind. We fished side by side in silence for about half an hour. Then Uncle Jeff took a deep breath and laughed.

"I do feel better," he said. "It's funny how Brian knows the right thing to do about a bad parent moment."

I wasn't ready to calm down yet. "Five miles Uncle Jeff, that's all we did today. I hiked that far the first time we went backpacking, and I didn't cry and scream for my mommy."

"Charlotte's only six years old. I think you were older than that, weren't you?"

"I was eight." I sighed. "I have it documented in my scrapbook."

"I guess two years make a difference at that age. I wouldn't know. I can't remember back that far." He pulled a fat trout off his line, put it in the bucket, and cast again.

"The memory is fading for me too," I said.

"So what's Alice's excuse?" Uncle Jeff looked back toward the campsite. "She's eight."

"Maybe she's just not a backpacker."

"I can't imagine any kid of mine not being a backpacker." He was almost snarling. "She doesn't like to garden either. Evelyn already knows most of her plants. She has a garden of her own the back yard. She planned it. She even brought a wildflower book for this region. Her mother took her to the bookstore and she bought it with her allowance. Unfortunately most things aren't blooming yet."

"Your girls are definitely different aren't they," I said feeling a little apprehensive about my impending twins. Maybe it was harder than it looked.

"Yeah, they're different."

When we arrived back at the campsite all three tents were pitched. Charlotte sat on my dad's lap watching a pot come to a boil on the camp stove. Alice was nowhere in sight, and Evelyn sat on the ground next to the campfire looking through her book on flowers.

"We brought dinner," Uncle Jeff set the pale of fish on the ground. "Where is Alice?"

"She and Drew went to explore that trail over there." He pointed into the forest. "Drew said he saw it from the woods. He thought there were some rocks to climb."

"She complained about hiking all day." Uncle Jeff sounded perplexed. "So now she's gone to explore rocks to climb."

"Hiking bores her, Jeff. Climbing rocks doesn't."

"Oh boy, trout," Evelyn had real enthusiasm in her voice. She stood up and looked into the pail. "Four of them," she said. "I can probably eat that big one by myself."

"Grampa is making instant Mac and cheese for Alice and me," Charlotte said.

"Grampa always knows what to do about a bad parent moment." I repeated what Uncle Jeff had said to me.

"Trying to make up for lost time, I guess." Dad looked up at me and we exchanged a smile.

The next day I picked up Charlotte's pack after the first mile. Then I carried Charlotte on my shoulders again for about two miles.

"Charlotte," Drew called from the trail up ahead. "Come and do sprint races with Alice."

"She'll beat me every time," she grumbled, but kicked my chest trying to scramble off my shoulders. "Let me down, Daddy."

"Stop kicking me, Charlita. You're knocking the breath out of me." I put my arms up and took her small hands to lift her off my shoulders.

"I'm going to stop for a minute." I told my Dad and Uncle Jeff who were walking beside me. "I need to stretch my shoulders."

"I'll stop with you," Uncle Jeff said. He'd been carrying Alice's pack for the last mile or so. "My shoulders are stiff too."

"Here, let me help you get her pack off," Dad said after he'd lowered his pack to the ground. He took Alice's pack off Uncle Jeff's back and put it down so that Uncle Jeff could lower his own to the ground."

"Why don't you let me carry her pack for a while," Dad said. "My conditioning has improved so much since I moved back here and became a dog groomer. You don't need to worry about my back anymore."

I looked at my dad. The transformation was impressive. His once soft sloping shoulders were firm now and appeared broader. I guess from the buildup of muscle. His chin still sagged a little, but he was leaner, and that made it appear smaller. His once bulging belly was flat.

"You look good, Dad." I smiled as I drank from my water bottle. "I guess life is agreeing with you."

"I love working with dogs all day. It's good for me, and I'm enjoying my nieces and grandchildren."

"And you're living with Mom," I said. It was the first time we had talked about it even though the pretense of him living over the nursery had stopped years ago.

"Yeah, she's great." He looked off into the woods.

"What I don't understand, Brian," Uncle Jeff said. "Is how can you stand the smell of dirty dogs when you can't stand the smell of clean dirt."

"Clean dirt," Dad teased. "Jeff, you're still a farmer. Do you know what an oxymoron that is? Clean dirt," he repeated.

"It smells fresh. Dirty dogs smell fowl."

"The dogs come into my shop smelling fowl, but they go out smelling like roses." He looked down the trail at Drew playing with the girls. "He's good with the kids. He's keeping them entertained. I guess we didn't think of attention span when we planned this."

"Do you think Alice and Charlotte are bored?" I asked. "Evelyn isn't bored." I looked at the spot where Evelyn was looking up at a wild shrub on the side of the trail. She held her open book in her hand. Her pack still sat securely on her back.

"That one's a chip off the old block." Dad laughed. "But look at Drew and Charlotte and Alice.

Drew stood about a hundred feet down a straight part of the trail with his hands stretched out at his side, palms showing. You could see his pack behind his head. Charlotte and Alice stood in starting position a small distance from us.

"Ready! Set! Go!" Drew called. Both girls took off to run and tap his hand. "Charlotte by a finger!" he called. "I told you kid. Alice may be older than you, but with those long legs of yours, it's a real close match."

"I'll win this time." Alice bounced up and down. "I wasn't ready when you said go."

"Okay." Drew took them both by the hand and started up the trail. "But we'll walk a length first. We have to stretch our muscles and catch our breath. Later we'll find an obstacle course of logs and stumps in the woods. How does that sound."

I put my water bottle into my side pocket and put the pack on my back. "I love my brother, Dad." I put my hand on his shoulder.

"You raised a nice son, Brian," Uncle Jeff said as we helped him secure Alice's pack to the back of his.

"You raised a nice son too, Jeff." Dad put his pack on and started up the trail.

"Well, it's not the Ritz," Alice said as we propped our packs outside our rooms at the bed and breakfast. "But at least I can take a bath and wash my hair." She and Evelyn and Uncle Jeff disappeared into the room that was across the hall from the one I would share with Charlotte.

"I want to go home," Charlotte whimpered. "I miss Mommy."

"You never call her Mommy. Why are you calling her that now?" I could feel my irritation rising. This trip had not gone the way I planned it at all.

"I want to go home," she cried and rubbed her eyes with her small fists. My irritation dissolved and I gathered her into my arms.

"I'm sorry, baby. Mom was right about this one. I guess I just wanted you to come with me so much I didn't realize it was too long for you to be away from her." I kissed the top of her head and rocked her in my arms. We sat on the side of the bed. I held her like that until her tears slowed down and her sobs became hiccups.

She sniffled. I wiped her nose and eyes with a tissue from a box on the bedside table. "I'm sorry, Daddy." She never called me Daddy either. She must be feeling very lost. "I wanted to come. Remember?" She sniffled again and buried her face in my shirt. "Now I want to go home."

"I'm sorry," I said. "I can't think of a way to go home. I guess we could take a bus to the airfield. I don't know how far it is from here by the road. I only made plans through the woods."

She started to cry again and I rocked her a minute longer. "We'll find a way, baby. If you want to go home, we'll go home." I remembered the aching homesickness I felt when I first went away to Harvard, and I was a lot older. How could I have not thought of this? Darla had thought of it.

"Why don't you take a bath," I said feeling lost myself. "I'll draw the water. I bet there's bubble bath. Then we'll call Mommy on the phone. Maybe hearing her voice would make you feel better."

"Okay." She hiccupped. She let me wash her and I wondered again, like I had when she was first born, at the perfection of her little body. What a beautiful little creature, and she'd come from me. How was that possible?

I toweled her dry and helped her put her clothes on. "I need to take a shower now. Then if you want we can call Mommy. Tomorrow we'll find a way to go home."

"Okay." She was using that word a little too much. It wasn't like Charlotte to be so agreeable. There was a knock at the door. I answered it. Evelyn and Alice stood in the hall. Their hair was wet and they smelled like soap. Their clothes were crumpled since they'd been packed in a backpack, but they were clean.

"You guys look refreshed," I said. "I was just getting ready to take a shower. We'll be down to dinner in no more than half an hour."

"Take your time, Bubba." Evelyn pushed past me into the room. "Charlotte," She bounced in excitement and took my daughters hand. "You won't believe where Drew and Uncle Brian are staying. They're in a train car in the back yard of the bed and breakfast. Come and see it. Can she come, Bubba?"

"It's soooo tacky, David." Alice rolled her eyes at me. "It's neat, though. There's a platform that you can climb up a ladder to and chairs to sit in and look out the window. I guess to watch where the train is going, if it was going anywhere."

"Can we take her while you shower, Bubba?" Evelyn asked. "We won't let anything happen to her."

I looked at Charlotte. Her eyes had brightened at the enthusiasm of her cousins. "Do you want to go with them, Charlita, or would you rather stay here with me? I'll only take a minute in the shower."

"Come with us, Charlotte." Alice took her other hand. I wondered if she could tell that Charlotte had been crying. She put her small arm across her shoulders in a comforting gesture. "Dad and Drew and Uncle Brian are having beer. They got Coke and Sprite for us. They have chips too, but we can't eat too much before dinner."

"No Coke," I said.

"It's decaffeinated, David." Alice rolled her eyes at me again. She must practice that in the mirror, I thought.

"Come with us, Charlotte," Evelyn encouraged.

"Okay," she said it with a reluctant smile this time, and I watched the door close behind the three little girls.

That night at dinner Alice was happy that the group was so big. The restaurant was family style. We took up a whole table.

"I'm so glad we didn't have to sit with strangers," she whispered loudly to the group. She lifted her nose to look around the crowded dining room.

"Don't be a snob, Alice," Uncle Jeff said. "Strangers can become friends."

"Not when you're only staying one night." She put her napkin in her lap with a dramatic flourish. "Charlotte," she addressed my daughter. "There are a lot of really quaint little shops in town. Dad said that we could stay until after lunch tomorrow and shop before we get back on the trail."

"Okay," Charlotte said again. Her eyes were big and a little bit watery, but she was smiling at her cousin.

Evelyn who sat beside her sister across the table from us said, "You don't have to just shop with her if you don't want. There is also a nursery and a small botanical garden in town. We could go see them. There will be different flora from what we see in Georgia."

"Different flora," Uncle Jeff said with an exaggerated pronunciation.

"Don't make fun of me, Dad." Evelyn frowned. The expression looked odd on her face. She never frowned. She didn't smile a lot either. "We can do both, can't we?" she asked.

"I don't see why not."

When we returned to the room that night we called Darla. Charlotte cried for a few minutes when she first got on the phone. Then she started to tell her mother about what we'd done. She talked about beating her older cousin in a race and the shopping trip planned for the next morning.

"Grampa brought instant Mac and Cheese. So Alice and I don't have to eat trout every night." Her voice sounded lively when she said that. I could hear Darla laughing on the line. Charlotte's chin quivered a little when she said, "I'll see you in two days." She handed the phone to me. She didn't cry.

"Is everything alright, David?" Darla asked when I greeted her.

"Yes, we're fine. I'll tell you all about it when we get home. I'll call you tomorrow before we get back on the trail. I love you." I made myself sound very calm as I said goodbye and hung up the phone. "You said you'd see her in two days. If you want to go home, we'll just explain to the others."

"I want to go home," she said, "but I can wait two days."

That night she slept soundly in my arms all night long.

We shopped the next morning. The warning to buy only things that could be carried on your back had to be repeated several times, but the girls had fun, and it was a good break from the woods.

Everyone carried their own pack that afternoon when we hit the trail. That evening we settled around the campfire. Uncle Jeff and I didn't even bother to fish. We ate dehydrated Chili Mac and fresh tomatoes and avocado that we'd bought at the market next to the bed and breakfast.

"I don't think I could have eaten another trout," Evelyn said.

"I thought you loved trout." I looked down at my quiet little cousin. She was running her finger around her bowl of chili Mac to get every last drop.

"There's another bag we can mix up in a just minute if you're still hungry."

"No, I'm good, Bubba." She smiled up at me exposing white but slightly crooked teeth. A few of them were missing. We were sitting alone at the campsite. The others had wandered up the stream we were camped beside for an after dinner stroll. "I do love trout, but not every day."

"Evelyn, you're so quiet and so easy. Do you get enough attention?"

"One of us has to be quiet. If we were both like Alice I don't think Mom and Dad would survive."

"She is a lively girl," I laughed. "But Evie, you need some attention too. Maybe you should make a little more noise."

"I don't really like being the center of attention." She stood and went to the stream to wash her bowl. I joined her with the other bowls that I collected from around the fire, and we set to work washing and drying.

"We make a pretty good team," I said when we'd finished. "We worked like an assembly line. You washed. I dried."

"That's the way Mom and I do it at home."

"Alice and Uncle Jeff don't help?"

"We alternate." She gathered all the dishes and spoons and helping me carry them back to the campsite. "We alternate partners too, but it gets done the best when Mom and I do it."

I could envision my uncle's quiet wife and quiet daughter working together like an efficient machine. Then I thought of the fiery tempered Alice and I laughed. "I guess Alice presents a challenge to any partner."

"Yeah, sometimes I just have to leave the room."

"Why don't you like being the center of attention?"

"I don't know. I just don't. I'm glad I share a birthday with Alice. It would be awful having to blow out those candles by myself with everyone looking at me."

"That *would* be terrible," I laughed.

"Don't make fun of me, Bubba." She sounded really hurt. I was about to apologize when she tripped over a stone and fell onto her knees on the rocky stream bed. The plates went everywhere and Evelyn scrambled to gather them up.

"Don't worry about the plates," I said. "Did you hurt yourself?" I knelt down beside her.

"I skinned my knees and tore my pants." She sat up and looked at her bleeding legs. Tears ran down her face. She sniffed and scrubbed at her cheeks.

"I'm sorry, honey. I didn't mean to make fun of you. Don't be mad. I'll get the first aid kit." I felt awkward and I was babbling.

"What happened?" Alice and Uncle Jeff said at the same time as the group came into the campsite.

"Evelyn fell and skinned her knees." I felt strangely guilty.

"Ev, are you alright?" Alice knelt on the other side of her sister and put her arms around her. Evelyn buried her face in her sister's shoulder and cried softly.

"I tore my pants," she said between sobs.

"Don't worry about your pants," Uncle Jeff said. "Sweetie, you really skinned your knees up." He bent over to kiss the top of Evelyn's head. "I'll get the first aid kit."

"It's alright, Dad," Alice said. "Come on Ev. Let's go into the tent where everyone isn't staring at you. We'll clean up your knees."

I looked around the clearing, and sure enough, everyone was standing around staring at the two little girls on the rocky shore of the creek. I looked back and watched Uncle Jeff pull Evelyn to her feet. Alice put her arm across her shoulders. They walked quietly to the tent.

"Do you need my help, guys?" Uncle Jeff called to them.

"We'll let you know if we do," Alice said as they disappeared into the tent.

"You looked guilty when we came into the clearing," Uncle Jeff said. "The two of you weren't fighting, were you? I thought the age difference would eliminate the problem of sibling rivalry." He laughed, but he sounded serious.

"No, we weren't fighting. In fact we had a really good visit with each other. I did tease her about something, though. She accused me of making fun of her."

"She hates to be made fun of."

"She's so quiet and serious. I didn't realize how sensitive she is." I looked at Uncle Jeff. He was looking at the tent where we could see the flash light hanging from the top and the silhouette of the two little girls.

"She's sensitive about some things and not about others. She has a good sense of humor if you tease her about some things. You just have to know what they are."

"I guess I need to know her a little better," I said. I was worried, but I wasn't sure why. "Should you go in and help them?"

"No, they'll let me know if they need me. With things like this it's better to let them take care of each other." He turned his head to the campfire. "Let's open that bottle of wine we bought in town, what do you say?"

"Sounds like a good idea." I sat down on the ground next to the fire.

Uncle Jeff uncorked the bottle and poured some into the coffee mugs we would drink from in the morning. He handed me one and sat down beside me. Dad and Drew joined us and Charlotte crawled into my lap.

"They've got that twin thing, David." Uncle Jeff put his hand on my shoulder and sipped. "I understand because I'm a twin. Your dad and I haven't always been together on things, but we still have the twin thing, don't we Brian."

"Yes we do."

"I guess I'm getting ready to learn about it firsthand."

"You will, but you'll never quite understand it. I know that Alice and Evelyn are very different from each other. Believe me they can fight as well as any siblings, better than most." He laughed. "But if one of them needs the other, that's where she'll be."

I wasn't sure it had always been that way for my dad and my uncle. In fact, I knew it hadn't. But it had been that way once, and it was that way now.

I looked at the two of them sitting side by side watching the leaping flames of the fire. They looked so much alike and yet so different. I looked back at the silhouette of my two little cousins on the tent wall. One was bent over the others knees. The other was loudly blowing her nose.

"I hope it lasts a lifetime for them," I said.

We hiked off the trail the next morning with Drew carrying Alice on his shoulders. My dad had Alice's backpack strapped to his own. I was carrying Charlotte and her pack. Uncle Jeff was carrying Evelyn's backpack.

He'd had to argue with her to get it. She didn't want to give up, but she did look pitiful limping beneath it with her bandaged knees and her torn pants. At first he had carried Alice and both packs. Drew and Dad insisted on relieving him of his load when he started to turn pale under the weight of it.

"I guess it's a good thing we didn't plan another day," I said as we loaded the packs into the bus that would take us to the air strip. "We debated, remember?"

"Yeah," Uncle Jeff laughed. "You and I wanted to, but Brian and Drew overruled us. Thanks guys."

"You're welcome," Dad said. "Next time I'll bring Nip and Tuck too. You guys overruled us on that one. But you were wrong. They'd have been good to have along."

"That's what was missing on this trip," Alice said. "Dogs, why didn't we bring Nip and Tuck? Why didn't you bring Dolores, Dad?"

"Dolores doesn't travel well. I figured she'd puke on David then he'd puke on her," he said.

I tossed a glare at him across the aisle of the bus as we all filed in and found seats.

"I figured with this many first time packers Nip and Tuck would be in the way." Uncle Jeff said. "Besides, do Shih Tzu's hike well with all that long hair."

"I gave them their summer cuts last week. But when you and David didn't want them to come, I left them at home with Charlotte and Farnsworth."

"I wonder why Mom named the new Afghan Farnsworth," I said.

"He came with the name." Dad laughed.

"I still can't believe you have frufrus, Dad," I said. "I was just as happy not to have them here. They're such yappy little things."

"Don't be a snob, David. I'm a frufru professional. They advertize my business. Anyway since when do you have a problem with dogs? Just think of the entertainment capability they'd have had on this trip." He nodded his head at Charlotte and Alice.

"Dad hates dogs," Charlotte said. "He won't let us have one. I like my cat, but you can't take a cat hiking." She giggled and it sounded nice, like her mother's laugh. I realized I was missing Darla too.

"I don't hate dogs, Charlita."

"Can we have one then?"

"No!" The rest of the bus ride was silent.

CHAPTER NINETEEN

"Mommy!" Charlotte ran from the truck into Darla's arms and dissolved into tears. Darla looked at me over my daughter's head as she collapsed on the mound of her mother's belly. I shuffled my feet feeling guilty and knowing I looked it.

Darla sat on the step of our front porch with Charlotte in her arms and spoke softly to her.

"Daddy!" Veronica raced out the door and tackled my knees. I bent and pulled her up to my hip, happy for the distraction. Darla looked up at me, and I knew the meaning of the phrase 'if looks could kill.'

"Did you miss me, vroom vroom?" I laughed as she covered my face with kisses. "I didn't think about you at all." I held her close enjoying the feel of her soft cheeks.

"I'll unload your packs, David." Uncle Jeff squeezed my shoulder and kissed Veronica's cheek. "It looks like you've got some family business to take care of." He looked in the direction of my sobbing daughter and my seething wife.

"Thanks," I said. I looked back at the truck. My two small cousins were watching the scene on my front porch with big eyes and solemn expressions.

"What's wrong with Charlotte?" Veronica asked. "Did she get homesick? Mom was afraid she would."

"Yeah," I said. "I guess your mom was right on this one. She was a little too young for this long of a trip."

"She's six. I'm going next year and I'll only be five." She put her small hand on my cheek and turned my head to look at her. "You promised I could go next year."

I kissed the tip of her nose. "We'll talk about that next year, vroom. Let me get through this year first." I set her on the ground and started up the walk holding her hand. "Let's go inside. Thanks, Uncle Jeff," I said to him on his way out the door. "Thanks for everything. I'll call you next week."

I looked down at Darla. She was still holding a sniffling Charlotte. She looked up at me. She wasn't glaring anymore but her eyes were wet.

"What do you want me to do, Darla?" I shifted uncomfortably. "Say you were right? Beg forgiveness? Grovel?"

She looked back down at Charlotte and kissed her forehead. She smoothed her tousled hair away from her face. "Let's go inside nd get you cleaned up, Charlotte." She struggled to her feet and Charlotte walked quietly beside her holding her hand. "Did Daddy even brush your hair while you were gone?"

"I brushed my hair." Charlotte's voice quivered pathetically.

I tried to remember brushing her hair. I couldn't. I was pretty sure I did, though.

"Maybe you'd feel better if you said I told you so." Darla and I were sitting in the living room after we'd had a very quiet dinner. The silence was only broken by Veronica's chatter and that stopped eventually too. The girls were asleep now.

"Charlotte ate like she was starving," Darla accused. "Didn't you feed her?"

"She didn't like trout."

"She's only a little girl, David. Of course she didn't like trout."

"Look, P.H." I rose and turned out the light beside my chair. "You can keep being mad at me about this if you want to, but the truth is, it wasn't a bad trip. I fed her. I protected her. We had a good time. She missed you. That's all. You expected her to miss you."

She looked up at me. "She says she'll never go backpacking with you again. She doesn't have to, David."

"No, she doesn't." I held out my hand to her. "Let's go to bed, Darla. We're both tired, and there's been enough drama for one night."

"I'm worried, David." She took my hand, and I helped her to her feet. "This wouldn't be a good time for me to be away from her again, and I had a contraction a while ago."

I looked at her startled. "It's too early, P.H. "You're not due for another month."

"Maybe it was just one of those false alarm contractions."

"How long ago did you have it?"

"Right after dinner ..."

"And you haven't had another one? It's probably nothing." I continued down the hall to the bedroom.

"You're probably right." She didn't sound like she believed it.

❁

I lay in bed until Darla's breathing became steady with sleep. Then I went to my computer room with my camera. I booted up my computer and plugged in the memory chip full of pictures of the trip. I titled the new album "Appalachian through the eyes of my children." Charlotte may never go again, but this time would be documented.

I organized the pictures in files. I separated the pictures of the kids from the pictures of adults. I made a file of group pictures. Then I put all the ones of just Charlotte in one file. I'd start there. All of the pictures needed some editing. There were a lot of Charlotte. She looked happy in most of them. I smiled at the thought of showing Darla that she hadn't been miserable the whole trip.

"David." I jumped at Darla's voice behind me. She put her hand on my shoulder and I covered it with mine.

"Look at her face, P.H." I pointed to the picture on the computer screen. "See, she had fun."

"I'm glad, but David, it's not a false alarm. The contractions have really started and something is wrong. David, I'm scared."

I turned and looked at her in the dim light. She clutched her belly and doubled over. I caught her as she slid to the floor. "The pain is wrong. It's not like before," she said.

I knelt beside her. "What should I do?" That's a stupid question, I thought.

"Call someone to stay with the girls, David. I need to go to the hospital."

❁

"It's like the babies are fighting to get into the birth canal." The doctor smiled at me over Darla's extended belly.

I didn't smile back. "Explain that to me," I said.

"The female fetus has her head down and is trying to get into the birth canal, but the male fetus's feet are in the way. Shades of things to come, I guess." He laughed.

Darla moaned, and I looked into her eyes. They were glazed with pain and fear. "What are we going to do, Dr. Rhomert?" she asked.

"That's right." I sounded angry and I was. How could he be laughing about this? "She can't go on in this kind of pain. Can we move the boy out of the way?"

"No, we'll have to do a C-section. The male fetus is showing signs of distress." The doctor stood and walked to the door. "I'm having a surgery suite prepared. Don't worry. Everything will be fine." He opened the door and was almost through it when the ultrasound technician called to him.

"Dr. Rhomert, look at this!" She sounded anxious. He hurried back over to the monitor of the ultrasound machine. He looked at the nurse that stood on the other side of the bed.

"Get her prepped fast," he said and looked at Darla and then at me. "The male fetus is in serious distress. I'm not sure what is wrong, but we need to get him out fast. The female is in front of him. She'll have to be delivered first.

I couldn't say anything. I could feel Darla squeezing my hand. I looked down at her. She was covering her mouth with her other hand. She started to gag and the nurse helped her turn and vomit into a basin.

"Mr. Landrum," Dr. Rhomert said from the door. I hadn't been aware that he had moved. "You can come into surgery with her if you want. We'll do the surgery under an epidural anesthetic. She'll be awake for it. You'll need to scrub." Then he was gone.

I was aware of people in hospital attire wheeling Darla out of the room. I had a glimpse of her tear stained face looking up at me as she went by. I couldn't seem to move my feet.

"Mr. Landrum, if you want to scrub and go in, come with me." A young male nurse took my arm. When I looked at him with my mouth still open, he pulled me in the direction of the door. "Come with me," he said.

"Alright," I said, but I don't think I said it out loud.

It seemed like hours later when we heard the cry of our new daughter. It was only minutes I know, but the surgical birth was so different than the others. There was no pushing, no hand squeezing, and no breathing for me to coach. I just sat there and looked at Darla's drawn face.

The pain had stopped with the application of the epidural anesthesia, but the pain I could see in her eyes hadn't subsided. Neither one of us said anything. I just held her hand until we heard that cry. Then for just a minute we both smiled and looked at the doctor as he held our tiny daughter over the sheet for us to see.

"She's perfect," he said. "A little bit small, but that's to be expected with twins." He handed the baby to the nurse. She took her out of sight to weigh her and measure her and suction the mucus out of her nose and mouth.

"She has a healthy wail for such a tiny thing," Dr. Rhomert said as he started back to work delivering our little boy. "We still have a heart beat," he said. "I'll have the other twin out as quickly as I can. Oh no, here is our problem." I could see the concern in his eyes above his mask.

"What is it?" I asked. "What is it?" This was a demand.

"What's wrong?" Darla cried. It was the first thing she'd said since we'd gone in to surgery. Her voice sounded raspy.

"The umbilical cord is wrapped around his neck. That wouldn't worry me much. They get their oxygen through the cord until they're born. But it seems to be crimped under his chin. That would stop the blood flow. He's blue. He's been robbed of oxygen, but he still has a heartbeat." He was speaking rapidly. He looked down at the surgery site as he worked on delivering my son. I held Darla's hand. She squeezed mine. I was glad that he was telling us everything.

"I've freed him of the cord. Here he is. He's free of the womb. Becky..." He signaled a nurse. "He'll need a respirator quick." He handed the baby we hadn't seen yet to the nurse, and she hurried away. Dr. Rhomert walked around the sheet that was set up between the surgery sight and us.

"I don't know how long he went without oxygen. I'm pretty sure we can revive him, but I'm also pretty sure there will be some brain damage. We won't know how much until we can stabilize him and do a CT scan. Even then we won't know how much he'll be affected."

"So he'll be handicapped," I said.

"I'm afraid so. He's big too, much bigger than the girl. Sometimes that can indicate that some of the blood flow was misdirected in the womb. That can sometimes lead to retardation. I'm sorry." He looked over at the nurse holding the baby girl.

"Four pounds eight ounces," she smiled, "seventeen inches long. She'll have to go into an incubator until she's five pounds, but I think you can hold her for a minute."

The doctor returned to finish the surgery, and the nurse put the infant down on Darla's chest. I put my arms around both of them. "She's beautiful," I whispered to Darla.

"Yes, she is." The tiny creature spit and pulled her lips up at the corners.

"Darla, look," I said. "She has dimples."

Darla pulled the baby up to her chin and started to sob quietly. I'd heard her cry a number of times over the years, but this was the first time I noticed that just like when she laughed; I was reminded of wind chimes. It didn't make me smile.

✦

Darla came home five days later with one baby. Brandon, our newborn son was healthy and gaining weight rapidly. He'd weighed seven pounds four ounces at birth. Not a big baby, but big for a twin and certainly bigger than his womb mate, Belinda. The pediatrician assured us that she would be big enough to bring home before another week was up.

"Are you sure you'll be alright if I go to soccer practice, P.H." I asked as I packed my duffle bag. "I could come straight home after work. After all, you've only been out of the hospital for three days, and you had abdominal surgery. That takes recovery time."

"I'm fine, David. I'm tired of everyone fussing over me. It's the babies that aren't fine. I did a terrible job carrying twins." She sniffed and scrubbed at a tear. She was never far from tears these days.

"Okay, I'm not going to soccer." I sat down on the bed where she was giving Brandon a bottle and ran my finger down her cheek. "Darla, we've talked about this. What happened with the twins didn't have anything to do with you. Maybe Dr. Rhomert was right. Maybe you should talk to someone."

"I'm not going to a psychiatrist, David. I'll work this out. It's just a matter of forgiving myself."

"There is nothing to forgive yourself for." I stood up and started to pace. I hated the fact that this made me angry, but it did.

"I know I didn't do anything wrong, David, but it's still my failure. Now please go to work and then go to soccer. I don't want you staying home because of me. It doesn't make me feel better. It makes me feel worse. Now go."

"Mom," Charlotte said from the doorway. "Is Gramma coming over while Dad's at work and Veronica and I are at school?" She looked up at me. "I don't want her to be alone yet, Dad."

"Come here and give me a hug, Florence Nightingale." Darla smiled more brightly than I'd seen her smile since she got home. She put the baby across her lap on his belly and held out her arms to Charlotte. "I'll be fine, but yes, Gramma is coming over. She'll help me if I need anything." Brandon burped loudly and Darla and Charlotte both laughed.

"Gross," Veronica said from the doorway. "I'm never having a baby. They're disgusting." She turned her attention to me. "Dad, if we don't go now we'll be late to school."

I smiled at Darla. At four and a half years old, Veronica was already a scholar. "It's only pre-school, vroom. I'll go in and explain."

"You do that every day. It's embarrassing. I just want to be on time for once."

"You two run on down and get your book bags. I'll only be another second." The two girls left the room. I looked at Darla. Some of the strained look had left her face.

"I'll be fine, David." She picked the fat baby up and put him over her shoulder. "Don't make the girls late for school. Have a nice day at work, and please go to soccer practice after you get off. The team really needs you now that I'm out of commission." She smiled, but her dimples didn't quite show. I leaned down to kiss her. She turned her cheek to me.

"I'll call you," I said. She hadn't kissed my mouth since long before the babies were born. Was my breath bad or something?

"David, can you give us a short marketing report?" Jane Fox, my employer asked in our weekly staff meeting that morning.

"Not much to say." I smiled at the faces of my co-workers and thought once again how much I loved my job. "We're pretty much at the top of all the subscription lists, and the advertising sales are great. I think we're supporting ourselves very well. I plan another sales trip next month. I think we'll try to expand ourselves in the U.K. We do alright there, but we can do better."

"That's great," she said as she stood up. "Once again, good work everyone. You've all made me proud. This has been an exciting venture." She stopped as she got to the door. "David, could I see you in my office, please?"

My heart started to pound as she left the room. I realized that my mouth was open, and I clamped it shut. The old fear of rejection was never far from the surface.

"Uh-oh," Mark, the director of art and design for the magazine said. "You've been called to the principal's office."

"I wonder what I did wrong. I guess I could have prepared a more formal report."

"I wouldn't worry about it, David. With the birth of twins and backpacking trips and all, nobody expected you to get a lot done for this meeting." Grant, another one of my co-workers said.

"There's no excuse for not doing my job."

"You're doing your job, David. Don't worry about it. She probably just wants to give you a baby gift. How are the babies, anyway?" Michael asked. He was the magazine's photographer and Grant's brother. The magazine where I worked was like a big happy family.

I looked around the room. No one had left even though the meeting was over. They were all looking at me with genuine interest on their faces. They cared about me, and I cared about them.

"Here, David." Christine, the dietician, smeared yogurt spread on a whole grain biscuit and handed it to me. "You didn't eat a thing and you didn't bring anything in either. Don't tell me I've lost my competition."

"No." I took the biscuit from her and realized how hungry I was when my stomach grumbled loudly at the first bite. "This is great Christine. I need that recipe. I just haven't had time to cook in the mornings since the twins were born. I've been taking the girls to school for Darla. She's exhausted. That pregnancy was hard on her."

"I'm sure it was," Mark said. "When will the little girl come home from the hospital? Did you say her name was Belinda?"

"That's right, Brandon and Belinda. I didn't want matching names, but Darla liked the idea that the first letters were the same. I like the names." I took a drink of the orange juice that Christine handed me.

"They're great names," Michael said.

"I'm hoping Belinda will come home tomorrow. She's growing like a weed. She only has to be five pounds for them to let her come home."

"How's Brandon, do you see any evidence of his handicap?" Grant asked.

"No, not yet anyway, he's about the happiest baby I've ever encountered. He doesn't even really cry. When he's wet or hungry he just, kind of, calls out to us. He's beautiful too. He has dimples in his cheeks like his mother. Belinda has them too. I'm happy about the dimples." I looked around the room. Everyone was smiling at me. "I guess I'd better go see what Jane wants with me. Thanks guys, for the support." I stood to leave the room.

"David, anything we can do..." Grant said.

"Listen," Michael said. "When they get a little more settled in we'd love to see those babies."

"You bet," I said as I left the room. I walked down the hall to Jane's office and knocked on the half open door. "You wanted to see me."

"Come in, David." She smiled from her seat behind the desk. "Close the door."

"Am I in some kind of trouble?" I heard my voice shake as I sat in the chair across from her. I felt like a guilty child.

"Of course you aren't." She looked startled and laughed. My shoulders relaxed and I took a deep breath. "I'm sorry if I made you think that."

"It's not your fault." I laughed and rubbed my eyes. "I guess I'm just a little jumpy right now."

"I guess you are. How is Darla handling things? I know it didn't go exactly the way you'd like it to. How are the babies?"

I took a deep breath and sat back in my chair. "Belinda is doing well. She's in an incubator because she was very small. She's growing fast, and her blood work and everything is excellent."

"That's comforting. When will she come home?"

"I'm hoping she'll come home tomorrow."

"And the little boy?"

"Big, strong, healthy as a horse and incredibly happy, the CT scan showed brain damage on the left side of his brain. I'm studying what that means. I have all sorts of pamphlets, but I really can't tell you much at this point. It's hard to believe there's anything wrong. He's such a pleasant baby."

"That's great. Maybe the damage won't be significant. How's Darla?"

"She blames herself, but she seems to be alright. I guess it's just something we have to work out." I looked across the desk. "I'm sure this isn't why you wanted to talk to me. What's going on, Jane?"

She smiled and leaned across the desk toward me. "I'm planning to semi-retire, David." She stood up and walked to the window to look out. "I want you and Grant to take over my duties." She turned and looked at me. "I've already talked to Grant about this. He's been my second in command up until now. This change would put the two of you on the same level. You'd be working together as a team."

"A team?" I felt the stupid expression on my face and tried to adjust it.

"That's right. The two of you are really the ones running this business. Now I want you to take over. I will no longer take a salary. I'm set up pretty well for retirement. So there will be a significant raise involved."

"Jane, you've directed us every step of the way. I'm not sure we can do it without you."

"I'm a good director, but now that I've set everything up, I think you and Grant can take over." She laughed and sat back down behind her desk. "Of course, I'll keep my office and be in from time to time. You're not getting rid of me, David." She leaned forward again. "I want to travel with Gordon. I can't believe that we've been married for almost ten years, and the only time we've been away was on our honeymoon. I travelled in my work before I started the magazine, so I didn't have the wanderlust. But Gordon didn't travel. You know he had that huge family and the business in this community. There are places I'd like to see with him."

"I understand, Jane, but are you sure you want to give this to me? What about Michael. After all, he and Grant are brothers."

"Michael isn't a leader or a manager. He's an artist. I've talked to him about this. He's fine with it. He has his share in the company. David, you're the one for this job, co-president with Grant. I'll give you time to think about it, but I hope you'll agree."

✺

"Well." Uncle Jeff fell in beside as I walked from my car to the soccer field. "You're shining like a new penny, son." He put his hand on my shoulder. "Everything must be going pretty well. Darla's settling in? The babies are well?"

"Actually, we've got some adjusting to do in that area. Darla's blaming herself for Brandon's problems, although I haven't seen any evidence of problems. He's the sweetest baby, Uncle Jeff. I didn't think I'd feel the same about a little boy as I do about the girls."

"I told you you would. I'll never forget the first time I held you in my arms."

"It's hard for me to relate to that now." I laughed and he laughed with me.

"How's Belinda?"

"She's growing like a weed. I went to see her at lunch today. I'm hoping to bring her home tomorrow."

"It's tough leaving one at the hospital. We had to leave Alice for a week after her heart surgery. That was a long week."

We arrived at the bench beside the field. I put my water bottle and towel down. "Hey, Jimmy." I greeted him as he approached us.

"Hey, you look happy," he said. "Did you have a good day?"

"Yeah, it started out a little bumpy, but I have something to tell you both. It's big news for me."

"Tell us," they said together.

"Jane has offered me a position as co-president of the magazine. She's retiring, and she wants Grant and me to run it together. I never dreamed I'd have my own magazine, I mean with a partner."

"That's great." Jimmy slapped my shoulder. "Congratulations, man."

"I'm proud of you, David. You've really done well." Uncle Jeff wrapped me up in one of the bear hugs I'd grown to love. "Jane is alright isn't she?" He stepped back and looked at me suddenly concerned. "She isn't sick or anything. It's not like her to give up control."

"She's fine." I laughed. "She wants to travel with her husband. I guess she's seen a lot of the world. Now she wants to show it to him. I imagine she'll still have some input."

"Well, that's great, David. I guess Darla's happy about it."

"I haven't told her yet, but I know she will be. She's wanted to finish the rumpus room above the garage for a while, but we really couldn't afford it. This promotion will involve a raise. That'll give her a project to focus on. Maybe take her mind off other things."

"You mean like feeling guilty about Brandon." Jimmy sat down on the bench to change into his soccer shoes. I sat down beside him.

"I guess Meryl filled you in on that."

"What's going on?" Uncle Jeff asked.

"Well, like I said before, Darla blames herself for what happened during the birth process, you know, the brain damage. Honestly, I'm a little worried about her feelings for Belinda. I'm afraid she might be blaming her a little bit too. It took longer to get to Brandon because Belinda was in the way."

"She can't blame an unborn baby for her position in the womb," Uncle Jeff said.

"No, consciously she never would, but maybe deep down."

"Meryl is really worried about that and about Darla's state of mind too." Jimmy stood up and started to stretch his legs. The rest of the team was assembling. I stood up too. "Meryl tried to take her to the hospital to see Belinda today, but she wouldn't go. She said she didn't need to because she isn't nursing the babies. Why isn't she nursing the babies, David? She breast fed the girls."

"She wouldn't tell me. I think she doesn't trust herself." I looked at the soccer field full of my team mates and suddenly didn't feel like playing soccer.

"Come on, David." Uncle Jeff put his hand across my shoulders and walked onto the field with me. "A good workout will do you good. Then you can go home and face your challenges."

"Hey Mom," I walked into the kitchen from the garage to find my mother standing at the sink washing dishes. "Is everything alright?"

"At the moment it is." She dried a plastic cup and put it on the shelf next to the sink. "Brandon is asleep. That is the sweetest baby, David. He smiles and I swear it isn't gas. I know people say a baby that young can't smile. But tell me, David, did having gas ever make you smile?"

"No." I laughed. "I usually just leave the room if I have gas." I kissed her on the cheek, and she smiled down at the dish she was washing.

"You said at the moment everything is alright. Has there been a problem?"

"Not really, Darlene was here. She spent a long time with Darla. It seemed to cheer her. She's so depressed, David. Did she have post-partum depression with either of the girls?"

"No. I don't think it's post-partum. Well, I guess it is, but not for the usual reason." I dished myself up a bowl of tuna casserole. It was obvious that Mom had cooked. It tasted great, comforting. "So, you and Darla's mom managed to be in the same house without fireworks?"

"Now, David, you know we've called a truce since the girls came along. She doesn't even seem to mind that Charlotte and Veronica look like me." Mom smiled and picked up the towel to dry the plate. "She does remind me frequently that Veronica has blond hair and blue eyes." She laughed. "I have to say, I was really happy to see her today. I just wasn't getting through to Darla. We've never had a problem talking before. I hope this passes soon. I miss her."

"I do too." I looked around. "Where is everyone?"

"Darlene took the girls home. She said she and Jason would get them to school tomorrow. She told me she knew you needed a rest. She's okay, David. I think she's accepted us."

"She definitely loves those girls." I looked around again. "Where's my wife?"

"I'm right here," Darla said as she came into the room. Her hair was wet and she smelled like soap. "Your mom said she'd stay and listen for Brandon while I took a shower. I hope you don't mind me letting Mom take the girls."

"Of course I don't, baby. Your mother can take care of them. I'm glad the three of us have a few minutes alone. I have some news."

"You do?" Darla looked up at me from under her brows. I hated that look. I'd never seen her do it until recently. It was like she was hiding, ashamed.

"What's your news, David?" Mom asked.

"Jane has asked me to be co-president of the magazine with Grant. She's going to semi-retire. It's a really nice promotion."

"That's wonderful, honey." Mom hugged me and stepped back.

Darla crossed the kitchen and put her arms around my waist. She buried her head in my chest, and I kissed the top of it. We were back to normal for just a second. "I'm so proud to be your wife, David. Congratulations sweetheart," she said and pulled back to look up at me. Her eyes were swimming with tears. She sniffed and scrubbed at her eyes with her fists.

I exchanged a look with my mom over Darla's head. "It will include a substantial raise, P. H. I think we can afford to finish the room over the garage now."

She looked up at me. There was hope in her eyes for the first time in days. I took a deep breath and my shoulders relaxed.

"That will be so nice," she said and pulled away. "Isn't he great, Charlie?" She smiled at my mother and Mom smiled back. Maybe this was going to distract her for a while.

We brought Belinda home on my birthday. Dad and Mom and Uncle Jeff and his family were there. Jason and Darlene had brought dinner. Something they had brought from the To-go Gourmet in mid-town. Jimmy and Meryl came with Heather, James, Jr. and Marissa.

"Charlotte was born a few weeks before your birthday, David," Jimmy said. "The twins were born a few *days* before. You'll have to have another to see if you can hit it bang on." We all laughed a little nervously and looked at Darla.

"No more," she smiled sadly. "David only agreed on three."

"But P. H. wanted four, and she always gets her way." I put my hand on her shoulder and kissed the top of her head.

She smiled down at Brandon who was sleeping in her arms. Belinda started to cry from her cradle in the corner of the living room. I went over and picked her up.

"She's so tiny it's almost scary," I said to the room as my mom came in carrying a tray of full champagne glasses. Belinda started to whale loudly. "But she's got a strong set of lungs on her. Her brother has never made a noise like that."

"I'll go get her bottle." Mom set the tray on the coffee table and hurried from the room.

"It's been every two hours all day long. I guess it's going to be a busy night."

"Busy nights for a while I'd say," Darlene came across the room and took Belinda from me. "I'll give her the bottle, David. I think we're getting ready to toast your birthday and your promotion."

I reluctantly handed my tiny daughter to her grandmother and picked up a glass of champagne. When everyone had one Uncle Jeff said, "Congratulations David, on turning a grand thirty four. God, Charlie," he said to my mom. "If he's that old what are we?"

"Older," she laughed.

My dad put his arm around her and kissed her cheek. "We've produced quite a brood, haven't we sweetheart?"

"We helped," Darlene said. "And Charlotte, I can forgive you for the girls looking so much like you now. This little thing looks just like me." She looked down at Belinda who was sucking loudly on the bottle. "And her brother is the image of his maternal grandfather."

I looked around the room. It was a happy gathering. Everyone was smiling and chatting. I looked at Darla. She was smiling down at Brandon. Maybe she would be alright. Then she looked up at me, and I saw the sorrow in her eyes. I didn't know what to do to make it go away.

"You can have some champagne, Darla. You're not nursing." Mom handed her a glass. She took it and thanked her. She took a sip.

"Congratulations on your beautiful new babies, too, David," Jimmy said, "and on your promotion."

We all drank champagne. The kids sipped ginger ale. Then they put their glasses down and ran outside for a game of kick ball.

"I guess I'll take feeding detail tonight, Darla." We were in our room getting ready for bed. The girls were asleep. The dishes were done. Brandon was sleeping like the good baby he was, and Belinda had quieted down after a screaming bout like none we'd seen with any of the others.

"No David," Darla yawned. "You have to work tomorrow and with your new position you'll need to be well rested."

"It's not going to be that different, P. H, and it hasn't started yet. Jane is just going over everything she does. I'm amazed how much it is. I guess I thought I was doing more than I was."

"No, I'm sure there's just a lot to do. Will you hire someone for your position?" She sat down on the bed and hung her head. She looked so defeated. I sat down beside her and pulled her into my arms.

"I don't think we'll have to hire anyone else. Grant and I will split Jane's duties, but if we have to hire someone we can." I squeezed her a little tighter. "Darla, let me feed the babies tonight. You're still getting over surgery, and I don't sleep much anyway."

"How do you do it, David?" She spoke in a monotone as if she lacked the energy to talk. "You're so successful. You're a wonderful father, the perfect husband. You play soccer and work with troubled children and all on no sleep."

"I'm not that great, Darla. You're blowing it out of proportion. Don't put me up on a pedestal. I'm sure to fall off."

"No you are that great, David. I can't do anything. I can't even feed my own babies. What's wrong with me, David?" She looked up at me with a look of pure pain. Her eyes pleaded with me to relieve it. I couldn't speak for a minute.

"P. H. please snap out of this. I can't stand it."

"I'm sorry, but it's who I am. I can't do anything. I'm a failure, David. I'm a weight around your ankle. I don't want to be here anymore. I wish I could just go to sleep and not wake up. I wish I could die."

"Don't talk like that, damn it." I stood up and walked to the door.

"It's true," she whispered.

"Then go ahead and do it. Kill yourself." I regretted saying it as soon as it was out, but I walked through the door and slammed it behind me. I heard Belinda's startled cry as I stormed to my office. It made me furious when she talked like that. She'd said that a couple of times since the babies were born. I sat down at my computer and booted it up. I could hear Belinda screaming and now Brandon was crying too, which was rare. I couldn't leave Darla alone with that. Pretty soon they'd wake up the girls.

I stood and went back to the bedroom we shared. "I'm sorry, Darla." I crossed the room and picked up Brandon. "I shouldn't have said that." She was holding Belinda. It was the first time she'd held her all day. The look on her face was unreadable. I put Brandon over my shoulder and he quieted.

"She's beautiful," Darla said it so quietly I almost didn't hear her. The baby started to quiet down. Darla held her to her chest and tilted her head to look more directly into the tiny face. "David, I do love her. I was afraid I couldn't."

I'd been afraid of that too. I didn't say so. I crossed the room with my son to stand next to my wife and daughter.

"It wasn't her fault." Her voice was just a breath as she kissed the baby's soft cheek.

"No. It wasn't your fault either." I was afraid to say more.

"No." Her mouth formed the word, but she made no sound.

"You look surprisingly rested, David, for a man who has infant twins," Jane said to me as I entered the break room at the magazine with a breakfast casserole in my hand. "And you've brought breakfast for our meeting."

"Christine is bringing the bread. I think it's going to be agave glazed cinnamon rolls. We coordinated this time so we wouldn't have too much. I have a bowl of fruit salad in the car." I hurried out the door to get the fruit.

"So explain why you look better than you usually do when you should look exhausted," Jane said as I came back into the room with the bowl. "Surely you're not making Darla do all the night duty. It can't be easy with two of them. They're what, a couple of months old now. Do they sleep through the night?"

"Sometimes Brandon does but not Belinda. Darla nursed the other two and that's great, but there wasn't much for me to do. We're bottle feeding the twins. She's pretty stingy with Brandon. I think she feels like she has to give him special attention with his problem, although I haven't seen any evidence of a problem yet." I set the bowl on the table and went to the cabinet to see what we had in the way of paper plates and plastic tableware.

"So you do night duty with Belinda."

"Yeah, Darla gives her a lot of time during the day. I think they're bonding alright. I was worried about that at first. But if Brandon gets up she feeds him. If he doesn't, I let her sleep."

"That's nice of you. You're a good husband." Jane looked at her watch. The meeting would start in about five minutes.

"Well, that's nice of you to say, but it's not entirely unselfish. I never realized the serenity of feeding a baby in the middle of the night. I know that sounds poetic, but it's true. Everything is so quiet, and the baby is so peaceful in your arms sucking on that bottle. The only time in my whole life I've achieved complete contentment is feeding my baby in the middle of the night."

"That's a beautiful way of putting it," Michael said as he came into the room. "I felt that way myself when my kids were little."

"I still don't know why you look more rested," Jane said as the rest of the group filed in. "You're still up instead of sleeping."

"I sleep better when she goes back to sleep. I don't sleep for long, but I sleep more deeply than I ever have before." I frowned remembering for a second how soundly I slept in Anna's arms. I cleared my throat to clear the memory. "I wake up more rested." I went across the hall to retrieve my marketing report and to remove myself from the conversation for a minute.

"And after feeding an infant in the middle of the night," Jane was saying to the group assembled around the conference table as I came back into the room. "David was still able to get up in time to prepare breakfast. Christine did her part too. We thank you both."

We all went to the buffet table to fill our plates and sat down to start our weekly staff meeting.

"Excuse me," Celia our receptionist knocked on the door and peered into the room around it. "There is a phone call for you, Mr. Landrum. It's your wife. She says it's urgent."

My heart started to pound. I left the room without saying anything. I hurried across the hall to my office and picked up the phone. "What's going on, Darla?"

"It's Brandon." She was crying. Her voice sounded frantic. "He must be having a seizure. David, his legs and arms are stiff, and he's sort of paddling them."

"I'll be right there."

"No David, my mother and yours are on their way to watch the girls. I've called an ambulance. The ER doctor I talked to told me to turn him on his stomach to keep him from choking on his tongue. I can hear the ambulance. It's here. Meet me at the children's hospital." She hung up the phone before I could say anything else. I grabbed my keys and crossed the hall.

"I have to go," I said to the room full of people and left before anyone could ask a question. I don't remember the drive to the hospital. It was closer to my office than it was to my house. I waited for what seemed like hours, but was probably only minutes, for the ambulance to arrive.

"Darla!" I called across the crowded ER and ran to her. She held Brandon in her arms, and he was very still. "Is he..?" I don't know how I was going to end that question.

"He's alright now," she said. Her voice was weak.

I looked down at him in her arms. His cheeks were flushed pink. I expelled a breath I hadn't been aware of holding.

"He's sleeping," Darla whispered.

"The seizure was pretty much subsiding when we arrived, Mr. Landrum." The ambulance attendant told me. I hadn't noticed him until he spoke. "We didn't have to give him any valium. That's good because the doctor can make a better evaluation that way. He'll sleep soundly for a while. We'll need to check him into the hospital. They'll want to observe him." He guided us to a check-in window as a nurse came to take Brandon to the back.

"No, please don't take him from me." Darla turned her back to shield the baby from the nurse.

"Ma'am, please give him to me. I need to take him to be examined. You can come along." The girl looked up at me for support.

"Give Brandon to the nurse, Darla, so she can make sure he's alright. You go with them. I'll check him in." I sounded in charge, but my heart started to pound again, and my knees felt weak as the doors closed behind them. I couldn't see my son anymore. I had to get back there fast. I wanted him in my sight.

✺

"He slept through the night last night," Darla spoke as if in a dream. "He usually wants to eat early when he does that, but this morning he didn't call me. I wonder if that was leading up to this. I woke up at seven because Belinda was crying. I guess you fed her in the night." She looked at me. Her face was expressionless. We were in the hospital room with Brandon. He had slept for several hours and we sat in chairs on either side of his crib.

I nodded. "She still hasn't slept through a night."

"Poor thing, she didn't get a bottle until your mother got there, but she quieted down really fast when I realized something was wrong with Brandon. It was like she knew. Before I went to her I looked in his crib to make sure he was alright. It was eerie, David. He wasn't asleep. He was just staring at the ceiling. I called his name, and it was like his head sort of wobbled in my direction. He tried to look at me, but he didn't. I mean his eyes looked at me, but I don't think he saw me."

"He had an aura," I whispered it.

"What?" She looked at me and her eyes questioned.

"I'm not sure babies that age can really focus anyway." My mother's voice came from the end of the bed. Darla and I both jumped and looked at my parents. All three of them were there, Mom, Dad and Uncle Jeff. We hadn't even heard them come in.

"He's looked at me more clearly before," Darla continued without asking when they had arrived. "What do you mean an aura, David?"

"It's like a warning that a seizure is coming. I had one when I was in high school."

"You had an aura?" Uncle Jeff asked.

"Yes," I said. "And I had a seizure. Who's watching the girls?"

"Darlene and Jason," Mom said. "We tossed a coin."

"He had a seizure?" My dad looked at Mom. It was the first time I'd ever seen him look angry with her. "Why didn't I know about this, Charlotte? I'm his father. Don't you think it was something I should know?"

"I didn't know either, Brian." Uncle Jeff sounded upset too, but he wasn't looking at Mom. He was looking at me.

"You aren't his father." Now Dad was angry with Uncle Jeff.

"No, but I raised him."

"You're going to throw that in my face at a time like this." I looked at all three of my parents. They were about to fight with each other. The tension in the room was unbearable.

"Hey," I raised my voice and Brandon stirred. It was a relief. He'd been so still. "This isn't about me," I said. "It's about my son." I looked at Darla. "I hope it isn't hereditary. Maybe I'm not the perfect genetic compliment you thought I was. I guess I should have told you about the seizure."

"I knew about it. Teresa told me." She looked down at our sleeping son. He balled his little fists and stretched his arms over his head. "Anyway, I'm sure it isn't that. It has something to do with the lesions on his brain."

She was determined to blame herself for everything.

"Anyway, even if it is hereditary you never had any more seizures," Mom said. "You didn't, did you, David?"

"No, I had migraine headaches. They start with an aura too. It's a little different, though."

"Migraine headaches?" Mom put her hand on my shoulder. I looked up at her.

"We'll talk about this later," Dad said.

"Yes we will." I looked at Uncle Jeff. He didn't look angry. He looked hurt. Mom looked concerned. Dad looked mad. I shrugged. We'd deal with it later.

The door opened and the doctor came in. "How's our boy?" He walked to the crib and looked down just as Brandon opened his eyes. "Good, he's awake." He looked up at the rest of us and smiled. How can doctors smile at times like this, I wondered?

"They frequently sleep deeply after a seizure and seem to feel very good for the rest of the day," he said. I remembered the doctor saying that about me after the seizure. "I sent for his records from the women's center where he was born and had a look at them. He does have some lesions from the problem at birth. This is probably due to that, but you'll need to take him to a pediatric neurologist for tests."

"Could this be hereditary?" I asked.

"Why do you ask? Have any of you had seizures?"

"I have. I had one a long time ago. I never had another so we blamed it on stress."

"I guess they called it idiopathic."

"That's right. What does that mean?" Mom asked. "They told me at the time, but I don't remember."

"Just what it sounds like, we're idiots." He laughed. "We have no idea why he had a seizure."

I remembered the ER doctor saying that to me all those years ago. I didn't think it was funny then or now.

He looked at me and sobered. "I'm sorry," he said. "I know none of you feel like laughing right now. I suppose this could be hereditary, but I'm not a neurologist. I'm going to refer you to a very good one who will do further tests and give you a better idea of what is going on here. In the mean time you'll need to watch him closely for more seizure activity. You handled it very well today," he said to Darla.

"Can we take him home now?" Darla asked.

"I think I'm comfortable releasing him." He looked down at Brandon. The baby was smiling up at us and holding his left foot with his tiny left hand. "Look at him," the doctor said. "He's a little young to be holding his feet. I guess with the left brain out of the way, the right brain develops fast." He looked up at us. I resolved to go home and read all those pamphlets on brain function we'd gotten when he was born. "I'll send a nurse in with release papers to sign and a referral to the neurologist."

◊

"Jane Fox," my boss answered the phone the next morning.

"Hey," I said. "It's David. I need to work from home today," I said. "I know you were planning to run over some things with me this morning, but Darla is afraid to be alone with all the kids after yesterday. I'm hoping this won't last long."

"I understand. Would it be alright if I came by a little later? Why don't I bring lunch? We could run over some of my notes, and I'd get a chance to see those babies. How is Brandon today?"

"He's happy as usual. He felt great after his long sleep yesterday. We haven't seen any sign of more seizure activity. I'm hoping it will be a one time thing. We go to the neurologist tomorrow and I think Darla will feel better after that."

"Do you think she'll mind me dropping by today?"

"No, but she may not come out of her room. You may not see her."

"I hope I will. I've missed her, but if not, that's okay too. See you around noon." I hung up the phone and the doorbell rang. I opened the door to all three of my parents and they all looked intense.

"I can't believe the three of you are going to attack me at a time like this." I turned and walked back to the kitchen where I had coffee brewing and a banana French toast casserole in the oven."

"We didn't plan it." Mom followed me in and put down her purse. She kissed my cheek and poured herself a cup of coffee. "We all came in different cars. Your dad and I didn't even talk about it when we left the house. We were half way here before I realized he was following me." She laughed and started gathering plates and flatware to set the table.

"I guess we all kind of think alike when it comes to you, David." Uncle Jeff poured two cups of coffee and handed one to my dad.

"I figured I'd take the girls to school this morning. I don't have a fitting until nine," Mom said. "I don't have to stay for the scolding. I've already had mine."

"You guys can't blame Mom for not telling you about that seizure. She was just honoring my wishes," I said. "And you'd be a hypocrite to be mad at her, Uncle Jeff. After all, you didn't tell her about the waterfall incident."

The room fell silent and everyone looked at me. "Shit!"

"The waterfall incident," Mom said ominously.

"What waterfall incident?" Dad asked.

"The subject of this conversation is the seizure," Uncle Jeff squirmed and served himself some of the hot casserole I'd put on the table. "Why didn't you want me to know you'd had a seizure, David? Don't you trust me?"

"What does it have to do with trust?" I sat down and dished up two plates of casserole for the girls. It was hot and needed to cool before they got down for breakfast.

"I just feel like you thought I'd judge you for it or something. Didn't you realize I just cared about your well being?"

"I don't know why I didn't tell you, Uncle Jeff, but it wasn't a lack of trust. I always knew you loved me ever since you pulled me out of that waterfall. Shit!" I said again and looked at my mom.

"We're going to talk about that waterfall."

"I'm not here to scold you, David," Dad said. "I know why you didn't trust me. I'm here to apologize for abandoning you the way I did."

"Please don't." I ran my hand through my hair and recognized the gesture as one of my uncle's. "Look, it wasn't a matter of trust. It was embarrassing. It happened at school. I had to go out of there in an ambulance. My teacher rode with me. Even though I don't remember it, I guess she saw me twitching and jerking. I hate the thought. I didn't want anyone else to know. It never happened again so what difference does it make?"

The room was quiet. "Okay," Uncle Jeff said.

"Yeah, I guess I understand," Dad said.

"Tell me about the migraine headaches," Mom said.

"I had one the night you and Uncle Jeff left me at Harvard. I thought it was another seizure at first, but the dorm mother recognized the signs of migraine. She took me to the infirmary. I spent the night there. I was sick all night but fine in the morning."

"You didn't tell us before we left the next day," Uncle Jeff said.

"It was over. You didn't need to know."

"Do you get them often?" Dad asked.

"No."

"Yum, banana French toast," Charlotte bounced into the room with Veronica right behind her. "Will one of you stay with Mom while Dad takes us to school?" She looked around the table at her grandparents. "She shouldn't be alone with the babies right now."

"You take such good care of your mother." Mom kissed both girls on the tops of their heads. "I'm taking you girls to school. Eat up." She looked across the table at me. "We'll talk about the waterfall later."

CHAPTER TWENTY

"There are no changes in his CT scan since birth," Dr. Sedwick, the pediatric neurologist said. We had spent the morning at the hospital having tests and had come back that afternoon to discuss the results.

"So this could be something he inherited from me?"

"Probably not," he said. "Considering the circumstances, I think it probably has something to do with the lesions on his brain from birth."

I looked at Darla. She was holding a sleeping Brandon in her lap and looking down at him with an unreadable expression. I'd seen that expression so many times since the twins were born. It worried me. I'd almost hoped we could blame this on me.

"But you can't rule it out," I said.

"No, but I can't call it idiopathic either. I'm going to give him the diagnosis of epilepsy. It's just a matter of finding out how severe it will be. It's a good sign that he hasn't had another seizure in this many days. Sometimes they come in clusters and that can have a pretty severe prognosis."

"So he may not have another one."

"It's possible, but I expect he will." The doctor walked around the exam table and looked down at Brandon sleeping in his mother's arms. He stroked the soft cheek with the back of his forefinger and Brandon smiled in his sleep. "He sure is a beautiful baby."

"Yes he is," Darla said quietly.

"Hopefully, this will be a mild case. I don't think I'm going to recommend any drug therapy at this point. This baby will have developmental challenges as it is. It will be better if we don't throw drugs into the mix. If we can help it, that is. I'll give you very mild valium in suppository form in case of a bad seizure, but you may not need it. I've interviewed the paramedic who treated him. He told me the seizure was resolving on its own when he arrived at your house."

"It seemed pretty bad to me," Darla's voice was so quiet the doctor didn't seem to hear her.

"It seemed bad to her," I repeated it louder.

"I know it did. When you aren't used to seeing these things they're frightening, especially when it's your own baby." He went to the door of the exam room. "I'm going to get you some pamphlets to read and a list of support groups around town. "Dealing with these things is always better if you can talk to people who have been through it."

I looked at Darla. She didn't look back. Her eyes never left Brandon's face.

"I highly recommend a support group," Dr. Sedwick said to me. Darla didn't seem to be responding. He looked at her then back at me. "I'll bring a list of therapists that help with these things as well. They lead the groups. They do one on one therapy too. I highly recommend it." He repeated, glanced at Darla again and left the room.

"I don't need a group or therapy," Darla said without looking away from Brandon.

I went across the room and reached for my son. Darla turned and shielded him from me. "He's my baby too, Darla." I pulled Brandon from her arms. "I need to hold him sometimes. You aren't thinking of anyone but yourself. This isn't just about you."

She looked up at me, and we glared at each other. Brandon stirred. I bounced to calm him and turned away.

"I'm sorry. I'll try to be more considerate," she said, still in a whisper. I didn't turn to look at her.

I pulled my front door shut behind me, turned the lock, and buried my gloved hands in my pockets. It was just before midnight in late October. I had resumed my midnight walks when Belinda started sleeping through the night in the early fall. The twins were six months old now and the night duty had slowed to only occasionally, and once again, I wasn't sleeping very well.

The air was crisp as I walked up the path to the road. Our neighborhood was quiet, and I felt safe walking late at night. I stayed close to the streetlights, though. We did live in a big and dangerous city.

"David," I jumped as I heard my name spoken from behind me. My heart rate slowed as I recognized the voice. I turned around.

"Jimmy, you scared me to death," I said. "What are you doing prowling around here in the middle of the night?"

"I'm waiting for you," he said. "I figured you still took your midnight walk. I wanted to talk to you."

"Well, I don't still walk. I'm walking again since Belinda is sleeping through the night. I slept like a baby after feeding my baby, but I'm back to my old coping mechanism now."

"Well, don't smoke that stuff while I'm here."

"You know I won't."

"But you do when …?"

"Drop it, Jimmy."

"Right …"

We walked in silence for a few minutes. "So what did you want to talk to me about?"

"A couple of things …" He blew on his hands. I could see the steam from his breath in the cold night air. "Is it usually this cold this early in the fall? It seems to me this is unseasonably cold."

"You stalked me in the middle of the night to talk about the weather," I teased. "Well yes, I think it is unusually cold out tonight. I wonder why."

"That's not what I came to talk to you about, but I wish I'd worn a warmer jacket."

I stopped and looked at him. He was wearing a windbreaker and his hands and head were bare.

"Let's go back to the house, Jimmy. You really aren't dressed warm enough."

"Will you be able to sleep if you don't walk?"

I smiled and put my hand on his shoulder to turn him toward the house. "I'll be alright. I have some hot buttered rum on the stove. Have a mug with me and I'll sleep just fine."

"Will I be able to drive home?"

"I only made enough for me. We'll split it and you'll be fine."

"You haven't switched to alcohol to make you sleep have you, David? I'm sure that isn't a good idea."

I laughed. "You worry about me too much. I'm fine, Jimmy. I hardly ever drink anything. I just had a hankering tonight, and I'm trying a new recipe. Did I tell you I'm writing a cookbook?"

"No, but that's a great idea. You're a good cook."

"Yeah," I let us into the front door and led Jimmy down the hall to the kitchen. "I'll have to pour the whole thing into a steaming mug and take a picture before I divide it up. I like a cookbook with pictures."

Jimmy laughed and sat down at the kitchen table while I poured, snapped the picture and then divided the drink into two smaller cups. I placed one on the table in front of him then sat down with my own across from him.

"What's on your mind?" I asked.

"Well, good things first, James, Jr. is playing tennis in the State Championships on the high school level. He's the youngest student to ever make it that far."

"That's fantastic. When is it? I want to be there."

"I bought you a ticket. I got one for Darla too. In fact I have a bunch of them. Everyone I know is going." He sipped his mug of rum. "This is really good, David, and if it's having the same effect on you as it is on me, you'll sleep fine tonight."

I smiled and sipped. "You said good things first. Is there something wrong?" I suddenly felt nervous and leaned forward. "Is Heather alright, Marissa? I haven't seen much of your family since the twins were born."

"They're both fine. Did I tell you that Heather got into Harvard for next fall?"

"You're kidding. Is she at that point already?" I sat up straight and looked at Jimmy. Pride was shining all over his face.

"She's finishing early like you did."

"I remember you telling me at some point that Heather was easy because she was middle of the road. You said she was smart enough but not too smart."

"Maybe she's smarter than I thought. She's definitely driven. She wants to be a doctor. Can you imagine? A child of mine wants to be a doctor."

"I can imagine. You're a smart guy, Jimmy. You just had a tough break."

"I had a tough break that I passed on to my son. But he's doing alright. He'll never be a scholar like his sister, but he does okay, thanks to you."

"Thanks to all of us, Jimmy, so what's the bad thing you wanted to talk to me about?"

He looked over his shoulder and listened to the silent house for a minute. Then he stood up and closed the kitchen door. "I'm worried about P. H.," he said as he sat back down at the table.

I leaned back and studied his face. "Why? Has she talked to you? Has she talked to Meryl?"

"No, that's the problem. She doesn't talk anymore. Meryl noticed it first, of course. She and Darla have always been so close. I told her not to worry about it, but she persisted. Yesterday she talked me into doing a really silly thing. She asked Darla to lunch. She had to come to the house with Darla's mother in tow to babysit the twins. She said it was like pulling teeth to get Darla out of the house. Then I acted like I just happened by the café and saw them. We tried to have a fun lunch with her like we used to do when you were away."

"When I was in prison?" I asked.

"Yeah," he looked embarrassed. "Or when you were at school or when you were with Teresa. There were a lot of times when Darla and Meryl and I were a threesome. But Darla didn't talk this time. She used to be the life of the party. She has a strange expression on her face. It's almost like no expression at all. She's not getting over this thing with Brandon. How sick is he, David?"

I drained the last of my drink and took a deep breath. "We won't know for years how bad the brain damage is, Jimmy. But he's the happiest baby we've ever had. He's developing a little bit lop sided. The muscles on the right side of his face are a little weaker so his smile is crooked, but it's cute, and at least he's smiling. He grabs his left foot, but can't quite get the right foot. They're six months old now. Belinda is up on her hands and knees. It won't be long before she's crawling, but Brandon isn't sitting up yet. I think his balance is a little bit compromised. I mean with the lopsided growth you can understand. I'm hoping he'll be able to overcome that."

"What about the seizures?"

"They're mild. He didn't have one after that first one for three months. We were hoping that would be it, but he's had four in the last three months. They've all been over before we could get the valium suppository into him, except the last one. He came out of it fast like the others. Then he went back into it. We gave him the medication that time. He slept eight hours that night." I rubbed my eyes. "Darla didn't sleep at all. She usually doesn't have trouble sleeping."

I looked at Jimmy. He didn't say anything.

"She won't go to a support group. I went a few times, but it didn't seem like I was the one that needed it."

"Did it help at all?"

"It did, I think."

"Maybe you should go back. Maybe you going will help her or help you help her."

"Maybe," I said. I rubbed my eyes again. "You know what, Jimmy. I'm sleepy. You think you're alright to drive."

"I'm good." He stood up and put on his jacket.

"At least let me give you some gloves and a scarf." I went to the hall closet and got out the box of warm wear.

"David," Jimmy said as I wrapped a scarf around his neck and pulled a stocking cap over his head. "You don't have to talk to me anymore about this right now but don't ignore it. I think P. H. is in trouble, and I think you're the only person who can help her."

"David," Darla woke me out of a sound sleep the next morning. Jimmy was right. That midnight hot rum did make me sleep. You could get used to that. "What babe," I mumbled.

"Did you drink last night? I smelled alcohol on your breath when you came to bed."

"I'm sorry. I was trying not to wake you up." I sat up and looked at the clock. "Whoa, I slept until seven thirty. I never sleep that late."

"You were passed out."

"I was not passed out," I laughed. "I made one hot buttered rum drink to try out for my cookbook, and I split it with Jimmy. It did relax me though. I can see how bad habits form. I won't do that again for a while."

"Why was Jimmy here?" She got up out of the bed and walked to the bathroom. I heard her turn on the water and start to brush her teeth.

"Sometimes he meets me for my midnight walk. It's kind of a male bonding thing I guess." I followed her into the bathroom and put my arms around her from the back. "Are the kids still asleep? We haven't stayed in bed this late since the twins were born."

"No, they're up. I didn't wake you. I've fed all four of them and the girls are playing in their room. Both twins have dozed back off, but I don't think that will last for long so …" She gently eased herself out of my arms. "… don't start something you can't finish."

"What makes you think I couldn't finish it?" I picked up my toothbrush and took her place over the sink. I looked at myself in the mirror. My hair was sticking out in odd directions and my eyes were bulgy. There were marks on my face where I'd slept on my hand. No wonder she didn't want to snuggle up to me. Come to think of it, we hadn't had sex since the twins were born.

"Why don't we make love anymore, P. H.?" I asked as I started the shower.

"Don't worry about it, David. We've been preoccupied with things. Anyway, you haven't wanted it any more than I have." I looked down at my body and realized she was right. She stepped into the shower behind me, and I felt a little better. At least we were still that intimate.

"Move over and let me wash, David. The twins will be up any minute."

"Yes ma'am," I said and moved out of her way.

"I wanted to talk to you about something. That's why I woke you up." She tilted her head under the shower and closed her eyes. "I want to fix up the room above the garage. You know. We've talked about it. I think I need a little project to distract me from Brandon's problems. It isn't good for him to have me hovering over him the way I do." She rinsed her hair and opened her eyes to look at me. The expression on her face had changed. She looked animated for the first time in months.

The tension in my neck started to ease a little. I hadn't even realized it was there until now. "You look like yourself again, baby."

"I woke up feeling like myself, only a little, but better than I have for a while." She moved around me easing me into the shower and herself out of it. She stepped out of the curtain and I could hear her pull the towel off the rack. "I need your help though, David. I'll need you to give me a budget on the project like you always do. And I'll need you to do the plumbing for a bathroom up there."

"Why do we need a bathroom up there? The powder room is at the bottom of the steps next to the kitchen." The hairs on the back of my neck were prickling. I'd had that feeling before. It was some kind of instinctive reaction to fear.

"I want a full bath up there."

"I thought it was going to be a play room for the kids."

"We'll see how it goes." She was in the bedroom now. I got out of the shower and grabbed my towel.

"You're not planning to put a kitchen up there are you?" I asked as I came into the room. Darla was dressed and brushing her hair at her small vanity table.

"Of course not," she laughed. "What would we need a kitchen for? There's the most perfectly appointed kitchen just down the stairs." She stood and stretched up to kiss me on the cheek. "I'll give you a list of the things I need, and you can make up a budget for me. I know how you like to have everything planned." She hurried out of the room and sounds of happy baby babble came from the direction of the nursery.

I stretched my shoulders in to ease the tension that had returned to my neck. Something wasn't right about this, but Darla was smiling and motivated. Maybe I'm just imagining things. She's happy, I thought. Just let her be happy.

She wasn't happy for long.

"Why do we need a hardwood floor in a playroom?" I asked Darla. We were sitting in the living room going over the budget for the room above the garage.

"Shhhh ..." she said. "You'll wake the girls up."

She had given me her list of supplies for the project after we had bathed the girls and put them to bed. The twins were settling down in the nursery above us. You could hear them cooing happily as they readied themselves for sleep.

"Okay," I lowered my voice. "But P. H. a hardwood floor isn't durable enough for a play room. If you like the look why don't we use a laminate floor? It's looks very real."

"I don't want laminate, David. It's fake. I want hardwood."

"... but for a playroom?"

"David," she took a deep breath. "It isn't going to be a play room."

My heart started to pound. I had anticipated this, and I didn't think I could stand it. "Baby, please don't tell me you plan to move out of our room and live up there. I don't think I can stand it if you do."

She looked up at me. Her eyes were wide and startled. "Oh David," she stood and came to me. "Of course I'm not planning that." She climbed into my lap, straddling me. "I'm sorry I've been so awful since the twins were born. I've hurt you, and I didn't mean to." She buried her face in my chest. My arms went around her, and I felt myself relax for the first time in months.

"So if you aren't planning to make the place a playroom, and it isn't going to be your bedroom, what is it going to be?"

"An office," She leaned back and looked into my eyes. "David, I want to start a business, my own business out of the house."

"Your own business ..?"

"Yeah, I was thinking about those albums you make. I thought you could teach me how to do it, and I could make family albums for people. I sent out a survey in the last newsletter at the elementary school and the response was good."

I guess my face didn't show enthusiasm because she jumped off my lap and stomped back to her chair.

"I can see that you think it's a stupid idea. I knew you wouldn't support me. That's why I didn't tell you in the first place." She sat down and looked away from me. "Well, you don't have to teach me anything. I'll take courses. I'm not stupid you know."

I could feel my mouth hanging open and shut it. Why couldn't I respond? I didn't think she was stupid. "I thought you wanted me to support you, I mean financially." Why did I say that? I thought. Maybe I am stupid.

"I don't want to think you have to support me."

"I don't have to. You were doing fine without me. But my support was part of the deal when we got married." That was another stupid thing to say.

"A marriage isn't supposed to be a deal."

"This isn't a deal, baby. I love you. This is a marriage." I stood and went to her chair. I knelt in front of her and tipped her chin to look at me. "I'll teach you. God, Darla, I thought you didn't want to be with me anymore."

She smiled, showing her dimples. "It isn't that. I just need to know I can take care of myself." She looked down at her hands clasped in her lap. "Then maybe I'll feel like I can take care of my children."

I leaned forward and touched my lips to hers. She responded. I put my hand on the back of her neck and pulled her out of the chair to the floor beside me. She wrapped her arms around my neck, and we fell together to the rug. Suddenly she pulled away and sat up. She turned her head to the stairway. I heard the cry from above.

"It's Belinda." Darla struggled to her feet. "She makes that sound when Brandon is going to have a seizure."

"You've noticed this before?" I asked as I jumped to my feet and followed her up the stairs.

"I guess so." She ran down the hall to the nursery. "I only just now realized it." She turned back to look at me as she put her hand on the door knob. "They feel each other," she whispered. "She knows."

"Hello big brother." Drew's voice sounded through the phone on my desk. I turned off the speaker phone and picked up the receiver.

"Hey Drew,"

"I'm in town," he said. "I was hoping we could get together for dinner. I have news."

"I have a support group tonight. Darla is taking the kids to her parent's house for dinner. I'll pick her up after the group. I guess we could have an early meal somewhere. I was planning to work up until the meeting then grab something later at home."

"What kind of group?"

"It's for parents of epileptic children."

"Darla isn't going with you?"

"No. She won't budge on that. She says she doesn't want to talk to a bunch of strangers about her problems."

"Is it helping you?"

I hesitated. "Yes," I took a deep breath. Held it for a minute then blew it out slowly. "It is helping me," I said. "There are even people there who have had problems with their wives and husbands about it. I guess misery really does love company."

"Brandon doesn't really make you miserable, does he, David?"

"No, Brandon makes me very happy and so does Belinda."

"Can I go to the group with you?"

"Why would you want to? You don't have an epileptic son."

"I have an epileptic nephew. Uncles count. Your uncle raised you."

"That's true," I said. "In fact, I'd enjoy the company. I'm feeling kind of lonely these days."

"What time is the meeting?"

"It's at seven thirty."

"I'll come around five then. That will give us time to have a nice meal and a good talk. The meal is on me so think of an inexpensive place to go. Then we'll go to the meeting."

"Aren't you a school teacher or something? How can you afford to take me out to dinner?"

"I can't but I'm doing it anyway. I have some really big news."

"I can't wait to hear it." I hung up the phone and stood to stretch my shoulders. I'd been at work at my computer for hours, and I was very stiff.

✦

"Okay, I couldn't work much this afternoon wondering about your news." I said to my brother after we'd been seated in a booth at the sushi restaurant around the corner from the office.

"I'll bet you can guess." He smiled and it was written all over his face.

"You're getting married."

"Right," He leaned forward grinning from ear to ear. "But that's not all. I got a job here in Atlanta in the public school system. We're going to be neighbors."

"That's fantastic, Drew." It was the first time I'd felt excited about anything for a while. "Tell me about your girl?"

"Ahhh ..." he leaned back and rolled his eyes to the ceiling "Lizzy ..." His smile was deliriously wide, but he leaned forward quickly. "Her name is Elizabeth, and if you shorten it in any way she'll slap you." He leaned back with that stupid grin on his face again. "But she lets me call her Lizzy."

"You are absolutely goofy about this girl."

"She's not a girl," he said sitting up a little straighter. "She's thirty years old, two years older than me. And I'm not goofy. I'm in love."

"I didn't mean to insult you, Drew. I was only teasing. I'm happy for you."

"Get this, David. She's a psychotherapist."

"And she's marrying a school teacher."

"Hey, it's special education. That's how we met." He stopped talking long enough to order his dinner. I ordered mine. Then he went on. "In fact, she was leading a parent's group. I joined to get an idea of the parent's needs, you know, the parents of learning disabled kids."

"Kind of like the one we're going to tonight."

"That's right. These support groups are great David. They really help. You should try to get Darla to go." His face sobered and he leaned forward. "I talked to Uncle Jason. He told me what a hard time she's having."

"I'm surprised. Jason doesn't usually notice things like that."

"He's not comfortable with feelings, David. But he loves his daughter."

"I know." I sipped the water the waitress put down in front of me. "So tell me about the job."

"Okay, we'll talk about Darla more when we get to the group."

"I'm beginning to wish I hadn't invited you."

"Well, you did." He smiled displaying his family's dimples. "Now, about the job, I'm so excited about it. It's at one of the schools in Dakalb County. Elizabeth is really just getting started. She's been in school a long time, you know. She got her doctorate and all. She has a friend here in Atlanta that she's going to share office space with. Won't it be nice to live in the same city, David?"

"Yeah, it will." I smiled at my brother's beaming face. It would be nice.

✦

"You couldn't get Darla to come so you brought her brother. It has to be with all that blond hair and blue eyes, and the dimples in his cheeks." Jennifer, the group leader, said.

"You've met Darla?" Drew said looking at me. "I thought she wouldn't come."

"He talks about her a lot," Jennifer laughed.

"This is Drew," I said. "He's Darla's cousin. He's my brother."

"You married your cousin?" She raised a brow at me.

"No, it's a confusing family." I said, declining further explanation.

"How is Darla doing this week, David?" Carol asked. Carol and Ed came to the meetings once a month. They had an eight year old epileptic daughter who was doing very well. They came to provide support for new members.

"I don't know. She doesn't talk to me anymore."

"Last month when we came you said she was getting excited about fixing up her office," Ed said.

"She backslid," Denise, the mother of a six year old epileptic boy said. "Apparently Belinda can sense Brandon's seizures. When Darla discovered it she went back into her depression."

"Is that right?" Drew looked at me.

"Yeah, it was strange. We had talked about the room above the garage. She told me about her ambition to start a scrapbooking business.

She smiled that night. It was the first time I'd seen those dimples in her cheeks in months."

"I know how much you love those dimples. The first thing you said to me when the twins were born was that they both have dimples." Drew put his hand on my shoulder and I felt the warmth of contact.

"Yeah, they're beautiful babies." I felt my grin. "Anyway," I sobered. "I was about to kiss her when Belinda started to cry. But it wasn't actually a cry. It was more of a keening sound. It was the first time Darla had realized that she makes that sound every time Brandon has a seizure."

"Wow," Jennifer said. She looked around the room at the eight people attending. "Have we ever had twins in this group before?" she asked.

"I've been here the longest," George said from across the room. "Ellen is twelve, and I don't ever remember twins."

"So that twin connection you hear so much about is real," Jennifer said.

"Oh yeah," Drew leaned back in his chair. "Our father, David's and mine, is a twin. Sometimes he and Uncle Jeff don't even have to talk to communicate."

I looked at Drew. He had a different perception of the relationship between Uncle Jeff and Dad. I was more aware of their problems.

"Isn't that right, David?" He looked at me for backup.

"They've had their problems, but they are very close. The ones that really pointed it out to me were our twin cousins. They even talk about themselves as we."

"That's right," Drew said.

"So what bother's Darla about Belinda being able to tell when Brandon is going to have a seizure?" Ed asked. "I think it would be nice to have a warning."

"Like I said, she won't talk to me about it, but that night before she had time to stop herself she said, "She's too young to have that responsibility. It isn't fair."

"It isn't a responsibility." One of the newer members of the group said. I'd have to ask his name later. "It's a connection. It's beautiful actually."

"It is beautiful," I said.

"What happened to the plans for the office, the plans for the business?" Jennifer asked.

"Nothing, the list of supplies is still sitting on the living room coffee table where I left it. It's been weeks and she hasn't done anything."

✦

"That was enlightening, David," Drew said as we got into my car to go back to the office to pick up his. "I think Darla is really in trouble."

"I know, Drew, but I don't know what to do about it."

"I'm going by the house tomorrow to talk to her. Is that okay with you?"

"Sure, maybe you can help."

"Maybe," he said, but he didn't sound too sure.

I watched Meryl dribble the soccer ball down the field toward my goal. We had just started pre-season practice. I was poised to catch it when I was distracted by something out of the corner of my eye. I had a fleeting irritation at myself for not being able to filter it. I was usually pretty focused when I played soccer.

"David ..." I recognized the sound of Drew's voice and turned to see him and my mother running toward me. Mom was holding Belinda on her hip. I registered the strangeness of this. My mother was not my brother's mother, and where was Brandon?

"David," Mom said as she approached me. I stood up straight and felt the soccer ball whiz by my left cheek. Mom was out of breath, and Belinda was tearstained and fretful.

"What's wrong?" I asked.

"David," Mom said again and put her hand on my arm. "Darla is gone."

"Darla's gone," I said stupidly.

"She took Brandon," Drew said.

"That's alright," I said. "Brandon is her son."

"David," Mom said. "She left a note."

"She left a note," I said sounding stupid again.

"A suicide note," she said. "She wants to die and she wants to take Brandon with her."

"P. H. wouldn't do something like this," I said. We were at home. Charlotte and Veronica were at Darla's parent's house. Belinda sat in my lap. At nine months old she was a pretty sturdy little armful. She was still small for her age but solid. She'd been fussy since I got home.

"Let me take her for a minute," Mom said.

"No," Mom pulled back her outstretched arms. She looked startled at my refusal to let my daughter go. "I'm sorry, Mom," I said. "I just need to hold on to this baby since my son is out somewhere on the coldest night of the year."

"I understand, honey."

"Besides she's upset. You know how connected she is to Brandon."

"David, can you think of any place she might go. She didn't even take her car. Is there some favorite hiding place she has that's within walking distance?"

"Not that I know of and she says very clearly in the note not to look for her because we won't find her. We'll just have to wait until she comes home." My mom and my brother exchanged looks of concern. The doorbell rang and Drew went to answer it. I looked back down at the note on the table.

> *David,*
>
> *I'll start by saying I'm sorry. I really am you know. I can't say it out loud to you because you'll object, and I just need to say it, without objection. I am sorry. I've let you down, and I've let Brandon down, and now I know I've let Belinda down too.*
>
> *I couldn't take care of both of them in the womb, and I can't take care of both of them outside of it. This was not a decision I made easily, but I have to do it.*
>
> *Brandon has no future in this world. A retarded child who has seizures has no place here. And Belinda has no future with him here either. And she deserves a future.*
>
> *I'm asking you to trust me, David. This is the right thing to do. I promise I won't let him suffer. I have the sleeping pills. I haven't taken any of them, and I've refilled the prescription every month since the twins were born. There will be enough for both of us.*
>
> *Don't try to find me because you won't. I've planned this well.*
>
> *Again David, I'm sorry. I love you. Take care of the girls, all three of them.*
>
> *Trust me on this.*
> *Darla*

"David," Uncle Jeff came into the room with my Dad. "I came as soon as I heard.

Do you have any idea where she could have gone?"

"What happened?" My dad asked Drew.

"I came over about 2:00 this afternoon to talk to Darla," Drew said. "I was worried after David and I went to the support group last night. I wanted to talk to her and see if there was anything I could do. But she wasn't here. Charlotte was here minding Belinda and waiting for the girls to get home from school. I decided I'd just stay until they got home and visit with them until Darla got home."

"Only Darla never came home," Mom said. "When it started getting late I called Darlene and Jason to come and get the girls. I kept Belinda, though. I just needed to keep her."

"I went up to your bedroom, David, when we started to get worried. I found the note on your pillow. I guess she figured you wouldn't find it there until it was too late."

"Should we call the police?" Dad asked.

"No!" I said it firmly and everyone jumped. Belinda started to cry. I stood up and put her on my shoulder. I walked around the room bouncing her until she quieted.

"David," Uncle Jeff put his hand on my shoulder. I shrugged it off.

"She won't do it," I said. "She's asked me to trust her and I do. She won't kill her own child. She won't kill herself."

"David," Dad said. "The Darla we all know won't do this, but she's not herself. She's so distraught. I can't believe I didn't see it. I can't believe it got this bad without me seeing it."

"I saw it," Mom said. "I just didn't know what to do."

"None of us knew what to do," I said. "But I know what to do now. She's asked me to trust her. I do. She won't do this."

"David," Uncle Jeff said. "I really think we have to notify the police."

"No police!"

"Then we should look for her," Dad said.

"We won't find her," I sat back down at the table. "We have to wait for her to come home."

✧

I sat on the couch in my living room. It was well past midnight. Charlotte and Veronica had gotten home a little before 10:00. Jason carried a sleeping Veronica upstairs. Charlotte asked where her mother was. I told her she had taken Brandon for a little trip and that she would be back. She had finally fallen to sleep around eleven o'clock.

It was hard to convince Darlene and Jason to go home. They were consumed with worry. It had been hard to convince my parents and brother to leave too. But reluctantly, everyone had finally left me alone with my children. I needed to be alone with them.

Belinda continued to fret until she finally fell asleep. I arranged pillows around her on the sofa beside me. I put my head back and closed my eyes. I must have dozed because I was awakened by a blast of freezing air. I looked up.

Darla stood in the open doorway, a bundle of blanket in her arms. "Help me, David," she whispered.

I moved from the couch to the door in a second and picked her up in my arms. I carried her and the warm bundle I knew to be my sleeping son to a chair and pulled them both close, rocking them gently.

"I couldn't do it, David. I couldn't go. I couldn't take him. But I can't stay." Her voice was softer than a whisper. "Help me, David. I don't know what to do."

"It's okay, P. H. We'll figure it out."

"Tell me you'll help me, David, please."

"I'll help you."

"All set?" Uncle Jeff's familiar greeting sounded from the open front door.

"I guess so," I answered reluctantly. It was spring break and we were going packing on the Appalachian Trail.

"You sound a little reluctant," he squeezed my shoulder.

"Well, it's hard to leave the family when we're just getting back to normal."

"I'll be alright, David." Darla approached me from behind and put her arm around my waist. "And you need the break. You and I have been attached at the hip for the last two and a half months."

"That hasn't been a hardship, P. H." I kissed the top of her head.

"For me either," she smiled up at me and I smiled back. "But we need some time, and it'll be nice for you to have some one on one time with Veronica."

"I'll miss Charlita," I said. "But she's determined to stay home and take care of you."

"Yes and Uncle Dad and Charlie are staying with us, so we'll be fine here."

"Bye, Mommy," Veronica stretched her arms up to Darla and Darla leaned to receive the embrace. Veronica gave her a loud kiss on the cheek and scampered off to climb into the truck with her cousin Evelyn.

"She isn't even six years old yet," I said, feeling a little panicky. "I hope this goes okay."

"I think she'll be fine," Darla said. "I hope she misses me at least a little bit."

"I'll miss you, Daddy." I felt Charlotte's soft hand take mine, and I looked down at her tearful face.

"Oh Charlita," I scooped her into my arms. "I'll miss you too. But it's only four days this time." We thought after last year we should start a little slower with Veronica. "I'll be back before you know it." She buried her face in my shirt and sobbed. I exchanged a helpless look with Darla.

She smiled reassuringly at me and pulled Charlotte off my shoulder. "Give us a call anytime you pass a phone, David. We'll want to hear from you."

I got into Uncle Jeff's truck and waved to my wife and tearful daughter. The twins sat on a blanket in the yard, Brandon leaning a little to the right and propped on a pillow. I waved to them. They squealed and didn't wave back.

"You sure you're okay with this? We could wait until summer." Uncle Jeff said as he pulled the truck away from my house.

"You promised, Daddy." Veronica called from the back seat.

"I'll be fine." I laughed. "If I get homesick, Vroom will comfort me. Won't you Vroom."

"I'll take care of you, Daddy." I heard her own version of her mother's tinkling laugh.

"Just don't go to sleep, Bubba," Evelyn said. "We don't want you to throw up. Did you know your dad gets carsick if he sleeps in the car?" she asked Veronica.

"Really, Daddy?"

"Really," I laughed. "So you'll just have to keep me entertained. Why didn't Alice come along? Last time I talked to her she said she was going to."

"She has an infection so Mom wouldn't let her."

"Is she alright?" I looked at Uncle Jeff.

"Nothing major," he said. "She had strep throat last week. Amanda didn't want to let her out of her sight for a while. We worry a little more about the infection spreading with her."

"Yeah, I'm not at risk," Evelyn said.

"Did you have strep throat too?"

"Yeah, but I'm not contagious anymore. I'll miss Alice, though."

"Dad is staying with Darla, and Drew is spending spring break with Elizabeth's family," I said. "So it's just the four of us. This will be nice."

✦

"First things first," Uncle Jeff said as we unloaded our backpacks from the trunk of the cab that had brought us from the airstrip we'd flown to. "David, you and Veronica sit down at the picnic table. I've got soda and crackers."

"I didn't know you'd get sick from falling asleep in the airplane, Bubba," Evelyn sat next to Veronica and bathed her pale face with a bandana she'd dipped into the water fountain. "And Veronica did too, just like you."

"I'm not sick!" Veronica cried too emphatically. I looked at her pallor and thought we were lucky there wasn't vomit on anyone.

"Sip this," Uncle Jeff popped open a Cola and put it to her lips. She avoided it. "I promise it will help." She took it from him and sipped. He handed me one then dug through his pack for crackers.

"Do you like cheese or peanut butter," he asked her. "Your dad likes peanut butter." He handed me a package and I smiled at him.

"Thanks, Uncle Jeff, you're a life saver." I handed my daughter a cracker. The color was returning to her face. She took the cracker and stuffed it into her mouth.

"I'm not sick," she repeated, spraying crumbs on the table in front of her.

"Well, I am," I said. "Don't let me go to sleep on the way back."

"I won't," she said and got up to go to the edge of the creek with her cousin.

"You always denied it too," Uncle Jeff laughed.

"I remember." I watched the two girls jumping from rock to rock in the stream. Evelyn was nine years old now. Veronica was only five and a half, but with her height they weren't that different in size. Evelyn did take care to help Veronica in certain spots in the stream.

"You're starting to get some color back, David," Uncle Jeff interrupted my thoughts. "They look good. Are you ready to go?"

"Sure," I stood and put on my pack. "Come get your pack, Vroom," I called. "I think we're ready to go."

"There is a campsite about a half mile from here," I said. "Do you girls want to stop there, or do you want to get a couple of miles behind us before dark?"

"Let's go farther, Bubba." Evelyn looked at Veronica. "I mean unless you get too tired, Veronica."

"I won't get too tired. Let's go farther, okay, Daddy, Uncle Jeff."

"Whatever you girls say." We started off down the trail and didn't stop for two miles.

"Daddy look," Veronica squealed. I looked up startled and caught the movement of a white tailed deer running away from us through the woods. "It was just standing there," Veronica whispered. Her eyes were wide. "Do you think it ran away because I screamed?"

"Maybe, they're really shy. It might have run anyway."

"I won't scream if I see another one." She walked on, almost tiptoeing. I smiled and caught Uncle Jeff's eye. He was smiling too.

"Dad, look at this plant." Evelyn had her wildflowers of the region book in her hand. "It's too early for it to bloom, but do you think it's this? She pointed to a picture in her book.

"Let me see." Veronica pulled the book down to look. "I think it is. Maybe we could come back in the summer and see the bloom." She looked up at Uncle Jeff and me.

"Maybe we could," Uncle Jeff said.

We hiked for two more miles. Veronica pointed out plants along the way and asked Evelyn to look them up. We found a campsite beside a stream. Uncle Jeff and I caught a couple of trout and pan fried them on the fire. Both girls enjoyed a generous portion but didn't complain about a serving of instant mac and cheese. Veronica fell asleep in my arms beside the campfire, and I put her to bed in her sleeping bag in the tent we would share.

I crawled into my sleeping bag and listened to the soft rise and fall of my daughter's breathing. I could hear Uncle Jeff and Evelyn talking quietly in the tent they were sharing. It had been a nice day, but I had to admit I missed Charlotte. I missed Alice too. I missed Darla and the twins. "Oh man," I whispered to myself. "This time I'm homesick."

"Daddy," I woke to the sound of my daughter's whisper. I opened my eyes. Her face was an inch from mine.

"What's wrong, Vroom. Are you scared?" It was very dark in the tent. I sat up and pulled her into my arms. "Uh oh," I said when I encountered her wet pajamas.

"I peed in my sleeping bag," she said and dissolved into tears. "I'm sorry, Daddy."

"You never wet the bed. What happened?"

"I think it's the river." She whimpered into my chest.

"Oh yeah," I listened to the babble of the nearby creek.

"What will I do, Daddy? I don't have any place to sleep."

"Don't worry, vroom vroom." I kissed the top of her head." You can sleep in my sleeping bag with me. It's big enough for both of us. But first let's go outside and make sure you've peed as much as you can. And while we're out there, I'll pee too."

I took her by the hand and led her to a tree then stepped behind another to empty my bladder.

"Don't leave me, Daddy. It's scary out here."

"I'm right behind you." We walked back to the tent. "Take off your wet PJs out here," I said. "I'll get the wet bag out of the tent." I pulled the bag out of the tent and draped it over a tree branch. When I turned back to the tent, Veronica stood shivering and naked.

"Go inside and put something on. You'll freeze," I said.

"I'm sorry." I could see her chin begin to quiver. I picked her up and crawled into the tent with her in my arms.

"Don't worry about it, vroom. Running water makes me want to pee too." I turned on the flash light and hung it from the tie at the top of the tent. "Let's see what else you have to put on."

"I only brought one pair of pajamas." She snuggled down into my sleeping bag.

"Well here, you can put on my flannel shirt." I pulled her out of the bag and put the shirt on her and buttoned it up. I leaned back and looked at her. The arms hung down to the ground and the shirt tail was around her ankles.

I smiled and she giggled.

"You look great, vroom. Now let's crawl back into this bag and warm each other up." I curled up with my daughter, and as I fell back to sleep listening to the rushing water outside the tent, I crossed my fingers that neither of us would pee in this bag.

"Well this is a new one," I said to Uncle Jeff the next morning. "It's hard to believe that in all the years you and I have been backpacking we've never had to deal with a peed in sleeping bag before."

"No, and we should be grateful for small favors," he laughed. "Now," he took out his map of the Trail. "According to this map there is a visitor's center about a mile down this trail." He pointed to a curvy line on the map. "It looks like it will be about two miles till we get to the turn off. Of course that will add about two miles to our hike, but we can make it up tomorrow and the next day."

"Do you think there will be a place to wash this stuff there?"

"If not they can advise us."

"Let's get started, girls." I called into the woods where Evelyn and Veronica were examining more plants.

"I'm coming Dad," Evelyn scampered over. She moved as if there was no pack on her back. I had noticed that she carried her own sleeping bag this year. She was shaping up to be a real backpacker.

Veronica followed sheepishly behind her cousin. She didn't seem to mind her pack either. There wasn't much in it, but still, Charlotte had complained the whole time.

"Is something bothering you, Veronica?" Uncle Jeff stooped before her and tilted her chin to look at him.

"I'm sorry I ruined our plans."

"There aren't any ruined plans." He kissed her cheek and stood taking her hand. They started down the trail together. "Did I ever tell you about the time your dad had to move out of the front bedroom because there was a display of fountains outside the window, and it made him feel like he had to pee?"

"My dad?" She looked back at me and giggled.

"Yeah, oh it was long before he was your dad. He was older than you, though." I watched as the two of them went down the trail, Uncle Jeff laughing as he told his story. Veronica was listening intently.

"He'll make her feel better, Bubba." I looked down at Evelyn. "She feels bad about wetting her bed."

"She's never wet her bed before." I said, feeling defensive.

"You know what I do when we camp next to water?" she asked.

"What," I looked down at her and felt a ripple of anxiety. There were circles under her eyes.

"I just don't sleep." She started down the trail. I took a deep breath and followed her.

"Daddy look," I lifted my head from the pajamas I was folding on the picnic table outside the welcome center.

"Oh, my God," I said. Veronica waved at me from the back of what looked like a buffalo. The creature flared its nostrils and stomped a front foot.

"That's Precious," Uncle Jeff said. "The buffalo, it's actually a bison. Laura, the ranger on duty, told me about it. She said that precious loves kids. Riding Precious is a big attraction for the park. That's Laura," he pointed to the girl who stood at the buffalo's head with the lead in her hand.

"Sorry," I said. "It was a shock to see her on that creature's back. I didn't notice Laura."

"I know where you're coming from," Uncle Jeff squeezed my shoulder. "Trust me."

I looked down at my laundry. "It should only be another twenty minutes or so before the sleeping bag is dry," I said. "Then we can get back on the trail. It was nice of the rangers to let us use their laundry facility. They didn't have to, you know?"

"No they didn't, but if they weren't nice people they wouldn't be doing this job."

"I wonder if there's some place around that I could get some waterproof pants for her to sleep in. I doubt we'll be lucky enough to run across more washing facilities." I looked around. We were in the middle of the woods.

"Don't, David," Uncle Jeff said. "It would humiliate her."

"Yeah, I'm sorry I thought about it."

"It was a reasonable thought but put it away. We'll make sure she empties her bladder before bed and hope for the best."

"Yeah," I sat down on the bench and watched as the ranger led Veronica around on the bison. Evelyn was sitting on the fence rail calling something to her cousin.

"Is something wrong, David?" Uncle Jeff asked.

"I think I'm missing Darla. I'm a little worried about her anyway."

"That's understandable." He put his hand on my shoulder. "Do you want to tell me what happened the night she brought Brandon home? I haven't wanted to pry, but I am interested."

"There isn't much to tell. I knew she'd come home and she did. It's strange. I was asleep on the couch with Belinda. She had been fretful of course, but both of us had finally gone to sleep. It was just about midnight. That's strange, Uncle Jeff. I never sleep before 1:00 am."

"Worry and fear are tiring."

"I guess so. Anyway, she came in holding Brandon in a blanket. I picked them both up and carried them to a chair. I just needed to hold them. She asked me to help her and I said I would. That's about it."

"And you've been going to the support group together ever since."

"Yes and we've started couples therapy."

He looked at me sharply. "Is something wrong with your marriage?"

I shook my head but looked in the direction of the laundry room. I was glad that the buzzing of the dryer had distracted us. "No," I said. I wasn't going to tell him that we hadn't had sex since before the twins were born. Some things you just don't share with your parents.

"I think since the twins were born and with Brandon's issues, we've just had a little trouble talking to each other. We just don't seem to move together like we used to." I got up and went to check the sleeping bag. It was dry. I pulled it out of the dryer and took it back to the picnic table where Uncle Jeff waited for me.

"I guess that's understandable," he said. "I'm glad you're doing something about it. Maybe you should call Darla while were here at the visitor's center. I think I'll call Amanda and Alice. I hope Alice is feeling better."

"I hope so too. I think I will call home. Darla said we should call every time we passed a phone. I hope it doesn't make Veronica homesick." We both looked in the direction of the petting zoo. Our daughters were in hot conversation over a group of bunnies. Veronica was holding one and Evelyn was petting it.

"I don't think she's the one that's homesick." Uncle Jeff laughed and went to join the girls. I finished folding the sleeping bag and stuffed it into its sack, then into my backpack.

"Hey guys," I called. "Let's get some lunch and get back on the trail."

They all looked up at me and smiled. Veronica ran toward me, and the other two followed more slowly.

"Dad," she called. "Did you take a picture of me on the buffalo?"

"No, but maybe after lunch Laura will let you get back on, and we can take one."

"I want one of me too, Bubba." Evelyn said. "Is that alright, Dad?" She looked at Uncle Jeff.

"Sure, it's a bison, though." Uncle Jeff was always teaching. "Not a buffalo."

"Can we call, Mommy?" Veronica asked. I tensed. She didn't usually call Darla Mommy. Charlotte had lapsed into that last year. Was Vroom getting homesick?

We hiked three more miles that day. The progress along our route was only five miles, which in itself was impressive with a five year old. But with the detour to the welcome center it was a total of seven miles.

"We knew Evelyn was good," I said as we stopped at a campsite next to a small but noisy stream. "But Veronica is amazing."

"Your face is beaming with pride, David." Uncle Jeff took off his pack. We were watching the girls crouched next to the stream splashing their faces with water.

"She didn't even cry when we talked to Darla. She just chattered about the petting zoo and the plants that she and Evelyn had identified along the trail."

"You didn't cry either," Uncle Jeff laughed. "I was proud of you."

I laughed as I took off my pack. "Charlotte cried," I said. "She misses me. She's a nurturer, that one. I hope life isn't too hard on her."

"If you're not worried about one it's the other," Uncle Jeff said. "I was glad to hear that Alice was feeling better. We knew she was out of the woods, but it's still scary with the heart problem and all."

"I know how you feel." I thought about the relief I'd felt when Darla told me all had been well with Brandon and Belinda.

"Ladies, don't get your selves too wet," Uncle Jeff said. "The sun is going down, and it will be getting cold. Remember we're further north than Georgia." He turned to me and we started to collect kindling. "Let's get the fire going."

I looked at the stream and the clearing where the campsite was. The babbling sound of the water seemed to get louder. I looked over at the girls and remembered the circles under Evelyn's eyes.

"Uncle Jeff," I put my hand on his arm to stop him from unpacking his bag. "Let's camp behind that stand of rocks over there." I pointed into the forest away from the stream. "It looks like there's a clearing on the other side."

Uncle Jeff looked at the large stand of rocks then back at the stream. He smiled. "Good idea," he said.

CHAPTER TWENTY ONE

"You're sure you'll be okay alone with the twins," Darla looked up at me from the deck around the swimming pool. I was on the roof of the pool house cleaning the gutters.

"I'll be fine P. H. It's not like I haven't watched them before. They're six years old."

"You can't watch them from the roof, David. We just opened the pool and Belinda doesn't know how to swim yet. What are you going to do from up on the roof if she falls in?"

"I'm finished up here. I'm coming down right now." I stepped onto the ladder that I had ready and climbed to the deck beside her. "I'm down now. Anyway, Brandon swims better than I do. He won't let Belinda drown."

"Come on, Mom," Charlotte called from the back door of the house. "I'll be late for band practice."

I looked in the direction of the house. "I can't believe she's only twelve years old," I said. "She looks about twenty."

"It's her height and her full figure," Darla said, sounding as unnerved as I did.

"It's scary and Veronica is right behind her. I think it's worse with Vroom, though, with the blond hair and blue eyes."

"Either way it's scary," Darla stood on her toes to kiss my cheek. I turned her face and kissed her mouth. "I have to run," she said. "I have to drop Charlotte at the school for band practice and then Veronica goes to the soccer field. Saturday is the last game of the season and this is her last practice. I'll be glad when the school year is over and things settle down for a while."

"I will too." I looked around. "Where are the twins anyway?"

"They're in their room. I told them to stay there until you came in. Don't leave them too long," she said as she hurried toward our waiting daughters.

I put the ladder away and went into the house. I washed my hands and headed upstairs to the room the twins shared. Darla had talked about separating them soon, but they had such a bond I didn't want to do it.

"Don't drool, Brandon." Belinda was wiping her brother's mouth with a tissue when I entered the room. "People will think there is something wrong with you and there isn't. So remember, don't drool."

Belinda enunciated her words so dramatically, I had to smile. She'd learned to talk before she could walk. She'd spoken whole sentences by the time she was two years old. There had not been one hint of baby talk from her.

Brandon, on the other hand, was still hard to understand. Although, Belinda always knew what he was saying. But he had walked before he'd crawled and was running soon afterwards. He could swim like a fish by the time he was three years old. He limped slightly on his right side, and that side was a little bit smaller than the other. The drooling problem that Belinda was so determined to control was only on the right side of his mouth. He tended to smear food on that side too.

"You guys want to go out and have a swim before dinner? It's warm enough outside, and I checked the heat on the pool. I think it's comfortable." They both tuned to smile at me displaying identical dimples in their cheeks. Brandon's a little weaker on the right side but still charming enough to make my insides quiver and put a smile on my own face.

Besides the dimples and the blond hair and blue eyes they were very different. Belinda was tiny. She couldn't have stood more than three feet tall and every part of her body was petite. Brandon was tall like his older sisters, but instead of the lean wiry build they'd had growing up, he was husky, not fat, husky. You might even call him burly.

"Ahh wanna … fwim," he said. He was already dressed in his trunks and he headed for the door.

"Wait for me, Brandon," I put my hand on his shoulder to stop him. "Your sister hasn't put on her suit yet."

"Huwy up, Binda." He sounded so disgusted Belinda and I exchanged a look and laughed.

"I'm sorry, Brandon, but it's hard to put on this suit with all the floaty things in it." She looked up at me. Was she blushing? "Can you help me, Daddy?"

"No problem, bring me the suit. Aren't the swimming lessons helping at all, Beeta?" I asked. For some reason I hadn't shortened Brandon's name, but Belinda was just too big a name for my tiny little daughter.

"No, and I'm frustrated, Daddy. I just sink to the bottom of the pool no matter how hard I kick."

"Well, nobody is good at everything." I turned her around and looked at her. The bathing suit bulged all around her middle and under her arms with floating devices. It couldn't be comfortable. "This year we'll figure out something. We'll work on it together, okay?"

I took both kids by the hand and we headed for the pool. "Where did you learn a word like frustrated, Beeta?" I asked. "That's a mouthful for a six year old."

"I said it right, didn't I?"

"Of course you did. You say everything right."

"What did she say?" I jumped at the sound of Uncle Jeff's voice as we went out the back door. He and Evelyn and Alice came around the side of the house. "We were in the neighborhood looking at a landscape job, and the girls insisted on dropping by."

"We haven't seen you in ages, David." Alice flung herself into my arms nearly knocking me over. I let go of the kid's hands and swung her around. Setting her back down on the ground I reached for Evelyn. She put her arms around my waist, and I leaned down to kiss the top of her head.

"What a nice surprise," I said looking in the direction of the pool. Brandon was already in the water and coaxing his sister to go down the steps. "Did you guys bring your suits?"

"No," Uncle Jeff said. "We'll only stay a few minutes. Amanda is expecting us home for dinner. So what did Belinda say that was so impressive?"

"She said she was frustrated. Don't you think that's a big word for a six year old?"

"Yeah, but it reminds me of you. You were always surprising me with your vocabulary."

I smiled at him. I looked at his face and felt a sudden urge to hug him. His skin was weathered, but I knew every line, the ones around his eyes and his mouth. I could remember all the smiles that had put those lines there and some of the frowns. How old was he now? Early sixties? Mid sixties? I swallowed the lump in my throat and looked again in the direction of the swimming pool. Evelyn and Alice sat on the edge of the pool with their shoes off and their feet in the water, two dark haired beauties with their father's dancing blue eyes. They laughed at something Brandon said.

"They're young women now," I said brushing aside the nostalgic moment. "Not children anymore."

"Actually, they're children in women's form." He shuddered slightly. "It's terrifying."

"I was just thinking the same thing about Charlita, and Vroom is right behind her. Are we up to this, Uncle Jeff?"

"We'd better be." He sat down in a chair. I sat in the one beside him. One of the girl's cats jumped into his lap, and he started to stroke it. "Which one is this?" he asked.

"That's Furry," I laughed at the sight of him stroking the arched back of the purring cat. "Soft has three colors and she's not as nice as Furry."

"You still call them Soft and Furry?"

"Those are their names."

"Brandon, I'm too deep!" I heard Belinda's panicked call from the pool and sat forward to see where she was. Brandon streaked across the pool in a perfectly executed butterfly stroke and gently put his hand under his sister's arm pit to guide her back to the shallow water.

"He swims pretty well," Uncle Jeff said.

"Physically he's amazing," I said. "He's in speech therapy, though. Sometimes I can't understand him at all."

"Can't sink, Binda," I heard him say. "Fwoaties …" He pulled slightly on one of the floating devises embedded in Belinda's swimming suit.

"I know but it's scary when it's deep," she whimpered. She climbed up the stairs at the shallow end of the pool and Brandon followed her. They both picked up a towel and wrapped themselves in it. They sat down on the deck and my cousins joined them. Soon they were all engaged in conversation. No one seemed to have any trouble understanding Brandon.

"They're so different," I looked back at Uncle Jeff who was still petting the cat.

"But they're so connected." He laughed.

"Uh oh, Daddy," Belinda called and I looked up to see Brandon crawling shakily toward a lawn chair. He crawled between the metal bars that supported it and sat cross legged with his head down as it began to bob. Belinda went to the chair and sat in front of it with her hands on his knees.

"He's having a seizure," I said as I stood and went to my children. I knelt down behind the chair and putting my hands under Brandon's armpits started to lift him out from under it.

"He feels safe under the chair, Daddy," Belinda said. "Leave him."

"It's made of metal, Beeta. I'm afraid he'll bang his head."

"He won't, Daddy, leave him." She reached forward and put her hands on Brandon's arms just as they started to flail. He smacked her in the face with the back of his hand and looked up. His head wobbled but he was looking in her direction.

"Ahhh … sooowy …"

"It's okay, Brandon." She looked past him to meet my eyes. "He worries about me."

I looked at my two children in wonder. I hated the seizures, but the relationship was beautiful. "Are you alright, honey? Your face is a little red where he hit you."

"It hurts a little but it maybe should."

"What do you mean ..?"

"He's getting better, Daddy. We should take him inside. He likes to sleep after he has a seizure." Belinda had stood and was trying to pull Brandon out from under the chair.

"I'll get him from back here, Beeta. You stand back now." I pulled Brandon out from under the chair and picked him up. He looked at me and I smiled. "You feeling better, son?" I asked.

"... fleepy ..."

"We'll get you to bed. You can have a nap before dinner."

"Binda ..." he stretched his hand out to his sister.

"I'll come up too," she said to him then looked at our guests. "Uncle Jeff, please don't leave until I get back. He'll be asleep in just a minute."

"The perfect little hostess," Uncle Jeff said. I felt his comforting hand on my shoulder. I looked at the solemn faces of my twin cousins.

"Everything is alright guys," I said. "Come inside and get something to drink. We'll be back in a minute." I looked down at my son clasping his sister's hand. He was already asleep nestled in my arms.

"Belinda," I snagged her arm as she tried to walk by me to the stairway. "We need to talk." We had just said good bye to Uncle Jeff and the girls. Darla, Charlotte and Veronica weren't expected home for at least another half an hour, and Belinda was skimming by me to go up the stairs to check on her brother.

"I need to check on Brandon, Daddy." She tried to squirm out of my hold.

"He's still asleep, Beeta. He'll sleep for at least another hour."

"Well," she licked her lips. "You go and start dinner, and I'll go up and check on him. Mom and the big girls will be expecting dinner. You did agree to cook tonight, remember."

"Not a problem, Beeta," I said as I pulled her toward the stairs. "We'll check on him together and then we'll cook together." I swung her onto my hip and went up the stairs two at a time. We looked into their bedroom and everything was quiet. I looked at her. She avoided my eyes. I carried her back down the stairs and into the kitchen, set her in a chair, and went to the refrigerator to get out the steak I had been marinating since lunch time.

"Why did you get home so early today, Daddy?" she asked all innocence. She was trying to draw my attention away from what had happened this afternoon.

"Mom said she needed me to stay with you and Brandon while she ran the girls around, and I jumped at the chance to be with you two guys. I'm glad I did or I would have missed Uncle Jeff and the girls too."

"It was nice to see them. I just love Uncle Jeff." She sounded so dramatic that I couldn't help but laugh. I looked at her sitting at the table. Her head was barely above the surface.

"It won't work, Beeta. I heard you say that maybe you deserved to hurt when Brandon hit you. We're going to have to talk about it."

"Brandon didn't hit me on purpose, Daddy. You can't blame him. He was having a seizure."

"You know I'm not blaming him. Why do you think it's okay for him to hurt you, even if it is accidently?"

She looked down at something below the surface of the table. Her face disappeared below the side, and all I could see was the top of her head. "It's my fault." She said it so quietly that I almost didn't hear it. I had to wait a minute for it to be processed in my brain. I walked over to the table and sat down beside her. I lifted her face and made her look at me.

"What is your fault?"

"It doesn't take a scientist to figure it out, Daddy." She said it so emphatically that again I was tempted to laugh. I resisted the urge.

"What have you figured out, scientist?"

"Brandon has seizures because he didn't get enough oxygen when he was born. I heard you and Mom talking about it. Charlotte and Veronica said so too. That's why he drools and why he can't talk good."

"That's right. I won't deny that. If you have questions about it, all you have to do is ask. What do you want to know about when you and Brandon were born?"

"I don't have questions." Her look was defiant and determined. "I was born first. He didn't get enough oxygen. I took his oxygen. It was my fault."

I closed my eyes. My heart was pounding and for a minute I couldn't breathe. Oh my God, she blames herself.

"Daddy," my daughter pulled on my arm. "Are you alright?"

"I'm upset, Beeta." I opened my eyes. "Your mom blames herself too. This isn't anyone's fault, honey, not yours, not your mom's, not mine."

"Daddy," she put her hands on either side of my face and forced me to look at her like I'd just done with her. "I know I didn't do it on purpose. I was just a baby."

I focused on her tiny face. Her small soft hands were caressing my cheeks. I took one of them in my hand and held it to my mouth. "Beeta, don't do this to yourself. Brandon is alright. He's going to be fine."

"I know," she said. "I'll make sure he's fine."

"Baby, it isn't up to you to ..."

"Daddy," Brandon bounded into the room. "Ahh ... hungwy ..."

"We're cooking dinner, Brandon." Belinda jumped up and grabbed his arm. She guided him to a chair. "I'll get you a before dinner snack. Oh ..." She looked in the direction of the garage as we heard the sound of the door going up. "Mom and the big girls are home. Here, Brandon." She went to the pantry and pulled out some soda crackers. "Eat these until dinner is ready."

I watched her pull crackers out of the package and hand them to her brother. My heart fell. She's too young to feel that kind of responsibility, I thought. Then I looked at the door to the garage as my older daughters and Darla came in. Darla looked at me and smiled then she looked closer and our eyes met.

"Run upstairs and clean up for dinner, girls," she said to Charlotte and Veronica. They both kissed my cheek and left the room. They were chattering about school as they disappeared around the corner.

"What's going on?" Darla asked me.

I looked at Belinda. "Brandon had a seizure." She told her mother then stared at me intently. "It wasn't a bad one." She smiled. "Everything is good now. Don't drool, Brandon." She wiped the right side of Brandon's mouth with a napkin.

"She's too smart for a six year old." I told Darla as we drove toward our couples counseling session the next afternoon. Darla's parents had come with fast food to stay with the kids. "Charlotte was furious that you wouldn't leave her in charge and honestly, P. H., I think you could leave Belinda in charge. She knows exactly how to take care of Brandon."

"My parents need to spend time with the kids too. Besides, like you said, she's too young to have that kind of responsibility."

"I said Belinda was too young to be that smart."

"She is smart," Darla leaned her forehead against the closed window of the car. "I think she got everything Brandon didn't get."

"I don't know. Brandon is exceptionally athletic for a six year old and artistic too."

"He is." She grinned with pride.

We arrived at the psychologist's office and went inside. We sat quietly in the waiting room until Dr. Watson came to get us. We went into her office and sat in the places where we always sat.

"So what's going on this week?" Dr. Watson asked. She was an attractive woman, probably fifty years plus. She seemed to exude calm. Darla and I had both commented on how easy she was to talk to.

"I want to bring something up," Darla said before I could respond. I had planned to talk about the problem we had with Belinda. I'd discussed it with Darla the night before after all the kids were either asleep or in their rooms. I guess she had the same plan.

"I think we should get Brandon a seizure dog," she said. I felt my mouth drop open as I gaped at her. "I'm sorry, David. I've wanted to talk to you about this for a while, but I knew you wouldn't listen."

"P. H. you know how I feel about dogs. I will never have another one." I looked at Dr. Watson. "Now what I wanted to talk about was Belinda. I need to tell you about what happened yesterday."

"I want to hear what happened yesterday, David. But we can't just ignore what Darla has just said. We need to talk about that first," she said. My heart began to pound.

"I don't want to talk about it." I said. I felt stupid. I felt cornered. I just wanted to leave the room. I stood up and walked to the window.

"We haven't talked about dogs before," Dr. Watson said.

"David had a bad experience with his childhood dog," Darla said. I could feel her coming toward me. She put her hand on my arm. I shrugged it off. She grabbed my arm firmly and squeezed. I looked out the window determined not to respond.

"I'm sorry," Dr. Watson said. "Darla, why do you think it's worth digging up now?"

"I've studied it," she said pulling me away from the window and back to the couch beside her. I couldn't speak. I could only follow her.

"I found a group that trains seizure dogs for children. Most seizure dogs are only trained for teens and adults but this group works with kids." Darla had never let go of my arm and she turned to me now. She looked straight at my face. I tried to avoid her eyes, but I couldn't. "David, I know this will be hard for you, but it will help Brandon. Not only that, it will help Belinda. If we can get her some relief maybe she won't feel so responsible."

"We help her," I said, sounding like a robot. "Charlotte and Veronica do too."

"Yes but, David, you of all people should know that a dog can relate to a child better than a parent sometimes, better than a sister."

"He has the cats."

"And he loves the cats, but these dogs are special. They have special abilities and training. This can help, David. We need to at least look into it."

I closed my eyes, and I saw Charlotte, my dog Charlotte; the little brown fuzzy creature that slept in her own bed beside mine when I was a kid. I saw the image I'd seen of her so many times since, dead in my abandoned bed, my abandoned dog.

"She died of a broken heart," I whispered.

"This dog won't, David." Darla squeezed my arm. "We won't let it."

The room went black. My ears were buzzing, but I was beginning to make out some conversation around me. Darla and Dr. Watson stood on either side of me. My face was in my hands.

"I'm alright," I said, not lifting my head. "Could I get a glass of water?"

"Sure," Dr. Watson said and left the room. Darla sat down beside me.

"Did you faint?" she asked.

"I don't faint," I said sitting up and stretching my back. "I'm a man. Men don't faint."

"You turned white and put you face in your hands. It took a full two or three minutes to get you to respond. I think you fainted." She laughed and I heard wind chimes.

I looked at her. Her dimples were showing and I smiled. "I did not faint," I said. "I just needed a minute."

Dr. Watson came back into the room and handed me a glass of water. I took it and drank. "Thank you," I said. She sat back down in her chair.

"I've been meaning for a while to talk to you about a change in your therapy," she said. "I think you both should pursue individual therapy."

"You don't want to see us anymore?" I felt shocked.

"No, I want to continue to see you, but I think once a month for couple's therapy and once a month for the support group is enough. You're both ready to deal with your individual therapy. I think you'll really enjoy it."

I looked at her. Her face was animated. "You make being crazy sound fun," I said.

"I don't know what the definition of crazy is." She laughed. "What I'd call the two of you is human. I think you'll be glad to get to know yourselves."

❖

"I have brochures I want you to look at and an article I printed off the internet," Darla said after we'd said goodnight to Jason and Darlene.

"Nothing was decided tonight but that I would go into individual therapy and work on this, Darla. We're not getting Brandon a dog."

"If we wait until you have yourself straightened out, Brandon will be an old man with no past because he didn't have a dog."

"Thanks for the vote of confidence."

"I am confident that you'll work this out, but we can't wait for that. We're going to deal with this right now, David. I will not give up."

I looked at her determined face. No, I thought, on some things you just have to stand firm. "We are not getting Brandon a dog!" I said.

"We're getting Brandon a dog?" Veronica walked into the room with Charlotte right behind her. "Woo hoo …" She jumped up and down in excitement.

"I said we are not getting Brandon a dog." The sinking feeling in my chest told me I'd already lost this battle. "Weren't you listening?" I looked at Veronica, bouncing with excitement, then at Charlotte who looked disgusted.

"But Mom said we are and that means we are." Veronica ran to her mother and hugged her picking her up off the ground. At ten years old she already stood an inch taller.

I looked back at Charlotte. Maybe she could help me.

"It hardly seems fair," she said. "When I asked for a dog the answer was firmly no. You didn't fight for me." She looked defiantly at her mother.

"Maybe I should have, Charlotte," Darla said. She handled the confrontation so smoothly I had to smile. "I've learned my lesson. This will be a seizure and therapy dog to help him with his problems and to take some of the pressure off of Belinda." She went to Charlotte who stood four inches taller than her and handed her the brochure. "It's amazing what they can do with these dogs, and this group will work with Brandon and the dog together."

Charlotte took the brochure and looked at it. I saw the battle she fought to maintain her defiance in the face of interest. She looked over the brochure and handed it to me.

"But this will still be a family pet. We all live here together," Darla said. "That's why I want the whole family to go next week to see the facility and look at the dogs they have available. The chemistry has to work for all of us." She looked into my eyes, and I knew I had no choice. "Now that school is out we'll have plenty of time."

"I have plans for next week," Charlotte said, defiance returning. I guess there was some sort of hormone rampaging through her.

"If we have to change your plans we will," Darla said so firmly that we all knew there would be no discussion.

"Woo hooo ..." Veronica said again. "Can I go talk to Brandon about it? Maybe he'll let me help pick out a name."

"We're not naming the dog Fuzzy or anything like that." My voice broke as I admitted my defeat. I looked at Darla. She smiled at me and crossed the room to stand on tip toe and kiss my cheek. I turned her head and kissed her mouth.

"Veronica wait!" Darla called as Veronica headed for the stairs that led to the bedrooms. "Let Dad tell him about it."

"No, Daddy!" I was sitting on the double bed that the twins shared. Brandon had night terrors if he slept alone. Belinda stood in front of me. Her small hands balled into fists and placed squarely on her hips. "I don't want to get Brandon a dog, please," she said.

"Why not, Beeta?" I was completely taken by surprise. What kid says no to a new dog? "It will help you out with taking care of him. These are special dogs. They can sense seizures, and they can help him to socialize with other kids and all sorts of things. Look at this." I handed her the brochure I still had in my hand.

She took it and looked at the cover then up at me. "You know I can't read this good. How do I know what it says in here?"

I took the brochure back feeling stupid. I sure was feeling stupid a lot lately. "Why don't you want a dog, Beeta? Brandon wants one don't you, Brandon?" His eyes had lit up when I'd told him about it. Then they had gone blank with confusion when Belinda vetoed the idea so emphatically.

"Ahhh ... do ... Binda ..."

"No you don't, Brandon!" She turned on her brother, her tiny fists still planted on her hips, and her head tilted up to look at his face. "Dogs bite and they jump on people. I hate dogs." She turned back to me. "You do too, Daddy. You always have."

What have I done to this child? I thought. "I don't hate dogs, Beeta. I love dogs. I've always loved dogs. You don't hate them either. You like Gramma Charlie's dog and Grampa's little dogs and Uncle Jeff's. They don't bite."

"That's different." She stormed across the room and climbed into the window seat. She crossed her arms and legs and looked out the window. "Daddy, I don't want Brandon to have a dog."

"Can I come in yet?" The door to the twin's room opened a crack and Veronica stuck her head in. "Aren't you excited, Brandon?" She danced into the room, scooped her little brother up and swung him around. "Can I help you think of names?"

"Binda ... say ... noooo dog." Brandon said as he staggered to regain his balance when Veronica put him down.

"What?" Veronica looked at Belinda sitting in the window seat. "What's your problem, party pooper?"

"I hate dogs. I don't think it will be safe for Brandon."

"Well, I wonder whose fault it is that she hates dogs," Charlotte said coming into the room, her hormonal tirade turned toward me now. "You've banned dogs from this house all of our lives."

"I didn't ban dogs from the house. I just said we didn't need to have a dog for a pet. You've had fish, hamsters, gerbils, frogs and cats. What's wrong with Soft and Furry?"

"Nothing," Charlotte crossed her arms very much like her defiant younger sister. "We love Soft and Furry and we've loved all the others. We just wanted a dog too. But no ... you wouldn't let us. Why do you hate dogs so much, Dad? Did one bite you or something?"

I looked around the room at all of my children. Two were angry, one was excited but looking a little worried, and one was very confused. My ears were ringing, and I looked at the door as Darla came into the room.

"Okay guys, that's enough," she said and all eyes turned to her. "I have made an appointment for the whole family to go to the companion dog facility on Tuesday of next week." She turned to Belinda. "Why don't you want us to do this, Belinda? It could be very helpful to Brandon, and it will take some of the pressure off of you."

"I like taking care of Brandon."

"You and Brandon both start school in the fall. We held you back one year, but we can't hold you back again. You have to go, and you won't be able to take care of him then. It's important for both of you to learn to be apart a little bit."

"You said we'd go together." Belinda got up from the window seat and ran across the room to Brandon. She wrapped her arms around him and he hugged her back. His cheek rested on the top of her head.

Darla was right, I realized. They needed some independence. Belinda had set herself up as Brandon's caretaker for life, and though it wasn't as obvious, Brandon took care of her too. They were twins, but they also needed to be individuals. We had to do something. Maybe this dog was a start.

"You will go to kindergarten together." Darla continued. "We've arranged for that, but in school you won't be able to be with him all the time. Belinda, he has to learn how to take care of himself. You have to help him learn that."

"Ahhh ... care ... Binda too." Brandon said echoing my thoughts.

"Yes you do, Brandon." Darla said. Her face softened when she talked to him. Her dimples showed. She'd looked very stern when she talked to Belinda. "And you have to help Belinda learn to take care of herself too."

"He won't be able to take a stinky old dog to school with him." Belinda mumbled into Brandon's chest.

"No, but it can help him gain some confidence outside of school. That will help in school." Darla said. The room fell silent. "I don't plan to let the dog stink, Belinda."

"We'll see how it goes on Tuesday, Beeta," I said. "If we don't find a dog that we all like. We won't bring one home."

"Then we won't get one because I hate dogs."

"You know, Miss Sassy Pants," Veronica said. "You're not in charge of this family, and the rest of us want a dog."

"That's right." Charlotte sulked. "Even though it won't be my dog, at least I can still be friends with it."

"It will be a family pet," Darla said. "Belinda, do you want to talk a little more about this with me in private?"

"No!" She stalked back over to the window and stood looking out barely able to see over the window sill. Brandon followed her.

"Binda?" he said. She turned and gave him a reluctant smile then looked back out the window.

✧

"What have I done?" I said to Darla after all the kids had gone upstairs. The older girls were in their separate rooms doing whatever they did before bed. The twins were asleep, at least Brandon was. I suspected that Belinda was pretending. "I didn't realize my own neurosis about dogs was having such an effect on my children."

"Don't blame yourself too much for this, David," Darla said. She came across the room and climbed into my lap. It was the first time we'd sat like this in years, and it felt good. "I should have objected. It was just that with four kids and two cats and with Brandon's problems and all. I just didn't think we needed a dog. I guess I was wrong. Charlotte seems to feel very deprived."

"Something tells me Charlotte wouldn't be happy with us right now if she'd had dogs all her life."

"You're probably right." Darla leaned her head on my chest, and I kissed the top of it. "You know she started her period last month."

"Yeah, you told me. It's kind of hard to take all that anger. She used to think we were great."

"Well, get used to it. I think it's a while before that comes back around."

"… And Vroom is right behind her."

"Something tells me it won't be so bad with Veronica. She's always been a jollier person than Charlotte. Maybe it's the first child thing. Although, Charlotte wasn't an only child for long. Veronica is only sixteen months younger than her."

"Yeah …" I was quiet for a minute. "P. H., why don't we make love anymore?"

"David," she sat up and pulled away from me.

"Don't go." I reached for her. She dodged my grasp and sat down on the couch across from my chair. "I'm not going to press you." I said feeling cold where Darla's warmth had been a second before.

"That's because you aren't any more interested than I am," she said.

"No," I leaned my head back on the chair. "I guess not."

"I think it's just a stage in the development of our family, David. I mean it's just not the time for a lot of intimacy between you and me."

"I guess," I said. "Is that why you spend most of your nights in your office above the garage? You know I've noticed that you're moving your clothes up there. I wondered why you wanted to put that huge walk-in closet in a combination office and guest room."

She smiled. "I wondered if you'd noticed. You didn't say anything."

"Don't you love me anymore, Darla?"

"I love you, David." She said it, but she didn't come back to my lap. "I've always loved you and I always will."

As a friend, I thought, hating the sound of it and knowing that I felt that way too. "Sleep in our room tonight, P. H." I heard the hope in my voice

"I thought I would," she said. "With all the turmoil I want to be close to the kids if they need me. David," She leaned forward. "Don't be hard on yourself about the dog situation. I think your feelings are just the excuse for Belinda."

"What do you mean?" I sat forward and looked at her.

"I agree with Charlotte about not getting her a dog. It wasn't fair. She's always wanted one. You do need to work on the feelings you have about Charlotte. I mean your dog Charlotte." She laughed. "I guess that's why Dr. Watson wants us to go into individual therapy. I have issues to work on too, most urgently my feelings about my youngest daughter."

"You don't like her as much as you like the other kids," I said.

She looked up at me sharply. "I love her with all my heart, David. She's my baby just like all the rest of them."

"I didn't say you don't love her. I said you don't like her. I can see it in the way you talk to her, the way you look at her when you talk to her."

"I suppose it seems that way, and I'm sorry that it does. But it isn't that. I do like her. In fact I'm in awe of her. She's so brilliant and so in touch with her brother. He doesn't need me the way he needs her."

"That's not true, P. H. They both need you. They're children. They need their parents to take care of them."

"I don't know, David. With those two I think the rest of us could disappear tomorrow, and they'd be just fine. Brandon would keep her physically safe, and she'd keep him mentally safe. They don't need either one of us."

"You're jealous."

"That's right," she laughed and I laughed too. "And that's why Belinda doesn't want Brandon to have a dog. She's jealous."

"You think so?" I stood up and put out my hand to pull her to her feet.

"Yes, I do think so. She's used to having Brandon all to herself. She's used to him needing her and her alone. It's alright for them to be close, David, but they need to be able to have their own lives too."

"You're wrong about one thing," I said as we went up the stairs toward our bedroom.

"What's that?"

"They do need you. They need us both to teach them independence from each other. I'm not sure exactly how we're going to do it but we will. We have to."

"We'll start with a dog."

I woke up a couple of hours later. Darla and I lay in our bed back to back facing opposite sides of the room. Things had changed from the days when we slept in each other's arms. Don't get sentimental, I thought. With my nocturnal ways we hadn't slept in each other's arms that much.

I tiptoed out of the room. I didn't want to give Darla an excuse to go to the garage room. I moved silently down the hall toward my office, pausing for a minute at the twin's door. It was quiet, but something almost static in the air alerted me to activity inside. We always left the door slightly ajar. I pushed it open and looked in. Belinda sat up in the bed looking down at her sleeping brother.

"Is everything alright?" I whispered as I approached the bed and sat down next to her.

"Um hm," she said without looking at me. "He talks in his sleep," she whispered. "It's funny cuzz he talks better when he's asleep."

"He does? I wonder why."

"He gets too excited when he's awake."

I looked at her small profile in the light from the window. She was still looking at Brandon. What a bright intuitive child. My heart fluttered as I realized the how talented she was. Darla was right. I was in awe.

"You're a smart kid, Beeta," I said. "But smart kids need their sleep. Does Brandon wake you up when he talks in his sleep?"

"No," She finally looked at me. She crawled under the covers. "I never sleep till later anyway."

"You don't? Why not?" She probably has my sleeping problem, I thought, feeling guilty.

"I don't know." She rolled on her side facing away from Brandon. "Night night, Daddy." She dismissed me. I smiled in the darkened room.

"Goodnight, sweet girl," I said. I brushed her white blond hair aside and kissed her cotton soft cheek.

"I'm nervous," I said to Darla as we all walked from the car to the seizure dog facility.

"David, you know how to deal with dogs. Even though you haven't had one for a while you've been with your parent's dogs."

"I know but for some reason I really don't understand I'm nervous."

"Well, take a deep breath and exhale all the way. Then we'll go in." She put her hand on my back.

"Are you alright, Dad?" Charlotte asked. Even with the mood swings she was always concerned about the people around her. She'll make a good mother, I thought. I shivered. It was too early to think about that.

"I'm fine, honey."

"Dad, when I asked the other day if you got bitten by a dog or something it dawned on me. Maybe you did. I can live without a dog if this is really going to upset you," she said. "We all can."

I looked around at my family. We all stood outside of a large building with glass doors. There was a button beside the door and a sign that said "Buzz for Reception." They were all looking at me with concern. I smiled. "I've never been bitten by a dog, Charlotte. I just lost one once and it really hurt. I'll tell you about it one day if you want, but right now let's go inside and see what this place has to offer."

I pressed the buzzer and someone came to open the door. "You must be the Landrums," A middle aged woman ushered us inside. She was a little heavy set with a big smile.

I stood back for the rest of the family to go in. When I started inside I felt a tug on my pants and looked down at Belinda. She was looking up at me. Her eyes were filled with tears and her bottom lip quivered. I picked her up. "Are you nervous?" I whispered.

She nodded her head then buried her face in my neck.

"So am I. I don't know why I'm nervous though. Why are you?"

"I don't know," she whispered. Her mouth was just below my ear. I could feel her warm breath on my neck. I could smell the salt in her tears.

"Stay close to me," I said. "We'll get through this together."

"You must be Brandon," the woman said. "I'm Gail. I understand you are the one interested in looking at a companion dog."

Brandon looked at the woman speaking to him. His eyes were wide and his mouth was slightly open. There was a small drop of saliva glistening on the right side of his mouth. Belinda squirmed out of my arms and went to him. She pulled a tissue out of the pocket of her pants. Standing on her toes to lean close to his ear she whispered, "Don't drool, Brandon." He made a slurping noise as she wiped his face. He smiled shyly up at Gail.

"I'm Brandon's mother," Darla stepped forward and extended her hand. "And these are our other children, Charlotte, Veronica, and Belinda. This is my husband David."

Gail shook hands with us all. When she got to Belinda she said. "I heard that you were twins. This will be fun for me. I've never worked with twins before."

Belinda smiled but didn't speak.

"Have you all read the brochure and the information packet I sent you?" Gail asked.

"Brandon can't read." Belinda broke her silence. "And I can't read little writing."

"No," Gail smiled, her eyes lighting at Belinda's speech. "But I'll bet you can read big stuff pretty well for your age."

"I know the alphabet and I can spell my name. I can read okay, but I think I'll be better when I go to school."

"I'm sure you will," Gail smiled at me and then at Darla. "Brandon has quite a twin," she said.

Darla looked angry and was about to say something, but Veronica interrupted. "I read the brochure and all the information. I can't wait to see the dogs."

"I read it all too." Charlotte said. "I'd really like to see the facility. I was thinking of doing a school project on it next year. I start high school in the fall. Would it be alright if I talked to some of your counselors?"

"Absolutely," Gail said. "We love to help with school projects. It lets people know what we do here and helps to support us. Call me when you get ready to do the report, and we'll make arrangements. Now," she looked around at the rest of us. "Shall we start with a tour of the facility?"

"That sounds great," I said. I was relieved. I'm not sure what was about to happen with Darla and Belinda, but I was glad it had been avoided.

"We work with teens and adults as well as children," Gail said. "I know that the reason you started here with us is that there are very few services like this that will adopt to children. We started with teens and adults just like all the others, but when we realized that most of the calls we got were for children who have seizures we knew that there is a need and we determined to meet it.

Finding a therapy dog for a child is very different than finding one for an older person." She paused at a room with a large window exposing the inside. "This is one of our training rooms. We're working with a teen today." She waved at the young man in the room. A golden retriever sat in front of him watching closely as the young man made a signal to him with his hand.

"Children are not able to do the intensive training that we do with a seizure response dog, like teaching them to go for help or dial 911 or other things. What we do with children is train the dogs to be close companions. We train them to tune in to the child's feelings and to help with adjustments in social situations as well as at home. For instance, some children who have seizures are afraid to sleep alone." She looked at Brandon as we walked down the hall.

"Brandon doesn't have to sleep alone," Belinda said. "I sleep with him."

Darla and I exchanged a look. I was sure we both looked guilty. We had talked about getting them different beds. We knew we would have to eventually, but we were both more comfortable knowing Belinda was with him. I looked up at Gail and she smiled reassuringly.

"This is one of our kennel rooms," she said as we stopped at another window. The room was full of dogs. They weren't in cages but lay on beds that were spread throughout the room or walked around. Some were playing with each other. Others were standing alone.

"We don't cage them," Gail answered my question before I asked it. "These dogs need to be good with other dogs as well as people. We train them not to chase cats and other small creatures as well. If we can't train them, we know they aren't right for what we do and we adopt them out as pets."

"So," Darla said. "You don't train the dogs to sense seizures and go for help."

"Well, for one thing, we can't train dogs to sense seizures. Some of them just do. In fact most of them do. What we think is that there is a chemical given off before a seizure begins that dogs, with their hyper sense of smell, can detect."

"You mean they smell a seizure?" Charlotte asked.

"Actually," I said. "I think they smell the aura." I remembered faintly smelling something as I walked down the aisle toward my teacher in high in school.

Gail looked at me. "Do you have seizures too, Mr. Landrum?"

"I had one once."

"You had a seizure, Dad?" Charlotte asked, concern drawing her brows together.

"A long time ago, honey. It never happened again."

"I know when Brandon is getting a seizure," Belinda said and I was happy for the interruption. "I don't smell anything."

"How do you know then?" Gail asked.

Belinda shrugged her shoulders. "I just do." It dawned on me that Belinda had no problem admitting that she didn't know something. I smiled and took her hand.

We all fell silent as we filed into a large room with chairs set up in a semi-circle.

"Anyway," Gail continued. "To answer your question, Mrs. Landrum, we don't train any of the dogs to sense seizures. Some do. Some don't. We only use the ones that do for adults and teens. But for children we find that a properly trained dog can provide support and confidence and a number of other very positive things. Even if they don't detect the seizure before it happens. But there always has to be an adult close by."

"As with all children," Darla said.

Gail pointed to the chairs. "Make yourselves comfortable. I have a number of dogs picked out for you to look at. We like for the chemistry to be right. If none of these seem to work we have a full kennel. We will just keep looking until we find the right dog for all of you."

We all sat. Charlotte and Veronica sat on one side of Darla, the twins in the middle, and me on the end.

Chapter Twenty One

"We rarely work with mixed breeds," Gail said. "It isn't that we have a problem with them, but certain pure breeds are well suited for this kind of work. However, the first dog I'm going to bring in is a mix. One of our counselors volunteers at the humane society. She noticed this dog and brought it to us. The reason she noticed it is because she has seizures, and this little dog detected one when she was there one day. It warned her, and she was able to go to a safe place. She already has a seizure detection dog at home, so she brought this one here. He's very smart and has learned his obedience very well."

She left the room and returned a minute later with a small scruffy dog. He probably weighed about thirty pounds. His legs were long so he stood fairly high. He was lean and wiry looking. He was a blond color with lighter streaks through his shaggy coat and golden highlights that showed up when he walked in and out of the light.

He didn't bound over to us as I had expected. I guess I had hoped he would. He walked sedately over to the group and sniffed each one of us. He wagged his tail as we extended our hands to him. He sat down in front of us, and his tongue fell out of his mouth in a smile of greeting.

"What's his name?" Veronica asked. She sounded shy.

"We train them with commands. We'll give you a list of them and teach you all how to use them, but we don't really name the dogs. We've called him Scruffy when talking to each other about him."

"That will have to go," I said. "Come," I held out my hand to the little dog, and he got up and came over to me. He let me pet him and then moved to Brandon who sat on my right. Brandon put his hand on the little dog's head and smiled. The dog leaned against his legs and propped his chin on his knee.

Brandon stroked the dog's head. "Binda?" he said and Belinda looked away.

"Come here, little dog?" Veronica held out her hand. The dog went to her and accepted her caress then he went to Charlotte and Darla. They all smiled at him.

"He has awfully long hair," Darla said. "Will he let you brush him?"

"He loves to be brushed," Gail said and producing a brush. She gave it to Darla. Darla ran it through his coat a few times then handed it to Charlotte who did the same. I could tell they were falling in love with him.

"You said you had more dogs to show us," I said. We didn't need to make a snap decision.

"Yes, I do," she said. "Are you ready to see the next one?"

Before she could signal, the little dog walked over to Belinda and stood on his hind legs with his paws on the side of her chair. Belinda pulled back away from him, and I reached to pull him away. Before I could, he licked her on the neck just below her ear. She giggled.

Darla and I exchanged a look that said. He's got us. This is the one. "We're ready to see the next one," I said.

◈

"So," I said an hour later. "You're sure none of those Golden Retrievers or Labs will do. How about the German Sheppard? He was beautiful and so well behaved."

"They were all well behaved, Dad," Charlotte said. "They've all been trained."

"Binda ... like ... de haiwy dog." Brandon was in charge.

"I didn't say I liked him, Brandon. I said I thought he would be safe. He's little." Belinda was not going to give in easily.

"Gail," I called signaling her through the window to come back into the room. She had left to give the family time to talk. "I think we would like to start adoption procedures for the first dog we saw."

"That's wonderful," she smiled. "I hoped you would take him. As good as he is, most people want a purebred, especially when they pay this much."

"We don't care about breeding," Darla said. "Can we take him home today?"

"No," Gail said. There was a collective sigh of disappointment from my family. "I know," she continued. "But we have to check out your house and all first, and we like to do two training sessions with the parents and the child first, children in this case." She looked at the twins. "I know you're wonderful people, but we have to be sure to place them properly. We want this to work."

"Can we see him again before we go?" Veronica asked.

"Of course, I'll go and get him.

This time the little dog did bound into the room. He headed straight for Belinda's chair and stood to lick her earlobe. She giggled again and reluctantly put her arms around his neck. He jumped down and leaned up against Brandon then greeted the rest of the family.

"So what will we name him?" Veronica asked.

"What do you think, Brandon?" Darla asked. "What do you want his name to be?"

"Haiwy Dog ..."

"No," I said. "I will not have a Soft Cat, Furry Cat, and Hairy Dog living in my house."

"We'll spell it H-a-r-r-y, David," Darla said as she stood to gather her purse.

"Yeah," I smiled feeling stupid again. "Harry, I can live with that."

CHAPTER TWENTY TWO

"Hode de pecil like vis, Binda," I stood at the door to the twins' bedroom. Belinda was sitting at the desk we had put by the window for her. Brandon's desk was across the room, but he was standing next to her demonstrating the way he held his paint brush in his left hand. The twins had been in school for two years. We'd managed to talk the school into putting them in the same class each year, but the adjustment had still been difficult for everyone.

"Brandon, don't talk like that." She put her forehead down on her desk and dramatically rocked her head back and forth. I had to cover my mouth to suppress a laugh.

"I hate it when you pretend to be stupid." She looked up at him. "Now say it right."

"I'm not pretending," he said seriously. Then his face crumpled into a grin, and he dissolved into laughter.

"Say ... it ... right!" Belinda repeated.

"She has no sense of humor," Darla whispered from behind me. I jumped. I hadn't heard her approach.

"Brandon sure does though," I whispered back.

"Say it right, Brandon," Belinda demanded.

"Hold the pencil like vis."

"This ... T ... H ... th ... th ... th."

"Th ... th ... this," Brandon laughed again.

"That's a paint brush, Brandon." He put the paint brush down and picked up a pencil, demonstrating the same hand position.

"I can't," she said as she struggled to imitate his hand position around her pencil. "And besides, Mrs. Wafford says I have to use my right hand."

"Vat's stupit," Brandon said. "Watch vis." Th seemed to be hard for him. He put his hand down to the paper Belinda was writing on and made some kind of a mark. Belinda looked down at it for a minute and then burst into tears.

"Hey, what's the problem here," I said. It was time to stop spying on my children and get involved. I walked over to the desk and looked down at the paper. I sucked in my breath in shock. *Brandon Jeffrey Landrum* was written in perfect cursive.

"Do you know what that says, Brandon?" I asked.

"It's my name."

"Read it to me," Darla said.

"B r a n d o n," he said it slowly but that was all he said. Darla and I exchanged a glance.

I looked up at the painting of Harry that I'd had framed. Brandon had done it with a set of children's water colors shortly after we had brought the dog home. It was a perfect likeness. I became aware of pressure on the lower part of my leg and looked down. Harry was standing between me and Belinda. I looked at my daughter with her head on the desk crying. Harry licked her hand and she distractedly stroked his head.

"What's wrong, Beeta?" I put my hand on her shoulder and stooped beside her. She looked up and met my eyes.

She whispered. "He can write it, but he can't read it. It scares me." I put my arms around her.

"And look at mine," she whispered into my neck. I looked at the paper. *Belinda Brian Landrum* was scrawled in broken almost unreadable print.

"Did you do this with your right hand?" I asked, looking up at Darla. "She's left handed. It's clearly genetic. They're both left handed."

"David," Darla said defensively. "I've discussed it with Mrs. Wafford and with the principal. They said they wouldn't make her use her right hand anymore."

"Does she make you use your right hand?" I asked Brandon.

"She doesn't care what hand I use." Brandon wasn't laughing anymore. He was stroking the little dog's back and looking at Belinda with concern.

"Anyway, it doesn't matter," Belinda said. "I did that with my left hand." A new wave of sobs erupted from her, and I felt the wetness of her tears on my shirt. "I can't do it," she whispered to me again. "And it scares me."

"Beeta," I said, easing her back into the chair and looking into her eyes. "You don't have to be afraid of anything. If writing is hard for you, Mom and I will help. Brandon will help."

Belinda looked up at her mother. Darla was scowling but her features smoothed, and she put her hand on Belinda's head, gently prying the straight blond hair off her wet cheek.

Belinda stiffened. I guess she had seen the scowl. She looked back at me and said, "Brandon doesn't write, Daddy. He sketches."

"Is it so different?" I asked. "You help him with his speech. Let him teach you how to sketch."

"I don't want to sketch. I want to write."

"Same fing, Binda," Brandon said. "You just sketch letters." He smiled again, and I felt the squeeze on my heart that happened every time I saw the dimples in his cheeks. I looked back at Belinda. Her dimples didn't show as often as his did.

"Hold ... the ... pencil like th ... is," he said. "Try it. It works." He spoke clearly but obviously with an effort.

I wiped my daughter's eyes with my shirt tail. "Gross," she said and picked up her pencil. Brandon took my place next to her, and Darla and I left the room.

"They're eight years old and he can't read and she can't write," Darla said when we got to the kitchen. "I feel like such a failure."

I went to the refrigerator and took out the chicken I was planning to barbecue for dinner. I pulled out the spinach I had washed earlier and tossed it onto the counter. Then I went to the back door and slammed it behind me as I went out. It was childish and stupid, but it felt good. I went to the grill we had on the back deck and began the starting procedure.

Darla came out the door and stood behind me. I couldn't see her, but I was sure she had her arms crossed. "I guess you must think I'm a failure too. Otherwise you wouldn't be so mad at me."

"Shut up, Darla," I said.

She gasped. "I can't believe you said that to me."

"Shut up, Darla."

"What did I do? You're the one that's always telling me this isn't my fault. I couldn't do anything about the birth process that damaged Brandon. We went to therapy about it. Why are you mad at me now?"

I turned around and looked at her. For the first time ever she didn't look good to me. I looked a little closer. Same features, not heavy, she actually looked great right now. But she didn't look good to me.

"What are you looking at?" She dropped her arms to her side and balled her fists defensively.

I shook my head and bit back a bitter response. "Darla, this isn't all about you."

"Oh, I'm being selfish. Excuse me, David, but I've been through hell since those twins were born, actually since they were conceived."

"Hey, you were the one that wanted four kids."

"We compromised, David. I couldn't have planned twins, and besides, you know you were as ready to try again as I was."

"Yes," I turned back to the grill. "Yes, I guess I was." The silence stretched between us for a few minutes.

"And ... You're just not going to talk to me now? You've got more to say. I know you, David."

"I didn't know trying for the last child would be the last time you'd touch me," I said.

"Oh, that's what this is all about." She put her hands on her hips. "You're horny."

I looked at her again. She looked good this time. The sky seemed to brighten around her. "I guess I am, but more than that I'm lonely."

Darla put her hands on her eyes. "I'm sorry, David," she said. "But I don't know why you'd want to touch me. I've made such a mess. And I can only seem to keep making it worse."

"Like I said before," I bit back the fury. "This is not about just you. Those kids are not a mess. They're beautiful. God, Darla, you can't even touch your own daughter. You can touch Brandon. He's the one with the brain damage."

"I touched Belinda," she said, but she put her hands to her face again and crumpled to the deck floor. I watched her roll to her side and curl into a ball. "I touched her. I love her. I swear I love her."

I closed the lid on the grill and went to her. "P. H. stop, please. I'm sorry." I pulled her into my arms.

"Why would you want me, David?" She sobbed into my shoulder.

"I do, P. H. I want to hold you and I want you to hold me too." She put her arms around my neck and kissed me full on the mouth. I felt my fly stretch and looked back at the house nervously.

Darla sat up and looked around. "The pool house, David, carry me, I'm not sure I can walk."

I picked her up and looked back at the house again.

"The twins are busy and Harry is with them," she said. "Charlotte and Veronica won't be home for an hour. Take me to the pool house. Please."

I don't remember the trip around the pool. I put Darla down on a lounge chair and closed the French doors behind me. "I'm glad you insisted on these bamboo blinds."

"You didn't think we needed them." She laughed as she stretched her arms out to me.

"I was wrong." I hurried to the lounge chair and pulled off my shoes. Then I pulled off Darla's and ran my hands up her legs under her slacks. She tugged at the buttons on my shirt then lost patience and popped one off. It hit the floor and bounced who knows where. We laughed and I stretched out on the lounge beside her. I kissed her mouth and she kissed mine. I remembered the perfect pressure of our lips and tongues together. It had been too long since we'd been together like this.

"I love you, Darla," I whispered. "I've missed you so much."

"Hurry, David." She struggled with my fly and tugged at her slacks at the same time.

"Hurry?" I laughed. "That wasn't the response I expected." We both struggled out of our clothes and returned to the lounge naked.

"You know I love you, David. But right now I want you, and I'm not sure how much time we have."

"Mmm," I kissed her again and moved my hand between her legs. She was not quite ready. I slid down to the end of the lounge on my knees and licked the warm sweetness between her legs. She moaned and I submerged my tongue. She was ready now. I moved up over her. She reached down to guide me inside.

I could hear us both moaning our pleasure. It was heaven. We moved together in perfect harmony. It had been years, but we still knew each other's bodies. We still knew each other's rhythm. I felt her shudder just before I knew I couldn't go on much longer. Then I poured myself into her and we collapsed. Hearts pressed together and pounding.

"I needed that," Darla kissed my shoulder, eased out from under me, and started to dress.

"Me too," I didn't move. My heart was still pounding. "I think we should sleep together tonight."

"We'll see."

"We'll see?" I said. "I thought you said you needed that."

"I did." She leaned down and kissed my mouth. "Now get up. The girls will be back any minute. I'll go check on the twins."

She closed the French doors of the pool house behind her, and I got up to put my clothes on. I changed my mind and went to the dresser we kept out there with bathing suites. I pulled one out and put it on. It was early fall, but the pool was heated. I dove into the cool water and started to swim laps.

❖

"You know, Darla," I said an hour later when we were both dressed, and I was standing at the barbecue flipping the chicken.

"What?" She was sitting on a stone bench at the edge of the garden drinking a glass of wine.

"When we were having all those babies, and you said we were the perfect genetic compliment, I kind of felt like a stud for hire." I closed the lid and went to the bench to sit down beside her. "Today, I feel like a whore."

I smiled at the sound of wind chimes in her laugh. She put her arm around my waist and leaned her head on my shoulder. I stretched my arm across her back.

"You're very good at both roles, David."

"I want to be your partner. I don't want to play a role."

"I'll sleep with you tonight." She looked up at me and I kissed her. She put her other arm around my neck, and we held each other for a minute. We moved apart at the sound of the back door closing and looked up as Charlotte and Veronica came down the path to the pool. They had on their bathing suits.

"I think it's a little cool to swim," Darla said.

"We're getting in the hot tub," Veronica called back as the two of them went around the pool and climbed into the Jacuzzi.

"They're gorgeous women," Darla said. They were fourteen and fifteen years old now and had the height of my mom with the shapely curves from Darla. Veronica was platinum blond like her mother with the clear blue eyes from both sides of the family and Charlotte had matching brown hair and eyes that reminded me of cinnamon.

"Scares me to death," I said.

"I have to say, parenthood has been scarier than I thought it would be."

"Yeah," I stood and went back to the grill. "Darla, before when we were fighting you said we'd gone to therapy about the problems with the twins. I don't think we did enough."

She was silent behind me.

"Dr. Watson gave us names of psychologists to see individually. She gave you one that could work with you and Belinda. But you didn't go."

"You didn't go either." She looked into her wine and swirled it around the glass.

"We didn't even go back to her," I said.

"I thought I could handle it myself." She didn't look angry as I had thought she would. She looked sad.

"Me too," I closed the grill and went back to sit beside her.

"We can't." She leaned her head on my shoulder and I put my arm around her again.

"I'll go if you go." I laughed.

She looked up at me and smiled sadly. "It's been two years. I don't have the names anymore. Let's go back to Dr. Watson. She'll tell us what to do."

"Sounds like a plan."

She did sleep with me that night. We made love all night long. Just like the first time, I was surprised at my stamina.

The next morning was Monday. I stood at the front door and watched my family drive away. I felt ill at ease to say the least. Charlotte was in the driver's seat. She had gotten her learner's permit the previous spring. Darla was sitting beside her. They were having an animated conversation. They'd left the house arguing about some after school activity that Charlotte wanted to squeeze into an already full schedule. Veronica sat in the far back seat of the minivan arranging some papers in her notebook and scowling about something. But the eight year old girl sitting in the middle seat crying with her brother's arm stretched across her shoulders was my greatest concern.

I knew something had to change. Belinda was an eight year old nervous wreck. She worried about everything. She felt responsible for her brother's problems, and she was so critical of herself that she couldn't tolerate anything short of a perfect performance. Her mother couldn't touch her, and she knew it. I was glad Darla had agreed to more therapy, but I worried it would be too late.

I felt something brush my leg and looked down at Harry's scruffy smiling face. He wagged his tail, and I reached down to pat him on the shoulder.

"I'll take you for another walk before I go to work. Does that sound good?" He wagged his tail again and I thought about how much I'd missed walking a dog. Why had it taken all these years and a brain damaged child to allow myself this pleasure again?

The phone rang shaking me out of my thoughts. I went back to the kitchen to answer it. The caller ID showed Uncle Jeff's name and number.

"Hey," I picked it up.

"Uh uh ... hey," he said and we both laughed. "I can't get used to people knowing who you are before they answer the phone. Technology is moving a little fast for an old guy like me."

"You keep up pretty well for an old guy like you." We laughed again. "What's going on?" I asked.

"I have a favor to ask of you. I'm having a sales promotion day at the nursery, and I've committed to a brunch buffet. I was planning to hire a caterer and then I thought about you. You make the best breakfasts in the world. Do you think you could do it?"

"Wow," I sat down. What was that feeling in my chest? Was I having a heart attack? No, my heart was pounding with excitement. This sounded like fun.

"David," Uncle Jeff said. "Are you still there?"

"Yeah," I laughed. "I've never done anything like that, Uncle Jeff. How many people do you think it would be?"

"We're just a nursery, David. It's not like a big department store or anything. I was planning to tell the caterer a hundred people."

"A hundred people," I sounded breathless even to myself.

"Maybe it's not such a good idea," Uncle Jeff sounded disappointed. "Forget I asked."

"No, wait," I said. "You just took me by surprise. I'd like to try. I've never cooked for that many before, but it sounds like fun. I might mess it up. Are you sure you want to take a chance on me?"

"I have complete faith in you, David. Alice wants to help you. She's planning to come by to talk to you at the office at lunchtime. She's driving me crazy."

"She's always driven you crazy." I laughed.

"That's right. She was born with a heart problem. The doctors corrected it, and she's been giving me a heart problem ever since." I could hear the love through his complaint.

"And you wouldn't change her if you could."

"No, I guess not. I have to say, though, I appreciate Evelyn. She plans to go to the University of Georgia in the fall and study horticulture just like her old man. She wants to take over Landrum's when I retire. She's so easy."

"You're never going to retire."

"No, I probably won't. But I'll cut way down and Evelyn will take over. I'm glad she's so steady. Two of them like Alice would kill me."

I wondered for a minute if Evelyn ever got the attention she needed. I'd wondered that before. Alice was so dynamic.

"Anyway," Uncle Jeff continued. "Alice has this crazy scheme. She'll tell you about it at lunch. Will you be at the office?"

"Yeah, I'm getting ready to go in now." I looked across the room at Harry standing beside the back door. "After I walk the dog, that is."

"You're going in a little later these days. It seems when you started this career you were in before the sun came up."

"I hired a new editor and he's taking over some of my duties. I'm almost starting to think they don't need me around there anymore."

"I'm sure that's not true. The promotion is for the holidays. That season has been a little slow for the past few years. I'm trying to spice it up. I'm thinking mid November. See if you can come up with a menu and let me know what kind of funds you need. Talk to you later, David."

I hung up the phone and grabbed Harry's leash off the peg by the door. "Let's go," I said and felt the tension releasing from my shoulders as I walked the happy dog around the house and down the street.

✧

I arrived at the office a little bit before nine o'clock. Stan Crenshaw met me at my office door with his marketing plan for the new year.

"I know you want to look it over before I present it to the board on Wednesday," he said.

"You're right," I laughed, taking his folder and putting it on my desk. I hung my sweater on the hook behind the door and sat down. "I think you're ready to do this on your own, but I don't think I'm ready for that yet."

"I still need your input." Stan laughed and left the room closing the door behind him. I opened the folder and started to read. It was a beautiful plan and Stan had mapped it out for a very good presentation. There was a slight sinking feeling in my chest along with a feeling of awe at the perfection of his work. Was my work that impressive? Had it ever been? It was a long report and I lost myself in the reading of it.

"David," I looked up at the sound of Drew's voice. He stood at the door to my office. "I didn't mean to interrupt," he said. "You look really intense. I was hoping we could have lunch, but if you plan to work through …"

"He isn't going to work through lunch," Alice skimmed past him through the door and bounced over to sit on my lap. "He's going to go to lunch with me. Do you want to join us, Drew?"

"Sure, I didn't know you had a lunch date with each other. Would I be intruding?" he asked.

"On what," I said, standing up and setting Alice onto her feet. "Uncle Jeff says she has some crazy scheme to tell me about. I'm sure you would enjoy hearing about it too."

"Dad thinks anything that doesn't have step by step instructions is a crazy scheme." Alice went over to the door and got my sweater off the hook. "I like to think outside the box." She handed it to me and I put it on.

"Do you want to go with us, Drew?" I asked.

"I would like to, but I want equal time," he said. "I wanted to talk to you about the twins. I have a suggestion."

"About Evelyn and me," Alice said. "What kind of suggestion do you have?"

"No, toots," Drew pinched Alice's nose. "The world doesn't revolve around you and your twin, you know. I was talking about Brandon and Belinda."

"Bite your tongue, Drew. The world does too revolve around me, not Evelyn, but certainly me." Alice laughed and I smiled at her animation.

She and her sister were small like their mother, not tall like Uncle Jeff or my girls. She looked at me and said, "I really want to talk to you, David, but if you and Drew need for me to leave after we talk, I will. I don't want to intrude."

"There isn't anything we would say that can't be said in front of you, Alice." I picked up my keys out of the dish on my desk. "Where would you like to go for lunch?"

We went to the mall, but instead of the food court we chose a quiet booth in a restaurant on the outside. I sat down across the booth from Drew and Alice and looked at the two of them.

"You know," I said. "I've never noticed it before, but you two have a family resemblance. I've always thought of you as polar opposites; you with your dark hair, Alice, and Drew being so blond."

"It's the eyes, David." Alice looked at Drew and back at me. "Not only are they blue but they have the same set and shape. They're Jeffrey and Brian Landrum eyes."

I looked closer. "You're right."

"Yours have the same set and shape but they're brown like your mom's."

"Is that right," I said. The waitress came and we all looked quickly at the menu and ordered. "So, who wants to start?" I asked.

"I do," Alice said. "I have a date with a friend for the afternoon, so I'm pressed for time."

"Go ahead then, by all means," Drew said. "I only have to go back to work."

Alice grinned, acknowledging the jab. "David," She looked at me intently across the table. "I want to be a chef and own my own restaurant. I love to cook, David. I'm like you. I think it's in the blood."

"I don't have a problem with that. Does your dad have a problem with it?"

"Yes," she said and drew her brows together. "He says if I still want to do that after I get a bachelor's degree he'll be behind me all the way."

"Well," I paused to collect my thoughts. "I have a great respect for education. I don't think a bachelor's degree could hurt you. Couldn't you study cooking or something, home economics?"

"I don't want to study home economics," Alice pouted and I laughed. She was so good at it. She tilted her eyes up at me and I swear they glowed red. "I won't do it, David." She looked at Drew. He held his hands palm up in submission. "I'm not going to the University system, and I'm not going to a private college. I won't! I won't!" She looked down at her plate as the waitress put down her meal, then Drew's and mine. Drew and I exchanged a helpless look.

"I didn't realize you felt so strongly about it," I said after we had all taken a first bite in uncomfortable silence.

"Well, I do," she looked up at me and I smiled. We all took another bite in more uncomfortable silence.

"Maybe you should tell me about this crazy scheme," I said.

"I knew you'd give me a chance to talk, David." She looked at Drew. He raised his eyebrows innocently. "I don't care what you think!"

"I didn't say a word." Drew looked back down at his plate.

"Dad and I have compromised on Culinary School. There is a school for the arts that has a good program out near where we live." She looked directly into my eyes. "I think Culinary School is stupid. Everyone in the business knows that most people out of school can't cook. It isn't something you have to learn. You didn't go to school, and you're the best cook I know."

"Thank you." I said. "I hear what you're saying, Alice, but I cook for fun. I think I'd enjoy learning the right way to do it. Not only that, but if you want to make a living at it, it's always better to have some credentials."

"When was the last time you went into a restaurant and asked for the chef's credentials?"

"Okay, I've never done that, but if I was hiring a chef I'd want credentials."

"I want my own restaurant. I want to be my own boss."

"Yeah, but you can't start that way."

"Yes, you can." She looked across at me and again. Her gaze was intense. "David," She sat back and took a deep breath. "I've been thinking that you should open a café at Landrum's. I thought we'd give it a try with that sales promotion that Dad has planned. I was the one that suggested you prepare the food."

"I hope you didn't force Uncle Jeff to agree." I was disappointed that he hadn't thought about it himself.

"Of course I didn't. He thought it was a great idea too." She was oblivious to my feelings. I was glad. "We could renovate the kitchen in the apartment upstairs. Nobody lives there now, and I don't think anyone ever will again. Well, Evelyn has talked about it, but she won't get in my way when I tell her about it. I just wanted to talk to you first."

"Alice, I have to tell you that I've worried over the years if Evelyn gets enough attention with you being so demanding of it."

Alice took a deep breath. She leaned back in the booth and looked at me, then at Drew. "I worry about that too."

I smiled. "You never fail to surprise me, kid."

"Evelyn is the best part of my life, and my life is good. Mom and Dad are great. I have you two, but Evelyn is the best." She looked back and forth between us. "We'll compromise. There's lots of room up there. It's a three bedroom apartment, and I was thinking of putting a stairway down to the fountain display with tables and all. David," She looked at me dramatically. "Think about it. You handle breakfast and brunch on Sunday. I handle dinner through the week. At first we'd only do lunch on the weekends. Then, if things go as well as I plan, we could do lunch all week. It would work. You'd love it and so would I."

"What about the job I already do?" I asked.

She grinned. "I know you. It's time for a change."

I looked at my empty plate. I'd eaten everything. There was no rescue there. "I hate to admit it, but it sounds good to me."

"Just sit with it, David. Culinary School is two years, and I promised Dad I would finish."

"Okay," I said. "I'll sit with it."

"I guess that means it's your turn," Alice smiled at Drew.

"My turn for what?" Drew's face looked blank.

Alice and I both laughed. He shook his head and laughed with us. "I can see why Uncle Jeff always looks a little confused. You're a whirlwind, Alice."

She grinned, pleased with the description. "You were going to talk about Brandon and Belinda."

"That's right," Drew leaned forward a little and made eye contact with me. "David, public school isn't going to work for those two."

"I know." I said. "I had pretty much come to that conclusion myself. It was sad watching them leave for school this morning. Belinda was crying, and Brandon was trying to comfort her. We have to get her some relief, and I don't think Brandon is getting the attention that he needs either. But I have to look into the alternatives."

"Did it ever dawn on you to ask me about it, David? I'm a special education professional and so is Lizzy."

I looked back into his eyes. It hadn't dawned on me. Drew and Elizabeth had been at our house a lot in the past few years. They loved the kids but hadn't had any of their own. Darla and I had wondered if they couldn't for some reason. All they said to us was that they were devoting their lives to helping other people's kids through their work. Maybe that was true. They were both very happy in their carriers.

"Stupid of me," I said.

"Yeah, or do you just not think of me as capable because I'm your little brother?" I looked directly into Drew's eyes and he held my gaze.

"Okay, you two," Alice said, "Enough with the sibling rivalry."

I broke the stare and looked at her then back at Drew. "I don't know why I didn't think of asking you, Drew, but I'm pretty sure it wasn't sibling rivalry."

"That's what Lizzy said. She said I was being too sensitive, and it was time for me to break my silence and talk to you about this."

I leaned back in my booth and met his eyes again. "I'd say it's past time for you to break your silence. Am I that hard to approach, Drew?" I said. "I need your help here. Maybe I didn't realize it before, but I'd have been open to it anytime you'd given me the chance."

"Hmmm ..." Alice said. "I wish I could hang around for the rest of this, but my date is here." She waved in the direction of the door.

I turned and looked. A young man, probably about her age but looking a bit younger, waved back and started toward our booth. "How did he know we were here? Did you have the restaurant planned too?"

"No," she said as the young man approached. "I called him on my cell while we were waiting to be seated. Daniel," she said. "This is my cousin, Drew, and my brother cousin, David."

"Nice to meet you, sir." The young man held his hand out to Drew. "Brother cousin?" he asked as he shook my hand.

"I'll explain later," Alice nudged Drew to let her out of the booth. "We have to go, guys." She leaned down and kissed my cheek then hugged Drew. "Don't be too hard on him," she said. "He didn't grow up with siblings so he doesn't understand the rivalry." She looked back at me. "Think about my idea, David." Then she was gone.

Drew sat back down. He looked down as the waitress picked up our plates. "Will there be anything else?" she asked.

"I'd like the chocolate lava cake," he said, "with Ice cream. Bring two spoons."

We sat in silence for a few minutes. "I'm sorry if I've insulted you, Drew."

He looked up at me and took a deep breath. "You really didn't know, did you?"

"That I suck as a brother?" I asked and laughed. He laughed too. "No, I really didn't know."

"Well, you do." He leaned back as the waitress put the desert down in front of us. "You're going to eat some of this aren't you?" he asked. His look was so intense that I picked up my spoon and dug in. "I guess I suck as a brother too. I've worried about this for years, and I suppose I could have talked to you about it."

I took another bite and didn't say anything. I looked into his eyes.

"Lizzy told me I should talk to you about it." We ate in silence for a minute then I put my spoon down and looked at him.

"Why didn't you?"

"I wanted you to come to me because you admired my expertise."

I looked at him. "Punch me," I said. "I'm an idiot."

"No, you aren't." Drew laughed. "You were caught up in your own family which is large and distracting." He put down his spoon. "I feel a little foolish for being so self absorbed."

"Don't," I tapped his hand and picked up my spoon to dig into the rich chocolate again. "We were both caught up in something, and we didn't communicate. We should learn from this. You should know you can talk to me, and I need to realize how capable you are. Help me with my kids, Drew. I don't know what to do anymore."

He looked into my eyes and smiled. He picked up his spoon and we finished the desert in silence.

"That was good," he said.

"It was. Thanks for ordering it."

"Okay, here's my expertise." He looked at me across the table. "I'm about to change jobs."

"Really, I thought you were happy in the public school system."

"I have been but it can be frustrating. I hate that they get in my way, but I haven't wanted to abandon the kids who need me. But a friend of mine and I have put together a school devoted to special education. It's located north of Atlanta a little, between where Uncle Jeff lives and where you and Darla are. It'll be a bit of a drive for you, but we have a dorm so we can board."

"No way, Drew. I'm sure it would be a good environment for them, but I'm not sending my eight year olds to boarding school."

"I didn't think you would." He laughed and leaned back in his booth. "I figure I can take them with me every day. I'll be going, and we don't live far from you."

I looked around the room. I had an uneasy feeling. I wasn't sure why. "What about Belinda. She isn't handicapped. She doesn't need special help."

"She's gifted, David. All your girls are smart, but she's brilliant. I hate to say it, but in the public schools that can be a handicap. We're setting up a gifted program as well. She'll fit right into it. Not only that, but she's left handed. I know how hard that is. No one will ever tell her to use her right hind in my school." He looked down at his left hand, flexed it, and spread the fingers.

"Are you left handed?" I asked, knowing the answer without ever having observed it.

"You bet," he laughed.

I didn't say anything. My cell phone rang and I picked it up. It was my office. I told the receptionist to reschedule my afternoon appointments and hung up. I looked across the table at my brother.

"You don't trust me ..." he said.

"It isn't that, Drew. I'm scared and I'm not sure why." I clasped my hands together and put them on the table. I looked down in silence. Drew didn't break it.

"Brandon has seizures," I said. "Not that often but at least one or two a month and you never know when they'll happen. How will you handle that?"

"All of our employees are CPR certified. We have a registered nurse on staff and there is a hospital two miles from us. David, he can bring the dog." Drew leaned forward and put his hands on my clasped ones. "I love those kids as much as you do, David."

I looked up at him, and I could feel the emotion in my eyes.

"Probably not as much as you do," he said, quickly. "I've never been a parent, but I love them very much. I won't let them be hurt. Trust me, David. I think we can help them."

"I don't know what Darla will say."

"I want you two and the twins, the girls too, if they will; to come up to the school. We opened this past fall with a pretty full roster. I had some loose ends to clear up in the county school, but I'll be there full time in two weeks. Oh, and David, I have to tell you. We're offering scholarships to kids that can't afford it. We can only do that if we charge a good bit of the people that can afford it."

"I can afford it, within reason of course."

He grinned. "I know you can, and I'll assign a kid or two to you to sponsor. You can keep tabs on them as well as your own. I think you'll enjoy that. You've had to give up your big brother activities with the large family and all."

"You're right. I have and I miss it."

"So you'll come to see the school. I was thinking Saturday. We can see the facility without all the activity. Only the boarders will be there. We have about seventy five at the moment. It's a beautiful campus. I think the family will enjoy the fresh air and we'll have lunch in the cafeteria. Our dietician is excellent."

"I'll have to talk to Darla about it," I said.

"Truth is, I'm hurt that she didn't think of me either. I've known her longer than I've known you."

I looked up into his eyes. He didn't look too hurt.

"She's preoccupied just like me."

"I know. Listen, if she wants, Lizzy and I would love to talk to you guys about it. We could have dinner out. I'm sure Charlotte and Dad would babysit. Darlene and Jason would too. We haven't gotten together just the four of us in a long time."

I thought about how long it had been since Darla and I had gotten together just the two of us, before the last afternoon that is. Relationships are important and they need maintenance. "Let's do it, even if we don't have to talk about the twins."

"That sounds good to me."

◊

"Hello, sweetheart," I kissed Darla on the top of the head when I got home that night.

"Hello David," She was standing at the stove stirring something in a large pot. It was emitting an aroma that made my salivary glands tingle. She didn't look up at me so I couldn't kiss her mouth.

"Spaghetti, Brandon's favorite," I said. "Is everyone alright?"

"No." She didn't say anything else.

"Is somebody at the hospital?" I asked, hearing the panic in my voice. "Is somebody dead? Give me the news, Darla."

She turned and looked at me. Her eyes were sad, almost defeated. "Nobody is hurt, at least not physically. Brandon had a seizure in school today. He's been expelled." She turned back to the pot and began to stir again. "So has Belinda."

"They can't expel him for having a seizure. What did Belinda do?" I stormed to the stairs. "Where are they? Are they okay?"

"Be quiet, David. Brandon's sleeping the way he always does after a seizure. Belinda is with him and Harry is with her. I swear I think that dog is more hers than his." She looked at me then. "Please don't upset them more than they already are."

I took a deep breath. "Okay," I said. "Why don't you tell me what happened so I'll know all the details when I go in there tomorrow and tear the place up."

She went to the refrigerator and poured herself a glass of wine. "Will you join me?" she asked without turning around to look at me.

"Yes."

She poured another glass and sat down at the table, setting one glass in front of her and one in front of the chair across the table. I sat down.

"I guess I shouldn't have described the situation to you that way. I was angry. I'm sorry, David."

"I forgive you. Now tell me what happened."

"Apparently he crawled under the teacher's desk. You know how he goes to a place he thinks will be safe when he's about to have a seizure?"

"Yeah," I smiled, remembering times when he'd crawled under furniture in the house.

"From what I can gather from the hysterical teacher and the hysterical principal, Belinda went under the desk with him and held his arms. You know how she does? It's a new year and this was the first time Mrs. Wafford had dealt with one of Brandon's seizures. She tried to pull Belinda out and she kicked her."

"The woman kicked Belinda!" I shouted. I stood up and stormed toward the stairway.

"No David, stop," Darla jumped up and ran to bar my way. "Belinda kicked Mrs. Wafford, made a huge welt on her shin. The woman acted like a child with a skinned knee. She was in the infirmary with her leg propped up when I got there. She said she wouldn't have either of them in her classroom again."

"We'll see about that." I sat back down at the table and sipped my wine. "Where were the twins when you got there?"

"Brandon was sleeping it off in another room of the infirmary, and Belinda was sitting with him. She was just sitting there on the cot. She had one of Brandon's hands clasped in her tiny little fists, and she was staring at her lap." Darla started to cry. "She's such a sweet loving little thing, David. Why have I been so awful to her?"

"You haven't, P. H. This situation is just bigger than the two of us. It's bigger than the four of us." I pulled Darla into my lap and held her in silence for a minute until her sobs calmed and she rested on my shoulder.

"I had a hard time being comforting to her even then. I'm crazy, David, and I'm hurting my little girl."

"You aren't crazy. But we need to get Belinda some help, and Brandon needs help too." I took a deep breath and put her back in her chair. I stood and went to the back door to look out at the yard. Charlotte and Veronica were sitting at the table by the pool with their school books spread between them. Fall leaves were scattered on the table and lawn. The weather was warm with a cool breeze. The girls were not studying. They were having an animated conversation. I admired the beauty of them for a minute. It made me smile, and I turned back to the kitchen.

"Darla," I said. "I had lunch with Drew today. He and a friend have opened a school for handicapped and learning disabled children. He wants us to send the twins to him."

She was silent for a minute. "I saw Elizabeth about a month ago. We had lunch together. She told me about it, but she said it was a boarding school. I won't send them away, David. I couldn't stand to let Brandon go and live somewhere else. Oh God," she put her face in her hands. "...Or Belinda, or Belinda."

"I said the same thing." I went back to the table and sat down. "We don't have to board them. In fact, Drew said he'd take them with him every day. I don't know about that, but we'll work out the details. They want to have dinner with us on Friday night, Drew and Elizabeth. They want to talk to us about it. Then we could go on Saturday to see the school."

The back door opened and Charlotte came in with Veronica right behind her. They both carried their books in their arms. "Mom, Dad," Charlotte said. "The twins can't go back to that school. Veronica and I have talked about it, and we'll give up our afternoon activities to take care of them."

"Maybe you could home school them, Mom," Veronica said. "We could help. It's all fresh in our minds."

I reached for Darla's hand across the table, and she squeezed mine with hers. "That won't be necessary, Vroom, Charlita," I said. "Although, your mom and I really appreciate the offer. They aren't going back there. We'll find a better place for them. Would you two be up for a little family field trip on Saturday? We have a new school to look at."

"I was going to the movies with Lana," Charlotte said, "but she and I can go on Sunday instead."

"Daddy!" Brandon launched himself at me from the bottom of the stairway. I was always surprised by the size and substance of him. He wrapped his arms around my neck and covered my face with sloppy kisses.

"Brandon," Belinda said as she came up to me with a tissue in her hand. "You've slobbered all over Daddy." She handed me the tissue to clean off my face.

"Don't I get a kiss from you?" I asked her.

"Not until you clean up the slobber." She waited patiently until I had dabbed my face dry. "Daddy," she said as she kissed me on the cheek. "Please don't make us go back there. Mrs. Wafford won't let me help Brandon and I have to help him. I don't care about the *stay in your seat* rule."

I looked at Darla. She had tears in her eyes. I looked at Charlotte and Veronica. They had tears in their eyes too. Mine were starting to sting.

"You won't be going back there, kids. We'll work it out."

I looked in on the twins about midnight. They were both asleep. It wasn't unusual for me to find Belinda awake. More and more though, since Harry had come, she was getting to sleep before the clock struck twelve. She had this night.

Harry slept with Brandon. I think that took some of the pressure off her. She had gradually learned to trust the dog to know when a seizure was coming on. Sometimes the dog would run from the other room to

Brandon when he was going to have a seizure. It was amazing. The twins slept in different beds now. That had been a big step.

The little dog tapped his tail gently on the bed when he saw me, and I signaled him to come to me. He jumped quietly down from the bed and came to the doorway where I stood.

"I think I can borrow you for a while." I whispered. "Do you want to go for a walk?"

Harry wagged his tail again and walked in front of me down the hall to the steps. I had the feeling that he wouldn't go with me if Brandon was going to have a seizure. I laughed quietly. Surely I was overestimating his abilities. Still it was a comforting thought.

I closed the front door and turned to lock it. When I turned around there was a man standing a few feet away from me leaning down to pat Harry.

"Ahhh..." I jumped and felt my heart start to pound. "Jimmy, are you trying to kill me. Tell me when you're going to join me for my walk. You scared me to death."

"Look again, Uncle David." The man straightened standing considerably taller than Jimmy.

I looked closer. He was taller than Jimmy, but his features were the same. "James, Jr." I said and wrapped him in a bear hug reminiscent of Uncle Jeff's. "What in the world are you doing on my doorstep at midnight?" I asked. Then feeling suddenly concerned. "Is everything alright? Is your dad alright?"

"I'm fine, David." Jimmy stepped out of the shadow of a shade tree. "Jamie wanted to talk to you, and I told him this was the best way to do it. It's hard to get time with you anymore these days. You're a busy man, but you always take a walk at midnight."

"Shall we go?" I started down the street toward the small park that the homeowner's association kept up. The Jameses fell in beside me. Harry led the way trotting at the end of his leash.

"It's good to see you walking a dog again," Jimmy said. "Did you finally decide to forgive yourself?"

"I guess so."

"What did you have to forgive yourself for, Uncle David?" James, Jr. asked.

"I had a dog when I was a kid. I felt responsible for her death," I said. "But let's not talk about me. Tell me your news."

"I'm finally going to go to college." He sounded ambivalent.

"I thought you were happy teaching tennis. You know, Jamie, a college degree isn't a statement of your worth." He'd struggled with his decision not to go to school. We'd had a number of conversations about it.

"I know, Uncle David, but I can't make enough to support a family doing this."

"Are you trying to tell me you're getting married?" I put my hand on his shoulder and squeezed.

"No, not right now anyway. I'll want to someday, though."

"Anyone in particular?"

Jamie looked away. I couldn't see the expression on his face in the dark, but I could feel his discomfort. "Not really, but with Heather getting married it made me start thinking. I want to be able to have a family and a home someday too."

"Heather is getting married?" I stopped and looked at Jimmy. "We really haven't gotten together enough lately. When did this happen?"

"We just found out about it. I was going to tell you tonight." Jimmy smiled broadly. Even in the moonlight I could see his happiness.

"You must like the guy."

"Yeah, they met in medical school. You know she finishes her internship in the spring. Then they both will be going to the Mayo Clinic for a residency in internal medicine. Imagine a child of mine being such a scholar."

"Don't get too excited, Dad," James, Jr. said, but he didn't sound unhappy. "You still have me."

"And you are a tennis pro. If we can get Marissa through school we'll be set."

"Is Marissa having a problem in school?" I asked.

"No, she's doing really well. She's in the gifted program. I just wish she could have gone to school with Charlotte. They were good friends before school separated them."

"I think they're still good friends. So tell me about your decision to go back to school, Jamie," I asked feeling bad to have gotten off his subject.

"Well, I've got a tennis scholarship to Georgia State. My high school grades were good. Thanks to you mostly. So even after five years off they were willing to give it to me. I'll work as an aid on the tennis team, but I think they'll take advantage of having me there to teach. That's what I want to do eventually. Teach tennis in the university system. It would make decent money. I won't be rich but the benefits are great. I don't have benefits now."

"It sounds like you've really thought this out."

"I have." He looked down at the path in front of him as we entered the park. "I have to take the core curriculum before I get to my major subjects. I'm nervous about it."

"I'm sure you'll do fine." We walked in silence for a few minutes. I could feel the tension in the air. "What's wrong, Jamie?" I asked.

"I don't think I can do it without your help. I know you don't have time anymore. You work so much and you've got your own kids. The twins need a lot of attention." His voice quivered and he whispered. "I really need your help."

"Jamie, you can call me any time." I stopped walking and turned to put my hands on his shoulders. When had he gotten so tall? We were looking eye to eye.

"That's what I told him. I told him about how I could call you in the middle of the night and you'd help me," Jimmy said.

"Well you can too, Jamie, but why do you feel so insecure. I didn't get you through high school. You did it yourself."

"I was hanging on by a thread, Uncle David. Every direction I went in I hit a brick wall. I'm just afraid I won't be able to do this, and I really want to. I want a future."

"You have a future. I'll help you, son. But I want you to work on your self confidence."

"It's really only school." Jamie pulled away from me and started back down the road toward my house. "I'm confident about other stuff. I mean tennis and, you know, the business end of it and all. It's really just school that gives me the willies, and girls, well women."

I looked at Jimmy. He smiled and shrugged. We followed James, Jr. back to the house. I hadn't noticed that there were two cars parked in the driveway. James, Jr. walked to one of them. I followed him.

"When do you start?"

"Winter semester," he looked sad.

"Hey, don't worry. I'll help you. In fact I'm excited. I was starting to feel like I was in a rut. I need a new project."

"Well, I'm glad I could provide one for you."

"When you get registered for your classes let me know. We'll work out a plan. You'll do great, Jamie. I can't wait to see you in your cap and gown."

He laughed then. He wrapped his arms around me for just a minute then got into the driver's seat of his car. He rolled down the window. "Thanks David, I do feel better now knowing you're on my team."

"I'm always on your team." He pulled out and I looked over at Jimmy.

"I think he's in love." Jimmy walked over to me and stooped to pet Harry. "I think that might be one of the reasons that he's feeling so insecure."

"I thought he'd gotten over that. I mean he's seemed so self confident for so many years."

"You know what love does to you."

"Is the girl pushing for marriage or something?"

"I don't think it's gone that far, David." He stood and shifted back and forth on his feet. "I don't know how you're going to feel about this."

"What?" I said feeling a shiver of anticipation. "He doesn't have a thing for Charlotte or Veronica, does he? They're way too young for him."

"David, he's twenty three years old. That would be robbing the cradle. And besides, they're like sisters."

"Good," I expelled a breath I hadn't known I was holding.

"He hasn't talked to me about it, but I think he has a thing for Evelyn."

"Evelyn!" I jumped. "She's not that much older than Charlotte."

"I know, I know," Jimmy said and paced away from me. "I probably shouldn't have told you. It's just a hunch. He's been teaching her tennis for about a year now. There is just something about the way he talks about her that makes me suspect."

"What does he say?" I demanded.

"Just how smart she is and how she listens and how her hair has red in it when she stands in the sun …" his voice trailed off.

"Oh …"

"How old are Alice and Evelyn now?" Jimmy asked.

"Seventeen I think, eighteen in March."

"So it would still be statutory …"

"Don't even say it, Jimmy. Whoa." I picked up the little dog at my feet and buried my face in his fur.

"David, Jamie is a good kid. He won't take advantage of a young girl. You can trust him."

"I know that but I was his age once." I actually started a lot younger, I thought. I started up the walk to the house. "I need to go inside, Jimmy."

"Are you upset, David?"

"I don't know. I just hadn't thought about the twins as women yet."

"Have you looked at them lately?" Jimmy asked as I walked to the door. He got into his car and drove away.

CHAPTER TWENTY THREE

I hurried home from work on that Friday. I had run into a problem at the office with a marketing trip we had planned for a time when neither Stan nor I could go. I had to get the receptionist to work on changing reservations, and we'd had to plan the whole thing over again. We were supposed to meet Drew and Elizabeth at the restaurant in an hour, and I needed to shower and change.

I parked the car in the garage and hurried through the door into the kitchen. I stopped short and looked around to be sure I was in the right place. There was a girl sitting at the table alone. I'd never seen her before. She looked to be about the twin's age. She had straight red hair pulled into a braid that fell to her waist, and she was tall, maybe as tall as Brandon.

She looked up and saw me. Her eyebrows and lashes were as red as her hair. She smiled displaying a mouth full of braces and stood to come toward me. "You must be Mr. Landrum," she said holding her hand out to shake mine. "I'm Sivon. It's nice to meet you."

I took the delicate hand and shook it gently. "It's nice to meet you too. Did you say your name was Sivon?"

"Yes, and we might as well get the name business over with up front," she said and I had an urge to say, "Yes ma'am."

"My name is actually spelled S i o b h a n. My mother is Irish." She explained. "You would pronounce it Shivon, but no one can get it right, except for my mother of course, and Dad does alright too. So I've changed it to Sivon, which is what everyone calls me, and I like the way that sounds better anyway."

"How do your parents feel about that?" I asked. My hurry was forgotten with this delightful unexpected guest.

"They don't like it too much. I've agreed not to change it legally. It's a family name you see."

"I see," I said and looked around. "Speaking of family, where is mine?"

"They're upstairs having an argument. Charlotte wants to babysit for the twins, but Mrs. Landrum thinks it would better if her grandparents came."

As she finished her sentence I heard the commotion of my family coming down the stairs. "Sivon, are you still here?" Darla said as she came into the kitchen. "Won't your parents be looking for you?"

"I called them when you all went upstairs. I'll go in a minute. I just wanted to see how things turned out. Is Charlotte going to babysit?"

Darla looked at the girl with a completely blank expression. I laughed and she looked at me. She laughed too. "Oh David," she said. "I'm glad you're home. I called Drew and Elizabeth. They've changed the reservation to 8:00, so you have time to shower."

"Good," I said, feeling like I'd been dismissed. I wanted to stay and see what happened next. "I was just getting acquainted with Sivon. Are you our new neighbor?" I asked the child. The house next door had recently sold.

"Yes, the moving truck came today and I didn't want to be over there so when I saw Brandon in the back yard I asked if I could come over and he said that would be alright." I don't think she took a breath before the end of that sentence.

"This is Sivon," Brandon said.

"Can Sivon stay for dinner, Daddy?" Belinda asked.

I looked between the two of them. It was surprising. They had both talked about friends in school, but neither one of them had ever asked to have a guest. It worried me at times. I'm not sure that tight a bond is healthy.

"Well," I looked at Darla.

"Not tonight, kids," she said. "I talked to Sivon's mother. Her name is Christina although she spells it differently." Darla looked a little bit confused. "I've invited you and your parents for a picnic dinner on Sunday evening, Sivon. They said they would come, so we'll all get to know each other then."

"Aw Mom," Brandon said.

"Brandon," She stopped him in mid objection. "Tonight is Charlotte's first night to babysit, and I'll worry more if there is an extra person here."

"Yeahhhhh..." Sivon jumped up and down. "You won, Charlotte."

Charlotte smiled and put her hands on Brandon's shoulders.

"Well, she's not in charge of me, Mom." Veronica didn't sound happy. "I don't need a babysitter."

"No, you don't. You can take care of yourself, but you will still cooperate with Charlotte. She is in charge of the twins. Don't worry,"

Darla said before Veronica could object. "You'll get your turn." Turning to our small guest, she said, "It's time for you to go on home now, Sivon. We won't be here tomorrow, but we'll see you on Sunday."

"Okay." The child bounced to the back door. "It was nice to meet everyone, especially you and Belinda, Brandon. I'm so lucky, not just one kid my age but two." She let the door slam behind her.

"What an extraordinary child." I realized I hadn't done much talking since I'd been home.

"She certainly is." Darla said. I wasn't sure she sounded happy. "Veronica, watch out the back to make sure she gets home alright. You'd better take that shower, David."

"It's so good to see you." Elizabeth hugged Darla and kissed me on the cheek. I put my hand on her shoulder and shook Drew's hand. They had been waiting for us in a booth in a dark quiet corner of the restaurant. The waitress seated us and handed us our menus.

"We don't get together enough," Elizabeth continued. "Drew and I have determined that we will change that."

I looked across the table at my brother's wife. I remembered the first time I'd seen her. I'd wondered why he was so in love. She had brown hair, but not the sparkly cinnamon color that Charlotte had or the honey highlighted brown hair that my mom had. It was truly dishwater brown. Her eyes were somewhere between grey and blue, and her skin was a little bit pasty looking. She was plain. Then she smiled and spoke. Her smile made you forget anything but feeling good, and her voice was a rich and husky. It was mesmerizing.

"I'll hold you to that," I said. "We just get so caught up in things; we forget that family and friends need time too."

"That's right," Darla said. "But we aren't here just as family and friends. You said you'd help us with the twins, and we are in desperate need of help."

"You are not as desperate as you think, Darla," Drew said. "Elizabeth and I agreed with your decision to put the twins in the public school system at first. It might have worked. It might have been the best thing you could do."

"But it wasn't," I said.

"I'm not so sure it wasn't. Every experience we have is just a step toward where we're going. Whatever you and Brandon and Belinda went through was necessary to get you where you are now."

"So, I guess you're saying, let's accept what is behind us and move forward."

"Exactly,"

"I've thought about home schooling. We have a new neighbor, a child the twins' age. I talked to her mother today. She home schools, and she was telling me that there's an association that guides the parents and helps the children get the proper social skills at the same time."

"I'm very encouraged by home schooling. I have a number of children that I see who are having a very good experiencing with it ..." Elizabeth smiled at Darla and there was something in her eyes that told me she didn't think we should home school.

"But ..." I said.

"I don't think it's the right thing to do with your kids. The relationship between the four of you is too strained already. I think it would interfere with their education and their socialization."

"The relationship is strained between me and Belinda," Darla said. She sat back and looked at the empty plate in front of her. "David and Brandon are just fine. David and Belinda are just fine. I'm the one with the problem."

"P. H." I said. "Nobody is attacking you."

"I know that but it's true. I'm the one with the problem."

"And well you should be." Elizabeth reached across the table and put her hand on Darla's. "But it's a family, Darla. If one member has post traumatic stress so does everyone else."

"Post traumatic stress?" Darla looked up, and for the first time in a while, there was hope in her eyes."

"That's right. I shutter when I think about what you went through the night the twins were born. David described it to us when we came to see the babies. I know you and David did some couples therapy, but this is something that you have to deal with inside of you, Darla, and you can't do it alone."

"What is it? What is post traumatic stress?"

"In short," Elizabeth said. "It's an anxiety condition caused by being exposed to a near death experience. It doesn't have to be your own death. It could be watching a loved one die, or it could be the near death of a loved one. We see it in a lot of war veterans but, it happens in everyday life too. What you went through that day, on top of the nine months of a very difficult pregnancy, was enough to traumatize anyone."

"So I didn't just go crazy." Darla was whispering. I put my arm across her shoulders and pulled her close to me. "I thought I had gone crazy." She still whispered, but we all heard.

"No," Drew said. "You suffered terribly. You've handled it better than a lot of us would have."

"What about Belinda? She's an eight year old that worries about everything. She's a nervous wreck. It scares me to death." I said.

Darla looked at me startled. "It's because of me, David. I haven't given her the love and support a mother should give her child. We all know that."

"Give yourself a break, Darla," Drew said. "This isn't your fault. Your relationship with Belinda goes two ways just like with everyone else."

"What do you mean?"

"Belinda is suffering from post traumatic stress too." Darla just stared across the table. She and I moved slightly apart, and we both looked at Elizabeth as she continued.

"We have become aware in psychology that infants, even fetuses, are more aware of their surroundings than we had originally thought. I have a couple of articles I'll email to you so you can understand better.

"I'm going to describe to you what Belinda went through in the birth process. It seems brutal, but Drew and I have talked about it and we agree that you need to understand. Do you want to order dinner and talk about it another time? I hate to ruin the first time we've seen each other in months."

"No, I need to hear it now," Darla said. "What about you, David?" She looked up at me and again I saw hope. I realized that she'd taken on a look of defeat since the twins were born. Her eyes still looked sad, but there was hope behind the sadness.

"Please go on," I said. "But I think I'll order a martini and a starter. Would that be alright?" I looked at Darla.

"Yes, I'll have a martini too."

When we had ordered and our drinks had been brought out. I leaned back and looked across at my brother and his wife. "I love you, Drew," I said. "I wish we'd grown up together."

"I feel the same way, but that is a subject for another day."

"That's right," I smiled. "Please go on, Elizabeth." I looked down at Darla she was looking into the swirling clear liquid in her glass.

She looked up at the silence. She looked at me then across the table. "Yes, please go on."

"We've noticed a trend with c-section babies in our research. It doesn't seem to happen in planned c-sections; but if labor has started, and the surgery is an emergency procedure, the children seem to be predisposed to certain anxiety disorders. They have a fear of failure. As a result they struggle for perfection, and they don't like to finish things. Theoretically that is because they weren't able to finish the birth process."

"Brandon doesn't have anxiety ..." Darla said.

"No, all babies don't, but Belinda was the one trying to get into the birth canal. Once labor starts it is instinctive for them to try to be born. They turn and push their heads into the birth canal."

"Only she couldn't get there," Darla whispered.

"Then she was abruptly pulled from the warmth of the womb and the comfort of her brother. We've seen ultrasound pictures of twins holding each other in the womb, and I know without doubt that Brandon and Belinda did. Their bond didn't form at birth," Elizabeth said.

"Then," It was Darla speaking now, in a whisper. "We held her for a few minutes, and they took her away and put her in an incubator. She was too small to stay with me. I wouldn't have been any good to her if she could have. She was abandoned. I didn't even visit her in the hospital. Oh God, David, our baby," She turned and buried her head in my chest. I put my arms around her. "I didn't know," she said.

"How could you know, Darla," Drew said. He reached across the table and put his hand on hers. Elizabeth sat silently as our starters were placed before us. The waiter didn't wait to take our dinner order but hurried away.

"I need to go home." Darla pulled away for me and looked for her purse under the table. "I need to see Belinda."

"I understand," Elizabeth said.

As Darla pulled her purse from under the table my cell phone rang. I answered it.

"Dad," It was Charlotte. "Everything is fine, don't worry." She said it quickly knowing, I'm sure, that her call had sent chills up my spine. "The twins wanted to say goodnight and tell you they're fine. Here's Brandon."

"Daddy," My son's voice piped over the phone. "Charlotte let us play computer games and I won twice. I'm fine I didn't have a seizure. Now we're going to bed after Charlotte and me walk Harry."

"That's great, son," I said.

"Can I talk to Mom?"

"Alright," I handed the phone to Darla.

She listened to Brandon's excited voice then said. "I love you, Brandon." I could hear through the phone when he said he loved her back.

"Can I speak to Belinda?" Darla asked. She wiped her nose and eyes with her napkin in an effort not to sniff. She listened in silence while Belinda said that Brandon was fine and she said goodnight. As usual her voice was more subdued than her brother's and her conversation was about his well being. I could hear it through the phone.

"I love you, Belinda," Darla said. There was silence on the other end of the line. "I love you, baby," Darla said stifling a sob and Belinda said. "I love you too, Mom." Darla handed the phone to me and buried her face in her napkin.

"Brandon is fine, Daddy," Belinda said. "Is Mom okay?"

"She's fine. Are you fine too, Beeda?" I asked.

"Of course I am."

"How about Veronica?" I asked. I thought it would deflect some of the feelings flying around. We hadn't spoken to Veronica.

"She's in her room. I think she's mad at Charlotte, but they aren't yelling or anything."

"Good," I said. "Go to bed when Charlotte tells you to. Goodnight."

When I hung up the phone all four of us used our napkins to dry our eyes.

"I think I can eat dinner after all," Darla said. Her eyes were glistening with tears and full of hope.

That night I checked the twins, borrowed Harry, and took my midnight walk. When I returned I started toward my office to work on an album I'd begun when the twin's started school. I looked into our bedroom at the empty bed and felt sad. Darla had stopped sleeping with me again.

I looked in the direction of the stairs to the garage room. You could see them across the open foyer. There was no light coming from under the door. Darla was probably asleep. I turned toward my office again then swiveled back around.

"What the hell," I said out loud. "I'll wake her up."

I glanced into the twin's room again on the way by. Harry had resumed his place at the foot of Brandon's bed, and the heavy, even breathing that came from Belinda's bed told me that she was asleep.

I crept quietly up the stairs and opened the door. I could see the form of her body under the sheet on the bed. She'd thrown off the blanket. We were only mid forties, but she had already complained of hot flashes. I hoped it wasn't too late for what I wanted to ask her.

I took off my clothes and slid under the sheet and up next to her. I slid my hand over her bare hip, smiling to find her naked. She put her hand on mine.

"David?"

"Who else would it be?" I whispered. She turned and I kissed her mouth.

"Let me brush my teeth," she said.

"No need." I kissed her again and slid my hands along the sides of her body. Her arms came around my neck. Her knees slid up on either side of me and I rested between them.

"Darla," I whispered. "Let's have another baby."

She stiffened and arched her back, pushing me slightly away from her with her thighs. Then she relaxed and I entered her gently. I kissed her neck and she slid back and forth, her warmth gliding over me. We rocked together silently looking into each other's eyes. She rolled me over and mounted me without breaking contact. Then I watched the muscles in her thighs as she rose and fell above me. We came together. Her head fell back and she shuddered as I closed my eyes in climax.

She leaned down to my chest and kissed my jaw. "We can't," she whispered. "I had my tubes tied when the twins were born. Remember?"

"Oh yeah," I stroked her hair. Her head was on my chest and she lay beside me now. "What were we thinking?"

"We thought we'd had enough kids."

We lay in silence for a minute. "We could adopt," I said.

She propped herself up on her elbow and looked closely at me. I smiled up at her. "You're serious aren't you?" she said. "David, you were the one that wanted to stop at two."

"That was before I'd ever had any kids. Now I want a dozen."

"You love being a father, don't you?"

"Yes, I do."

She lay down on her back and we stared at the ceiling together. "I'm maxed out, David. I don't want to adopt."

"I guess I expected you to say that. I guess I'm maxed too." I kissed her cheek and rolled over to sit up on the side of the bed. "Maybe I was just trying to find an excuse for you to sleep with me again."

She didn't say anything as I gathered my clothes from the floor. I pulled on my underwear and t-shirt and picked up my pants and shoes.

"David," she said as I reached the door. "Why don't you sleep here with me tonight?" I looked back at her then at the closed door. "The kids will find us if they need us," she said.

I did sleep with her that night. We made love again in the morning when her alarm went off to start the busy day.

"Why did you sleep upstairs, Dad?" Brandon asked at the breakfast table.

"Just for fun," I said.

"I can't remember the last time I was this nervous," I said as I put a steaming pan of banana bread French toast down on the buffet table Uncle Jeff had set up in front of the fountain display at the nursery. There were tables set up around the patio display with cloths and knives and forks. I had baked two hundred muffins that morning and the day before. There was fruit compote and fruit salad. Besides the French toast there was a vegetable frittata and a large pan of chicken sausage. I smiled at the smells that came from the table and from the open window of the apartment above.

"I hope there's enough," I said to Uncle Jeff as he unfolded another chair.

"There better be enough," he snapped. "I gave you enough money for supplies."

"Whoa, this isn't a good day for you to be grumpy." I looked at him and saw unusual frown lines between his brows. "Are you nervous too, or is something wrong? It isn't like you to be rattled about something like this."

"I am not rattled about a stupid open house, David. I've been in this business for a long time. It's not the first time I've done this." He turned and stormed toward his office. He hit the door with the palm of his hand, and I could hear it bounce off the wall behind. I looked at my uncle's partner as she came around the corner.

She walked toward me looking concerned. "He's been like that all morning. We'll be opening the doors pretty soon. I hope he can keep from offending any customers."

Alice came through the door carrying paper plates and napkins. "He's been like that ever since he got up this morning," she said. "I think he and Mom had a fight. I heard raised voices coming from their room last night. He's been miserable all morning. I tried to talk to him, but he bit me so I quit trying."

"Yeah," Evelyn said. She was right behind Alice carrying plastic glasses and champagne flutes for mimosas. "He snapped at me while we were putting together the garden displays."

"That's unusual," Alice said. "It isn't strange for him to snap at me, but he never gets upset with Ev." She turned to her sister. "He didn't hurt your feelings, did he?" I was surprised at her concern. Where was the sibling rivalry between these two?

"I'll try to talk to him," I said heading toward the closed office door. I turned back and said. "If I don't come out in ten minutes, come in after me." We all laughed and I knocked on the door.

He didn't answer so I eased it opened. Uncle Jeff sat at his desk looking out his office window at the cars gathering in the parking lot. "I'm sorry, David," he said without turning around. "I shouldn't have snapped at you like that. I'm sure you are nervous. You told me you'd never cooked for so many people before."

"It's okay." I came into the room and sat down in the chair across the desk from him. He continued to look out the window. "Do you want to tell me what's bothering you?"

He was silent for so long that I wondered if I should repeat my question. Then he turned the swivel chair and looked at me across the desk. "I got up at about midnight last night. I was thirsty. I thought I'd just go down to the kitchen and get some lemonade. There is nothing like a glass of lemonade to quench your thirst in the middle of the night." He didn't say anything else, just looked at me.

"Were you out of lemonade?" I asked.

"No, I forgot about the lemonade when I passed the window on the stairs. You know that goldfish pond that you can see from that window?"

"Yeah,"

"There was a full moon last night. It was lit pretty brightly."

"Yeah," I said, wondering where we were going with this.

"Sitting on that lovely stone bench beside the fountain was James Parnell, Jr. and he was kissing my youngest daughter."

"Oh," I said. I could feel myself squirming in my chair. "Evelyn is only a few minutes younger than Alice." Why did I say that?

"That's not the point." He stared at me again. First he looked intent then realization dawned. He leaned back and took a deep breath. "You knew about this and you didn't say anything to me. How long has this been going on?"

"Uncle Jeff, I didn't know anything was going on. I mean I'm sure nothing is going on." I took a deep breath to try to stop saying stupid things. "Jimmy told me a few days ago that he thought James, Jr. had a crush on Evelyn. He's been teaching her tennis. I'm sure it's all very innocent."

He stared at me and his features relaxed just a little.

"Uncle Jeff, they're beautiful girls. I'm sure that's not the first time she's been kissed. You had to be prepared for that to happen eventually."

He turned back to look out the window. "That's what Amanda said, but he's too old for her. He's got to be twenty two years old, at least."

"He's twenty three, and you're right, he is too old for her, but he's a good boy. He knows he's too old. He won't take advantage of her innocence."

"That's what Amanda said."

"What else did Amanda say?" I asked.

"She reminded me that I'm five years older than she is. But if Jamie is twenty three that makes him six years older than Evelyn."

"I know when both of their birthdays are, and I think it's more like five and a half."

He looked at me. His features relaxed and he rubbed his eyes with both hands. "You do see that five years difference doesn't matter in your forties and fifties. It's a lot different in the teens and twenties." His voice was muted from speaking through his hands.

"It is different, and with my own girls right behind yours, I can understand the way you feel. But Uncle Jeff, I don't think there's anything you can do but trust her, trust him."

He lowered his hands to his cheeks and looked at me over his fingertips. "That's what Amanda said."

"Amanda is pretty smart." I smiled and stood up. "I guess you didn't say anything to Evelyn. She couldn't explain your bad mood any better than the rest of us."

"What could I say? Ev, honey, I spied on you necking with your boyfriend last night."

"So you feel a little bad about it?"

"Yeah, I just wish I'd gone to the bathroom for a cup of water."

"Well, I made too many muffins," I said to Alice as we surveyed the empty buffet table. It was 2:00 and all the food was gone but the muffins, and there were about fifty left. The nursery would be open until 5:00 pm, but Uncle Jeff had suggested that we start cleaning up from brunch.

"That's not a problem," she said. "I plan to sell them at the coffee stand that Victoria and Dad always have during the week. We're on our way, David. This was a great success."

I looked at her beaming face. "We're on our way?"

"I hope you've been thinking about my suggestion," she said as we folded the table cloth together.

"Actually, with the twins changing schools and Charlotte in the band and Veronica playing soccer, I haven't had time to think about it. You said we had time. You won't start culinary school for almost a year. Then it's two years before you're finished. We have time."

"I want to get the kitchen renovated before I finish, and I hope to have you opened for breakfast by the end of next year. Once you get things started it'll be easy for me to move into a lunch and dinner schedule."

"Wait a minute, Alice. You didn't say anything about getting started in a year. I have a job already. I love my job."

She was tying a garbage bag to take to the dumpster. She stopped and looked at me. "Do you love your job, David?"

"Yes, I do." I looked back at her. She just stood there silently. "I do love my job," I said.

"… but,"

"I do love my job."

"… but,"

I took a deep breath and went to the other garbage can to tie the bag and remove it. When I had finished I looked at my cousin. She was still watching me.

"You're right," I said. "Why are you so smart?"

"I'm smart, but I also know you better than most people do. I think you and I are a little alike. I've seen that look on your face. You're restless. You looked like that about a year before Brandon and Belinda were born. I'm guessing Darla doesn't want any more kids."

"Alice!" I turned feeling my face flame. "What are you doing, spying on me?"

"I don't have to spy on you, David. I know you. You're ready for a change. You're ready for a new challenge."

I turned to begin folding the tables. I worked silently until they were all folded and stacked in the classroom. I thought about Alice and a restaurant. My eyes kept going to the window of the kitchen in the upstairs apartment.

"You're making plans for the kitchen aren't you?"

I looked at Alice and laughed.

"It's going to be so fun," she said. "We'll all work together. You and me upstairs, Dad and Evelyn right down here."

I didn't say anything.

"Come on, David," Alice said.

"I'll need to talk to Darla about it. If it isn't alright with her it won't happen."

"She won't have a problem."

A gust of cold air came through the door to the growing yard. I looked to see who had come in. Evelyn and James, Jr. stood in the doorway looking at each other. No question about it. They were seriously attracted. My heart started to pound a little at the memory of first love. They walked together toward Uncle Jeff's office. The nursery was crowded. Uncle Jeff had been on the floor until just a few minutes ago. I had a pretty good idea why they were going there. I wondered how it would go.

"I guess she's finally going to tell him," Alice said.

"Tell him what?" I asked. My sincerity sounded false even to me.

"They've been dating ever since about her third tennis lesson. She's in love with him, and I'm pretty sure he feels the same way." I looked at her. There was something about her expression that worried me.

"You don't sound happy about it."

"I am ..." She paused. Her voice had broken a little. I think she was trying not to cry. I put my arm around her shoulders. She put hers around my waist and buried her face in my shirt. I could feel her struggle as she collected herself.

"He won't try to come between you I'm sure. He knows how close you and Evelyn are."

"I know." She sniffed and pushed away from me to wipe her eyes. "What a cry baby. I don't know why it upsets me so much."

"There isn't anything wrong with your feelings, Alice." She looked up at me and smiled. A customer touched her arm and asked her a question. She moved off to help her, and I looked at the closed door to Uncle Jeff's office. Then I went to the stairs to the apartment. I wanted to have a look at that kitchen.

✦

"I guess it's a good thing we aren't having another baby," I said to Darla that night after dinner. Charlotte and Veronica were in their rooms doing homework and the twins had gone to bed. We always enjoyed a couple of hours together in the evening before we went to our separate offices.

"I think it is, David. We aren't getting any younger and we have a long way to go with the kids we have."

"We do and I'm not sure what kind of a toll the dating stage is going to take on me, on us."

"Why do you say that? Is one of the girls dating and nobody told me?"

"No," I laughed. "But James, Jr. and Evelyn are dating. I know she's seventeen years old, but it still took me by surprise."

"I knew they had an interest in each other. Meryl told me. I didn't realize it had gone as far as dating. Meryl was worried about the age difference."

"So was Uncle Jeff. Apparently he saw them in an intimate embrace, and until that he'd had no idea. He thought Jamie was just teaching her tennis."

"Poor Uncle Jeff, that must have been upsetting."

"He was in a foul mood in the morning. Then Jamie and Evelyn went into his office to talk to him about mid afternoon, and he seemed to relax a little bit after that. I hate to admit it, but I was eaten up with curiosity about what went on. I didn't feel like I could ask."

"I guess not." Darla stretched her arms and lay down on the couch with her head on a pillow. "So the brunch went well I guess. It looked like you were doing pretty well when Charlotte and I came by at noon."

"It went great. I made too many muffins, but I'll learn how to estimate better with practice."

"What do you mean practice?" She sat up and looked at me. "Are you thinking about opening a catering business or something?"

"Or something," I said. "Alice has this crazy idea. Uncle Jeff calls it a crazy idea but I'm intrigued."

Darla looked at me. She tilted her head and said. "Tell me about the crazy idea."

"Alice is going to culinary school," I said. "She wants to open a restaurant in the apartment above the nursery. She's even talking about serving in the patio around the pond and fountain display."

"Sounds great to me," Darla said. She looked me in the eye. "Why is that a crazy idea?"

I stopped and looked around the room. "You're right. It isn't a crazy idea. The thing is, she wants me to join her in the venture."

She pursed her lips and looked back at me. "Explain," she said.

"She wants me to start the place with breakfast during the week and brunch on Sunday. She wants me to oversee building the kitchen out to serve a café and start the place up in the mornings. Then she plans to do lunch and dinner when she gets out of school."

Darla didn't say anything. She just looked at me.

"She doesn't really want to go to culinary school. She's just doing it to make Uncle Jeff happy."

Darla still said nothing. I waited, but the silence became too much.

"Say something, P. H.," I said. "I have to admit it sounds like fun to me."

"I thought you were happy at the magazine," she said finally.

"I am," I said. I put my hands on my eyes and remembered Uncle Jeff doing the same thing earlier. "I am."

The room was silent. I squirmed and peaked through my fingers. Darla met my eyes. "David," she said. "I know it isn't fair for you to work when I don't, but when I proposed to you, I told you I wanted you to support me. That hasn't changed."

"I know." I lowered my hands and looked at her. "I'll always support you."

"I mean financially. David, we have four children. The twins are doing well in their private school. I know Drew is your brother and my cousin, but we can't ask him to do it for free, and the older girls will be going away to college soon. I work hard at my scrapbook business, but it only gives me spare money for gifts and stuff. I can't pay for their school."

"I wouldn't do anything that would make me unable to support my family. Come on, P. H., you know I wouldn't do that."

She took a deep breath and crossed the room to sit on the arm of my chair. "You're right. I'm sorry I doubted you. So you think you can do this and still support the family?"

I put my arm around her waist. "I own part of the magazine. I know you never wanted to know the details of my work or the finances, but one of the incentives of working for Jane is that she's given me interest in the magazine as it progressed. She couldn't pay me a lot at first. I won't lose that interest, and I'll continue to work there on a consulting basis. It'll still provide income. I love it. It's been a very good place for me."

"What about the overhead on the café?"

"We own the property. I mean Uncle Jeff does. He'd do this for Alice anyway. He'd do it for me anyway. I think we can make a go of it. I really do." She put her arm on my shoulder. I leaned my head against her. "I've planned well for the kids' educations. I promise they'll have what they need."

"And you'll have what you need," she said.

I looked up at her. "I won't think about it anymore, Darla, if it isn't alright with you."

"It's alright with me, David," she said and stood. I stood with her and put my arms around her. She hugged me for a minute then pulled away.

"I have an album to finish tonight." She turned and headed for the stairs to the room above the garage. "I'll see you in the morning."

"All set," Uncle Jeff said. It was the second week of summer break and we were going to the Trail in Maine. Uncle Jeff and I were going. Dad and Drew were going. Alice and Evelyn were going too. Charlotte had decided at the last minute to go and Veronica always came with us. Brandon was making his second trip. The twins had started backpacking later than the older girls had. Darla'd had a hard time letting Brandon go with his problems. Belinda hadn't wanted to start without him.

I looked back at the front porch of the house and said. "I'm just not sure I can do it." Brandon sat on the step next to Belinda. His arm was around her. She was dressed in her pajamas, and Darla stood next to the two of them. Belinda was crying, and Brandon was saying something into her ear.

"David," Uncle Jeff said. "I told you we could put it off, or we could just skip it this year."

I looked at him. He was smiling in that supportive way I'd known all my life. "No," I said. "If I don't go and take Brandon, Darla will think I don't trust her to take care of Belinda. I just feel bad that Belinda is sick and can't come with us." I looked back at my tiny daughter. She was still smaller than all the kids in the family. She was brilliant, but physically she was tiny and delicate health wise.

"You aren't even a little bit concerned about the relationship between them?"

I looked at him. "You know I am, but Darla is her mother. I have to trust her." I took a deep breath. "Remember, I trusted her when she took my son into the night and left a note that she was going to kill them both." I dropped my chin to my chest and breathed. I hadn't thought about that for a long time.

Uncle Jeff put his hand on my shoulder and I felt the comfort from it. "I'm just worried about the toll this will take on you."

"Hey," I smiled. "Look at the group of people I'm going with." I looked back at the truck and the van that Dad used as a mobile groom shop. He had removed the equipment for the trip to the air field. "I'll forget the worry as soon as we're in the air." I looked back at Darla as she hugged Brandon and sat down on the porch next to Belinda. "I do trust her, you know. They've been in therapy together for months now. They still have their ups and downs, but overall, things are improving."

"Dad, Brandon," Veronica called from the cab of the truck. "Come on, let's go. Sam is waiting at the airfield. We want to get to the bed and breakfast before too late. We'll need to get dinner and get to bed early so we can start first thing in the morning."

I looked down as I felt Brandon take my hand. "Come on, Dad. Don't drag this out. The women are crying." He smiled up at me. His expression held appropriate concern for his mother and sister, but he also looked genuinely excited about the trip ahead. I looked back one more time to see the backs of my wife and daughter. Darla had her arm around Belinda's shoulders. She kissed the top of her head as they disappeared into the house.

"I trust them both," I whispered.

"Me too," Brandon said as he pulled me toward the van where we would ride with Dad and Drew. Uncle Jeff had all the girls.

"It's just us guys in this car," Brandon said as he jumped into the middle seat of the van. Harry leaped into the back seat and I sat beside Brandon. He pulled a tissue from his pocket and dried the right side of his mouth. I smiled as he tucked it back in. Belinda was with us in spirit.

"I feel bad for Nuncle Jeff." Brandon could speak pretty clearly now. He'd been in speech therapy since he was six years old. But *Nuncle Jeff* had become an endearment. Even the girls called him *Nuncle Jeff*.

"All those women," Brandon said. "I hope they don't get carsick."

"From what I hear it's your Dad that gets carsick," Drew said.

"Not since I came along." Brandon stuck his bony elbow into my side and I grunted. "I won't let him go to sleep."

"No you won't, and I appreciate it very much." I put my arm around him and rubbed my knuckles on his head. "I hope someone does that for Vroom. She has the same problem."

"I told Charlotte to. I think Evelyn will help too. She and Vronie have backpacked together for a long time." Brandon chattered. He had a tendency to nick name like his old man.

"I was surprised Charlotte wanted to come," I said. "Alice too, they haven't been interested in the Appalachian hikes. They usually only do overnights."

"I asked Alice about that," Dad said. "We're getting near the end. Only thirty more miles and we'll do fifteen of them on this trip. I think they'll come next year too. Like crossing the finish means they did the whole Trail." He laughed.

"I'm gonna do the whole trail," Brandon said. "Me and Sivon already talked about it."

"Sivon and I already talked about it." I corrected his grammar.

"Sivon already told you?" He looked at me innocently.

"No, I was telling you how to say that correctly."

"Oh." He looked confused for a minute then looked out the window excited as we pulled up to the airfield. Dad parked the van, and we all jumped out and started loading our backpacking supplies into the plane.

I thought about our conversation while we worked. Sivon had been a regular guest at our house since that first meeting. At this point she had become a member of the household. She went home to eat dinner with her parents and slept there most of the time. She was homeschooled, so her mother spent a lot of time with her. But there were many weekend nights that she ate and slept with us. She always slept in the guest room. It was almost like she had moved into it. She even had posters on the wall and a dry erase board that she wrote notes and phone numbers on. She'd been very respectful and asked permission for this.

Darla and the twins had all agreed that Sivon should have her own room. We had plans to move Belinda into it when we and her therapist deemed it time to try to separate them. I wondered if Sivon having already occupied it would cause a problem. It made me nervous to even think about the separation process. Anyway, Sivon had bonded completely with both twins and had very gratifying and supportive relationships with them. I don't know if I was completely comfortable with this, but I couldn't help but be impressed by it. Neither Darla or I had managed to develop relationships with either of them that didn't carry at least some baggage. Our therapists assured us it was understandable.

"Earth to Dad," I looked in the direction of the voice. It was Veronica who would turn fifteen next month. She stood five foot ten inches tall. In other words, I didn't have to look down very much to talk to her. Her sister at age sixteen was six feet tall.

"You were off in never never land, Dad," she said and took my arm to pull me toward the airplane. "We're all loaded and ready for takeoff. You'll forget about Mom and Belinda once we're in the air."

"That's right," Charlotte said. "Trust me, Dad. Mom won't kill her no matter how much of a brat she is. Mom is trying to prove something here."

"I wasn't thinking about them," I said. I sounded guilty, but the truth was, I hadn't been thinking about them. "And Belinda is not a brat."

"Not from your perspective I guess," Veronica said. She and Charlotte and Brandon all laughed.

I looked at the three of them. I wanted to defend my tiny, dimple cheeked daughter, but their expressions were benevolent. I could see that they cared about her.

"She is not a brat," I said again as I climbed into the airplane. Harry jumped into my lap and I buried my face in his furry neck. "Belinda just has a lot going on."

✦

We had hiked most of the Trail since Pennsylvania in the summer. It was cool in the northern states in the spring. Not only that, but most of the northern states closed the Trail in the spring. It was the most vulnerable season because of the melting snow.

The hikes had been pretty easy for the past few states. Pennsylvania had the description of "where boots go to die." It was true. I had worn out two pairs of hiking boots. The ground was very rocky. It was not hard to hike though. Most of the Trail was along ridges.

New Jersey was not too difficult. There was considerable bear activity there. We had seen three on our trips. Two when Uncle Jeff and Dad and I were without the kids. On one trip Evelyn and Veronica were along. You should have seen that bear running away at the sound of their screams. There were metal bear proof garbage cans at all the shelters. We didn't use the shelters. We preferred to camp, so we hung our packs in trees far from our campsites.

New York had very little elevation change, but it was a pretty hard hike anyway. It had a number of short but nearly vertical ledges with very sheer drops. It made me very nervous to see the girls on those parts of the trial. I insisted that they wear rock climbing gear. They objected loudly, but in the end they indulged me.

Uncle Jeff and I did Connecticut in three days. It has only 52 miles of the Trail. We were by ourselves that time and we got through a good bit of Massachusetts as well. I loved having my family with me on the Trail, but I have to admit, those hikes with just the two of us were nice.

It took a couple of years to get through Vermont and New Hampshire. There was more of the Trail in those states, and toward the end in New Hampshire the terrain became very difficult as we entered Maine. Maine is considered by most hikers as the most difficult part of the Trail. At the start you have to go over a series of boulders that lasts at least a mile. This is considered the Trail's hardest mile.

The Trail also crosses a river at a point that is two miles wide. We had to cross in a boat. There was also a long stretch of wilderness. It was called the "100 mile Wilderness" and is the most remote section of the trial.

We had seen a moose on Brandon and Belinda's first trip. It was the first time I'd ever seen Brandon get really mad at his sisters, Belinda and Veronica, Evelyn too. He'd had his camera out of his pack in a second, but he'd only got a shot of the moose's rear end as it ran from their screams.

Neither of the twins got homesick on that trip. As always they were fine if they were together.

I looked at our campsite the next day. We had hiked five miles. Our plan had been to do seven the first day, but it started to rain, and we decided to stop and pitch the tents before we got too wet. We found a flat spot on the top of a hill so the water ran away from the tents.

All four girls were sleeping in a three man tent. I was a little worried especially since my girls were so big. But Uncle Jeff's girls were as small as mine were big. Maybe they wouldn't be too crowded.

Uncle Jeff and Brandon and I were in another tent, with Harry, of course. Dad and Drew had a tent of their own. I smiled. Things had changed since it was just Uncle Jeff and me.

We had all piled into our tents for a couple of hours to wait out the rain. I could hear the girls chattering in theirs. Dad and Drew were quiet. I suspected they were reading. They had both brought their electronic readers. They were very proud of their new gadgets. Brandon had fallen asleep with Harry curled beside him, and Uncle Jeff dozed beside them.

The rain stopped, and I went outside to see if I could gather some wood that wasn't too wet for a campfire. The sun was going down, and I thought it would be nice to have some supper over a fire. The fallen trees and branches that were buried beneath enough leaves were fairly dry.

Chapter Twenty Three

When the fire first lit the water snapped and popped, but eventually the wood started.

I looked up as Brandon and Harry emerged from the tent. Brandon was crying and Harry looked very concerned.

"What's up, son?" I asked as he came over to me. He wrapped his arms around my waist and buried his face in my shirt. I picked him up and sat down on a tree stump that I had put a dry pad on. He curled into my lap and I rocked back and forth. Harry wined and I stroked his blond head.

"I miss Binda," he said. "I want to go home."

The twins had backpacked with me for three years now. Neither of them had ever gotten homesick. Even Brandon, as tightly bonded as he was with Darla, was fine as long as they were together.

"I'm sure she misses you too, Bran, but we can't go home now. We've got three more days."

"I want to go home," he cried and a new wave of sobs began. Uncle Jeff came out of the tent. I saw the flaps of the other tents open and the tentative faces of our fellow campers peeked out.

"I've never seen you get homesick before, Brandon," Uncle Jeff said. Standing beside us, he put his hand on Brandon's back.

"I'm not homesick." He sniffled. "I'm Binda sick."

"I know how you feel, Brandon," Evelyn came out of the tent with Alice right behind her. "When I go on these trips without Alice I get Alice sick."

"And I get Ev sick," Alice said.

Uncle Jeff smiled up at his daughters. "It's the twin thing," he said as my Dad approached nodding his head.

"Most of the people here understand how you feel, Brandon. This is a crowd full of twins."

I looked down at my son. His sniffles were drying up, and he pulled the tissue out of his pocket to dry his eyes and wipe the side of his mouth. I was always amazed at how easily he displayed his emotions. He wasn't at all self conscious.

"How do you cure it?" he asked.

"You can't cure it," Evelyn said. "But you can distract yourself with something you like to do. I get out my book on plants and try to identify the local flora."

"I don't read that good," Brandon said.

"You don't have to do that," Alice said. "Did you bring your sketch pad and pencils? You love to draw."

"Yeah, I brought em." He jumped up and ran toward the tent. He stopped about halfway and ran back. He put his arms around my neck and kissed my cheek then hurried to the tent to get his treasures.

"Thanks, guys," I said. "I'm not sure I could have handled that myself. I'm not a twin."

"Yeah, it must be a twin thing," Charlotte said. "I've never been Veronica sick."

"I've never missed you either," Veronica said and they walked toward the stream at the bottom of the hill. They were laughing and chattering as they went. They might not be twins but the sister bond was pretty tight.

Alice watched Brandon until he was in the tent ruffling through his pack. She turned back and smiled at Evelyn. "Let's go to the creek with the cousins," she said and the two girls hurried off.

"Well, I'm not a twin either," Drew said. "But I spent most of my life being David sick." He slapped me on the back. "I think I'll join the girls at the stream. There's a trail along it I'd like to explore."

"Bring them back before dark." I called after him.

"I'm going with them," Dad said. "I'll make sure they get back before dark."

I looked across the fire at Uncle Jeff. He was sitting on another stump and was stirring the flames. He must have felt me looking at him because he looked up and smiled.

"David," he said. "I know it isn't right to ask someone about their therapy. I've tried not to, but …"

"Uncle Jeff, you can ask me anything. If I don't want to tell you about it I'll say so."

He didn't say anything, but the way he looked at me made me laugh. "What do you want to know?"

"I'm not asking about yours or the couple's therapy you and Darla have. I just wondered about Darla and Belinda. I know things have been rough between them. Is it really possible to bridge that gap?"

"I'm hopeful. It really has been an interesting process. Apparently, there is a problem with caesarian births, especially if labor has started and the fetus has moved into the birth canal. I'm not a doctor, but from what the therapist and Elizabeth explained, the baby actually goes through an instinctive process to be born. If that process has been started and then is interrupted by surgery, the child is frustrated and there's trauma."

"So," he said. "If the C-section was planned and the mother never went into labor, it wouldn't be a problem."

"It doesn't seem to be."

"What about Brandon? I don't think he has any trauma." He smiled and looked in the direction of my son. Brandon had put his plastic pad down on the edge of the hill and sat busily sketching something he was looking at below. Harry sat beside him scratching behind his ear and looking in the direction Brandon was looking.

"No, I don't know. Maybe it's the brain damage or maybe it's because he was never in the birth canal. Belinda was trying to get there, but Brandon's foot was in the way." I laughed.

"How bad is the brain damage?" Uncle Jeff was still watching Brandon. "I remember at the time they said we wouldn't know until he had developed a little."

"Well, outwardly you can hardly tell. He drools a little out of the right side of his mouth. Belinda insists that he carry a tissue, and he has become very good at not letting it build up. He walks with a limp. The left brain controls the right side so it didn't develop quite as well as the left. The left brain is where the damage is. He can't read much at all and math is a complete bust. But he's brilliant at social studies. I mean, he retains information like history, literature. He can't read it, but you can get most of that stuff on CD these days. He can spin a tale and with voice activated word processing I think eventually he'll be able to write. Not with his hands though. I mean he writes beautifully, but it's really just a sketch of letters. He can't read it."

"Obviously he's very artistic. How are the seizures? Is there any chance he'll grow out of them?"

"It doesn't seem likely." I shook my head. "We didn't put him on medication when he was young because we didn't want to interfere with his development, but we have him on a new medication now. It doesn't interfere with his development. He still has seizures, but they aren't as often or as severe. They were never too severe anyway."

We watched Brandon in silence for a minute. He turned and saw us. He waved and turned back to his work. Harry licked him on the face and he giggled. The little dog jumped up then and ran down the hill out of sight.

"So do you think you would mind describing the therapy process for Belinda? I mean you don't have to tell me anything personal just the theory."

I looked back at him and smiled. "Uncle Jeff, I don't mind telling you much of anything."

"Good,"

"At first Darla and I both went. Well, at first Brandon and Darla and I went with Belinda. But right away the therapist said that Brandon didn't need to come. Maybe that could be the start of teaching them to be separated from time to time."

"So then it was you and Darla and Belinda."

"That's right. There were games and exercises that we did to simulate the birth process. I think it was to try to help her feel that she had completed it. I thought it was silly at first. You know, Dr. Alvarez had Darla and me form a tunnel on our hands and knees for Belinda to crawl through. It seemed really stupid, especially given the difference in our sizes." I laughed and Uncle Jeff laughed too.

"But the first time Belinda tried to crawl through it she got just past Darla's hip and collapsed to the floor in tears. Darla and I both scrambled to pick her up. We wanted to stop the tears, but Dr. Alvarez said it was important to let her cry. The tears meant that we were dealing with a memory."

"So did she ever get through the tunnel?"

"She did but it took a while. After a few months we had completed all the exercises, and Dr. Alvarez said it was time for Darla and Belinda to work together without me. I felt a little rejected at first, but in my own therapy I realized that my relationship with Belinda was pretty good. I can't really tell you about what goes on with Belinda and Darla in therapy. I can tell you that they're making progress."

"I'm glad, David."

"I'm starved," Brandon said as he approached us and handed me his sketch pad.

I looked at the drawing. "You never cease to amaze me, kid," I said. It was a drawing of the stream below the campsite. In the middle of the stream standing on a rock was a perfect likeness of Belinda. She was looking up and waving, I guess at Brandon. Harry was standing on the bank of the stream. He was looking in her direction, his tail flung to the side in a wag. "Look at this, Uncle Jeff." I handed the pad to him.

"I guess you've got her with you now, haven't you, Brandon?" he said.

"Yeah," he smiled and my heart thumped.

The next day we hiked eight miles. The terrain was very rough. We were all tired at the end. We made up for lost time with the rain and tent confinement of the day before. We stopped for lunch and ate sandwiches and chips next to a pond. There were loons swimming on it, and we could see fish beneath the surface. There was a log in the middle covered with turtles. It was a beautiful spot. Then we hiked another four miles to a campsite next to another stream. No one in the crowd had a problem with running water anymore. I smiled at the memory.

"What's the problem, Jeff?" I looked up when I heard the concern in Dad's voice. The kids and Drew had gone for a walk by the stream. It had become their evening routine.

Chapter Twenty Three

Uncle Jeff sat on a log rubbing his right knee. "I don't know. My knee's been giving me trouble lately. It was hurting for the last couple of miles today. That's the first time it's hurt just from walking. It's usually only when I stoop and stand."

"I noticed you were limping a little." Dad sat down beside him. "Roll up your pants and let me see it."

"You're not a doctor. You're a lawyer." Uncle Jeff pushed him with his elbow. "Leave it alone. It'll be fine in the morning."

"I'm not a lawyer anymore. I'm a pet groomer. Let me see your knee."

"Neither of those things qualifies you to look at my knee."

I laughed at the two of them. "You're worse than the kids," I said. "I'm a marketing rep and a cook." I stooped in front of Uncle Jeff and started to roll up his pants. "Let me look at your knee."

"Oh alright, I don't think either of you know anything about knees, but if it will make you leave me alone, I'll let you look at it."

When the knee was exposed, Dad and I both drew in a breath. It was swollen and red. There was obviously something seriously wrong.

"Uncle Jeff," I said. "You can't hike on that leg."

"I don't see where I've got a choice, do I? I don't think I'll do the day hike though." We had planned a day hike off trail the next morning. Then we planned to do the last three miles. We had a reservation in a bed and breakfast for the last night, and we'd fly back the following morning.

"I wonder if they can get a jeep out here," Dad said.

"I don't need a jeep," Uncle Jeff protested and rolled his pants leg back down.

"What's wrong, Dad?" Alice said. She and Evelyn came out of the woods and sat on either side of him.

"Nothing," he put his arms around both of them and kissed Alice's cheek. "I'm old, that's all."

"It's his knee," Evelyn said. "It's been bothering him for a while. You said hiking wouldn't hurt." She looked at him sharply.

"You knew he had a problem and you didn't tell me?" Alice said to Evelyn looking past Uncle Jeff.

"Hey, you two," Uncle Jeff laughed. "I'm sitting in between you. Don't talk about me like I'm not here."

"I do wish you'd told us you had a problem, Uncle Jeff." Drew joined us. "We could have planned a shorter trip."

"I don't have a problem, and this trip is about the shortest trip we've done since David and I started." He stood up, almost knocking the girls off the log, and limped to the tent to disappear inside.

After two miles the next day, Uncle Jeff took off his pack and sat down in front of a tree. He stretched his legs out and rested his head on the tree. His eyes were closed. I could see the pain in the expression on his face.

"I'm not going to make it," he said. I could hear pain in his voice too.

"The ranger station is only about a mile," Dad said. "I'll go on ahead and get a jeep. I'm sure they have a four wheel drive vehicle that can make it out here. Take this, Jeff," Dad searched through his pack and pulled out a bottle of ibuprofen. "It'll help at least a little."

"I'll stay here with Dad," Alice said. She sat down next to him looking very concerned.

"I'll go with Uncle Brian," Evelyn said. "I hike faster than him. I'll get there quicker."

It was decided that Brandon and Charlotte and Veronica would go with Brian and Drew and Evelyn to the ranger station and find transportation for Uncle Jeff. Alice and I would stay here.

"I'm surprised Evelyn didn't stay too," I said. "You guys are pretty protective of your dad."

"She's hoping there will be a phone she can use to call Jamie. She hasn't been able to get a signal on her cell since we started hiking." Alice watched the group of hikers go out of sight as the Trail curved. Evelyn was in the lead.

"I've been replaced," Uncle Jeff said without opening his eyes.

"So have I." Alice sat down next to Uncle Jeff. He put his arm across her shoulders. I sat cross legged next to them.

"So they're still dating?" I knew they were. I had worked with James, Jr. for the entire semester. He still struggled, but with hard work he'd done very well.

"Yes, but I'm okay with it." Uncle Jeff still had his eyes closed. "Jamie makes a point to talk to me about it. He always assures me that he will not take advantage of her innocence. I think he makes her happy. I have to admit though, I'm glad they'll be separated when she goes to the University in the fall. I think she's a little young to be too permanently attached."

"That's the only reason why I don't mind. I guess I always knew we'd go our separate ways, but sometimes I miss her. I guess I need to get used to missing her since we aren't going to school together." Alice looked at me. "She is happy though. Evelyn has always known exactly what she wanted."

"I don't know how I'm going to handle it when my girls actually have a boyfriend. Charlotte has gone out on a couple of dates, but she hasn't gotten attached to anyone. Darla won't let them date until they're sixteen so Vroom hasn't gone out. There is a young man she goes to school with that comes to the house sometimes. I get the idea that he's more interested in the swimming pool than Veronica though."

"Stupid kid," Uncle Jeff leaned forward and rubbed his knee. "I'm sorry about ruining the trip," he said.

"You didn't ruin anything, but I hope you'll go to a doctor when we get home and find out how to fix this," I said.

"That's right, Dad," Alice said. "You shouldn't have ignored it."

"You're right. I shouldn't have. Evelyn said the same thing."

Uncle Jeff leaned back against the tree again. In a few minutes he was snoring lightly. "I guess pain is tiring," I said.

"Yeah, so David, how is the kitchen renovation going? I looked in on it about a month ago, but I've been busy with exams and all. I haven't had a chance to get by again."

"It's going really well," I said. "I can't wait to open. I'm planning on October. That way we can get started and be in top form for the holidays. I've about gotten all of my duties at the magazine turned over to Stan. All I'll need to do is go to meetings on Wednesday morning. I plan to hire an assistant manager so I can do that and have a day off now and then."

"I'm glad you're excited about it. I thought you needed a change."

"I think it's a midlife thing. I remember when your dad was my age. He got restless too. He had to make a change. That's when you and Evelyn came along."

"Dad was fifty when we were born. How old are you?"

?"I'm forty three but I'm ahead of my time. I'll keep my hand in on the magazine though. I have loved that work."

"So have you got your menu done yet?"

"I have but I keep changing it. I probably will until we open. Call it poetic license."

CHAPTER TWENTY FOUR

I opened the back door and looked at my kids. It was mid August, and they were all gathered around the pool. The weather was hot, and the only way to be outside was to be either in the pool or close to it so that when the heat got to you, you could plunge in.

Veronica and Charlotte were swimming laps. They had both become very conscious of their figures, and they were avid exercisers. Not only did they swim, they rode bikes, and ran too.

Belinda was sitting at a table next to the pool with Sivon. Brandon sat with them under the umbrella with his sketch board in his right hand. He was drawing frantically and looking at the hill in our back yard. When we had moved into the house I'd made plans for that hill. It was steep, but I thought it would make a nice rock garden. Time had played against me though. With the big family, and work, and my small internet business, the hill had grown wild. It was thick with brush and weeds. Every time I looked at it I winced, but it was low priority on my list of things to do.

"What are you doing, Beeta?" I asked as I approached the table.

She looked up from her computer and blinked her eyes. I guess her concentration was so great it was hard to break through. "I'm getting a jump on my science class for fall," she said. "Uncle Drew says that I can be on middle school level by winter semester if I try. I want to. I'm getting board with all this kid's work."

I laughed. "You're a chip off the old block. What are you two doing?" I turned to Brandon. Sivon was looking over his shoulder at his drawing."

"Brandon is drawing a gazebo on the top of that hill. After he draws it, I'm going to design it, and we were thinking that you and my dad could build it." Sivon didn't look up at me as she talked.

I looked at Brandon's sketch board. "How are you going to design that?" I asked. It was a picture of a building at the top of the hill. It must have been six sided judging by the front of it. There was a winding stairway up to it with landscaping all over the hill. "That's a beautiful picture, Bran, but how is Sivon going to design it, and how am I going to build it? I've never built anything."

"Sivon has a computer program. She's gonna be a architec when she grows up," he said without looking up from his work.

"Well, I'm already grown up, and I'm not a builder."

"I'll help you, Dad." He looked up from his drawing then. His eyes were sincere and encouraging.

"Okay," I said. "Now that you mention it, I think it would be nice for you and me to work on a project together."

"I hope you don't mind if my dad helps." Sivon broke in. "He's excited about working on a project with me too. We don't see enough of each other."

"I think we'll make a great team. Who will do all this gardening on that hill?" I pointed to the drawing.

"Nuncle Jeff, of course," Brandon said.

I took a deep breath. I was worried about Uncle Jeff. Ever since the camping trip he had been depressed. He went to the doctor, and they tried cortisone treatments in his knee. I didn't think they were working very well. He still walked with a limp, and he'd stopped going out with the landscaping crew.

"See this trellis in front of the gazebo, Dad. Me and Sivon are getting married there." My thoughts jumped back to the conversation.

"Sivon and I are getting married there." I corrected him.

"You can't marry Sivon. You're already married to Mom," Brandon laughed.

"I was correcting your grammar. You and Sivon can't get married. You're only nine years old."

"Not now, silly," Brandon and Sivon both laughed. I didn't really feel like laughing. "When we're grown up we'll get married there."

"Did you already propose to her?" I asked Brandon.

"No, she asked me and I said yes." That sounds familiar, I thought.

"How do you feel about this, Beeta?" I looked at her. She had looked away from her computer when this subject came up.

She frowned and looked at Brandon. "I guess I don't mind if he marries Sivon. I wouldn't want him to marry anyone else, though."

We were making progress with the twin's independence, but we still had a ways to go.

✧

I knocked on the door to Uncle Jeff's office. I knew he was here because his truck was in the parking lot, but he didn't answer. I looked around and didn't see him on the floor. He could have been in one of the greenhouses. I knocked again and then opened the door slightly to look in. He was sitting at his desk with his head down on his crossed arms.

"Uncle Jeff," I said as I came into the office and closed the door behind me. "Are you alright?"

He looked up at me. I could see the pain and the sadness on his face. "No, I'm struggling, David."

I crossed the room and put my hands on his arms. "What's going on? Is the knee not getting any better?"

"No, it's worse. My orthopedist says I need to have a knee replacement. I guess I won't be finishing the Appalachian with you. I can't even work."

"Won't a knee replacement help? Why else would they do it?"

"I don't want a knee replacement. I don't want any surgery. I just want to quit. I'm tired of the struggle. I don't have the energy for this anymore. I'd like to retire, but I can't until Evelyn is out of school. Maybe I could leave the business with Darcy. She's been a good manager."

"Uncle Jeff, you don't want to retire. You just need a break. Remember when you went to Peru on that bike trip. Take Amanda and go on a long vacation when the girls go to school."

"I can't even walk, David. I certainly can't ride a bike."

"I'm sorry. That was a stupid suggestion, but you are going to have the surgery, aren't you?"

He didn't answer me. He put his head back down on the desk.

I looked up at the sound of the door opening. His wife Amanda stood in the doorway. She met my eyes. Hers were filled with concern. "Jeff," she said and walked around the desk to massage his shoulders. "Please snap out of this. You have to have the surgery. Then things will get better."

"I just don't believe it." His voice was muffled from talking into his arms. "I've known people who had that done. They're never the same."

"You'll never be the same if you don't have it done either," she said.

"Uncle Jeff, they can do great things in medical science these days."

He stood up and limped to the door. "Leave me alone. Just leave me alone." He closed the door hard as he left the office. Amanda sat down in the chair he had just vacated and put her face in her hands. She cried quietly. I'd never seen her cry. We had worked together at the magazine until she retired a few months ago. She was always very calm, very much in control. I reached across the desk and wrapped my hand around her arm.

"How long has he been like this?" I asked.

"It started right after the backpacking trip, and it's gotten progressively worse." She pulled a tissue out of her purse and dried her eyes. "His doctor says depression is not uncommon in these situations. He gave him a prescription for an antidepressant, but he won't take it. I filled it but he won't take it. I'm afraid to leave him alone. The girls are both scheduled to go off to school in two weeks. They're afraid to leave. I've had to talk both of them out of withdrawing."

"Did you tell him that?"

"No, I don't know if I should. I'm so worried I can't think right. I don't know how to help him."

I stood up. "I'll talk to him. I'll trap him in the greenhouse and won't let him out until we've done something about this. Stay here. Don't go anywhere until one or both of us come back."

"What can you do about it?"

"I don't know but I'll think of something." I left the office and stopped an employee on her way by. "Did you see where my uncle went?"

"He's in the potting shed. I had to leave because he bit my head off, and I could see it was going to happen again. Good luck!" She called after me as I headed in the direction of the shed.

I found him sitting at the work table. His back stiffened when I came in, so he knew I was there.

"Look, Uncle Jeff," I said. "Let's talk about this. Maybe it will help."

He didn't say anything.

"Amanda says the doctor told you depression goes along with this. Why don't you take the pills and relieve some of the tension."

"Didn't I say leave me alone? Do you want me to explain what that means?"

"No, I know what it means. You want me to let you wallow in your own misery. Well, I won't do it. You made Amanda cry. I've known her for a long time, and I've never seen her cry."

"I've seen her cry. It's not that big a deal."

"You are such a selfish bastard." He looked up at me then. He was angry. I was glad to see some feeling instead of the flat affect of depression. He got up and limped toward the door to leave. I moved between him and escape. He glared at me.

"Did you know that Alice and Evelyn have both told Amanda they want to withdraw from school?"

He looked surprised and again, angry. "They damn well better not. Alice and I had a deal. I wouldn't have done all that renovation to the apartment if she hadn't agreed to go to school. And why would Evelyn want to quit. She's wanted to study horticulture all her life."

"They're afraid to leave you."

"Oh." He sat back down on the stool and resumed his sad expression.

"Uncle Jeff, you're only thinking of yourself right now. I understand why that is. It's hard to think of anything else when you're in pain. I remember when Anna left me and I took all those sleeping pills. I was only thinking of myself then. It was selfish, and it hurt a lot of people."

"I haven't thought about that in years." He rubbed his knee. "I didn't mean to hurt the girls. I didn't mean to hurt Amanda. I didn't mean to hurt you either, David." He looked up at me. There were tears in his eyes. One escaped and ran down his face.

I walked over to him and put my arms around his shoulders. He rested his head on my arm and sobbed only one time. Then he sat up straight and rubbed his wet face with a towel that was lying on the table. He looked up at me and I smiled.

"You've rubbed dirt all over you face."

"I think I'll let it stay there. I deserve to have dirt on my face." He took a deep breath and limped over to the hose on the wall. He wet the towel and cleaned his face with it. "I don't know if I can do it, David. I thought with all the physical activity I do in my work I wouldn't have these problems as I aged. I was wrong. I hate being wrong." He limped back over to the stool and sat down again. "I've been depressed before, but in my whole life I've never been this depressed. I don't think I can pull myself out of it this time."

"Then accept some help. Take the pills, Uncle Jeff. They'll help I'm sure. Then schedule the surgery."

"David," he looked up at me. His eyes were pleading. "Will you go with me? There's this class that they want Amanda and me to go to. It's to explain the procedure and the recovery. I think I would feel better if you came along."

"Of course I'll go. Just let me know when."

"It's Wednesday. The surgery is scheduled for the following Monday."

"So you've already scheduled it. I'm pretty sure Amanda doesn't know that."

"I haven't told her yet. I just got off the phone with the hospital when you came in. I guess I needed to wallow a little longer."

"That was mean, Uncle Jeff."

"I know. Will you help me back to the office? I don't think I can make it by myself. I need to beg some forgiveness."

"Of course I will." I put my arm around his waist and shouldered his weight as we made slow progress toward the office.

"Hey, Alice," I said as I entered the newly renovated kitchen. She stood at the window looking out onto the parking lot. "I've got good news."

"Good," she smiled sadly. "I could use some good news."

"Your dad has scheduled his surgery."

"Really?" Her face lit up. She ran across the room and threw herself into my arms. "How did you talk him into it?"

"I didn't," I said. "He had already done it when I got to his office."

"Oh, David," Alice sat down on a work bench. "I've been so worried about him. We've all been worried about him. Mom has been beside herself, and you know it's hard to ruffle Mom's feathers. Even Ev wanted to withdraw from school, and she's been planning this all her life."

"I know, but he did the right thing without me having to rope him into it. He's even admitted that he was being selfish and wallowing in his own misery."

"You're kidding." She laughed. "I'm sure you had something to do with that."

"Yeah, I pointed it out to him." I walked to the window to look out. "I don't think the crisis is really over yet. I'm sure the whole ordeal will be tough, but eventually it will be over. I'm sure he'll adjust to any limitations he's left with."

"What a relief. Do you think I could go down and see him or should I wait?"

"Maybe wait a minute or two. I left your dad wrapped in your mom's arms. They were both crying. Give them a minute. Then be sure to knock on the door before you go in." I looked back at her. She was smiling candidly. At least some of the worry had been eased.

"When will the surgery be?" she asked. "I hope I can get time off from school. I won't be able to concentrate, I'm sure."

"It's a week from Monday. When does school start?"

"Not until the following week, but I think Mom will need help. Dad won't be an easy patient."

"The art school doesn't have dorms does it? You'll be at home in the evening."

"Actually, I've rented an apartment with another student. I found her on the internet. She's from Florida and will need a place to stay. I wanted to leave home like Ev. I think I'll miss her less if I'm not at home."

"Really, well you'll be close enough to help if your mom needs you. They may enjoy some time alone together. It's called empty nesting. They can renew their relationship." I looked back out the window.

"That's true. I hope they'll miss us a little."

"They'll miss you a lot, but they'll be gratified by how well you girls are doing. I'm gratified by it. I hope you know that." She didn't say anything. "Oh look," I said. "Evelyn just pulled into the parking lot. Maybe you should go down now and give her the good news before she busts in on your mom and dad."

"Thanks, David." She stood on her toes to kiss my cheek. Then she ran out the door and down the steps to intercept Evelyn.

◊

"You should come by and see the café." I told Darla that night after the kids had retired to their rooms and Sivon had gone home. "It's really coming along. They've about finished the kitchen, and they've torn down the wall between one of the bedrooms and the living room. There will be room for plenty of tables. We'll use one of the other bedrooms for private party rentals. The other bedroom will be an office for Alice and me to share."

"It's nice to see you so excited about this, David. I guess you had gotten a little burned out at the magazine." Darla stretched out on the couch and yawned.

"I don't know if I was really burned out or if I just need a little change. I've hired a kitchen manager and a couple of waitresses. I'll need more. I plan to be open seven days a week, but I can't work that many days. I need to be at the magazine on Wednesday for the staff meeting. And of course, I need time with my family."

"That brings up something I wanted to talk to you about." Darla sat up and looked at me seriously.

"Uh oh," I said. It was scary when she looked at me that way.

"It's nothing bad. I just want to change the twin's school situation."

"Why?" I sat forward. "They're doing so well with Drew. I'm going to have to object to sending them anywhere else."

"Oh no," She laughed lightening my mood like her laughter always did. "I don't want to change their school. I just don't want them to be there all day anymore. With Charlotte driving now, she can take Veronica to school and any place she needs to go in the afternoon. That way I can take the twins and pick them up. They're awfully young to be away from home from six thirty in the morning to five o'clock in the evening."

"Oh good," I relaxed. "I agree. I hope you didn't think I would object to that."

"No, but you might be more on call for Charlotte and Veronica. They may be getting more independent, but they still need parental guidance."

"That's true. I don't mind being on call. The café will close on the week days at noon. I'm only starting with breakfast. I have other things to do with the magazine and my internet activity, but I'll be available for them if they need me."

"Actually, David, I want you to do a little bit more than be available. I want you to check in with them. Make sure they're doing what they should be doing and relieve Charlotte if their activities conflict with each other."

"I can do that," I said feeling a little bit uneasy. I had left most of the activity with the kids to Darla. I wasn't exactly sure what all she did.

"I'll make a list for you at the beginning of each week." Darla came over to my chair and climbed onto my lap. We hadn't sat like that in a while. It felt familiar and comforting. "I hope this isn't too much to ask, David. I know the kids and the house were supposed to be my job. I just really want my babies home in the afternoon. I can help them with their homework instead of them getting it done while they wait for Drew. They're the last ones I'll have. I want to experience all of it."

"It's not too much to ask. I'm their father, P. H. I'm excited about it. It'll be nice to spend more time with Charlita and Vroom." I pulled her closer to me. She rested her head on my chest.

"I'm glad you feel that way."

The café opened on the first of October. We called it Alice's Place. It was a hit from the beginning. I couldn't believe how many people wanted to have a cup of coffee with biscotti while they browsed through the nursery. Just as many people wanted to sit around the fountains and have breakfast. Most of our business was done downstairs at this point. We had a large dining room upstairs with windows that looked out over the planting gardens and the greenhouses. Some people wanted to sit up there, but I figured it would be used more when Alice opened for lunch and dinner. We were doing a pretty good business, though. I was pleased.

Uncle Jeff's surgery went well. His depression worsened in the first days of recovery, but he gradually pulled out of it as his leg strengthened. He backslid a little when he first started walking at the park. I asked him what was bothering him one day. He said it was hard to adjust to having a foreign object inside his body. But he got over that pretty fast when he realized he was walking without pain.

Amanda and I took turns taking him to physical therapy until he didn't need us anymore. It was interesting to feel the subtle reversal of roles. Uncle Jeff had always been my rock, along with my mom, of course. Now he was looking to me for support. I didn't mind. In fact I was glad he'd come to me for help. I just hoped I would be equal to the task.

We had another setback when he became aware that one leg was shorter than the other. It caused pain in the other knee which scared him to death. His orthopedist assured him that this was not unusual, and he was fitted with a shoe insert that made up the difference. All in all, he healed pretty quickly and very well.

"What are you thinking about, Dad?" Brandon stood at my shoulder. I jumped at the sound of his voice. I hadn't heard him approach. I sat at the kitchen table. I'd just gotten home from picking up Veronica from soccer practice. She played in the goal, but she'd never minded it like I had at first.

"I was thinking about Uncle Jeff," I said. "But I should have been thinking about dinner."

"Can Sivon stay?"

"Not on a school night, Brandon. You know the rules."

"Yeah," He flashed his dimples at me. "I just wanted to see if I could slip it by you. I don't even try with Mom."

"You thought you could railroad your old man, huh?" I pulled him into my lap and tickled him.

"Not really," he laughed. "I figured you wouldn't want Mom to kill you when she got home and found Sivon eating dinner."

"Where is Sivon, anyway, upstairs with Belinda?"

"Yeah, Binda is helping her with her computer program. Sivon is smart but Binda is smarter. We hit a snag on the plans for the gazebo. It was hard, but we managed to get her to stop studying for a minute to help. Binda's a nerd." He laughed again. He was still the happiest person I'd ever known.

"Belinda is not a nerd," I said, realizing how often I defended my tiny daughter.

"It's okay, Dad," Belinda came into the room with Sivon behind her carrying a computer print out. "I don't mind being called a nerd. I'm okay with being smarter than everyone else." She smiled too, but the smile didn't quite reach her eyes. Her dimples did show, however. If Brandon was the happiest, Belinda was the most serious.

"We finished the plans, Mr. Landrum," Sivon said as she spread them before me on the table. They were elaborate and definitely over my head. "How am I supposed to follow those plans? I can't make heads or tails of them."

"My dad will help you. He's studied them already."

"I thought you said you just finished them."

"He helped me with them. He's built stuff before."

"I thought your dad was a doctor." I looked up at the red headed girl standing next to Brandon. They were both tall, but Brandon seemed to be growing very fast these days. He was taller than Sivon now. Belinda hit him about shoulder height, and she hit Sivon at about her chin.

"He is, but that's not all he does. He has a workshop in the basement. It's his hobby."

"Good, I'll need directions."

"Me too," Brandon said. "I can't understand those plans either."

"It's okay, Brandon," Sivon said and kissed him on the cheek. "You did your part when you drew the picture."

"Yuck." Belinda turned her face away. "Don't kiss in front of me."

I looked again at Brandon and Sivon. I'm pretty sure they're only nine years old, I thought. I wondered if there was reason for concerned.

Brandon laughed and rubbed the spot she had kissed with his hand. "I can build, though. I can hammer nails and stuff. I think I might even be able to use a drill."

"Good, we'll need that." Sivon gathered the plans and went to the door. "I have to go. Dad's coming home early today, and I want to show him the finished plans. He'll call you when he's ready to get started."

I watched her go out the door and sprint across the back yard to the gate. "She sure is a confident little thing."

"Yeah, Sivon is great." Brandon clipped the leash to Harry and started for the door. "I'm taking Harry for a walk before we eat. Come with us Binda." He took his sister's hand and headed for the door.

"I need to study some more."

"You need to walk some more." He tugged and she reluctantly followed.

"Dad," Veronica came into the room. I looked up at her. She was absolutely beautiful. All my girls were pretty but Veronica sparkled. Charlotte had a more subtle beauty, and it was hard to get past the serious look on Belinda's face.

"You've grown into a very lovely lady, Vroom." I stood up and went to the refrigerator.

"Dad, would you take me over to Billy's house? We're working on a science project together, and I think we could work for about an hour before supper," she said.

"I don't know. Your mom doesn't like for you to go out on week nights."

"I'll be back for supper, Dad. Mom and Charlotte won't be back until six thirty. They had a meeting at the school. Please Dad; it's a school project I swear."

"I believe you." I took the keys off the rack on the wall. "I guess it's alright, but I'll pick you up at six fifteen. That gives you an hour and fifteen minutes."

"Thanks, Dad." She kissed my cheek. "I'll get my notebook."

"Vroom, have we measured you lately. I swear you're almost as tall as I am."

"Yeah, I'm going to be an Amazon like Gramma Charlie. Thanks for that feature, Dad." She frowned.

"You don't like being tall?"

"Not much but I guess I'd better get used to it. I get the feeling I'm going to top Gramma Charlie and Charlotte. I can feel myself growing." She laughed. "I'll meet you at the car." She took the steps two at a time and almost beat me to the car.

◊

"It's almost like old times," Uncle Jeff said, "going hiking, just the two of us."

"Brandon and Belinda and Sivon are along too." I reminded him.

"Yeah, but they're so caught up in each other they leave the two of us alone."

"It's a good thing we like each other," I said. We were sitting on the ferry crossing the sound to Cumberland Island. We were going to hike the entire island, fifteen miles and back. Uncle Jeff had started hiking again about six months after his surgery. We tried to stay on flat ground at first. Then we had gradually added some hills. In the past three years we had hiked hundreds of day trails. In the last year he had started carrying a pack again for overnight trips. This was our first extended trip, and we had decided Cumberland was the perfect place. It was flat, easy hiking terrain, and there was help if we needed it.

"Sivon sure has endeared herself with your two kids." He nodded in the direction of the kids and I looked. Across the ferry Sivon stood between Brandon and Belinda. They were holding tightly to the rail and squealing in unison at the salt spray as the boat rode the waves.

"Look, it's a shark." Sivon let go of the rail long enough to point out to sea. Then grabbed it again as the boat took a particularly rough wave.

"That's a dolphin," Belinda said. "Sharks don't come up out of the water like that. Their tail fins go from side to side, and Dolphin tail fins go up and down."

I smiled at Uncle Jeff. "She's always teaching."

He smiled back. "She says she's going to be a doctor. I think I believe her."

"I'm sure she will. She plans to be a neurologist." I felt my brows draw together as I looked at my little girl. "She just can't seem to stop feeling responsible for Brandon's problems."

"As far as I can tell, Brandon doesn't have any problems." We both laughed.

"As far as he's concerned he doesn't. He's completely happy with life and can you blame him. He has two beautiful girls who are very interested in his well being." I looked at the three kids laughing and chattering at the rail of the ferry. "Uncle Jeff, do kids have sex at the age of twelve."

"I suppose they could," he said looking concerned. "Why do you ask?"

"Sivon and Brandon are planning to get married when they grow up, with Belinda's blessing, of course. Do I need to be concerned about chaperoning them at this point?"

He looked back at the kids. "I don't know, but I'm glad we have two tents. I think the guys should sleep in one and the girls in the other."

"I think you're right. I hope they don't get scared."

"Maybe we should have brought Harry after all. I'm sure you could have gotten permission with him being a seizure dog."

"I didn't want to risk him getting eaten by an alligator. He likes to swim," I said.

"Good point." Uncle Jeff looked back at the kids. Brandon had his arm resting across Sivon's shoulders. "We'll pitch our tents close together."

The girls did fine in their own tent. The first night Belinda called out after we'd all retired to our tents. She asked if there were bears on Cumberland Island. I told her no and that satisfied her. I didn't tell her about the bob cats or the feral pigs.

The third night we camped at the end of the island. It was August and the weather was hot, but the hike in the jungle was shady, and there was a sea breeze. We were comfortable. Our third campsite was just behind a dune. There was a path to the beach. We arrived about mid afternoon and walked to the shore. The kids played in the surf. Uncle Jeff and I went in for a short swim. Then we sat down on the sand to watch the kids.

"David," Uncle Jeff said. "I think I'm ready to finish the Trail."

"I think you've been ready for a while, but I didn't want to push you."

"Thanks, David. I can't believe it's been three years since we've been to the Trail. I think that's the longest we've been away from it in twenty years."

"It was worth the wait. I wouldn't have wanted to finish it without you, and I wouldn't have wanted you to hike it until you were ready."

He put his arm around my shoulders and pulled me to him in a hug. "You've been very good to me in the past couple of years. I probably didn't deserve it. I know I've been difficult."

"After all you've done for me in my life. I was glad I could return a little of it."

"You've always returned it. I love you, son. I'm glad I've been able to be a part your life."

We sat in comfortable silence for a minute. The kids were floating in the shallow water and chattering about something.

"So when do you want to go. I know the girls will want to come with us. Alice and I will have to plan it. We have an assistant manager who can relieve us for a week. So that won't be a problem, but the other kids are in school. I guess spring break would be the soonest we could do it."

"I think summer will be soon enough." He stood and brushed the sand off his suit. "Remember we're going north to Main. It might be too cool at Spring break. Besides they close the Trail in the spring in Maine, remember."

"That's right. I forgot."

Oh no!" he said.

I followed the direction of his stare. The kids had gone a little deeper into the water. Between them and the shore two fins moved through the water in a side to side motion. I broke into a full run toward the water just as I heard Brandon squeal. He stood and ran through the water strait toward the shark.

"No, Brandon," I yelled. Miraculously the shark moved along the shallow waters of the shore, around the children, and out to sea. I plunged into the water gathered all three children in my arms and pulled them to shore. I could feel Uncle Jeff's hand on my arm helping me fight the current. I collapsed to my knees in the sand. The three kids stood around me in silence while I caught my breath.

"Now that was a shark," Belinda said. "Did you notice how it moved from side to side not up and down like the dolphin?"

The other kids remained silent.

"Brandon, why did you run toward it?" I asked, still panting to catch my breath and slow my heart.

"I didn't want it to eat Binda or Sivon."

"You wanted it to eat you instead."

"No," he said. "I think I could have beat it up. It was a little shark."

"It was not little," Sivon said finally finding her voice. "It was huge."

"No it wasn't," Belinda said. "There couldn't have been more than two feet between the fins."

I looked up at Uncle Jeff. He nodded. I looked back at the kids. "I thought it was about six feet long," I said. My heart rate was gradually slowing to a normal pace.

"How does the knee feel now?" I asked Uncle Jeff as we pulled into my driveway.

"It's a little bit stiff after sitting in the car for six hours, but I can work that out. All in all, I'm feeling much better. I can't wait to finish that Trail next summer. That will be such a triumph." He flashed that grin at me, and I noticed the lines in his face. They were beautiful, but they reflected his age.

"How old are you now, Uncle Jeff?"

"Why do you ask?"

"Just curious."

"I'm not checking out of this world for a while, David. I'll be seventy two this winter. Imagine hiking the end of the Appalachian Trail at Seventy two."

He looked so much better than he had three years ago. He'd scared me then, but it looked like we had weathered the storm.

The kids jumped out of the cab of the truck when it came to a complete stop and ran to greet Darla. She was standing on the front porch with her arms spread as the twins ran into them. Sivon turned her cheek for Darla to kiss.

"I guess you had a good trip." Darla smiled at me. There was something in her expression that alarmed me.

"We had a great trip," I said. Whatever it was we'd talk about it later.

"We almost got eaten by a shark," Sivon said.

"What?" Darla looked up at me startled.

"No we didn't," Belinda said. "Sivon, don't scare Mom like that." She turned to Darla. "It was just a little shark. Brandon was going to fight it off, but it got scared and swam away."

"Brandon was going to fight it off?"

Darla looked at Brandon and squeezed him a little harder. "Brandon, please tell me you didn't tangle with a shark."

"I didn't but I was going to. I wouldn't let a shark eat Sivon or Binda. I could have beat him up, but Dad scared him away when he came splashing into the water."

"Darla, it wasn't a big shark, and we didn't swim in the ocean after that," I said as I met her terrified eyes. "Trust me it wasn't as close a call as it sounds like."

"Anyway," Uncle Jeff said. He was carrying two of the kid's packs. I had unloaded mine and one of the kid's already. "You should have seen how fast David ran down that beach when we saw the fins. He plucked all three kids from the serf and carried them all back to shore. Really Darla," Uncle Jeff kissed her cheek. "It was a very small shark."

"It was not. It was huge," Sivon said. "Wasn't it, Mr. Landrum?"

"It looked big to me too, Sivon. But I think you and I have blown it out of proportion. We seem to be the only ones that were afraid of it."

"It wasn't big," Belinda said. "Believe me, Mom. Now I want to go and take a bath. I feel filthy."

"And I need to go home," Sivon said. "I hate to admit it, but I missed Mom and Dad." She picked up her small pack and headed next door. Uncle Jeff said good bye, kissed both the twins, and got into his truck. We all waved at him as he pulled away then we went into the house. The twins headed upstairs with their packs.

"Brandon," Darla called after them. "You can take a bath in the guestroom tub. You don't have to wait for Belinda to finish. She takes forever."

"Okay Mom, but I don't think I really need a bath," he called back.

"Oh yes you do." She looked back at me and smiled.

"I think I'll take a quick shower, too," I said. "I sure am glad I had that extra hot water tank put in a few years ago."

"With a family this size, we needed it." Darla turned and went into the kitchen.

"Where are Veronica and Charlotte?" I asked as I sat down at the table after my shower.

"Charlotte is out with Brad. They seem to be somewhat of an item. I think they're dating each other exclusively."

"Really, she told me they were just friends."

"She told me that too, but I think it's changed." She poured me a cold beer, herself a glass of wine, and sat down across from me at the table.

"Have you given her the safe sex talk?" I asked.

"I'm hoping it hasn't gone that far, but I did talk to her a few years ago when she first started to develop. I reminded her of it recently too."

"Should I talk to her?" I asked. I felt nervous about it. "When I was a kid, Mom, Uncle Jeff, and Dad all three talked to me."

"Did it stop you from having sex?"

"No, but it did help me to be careful."

"I guess it's up to you," she said. "Talk to her if you want to." She took a sip of her wine. Her hand was shaking.

Veronica came into the room and went to the refrigerator to pour a glass of lemonade. Her face was clearly tear stained and she was sniffling.

"Okay, what's going on?" I said looking around the room. "Did something happen to Harry?" The dog bed in the corner of the kitchen was empty.

"Harry is fine," Darla said. "I'm sure he's upstairs greeting the twins. He missed them terribly."

"So what's wrong?" I looked at Veronica. She sniffed and sat down at the table.

"Tell him, Mom," she said. "I'm sure Gramma Charlie won't mind."

My heart started to pound. "What is it? Tell me. You're scaring me to death."

"David, your mom has been diagnosed with cancer."

"Cancer? They can cure it thought, right. They'll do chemotherapy won't they?" My ears were ringing now. I almost couldn't hear Darla's response.

"No, David, they can't cure it. It's a rare cancer. I'm not sure how to explain it. I'll let your mom explain. She wanted to tell you herself, but I told her I didn't think I could keep quiet about it. I found out on Friday after her CT scan. We had lunch, and I knew there was something wrong."

"What do you mean they can't cure it?"

"All I know is that the doctor told her it was terminal. He said chemotherapy and radiation treatment can buy her some more time, but she says she won't do it."

"Yes she will do it." I said. My voice broke and I put my face in my hands, swallowing hard at the lump in my throat. Veronica came around the table and put her arms around me. I lost control then and we cried together. Darla put her hands on mine across the table.

"I have to go." I stood up. I wrapped my arms around Veronica and kissed her cheek, noticing again how tall she was. "I have to go to see her right now." I looked at the two of them.

"I understand, David." Darla reached up to kiss me. Our lips met for one comforting moment, then I hurried to the garage.

CHAPTER TWENTY FIVE

"This can't be happening." I sat at my mom's table with both of my parents. Dad held Mom's hand. His face was tear stained just like mine. Mom was surprisingly calm.

"I know this will be hard on the two of you," she said. "That's my only regret. But I'm alright, David. You know how devout a catholic I am. If it's my time to die, the Lord has a reason for it, and I trust him."

"Please do the chemotherapy, Mom, please." I begged and took her free hand. "Maybe they'll have discovered a cure by the time you finish the treatment."

"No, David, they won't have. The problem is that it's secondary cancer. The doctor called it metastatic. That means it's spread from someplace else. Try as they might, they can't find the original cancer. It rarely happens this way, but when it does the prognosis is always bad."

"Why won't you do the chemotherapy? It could prolong your life. Don't you want to stay with us longer?" My voice broke, and a tear ran down my cheek. I brushed it away.

"I want to stay with you forever, but if the Lord thinks it's time for me to go; I won't try to defy Him."

"Do it for me, Mom, please." I put my hands to my face and rubbed my eyes trying to stop the tears.

"I would do almost anything for you, David. But I won't do that. If I only have a few months left in this world, I don't want to spend them nauseated and hairless. I want to feel good as long as I can."

"She wouldn't do it for me either, David." Dad got up and walked to the window. "I don't know if I can stand to watch you die, Charlotte."

"You don't have to, Brian. You've made me very happy in my life. If you need to pull away from me now, I'll be alright."

"I didn't mean that." He came back to the table and put his arms around her from behind her chair. "I couldn't possibly leave you. I love you."

"I love you too, Brian, and the wonderful son you gave me. I love you both so much." The room was silent for a minute. "Now I've got a challenge for you. Make my last few months on this earth the best few months." She stood up and went to the back door. She opened it and went outside to the small courtyard.

I looked at my dad. I could see the pain etched on his face. "Can we talk her into getting treatment?" I asked.

He looked at me and smiled sadly. "We can try."

I went into the café the next morning about an hour earlier than usual. I couldn't sleep, and I thought working on the menu would help me think about something else for a while. I was creating new muffins to serve. It was fun. I could bury myself in it. I guess it was some kind of artistic outlet.

"You're here early." Uncle Jeff came into the office I shared with Alice. "Are you doing alright, David? Your dad called me last night and gave me the bad news."

"I'm in shock," I said.

"That's understandable."

"I just keep thinking there has to be a mistake. She isn't even sick. They caught it on a yearly checkup."

"Yeah, it's hard to accept." He sat down at Alice's desk and started to straighten the stacks of papers. "Alice has always been disorganized."

"She is, but she gets things done. I'm amazed at how successful this place has been. It's a very good project for me. It was fun when I was alone, but working with Alice for the past year has been even better. She has so much energy and such a zest for life."

"She's happy too, and she's making a living. That makes me happy. Evelyn will be in school for probably four more years since she's planning to get a master's degree in landscape architecture. I've planned for their education, but it's still hard on the wallet." He turned and looked at me.

"I'm sure it is. I'm getting ready to find out. Charlotte is going to the university in the fall and Veronica the following year. She hasn't decided where she wants to go. It'll probably be some private school that costs a fortune." I took a deep breath and looked out the window. I wondered if Mom would live to see Veronica graduate from high school.

"It just keeps coming back at you, doesn't it," he said.

"I can get my mind on something else for just a little while then wham! It slaps me in the face again. I don't know how to deal with this. You know I've always been close to my mom. It was just the two of us for a long time. You were always there too. I don't mean to discount that."

"I know, son."

"But it was Mom and me in that little townhouse and always a dog or two. She and Dad don't have a dog now. They were going to travel. I guess that won't happen." I rubbed my eyes again and realized that they were sore. I put my hands down on the desk and looked back at Uncle Jeff. "How do you adjust to something like this?"

"I don't know. It's my first time too. My parents lived to a ripe old age, and Aunt Jean and Uncle Bill are still happy in assisted living."

"I guess we'll find out."

When the breakfast crowd had cleared out, I stopped by the office to say hello to Alice before I left.

"Your chia muffins were a big hit, I hear." She smiled, but I could see that she'd heard the news.

"People did seem to like them. I created them this morning. I couldn't sleep."

"David, I'm sorry about your mom. I don't really know what to say."

"I think *I'm sorry* is about all you can say. I'm still going to talk her into the chemo. I'm not ready to give her up. I need more time."

"I don't think forever would be enough time, David. You're very close to your mother. I'm close to mine too. So I know how hard this must be. I just couldn't stop hugging mom last night when I heard the news. I made her promise not to die any time soon."

I smiled. "Good for you, you should appreciate both your parents. They're great people."

"They are."

"Well, good luck on the dinner crowd. Maybe next year we'll open for lunch."

"I think that's a good plan."

Darla and I sat in silence after dinner. Charlotte was out again with Brad. Veronica was out with some of her girlfriends. They'd gone to a movie. The twins were in bed. Harry was with them. I stared ahead of me. I just couldn't do anything else. Darla was flipping through a stack of someone's pictures. She was working on a wedding album. The front door opened and Charlotte came in.

"It's early for you to be home," I said. "Is Brad with you?"

"No, I wanted to talk to you guys alone."

"Really," Darla looked up and smiled at Charlotte. "What's going on?"

"I know this isn't a good time with Gramma Charlie being sick and all, but it can't wait."

"Honey," I said. "Your concerns are always important to us. Tell us what you need."

"I need for you to be happy for me, Dad. I'm going to have a baby."

There goes that ringing in my ears again, I thought. I wonder what that is. I looked at Charlotte. She was standing in the doorway smiling at us. She actually was glowing. I looked at Darla. She was staring at Charlotte. Her mouth was slightly open.

"Aren't you going to say anything?" Charlotte asked. I noticed then that her hands were shaking.

"I don't know how many more shocks I can take," I said.

"How could this happen?" Darla said. "What about school in the fall?"

"You know how it happened, Mom." Charlotte crossed her arms and looked at her mother angrily. "You gave me the sex talk."

"It was a *safe* sex talk. Why didn't you listen?"

"I can't believe you're mad at me when you're getting ready to have your first grandchild." Charlotte sat down on a chair across from the couch and looked away from us.

"How far along are you?" Darla demanded.

"I said I'm going to have a baby so don't even think about abortion."

"We have to look at all the possible solutions."

"I'm going to have a baby. Brad and I are getting married. He's telling his parents right now. We'll live in their basement apartment, if they'll let us. If not we'll live somewhere else. He's going to Georgia Tech, and I'll work until he gets out of school."

"How are you going to work and take care of a baby too," Darla said.

"I was hoping maybe you and Brad's mom would help."

"I didn't have more babies because I didn't want to take care of more babies, Charlotte. You can't put this on me." Darla's temper was getting the better of her. I needed to step in, but I didn't know what to say.

"I'm glad I didn't bring Brad along to do this. You probably would have punched him or something." Charlotte looked at me. "You haven't said much, Dad. What do you think?"

"I don't think I would have punched him." I sounded stupid. It's strange how your children can make you stupid.

"What do you think?" Charlotte repeated.

"I think you're going to have to let me get used to this. I'm really not sure how I feel about it." The room was silent. Darla glared at me. I guess that's not what she wanted me to say. "I guess you won't be going to the university this fall."

"No, I've already withdrawn. There will be time for school later. Now I want to start a family."

"You're only eighteen years old."

"Uncle Jimmy and Aunt Meryl got married at eighteen, and they're still happy."

"That's true. I'm disappointed about school though." I had to admit I'd been excited about our first child going to college. It was like a milestone.

"I don't want you to be disappointed in me." She sniffled. I think she was going to cry.

"I could never be disappointed in you, Charlotte. You've been nothing but joy since the day you were born. It's just not what we had planned, and no matter how hard parents try, they can't help making plans for their children. You have to give us a chance to get used to this."

She sniffled again and took a tissue out of her pocket. "Alright, I'll give you time. But Brad and I are going downtown to get the license tomorrow. So don't take too long getting used to it." She got up to leave the room.

"Wait Charlita." I stood and went to her. I put my arms around her then held her at arm's length to take a good look. "Are you alright? Do you feel okay? Have you been to a doctor?"

"Yes Dad, I've been to a doctor. The same one Mom uses. I feel pretty good most of the time, but I throw up about mid afternoon."

"Your mom did that too."

"Only with the twins, God forbid," Darla said.

"My due date is February 18th but first babies are usually late. Wouldn't it be great if the baby was born on the 29th like Uncle Jeff? Next year is a leap year." She kissed my cheek and looked at her mother. "I think I need to give Mom a little more time." I looked at Darla. She was scowling. Charlotte ran up the steps. In a minute I could hear her talking on the phone. I turned back to Darla.

"I can't believe you're letting her get away with this," she said.

"What else are we going to do, P. H? She's made up her mind. It doesn't matter what we think. She's going to do this anyway. She can do it without our approval, you know. She's old enough. And anyway, I agree with her about abortion. It's our grandbaby, Darla. You don't want to kill it."

She took a deep breath and sat down. "No, I suppose I don't want to kill it. I don't know what I want. Maybe I just want this all to go away, your mom's illness, Charlotte's baby. I'm going to check on the twins." She hurried toward the steps. "I hope Veronica isn't in any kind of trouble."

"I don't know how long we'll be able to work in this heat," I said to Brandon. We were building the winding stairway up the hill first. When we got that finished we'd build the arbor and then the gazebo. It was early July, and we were getting record high temperatures.

"We can jump in the pool if we get too hot," he said. He was looking especially cute in his work clothes with his tool belt on. I'm not sure cute is the way to describe a five foot seven twelve year old. He was going to be tall like me and his older sisters. I looked down the hill at Belinda and Sivon sitting on the top step at the end of the pool. Sivon was getting tall too. But Belinda was tiny. I had the feeling she wouldn't even be as big as her mother. I looked back at Brandon. They were all cute.

"Dad's here," Sivon called out. Ed Sheldon opened the gate between our yards. He was carrying a small cooler. He put it down and waved at Brandon and me standing at the base of the hill. He went to the end of the pool and said something to the girls, then came over to us.

"Well, you've got the first two steps in. I love the flagstone. Will there be a rail?" he asked.

"Yeah, I think we need a rail. Brandon did include one in his picture. I'm just not sure whether it will be wooden or iron. The kids haven't decided, and this is their project.

Sivon and Belinda came over to the group, both wrapped in towels. "Let me go in and get my work clothes on, and I can help." Sivon hurried toward the pool house.

"I'm not helping," Belinda said. "This is Brandon and Sivon's project. I'm going to stay in the pool."

"Beeta," I said. "I don't want you in the pool when we're too occupied to watch you."

"I can swim."

"I know you can, but nobody should swim alone."

"Billy and I will watch her," Veronica said, approaching us with Billy in tow. I looked at the two of them. I hate to admit it, but our recent experience with Charlotte had made me suspicious of every young man that hung around my girls. This kid was a good six inches shorter that Veronica. But I guess a six foot two woman has to be happy with someone shorter than her. She doesn't want to narrow the field too much.

My expression must have given away my thoughts because Veronica said, "Don't worry, Dad. I had the safe sex talk too, and I listened. I'm not going to be stupid like Charlotte."

I looked at her, startled and a little embarrassed. "I didn't say a word."

"You didn't have to." Veronica put her hand on Belinda's shoulder and guided her toward the pool. "Come on Beeta, we'll watch you swim."

"I don't have to be watched. I can swim fine."

"I know, but nobody should swim alone, Miss Sassy Pants." Veronica laughed, and Billy walked beside them back to the pool. He hadn't said a word, but his face had gone red when Veronica made her statement. I wondered what that meant.

"Let's get to work," Sivon ran across the yard from the pool house. I smiled at her. She looked cute in her work clothes too.

"First," Ed said. "Brandon can you run get that cooler. It's full of cold water. We don't want any problems with the heat out here."

"Okay." My strapping son ran to the cooler and picked it up easily. He loped across the yard and put it down next to the work bench. He picked up the shovel and started digging into the hill just above the last step.

"We dig out a step," he said. Th... then we put a flag stone on the bottom part and one on the back part. Th.,. then Dad puts this little brace fing in the dirt to hold it in place." Brandon was so excited he tripped over his words, but it didn't slow him down.

"That seems to work very well," Ed said. "Don't you want a stone that's close to the same length for the back as you have for the front?" Brandon was putting a considerably smaller stone in place. "Here's a measuring tape, Brandon. See if you can't match them better."

Brandon looked blank. "I can't use a measuring tape," he said.

"Sure you can," Ed said. "Just try it."

I tensed. I knew Brandon couldn't do it. I was about to tell Ed, but Sivon beat me to it.

"Dad, I told you. When Brandon says he can't. He can't. It has nothing to do with trying. Brandon is just smart enough to know what he can do and what he can't do. It keeps him from hurting himself or making a mess. Isn't that right Brandon?"

"Right," Brandon smiled. I think it was the first time I'd ever seen him look bashful. I guess he enjoyed being called smart. I realized for the first time that Sivon was right; Brandon was smart enough to know his own limits. I smiled and ruffled his hair.

"I hate when you do that," he said as he tried to smooth his hair back in place.

I laughed remembering the same conversation with Uncle Jeff. "I'll try to remember that."

That afternoon I showered the grime of physical labor off and dressed in shorts and a clean shirt. I went down the stairs to the kitchen for a glass of water. We had almost completed the stairway. Ed had taken Brandon at his word for the rest of the day. If he said he couldn't do it. He just gave the job to someone else. As usual Brandon's spirits were not dampened at all by it.

I sat at the table enjoying the air conditioning and the cold water. The feeling of being clean and cool after a long day of physical labor was very satisfying. I could understand why Uncle Jeff had enjoyed his work in the landscape business. Darla came into the room looking fresh and beautiful. I smiled at her.

"Come and sit on my lap," I said. I held out my arms to her, and she settled comfortably on my legs. "I love to sit this way with you," I said.

"I like it too." She leaned her head on my chest, and I kissed the top of it. "Are you going to see your mom?" she asked.

"Yeah, I thought I could spend a couple of hours with her before dinner. I'm planning beef tenderloin. I was hoping I could talk Dad and Mom into coming over for a barbecue."

"Can I come with you? I haven't seen either one of them for a few days and time is precious."

"Yes it is. Sure, come along. They haven't wanted to go out much since the bad news. I think a little outing would be good for both of them."

"I agree. Maybe between the two of us we can talk them into it." She jumped up and headed for the steps to her room above the garage. "Just let me get my purse."

When we arrived at the townhouse, Charlotte's car was parked in the driveway. I looked at Darla. She shrugged. We both got out of the car and headed for the front door. Just as we were about to ring the bell the door opened, and we were face to face with Charlotte and Brad.

"Oh." Charlotte was startled. "Mom, Dad, what are you doing here?"

"Visiting Gramma Charlie," I said. "Hello, Brad." I held out my hand reluctantly. It was the first time we'd seen him since we'd heard the news. He took my hand. The boy had a firm handshake. I looked at his face. He was obviously uncomfortable. He stood about an inch taller than Charlotte. She had topped out at six feet even.

"Hello, Mr. Landrum," he said. "I'm sorry I didn't ask you formally for Charlotte's hand in marriage." He looked down at his feet.

"I understand," I said, "under the circumstances." I found myself looking down at my feet too.

Charlotte pushed Brad out the door and stepped out closing it behind her. "Good news, Dad." She was truly radiant. I was coming to understand that, as hard as this was for us, it was really a good thing that was happening.

"What's the good news?" Darla asked. "And why did you close us out here."

"I don't want Gramma Charlie to think we're plotting anything."

"Okay, tell us."

"I think I've talked her into having the chemotherapy. She wants to live to see her great grandbaby."

I felt a weight lift from my chest. "Really, Charlita?"

"Yes, I couldn't get a commitment from her, but I think she'll do it now. She was really excited. She's coming to the wedding too. Are you guys?"

"Of course we're coming to the wedding. Don't I get to give you away?" Ouch, it hurt to say that.

"I'd like that, Dad."

"I'd like that too, Sir," Brad said.

"When is the wedding?" Darla asked. She sounded small and frightened. I looked at her with concern. "Don't I get to help plan my own daughter's wedding?"

"I didn't think you would want to."

"Of course I want to."

"Good." Charlotte tugged on Brad's hand and they headed for her car. "We've set the date for July 25th."

"That's so soon." Darla followed them to the car. "Do you have a place in mind?"

"We could just go down to the justice of the piece. We don't have much to spend. But I was hoping, if you guys got over being mad at me, we could do it at the house. I like Sivon's idea about the arbor at the top of the steps, if you can finish it that is, and if Sivon and Brandon don't mind. They're planning to get married up there." She laughed. "Could we talk about this tonight? Brad and I are going to buy the rings." Darla stepped away from the car, and Charlotte backed out of the driveway. We waved, and they drove off.

"They're happy," Darla said.

"I think they are. Even Brad seemed excited, although I think he was a little bit afraid of me." I laughed. "I wasn't going to punch him."

"I guess we should be happy for them." Darla took my hand, and we walked toward the front door of the townhouse.

"We might as well. We can't change it. And I'll be grateful if it's changed Mom's mind about the chemo."

"I will too."

◊

My mom called the doctor that Monday morning. She arranged to begin the chemotherapy the following week. They told her that they had medication that could help with the nausea. She would still feel tired and weak for a few days after every treatment, but she shouldn't be sick.

She started going out again. She and Darla spent time together with Charlotte planning the wedding. It would be only family and a few close friends. Brandon, Sivon, Ed and I worked every spare minute on completing the steps and the arbor at the top of the hill. The gazebo would come later. We managed to get it finished, and Uncle Jeff was even able to do a little bit of temporary gardening to make the hill look festive.

The day of the wedding I stood in the pool house with my oldest daughter. She was nervous but she looked beautiful. Her wedding dress was not long like most. It came to just above her knees. It was fitted with small straps on her lovely broad shoulders. Her pregnancy didn't show yet. Her stomach was still flat. I couldn't help but be proud of the beautiful woman that stood before me.

"You're looking at me funny, Dad," she said. "Is something out of place?"

"No," I smiled at her beaming face. "Everything is exactly where it should be. I was just feeling proud that I created such a beautiful woman. The world is lucky to have you."

"Thank you, Dad. That was such a nice thing to say. I'm glad you're not mad at me anymore."

"I was never really mad at you, honey. I had a few negative thoughts about Brad." I laughed and Charlotte blushed. "But I'm over the shock of it now and I'm happy for you. You're happy. That's all that matters to me." I paused and looked into her eyes. "This path that you're taking could be tough at times. I hope you understand that."

"I know, Dad, but I can do it. I can make it work. Brad and I can make it work together."

"I believe in you, honey. But I want you to promise me that if you ever need me for anything, you won't be embarrassed to come to me." I knew I had to stop talking pretty soon, or I'd cry like a baby at my daughter's wedding.

"I promise, Dad." She kissed my cheek. "There's the wedding march. I guess we'd better go."

I walked out the door with my firstborn on my arm. My other two daughters were at the base of the hill dressed in matching blue dresses in the same design as the wedding dress. Sivon stood beside them dressed the same way. They were beautiful too, but as always, the bride stole the show. Brad stood at the top of the hill with his brother and Brandon as his groomsmen. They were waiting for us. The look on Brad's face was one of wonder. I remembered the way I felt when I saw Darla coming down the aisle in her wedding dress. I just hoped I could make it up the stairs without tripping and rolling down the hill.

"You know what would liven up this party," I said as we passed the pool, "If I pushed you in the water." I was trying to distract myself from the lump in my throat.

"I think it would be better if I pushed you."

We walked past my mom and dad, Uncle Jeff and his family, Darla's parents and Darla. Jimmy was there with Meryl and their kids. Brad's family was there. That morning in my own yard all my troubles faded away, and I felt like the luckiest man in the world.

In November Mom had her last chemotherapy treatment. The doctors were pleased with how well she had tolerated it all. She'd lost all of her hair, of course. There is no way around that, but she'd felt pretty well during the whole thing.

When we got the report it was good news. The doctor told her that the legions on her liver were not gone, but they had definitely shrunk and were not posing a threat to her liver function at this time. He also said that there was no sign that it had spread to any other organs.

I would rather have heard that the legions were gone, but I was happy with this. She would be with us for a little longer it seemed. Her doctor wanted to check her again in a few months. If the legions were getting bigger again, they would talk about radiation.

I called her from my cell phone as I pulled into the driveway of the townhouse. It was a crisp, cool November day a week before Thanksgiving. "Mom, I'm in the driveway. I have a surprise for you. Are you in the kitchen? Go to the backyard."

I walked around the house holding the Afghan puppy in my arms. She stood on the patio rubbing her arms in the cool air. Her face lit up when she saw what I was carrying. She ran to me to fold the puppy into her arms. He licked her face and she laughed. She looked so happy my heart skipped a beat.

"His name is Pepper," I said.

She smiled up at me from where she had stooped to let the little dog run around. "David, thank you. He looks just like Pepper. You wouldn't let me name Ruffles that."

"Ruffles was stupid. He was lovable, but he was stupid. Pepper was smart, and this little guy is smart too."

We watched the puppy romp around the small back yard. He played a lively game of chasing his tail. "Are you sure he's smart?" Mom asked as we laughed at the puppy trying to sneak up on the tail. Every time he got close to it, it moved away.

"I guess we'll have to wait and see." I looked at her rubbing her arms. "You don't have on a jacket. You must be freezing. Let's go inside."

"Can I bring Pepper in?" she asked.

"It's your house, Mom, and Pepper is your dog." She scooped the puppy up and went into the kitchen. She put him down. He scampered around the kitchen sniffing. He jumped when the dryer in the laundry room buzzed, and we laughed.

"Where is Dad?"

"He's gone to the groom shop."

"I thought he had hired groomers so he could stay home with you."

"He did, but they require management. He doesn't go in much, but I think he just needs to get away from me sometimes."

"I'm sure that's not true."

She smiled and went to the refrigerator. "Would you like some lemonade?"

"No thanks. I need to get back to the house. Vroom is expected home at 4:00 today, and Darla likes for me to make sure they do what they're supposed to. Well I guess it isn't *they* anymore now that Charlotte is living at Brad's house."

"I know you miss her, David. But she looks deliriously happy. She comes to see me twice a week. She's such a sweet girl. When I look at her I feel like I'm looking in a mirror. Only seeing a young me," she patted the scarf she was wearing on her head, "with hair."

"You look as beautiful now as you ever did," I said, "with or without hair."

"Thank you, sweetie. Anyway, Charlotte is big for six months. She says it isn't twins, but I'm not so sure. It's going to be a big boy. Are you excited about your pending grandparenthood?"

"Yes, I think it's going to be really fun to have a grandchild. You know I wanted to have another baby a few years ago, but Darla had it fixed so we couldn't when the twins were born. I wanted to adopt, but she said we were too old. I guess she was right. I think this is the perfect compromise. Darla has even said she'll help when the baby is born and Charlotte starts to work. She didn't want to at first. I think she was mad."

"Well, you weren't really prepared. I know it was a shock."

We sat in silence for a while. I was thinking about when the baby was born. I worried that Mom would give up after his arrival.

"I'll stay around for a while, David. I want to get to know my great grandson."

"How do you do that?" I said. "You know what I'm thinking. You've always been able to do that."

"You've always worn your thoughts on your face, honey." She laughed and reached down for the puppy. He was sitting at her feet with his big tongue hanging out of the side of his face. His brown eyes were staring adoringly at her. "I think we've bonded already." She pulled him into her lap and hugged him to her chest.

"You'll keep him after I'm gone, David. You won't find him another home or anything like that, will you?"

"Mom …" I started to protest. It was hard to hear her talk about being gone.

"I need to know you'll keep him, David. Your dad likes small dogs. He'd take him anyway, but I want you to have him."

"I was planning to keep him."

"So you've forgiven yourself for Charlotte."

I smiled and touched her face. Her skin was cool. She turned my hand to her mouth and kissed it. Her lips were warm on my palm.

"I'm forgiven," I said and looked at the puppy snuggled into her chest. "You manipulated that situation pretty expertly, though, even if I wasn't planning to keep him."

"How could you say no to a dying woman?"

Our grandson was born on February 12th. Charlotte was wrong about the first baby being late, in her case anyway. He was a big baby, a whopping 9 lbs. 3 oz. Charlotte had an easy delivery and looked excited but tired when we visited her in the hospital.

"Did you see him?" She was sitting up in bed when we got there. He'd been born at 2:00 am. Brad had called us. He was so excited he could hardly get the words out of his mouth. We let Charlotte sleep through the night then visited at about ten in the morning. Of course, we knew the hospital had her up at the crack of dawn.

"We saw him," I said. "He's beautiful."

Darla went to the bedside and took Charlotte's hand. "Are you alright? Did you have a hard time?"

"It was quite an experience," she said. "But everyone said it was an easy delivery. If that was easy I don't want to know what hard is." She and Darla laughed companionably. The tension between them was gone.

"I don't want to hear the details," I said going to the other side of the bed and taking her other hand.

"You wouldn't have a problem with it." Darla said. "You were with me during all of our kid's births, even the c-section."

"I know, but it's different with my wife than with my little girl."

"I'm not a little girl, Dad. I'm six feet tall."

"I still can't believe that." I looked around the room. "Where's Brad? He didn't let you do this alone, did he?"

"Of course he didn't, Dad. He even spent the night with me. That chair over there folds out into a bed, a very uncomfortable bed. He stayed until they brought the baby in. Elliot stayed in the nursery last night to let me rest from the delivery. They just took him to do some tests. They'll bring him back in a minute. Then he'll be rooming in with me until I go home tomorrow."

"I can't believe they'll let you go home in a day," Darla said. "When I was having babies they kept us at least three days. I stayed five after the c-section."

"I'm fine. I'm happy that I'm going home tomorrow. I can't wait to start being a mommy."

"What kind of tests are they doing?" I asked. "There isn't anything wrong is there?"

"No just standard tests. They prick his heel to test for bilirubin, whatever that is. I wish they didn't prick his heel."

"He won't remember it." Darla smoothed Charlotte's sleep mussed hair away from her face. "You look beautiful, baby."

"I'm really happy." She put her hand on her belly. "I can't wait to start working on getting my figure back."

"I don't see where you've lost it," I said.

"I at least need to firm this part up." She patted her belly again. "It stretched a long way."

There was a knock on the door, and Mom and Dad came into the room. I smiled proudly at them. "Did you see my new grandson Elliot?" Mom came to me and kissed my cheek. She looked so good. Her hair had grown back in. I wasn't sure, but it looked a little bit curlier. She had filled out some. She'd gotten thin during the chemotherapy.

"We saw him. The nurse said they were about to bring him in here. So maybe we can hold him."

"Wash your hands everyone," Charlotte said.

"A lot of things have changed," Darla laughed. "In my day they said don't be afraid of germs. Babies are covered by the mother's antibodies until she stops nursing."

"Well now they say wash your hands." Charlotte pointed to the sink beside her bed. "So get in line, everybody."

We left before Brad came back. We had passed Elliot around a couple of times. Charlotte had changed his diaper. I was a little embarrassed when Mom told Charlotte to be careful because when I was a baby I tended to pee in her face.

"Forgive me for that, okay Mom," I said.

"I was never mad at you for it. It just goes along with baby boys."

"Dad's blushing," Charlotte laughed, and all the people in the room thought that was hilarious.

As we were leaving, Uncle Jeff and Amanda were coming in. "Congratulations!" Amanda said. "You look very proud." She hugged Darla, then me.

Uncle Jeff hugged Darla, then shook my hand and slapped me on the shoulder. I could feel the big, goofy grin on my face. "Oh, that's not going to do," Uncle Jeff said as he wrapped me in one of his bear hugs. I hugged him back.

"We were just leaving. Mom and Dad are in there, but I think they're about to leave too. The baby is rooming in with Charlotte." I looked back at the room. "She'll probably let you hold him if you wash your hands."

On my birthday that spring, we celebrated in our backyard. The gazebo was finally finished. We had ceased working on it when the winter cold had set in. We'd had a cold winter for northwest Georgia. The spring had been cool too. But this day was sunny, cool in the shade but warm in the sunshine. We hadn't opened the pool yet, but the spring flowers were blooming, and the hillside garden was almost complete.

"Uncle Jeff and Amanda were there. Alice was there. Evelyn had come home from the University for the Event. I was glad it had fallen on a Saturday this year. Charlotte and Brad and Elliot were there. Veronica and the twins were there, and of course, the ever present Sivon. Her parents had come over for a short visit and happy birthday wishes. Jimmy and Meryl were there without children. It was strange to see them that way.

Mom and Dad were there too. Mom wore a scarf on her head. The legions on her liver had started growing again, and the oncologist had recommended another round of chemo instead of radiation. She was thin as a rail and hairless, but as always, she was smiling and happy to be surrounded by her family. Dad looked like death.

"Mom, come up and see the gazebo," I said. "You know I've never built anything before, and even though I had a lot of help, I'm really proud of it."

"Oh honey," she smiled up at me from the chair she'd been in all afternoon. "I wish I could, but I'll never make it up those steps."

"I'll carry you then. Mom, you have to see my gazebo."

She laughed and stretched her arms up to me. I scooped her up. She was light as a feather. My heart ached to feel the bones of her legs, her spine, and her ribs. I could feel Dad's eyes on my back as I climbed the steps.

"Jeff has done a lovely job on this garden," Mom said as we went. "I love the weeping red bud at the top. I don't think I've ever seen one of those."

"I like it too. And I really like the fact that he did most of it himself. His knee has recovered very well, and there's no sign of depression. He scared me to death with that depression."

"He scared us all," she said. I put her down in a wicker love seat that Darla had made cushions for. She started to struggle to her feet.

"Mom you don't have to get up." I tried to sit next to her, but she stopped me with her extended hand.

"I have to look at the view. I can walk, you know, but I might need some help getting up."

I pulled her to her feet and noticed that she may have lost weight and hair, but she was still tall and standing straight and proud. Her shoulders were still broad.

She walked around the six sided building stopping at each opening to look out. "I'm so glad you screened it in. It's nice to have a place outside where you aren't bothered by the bugs."

"Were the bugs bothering you down in the yard? You should have said something. I could have gotten you some spray."

"The bugs weren't bothering me. Darla sprayed the yard." She stopped at the opening of the gazebo that looked out over the group of people below. "What a beautiful sight."

"You're not going to give up now, are you, Mom?" I asked. There was a lump in my throat. I swallowed it down.

"Yes I am, David." She looked back at me, and I guess my expression told her of my grief. She came to me and put her arms around me. She rested her head on my shoulder. I put my arms around her too, and gave way to the tears.

"Oh, I'm still going to be glad for every day I have," she said. "And I'll still fight the weakness and the pain. But I won't have any more treatment. My life has been wonderful, David. But it's over."

"Don't say that, Mom."

"I guess you're right. It's not over yet." She let me go and went back to the window. I was suddenly cold. I rubbed my arms, feeling the warm places on them from her embrace.

"Mom, why don't you get depressed? Uncle Jeff sunk so deeply into depression, and all he had was a bad knee." I gulped and rubbed the tears off my cheeks. "Why aren't you depressed? You're going to die." I think it was the first time I'd said it. I think it was the first time I'd accepted it.

"Jeff had to find a way to go on," she said. "I don't. Come over here, David." She stretched her arm toward me, and I went to the window. "I'm going to die, but I'm not going to die today. Look down there, David. Look at my beautiful family, my wonderful friends, my dog named Pepper. How could I possibly be depressed?"

✦

My mother died in August of that summer. It was just a little over a year from diagnosis. She had rallied again after her last round of chemotherapy. Her hair grew back and she filled out. She even gained some strength. She enjoyed her visits from her grandchildren and her great grandchild.

My Dad's health suffered. His blood pressure went up, and he had to start taking medication. I worried about him, but most of my energy went into savoring every minute I had with Mom. Dad assured me that he was taking his medication, and he was under the care of a good physician. I had to be happy with that.

In mid July we learned that the legions not only had grown, but the cancer had spread to her lungs and glands. She went to bed then and didn't get up. In the beginning of August she asked to go to Hospice. I offered to get her a nurse to come into her house, but she refused.

On the third of August, Dad and I sat on either side of her bed. We each held a hand. She'd seen the priest. Darla, my kids, Uncle Jeff and his kids, had said their tearful goodbyes and left us. My brother and sister had both said goodbye too. She smiled and told them that she loved them. They had left then. I guess they knew this was something Dad and I needed to do together.

She looked at both of us. Her eyes seemed to penetrate me down to my heart, down to my soul.

"When I came into this world I was completely alone." Her voice was a whisper. "I lived the first twenty years of my life alone." She took a deep breath and looked at Dad. "Then I met you." She looked at me. "And you gave me David. Thank you." She looked back at Dad then stopped and closed her eyes for a minute.

"Mom ..." My heart was pounding. Was she gone?

She opened her eyes and tried to say something. Dad and I both leaned closer to hear her.

"It's time for me to leave this world now." She whispered. "And I am not alone."

She signaled for the nurse who had just entered the room. "I'm ready for the morphine now."

The nurse administered it with a sponge under her tongue and left the room. "Don't ever forget how much I love you both. And don't ever stop loving each other." She closed her eyes.

Dad and I sat next to that bed in silence for another hour holding her hands. I wanted to scream, *Mom don't go, don't leave me.* But I knew she couldn't stay. So I just sat there watching her breathe. After a time, Dad and I joined our other hands across the bed. We both looked up as she took a deep breath then stopped. She sat up a little and her chest collapsed. As the air blew through her vocal chords, I heard her voice for the last time.

Dad dropped his head on her hand and said, "Charlotte, Charlotte." I remembered that room where Pepper had died. Mom had done the same thing. She'd embraced the dead dog and said his name again and again. I had run from that room. I looked at the lifeless face of my mother, and suddenly, I had to run from this room.

I went to the lobby. Uncle Jeff and Darla were there. "She's gone," I said. They came to me and put their arms around me. We all cried, and I was not ashamed.

We didn't finish the Trail that summer. Dad and I were both too worn down, and Uncle Jeff understood. He was doing well. He exercised and ate right. He said he was going to dance at his daughter's weddings. Although he wished they'd go ahead and get married. He wanted more grandchildren. It made me feel good to know he saw my kids as his grandchildren.

It wasn't a good time for Charlotte to go to the trail. The baby was too young to leave behind and too young to take with us. She had embraced motherhood with an energy even Darla was amazed at. Brad started school at Georgia Tech that September. He wanted to be an electrical engineer.

I insisted on going to my Dad's follow up doctor's appointment. I talked him into letting me discuss his health with his doctor. I couldn't lose another parent anytime soon. It would be the end of me.

Talking to the doctor helped. She assured me that even though he was somewhat run down, which in light of his recent experience was understandable, he would be fine. He should take his medication, get onto an exercise routine, and eat right. Apparently, when Mom got sick, he started eating a lot of fast food and processed stuff instead of cooking his own healthy meals.

We decided to sell the townhouse. He didn't want to live in it without her, and I didn't want to rent it and have to manage it. I walked through it one last time after it was sold. I stopped in the doorway of the little room off the kitchen. The one she had used as her sewing room. I could almost see her sitting there. I could almost hear the whirring of the machine.

Pepper nudged my hand with his wet nose, and I looked down. I had brought him with me for the last walk through. It seemed right. He'd been good for her in her last months. I clipped the leash on his collar and locked the front door as I went out.

CHAPTER TWENTY SIX

We didn't finish the Trail the following summer either. My grief process went smoothly. It was painful, of course. I missed my mom very much. I knew I would always miss her. But after the anger and the guilt passed, the joy of her existence came shining through. I remembered her at the oddest moments, things she said to me, the clothes she made for me when I was a kid, the way she loved her dogs, and the graceful way she'd died.

Dad didn't fare so well. He rented an apartment close to the nursery. He came to breakfast every morning at first. I couldn't help but notice the circles under his eyes. His shoulders had begun to slope again. I remembered when he first came back to Atlanta. He'd been depressed then. His wife had left him. His children had moved on. His shoulders had sloped then too.

I asked him every morning how he was. He took a cup of coffee and biscotti, the sugary ones, not the whole grain. I tried to talk him into mixed fruit or a whole grain muffin. He'd just shake his head and look down into the black coffee in his cup.

After a while he stopped coming into the café. If I called him and asked him to dinner, he refused. I went to his apartment. It was a mess. He'd always been irritatingly neat. I invited him to move into the pool house so he'd have company. He refused.

"I'm worried about him," I said one day when I'd gone to Uncle Jeff's office to take a break from the counter. "I can't reach him. I've tried everything. I even told him to stop wallowing in his own misery. That worked for you. He said he was very comfortable with his own misery."

"I'm worried about him too, David. But one thing I know is that you can't deal with someone else's problems. I was ready to come out of that depression. You just gave me a hand. We have to let Brian get ready. I think that's all we can do."

On my forty eighth birthday we planned a party at our house like we usually did. Dad refused to come. I told him I'd cancel the whole thing if he didn't come. He agreed to be there, but he was only there in body. He sat at a table by himself nursing a beer and watching the bubbles rise to the surface. I'd had enough.

"Dad," I said. "Come up to the gazebo with me."

"Oh, I don't think so." He looked more closely at his beer. "I need to get going."

"You need to go back to your apartment to hide under the mess?"

"Don't be an ass, David. I'm grieving my wife."

I was angry enough to remind him that he'd never married her again, but I didn't. "I grieve for her too, Dad. But I'm grateful enough that I had her in my life to honor her memory."

"I honor her memory."

"You honor it by refusing to live?" I put my arm under his and pulled him toward the stairs. I practically dragged him up. About half way he pulled away from me and climbed the rest of the stairs himself.

He followed me into the gazebo and sat down. It was a warm spring day, and I turned on the ceiling fan. I sat down across from him and leaned forward.

"Mom and I came up here right after the second round of chemo. She was so weak I had to carry her."

"I remember. I watched you. I thought about following, but I figured maybe you needed some time alone together." He looked down at the floor.

"When we were up here, she stood up and shakily walked to every window to see the view. You're staring at the floor."

He looked up and met my eyes then returned his stare to the floor. "I was never good enough for her," he said. "She had such a zest for life. I loved her so much." He looked up at me, and I winced at the pain in his eyes. "Now she's left me just like I left her. Only she won't come back."

I swallowed the lump in my throat. "No, but it isn't that she won't come back. She can't come back. Dad, in so many ways she's still here. I have a lot of her in me. Sometimes it startles me. And Charlotte is the image of her. Even though Veronica is blond with blue eyes, her facial features are Mom's in every way. And she's six foot two. Where do you think that came from?"

"You and I are tall too."

"They stand up straight and tall. They're Amazon women who aren't ashamed. You told me once that was what made you fall in love with Mom."

He smiled at that. The smile was brief. It didn't reach his eyes, but it was something. I stood and went to the window that overlooked the yard. "Come over here, Dad." He didn't move. I went to his chair, put my hand on his arm, and lifted him to his feet.

"That's the second time you've forced me to move against my will, David. It's not nice to manhandle an old man."

"I'll keep doing it if you don't start cooperating a little bit." I pulled him toward the window. He shook my hand off and walked to the window himself. I smiled. There was still life in the old man.

"Mom and I stood at this window looking down at the same scene. It was just last year." I couldn't believe it had only been a year. So much had changed. "I asked her why she didn't get depressed. After all, Uncle Jeff had gotten so depressed about his knee. Here she was facing death, and her spirits were great."

"You know," he said. "I wondered that too. She never got depressed. She was sad sometimes but never depressed."

"She told me that Uncle Jeff got depressed because he had to figure out how to go on. She didn't. Then she told me to look down at the yard." My dad looked down at the gathering by the pool. "She said, look at my beautiful family. Look at my wonderful friends. Look at my dog named Pepper. Then she said, *how can I be depressed?*"

We stood in silence for a few minutes looking at the beauty of the gathering.

"You have the same family, Dad, the same friends. She made me promise to keep Pepper, but you can have him if it will get you moving again."

"She told me. Pepper was a memory that the two of you shared. I don't want to interfere with that."

"Dad, the point is that like she said. She didn't have to find a way to go on. You do."

He sat back down in the chair. "I don't have the energy, David. I'm too old to start over. I don't want to groom anymore, and I sure don't want to be a lawyer. I don't want to retire alone. I just want to give up."

"Please don't give up, Dad. I need you."

He looked up at me, and there were tears in his eyes. I knew mine were wet too. He stood and came back to the window. We put our arms around each other and cried.

"I'll try, David," he said. "I'll try."

He started coming to the Café again then. He let me talk him into switching to decaf after his first cup of coffee. He let me give him a whole grain muffin instead of biscotti, and on a few mornings, he took a bowl of mixed fruit. His eyes were still circled and his shoulders still slumped. But I was grateful for his progress even if it was slow.

Chapter Twenty Six

✦

"How are your parents doing, Darla?" I asked as we sat in the living room after dinner. The house was empty. Veronica had gone to the university. It was late summer, and she wanted to set up her dorm room before classes started the following week. The twins were spending the night with Sivon for a change. Harry had gone with them.

"They're doing really well," she said. "Why?"

"I was thinking today at the café how the roles have reversed between me my parents. The changes were so subtle I hardly noticed them. Then suddenly I was the care taker, and they needed me instead of the other way around. I'm glad I can give something back to them, but sometimes it's very challenging."

"I thought Uncle Jeff was doing pretty well."

"He is, but there was a time when he needed my help. I think there probably will be again."

"Is Uncle Dad still depressed?"

"Yeah, he's making an effort, but I can see it in his face and the way he carries himself."

"I'm sorry, David." She looked down at the photos she had in her hand. "He really loved your mom. She was his grand passion."

"Yeah," I said. "She was his grand passion."

"Well, my parents are doing well. I'm sure the time will come when they need me to take care of them, but now they don't. In fact, the last time I talked to them they were planning to buy a house at the beach. Dad said he wanted to do it while they were still young enough to enjoy it."

"That's great."

✦

"David," I looked up at Dad's voice. There was something different about him today. He still had circles under his eyes, but he was standing a little straighter. He sat down at the breakfast bar and asked for coffee. I put it down in front of him. He stared down into the black liquid. It must have been my imagination, I thought, wishful thinking.

"You want some fruit today?" I asked.

"No, I think I'll splurge and have biscotti."

Definitely wishful thinking, I thought. "You know, I make *this* biscotti with whole wheat and sweeten it with agave." I picked up the healthy one. "It's not bad for you though, so if you're trying to kill yourself, it won't work."

He looked up at me. At first his face registered anger, then he smiled reluctantly and looked back down. "I'm not trying to kill myself. In fact, I got up and took a walk this morning. I went almost a mile."

"Fantastic," I said and squeezed his shoulder.

"Listen, would you come down to Jeff's office with me. I have an idea I want to run by him. I'd like for you to be there for moral support." He looked up at me. I couldn't read his expression. Maybe he looked insecure, or maybe worried.

"Sure, just let me get Maggie out of the kitchen to mind the counter."

We went to Uncle Jeff's office. He wasn't there. I asked a clerk where he was, and she said he was in the far greenhouse. We walked out of the show room and around the growing field out to the greenhouse.

"I forget how big this place is," Dad said. He sounded wistful. "I remember when it was a farm."

I opened the door to the green house and signaled Dad to go in. Uncle Jeff was sitting at the far end talking to Evelyn. She had finished her graduate school in record time and was working full time at the nursery. They saw us and waved. Evelyn got up and hugged both of us then headed for the door.

"Honey, wait," Dad said. "I wanted to run something by your dad. Since you're working her now too, I'd like to get your opinion."

"Okay." She sat back down on the stool.

Dad turned and walked away from us a little. He was pacing. He really must be nervous, I thought.

"I sold the groom shop," he looked at us expectantly.

Uncle Jeff and I exchanged a look. "You told me you didn't want to groom anymore." I filled the silence. "Did you get a good price for it?"

"Yes, I did. I got enough to start a new business without going into my retirement. I was thinking of a bird food store. You know, you see them in those little strip malls."

"I love those stores, Uncle Brian," Evelyn said.

"I've never been in one," Uncle Jeff said. "Do they just sell bird food?"

"Oh no, Dad," Evelyn bounced on her stool. "They sell all sorts of things, bird feeders and bird baths. I got a small feeder for my apartment in one of those stores. It suctions to the window." Uncle Jeff smiled at her, but there must have been a silent communication because she stopped talking and looked back at Dad.

"I was wondering if I could claim a small corner of the nursery show room and devote it to wild birds. Don't answer me right now." He said it fast as if to stop anyone from saying anything. "Just think about it for a while. Call me when you decide." He turned and left the greenhouse.

We all looked at each other in silence for a minute. I looked at Uncle Jeff. "Don't you even think of saying no," I said.

"That's right, Dad." Evelyn got off her stool and went to stand in front of her father. "Uncle Brian needs us. Besides, I'd thought of that myself. All nurseries have a wild bird section. We need one."

Uncle Jeff laughed. "I wasn't going to say no. I was just a little shocked. Brian hasn't said two words in a row to me in months. Plus, I didn't want to seem too excited. I was afraid I'd scare him away."

❖

I clipped the leash to Harry's collar and then clipped one to Pepper's. The two dogs got along fine. Pepper, being a young dog, could get on Harry's nerves. But the older dog was very patient. I guess that's why he made such a good therapy dog for the twins. It was midnight, and I let myself out the front door.

"How old are you now, Harry?" I asked the dog as if he could answer.

"Talking to your dog?" The voice came out of the shadow of a tree. I jumped, knowing as I did, that it was Jimmy. Then I noticed his car parked a little way down the road.

"You just enjoy watching me jump, don't you? That's why you don't ever warn me that you're coming." He fell in beside me and took Pepper's leash.

"So how old is Harry?"

"We don't know exactly how old he was when we got him, but I'm guessing about nine or ten. He's still feeling good, though. He keeps up with the twins just fine."

"Does he still detect Brandon's seizures?"

"He sure does. Of course, so does Belinda. It isn't too crucial though. They're happening less and less. I'd like to think he's growing out of them, but it's probably the medication. That's okay too."

"Yeah, so tell me. Are you enjoying being a grampa?"

"Yes, it's great. Charlotte isn't stingy with Elliot either. We get to keep him all the time. I'm home in the afternoon, you know. Darla is still picking the twins up in the afternoon so she gets home late. Veronica isn't around much anymore, so keeping Elliot gives me something to occupy myself with."

"That's nice, but you never had a hard time occupying yourself." We walked in silence for a minute.

"So how do you like being a grampa?" I asked him. "Heather has two kids right?"

"Yeah, she has a girl and a boy. Just like us. I hope she'll stop now. It's hard thinking of your little girl having babies. It's even harder to think about her doing what she did to get them."

I shivered, even in the warm night. "I know what you mean."

"Anyway, I think being a grandparent is one thing that really is all it's cracked up to be."

"That's a great way to put it." We stopped for Pepper to deposit a large pile on my neighbor's lawn. I pulled the plastic bag out of my pocket and scooped it up. "Yuck."

"David," Jimmy said. "I wanted to thank you for helping James, Jr. with school. It was hard for him, but he made it through. He won't actually graduate until January, but I know he will. I can't wait to see him walk up there with his cap and gown and get that diploma. I know it's in a large part because of you."

"The brain was his. I just helped him organize it in a way that he could use it."

"Well, I just wanted to say thank you."

I put my arm across his shoulder and laughed. Jimmy was always a little shocked when I touched him affectionately. I felt him tense then relax in my embrace. I dropped my arm again and reached down to untangle Harry's leash.

"So how is he doing?"

"He got hired at Georgia State. He's on staff in the athletic department, an assistant coach. He wants to work his way up to faculty, but for now he's happy. Imagine a kid of mine in higher education."

"You could have done it if you wanted to."

"Not without you." The silence was a little awkward this time.

"Is he still seeing Evelyn?" I asked.

"Well, when they separated to go to school they kept dating for a while, but you know how hard long distance relationships are. I know that Jamie dated other people. I don't know about Evelyn, but she's been back for a while now, and I haven't heard anything about her. Of course, Jamie has his own place. I don't know everything he does."

"I guess the distance broke them up."

"It looks that way."

We had turned to walked back to the house. I stopped on the front walk and took Pepper's leash back.

"Thanks for walking with me, Jimmy. It's always nice to catch up, just the two of us."

I watched him get into his car and drive away. How long had I known him? I thought. ...Forever.

That summer was spent with Dad supervising renovations to the nursery. He wrote a cost analysis and studied where to order his merchandise. It was nice watching him work his way out of his depression.

He was thinking about buying a small house in midtown. Not far from the one of Amanda's that we had shared for a short time before he moved back in with Mom. He'd gotten himself a dog, a long haired dachshund. Mom was right. He liked small dogs.

Plans were made to finish the Appalachian Trail the following year in the summer. In the meantime we planned several overnight packing trips and some day hikes to get Dad back in shape.

"This is the first trail we packed." Uncle Jeff told Dad as we set off up the path. "David was eight years old, and he had decided he wanted to start back packing. We went to the outdoor store and bought equipment and a book. David chose this trail."

"It's a little rough for a first hike," Drew said. It was Uncle Jeff, Drew, Dad and me. None of the kids had come on this trip.

"It isn't bad now after a lifetime of hiking," Uncle Jeff said. "But that first time I didn't think I was going to make it."

"I didn't either, but I wasn't going to admit it." I laughed.

"You were a stubborn kid."

"I'm sorry I missed it, David, but I'm always glad when I hear how close you and Jeff were. You were a good father to him, Jeff. Thank you."

"Trust me, Brian. It was my pleasure."

The group fell into silence for most of the rest of the hike. We stopped to eat lunch on an outcropping of rocks. While we ate, we told Dad and Drew about the bear and the rattle snake. They were impressed. I noticed that Dad watched his step a little more closely when we started walking again.

When we were about a mile from the waterfall, Drew broke the silence. "I have an announcement to make." We all stopped and looked at him. "I was going to try to find a better time, but I can't hold it in anymore."

"Well, spit it out, son," Dad said. "Don't keep us in suspense."

"Lizzy and I are pregnant."

"You're pregnant?" I laughed. "Fantastic."

"Well, she's pregnant, but I get queasy at the smell of bacon frying. She doesn't seem to have a problem with it, though." We all laughed and patted him on the shoulder around his pack.

"Are you sure you should have left her?" Dad asked. "How far along is she?"

"She's fourteen weeks. That's about three and a half months. She was glad to get rid of me. I've been sort of a worry wart. We're not young, you know."

"You're young from my point of view," Dad said. He took Drew by the shoulders and kissed him soundly on the cheek. "How exciting, I thought I'd had all the grandchildren I would have."

"How old are you Drew?" Uncle Jeff asked.

"I'm forty three but Lizzy is forty five. They do some kind of test to all women over thirty five. It's called an amnio something. I guess there are some birth defects that are more common in older women. Lizzy had hers and the baby seems to be alright. But the risk for the mother is still greater at her age."

"But Elizabeth is in good condition so it reduces the risk again," Uncle Jeff said. "I know this first hand. Amanda was forty five when the twins were born. I was fifty. It's a great time to start a family."

"I guess it better be. We're into it now."

"Listen, Uncle Jeff." I cocked my ear in the direction of the sound. "Remember, you can hear the waterfall before you get to it."

"That's right," he said. "I think it's about a half a mile now."

We arrived at the campsite about an hour before dusk. We set up camp. Uncle Jeff and I were in one tent and Dad and Drew in the other. We sat down at the campfire, and Uncle Jeff pointed to the waterfall.

"Can I tell them?" He looked at me across the fire.

"Yeah, I guess it's about time."

"Don't tell me this is the secret waterfall incident." Dad laughed, remembering a long ago conversation.

"This is it," I said.

"David and I had arrived here and set up camp. I was building the campfire, and he waded into the water. I told him not to go very deep. Remember, he was only eight years old, and he was a little guy."

"You were a little guy?" Drew laughed.

"Believe it or not," Dad said, "he was."

"Anyway," Uncle Jeff continued. "I turned around, and he was sitting on that rock beside the waterfall." He pointed up the steep rock climb to the spot.

"Oh my God," Dad looked at me. "How did you get up there?"

"There's a path. It's an easy climb. I'll take you in the morning."

"Well, it scared me to death." Uncle Jeff continued. "I didn't know what to do. I didn't want to yell. I was afraid I would startle him into the water. So I signaled to him to come down instead. That was the wrong thing to do."

Chapter Twenty Six

"What happened?" Dad asked. He had an anxious look on his face.

"Don't worry, Dad. It's over and I lived."

He smiled and relaxed his shoulders. "That's right. So what happened?"

"Well, we told you about the bear we saw on the path. With my eight year old imagination, I thought he was telling me the bear was behind me. I jumped in alarm and slid into the waterfall."

"It looked to me like he just jumped into the waterfall for fun." Uncle Jeff was looking stressed at the memory. "I thought maybe he wanted to ride it down. He hit the bottom of the falls, went under, and didn't come back up."

"I was right under the falls. There was no way I could get to the surface. The rushing water just kept pushing me back down. Then Uncle Jeff's hands circled my waist, and he yanked me out of the water and into one of his bear hugs."

"I was frantic when I got to the falls," Uncle Jeff said. "I stuck my hands in where I'd seen him go under, but I couldn't find him. Luckily he was only a few feet to the left."

We stopped the story there. The rest was between us. But I smiled across the fire at him, and he smiled back.

"I have to say, David." Dad was shaking his head. "I'm glad I wasn't here for that."

"David?" Darla's voice came from the door of the little office that Alice and I shared.

I shook my head. I'd been so lost in thought that I hadn't heard her approach. "Hey, P. H.," I said. "What are you doing here?"

"I need to talk to you about a couple of things," she said and came over to stand behind me. She put her arms around my neck. "What are you working on? You were concentrating so hard you didn't even hear me come in."

"I'm working on the lunch menu. I try it all out at home first, so be prepared to taste test." I tilted my head so she could kiss my cheek.

"I can't remember ever saying, this isn't good; don't use it in the restaurant." She laughed, and I smiled like I always did at the sound.

"So what did you want to talk to me about?" I stood up and walked to the window stretching my arms and legs. At this age I seemed to stiffen up if I sat in one position too long. I turned and looked at her. She was worried about something. I could see it in her expression. "What's wrong?" I said. "Is Brandon ...?"

"Brandon is fine." She answered quickly. "In fact, when I left the house he was sitting out by the pool with Belinda and Sivon. They were making plans for their future. You know Belinda will graduate at the end of the coming school year. I'm so proud of her. I was so excited when Emory University accepted her so young."

"I was too. She's a brilliant kid."

"Like her father," Darla said. "Anyway, Sivon will spend her last year in public school to get her diploma. Then she goes to Georgia Tech. I think they've pretty well accepted her, tentatively anyway. Her mother tells me she's done very well."

I smiled and nodded. "Maybe they should get an apartment together."

"They talked about it, but when I told them they couldn't take Brandon with them, they decided against it. They plan to stay at home, and that's fine with me. I think our brain damaged child is going to do just fine. Aside from the fact that he's a brilliant artist, he has two women who love him and are determined to take care of him."

"That's true, but ..." I took a deep breath. "I just hope that Belinda will carve out a little bit of life for herself. It just seems to me she's too caught up in taking care of Brandon. Even with all that therapy, I think she feels guilty that she was in his way when the cord was around his neck. Like she had any control over that."

"Well, I can relate to her on that level."

"Sweetheart ..."

She held up her hand. "David, I didn't come here to talk about the kids. All of that stuff will work itself out in the long run."

I looked down at her. She was serious. I knew her well enough at this point. When she was serious, I needed to listen. "What is it, baby? Are you alright?"

"I'm fine. It's just ..." She looked away from me and walked to the small window to look out at the parking lot. "David, I've met someone. I think I may finally have found my grand passion."

I could feel my mouth fall open and my heart began to pound. I couldn't say anything.

"I want you to give me the chance to experience this." She still didn't look at me.

"Are you asking my permission to have an affair?" I found my voice. It sounded squeaky. My hands were shaking.

"No," she said. "I'm asking for a divorce."

"Divorce!" The word came out on a hiss, and I dropped into the desk chair.

Darla turned from the window. "Oh, David, don't look so hurt." She ran to the chair and climbed into my lap. Her knees were straddling me in our familiar position. She took my face in her hands. "It isn't that I don't love you anymore. I do love you, David. I…"

"Please don't say you love me like a friend."

"Well, that's part of it, but there is so much more. Here's the way I've worked it out. You and I were just meant to spend our lives together. We've created a fantastic family, and we've built a perfect relationship."

She sat back, the bones of her small flat bottom pressing into my legs. I settled her a little more comfortably.

"The way it feels to me is that you and I have just completed love. We've built it to its finish. Kind of like a house or a garden. Now all we're doing is living in it, and it's wonderful."

"But it isn't a grand passion." I put my hands on my face and rubbed my eyes. "I hate divorce, Darla. It tore me up when I was a kid."

"I know, David, but this won't tear up our kids. Please give me this chance." She pulled my hands away from my face and looked directly into my eyes. "If you really can't, then I'll stop talking about it and we'll drop the whole thing."

I looked into her beautiful face. She had her brows pulled together and was trying to look earnest. I smiled. "Darla, you will not drop the whole thing. You always get your way. We have four kids, don't we?"

"You can't blame me for that. Twins run in your family, not mine." She turned to sit in my lap sideways, draping her legs over the arm of the chair. "David, why did you marry me?"

I thought about that for a minute. Then I said, "Because I love you."

"Divorce me for the same reason."

I put my arms around her, and she settled her head on my shoulder. "How will I live without you, P. H.?" I asked.

"Fat chance you'll ever find out. I'm not going anywhere."

"Do I have to move out of the house?"

"Of course not, you own the house."

"We both own the house. Are you planning to get an apartment?"

"I don't see why anything has to change. I'm perfectly happy in my own little suite over the garage. I wouldn't want to break up the family. We still have children at home."

"You just asked me for a divorce." I was starting to feel hysterical. "You don't think that will break up the family?"

"This will be a divorce in name only."

Now I *was* hysterical. I tightened my hold on my little wife, and we both laughed. I laughed until my sides ached and my eyes ran. I reached for a tissue on the desk and wiped my face. Darla kissed my cheek and climbed out of my lap.

"What about a settlement?" I asked.

"Oh, I don't think that's necessary. You'll still be supporting me, unless Evan starts supporting me, and I doubt he'll be able to do it in the manner to which I have become accustomed. We can still share our retirement fund."

"Okay, who is this guy? Will I get to meet him?"

"Of course, I thought I'd bring him over to meet the family for dinner after the divorce is final. He's my hair dresser."

I looked at her hair and noticed, like I always did, how beautiful it was. "You've been going to that salon for years, P. H. How long has this been going on?"

"Evan is new. He started about a month ago. They called me to let me know that my appointment would be with him instead of Jenny, and I almost cancelled. I sure am glad I didn't."

"So, how well do you know him?" I couldn't believe how comfortable I was talking to my wife about her new boyfriend. She was right, as usual. We had built the perfect relationship. We hadn't slept together in years. Besides the fear of losing her, all I really felt was happy for her and a little bit sad for me.

"I would never cheat on you, David. That's why we're getting a divorce." She sat in the chair across the desk from me. "Evan and I have taken a couple of walks in the park together, and we've had lunch. We haven't even kissed. But my heart flutters every time I see him, and I think he feels the same way."

"I'm happy for you, P.H. You deserve this."

She smiled and those beautiful dimples danced on her cheeks. She had aged so well. The lovely girl I married had become a beautiful woman.

"Well, I hope so," she said. "And that brings up the second thing I wanted to talk to you about."

"No, not a second thing," I crossed my arms on the desk and put my head down on them. "I don't think I can take any more."

She put her hands on mine across the desk. "David, have you read the latest article on Anna Smart?"

I looked up at her in surprise.

"Don't try to deny it, David. I know you've followed her through the years. She's been very successful. Her clothing line is in all the stores. She has her own section in department stores, and she has stores of her own all over the country. People pay huge sums to go to her fashion shows."

"So, if you knew that I was keeping up with her, why didn't you say something?"

"Because it was your grand passion; I didn't want to interfere."

"Why are you saying something now?"

Chapter Twenty Six

"Well, if I'm moving on to a grand passion, I think it would be nice for you to have one too. I know how much you loved her."

"She dumped me twenty five years ago."

"She left you for a career. That last article says she's retiring and going to live in the suburbs. She's going to start a line of children's clothes and work out of her home."

"They're speculating that she's finally getting married," I said.

"The gossip columnists are speculating that. They've never gotten even close to knowing anything about Anna Smart. I may not have said anything to you about it, David, but I have kept up." She stood up and came around the desk. She stood behind me and put her arms around my neck again. "Go after her, David. Find out what's changed in her life. Maybe now the time is right for you to be together."

By the end of that summer Dad was in his new wild bird business. Alice and I had introduced a new lunch menu. And Darla and I were divorced.

I had put together a marketing plan for Dad, and his business was booming. The lunch menu at the cafe went over pretty well, a little slower at first than breakfast and dinner had been. But it was picking up. The divorce was a lot more complicated than we had thought it would be.

Charlotte and Veronica were both devastated. We hadn't anticipated that, but it was very hard to explain it.

"She's leaving you for another man." Veronica stood with her arms crossed." It's her hair dresser. I saw them in the park. They were practically making out."

"You're a slut, Mom," Charlotte said. "I can't believe you ever criticized me for getting pregnant. At least I wasn't married to someone else."

"Charlotte, don't ever say something like that about your mother again. You're not too old for me to punish."

"You never punished me when I was a kid. Mom did. Dad, how can you stand this? She's cheating on you."

"She isn't cheating on me. I know about the other man. That's why we're divorcing. She won't pursue that relationship until the divorce is final."

"So she is leaving you for another man." Veronica glared at her mother. "You're disgusting."

Darla was unusually silent.

"Vroom, same goes for you. You will be respectful to your mother, or you will leave this house."

Both girls were silent but continued to glare at their mother. Darla sniffed. I could tell she was fighting tears.

"Okay, let me see if I can explain this. Your mom is not leaving me. She is staying in her suite over the garage, and I'm staying in my bedroom here. We haven't lived any closer than that in years."

"So why are you getting a divorce?"

"Your mom has found someone that she thinks she can have a meaningful romantic relationship with. She won't break her vows, and I don't want to stand in her way."

"Now that is disgusting." Charlotte balled her fists at her sides.

"Your mother and I will always love each other. We're the best of friends and always will be, and we will always be together when it comes to you kids."

"I'm not listening to any more of this." Charlotte picked up my grandson, who was playing with blocks in the corner, and stormed through the front door.

"I'm just glad I go back to school in September. I don't want to be in the same house with people like you." Veronica stormed up the stairs and slammed her bedroom door.

I looked at the twins. They were fifteen years old now. They sat side by side on the couch watching the dramatic scene with very wide eyes.

"So what do you two think?" I asked.

"So, neither one of you are going to live somewhere else?" Belinda asked.

"You won't have to share us will you?" Brandon said. "John Burk's mom and dad are divorced, and he has to live with one of them at a time."

"No baby," Darla went to the couch and sat between them. "Nothing is really going to change. Dad and I haven't finished raising the two of you, and we want to do it together. And like Dad said, we'll always love each other."

"Then why are you getting a divorce?"

Darla looked up at me and I smiled. Neither one of us had anticipated having to provide an explanation to these two.

"I don't think it's something that you would understand right now," I said. "But we'd like for you to trust us."

"You can trust us, can't you?" Darla put her arms across their shoulders. It was a reach for Brandon. He was six feet tall at age fifteen.

"Brandon looked around his mother at Belinda. She nodded her head. "I think we can trust you."

"Yeah, we can trust you." Brandon repeated.

Chapter Twenty Six

They kissed their mother then came to me. Brandon kissed me on the cheek. I bent for Belinda's kiss, and they ran up the stairs to their separate rooms.

I watched them go. "Well, we won two and we lost two." I laughed and turned back to Darla. There were tears running down her cheeks, but she wasn't making a sound.

"Oh baby," I went to her and sat down putting my arm around her shoulders. "Don't cry. Charlotte and Veronica will come around."

✦

Uncle Jeff and Dad took the news surprisingly well. I went to Dad's apartment before I went to the café the next morning. He asked if there had been problems, and I told him there hadn't. I explained that there was a relationship she wanted to explore that had nothing to do with us. He looked at me oddly but didn't ask for details. I figured if Darla was going to bring another man on the scene, I should at least pave the way.

Uncle Jeff was a little bit more challenging. "What's the story, David? Talk to me."

"I don't know if you realized it at the time, but even though Darla and I loved each other when we got married, we weren't really *in love*."

"You'd been friends for a long time without actually dating. I did notice that, but when your marriage went so well, I figured that had changed."

"It did change. Darla asked me to marry her. At first I was shocked, but after she explained that she wanted a family and I did too, I wasn't so shocked. We were late twenties. Anna didn't want to make a family with me, and Darla was striking out in the field of love relationships. We were best friends, and I certainly didn't find her repulsive physically. She said we were the perfect genetic compliment." I laughed and Uncle Jeff did too.

"How could you argue with that?" Uncle Jeff squeezed my shoulder across the desk in his office.

"Obviously we did very well in that area. We had two kids in fast succession after we were married."

"I couldn't help but notice that Charlotte was born eight months after the wedding. Just an early baby, I'm sure." We both laughed.

"It happened the night Darla proposed." I looked down. I could feel myself blushing. "Anyway, after the twins were born, the … um … romantic relationship was pretty much over. We tried to maintain it for a while, but it didn't work. The way Darla explains it is that we went through all the stages of love to develop the perfect relationship. Now that we have it, all we have to do is enjoy it. It sounded crazy to me at first, but now I think she's right."

"So there is another man."

"Not yet, really. She came to me and told me that she was attracted to someone. She thinks it might be what she calls *grand passion*. I've always known that I wasn't her grand passion, and she's always known that Anna Smart was mine. She thinks this guy may be hers. She won't pursue it until it doesn't mean breaking her vows, and I don't want to stand in her way. I hated the idea of divorce at first, but she assures me that nothing will change." I looked into Uncle Jeff's eyes. "We haven't even shared a bedroom for years," I said. "And it was mutual."

He looked at me and smiled. "Will you move out or will she?"

"Neither. Like I said, nothing will change. She has a suite above the garage. It's all the privacy she'll need. We still have children at home."

"Will the new guy move in?"

I laughed. "He will if she wants him to. P.H. always gets her way."

✦

I went up to the café and put my key into the lock on the door. It was already unlocked. Alice must already be here, I thought. That was strange at this time in the morning. I went back to the office. Charlotte and Veronica were sitting at both of the desk chairs. There was a key at the house. I guess they used that.

"What a nice surprise," I said, dropping my keys in the dish on my desk. "Is there a reason for this visit?"

"Of course there is a reason," Veronica said. "And I'm sure you know what it is."

"I'm sure I know what the subject is." I sat down on the easy chair in the corner of the room.

"Dad, are you okay?" Charlotte asked.

I leaned forward and looked from one to the other. "What did I do to deserve such great kids?"

"The truth is that you're not a normal man," Veronica said. "You're much too nurturing."

"I'm glad you think that way, Vroom, but I'm not that great. I'm nowhere nearly as nurturing as Nuncle Jeff, and he was my male role model."

"That's true," Charlotte said. "So answer my question. Are you okay?"

I leaned back again and took a deep breath. "Yes," I said. "I'm okay. At first I was shocked and yes, hurt. I couldn't believe she wanted to break up the family. But she didn't. Do you want me to explain things to you? It might not be comfortable for any of us."

"We want you to explain," Veronica said.

I looked at Charlotte. She nodded. I took another deep breath. My head started to spin. I thought I'd better breath a little more evenly or I'd hyperventilate.

"Your mom and I got married because we were best friends. I mean the kind of friends that love each other completely unconditionally. And we both wanted a family. We were in our late twenties, and both of us were striking out in the grand passion field. That's your mom's phrase for falling head over heels in love." I smiled.

"We know," Charlotte said. "She's said that phrase to us too."

"Really?" I was surprised.

"Yeah," Veronica said, "in the safe sex talk. *You may think this guy is your grand passion.*" She mimicked Darla's voice perfectly. "*But think again.*" Charlotte was nodding her head.

I laughed. I couldn't help myself. It was a side of my daughters I hadn't seen. It was a side of Darla I hadn't seen.

"You do that very well," I said. "Anyway, we created exactly the family we wanted, and we did it together." I paused, feeling the warmth of the realization. "Not only that, but we were the perfect partnership. And none of that damaged our friendship. In fact it strengthened it. The best thing I ever did was marry your mother." I looked at my daughters. They both still looked angry.

"Our relationship will never change. But we love each other enough to move on individually, knowing it won't hurt our friendship or our partnership. Your mom thinks this guy might be her *grand passion*. Nothing will change between us, nothing that hasn't changed already. And nothing will change in the way we feel about our kids." I stood up and went to the desks. I kissed them both on the cheek. "We asked the twins to trust us, and they said they would. I'm asking you to do the same."

They both looked at me. I could see their shoulders relax. They looked at each other and then back at me.

"I guess I can trust you," Veronica said.

"Me too." Charlotte came around the desk and put her arms around my neck. She rested her head on my shoulder. "I can't stand the thought of her hurting you," she said.

"I appreciate that honey." I turned to pull Veronica into our hug. "But listen," I said, still holding them close. "I'm not condoning divorce. I hate divorce. I think married people should try to work things out. But sometimes, in rare circumstances, it's the right thing to do."

Both girls kissed my cheek, and both girls pulled away from me and smiled.

"You're always teaching, Dad," Veronica said.

In the end of August the divorce was final. The only thing that changed was that Darla and I didn't spend our evenings in the living room together any more. When the school year started she still took the twins out to Drew's school, and she picked them up in the afternoon. She supervised their homework and spent some time with each of them. They'd been in separate rooms for several years now.

After she was comfortable that the twins were alright, she checked with me to be sure I'd be home for the rest of the evening. Sometimes I had something to do, and she would spend the evening there by herself, just being available if the kids needed her. Veronica was at school, and they were our only concern, at home anyway.

When Thanksgiving came around, Darla said she was ready for the family to meet Evan. I was nervous. I couldn't quite identify the reason for the anxiety, but it was definitely there.

We were all gathered in the living room. I detected a little nervousness in the girls, but of course, Brandon was fine. Dad and Uncle Jeff were there. Amanda was at home nursing a cold. Darla's parents had moved to Hilton Head Island and were coming up for Christmas. They would meet Evan then. I was glad. I felt a little sorry for the pressure the guy must be feeling.

We all heard the front door open and stood to greet the new family member. I was surprised when they came into the room. Evan was possibly a couple of inches taller than Darla, which would make him five foot four or there about. He was slightly built and something about the way he moved made him just a little bit effeminate. Hmmm ..., I thought. I remembered Darla telling me she'd had a brief affair with Teresa. Oh well, it didn't really matter.

"Everyone," Darla said. "This is Evan." She was beaming. I hadn't seen her smile like that since the girls were born. She took his hand and pulled him around the room. "This is Charlotte, she's my oldest. Veronica is only sixteen months younger that Charlotte." She went around the room introducing him to everyone and ending with me. The girls had done a good job of shaking hands and seeming to be happy to meet him. He had nodded and shaken everyone's hand. He hadn't spoken yet, and I thought his silence was strange. Maybe he was shy.

"And this," Darla paused and smiled up at me, "is my husband, David."

I laughed at her reference to our marital status, but she didn't seem to notice. Neither did Evan. I held out my hand to him. "It's nice to meet you, Evan, and it's nice to see the smile that you've put on Darla's face." I was glad to note that his handshake was firm. I hadn't expected it.

"It's nice to meet you too." I almost jumped I was so startled. His voice was a rich baritone. What an interesting person, such a diverse collection of traits. I found myself wanting to get to know him.

"Darla has assured me that I have no need to try to compete with you," he smiled very pleasantly and took her hand. "She tells me that I couldn't possibly, even if I tried, so I shouldn't waist the effort."

I laughed and looked at Darla. "That's my girl," I said.

"That's our girl," Evan said. "I'll try not to let the green eyed monster raise its ugly head, but it still may from time to time."

Hmmm ..., I thought for the second time. He seemed to be a bit of a poet. "Can I get you a drink?" I asked and went to the wet bar in the corner of the room. I opened the liquor cabinet. "We have pretty much anything you might want."

"White wine," he said. "I'd love some Chardonnay."

We finished the Appalachian Trail that summer. I was forty nine years old. The group was tremendous. Sam had to hire a larger plane, a small jet, a Piper, I think it was called. Dad, Uncle Jeff, and I paid for it together. Charlotte and Veronica were there. Charlotte left Elliot with Brad and his parents. Brandon and Belinda were there. Uncle Jeff was there, of course. Surprisingly, Amanda had come along, Alice and Evelyn, Dad, Drew, and a surprise visit from my sister Kristina and her husband. Their kids were grown and living lives of their own. Sivon was with us. She was never far from Brandon and Belinda. And, believe it or not, Darla and Evan were there. I had never been able to get her to go with me, but apparently Evan had insisted. She didn't seem happy with the camping idea, but she was thrilled with Evan's assertiveness. I guess she found it sexy. With all these people our campsites looked like small villages.

We arrived at the ranger station where Uncle Jeff had been transported by jeep the last time we'd hiked on the Trail. From there he'd been taken to the hospital by ambulance. I laughed to remember how he had protested, but we'd all insisted, so off he'd gone.

We got out of the bus we had chartered for the trip from the landing field and unpacked our gear. After eating a short snack of peanut butter crackers and Coke, we stood, and I watched as the group put on their packs. Darla didn't carry one. I guess Evan was packing for both of them. That's my girl, I thought.

"Where are you going, Uncle Jeff?" I called. "This is the direction to the end of the Trail."

"I'll catch up with you later," he said. "If I'm going to claim I've hiked this Trail, I'm going to hike every step of it. I'm going back to where I crashed the last time we were here."

"Wait for me." I hurried after him. "But," I said when I'd caught up with him. "Do we have to take the packs?"

He looked back at me and laughed. "No, I don't suppose we have to take the packs."

Uncle Jeff and I hiked the mile back to the tree we'd rested against when his knee had gone out. It felt good to be just the two of us for a little while. It isn't that I wasn't thrilled with the family wanting to join us on this memorable event. It was just nice to get some time alone together. After all, we'd started the project alone together.

"How's the knee?" I asked as we turned to go back.

"It's not the same as it used to be," he said and leaned down to rub it. "But it'll do."

It took us three days to hike to the end of the Trail. It was only fifteen miles, but we took our time with the big group. Harry was with us. So was Pepper. Dad's long haired dachshund, Charlemagne, was along, too. Pepper was young. So was Charlemagne. They had no problem. In fact, they looked great together; the tall long legged dog with flowing hair and the small short legged dog with flowing hair, both were black and tan. They made an interesting picture.

Harry was older but in good shape. When he got tired along the trail, Brandon put him on his shoulders. He nestled comfortably between Brandon's neck and his backpack, still finding the energy to bark at anything that moved in the forest.

The Trail was strenuous at this point. Uncle Jeff had to rest his knee a lot. Amanda soaked it with a warm cloth in the evening when we stopped for the night. But he really wasn't the hold up. It was mostly Darla, she and Belinda. Darla complained from the time we started to the time we stopped. Belinda complained only slightly less. Their legs were tired. Their backs ached. Brandon took Belinda's pack. At this point he was almost as tall as I was. Belinda had still not reached her mother's height and probably never would. She was tiny. I looked at the two of them, mother and daughter, and noticed how much they were alike. Despite the problems they'd had over the years, they were almost mirror images.

"I'm beginning to understand why I never insisted that P. H. come on these hikes with us." I laughed as I pulled alongside of Uncle Jeff and Dad.

"And we appreciate that," Dad said.

Uncle Jeff laughed. "Evan has the patience of Job," he said.

"And he still maintains a good attitude." I watched as Evan smiled at Darla and said something that made her stop frowning for just a second and laugh reluctantly. "He has a great sense of humor," I said.

"And a sparkling wit," Dad laughed. "I hate to say it, but I like him."

"I do too," I said. "I call him my husband-in-law."

Uncle Jeff and Dad laughed. "Are they married?" Dad asked. "I didn't hear about it."

"No, I guess they don't have to be. Evan has moved into the suite over the garage with her though, and it's working fine. What a great family." We rounded a curve in the Trail to see the sign that announced the end. It was the beginning, of course, if that's where you were starting. Uncle Jeff and I stopped together and both sucked in a noisy breath.

"We made it," I said.

"Yeah, we did." Uncle Jeff grabbed my arm and turned me to look at him. We hugged. It was hard with the packs. They sort of collided with each other and bounced us back. We both laughed. I think we were almost hysterical.

"You two wait here," Dad said. "Turn around and look in the other direction. Don't look back until I call you."

"I wonder what they're planning." I asked as we watched Dad and the rest of the group head for the end of the Trail.

"Turn around," Darla called.

"Go ahead and cross the line!" It was Brandon's voice this time.

We turned to see a computer generated banner stretched between Alice and Charlotte, Uncle Jeff's oldest and my oldest. It said congratulations in huge letters of all different colors. We could see the heads of the rest of the group behind it. It had to be held pretty low to accommodate some of them.

"Let's go!" Uncle Jeff squeezed my shoulder. I smiled at the familiar embrace.

We crossed the line with the applause and the excited cheers of our family. Two of them snapped cameras. They blew bubbles at us from small bubble bottles and surged forward to give us hugs, pats on the back from the men, and kisses from the women.

What a finish!

CHAPTER TWENTY SEVEN

It was early December of that same year. Belinda had started school at Emory University and was really enjoying it. She'd gone directly in on a pre-med major. Darla and I had advised her to get her core curriculum out of the way and then decide what to major in. But she knew her own mind, and we didn't urge too hard. She had only started driving by herself the previous spring. I have to admit it made me nervous for her to drive all the way across town to school. I knew it was time to let go, at least a little bit, but I was glad she was living at home.

Brandon wasn't driving. It was probably something that he would never be able to do. He really didn't care, though. There were plenty of people who were happy to take him where ever he wanted to go. His parents, of course, and his sister; but mostly he was with Sivon. I had no doubt now that they actually would get married, and I believed that it would be a lifelong union. And it would be a happy one.

Brandon would get his certificate of attendance from Drew's school in the spring. The School of Art that Alice had studied culinary art in had accepted him on a handicapped status. He wanted to study visual art formally, and even though I hated the thought of his failing and being hurt by it, I had to let him try. After all, he had always known his limitations and accepted them. He didn't think this was a limitation, and if it was, I was sure he would accept it.

Sivon was in her last year of high school. She would finish in the public school to get her diploma. It had been a bit of a transition for her. She was home schooled all her life. It was a transition for her mother too. I could tell by the number of times I came home and found the pretty Irish woman with the attractive accent sitting in my kitchen talking to Darla. Sivon had plans to go to Georgia Tech and become an architect. I was confident she would do it and do it well.

Darla and Evan were still living above the garage, and as far as I could tell, they were very happy. The green eyed monster had raised its ugly head a couple of times. Darla had been true to her word that nothing would change. She still wrapped her arms around my waist in greeting and buried her head in my chest. I still kissed the top of it, and sometimes I caught a glimpse of jealousy in Evan's green eyes. Funny, he actually did have green eyes.

Sometimes Darla and Evan sat with me in the evening, but usually they went upstairs or out to a movie or something. Most evenings the twins sat with me and talked about their day. I think they worried about me. After a while they would go to the TV room behind the kitchen or up to their separate rooms, Belinda to study and Brandon to sketch or paint.

I would go up to my office and work on my small internet business or one of my albums. The business had gotten smaller over the years. But I still had a few customers, artists that wanted me to market them.

It was late fall, and tonight I had taken my walk early and had come in from the cold night ready to put on my flannel pajamas and fuzzy slippers. The dogs shivered too. They were glad to settle in their separate beds in the corner of the room.

When I was dressed in my PJs, I considered getting into bed. But that bed was way too big. Even for a giant like me it was lonely in there. I decided to get a smaller bed the next day and went down to the living room to read. I couldn't concentrate, so I turned off the light and just sat in the quiet of the night.

After a minute the light in the kitchen went on, and I looked in that direction. "Hey, David," Darla said. She was wearing her flannel nightgown and fuzzy slippers. We still matched. She came out of the kitchen holding two glasses of wine. "Are you alright? Why are you sitting alone in the dark, honey?"

"I'm fine," I said, reaching for the glass of wine. "Thanks, though, I could use something to relax me."

She looked over her shoulder. Then she looked back at me with an exaggerated smile. "Good, I'm glad I could anticipate your need." She handed me the glass.

"Oh," I said. "This wasn't for me." I glanced at the stairs that led to her suite over the garage.

"Well ...no, but it is now. Don't worry. It's a clean glass." She set her wine down on the table next to the chair I was sitting in and climbed onto my lap. She turned, plopped her bottom down, and swung her legs over the side of the chair. "What's going on, David? You never sit out here by yourself."

I glanced at the stairs to the garage suite again. "You think that if Evan comes looking for you and finds us like this, it won't bother him?"

She put her arms around my neck and kissed my cheek. "I hope it would bother him." She grinned wickedly. "Then it would give me another chance to make him see how things are around here. What's wrong?"

She laced her arms around my neck, and I looked into her eyes. "I'm not sure," I said. "I'm lonely I think. But I shouldn't be. I mean, I have you and the kids. Nothing has really changed."

"Are you unhappy about me and Evan?"

I looked at her radiant face. I could smell, faintly, the aftermath of sex on her. It didn't bother me like I thought it would. She was happy. She'd found her one and only. And she still cared about me.

"No, I'm very happy for you," I said.

"What the hell!" Both of us looked up as Evan's baritone interrupted our conversation. "What's going on here?" He demanded.

I scooped my arms beneath Darla's legs and tried to stand up.

"Don't you move, David!" Darla held tight to the chair, blocking me from standing. "David and I are having a loving moment," she said to the man standing before us in his bathrobe with his hair tousled. "I told you I'd always be close to him, Evan."

I laughed and gave up my struggle to stand.

"He looks like he's going to carry you away to bed." Evan stepped back and folded his arms across his chest.

"Well, he doesn't have any intention of that," Darla said, looking at me. "Do you, David?"

I looked at her pretty face and wondered why I had no intention of it. Why didn't I have the drive to run to bed with her anymore? Why didn't I have the stamina to make love to her all night? I used to.

"No," I said. "We love each other, but sex is behind us."

Darla kissed my mouth and smiled at Evan. "Darling, I'll be up in a few minutes, but I need to talk to David right now." She laughed at his grumpy scowl. "I'm glad it worries you, but I assure you it shouldn't," she said. "Pour yourself a glass of wine before you go up. I'll be right there."

She watched him go with a smile on her face, one that I didn't quite recognize. Then she turned to me. "David," she said. "I'm sure you see that I've found my grand passion. He won't leave because he found me in your lap. If he would, he wouldn't be my grand passion. I couldn't trust him if he didn't trust me."

"Are you sure he'll be there when you go back up?" I asked.

"Yes." She looked back at the stairway, then at me.

When she looked back at me, I knew what she was going to say. "I'm not sure Anna wants anything to do with me." I spoke before she could.

"You're not sure," she said. "If you don't ask you'll never know, will you?

Chapter Twenty Seven

I got off the plane and walked up the ramp to the airport. I could feel the cold air coming through the cracks in the ramp, but I couldn't see outside. It wasn't nearly as cold in Atlanta as it was in New York. I hoped I'd brought enough warm clothing.

I got a cab to the hotel and showered and shaved. Anna's last fashion show would start in only a couple of hours, and I wanted to be rested and clean.

I had a harder time finding a cab than I thought I would. I guess New York's cabbies have a better market. I was late to the show. As I walked down the corridor in the conference hall toward the room, I could hear her melodious voice announcing the models. My heart started to pound.

"Dear God, I still love her so much," I said under my breath. I walked into the room, and for a minute I couldn't breathe. She stood to the side like always, but her presence was the focus of the room. She hadn't changed much. Her body still flowed like a mountain stream. Her hair was the same, sculpted to her head, but in the light of the runway, I could see white sprinkled through the black.

I had the greatest urge to leap up on the stage and swing her into my arms.

"Sir, do you have a ticket?" I looked down at the woman standing in the doorway.

"Yes," I said and searched in my pocket for the ticket that Darla had gotten for me. She'd done it all. Darla had gotten the plane tickets. She'd booked the hotel. I looked at the ticket and showed it to the attendant. She ushered me into the door and asked me to keep my voice down until the show was over.

I listened to Anna's lilting voice as she described her outfits. She commented on the body types of her models and what the outfits would work for in the general public. When it was over, I went to the door that led backstage.

"I'd like to see Ms. Smart if I could," I said to the guard.

"I'm sorry. That's not possible," he said firmly.

"Could you just ask her? Tell her my name is David Landrum."

He looked at me, and I had the feeling I'd come up against a brick wall. "Sorry sir, Ms. Smart told me she would not see anyone tonight. She's retiring, you know."

"Carl." The guard and I both turned at her voice. "It's alright," she said. "David is an old friend."

The guard stood and looked at me menacingly. "Are you sure, Ms. Smart?"

"I'm sure," she said and extended her hand to me. "Come to my dressing room, David. It's been so long since I've seen you."

It seemed like we walked miles, but I'm sure it was only a couple of feet. We went through a door to a dressing room. She held my hand the whole way. When we had closed the door behind us, she let go. I felt the void immediately.

She turned and looked at me. "David, I couldn't believe it when I saw you standing there. You still remember me."

"How could I not remember you, Anna? You're my grand passion." I wanted to grab her hand back and hold it to my heart. I wanted to wrap her in my arms and hold her close to me.

"Grand passion?" She smiled up at me. "I didn't do right by you, David. Why don't you hate me?"

"I can't," I said. "I love you too much."

She looked up into my eyes for what seemed like eternity. Then she turned around and sat down at her dressing table. She picked up a washcloth that had been soaking in something wet and cleaned her face.

"I need to go home. I can't spend time with you right now, David. Will you be here tomorrow?"

I walked to her back and put my hands on her shoulders. "Do you want me to be here tomorrow?" I asked.

She met my eyes in the mirror and said, "Yes I do."

"I'll be here then. I need to ask one more question. Are the gossip people right? Are you finally getting married?"

She looked into my eyes through the mirror and laughed. "No, David, I'm not getting married."

"So, I still have a chance?"

"You have a family of your own." She smiled. "I've followed your life, David."

I laughed and looked back at her reflection. I could see that what she said was true. She'd followed me as closely as I'd followed her. "Then you would know that I'm divorced. I've never stopped loving you, Anna."

"It looks to me like you've never stopped loving your wife either." She turned back to the mirror.

"Not for a second," I laughed. "But it was never what I had with you. It wasn't for her either."

She turned away from the mirror and looked at me. Our eyes met and held. "Will you come home with me tonight?" she asked. "I want to show you something."

✧

"I'm sorry I was late, Ellie," Anna said when we opened the door of her apartment in the high rise building in New York. "I hope everything went alright."

"You know I would have called if it didn't." Ellie was a young woman, no more than a girl. I thought she was maybe late teens or early twenties. "Anyway," she said as she gathered her purse. "I'll go on downstairs if you're alright. Mom knows I'm okay, but she'll wait up for me." She eyed me as she said it.

"Oh, I'm sorry," Anna said. "David, this is my babysitter Ellie. Ellie, this is David Landrum."

"It's nice to meet you." I shook her hand and watched as Anna paid her. Then she went out the door and shut it behind her.

"Your babysitter?" I looked at Anna.

"Come in here." She signaled me to follow her. We walked into the bedroom of her small but luxurious apartment. It was dark. There was a baby crib set up in the corner and a double bed that had been shoved up against the window. She walked to the adjoining bathroom and turned on the light. It cast a quiet glow across the room, and I walked to the crib.

A child slept on his side in the crib. He was probably no more than a year old, maybe fifteen months.

"His name is Anthony," Anna whispered.

I looked at the child. He was black like Anna. His head was bald and shiny, and his lips folded in half as he whistled his peaceful sleeping cadence.

"Is he yours?" I asked.

"Yes," she said. "Actually, he's my brother's. Remember my baby brother Anthony?"

"I never met him." We were still whispering. "I remember how much you love him, though."

"He died four months ago."

I looked at her and saw the tears in her eyes. I took her elbow and guided her out of the room.

"I'm so sorry, Anna."

"I did." She sat down on her couch and put her face in her hands. "He and his wife had gone to a business dinner together. He was a lawyer, you know." She looked up at me. "They had a car accident."

"You put him through school."

"He'd done very well. He'd married, had a good job." She put her face in her hands again for one short sob. "It's not fair. If either of us should have died, it should have been me."

I sat down on the couch beside her. "I'm glad it wasn't."

She looked up at me. Her eyes were still watery.

"I'm not glad he died," I said hastily. "I'm just glad you didn't." I pulled her into my arms. "What do you plan to do now?"

"I've filed adoption papers." She rested back into my arms. "I remember how much you wished you could call your uncle Dad. I want him to call me Mom. I'll tell him the truth, of course." She looked into my eyes, and my heart started to pound again. "I'll make sure he knows his parents, but I want him to have something to hold on to, and that will be me."

We sat on that couch for at least an hour before either of us said anything again. "Anna," I finally broke the silence. "Let me be his father. Let him call me Dad."

"I can't wait for you to meet my wife," I said to Anna. She was sitting beside me holding Anthony in her lap. He slept peacefully to the hum of the engines of the passenger jet.

"I thought I was your wife." We'd been married at the justice of the peace in New York, and now we were flying to Atlanta to meet my family. She smiled up at me, and I noticed that she had dimples in her cheeks like Darla. That was what had always seemed familiar when she smiled at me. I didn't say so. I just smiled back.

"My ex-wife," I laughed. "It's a very interesting relationship, but I think you'll adjust to it easily. She's just a delightful person. I think you're going to love her."

"She's so different than me." Anna stroked Anthony's soft cheek. "I know that she came to New York to be an actress, but it didn't work. Other than that she's always been a stay at home wife and mom."

"You followed me as closely as I followed you," I said.

"Does that bother you?"

"No, it thrills me." I rubbed my hand over Anthony's bald head. "I wonder when he'll get hair."

"I wonder too. I'm thinking his father was about three years old before he got hair. I raised him, you know." She looked out the window of the plane, and I saw the sadness descend.

The baby started to fret. I took him from her and put him on my shoulder. I patted his bottom. He settled again. "He's so tuned in to you, Anna. The two of you have really bonded. He knows when you're sad."

She looked back and smiled. "You certainly are good with him."

"I've had a lot of practice. I have twin sisters slash cousins and four children of my own. I've raised a large brood."

"Are you sure you want to raise another one?"

"I'm one hundred percent sure."

The pilot announced that we'd be landing in Atlanta shortly and to raise our seat backs and buckle our belts. I put Anthony into the car seat on the aisle and buckled him in. He started to cry. I jiggled him a little, and he settled down to look around. He grabbed my hand and said, "Dada."

"He called me Dad," I said, and I could feel the grin on my face. "No matter how many I've raised," I said. "It's just as thrilling when they first call you by name."

Anna laughed. "I hate to disappoint you, but he's been saying that for a while. He says Mama too. I think those sounds are just easy to make."

"That's what Darla always said, but I don't believe it. He knows I'm his Dad."

The woman across the aisle from me said, "That child can't be your son."

I looked back at her firmly. "Yes he can," I said.

"David," I felt Anna's hand on my arm. "If that kind of thing bothers you, we'll have a problem."

I smiled at her. The place where she was touching me tingled, and I felt very happy. I turned back to the woman across the aisle. "He's adopted. Isn't he beautiful?" I said. He wasn't adopted yet, but he would be.

She smiled reluctantly. "I'm not sure I approve of inter-racial adoption. Won't it be confusing for him?"

"If it is, we'll help him understand it." I turned back to my family. I took Anna's hand and squeezed it in mine.

"I'm nervous," she said. "Will your whole family be at the airport to meet us?"

"Not all of them," I laughed. "I'm not sure the airport could stand it. My dad will be there and Uncle Jeff. I hope he'll bring Amanda. Won't you be happy to see her again?"

"Yes, I've missed her. She was the closest thing I've ever had to a friend."

I squeezed her hand again. "The girls won't be there. You'll meet them later, my cousins and my older daughters. Darla will be there and Brandon. I think Belinda and Sivon will be there. They never let Brandon far from their sight." I smiled thinking about that little love triangle.

"Gosh, that's a lot of people. I'm not a social butterfly, you know, David."

"You narrate fashion shows in front of thousands of people."

"That's different."

The plane stopped taxiing at the gate, and we carried our baby and paraphernalia off. The car seat that we used on the plane fit into a stroller frame to form the seat. I fastened Anthony in. Anna handed him a stuffed toy. He hugged it to his chest, and we headed for the baggage claim.

"David," I heard Darla's voice and looked over the crowd. Soon I saw her jumping up and down and waving at us.

"Over there," I took Anna's hand and pulled her in the direction of my family. "Oh, how could I forget my husband-in-law?" I said as we approached. "Evan is my wife's grand passion. I mean my ex-wife." I looked down at Anna. She was pushing the stroller with one hand and holding my hand in the other. She looked small and frightened. There was only one other time I'd seen her look that way. That time in the hospital bed.

"Don't worry, sweetheart," I said. "Everything will be fine." Then I was clasped in Darla's familiar hug, her arms around my waist, and her head buried in my chest. I kissed the top of it and returned the hug.

"David," Evan and I shook hands. I hugged my dad. Uncle Jeff gave me a huge bear hug, and I kissed Amanda's cheek. Then I turned to my oldest son. Brandon stooped in front of the stroller talking to Anthony. The baby was giggling.

"Daddy," I looked at Belinda. She stood next to me with Sivon.

"Baby," I picked her up and swung her. "I didn't see you there. You're such a tiny little thing."

"I'm not that tiny." She laughed and it sounded like wind chimes, just like her mother.

"Hello, Sivon," I kissed the girl's cheek, and she hugged my neck.

"Everyone, I want you to meet my wife." I propelled Anna slightly in front of me holding her securely by the hand.

"Anna, it's wonderful to see you again." Amanda broke the moment of silence that followed. She hugged Anna, and they held each other for just a minute, swaying slightly.

Uncle Jeff kissed Anna's cheek and said, "Do you remember me? We didn't know each other very long."

"I remember," Anna said shyly. I introduced her to my kids, and she greeted my Dad.

"Darla," I took my ex-wife's hand and pulled her forward. "I know this is a little awkward, but I want my wives to meet each other. I hope you'll be friends."

"Anna." Darla opened her arms and folded Anna into them. "I am so happy to meet you at last." I looked down at them. They were the same height, and they both had dimples in their cheeks when they smiled. Other than those two things they were polar opposites. My heart thumped against my ribs and I smiled.

"You're just going to love living with us. It's such an exciting household." I heard Darla start to chatter. She tucked her arm into Anna's and guided her over to the baggage carousel. Anna cast an anxious look over her shoulder to the baby.

"He'll be fine," I called to her. "Brandon is taking care of him." I looked down at my two sons. Talk about polar opposites. "Brandon, aren't you going to say hello to your old man?" I asked.

"I'm sorry Dad." He stood and embraced me. "I'm just so excited about having a brother at long last."

"At long last…" I laughed as Brandon stooped again to unfasten Anthony from the stroller and pick him up. "Where do you get phrases like that?"

"Probably from Sivon," he said. "Or maybe I got it from Binda. He carried the baby over to his sister. They were so different and yet so close. Sivon and Belinda played peek-a-boo games with Anthony. The three of them seemed so comfortable with each other.

"He's like his old man," Uncle Jeff said from beside me. "I remember asking you the same thing. You were always coming up with some phrase that just didn't seem to fit with a kid."

I smiled at him. "Brandon isn't so much of a kid anymore." I looked at my family and I felt good all over. "Why am I such a lucky man, Uncle Jeff?"

"You deserve it, son."

It was midnight. I sat at my computer working on the beginning of my album of Anna, Anthony, and me. I was usually in bed asleep at this time. My sleeping problem had ended with my marriage to Anna. I'd known all along it would.

I still took my walk at night. But now Anna took it with me. We went about 10:00, sometimes earlier. It was a luxury to have Darla and Evan in the house. They were almost always home at this time. Usually they sat in the living room with us in the evening, enjoying conversation or just companionship while reading or playing cards. We just had to ask them to listen for Anthony while we took our walk. They could even do it from their room with the intercom.

It was dark in my office. I liked to work in the dark. I had a small light over my keyboard, and of course the screen was lit. I was separating the pictures into files, Anna with Anthony, me with Anthony, Anthony alone, Anna with me, and the two of us with Anthony. It was slow going because I had to stop every other picture and think about how much I loved them.

"Come to bed, David." I jumped when Anna put her arms around my neck and spoke softly in my ear. "I don't sleep very well without you."

"Funny, I can't sleep without you either. I never could."

I closed my file and shut down the computer. I stood, put my arms across her shoulders, and we started for the door. The phone rang. I looked at my watch. "Uh oh." I said. "At this time of night it can't be good news." I went back to the desk and looked at the caller ID. It was Lenny. I looked back at Anna. She nodded.

I picked up the phone. "Hello, Lenny."

The line was quiet for a minute. "I can't believe you answered," he finally said.

"That's all behind us, Lenny."

"I'm glad."

Silence again. "I heard you're out of prison," I said.

"Yes, and I'm doing very well. Believe it or not, my books have been very successful. Financially we're good. I stay out of trouble because Carmen keeps me in line. She's the best thing that ever happened to me."

"I'm happy for you," I said. "I'm not surprised about your books. They're very good."

"You've read them."

"All of them."

There was another minute of silence. "I read about your marriage to Anna and Anthony's adoption. I'm glad for you both. I'm sorry I called so late. I hope I didn't wake him up."

"He sleeps soundly. A cannon couldn't wake him up."

We both laughed.

"Listen, Carmen and I are coming to Atlanta next month for a writer's convention. Maybe we could get together for dinner or something."

"I don't think so, Lenny. It's all behind us, even the relationship."

"I figured." My chest tightened at the sadness in his voice. "Do you think I could speak to Anna?"

I put my hand over the receiver. "Do you want to speak to him?"

Her eyes met mine for a minute. She shook her head. "I don't need to."

I looked at the tranquility of her smile and saw what I wanted to see. Any doubts I had ever had of her love were gone. Just as she was mine, I was hers.

"She doesn't need to."

More silence.

"Well I guess that's it then. Thanks for talking to me, David."

"No problem."

Chapter Twenty Seven

On my fiftieth birthday my family and friends gathered beside the pool in the back yard. It was a warm spring. We'd opened the pool early this year. I swam with my youngest son and played a rousing game of badminton with my oldest son. I bounced my grandson on my knee and hugged and kissed, and was hugged and kissed, by all three of my daughters.

My first wife was there with my husband-in-law. She waited on me, and Evan didn't seem to mind. He and I had a stimulating conversation about marketing. I think he was hinting for me to help him with his new salon. He'd opened one shortly after he and Darla had moved in together. I'd be glad to help him, and he wasn't going to pay me, but I'd make him sweat a little before I suggested it. I guess I'm a little bit jealous after all.

My current wife was mingling with the group. She had really warmed up and become a part of the family. We had raised the roof a story and built her a studio in the attic where she could work on her line of children's clothing. She and Darla got along beautifully. She convinced Darla to join a small theatre group, and she was coaching her on stage freight. Darla coached Anna on motherhood. Anna seemed to enjoy the support, even though she'd raised a boy already.

Jimmy was there with Meryl. Their youngest daughter Marissa was with them. James, Jr. sat beside the pool with his feet in the water talking to Alice and Evelyn. I wondered if there was something striking up again with Evelyn. I guess we'd just have to wait and see. Heather was living in another state with her family. She had called to wish me a happy day.

Dad was there with a new lady friend. He had assured me that it wasn't a date. He promised that no one could take the place of my mother. I knew that, but it didn't mean he had to be alone for the rest of his life. They didn't seem romantic though. Oh well, friends are important too.

Something caught my eye at the top of the hill. I looked up and saw Uncle Jeff standing under the arch. I handed Elliot to his mother and climbed the steps to join him. About half way up I realized someone was following me. I turned to find my dad on the steps below.

"I hope you don't mind if I join the two of you," he said.

"You know I don't." I continued my climb. I stood looking down at the crowd below. "Isn't my family beautiful?" I said.

"Very much so," Uncle Jeff said. "And being a part of that family, I want to thank you for the compliment."

"You're not that pretty, Jeff." Dad teased.

"Hey, I'm at least as pretty as you are." We laughed then looked on in silence.

"There's someone missing though." My voice broke and I cleared my throat. "I miss Mom so much." I pressed my eyelids with my thumb and forefinger. Both of my remaining parents put their arms across my shoulders, crossing them with each other's as they did.

"We all miss her son," Dad said. "But like you once said to me, she's all over the place down there."

"You're right." I cleared my throat.

"You know, David," Uncle Jeff said. "When you were a kid, you wouldn't cry for anything in the world. You didn't even cry when your dog Pepper died. I don't think you cried when Charlotte the pooch died either."

"I've gotten over that."

"We've noticed." Dad laughed. They removed their arms from my shoulder since we were beginning to sway, and we were dangerously close to the edge of the hill. We laughed again as we regained our balance.

"David," Uncle Jeff said. "I want you to tell me if you still smoke that stuff that got you into so much trouble."

"Does it matter?" I asked.

He and Dad were both looking at me intently. After a minute they both looked back at the crowd below.

"I guess not," Uncle Jeff said. Dad agreed with a shrug of his shoulders. We didn't say anything for another few minutes.

"I guess you got your fifth child." Uncle Jeff broke the silence. I followed the direction of his eyes. He was looking at Anna holding Anthony on her lap at the side of the pool.

"And you found your grand passion," Dad said.

"You know what?" I looked from one of them to the other. "It was all a grand passion."

I looked at my two wives. They were sitting together chatting happily with each other. I remembered a conversation I'd had with my stepmother a long time ago. She had said that she was Dad's ideal. Mom was Dad's grand passion. Darla was my ideal, the ideal partner, the ideal mother, the ideal friend. Anna was my heart.

"I understand you a little bit better now, Dad."

He followed the direction of my gaze and put his hand on my shoulder. "You carried it off a little better than I did," he said.

"I'd like to think so." I laughed and touched his hand. He laughed too.

"So what will you do next?" Uncle Jeff asked. "You've had two careers, three really. You've had two wives, still do really. You've had four, no five, children. You've hiked the entire Appalachian Trail. At fifty though, you're only half way through."

"That's right," Dad said. "Besides raise another kid and run a successful cafe, what do you have planned?"

I looked again at the gathering below. "I think I'll write a book.

www.ingramcontent.com/pod-product-compliance
Lightning Source LLC
Chambersburg PA
CBHW032057090426
42743CB00007B/151